≡ Controversies in ≡
CONSTITUTIONAL LAW

COLLECTIONS OF DOCUMENTS AND ARTICLES ON MAJOR QUESTIONS OF AMERICAN LAW

PAUL FINKELMAN
GENERAL EDITOR
Chicago-Kent College of Law

A Garland Series

ABORTION LAW IN THE UNITED STATES

Volume 3
Modern Writings on Abortion

Edited with an introduction by

Jenni Parrish

UNIVERSITY OF CALIFORNIA
HASTINGS COLLEGE OF THE LAW

Garland Publishing, Inc.
New York & London
1995

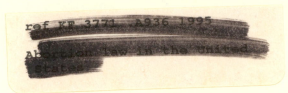

Library of Congress Cataloging-in-Publication Data

Abortion law in the United States / edited with an introduction by Jenni
Parrish.
    p.   cm. — (Controversies in constitutional law)
    Includes bibliographical references.
    Contents: v. 1. From Roe v. Wade to the present — v. 2. Historical
development of abortion law — v. 3. Modern writings on abortion.
    ISBN 0–8153–2183–X (alk. paper)
    1. Abortion—Law and legislation—United States.   I. Parrish,
Jenni.   II. Series.
KF3771.A936   1996
344.73'04192—dc20
[347.3044192]   95–30126
                                                    CIP

Printed on acid-free, 250-year-life paper
Manufactured in the United States of America

CONTENTS

Infanticide: A Historical Survey
William L. Langer 1

The History of Abortion: Technology, Morality, and Law
Joseph W. Dellapenna 15

Zig-Zag Stitching and the Seamless Web: Thoughts on
"Reproduction" and the Law
Marie Ashe 85

An American Tragedy: The Supreme Court on Abortion
Robert M. Byrn 115

The Law of New York Concerning Abortion and the Status of
the Foetus, 1664–1968: A Case of Cessation of Constitutionality
Cyril C. Means, Jr. 171

The Phoenix of Abortional Freedom: Is a Penumbral or Ninth-
Amendment Right About to Arise from the Nineteenth-Century
Legislative Ashes of a Fourteenth-Century Common-Law Liberty?
Cyril C. Means, Jr. 277

A Defense of Abortion
Judith Jarvis Thomson 353

Legal Reasoning from the Top Down and from the Bottom
Up: The Question of Unenumerated Constitutional Rights
Richard A. Posner 373

Unenumerated Rights: Whether and How Roe Should be Overruled
Ronald Dworkin 391

Acknowledgments 443

Contents of the Series 445

INFANTICIDE: A HISTORICAL SURVEY

WILLIAM L.
LANGER

Professor Langer's overview of infanticide in the West was originally written as an introduction to a projected reprint of William B. Ryan's Infanticide: Its Law, Prevalence, Prevention and History *(London, 1862). Since the reprint did not materialize, he has revised and documented the essay for readers of the* Journal. *He reminds us, however, that it still makes no pretence to being more than a historical review of an important subject which is only now beginning to attract the attention it deserves.*

Infanticide, that is, the wilful destruction of newborn babes through exposure, starvation, strangulation, smothering, poisoning, or through the use of some lethal weapon, has been viewed with abhorrence by Christians almost from the beginning of their era. Although often held up to school-children as an abomination practiced by the Chinese or other Asians, its role in Western civilization, even in modern times, has rarely been suggested by historians, sociologists or even demographers.

Yet in these days of world population crisis there can hardly be a more important historical question than that of the chronically superfluous population growth and the methods by which humanity has dealt with it. Among non-Christian peoples (with the exception of the Jews) infanticide has from time immemorial been the accepted procedure·for disposing not only of deformed or sickly infants, but of all such new-borns as might strain the resources of the individual family or the larger community. At the present day it is still employed by so-called underdeveloped peoples in the effort to keep the population in reasonable adjustment to the available food supply. Among the Eskimos of Arctic Canada, for instance, many babies are set out on the ice to freeze if the father or elder of the tribe decides that they would be a continuing drain on the means of subsistence.[1]

In ancient times, at least, infanticide was not a legal obligation. It was a practice freely discussed and generally condoned by those in authority and ordinarily left to the decision of the father as the responsible head of the family. Modern humanitarian sentiment makes it difficult to recapture the relatively detached attitude of the parents towards their offspring. Babies were looked upon as the unavoidable result of normal sex relations, often as an undesirable burden rather than as a blessing. More girls than boys were disposed of, presumably to keep down the number of potential mothers as well as in recognition of the fact that they would never contribute greatly to the family income. In the seventeenth century, Jesuit missionaries to China were horrified to find that in Peking alone several thousand babes (almost exclusively females) were thrown on the streets like refuse, to be collected each morning by carriers who dumped them into a huge pit outside the city.[2]

The attitude of the ancient Greeks in this matter is well reflected in the pronouncements of Plato and Aristotle. The former favored the careful regulation of all sex relations, so as to produce the most perfect type of human being, while Aristotle was more concerned with the problem of population pressure. With its limited resources, ancient Greece, according to a modern authority, "lived always under the shadow of the fear of too many mouths to feed." Neglect of this problem by many city-states was denounced by Aristotle as "a never-failing cause of poverty among the citizens, and poverty was the parent of revolution." He firmly contended that the size of the population should be limited by law and suggested that abortion might be preferable to exposure as a method of control.[3]

In Hellenistic Greece, infanticide, chiefly in the form of exposure of female babies, was carried to such an extent that the average family was exceptionally small. Parents rarely reared more than one daughter, with the result that there was an altogether abnormal discrepancy in the numbers of the sexes.[4]

The practice of the Hellenistic Greeks was continued under Roman rule and probably influenced Roman attitudes. After all, Rome itself was traditionally founded by the exposed youngsters, Romulus and Remus, who were saved from their certain fate by the nursing of a friendly wolf. Throughout the Republic and long after the authority of

2

the father over his family had worn thin, unwanted children continued to be disposed of in the accepted way. It was thought altogether natural that proletarians, poverty-stricken and hopeless, should protect themselves from further responsibility. As among the Greeks, there was a marked disparity between the sexes, which suggests that many bastards and a substantial number of female infants were abandoned if not murdered by drowning.[5] Seneca saw nothing unreasonable in this procedure, while Pliny the Elder defended the practice on the ground that the size of the population must be regulated. Edward Gibbon, writing in the late eighteenth century on *The Decline and Fall of the Roman Empire*, denounced this exposure of children as "the prevailing and stubborn vice of antiquity," and charged the Roman Empire with being "stained with the blood of infants." Lecky, writing a century later, speaks of infanticide as "one of the deepest stains of the ancient civilization" and as "a crying vice of the empire."[6]

A decisive change of attitude came with Christianity. The Church fathers were undoubtedly, in this respect as in others, influenced by Judaic Law which, while it did not mention infanticide specifically in the discussion of murder, was always interpreted by Rabbinical Law as an equivalent.[7] Philo Judaeus, the eminent Jewish-Hellenistic philosopher, denounced the exposure of children and declared it a form of murder. Increasingly, Christian leaders thundered against infanticide as a pagan practice and insisted that all human life be held inviolable. Yet it was only with the triumph of Christianity that the Emperor Constantine in 318 A.D. declared the slaying of a son or daughter by a father to be a crime, and only at the end of the fourth century that the Emperors Valentinian, Valens, and Gratian made infanticide a crime punishable by death.[8]

While the contribution of Christian theologians to the adoption of a more humane attitude is obvious, it should be remembered that the later Roman Empire apparently suffered from progressive depopulation, due to devastating epidemics, recurrent famines and general disorder.[9] Under the circumstances there was clearly no need to limit population growth. On the contrary, increased fertility was desired. Hence the repetition of the exhortation of the Bible: "Be fruitful and multiply." Until the late eighteenth century at least, when the great upswing of the European population set in, large families were the fashion, being regarded as the blessing of a benevolent deity.

Yet there can be little doubt that child murder continued to be practiced, even in the most advanced countries of western Europe. Lecky, in his *History of European Morals* (1869), speaks of the popular distinction in the early Middle Ages between infanticide and exposure, the latter offense not being punishable by law: "It was practiced on a gigantic scale with absolute impunity, noticed by writers with most frigid indifference and, at least in the case of destitute parents, considered a very venial offence."[10]

Until the sixteenth century, and in some places until much later, the unenviable task of dealing with the problem was left to the Church authorities. In the hope of reducing the exposure and almost certain death of newborn children (especially girls), foundling hospitals were opened in the eighth century in Milan, Florence, Rome, and other cities. But these institutions proved to be ineffectual, since most of the children had to be sent to the country to be nursed, and the majority soon succumbed either through neglect or more positive action on the part of the wet-nurses.

Infanticide by out-and-out violence of various kinds was probably always exceptional. Throughout European history the authorities were baffled and frustrated primarily by the many cases of reputed suffocation, the "overlaying" or "overlying" of an infant in bed by its allegedly drunken parents. This could and surely did occur accidentally, but the suspicion, always present and unusually warranted, was that of intentional riddance of an unwanted child. Since it was impossible to prove premeditated crime, the authorities contented themselves with the imposition of penance in the case of married women, who were condemned to live for at least a year on bread and water. The unwed mothers and the presumed witches, however, were to bear the brunt as examples and admonitions. A girl known to have committed infanticide in any form might be absolved by pleading insanity, but was otherwise condemned to suffer the death penalty, usually in the most diabolical imaginable manner. Medieval sources tell of women being tied in a sack, along with a dog, a cock, or some other uncongenial companion and thrown into the river for a supreme struggle for life. This method was probably never in general use, and in any case seems to have been abandoned by the end of the Middle Ages.[11] A detailed analysis of the court and prison records of Nürnberg from 1513 to 1777 lists by name eighty-seven women executed for infanticide, all but four of them unmarried girls who had committed violent murder. Prior to 1500 the penalty in Nürnberg as in most of Germany was burial alive, often with gruesome refinements. During the sixteenth century the usual method was drowning, and after 1580 decapitation. Hangings were quite exceptional. It was hardly worse, however, than being buried alive, being drowned or decapitated, penalties which continued to be practiced, though less and less frequently, until the nineteenth century.

In any case, overlaying continued to be a vexing problem until modern times. In 1500, the Bishop of Fiesole set fines and penalties for parents who kept babies in bed with them. In the eighteenth century, a Florentine craftsman designed a basket frame (*arcuccio*) which would protect the child from smothering. An Austrian decree of 1784 forbade having children under the age of five in bed with parents, and Prussian legislation of 1794 reduced the age of the infants to two.[12]

Government authorities were apparently no more successful than the clergy in checking the practice of overlaying, at least among married couples. One may safely assume that in the eighteenth and nineteenth centuries the poor, hardly able to support the family they already had, evaded responsibility by disposing of further additions. But by the eighteenth century another form of infanticide became so prevalent that governments were at their wits' end in their efforts to combat it. For reasons too complex and still too obscure, there was a marked increase in sexual immorality, in seduction, and in illegitimacy. The evidence suggests that in all European countries, from Britain to Russia, the upper classes felt perfectly free to exploit sexually girls who were at their mercy. As late as 1871, Mr. Cooper, the Secretary of the Society for the Rescue of Young Women and Children, testified before a Parliamentary Committee that at least nine out of ten of the girls in trouble were domestic servants: "in many instances the fathers of their children are their masters, or their masters' sons, or their masters' relatives, or their masters' visitors." To be sure, lords of the manor often recognized the offspring as their own and raised them as members of the family. But in the new factory towns foremen favored amenable girls for employment. Young aristocrats, too, were much to blame. When traveling they expected to find relaxation with the chamber maids of the inn. It seems to have been taken for granted that the upper classes were entitled to the favors of pretty girls of the lower classes and that fornication was looked upon as an inevitable aspect of lower class life.

Yet if a girl became pregnant, she was left to shift for herself. She at once became an object of obloquy and might well be whipped out of the village by the more fortunate members of her sex. Many sought anonymity and aid in the cities, where professional midwives would, for a pittance, not only perform an abortion or deliver the child, but would also undertake to nurse and care for it, it being fully understood that the mother would not need to worry further about it. Starvation or a dose of opiates would settle the child's fate in a matter of days.

Naturally all girls in trouble were not willing to resort to so drastic a solution. There was always the possibility, admittedly slim, that if the unwanted baby were left on the steps of a church or mansion, it might stir the sympathies of a stranger and be adopted by him, as was Tom Jones by Squire Allworthy. Many young mothers therefore bundled up their offspring, and left them at churches or other public places. In the late seventeenth century, St. Vincent de Paul was so appalled by the number of babies to be seen daily on the steps of Notre Dame that he appealed to ladies of the court to finance an asylum for foundlings. His efforts soon inspired others to similar action, and before long most large towns in Catholic Europe had established similar institutions. In England a retired sea captain, Thomas Coram, was so depressed by the daily sight of infant corpses thrown on the dust heaps of London that he devoted seventeen years in soliciting support for a foundling hospital. Eventually a group of his supporters petitioned the King to charter a Foundling Hospital so as "to prevent the frequent murders of poor, miserable infants at their birth," and "to suppress the inhuman custom of exposing new-born infants to perish in the streets."[13]

The story of the foundling hospitals is too long and complicated to be more than sketched here. For a time they were the favorite charity of the wealthy and huge sums were expended in lavish construction and equipment. Although the London and Paris hospitals were the best known, the establishment at St. Petersburg, actively patronized by the imperial court, was undoubtedly the most amazing. Two competent western observers of the early nineteenth century agree in their enthusiastic praise. It was housed in the former palaces of Counts Razumovski and Bobrinski and occupied a huge tract in the very center of St. Petersburg. By the mid-1830s, it had 25,000 children on its rolls and was admitting 5000 newcomers annually. Since no questions were asked and the place was attractive, almost half of the newborn babies were deposited there by their parents. A dozen doctors and 600 wet-nurses were in attendance to care for the children during the first six weeks, after which they were sent to peasant nurses in the country. At the age of six (if they survived to that age) they were returned to St. Petersburg for systematic education. The program was excellent, but its aims were impossible to achieve. Despite all excellent management and professional efforts, thirty to forty percent of the children died during the first six weeks and hardly a third reached the age of six.[14]

The chronicle of the hospitals everywhere was one of devoted effort but unrelieved tragedy. The assignment was simply impossible to carry out. Everywhere they were besieged by mostly unwed mothers eager to dispose of their babies without personally or directly committing infanticide. Even so, actual child murder appears to have continued to an alarming extent, due to the fear of many girls of being identified at the hospital. Napoleon therefore decreed (January 18, 1811) that there should be hospitals in every departement of France, and that each should be equipped with a turntable (tour), so that the mother or her agent could place the child on one side, ring a bell, and have a nurse take the child by turning the table, the mother remaining unseen and unquestioned.

Although it is agreed that Napoleon's provision of tours helped to diminish the number of outright child murders, it meant that the hospitals were swamped with babies. It was impossible to find enough wet-nurses for even a short period, and most of the infants had to be shipped

6

off to the country at once. Relatively few survived the long journey over rough roads in crude carts, and those happy few generally succumbed before long due to the ignorant treatment or the intentional or unintentional neglect of their foster parents. Small wonder that Malthus referred to the asylums as "these horrible receptables," while others spoke freely of "legalized infanticide." In the years 1817-1820, the number of foundlings in charge of the Paris hospital, many of them brought in from the provinces, and, interestingly, about a third of them children of married couples, was about equal to a third of all babies born in Paris in that period. Of 4779 infants admitted in 1818, 2370 died in the first three months. It would be unjust, no doubt, to put the entire blame for this situation on the foundling hospitals. Many of the infants were diseased or half dead when they arrived, and we may well believe that prior to the nineteenth century many newborn babies would in any event have succumbed to the methods of clothing and feeding then still in vogue.[15]

By 1830, the situation in France had become desperate. In 1833 the number of babies left with the foundling hospitals reached the fantastic figure of 164,319. Authorities were all but unanimous in the opinion that the introduction of the *tours* had been disastrous, that they had, in fact, put a premium on immorality. Thereupon the *tours* were gradually abolished until by 1862 only five were left. Instead, the government embarked upon a program of outside aid to unwed mothers. Presumably the growing practice of birth control and the advances made in pediatrics also contributed to the reduction in infant mortality.[16]

The story of the foundlings in England was no less tragic than that of France. The London Foundling Hospital (opened in 1741) was intended for the reception of London children only, but the pressure for admissions soon became so great as to give rise "to the disgraceful scene of women scrambling and fighting to get to the door, that they might be of the fortunate few to reap the benefit of the Asylum."[17] Under the circumstances Parliament in 1756 provided a modest grant on condition that the hospital be open to all comers, but that at the same time asylums for exposed or deserted young children be opened in all counties, ridings, and divisions of the kingdom. Parish officers promptly took advantage of the act to empty their workhouses of infant poor and dump them on the new hospices, while others had them shipped to London. By 1760, the London Hospital was deluged with 4229 newcomers, making a total of 14,934 admissions in the preceding four years. It was impossible to cope with the situation, and "instead of being a protection to the living, the institution became, as it were, a charnel-house for the dead."[18] In 1760, Parliament reversed itself by putting an end to indiscriminate admissions and returned the care of the provincial foundlings to the parishes. The London Hospital soon became more of an orphanage than a foundling asylum. By 1850, it had only 460 children and admitted only 77 annually.[19]

The parish officers were helpless in the face of the problem. A law of 1803 specified that charges of infanticide must be tried according to the same rules of evidence as applied to murder, while yet another law required that "it must be proved that the entire body of the child has actually been born into the world in a living state, and the fact of its having breathed is not conclusive proof thereof. There must be independent circulation in the child before it can be accounted alive." In other words, to kill a child by crushing its head with a hairbrush or hammer, or cutting its throat was technically not a crime, so long as its lower extremities were still in the body of the mother.[20] Since the required evidence was all but impossible to obtain, infanticide could be committed almost with impunity. In any case, juries refused, even in the most flagrant cases, to convict the offender, holding that capital punishment was far too harsh a penalty to pay when the real culprit was usually the girl's seducer. So infanticide flourished in England. Disraeli was only the most famous of several writers who maintained that it was hardly less prevalent in England than on the banks of the Ganges.[21] Dr. Lankester, one of the coroners for Middlesex, charged that even the police seemed to think no more of finding a dead child than of finding a dead dog or cat. There were, he asserted, hundreds, nay thousands of women living in London who were guilty of having at one time or another destroyed their offspring, without having been discovered.[22]

By the mid-century the matter had become one of public scandal. One doctor in 1846 commented on "the great indifference displayed by parents and others in the lower ranks of life with regard to infant life." Women employed in the factories and fields had no choice but to leave their babies in the care of professional nurses, sometimes called "killer nurses." who made short shrift of their charges by generous doses of opiates.[23]

Worse yet was the revelation that some women enrolled their infants in Burial Clubs, paying a trifling premium until, after a decent interval, the child died of starvation, ill-usage, or poisoning. They then collected £3 to £5 by way of benefit. Cases were reported of women who had membership for their babies in ten or more clubs, reaping a rich return at the proper time.[24]

The institution of "killer nurses" or "angel-makers" eventually became known as "baby-farming." By 1860, it had become the subject of lively agitation, both in lay and in professional circles. In 1856, Dr. William B. Ryan was awarded a gold medal by the London Medical Society for his essay on "Infanticide in its Medical-Legal Relations." He followed this two years later by an address on "Child Murder in its Sanitary and Social Bearings," delivered before the Liverpool Association for the Promotion of Social Science, presided over by Lord Brougham. He eventually published his findings in a book: *Infanticide: its Law, Prevalence, Prevention and History* (London, 1862), concluding: "We cannot ignore the fact that the crime of infanticide, as well as that of criminal abortion, is widespread and on the increase."

A survey of the British press in the 1860s reveals the frequent findings of dead infants under bridges, in parks, in culverts and ditches, and even in cesspools. The *Standard* in 1862 denounced "this execrable system of wholesale murder," while the *Morning Star* in 1863 asserted that "this crime is positively becoming a national institution." In Parliament an outraged member declared that the country seemed to be reveling in "a carnival of infant slaughter, to hold every year a massacre of the Innocents."[25]

In February, 1867, Dr. Curgeven, Dr. Ryan, and a formidable delegation of medical men from the elite Harveian Society called upon the Home Secretary with a lengthy list of specific recommendations for checking the increase in infanticide, with emphasis on the need for the registration of all child nurses and for annual reports on all "baby farms." The government acted with no more than its habitual alacrity, and it was only in 1870 that it was further pressed by the Infant Protection Society founded by Dr. Curgeven and when the country was shocked by the news that in Brixton and Peckham two women were discovered to have left no fewer than sixteen infant corpses in various fairly obvious places. The women were tried for murder and one of them was convicted and executed. Parliament at long last set up a committee to study the best means "of preventing the destruction of the lives of infants put out to nurse for hire by their parents." It can hardly have come as a surprise to the members that babies commonly died through being given improper or insufficient food, opiates, drugs, etc. In many baby-farms they were in crowded rooms, with bad air, and suffered from want of cleanliness and willful neglect, resulting in diarrhea, convulsions, and wasting away. The evidence was more than enough to induce Parliament to pass in 1872 the first Infant Life Protection Act providing for compulsory registration of all houses in which more than one child under the age of one were in charge for more than twenty-four hours. Each such house was required to have a license issued by a justice of the peace, and all deaths, including still-births, which had not previously been recorded, were to be reported at once. The penalty for violation of the law was to be a fine of £5 or imprisonment for six months.[26]

Less was heard or written about infanticide in the last quarter of the nineteenth and in the twentieth century. This was certainly a reflection of the beneficial results of the abolition of the *tours* in France, Belgium, and other countries, and of the increasingly stringent regulations in

9

Britain.[27] But credit must also be given to the growing public interest in maternity and child care, and to the progress in pediatrics which contributed to the reduction of the high infant mortality rate. Finally, consideration must also be given to the adoption and spread of contraceptive practices, even among the lower classes. Nonetheless, infanticide continued and still persists, albeit on a much lower scale. The ignorance and recklessness of many young people, and initially the expense and inconvenience of contraceptive devices made the unwed mother and the illegitimate child a continuing social problem. Only since the Second World War has the contraceptive pill, the intrauterine devices, and the legalization of abortion removed all valid excuses for unwanted pregnancy or infanticide. To the extent that these problems still exist, at least in western society, they are due primarily to carelessness, ignorance, or indifference.

William L. Langer is Archibald Cary Coolidge Professor of History, Emeritus, at Harvard University. The author of several books on diplomatic history, he is also the editor of the Encyclopedia of World History *(fifth edition, 1972) and of the twenty-volume series* The Rise of Modern Europe. *In recent years he has devoted himself chiefly to the furtherance of psychohistory and to the history of the European population.*

REFERENCES

1. Asen Balikči: *The Netailik Eskimo* (New York, 1970), chap. vii. I am indebted for this reference to my friend Professor Jerrold R. Zacharias of the Massachusetts Institute of Technology.
2. According to Dr. John B. Beck: "On infanticide in its relation to Medical Jurisprudence" (in his *Researches in Medicine and Medical Jurisprudence* second, revised edition, New York 1835) 13, this Chinese custom was still prevalent in the 1830s. Léon Lallemand: *Histoire des enfants abandonées et délaissés* (Paris, 1885), 606 ff. cites efforts of provincial governors as late as the 1870s to suppress infanticide. A basic work is P. Palâtre: *L'infanticide en Chine* (Shanghai, 1878).
3. Plato: *The Republic,* Books V and VII; Aristotle: *Politics* (Jowett Translation), II, 6-7; VII, 4, 16. The Greek attitude and practice is well discussed by A. R. Hands: *Aspects of Greek and Roman Life* (Ithaca, N.Y., 1968) 66 ff. Classical thought and attitudes were systematically discussed by M. de Gouroff (Antoine J. Dugour) in his *Essai sur l'histoire des enfants trouvés* (Paris, 1829), the first and only published volume of an exhaustive study the remainder of which was eagerly awaited by his contemporaries. See also Léon Lallemand: *Histoire des enfants trouvés et délaissés* (Paris, 1885) 71 ff.; William B. Ryan: *Infanticide: its Law, Prevalence, Prevention and History* (London, 1862), Part III. Recent studies are for the most part confined to medical and legal aspects of the problem, but see A. M. Carr-Saunders: *The*

Population Problem (Oxford, 1922), 256 ff.; John T. Noonan, Jr.: *The Morality of Abortion* (Cambridge, Mass., 1970).

4. For details, based largely on inscriptions, see W. W. Tarn: *Hellenistic Civilization* (third edition, 1952, 100-102); Hands: *op. cit.*, 68 ff. I am indebted for these references to my friend and colleague Professor Mason Hammond.

5. J. P. Balsdon: *Roman Women* (London, 1962), 196-197; Jerome Carpopino: *Daily Life in Ancient Rome* (New Haven, 1940), 77; Lallemand: *op. cit.*, 38, 53.

6. Beck: *op. cit.*, 11-12; John T. Noonan, Jr.: *Contraception* (Cambridge, Mass., 1965) 85.

7. Among the Hebrews, as among many peoples, the patriarch or head of the family had absolute power of life and death over members of his family, including the right to decide the fate of new-born babies. However, fruitfulness without limit was one of the very first commandments; hence infanticide was all but unknown. (Raphael Patai: *Sex and Society in the Bible and the Middle East* (New York, 1959), 136 ff. De Gouroff: *op. cit.*, 8, 12; Beck: *op. cit.*, 8, 12; Noonan: *op. cit.*, 86; Lallemand: *op. cit.*, 21 ff.

8. The attitude of the Christian Emperors was somewhat ambivalent. Constantine never explicitly forbade infanticide and the later Emperors did nothing to abolish exposure or the sale of exposed children as slaves. Not until the legislation of Justinian (529) was the subjection of foundlings to slavery forbidden. De Gouroff: *op. cit.*, 57 ff., 73 ff.; 85 ff.; Noonan: *op. cit.*, 86 ff.: Amédé Bonde: *Etude sur l'infanticide, l'exposition et la condition des enfants exposés en droit romain* (Paris, 1883).

9. A. E. R. Boak: *Manpower Shortage and the Fall of the Roman Empire in the West* (Ann Arbor, 1955).

10. William E. H. Lecky: *A History of European Morals from Augustus to Charlemagne* (London, 1869), II, 27.

11. H. Bode: "Die Kindestötung und ihre Strafe im Nürnberg des Mittelalters" (*Archiv für Strafrecht und Strafprozess*, LXI, 1914, 430-481). Y-B. Brissaud: "L'infanticide à la fin du Moyen Age, ses motivations psychologiques et sa répression" (*Revue Historique de Droit Francais et Etranger*, L. 1972, 229-256) concludes, on the basis of French records that this penalty, while it remained on the books as a deterrent, had disappeared by the fifteenth century.

12. Richard C. Trexler: "Infanticide in Florence" (*History of Childhood Quarterly*, I, 1973, 98-115). Mrs. Baines: "On the Prevention of Excessive Infant Mortality" (*Transactions of the Manchester Statistical Society*, 1868-1869, 1-20); Alfons Fischer: *Geschichte des deutschen Gesundheitswesens* (Berlin, 1933), II, 240; Arthur Thomsen: "Bankvavningen" (*Acta Reg. Societatis Humaniorum Litterarum Lundensis*, LVIII, 1960), with German summary, pp. 225 ff.; P. E. H. Hair: "Death from Violence in Britain" (*Population Studies*, XXV, 1971, 5-24).

13. The early history of the London Foundling Hospital was recorded by Jonas Hanway, an eminent philanthropist and one of the Hospital's governors. See his *Candid Historical Account of the Hospital for the Reception of Exposed and Deserted Young Children* (London, 1759), as well as the account of Hanway's biographer, John Pugh: *Remarkable Occurrences in the Life of Jonas Hanway, Esq.* (second edition, London, 1788). John Brownlow's *The History*

and Design of the Foundling Hospital (London 1868) is a basic treatment, but may be supplemented by M. Dorothy George: *London Life in the Eighteenth Century* (London, 1925) chap. v, and by the beautifully illustrated work by R. H. Nichols and F. A. Wray: *The History of the Foundling Hospital* (London, 1935).

14. See the glowing account of the eminent English physician A. B. Granville: *St. Petersburgh* (second edition, London, 1829), II, 290 ff.; and the enthusiastic observations of the well-known German traveler Johan G. Kohl: *Petersburg in Bildern und Skizzen* (second edition, Dresden, 1846), II, 72 ff. See also Bernice Madison: "Russia's Illegitimate Children" (*Slavic Review*, XXII, 1963, 82-95

15. The swaddling clothes, which generally equalled in weight that of the baby, were frequently too tightly wound. According to Dr. William Cadogan, chief physician of the London Foundling Hospital and author of one of the earliest handbooks of child care, the newborn babes were often "crammed with cakes, sweetmeats, etc. until they foul their blood, choak their vessels, pall the appetite, and ruin every faculty of their bodies." Cadogan: *An Essay upon Nursing and the Management of Children* (London, 1748; fifth edition, 1752), a book full of sane advice. Also Dr. John Theobald: *The Young Wife's Guide to the Management of her Children* (London, 1764).

16. The initial phase of the problem is competently treated in Shelby T. McCloy: *The Humanitarian Movement in Eighteenth Century France* (Lexington, Kentucky, 1957), 21 ff. and in Roger Mercier: *L'enfant dans la société du XVIIIe siècle* (Paris, 1961), 29 ff. Brief recent accounts may be found in the present author's articles: "Europe's Initial Population Explosion" (*American Historical Review*, LXIX, 1953, 1-17), and "Checks to Population Growth, 1750-1850" (*Scientific American*, February, 1972). The literature on the subject, now mostly forgotten, was generally by competent writers. The most important were:

Baron de Gerando: *De la bienfaisance publique* (Paris, 1829);

Jean Terme and J. B. Monfalcon: *Histoire des enfants trouvés* (Paris, 1837), a work crowned by the French Academy;

Bernard Remacle: *Des hospices des enfants trouvés en Europe, et principalement en France* (Paris, 1838);

Abbé Adolphe Gaillard: *Recherches administratives, statistiques et morales sur les enfants trouvés* (Paris, 1837);

Louis Benoiston de Chateauneuf: *Considérations sur les enfants trouvés dans les principaux états de l'Europe* (Paris, 1824);

F. S. Hügel: *Die Findelhäuser und das Findelwesen in Europa* (Vienna, 1863);

Ernest Semichon: *Histoire des enfants abandonnés depuis l'Antiquité jusqu'à nos jours* (Paris, 1880);

Léon Lallemand: *Histoire des enfants abandonnés et délaissés* (Paris, 1885).

The progressive abolition of the *tours* is analyzed in detail by Adolphe Baudon: "De la suppression des tours d'enfants trouvés" (*Le Correspondant*, XIX, 1847), 674-718.

17. John Brownlow: *The History and Design of the Foundling Hospital* (London, 1868), 7.

18. Brownlow: *op. cit.*, 14.
19. Nichols and Wray: *The History of the Foundling Hospital*, 36 ff.; 47 ff., 56 ff.
20. Dr. George Greaves: "Observations on Some of the Causes of Infanticide" (*Transactions of the Manchester Statistical Society*, 1862-1867, 2-24) quoting Archbold: *Pleading and Evidence in Criminal Cases* (fourteenth edition, 529-530); William B. Ryan: *Infanticide: its Law, Prevalence, Prevention and History* (London, 1862), Part I. These provisions were not changed until enactment of the Infant Life Preservation Act of 1929, making "child destruction" a crime (Nigel Walker: *Crime and Insanity in England* (Edinburgh, 1968), chap. vii.).
21. Disraeli, in his novel *Sybil* (1846).
22. *Daily Telegraph*, September 10, 1862; January 21, 1863.
23. The most popular tranquilizer was Godfrey's Cordial, a concoction of opium, treacle, and a bit of sassafras. In Coventry 3000 children were treated to this remedy, of which ten gallons, enough for 12,000 doses, were sold weekly. In one Lincolnshire town of 6000 a single chemist sold 25½ gallons annually. (Testimony of the eminent physician Dr. John Curgeven, to a Parliamentary inquiry, 1871). See also C. Fraser Brockington: *Public Health in the Nineteenth Century* (Edinburgh, 1965) 225-226.
24. Joseph Kay: *The Social Condition and Education of the People in England and Europe* (London, 1850), I, 433 ff., who added (p. 447): "There can be no doubt, that a great part of the poorer classes of this country are sunk in such a frightful depth of hopelessness, misery and utter degradation, that even mothers forget their affection for their helpless little offspring and kill them, as a butcher does his lambs, in order to make money by the murder, and therewith lessen their pauperism and misery."
25. A thick volume of newspaper clippings in the Harvard Law School Library contains a wealth of evidence.
26. Further refinements were added by the supplementary acts of 1897, 1908 and 1932. See Dr. George F. McCleary: *The Maternity and Child Welfare Movement* (London, 1935), 84 ff.
27. Only in 1938 did Parliament enact the *Infanticide Act*, which recognized infanticide as a crime distinguished from murder. The courts have become increasingly less punitive. In 1961-1965 seventy-two women were convicted of infanticide, but 68.1% of them were put on probation and only one imprisoned for less than six months (Walker: *op. cit.*).

THE HISTORY OF ABORTION: TECHNOLOGY, MORALITY, AND LAW*

by Joseph W. Dellapenna**

Those who understand evil pardon it; those who resent it destroy it.

G. B. SHAW

After the Supreme Court decided the cases of *Roe v. Wade*[1] and *Doe v. Bolton,*[2] some believed, or at least hoped, that the basic issue of the rightness of abortions had been settled. Instead, these cases have become a major focus of controversy extending to Presidential politics,[3] proposed constitutional amendments,[4] and arguments about the propriety of federal legislation under the fourteenth amendment.[5] The conflict persists in part because vocal minorities at the polar extremes will not accept any outcome less than complete victory. This controversy could not agitate the nation if a decisive majority would reach a consensus as to the rights and wrongs of abortion.[6]

---

* This paper was submitted in partial fulfillment of the requirements for the degree of Doctor of Juridical Science in the Faculty of Law, Columbia University. The author wishes to thank the members of the dissertation committee, Profs. R. Kent Greenawalt, chairman, Marvin E. Frankel, and Harold S. H. Edgar, for their valuable assistance.

** Professor of Law, Villanova University; LL.M., Columbia University (1975); LL.M. in Public International and Comparative Law, George Washington University (1969); J.D., Detroit College of Law (1968); B.B.A., University of Michigan (1965).

1. 410 U.S. 113 (1973).
2. 410 U.S. 179 (1973).
3. Several candidates in the 1976 primaries took stands on the question, and one (Ellen McCormack—one of the few Democrats who managed to survive the entire primary season without winning even one primary) built practically her entire campaign about opposition to *Roe* and *Doe.* The controversy then entered the final elections themselves.
4. Several amendments have been proposed. For advocacy of a complete reversion to a prohibition of virtually all abortions, *see* Byrn, *The Abortion Amendments: Policy in the Light of Precedent,* 18 St. Louis U.L.J. 380 (1974) [hereinafter cited as Byrn III]; Rice, *Overruling Roe v. Wade: An Analysis of the Proposed Constitutional Amendments,* 15 B.C. Indus. & Com. L. Rev. 307 (1974).
5. *Compare* Dellapenna, *Nor Piety nor Wit: The Supreme Court on Abortion,* 6 Colum. Human Rights L. Rev. 379, 412-13 (1975) *with* Rice, *supra* note 4, at 320.
6. Indeed the very lack of consensus, making both victory and defeat clearly possible for both extreme groups, accentuates the desire to impose victory through law. Aubert, *Competition and Dissensus: Two Types of Conflict and Conflict Resolution,* 7 J. Conflict Resolution 26 (1963). Just as with the prohibition of alcohol, if virtually everyone agreed the conduct in issue were wrong, law would be unnecessary, or at least secondary, Gusfield, *Moral Passage: The Symbolic Process in Public Designations of Deviance,* 12 Social Prob. 175 (1967).

The failure of the public to arrive at a consensus on the issue of abortion no doubt has many causes. One important cause is the uncertainty produced by the continually changing medical technology relating to birth processes. These changes played a significant part in the Supreme Court's consideration of *Roe v. Wade* and *Doe v. Bolton*. For example, while the Court's conclusions[7] were phrased in terms of limiting state action to the protection of the mother's health[8] or to the protection of a viable foetus, implementation of these allowable purposes was made to depend upon highly debatable medical conclusions[9]—debatable in part precisely because the relevant medical technology changes continuously.[10]

---

7.   Roe v. Wade, 410 U.S. at 164-65.

8.   But the state may not intervene at all before the end of the first trimester, *id.* Does this preclude state action against negligently or recklessly performed abortions occurring in high volume, high pressure, high profit clinics, as are increasingly reported around the nation? *See* TIME, Nov. 27, 1978, at 60.

9.   The Court defines viability as arising "between 24 and 28 weeks" gestation, 410 U.S. at 160. There is in fact even greater variance in medical opinion as to what viability is, when it occurs, and what is its significance. *See* L. HELLMAN & J. PRITCHARD, WILLIAM'S OBSTETRICS 493 (14th ed. 1971); Brodie, *The New Biology and the Prenatal Child*, 9 J. FAM. L. 391 (1970); Byrn, *Abortion on Demand: Whose Morality*, 46 NOTRE DAME LAW. 5, 12-14 (1970) [hereinafter cited as Byrn I]; Comment, *Viability and Abortion*, 64 KY. L.J. 146 (1975).

For some other medical puzzles not fully explored by Roe v. Wade, *see* Stone, *Abortion and the Supreme Court: What Now?*, MOD. MED. Apr. 30, 1973, at 37.

The Court reexamined the concept of viability in Colautti v. Franklin, 47 U.S.L.W. 4094 (U.S. 1979), but did little to clarify its views. There were three dissenters, *id.* at 4100, who argued that the majority merely added new confusions.

10.   These developments come in many fields, and frequently with no intent to enhance viability or otherwise befog the abortion controversy. For example, a team of German doctors has apparently solved the problem of monitoring the oxygen levels of newborns, even during the birth process, intending to eliminate birth defects caused by too much or too little oxygen, Altman, *Oxygen Monitor May Reduce Birth Defects*, N.Y. Times, June 13, 1976, at 1, col. 1. Such a development must enhance viability to some extent, since improper amounts of oxygen are the most common cause of fatal disease or serious injury in "pre-viable" foeti. Increased viability without increased risk of handicaps is occurring at earlier stages of pregnancy, Schmeck, *Study Finds Premature Babies are Surviving at Earlier Ages*, N.Y. Times, Mar. 16, 1975, at 44, col. 3.

Despite such rapid technological changes, the Court seems to have accepted the role of Medical Review Board; this position became most clear with the review of the prohibition of saline amniocentesis ("salting out") as a method of abortion by Missouri. *See* Planned Parenthood v. Danforth, 428 U.S. 52, 75-79, 95-99 (1976). This approach seems to freeze law in a pattern perhaps appropriate to a given point of technological development, but a point which has been passed by the time the case has reached the Supreme Court. The role of Supreme Medical Review Board is ill suited to a body which has no institutional competence for questions of health. *See* Wellington, *Common Law Rules and Constitutional Double Standards: Some Notes on Adjudication*, 83 YALE L.J. 221, 299 (1973). The Court seemed to seek a way of avoiding the role of Medical Review Board in Colautti v. Franklin, 47 U.S.L.W. 4094 (U.S. 1979), relying on the shibboleth of "void for vagueness" to strike down a statute seeking

This Article analyzes the role of medical technology in shaping the current dissention surrounding abortion.[11] By examining this narrow question we may better understand the impact of technology on the law generally,[12] and help to clarify the specific issues presented by abortion. Understanding the evolution of the current moral debate may present a more rational approach to a controversy that has thus far been characterized more by emotion than reason.

I.   MEDICAL TECHNOLOGY IN THE ROE OPINION.

Justice Blackmun's majority opinion in *Roe v. Wade* has many references to medical "facts." The majority also expresses surprise and concern at the lack of agreement among physicians.[13] In the face

---

to limit abortions by using the standards previously announced by the Court in Roe v. Wade, allowances being made for very small verbal changes. Whether this case presages the end of these standards, or merely a requirement of more careful drafting, remains to be seen. The latter will once again put the Court back in the role of Supreme Medical Review Board.

11.   This Article does not attempt to resolve the many other problems involved in the abortion controversy. The *Roe* opinion has been widely criticized for inadequate historical analysis, Byrn, *An American Tragedy: The Supreme Court on Abortion*, 41 FORDHAM L. REV. 807 (1973) [hereinafter cited as Byrn II]; Viviera, *Roe v. Wade: Substantive Due Process and the Right of Abortion*, 25 HASTINGS L.J. 867, 872-74 (1974); for having reached the wrong decision on the moral issues, Byrn II; Byrn III, *supra* note 4; Dellapenna, *supra* note 5; Rice, *The Dred Scot Case of the Twentieth Century*, 10 HOUS. L. REV. 1054 (1973); Rice, *supra* note 4; *and* Wellington, *supra* note 9, at 297-310; and for arrogating power over a sphere properly left to the state legislatures, Roe v. Wade, 410 U.S. at 172-77 (Rehnquist, J., dissenting); Ely, *The Wages of Crying Wolf: A Comment on Roe v. Wade*, 82 YALE L.J. 920 (1973); Epstein, *Substantive Due Process by Any Other Name: The Abortion Cases*, 1973 SUP. CT. REV. 159; Loewy, *Abortive Reasons and Obscene Standards: A Comment on the Abortion and Obscenity Cases*, 52 N.C.L. REV. 223 (1973); Viviera, *supra*. The opinion is so poorly written that even its defenders begin by apologizing for the difficulties in following the reasoning of the Court, Heyman & Barzelay, *The Forest and the Trees: Roe v. Wade and Its Critics*, 53 B.U.L. REV. 765 (1973); Perry, *Abortion, the Public Morals, and the Police Power: The Ethical Function of Substantive Due Process*, 23 U.C.L.A.L. REV. 689, 690-92 (1976); Tribe, *Forward: Toward a Model of Roles in the Due Process of Life and Law*, 87 HARV. L. REV. 1, 2-5 (1973). The Court itself has twice found it necessary to beat a hasty retreat from its overbroad language in Roe v. Wade, Sendak v. Arnold, 429 U.S. 968 (1976); Connecticut v. Menillo, 423 U.S. 9 (1975).

12.   For a recent study in a technologically unrelated field *see* Hagelin, *The First Amendment Stake in New Technology: The Broadcast Cable Controversy*, 44 U. CIN. L. REV. 427 (1975). Many other scholars have found a broadly based dependency of social values on technology. *See generally* K. BOULDING, THE MEANING OF THE TWENTIETH CENTURY (1964); J. ELLUL, THE TECHNOLOGICAL SOCIETY (J. Wilkenson trans. 1964); M. HARRINGTON, THE ACCIDENTAL CENTURY (1965); M. MEAD, CULTURAL PATTERNS AND TECHNOLOGICAL CHANGE (1961); E. MESTHENE, TECHNOLOGICAL CHANGE (1970); L. MUMFORD, TECHNICS AND CIVILIZATION (1934); THEORIES OF SOCIETY (T. Parsons *et. al.* ed. 1961); Kranzburg, *Technology and Human Values*, 40 VA. Q. REV. 578 (1964).

13.   Expression of this concern begins with the second paragraph of the opinion, 410 U.S.

of disagreement among medical technicians the Court makes an effort to avoid the appearance of resolving highly uncertain issues posed by medical technology.[14] Because of the difficulties in finding a coherent thread of reasoning in the opinion, and the uncertainties surrounding the word "technology," the effect of changing medical technology in shaping the Court's opinion has escaped observation until now.[15]

The term technology can be used in several senses. Some would limit its definition to the physical tools used to do something: technology is seen as machines.[16] It is clear, however, that technology consists of more than its "hardware." Often the "software" of ideas is even more significant in its impact on society. This Article uses the definition developed by Emmanuel Mesthene to describe both tangible and intangible tools. Mesthene defines technology as "the organization of knowledge for the achievement of practical purposes."[17] Thus existing abortion technology is not solely confined to the physical tools available for the performance of operations, but also includes the knowledge about abortion and medicine generally, and the ways in which the knowledge and tools are integrated and applied at a given time. A tool may exist for some time before its applicability to a problem is discerned. Conversely, a problem and its solution may be known for some time before the tools to effect the solution are developed. Only when both the tools and the knowledge coexist in an organized way can we say a particular technology has come to be.[18]

---

at 116. *See also id.* at 131, 142-44, 159-61. This concern was emphasized even more explicitly in Colautti v. Franklin, 47 U.S.L.W. 4094, 4096-97 (U.S. 1979).

14. Perhaps the most quoted passage in the opinion is: "We need not resolve the difficult question of when life begins. When those trained in medicine, philosophy and theology are unable to arrive at any consensus, the judiciary, at this point in the development of man's knowledge, is not in a position to speculate as to the answer." 410 U.S. at 159.

15. Only Robert Byrn makes a passing comment on this question, Byrn II, *supra* note 11, at 859. *See also* Byrn I, *supra* note 9, at 25-26.

16. ELLUL, *supra* note 12, at 3-7 sees the machine as the ideal, if no longer sole kind of technology. MUMFORD, *supra* note 12, at 9-12 distinguishes five elements in technology—machines, tools, utensils, apparati, and utilities—without ever mentioning intangible technics. This is surprising as he elsewhere stresses the primacy of ideologies and social structures, *id.* at 3-6, 18-22, 31-51, 182-85, 321-33, and 364-68. For a brief discussion of the problem of isolating technology from other forms of human activity, *see* Mitcham & Mackey, *Jacques Ellul and the Technological Society,* 15 PHILOSOPHY TODAY 102, 110-17 (1971).

17. MESTHENE, *supra* note 12, at 25. Ellul would add that the knowledge is organized on a model of mechanical rationality, ELLUL, *supra* note 12, at 6-7, 79. *See also* 1 M. WEBER, ECONOMY & SOCIETY 65 (G. Roth & C. Wittich eds. 1968).

18. *Compare* MUMFORD, *supra* note 12, at 4-6, 107-09, 139-42.

The majority opinion contains many references to the existing state of technology relating to abortion. The majority does not, however, place its historical review of abortion in this or any technological or social context. Without such a context, the one-third of the opinion[19] devoted to its historical survey seems pointless.[20] If the purpose of the Court's historical survey was to show an enduring consensus favoring abortion, it clearly fails. On the other hand, if its purpose was to expose the factors making for a changing societal attitude (and thus possibly a changing constitutionality), the necessary questions were not explored. There is neither discussion of the relevant levels of technology at any stage of history, nor of any other factors which might account for changing attitudes through time. Thus there is no means of relating the views on abortion of any previous period to today. Nor does this give us any means of determining that prevalent moral attitudes regarding abortion (whatever they may be) have achieved sufficient depth or breadth so as to acquire constitutional status.[21]

One is left with several plausible explanations of the Court's decision, none of which is explicitly adopted by the Court.[22] The Court does, however, rely heavily both in its reconstruction of history, and apparently in its later attempts to analyze the conflicting interests at stake, on arguments which are directly based on changes in relevant technology. This thesis is found in the arguments developed by the National Association for the Reform of Abortion Laws

---

19.   410 U.S. at 129-47. *Cf.* Byrn II, *supra* note 11, at 814-39; Quay, *Justifiable Abortion—Medical and Legal Foundations,* 49 GEO. L.J. 173 (1960), 395 (1961), for more thorough studies of these attitudes. For a brief review of the inconsistencies apparent even on the face of the opinion, *see* Dellapenna, *supra* note 5, at 381 n.15.

20.   The problem arises in part because of the necessarily contextual process of separating true descriptions of fact from ascriptions of value. For example, H.L.A. Hart has analyzed the problem of identifying a "cause" in law as one of sorting the understandings of the term between "facts" and "policies"—which last result in determining "cause" through value decisions rather than factual inquiries, H. HART & A. HONORE, CAUSATION IN THE LAW 2-7, 83-102, 126-27, 146-48, 365 (1959). Hart analyzes the entire problem of the relevance of foreseeability and risk to recovery for tort, and the interface of moral blame and tort law in these terms, *id.* at 230-76, as well as the relevance of causation to the principles of punishment for crime, *id.* at 348-63. Hart also summarizes similar analyses in continental jurisprudence, *id.* at 412-23. *See also* A. GOULDNER, THE COMING CRISIS OF WESTERN SOCIOLOGY 270-73 (1970); Jorgensen, *Ideology and Science,* 1974 SCANDINAVIAN STUD. IN L. 89.

21.   For a general discussion of the relation of law and morality in the context of abortion, *see* Dellapenna, *supra* note 5, and the sources cited therein.

22.   *See, e.g.,* Heyman & Barzelay, *supra* note 11; Perry, *supra* note 11; Tribe, *supra* note 11.

(NARAL),[23] particularly the published work of NARAL's legal counsel, Cyril Means, Jr.[24] One critic has concluded that the Court's wholesale acceptance of the Means thesis underlies the basic error in the opinion.[25] If that is true, that error can be traced directly to the Court's failure to appreciate the effect of technology on morality. Means' thesis is flawed in just this respect.

The highly influential Means thesis is simple to state.[26] He postulates that the only purpose for the criminality of abortion was to protect the life of the mother. Laws were first enacted when abortions required surgery—and surgery was highly dangerous because of infection and shock. Abortion is now simple and safe, safer than childbirth. Means argues that laws prohibiting abortion are now unconstitutional because they limit a woman's freedom to control her own body where the reason underlying the limitation is no longer valid.[27] The Court states this logic, but neither explicitly endorses nor rejects it.[28] This reasoning seems to be explicitly rejected in the companion case of Doe v. Bolton.[29] Nonetheless, the majority does make the protection of the mother's health the major touchstone of the state's power to regulate abortion.[30] The state may not act to restrict abortion during the first trimester of pregnancy

---

23. A book by the founder and long-time chairman of NARAL, L. LADER, ABORTION (1966) [hereinafter cited as LADER I] was cited seven times by the Court.

24. Means, *The Law of New York Concerning Abortion and the Status of the Foetus, 1664-1968: A Case of Cessation of Constitutionality*, 14 N.Y.L.F. 411 (1968) [hereinafter cited as Means I], cited three times by the Court; Means, *The Phoenix of Abortional Freedom: Is a Penumbral of Ninth-Amendment Right About to Arise from the Nineteenth-Century Legislative Ashes of a Fourteenth-Century Common-Law Liberty?*, 17 N.Y. L. F. 335 (1971) [hereinafter cited as Means II], cited four times by the Court.

25. Byrn II, *supra* note 11, at 814. Byrn devotes nearly half of this article to refuting Means, *id.* at 814-39.

26. Means I, *supra* note 24, at 418, 453, 511-15; Means II, *supra* note 24, at 382-84. *See also* Lucas, *Federal Constitutional Limitations on the Enforcement and Administration of State Abortion Statutes*, 46 N.C.L. REV. 730 (1968).

27. *See, e.g.*, Baker v. Carr, 369 U.S. 186 (1962); Abie State Bank v. Bryan, 282 U.S. 765 (1931); Chastleton Corp. v. Sinclair, 264 U.S. 543 (1924); Kansas City S. Ry. v. Anderson, 233 U.S. 325 (1914); Poindexter v. Greenhow, 114 U.S. 270, 295-96 (1884); Municipal Gas Co. v. Public Serv. Comm'n, 225 N.Y. 89, 95-96, 121 N.E. 772, 774 (1919). *See also* E. BODENHEIMER, JURISPRUDENCE 366 (1962).

Generally the rule that when the reason ceases, the law ceases, has not been applied because of technological changes. For an instance where it was so applied, *see* Nashville, C. & St. L. Ry. v. Walters, 294 U.S. 405 (1935) (railroad could no longer be required to pay for changes in roadways caused by the emergence of highspeed motor traffic).

28. 410 U.S. at 151-52.

29. 410 U.S. at 190-91.

30. Roe v. Wade, 410 U.S. at 162-65.

because it is then safer for the mother to abort than to carry the baby. Even during the third trimester, when the state may protect the "potential life" of the child, the mother's health must take precedence. Thus Means' criteria seem to prevail even without an explicit endorsement of his theory.

The Court, despite its obvious approval of Means' reconstruction of history, does not explicitly adopt his thesis. If *Roe v. Wade* is the result of technological changes inducing legal changes, the question arises as to whether the Court's analysis of technology and law is valid. Of course, the accuracy of Means' reading of history is not intrinsically important. Historical considerations need not determine today's constitutionality.[31] Whether in 1791 abortion was a liberty, a misdemeanor, or a felony, hardly precludes any decision now,[32] so vastly different is our society and our knowledge of gestation and abortion.[33] Nonetheless, one must determine the proper reading of the history of abortion if one is to answer the question: In just what ways, if any, did changing technologies effect changes in Anglo-American law? Only by answering this question, which the Court failed to do, can one determine how this history should affect the constitutionality of laws passed in previous legal-technical phases. Can the answer given be enduring if it is based on ignorance of history?

II.   Four Phases of the Law Governing Abortion in Anglo-American Law

This section will review seven centuries of Anglo-American history to discover correlations between changes in abortion law and abortion technology. Even a brief examination of the changes in the law and the technology of abortion and contraception will show that their relationship is not direct and unifactoral. To properly appraise this relationship one must further explore other technological changes which have had an impact on the value cluster relating to fertility control. General theories about the relation of law (or values) to technology will be alluded to only insofar as necessary to illuminate the specific relationship here considered.[34] This section

---

31. No doubt why the Court's historical ruminations reach no particular conclusion, merely expressing theories and doubts, 410 U.S. at 132-41, 151-52.

32. Means, however, insists on the contrary proposition, Means II, *supra* note 24, at 336, 351-54, 374-75, 410.

33. Even Means acknowledged these great changes, Means I, *supra* note 24, at 438-39.

34. Further studies of general theories of law and technology are planned to complete

will consider four phases through which the Anglo-American law regarding abortion has passed and will examine various factors to explain the transitions. These four phases and their approximate dates are: I (1200-1600)—Abortion Relegated to Ecclesiastical Courts; II (1600-1803)—Jurisdiction Over Abortion Captured by the Royal Courts; III (1803-1967)—Statutory Prohibition of Abortions; and IV (1967-Present)—The Legalization of Induced Abortions. The precise dates will vary somewhat in the several jurisdictions under study.

A. Phase I (1200-1600): Abortion Relegated to Ecclesiastical Courts

Study of the law, the relevant technologies, or of any other factor in this early period is difficult. The materials are sparse, and they are in Law Latin or in Law French. There have been few attempts to uncover the limited materials bearing on abortion written during this period.[35] Nor are there any standard translations of the scant materials which have been identified. Probably in both respects Cyril Means, Jr., has done more than anyone else to make the materials available, and his translations will generally be accepted here.[36] Nonetheless, serious questions arise as to the accuracy of Means' interpretation of this data—particularly in view of his role as legal counsel for a body involved in litigation where his scholarship figured prominently.[37] Means' data ultimately does not support his conclusion as to the state of the law during the various stages.

Prior to 1600, there is very little reference to abortion in either treatises or reported common law cases. The two fourteenth century cases are inconclusive as to the state of abortion law or the impact of abortion technology on that law. In the first case,[38] a man was

---

the study of which this paper forms the first part. In these studies attention will focus on the prospective impact on law of the emerging technologies of biomedical engineering in the human birth processes.

35. *E.g.*, in the general index to W. S. HOLDSWORTH, A HISTORY OF ENGLISH LAW (1903-1973) there is no entry for either abortion or miscarriage. This book is the definitive 17-volume history of English Law, and is in part edited by others. Apparently 3 HOLDSWORTH 315 n.6, contains the only direct reference to this problem in early times.

36. *See generally* Means I and Means II, *supra* note 24. Robert Byrn, in attempting to refute Means, also relied largely on Means' translations, Byrn II, *supra* note 11, at 814-39.

37. This fact is not disclosed by Means in either article, but proudly proclaimed on the front cover lining of L. LADER, ABORTION II (1973) [hereinafter cited as LADER II]. Means does allude to his arguments in lower courts, Means II, *supra* note 24, at 352 n.37, but without mentioning NARAL.

38. The Twinslayer's Case, Y.B. Mich. 1 Edw. 3, f.23, pl.28 (1327), *translated in* Means

arrested for beating a pregnant woman. One of her twins was still-born, and the other died two days after birth. The case was ad-journed without decision because the defendant was being prose-cuted on another, unrelated charge.[39] In another case[40] the action was dismissed because of lack of proof as to whether the defendant killed the child. These cases did not clarify the substantive law of abortion. A dismissal due to problems of proof or procedure does not make the underlying conduct lawful.

The treatises are no more helpful. Bracton[41] and Fleta[42] in the thirteenth century both classified abortion as homicide if the foetus was "formed and animated," while Stanford[43] and Lambard[44] in the sixteenth century concluded that abortion was neither a felony nor a misprision (misdemeanor). These authorities, while somewhat contradictory, are not as discordant as they appear. Stanford and Lambard are discussing Pleas of the Crown, that is, prosecutions before the King's Bench.[45] In assessing the law of England before 1600 one must also examine the body of canon law. Many matters important in modern law were then dealt with by ecclesiastical rather than royal courts.[46] One can no more assess the true state of

---

II, *supra* note 24, at 337, 338 n.4.

39. Means buries this part of the report in a footnote, discussing only the failure to prosecute for abortion. Means II, *supra* note 24, at 336-38. Contrast Byrn II, *supra* note 11, at 817-19. Remember, a felon can only "hang" once, and all felonies were then capital.

40. Fitzherbert, Graunde Abridgement, tit. *Corone*, f.268, pl.263 (1st ed. 1516), (Y.B. Mich. 22 Edw. 3 (1348)), *translated in* Means II, *supra* note 24, at 339 [hereinafter cited as the *Abortionist's Case*].

41. 2 H. Bracton, The Laws and Customs of England 279 (Twiss ed. 1879), *quoted in* Roe v. Wade, 410 U.S. at 134 n.23; Byrn II, *supra* note 10, at 816; Means I, *supra* note 24, at 419; Quay, *supra* note 19, at 431.

42. Fleta, Book I, c.23 (Selden Soc. ed. 1955), *quoted in* Byrn II, *supra* note 11, at 816; Means I, *supra* note 24, at 419; Quay, *supra* note 19, at 431.

43. W. Stanford, Pleas of the Crown, Book I, c.13 (1557), *translated in* Means II, *supra* note 24, at 340-41.

44. W. Lambard, Of the Office of the Justice of the Peace 217-18 (1st ed. 1581), *quoted in* Means, *supra* note 24, at 342-43.

45. *See generally* T. Plucknett, A Concise History of the Common Law 421-23 (5th ed. 1956).

46. Among the matters covered only by church law in fourteenth century England are marriage, wills, informal contracts, slander of ordinary people, and other matters without which modern secular law would be seriously defective. *See generally* 1 Holdsworth, *supra* note 35, at 65-77, 580-632; 3 Holdsworth 296, 408-28, 534-36; 15 Holdsworth 198-208; Plucknett, *supra* note 45, at 301-05, 483-98, 657-70, 727-46; 1 F. Pollock & F. Maitland, The History of English Law Before the Time of Edward I 88-114 (2d. ed. 1898); Means II, *supra* note 24, at 350-52. Judgments from church courts would be enforced by the King's sheriff, 1 Holdsworth 614-21, 630-32; 1 Pollock & Maitland 461-63; Means I, *supra* note 24, at 439 n.64.

English law at this time by ignoring canon law than one could do so by ignoring equity, admiralty, or the Star Chamber. While there appear to have been no royal prosecutions for abortion in this period, abortion after quickening clearly was a crime under canon law.[47] Bracton and Fleta presumably meant more than this, as theirs were books of the common law, but a common law still in its formative stages. Both, like judges deciding actual cases at the time, borrowed freely from Roman and Canon law to fill *lacunae* in the still immature common law.[48] The canon law supported their statements without necessarily contradicting Stanford and Lambard, if one speaks of English law as a whole, and not merely the common law.

These sparse materials lead to the conclusion that, at least prior to 1600, royal courts did not concern themselves about abortion, but that royally-sustained ecclesiastical courts did. Leaving abortion to church courts resulted in differences which suggest that, in modern terms, abortion prior to 1600, while perhaps a criminal homicide, was not considered the equivalent of murder. Murder at common law was a felony, and like all felonies was punished by death, forfeiture, and corruption of blood.[49] Ecclesiastical courts could only punish by fine, whipping, or excommunication.[50] Since excommunication was seldom imposed for abortion[51] (at least in the later Middle Ages), one might well conclude that abortion was thought to be less serious than murder.

---

47.   There are few discovered prosecutions for abortion in English ecclesiastical courts, Means I, *supra* note 24, at 439 n.63. Nonetheless many authoritative pronouncements of the Church proclaim post-quickening abortion a crime, *id.* at 411-12. *See also* B. DICKENS, ABORTION AND THE LAW 22 (1966); G. GRISEZ, ABORTION: THE MYTHS, THE REALITIES, AND THE ARGUMENTS 137-55 (1970); 1 J. STEPHEN, HISTORY OF THE CRIMINAL LAW OF ENGLAND 54 (1883); Means II, *supra* note 24, at 346-52.

48.   *See generally* 2 HOLDSWORTH, *supra* note 35, 236-44, 267-86; PLUCKNETT, *supra* note 45, at 261-65; 1 POLLOCK & MAITLAND, *supra* note 46, at 185-88. Judges, in deciding actual cases, also relied on Canon or Roman law at this time, 2 HOLDSWORTH 202-06, 353-57; PLUCKNETT 235-36; 1 POLLOCK & MAITLAND 110-14, 167-69; 2 POLLOCK & MAITLAND 473-76. Byrn II, *supra* note 11, at 816, perhaps means no more than this when he asserts that Bracton was a canonist. Clearly Bracton was a cleric, 2 HOLDSWORTH 232-34. If Byrn means more than this, he is wrong.

49.   11 HOLDSWORTH, *supra* note 35, at 556-66. For the evolution of the concept of murder at this time, *see* 3 HOLDSWORTH 310-16; 2 POLLOCK & MAITLAND, *supra* note 46, at 476-86.

50.   1 HOLDSWORTH, *supra* note 35, at 630-32; 2 POLLOCK & MAITLAND, *supra* note 46, 516-17, 542-43. Heretics might be burned, although there was much uncertainty in England, 1 HOLDSWORTH 614-16; 2 POLLOCK & MAITLAND 543-50. Excommunication at that time may well have been a "fate worse than death."

51.   Means I, *supra* note 24, at 439 n.63.

Given the considerable sanctions imposed for conviction of a felony, the common law early developed substantial procedural safeguards for the accused.[52] This quickly evolved to a system of presentation to a jury, a formal written indictment, and trial by petit jury, with presumption of innocence,[53] and a right against self-incrimination,[54] as well as many protective pleading technicalities.[55] In contrast, church courts followed a simple, largely written, roman-style procedure,[56] the central feature of which was the *ex officio* oath.[57] By this oath, one swore to answer all questions truthfully even if the answer should be self-incriminating. Thus the greater penalty was tied to the greater procedural safeguards,[58] and presumably to the greater certainty of guilt.

The reasons the royal courts gave for dismissal of abortion cases suggest that procedural considerations were more basic than any strong doubts as to the criminality of the act of abortion should it be proven. In the *Abortionist's Case*[59] the King's Bench gave only

---

52. *See generally* 3 HOLDSWORTH, *supra* note 35, at 607-23; 9 HOLDSWORTH 222-31; PLUCKNETT, *supra* note 45, at 424-41.

53. The presumption of innocence was already embedded in the writings of Fortescue in 1470, 3 HOLDSWORTH 620.

54. Although not fully developed until after 1660, the growth of a right against self-incrimination began somewhat earlier in common law courts, 5 HOLDSWORTH, *supra* note 35, at 193-96, 419-20; 9 HOLDSWORTH 197-203; PLUCKNETT, *supra* note 45, at 437. In the sixteenth century the accused came to be considered an incompetent witness, *id.;* 9 HOLDSWORTH at 194; *i.e.,* he could not testify even if he chose, but this practice was not always followed before the eighteenth century.

55. 3 HOLDSWORTH, *supra* note 35, at 621-23; PLUCKNETT, *supra* note 45, at 433-41.

56. 12 HOLDSWORTH, *supra* note 35, at 678-80. Very similar procedures were followed in the Star Chamber and other prerogative courts. *See* 5 HOLDSWORTH 167-96 for a lengthy discussion of the Star Chamber procedure. So similar were the practices and personnel of the Star Chamber and the High Commission (created in 1549 as the ultimate ecclesiastical court), that one often had difficulty distinguishing the two, 1 HOLDSWORTH 405-505, 605-11.

57. 1 HOLDSWORTH, *supra* note 35, at 609; 9 HOLDSWORTH 199-200; PLUCKNETT, *supra* note 45, at 185. *See also* I. BRANT, THE BILL OF RIGHTS 87, 107-08, 382-83 (1965). Putting the oath to the accused may not have begun until 1583, 9 HOLDSWORTH 200, but substantially the same practice was followed much earlier by putting the oath to compurgators, witnesses swearing, without examination, to the innocence of the accused, 1 POLLOCK & MAITLAND, *supra* note 46, at 426-27. The latter form was known as well to the common law, but died out in practice much earlier than in the church courts, 1 HOLDSWORTH 305-08, although it was not formally abolished until 1833. Both in royal and in ecclesiastical courts, this "wager of law" quickly became a farce unless backed by torture, 3 HOLDSWORTH 301; 1 POLLOCK & MAITLAND 426-27. The royal courts turned to other methods of trial. The more powerful of the church courts turned to torture, 1 HOLDSWORTH 605-11. Ordinary church courts became powerless, Means I, *supra* note 24, at 439 n.63.

58. As PLUCKNETT, *supra* note 46, at 438 points out, the true import of procedural technicalities is not always easy to judge.

59. Fitzherbert, *supra* note 40, *translated in* Means II, *supra* note 24, at 339.

25

two reasons for dismissal: the lack of a baptismal name on the indictment, and the difficulty of proving whether the defendant killed the child. The first reason is spurious, as many instances occurred of convictions for murder without a baptismal name for the indictment.[60] The second reason is more substantial. The common law was very severe in its treatment of persons culpable for the death of another, especially a deliberate murder.[61] One example of the rigor of the law concerning premeditated murders was that deliberate murderers were never subject to benefit of clergy, a form of protection which in later times evolved into a means for the general mitigation of the harsh penalties prescribed for nearly all felonies.[62] Because of this rigorous treatment the royal courts became very cautious not only about technicalities of pleading, but also in demanding certain proof of causation. One manifestation of this was the rule, apparently first announced about this time, that the deceased must have died within one year and one day of the act said to cause death.[63] As to abortion, difficulty of proving that the act of the abortionist caused the death of a person is the sole basis given by the later treatises for denying that abortion was a crime cognizable by the royal courts.[64] The difficulty was twofold. First, there must be proof that the child was alive when the abortional act was committed. Second, there must be proof that the abortion act caused the death—that there was not some supervening cause for a spontaneous abortion. Both of these difficulties are technological.

At all times relevant to the period we have been discussing, knowledge of gestational processes was extremely rudimentary. Not

---

60. STANFORD, *supra* note 43; Means II, *supra* note 24, at 340-41. Although this reasoning illustrates the highly technical processes of criminal justice in England at this time, and the ways in which it might protect an admittedly guilty person, the statement ignores that the very term "murder" in England meant a fine imposed upon the district (the "hundred") precisely where no one could be found to prove the deceased's identity as an Englishman, 1 HOLDSWORTH, *supra* note 35, at 11 n.11, 15; 3 HOLDSWORTH 314-15; 1 POLLOCK & MAITLAND, *supra* note 46, at 67-68, 545; 2 POLLOCK & MAITLAND 480-86. This usage of the term was ended only in 1340, PLUCKNETT 88, 444-45, eight years before the *Abortionist's Case* was decided.

61. The term *malicia praecogitata* (malice aforethought) occurs at least as early 1330, Fitzherbert, *supra* note 40, tit. *Corone*, pl.284.

62. *See generally* 3 HOLDSWORTH, *supra* note 35, at 293-302, 315; PLUCKNETT, *supra* note 45, at 439-41, 445-46; 1 POLLOCK & MAITLAND, *supra* note 46, at 424-40.

63. Fitzherbert, *supra* note 40, tit. *Corone*, pl.163 (1330). 3 HOLDSWORTH, *supra* note 35, at 315 notes that this rule might have been grounded in earlier, but increasingly obsolete, pleading rules.

64. LAMBARD, *supra* note 44; 1 W. RUSSELL, A TREATISE ON CRIMES AND MISDEMEANORS 618 (1819); STANFORD, *supra* note 43; Byrn II, *supra* note 11, at 819; Davis, *Child-Killing in English Law*, 1 MOD. L.REV. 203 (1937); Means II, *supra* note 24, at 340-43.

until 1824 was fertilization of an ovum definitely observed. Only then was the nature of conception known.[65] The prevailing view in Western Europe envisioned a child developing from male semen implanted into a woman, or from the female ovum independently of the male. Regardless of how this was thought to occur, the prenatal child was deemed alive (animated) forty days after conception if male, and eighty days after conception if female.[66] Very little was known as to the causes of miscarriages. Similarly, techniques for inducing abortions were extremely primitive. Not surprisingly, this uncertainty made royal courts very reluctant to convict a person for murder for performing an abortion; the royal courts instead relegated the crime to the less rigorous penalties of the church courts.

Ascertaining the state of abortion technology in this early period is very difficult. Judging from the few reported cases and the early legal treatises,[67] two methods were used: a physical beating, or a "noxious potion." Both methods were effective, but both were extremely dangerous and painful for the mother. The medical literature similarly discloses only techniques which might best be described as suicidal for the mother. Research into medical means of inducing abortions must also rely on scant materials, much of which is purportedly second hand.[68] The reluctance of doctors to write

---

65. G. WILLIAMS, THE SANCTITY OF LIFE AND THE CRIMINAL LAW 227-29 (Engl. ed. 1958), for some reason gives the date as 1854. *See* text accompanying notes 268-86 *infra*.

66. J. NOONAN, CONTRACEPTION 88-91, 203-05, 216-17 (1965); WILLIAMS, *supra* note 65, 149-52; Byrn II, *supra* note 11, at 816; Means I, *supra* note 24, at 411-12; Quay, *supra* note 19, at 426-31.

67. *See* the sources cited *supra* notes 38-44, quoted in the original language and translated in Means II, *supra* note 24, at 337-43.

68. *See generally* AVICENNA, LIBRI CANONIS MEDICINE (Gerard of Cremona trans. 1595), *and* RHAZES, LIBER AD ALMANSOREM (1497). These treatises were originally in Arabic, and upon translation into Latin became the standard medical reference works in Europe. These works are discussed extensively in N. HIMES, MEDICAL HISTORY OF CONTRACEPTION 139-51 (1936), and in NOONAN, *supra* note 66, at 201, 212. Both works suggest a widespread ignorance of contraceptive practices in medieval Europe, and limited actual use of contraceptives, HIMES, *supra* at 160; NOONAN, *supra* at 222-30.

For early works in English, *see* 1 COMPLEAT HERBAL 69-71, 94-95 (G. Swindells ed. 1787) [hereinafter cited as Swindells]; M. ETMULLERUS, DESCRIPTION OF ALL DISEASES INCIDENT TO MEN, WOMEN AND CHILDREN 563 (3d ed. 1712); J. PECHEY, COMPLEAT HERBAL OF PHYSICAL PLANTS 13 (1707). While each of these comes from the Phase II period, they do show the primitiveness of abortion techniques even 350 years after the *Twinslayer's* and the *Abortionist's Cases*. ETMULLERUS is a translation of a much earlier work originally in Latin.

The caution with which abortion and contraception was discussed in these early times is shown by the usual introductory phrase "it is said" prefacing descriptions of various alleged techniques, NOONAN, *supra* note 66, at 201-07, 217. These methods often did not work, *see* text accompanying notes 74-108, *infra*. There is little variation in the abortion techniques

openly of abortion itself shows either that the procedure was virtually unknown, or that it was not approved in the society. Nor is the popular literature any more informative.[69]

Legend asserts that primitive cultures had miraculous means to induce abortions.[70] Some primitive cultures still believe they have miraculous means. Modern research[71] generally shows that these miraculous means either did not work, or worked only too well—inducing death for the mother as well as for the foetus.[72] Techniques recommended by doctors, or by folk traditions, range from the wholly ritualistic, to internal attacks on the woman's body, to violent external attacks on her body. An example of a wholly ineffective technique is one recommended by Hippocrates, who advised a young lady "to jump in the air, striking her heels against her hips.

---

described in various sources over a period of six centuries—which is not surprising given the general lack of inventiveness about abortifacients among primitives, G. DEVEREUX, A STUDY OF ABORTION IN PRIMITIVE SOCIETIES 28 (1955). Science was in its infancy throughout this period, and much of abortion practice was ritual, not remedy.

69. A single apparent reference to abortion in Chaucer's *The Parson's Tale* may in fact be a reference to contraception. *See* NOONAN, *supra* note 66, at 215-16.

70. DEVEREUX, *supra* note 68, at 40-42, 171-358. *Cf.* B. MALINOWSKI, THE SEXUAL LIFE OF SAVAGES IN NORTH-WESTERN MELANESIA 168-69 (3d ed. 1932):

They never practise coitus interruptus, and still less have any notion about chemical or mechanical preventives.

But though I am quite certain on this point, I cannot speak with the same conviction about abortion, though probably it is not practised to any large extent. I may say at once that the natives, when discussing these matters, feel neither fear nor constraint, so there can be no question of any difficulties in finding out the state of affairs because of reticence or concealment. My informants told me that a magic exists to bring about premature birth, but I was not able either to obtain instances in which it was performed, nor to find out the spells or rites made use of. Some of the herbs employed in this magic were mentioned to me, but I am certain that none of them possess any physiological properties. Abortion by mechanical means seems, in fine, the only effective method practised to check the increase of population, and there is no doubt that even this is not used on a large scale.

. . . It is amusing to find that the average white resident or visitor to the Trobriands is deeply interested in this subject, and in this subject only, of all the ethnological problems opened to him for consideration. There is a belief prevalent among the white citizens of eastern New Guinea that the Trobrianders are in possession of some mysterious and powerful means of prevention or abortion.

71. *See generally* J. BATES & E. ZAWADZKI, CRIMINAL ABORTION 14-23, 85-91 (1964); DEVEREUX, *supra* note 68; W. SUMMER, FOLKWAYS 320-27 (1907); F. TAUSSIG, ABORTION SPONTANEOUS AND INDUCED 31-45, 352-57 (1936); Breitenecker & Breitenecker, *Abortion in German-Speaking Countries of Europe*, in ABORTION AND THE LAW 206, 218-20 (D. Smith ed. 1967).

72. This pattern is so common among primitives that one study emphasized the close link between suicide and abortion as alternative responses to an unwanted pregnancy, DEVEREUX, *supra* note 68, at 28, 149-50. *See also* Fisher, *Criminal Abortion*, in ABORTION IN AMERICA 3, 6-10 (H. Rosen ed. 1954) [the collection is hereinafter cited as Rosen].

She followed his advice and after the seventh (magical number) jump promptly aborted."[73] Other apparently ineffective, but frequently mentioned techniques included ingestion of such items as stewed bananas,[74] goat dung,[75] raw eggs,[76] acid food,[77] hops,[78] lavender,[79] marjoram,[80] parsley,[81] sage,[82] "ungrateful strong smells,"[83] and wine.[84] When these methods failed, a woman could ingest substances which would cause abortions, but only if taken in dangerous quantities.[85] Oil of savin for example, is a very ancient abortifacient. Frederick Taussig reports one study which found 21 instances of attempted abortions by means of this drug, in ten of which attempts there was an abortion. Unfortunately, nine of the "successful" women died, as well as four of the "unsuccessful" ones.[86] Other such drugs included assarabacca,[87] castor oil,[88] cloves,[89] ergot,[90] helle-

---

73. TAUSSIG, *supra* note 71, at 33. How Hippocrates reconciled this advice with his Hippocratic Oath is not entirely clear, although this method did not involve giving a woman "a pessary to produce abortion," as the Oath is translated in A. CASTIGLIONI, A HISTORY OF MEDICINE 148 (2d ed. 1947). *See also* L. EDELSTEIN, THE HIPPOCRATIC OATH 3 (1943). Devereux apparently found overexertion to be a credible abortifacient, Devereux, *A Typological Study of Abortion in 350 Primitive, Ancient, and Pre-Industrial Societies,* in Rosen, *supra* note 72, at 97, 116, 123-24. *Compare* Devereux *and* Breitenecker, *supra* note 71, at 219.

DEVEREUX, *supra* note 68, at 40-42, 171-358, lists other magical or ritualistic techniques. In the primitive mind most or all techniques might be conceived of as magical.

74. BATES & ZAWADZKI, *supra* note 71, at 22; DEVEREUX, *supra* note 68, at 297; TAUSSIG, *supra* note 71, at 43-44.

75. DEVEREUX, *supra* note 68, at 38, 279.

76. *Id.* at 38, 249.

77. ETMULLERUS, *supra* note 68, at 563; TAUSSIG, *supra* note 71, at 33.

78. V. SCULLY, A TREASURY OF AMERICAN INDIAN HERBS 120 (1971).

79. HIMES, *supra* note 68, at 170-71.

80. *Id.*

81. *Id.* at 13 n.47, 170; TAUSSIG, *supra* note 71, at 32. Parsley is a far more versatile herb than most people realize since it has been recommended for preventing as well as inducing abortion, *id.,* while it was also considered an aphrodisiac and contraceptive, NOONAN, *supra* note 66, at 208.

82. 1 Swindells *supra* note 68, at 94-95. This is recommended for helping conception and preventing miscarriages, as well as to induce abortions.

83. ETMULLERUS, *supra* note 68, at 563.

84. *Id.* Other herbs could be added to this list without changing its import. BATES & ZAWADZKI, *supra* note 71, at 16, report that the Greeks used enough different drugs to fill twelve pages—all ineffective.

85. *See generally* DEVEREUX, *supra* note 68, at 42-43; NOONAN, *supra* note 66, at 211; Breitenecker, *supra* note 71, at 218-19.

86. Taussig, *supra* note 71, at 353.

87. PECHEY, supra note 68, at 13 ("purge violently, upwards and downwards"); 1 Swindells, *supra* note 60, at 69-71 ("they weaken nature, nor shall never advise them to be used, unless upon urgent necessity.")

88. BATES & ZAWADZKI, *supra* note 71, at 89.

bore,[91] nutmeg,[92] quinine,[93] rue,[94] saffron,[95] sassafras,[96] tansy tea,[97] thyme,[98] and yarrow.[99] If none of these induced the abortion, one might ingest a variety of substances which were highly toxic even in small quantities.[100] These included aloes,[101] apiole,[102] arsenic,[103] cantharides,[104] cedar,[105] snake venom,[106] and a variety of metal salts.[107] Not all of these potions were available in England prior to the nineteenth century. These remedies do include those reported by the medical texts in use in England during this time. Assuming other potions were known to English folk medicine than those reported in the texts, there is no reason to believe that these would be any more effective or any less dangerous. Frequently even these highly toxic potions were not sufficient to bring on the abortion. In that case, those involved could resort to various manoeuvers of, or on, the body of the mother:[108] pressing or sqeezing the abdomen with

---

89. *Id.*

90. *Id.* at 88; TAUSSIG, *supra* note 71, at 353. Ergot is apparently ineffective even in large doses.

91. BATES & ZAWADZKI, *supra* note 71, at 89; SCULLY, *supra* note 78, at 120. Hellebore could produce sterility for life.

92. BATES & ZAWADZKI, *supra* note 71, at 89; SCULLY, *supra* note 78, at 120.

93. BATES & ZAWADZKI, *supra* note 71, at 88-89; TAUSSIG, *supra* note 71, at 353; Breitenecker, *supra* note 71, at 218.

94. BATES & ZAWADSKI, *supra* note 71, at 89.

95. *Id.*

96. *Id.*

97. TAUSSIG, *supra* note 71, at 353. Although quite popular, tansy is rather ineffective, and quite deadly. *See* C. MILLSPAUGH, AMERICAN MEDICINAL PLANTS pl.86 (1887).

98. BATES & ZAWADZKI, *supra* note 71, at 89; HIMES, *supra* note 68, at 170.

99. Which SCULLY, *supra* note 78, at 120, tells us is "not as dangerous as nutmeg."

100. BATES & ZAWADZKI, *supra* note 71, at 88 point out that much knowledge of modern poisons originated in the search for abortifacients.

101. *Id.* at 89; TAUSSIG, *supra* note 71, at 353.

102. A derivative of parsley capable of inducing nerve paralysis, TAUSSIG, *supra* note 71, at 353-54, but possibly ineffective for abortions, HIMES, *supra* note 68, at 13 n.47, at 170.

103. TAUSSIG, *supra* note 71, at 354.

104. Also known as "Spanish fly," BATES & ZAWADZKI, *supra* note 71, at 89; TAUSSIG, *supra* note 71, at 354.

105. *Juniperus Virginiana*, MILLSPAUGH, *supra* note 97, at pl. 166; Scully, *supra* note 78, at 120.

106. BATES & ZAWADZKI, *supra* note 71, at 90; TAUSSIG, *supra* note 71, at 355.

107. Including copper, lead, mercury, and phosphorous, BATES & ZAWADZKI, *supra* note 71, at 89-90; TAUSSIG, *supra* note 71, at 354-55. Mercury may have been used before 2700 B.C., BATES & ZAWADZKI 15; TAUSSIG 31. Copper and mercury are occasionally effective, but produce the abortion indirectly by poisoning the kidneys and intestines. Lead poisoning can induce death or blindness, as well as abortions. Phosphorous is somewhat effective, but always produces jaundice (and occasionally death) through liver poisoning.

108. BATES & ZAWADZKI, *supra* note 71, at 87-88; DEVEREUX, *supra* note 68, at 30-35;

hands, heavy objects, or sharp instruments; twisting the uterus through the abdominal wall; or striking the belly with fists, stones, or other objects, often until there was vaginal bleeding. Objects may be inserted into the vagina, although in medieval England this appears to have been limited to pessaries, rather than actual intrusion through the cervix into the uterus.[109] Not surprisingly such techniques usually injured the mother as seriously as the foetus.[110]

While no one can claim complete knowledge of the various techniques used in England folk medicine to attempt abortion prior to 1600, there is evidence, reinforced by anthropological studies of abortion techniques in other primitive medical systems, which allows one to infer a fairly clear picture of what a woman seeking an abortion would go through. First she would be asked to do some simple body manoeuvers (jumping, twirling, etc.), perhaps accompanied by ingestion of a harmless potion. When these failed, she might take increasingly more dangerous potions.[111] If these methods failed, as a final resort someone could strike blows upon her belly to kill the child.[112] The question arises, when and why would a woman undertake such actions? A woman would voluntarily persist in such a course only if she were willing to persist until success or

---

TAUSSIG, *supra* note 71, at 41-45, 355. DEVEREUX 171-358 quotes the existing anthropological literature for descriptions of abortion techniques for almost every ethnic group then studied (over 600). Bodily manoeuvers appear to be by far the most common method, if only because these might actually work if extreme enough. Simpler manoeuvers, like that recommended by Hippocrates, might be attempted, but these seldom succeeded. *See* note 73 *supra*.

109.   Pessaries are vaginal suppositories, in this case including drugs believed to induce abortions. Without intrusion through the cervix, where it is the intrusion itself which may induce the abortion, regardless of the drug, pessaries do not seem to have been effective. DEVEREUX, *supra* note 68, at 37; TAUSSIG, *supra* note 71, at 355-56. Pessaries were sufficiently dangerous for Hippocrates explicitly to condemn their use in his famous Oath, CASTIGLIONE, *supra* note 73. As to the effectiveness and dangerousness of intrusion into the uterus or the cervix, *see* BATES & ZAWADZKI, *supra* note 71, at 21-22, 85-87; DEVEREUX, *supra* note 68, at 36, 42-43; TAUSSIG, *supra* note 71, at 43, 355; Breitenecker, *supra* note 71, at 219-20.

110.   DEVEREUX, *supra* note 68, at 42-43. Note that in both reported cases from England in Phase I, the mother did not die, notes 38 & 40 *supra*, thereby presenting the problem of the legality of abortion squarely to the courts.

111.   The progression of remedies from harmless and ineffective to dangerous and deadly is common among primitives. BATES & ZAWADZKI, *supra* note 71, at 16-17. The pattern persisted well into the twentieth century in the United States, R. PALMER & S. GREENBERG, FACTS AND FRAUD IN WOMEN'S HYGIENE 158-75 (1936).

112.   Although striking blows upon the mother's abdomen appears in English sources as an abortion technique as early as 1327 in the *Twinslayer's Case*, *supra* note 38, and pessaries are mentioned in medical texts even earlier (see the sources cited in note 68 *supra*), there is no mention of inserting instruments into the cervix or the uterus in any English source before 1600. *Cf.* GRISEZ, *supra* note 47, at 149, reaching a similar conclusion about Roman times.

death, as generally one could succeed only through death,[113] or at least severe crippling.[114] The only other explanation for resort to such drastic methods was that it was done against the woman's will—which clearly would be a capital felony if she died, regardless of whether the foetus aborted. If the woman, or her assailant, desisted without procuring her death or the abortion, no royal crime at all was committed,[115] for at this time to attempt a felony was not a crime[116] except before ecclesiastical courts.[117]

Means infers that the common law, and even canon law,[118] did not really condemn abortion. Why else, he asks, were there so few prosecutions involving abortions before 1600? Even a brief examination of the techniques of abortion then in use leads one to ask "why so many prosecutions?," not "why so few?"[119] It is no wonder that royal judges were perplexed when confronted by the crime. The ancient texts illustrate this perplexity by their division as to whether a mother could appeal a trespass for an assault which killed

---

113. *See* note 72 *supra*. *Cf.* BATES & ZAWADZKI, *supra* note 71, at 16-17.

114. Again and again the researchers observe that non-fatal primitive techniques could only succeed on a woman already highly prone to miscarry, BATES & ZAWADZKI, *supra* note 71, at 85-91; TAUSSIG, *supra* note 71, at 35, 352-55. Confusion can easily occur if the woman is not actually pregnant, BATES & ZAWADZKI 90; TAUSSIG 357; or if the woman aborts spontaneously, as is probably true when abortion is "achieved" by less destructive means (or even by quite destructive means according to BATES & ZAWADZKI 85). *See also* Breitenecker, *supra* note 71, at 218-20.

115. Mayhem originally encompassed only injuries which interfered with a man's ability to fight, and in any event it had by the fourteenth century fallen out of the list of felonies, 3 HOLDSWORTH, *supra* note 35, at 317, 2 POLLOCK & MAITLAND, *supra* note 46, at 487-89, at least if one did not resort to an "appeal"—meaning trial by battle, PLUCKNETT, *supra* note 45, at 443, 456. As appeals were obsolete in practice, until late in the seventeenth century the most violent crimes against the person apparently were treated as misdemeanors punishable by fine and imprisonment, 3 STEPHEN, *supra* note 47, at 109.

116. 2 HOLDSWORTH, *supra* note 35, at 452; PLUCKNETT, *supra* note 45, at 453-54. Attempted murder was not made a felony until 1861, Offences Against the Person Act, 1861, 24 & 25 Vict., c.100, § 11; 3 HOLDSWORTH 315.

117. 2 HOLDSWORTH, *supra* note 35, at 258-59. The policy of punishing attempts was taken over by the Star Chamber in the sixteenth century. 4 HOLDSWORTH 273; 5 HOLDSWORTH 201; PLUCKNETT, *supra* note 45, at 459. In part this was because of the close affinity of church courts and the Star Chamber, 1 HOLDSWORTH 608-09, and also because the ex officio oath allowed both courts to probe intent. Later common law courts absorbed the rule as to the criminality of attempts, treating them as misdemeanors, 8 HOLDSWORTH 434; 11 HOLDSWORTH 532. *See also* 2 STEPHEN, *supra* note 47, at 223-24.

118. Means I, *supra* note 24, at 439 n.63.

119. Infanticide has always been preferred when the abortion technology is so primitive, Quay, *supra* note 21, at 406-10. One evidence of the prevalence of the problem of infanticide was the need to prohibit concealing the death of a bastard infant by treating concealment as murder, An Act to Prevent the Destroying and Murdering of Bastard Children, 21 Jac. 1, c. 27 (1623); 9 HOLDSWORTH, *supra* note 35, at 142. *See* text accompanying notes 232-51 *infra*.

her child. These authorities do not cite cases and ignore the fact that the action for trespass was in fact a major device for eliminating the appeal altogether.[120] When abortion was the problem, perplexity arose in two contexts. Given the very limited technology (both information and tools) available to perform abortions, the judges could not determine that the child was alive before the abortional act, or that the act caused the misdelivery. Even if the courts were willing to punish the criminal intent without the accomplished act, royal courts had no effective means of probing for this intent. Just as with other attempted but incomplete crimes, the royal courts preferred to leave the matter in the hands of the still effective ecclesiastical courts. There the claims of conscience through compurgation and *ex officio* oaths would allow access to the necessary evidence, while the lesser temporal penalties of these courts would offer some protection in case of mistaken judgment. If other, more easily proven crimes occurred (such as the killing of the mother), it would be enough if the felon hanged for that. Even this last alternative seems rare. Given the dangers, there probably were not many abortions in England before 1600.

These problems of proof beset ecclesiastical courts as well as royal courts. Since the moment of conception was not ascertainable, how could one measure 40 or 80 days? The ecclesiastical courts in England came to adopt "quickening" as the criteria separating homicidal abortions from others.[121] Quickening is the intrauterine movement of a child, felt and perceived as such by the mother.[122] This is a highly subjective test. The time of quickening varies with the vigor of the child, the sensitivity of the mother, and her awareness of the meaning of what she feels. Thus, quickening occurs at different times for different pregnancies in different women, or for

---

120. These authorities are discussed in Dietrich v. Inhabitants of Northampton, 138 Mass. 14 (1884). As to the availability of appeal for trespass generally (since trespass was an important device for eliminating the appeal altogether), *see* 2 HOLDSWORTH, *supra* note 35, at 360-61; PLUCKNETT, *supra* note 45, at 369-70; 2 POLLOCK & MAITLAND, *supra* note 46, at 526-27, 617-18. Means II, *supra* note 24, at 344 n.18, says that these authorities are "cases" which they certainly are not.

121. Means I, *supra* note 24, at 439 n.64. Ensoulment was also considered to be shown by two principals: knowledge and movement, WILLIAMS, *supra* note 65, at 151. For a discussion of the religious background of the development, *see* GRISEZ, *supra* note 47, at 130-55. By 1211 at the latest, church law had classified abortion of the "formed" foetus as homicide, and abortion of an "unformed" foetus as a serious sin but less than homicide, *id.* at 152-53. *See generally* R. HUSER, THE CRIME OF ABORTION IN CANON LAW 16-36 (1942).

122. BLACK'S LAW DICTIONARY 1415 (4th ed. 1951). *See also* Roe v. Wade, 419 U.S. at 160; Brodie, *supra* note 9; Byrn I, *supra* note 9, at 9-12.

different pregnancies in the same woman. Quickening may occur between the twelfth and twentieth weeks, though usually towards the end of that period.[123] This can only be established by the testimony of the mother—which would be unavailable or of little probative value at common law if she had been a party to the crime.[124] In church courts the *ex officio* oath could be used to coerce her testimony on the point. If the oath were taken seriously this evidence would be procured. The choice of quickening as the decisive point was itself dictated by the then available medical technology. Lawmakers apparently believed that the foetus was a separate life entitled to protection from the fortieth day after conception,[125] but the existing technology only permitted protection after the child had been felt to quicken. The problem and its supposed solution were known, but the technical means to accomplish the solution did not exist. The church courts penalized the action where existing medical technology permitted ascertainment of the essential facts.

Even after quickening, one could not be sure that the child was alive at the time of the abortional act, unless the child moved at the time of the act itself, or afterwards before the onset of the pain accompanying the abortion which would override maternal perceptions of foetal movement. Given the then primitive knowledge about miscarriages, one could seldom rule out the possibility of a supervening spontaneous abortion. Again, the existing technology (or, perhaps more properly, the lack of it) precluded the sort of certainty which was felt necessary to justify execution. This lack of certainty did not preclude the milder penalties of the church courts, which once again undertook to fill gaps in the common law.

Thus it appears that Means' inference that abortion was not thought to be either serious or criminal in this period is based on

---

123.   H. M. I. LILEY, MODERN MOTHERHOOD 37-38 (rev. ed. 1969); Means I, *supra* note 24, at 412; Means II, *supra* note 24, at 380.

In Roe v. Wade the Court characterized quickening as occurring between the 16th and the 18th weeks, 410 U.S. at 132. Byrn II, *supra* note 11, at 823, asserts that it may occur as early as the eighth week, but the authorities he cites discuss only foetal movement, not maternal perception.

124.   At least the mother would not be permitted to testify after defendants became incompetent to testify in royal courts. *See* note 54 *supra*. Even if unsworn testimony were accepted, such testimony was likely to be less reliable in an age of greater faith in the efficacy of oaths.

125.   Apparently the fortieth day was chosen to make certain that no lives were taken as one could not then determine before birth if the child were male or female, Means I, *supra* note 24, at 412; NOONAN, *supra* note 66, at 217.

faulty reasoning. Royal courts did not confront the problem primarily because abortions were rare, and when they did occur, the abortion was usually forced on an unwilling woman. Abortionists could
die just as easily for the crime against the woman as against the
unborn child, and the former crime was far easier to prove, given
the primitive state of the medical and legal technology available to
royal courts. Problems of proof and procedure were not so severe in
ecclesiastical courts, but even there cases involving only abortion
were few. Abortions simply were seldom done in this period in England.

B. Phase II (1600-1803): Jurisdiction Over Abortions Captured by the Royal Courts

After centuries of apparent indifference to abortion, early in the
seventeenth century the common law attitude towards abortion
changed. The leading commentators came to denounce abortion
after quickening as a great misdemeanor.[126] Justices of the Queen's
Bench in *Sims' Case*[127] announced a like opinion, although it was
unnecessary to decide the case before them. Before the end of the
seventeenth century this result would be reached in a case which
more clearly presented the issue of the legality of abortion.[128] In
reality, this "new approach" was not altogether new to England.
Rather, this represented a transfer of jurisdiction and penalties
which the common law had heretofore been content to leave to the
canon law. This section will first examine the nature and scope of
this restructuring of the law of abortion in England in the seventeenth century. We will then turn to an examination of the reasons
for the change. Finally, we will trace the evolution of the seventeenth century's response down to the next major shift in legal direction early in the nineteenth century.

Sims' Case was decided in 1601. The child involved was born
alive, but clearly showed the bruises left from an unsuccessful attempt to induce abortion by physical assault on the mother. The
child died. Rather than seeking a criminal indictment, the bereaved
parents brought an action in trespass. Only four of the eight justices

---

126. 1 W. BLACKSTONE, COMMENTARIES 129-30 (1765); 4 W. BLACKSTONE, COMMENTARIES
198 (1769); E. COKE, THIRD INSTITUTE 50-51 (1644); M. HALE, HISTORY OF THE PLEAS OF THE
CROWN 433 (1736); W. HAWKINS, TREATISE OF THE PLEAS OF THE CROWN 80 (1716); Byrn II, *supra*
note 11, at 819-24; Means II, *supra* note 24, at 343-51.
127. 75 Eng. Rep. 1075 (K.B. 1601), *quoted in full in* Means II, *supra* note 24, at 343.
128. HALE, *supra* note 126, at 429-30.

then on the Queen's Bench were present. Only two of them declared themselves. Both did announce that when the child is born alive showing the mark of the attack, and subsequently dies, it would be murder, for then it would be possible to know if the assault were the cause of death.

The precedential effect of such a decision is unclear.[129] In 1601 such a pronouncement by a clear majority of the Bench probably would have been more than mere dictum. Trespass was originally a criminal writ with civil damages tacked on in order to enlist private enforcement in place of the nonexistent police.[130] In early days double and even treble damages would be given as an incentive to private persons to enforce the King's peace.[131] For a long time loss of an action of trespass left the defendant open to minor punishments without further proceedings.[132] The adverse judgment could serve in place of a presentment and indictment.[133] The practice of indicting minor trespasses for trial before local justices of the peace emerged in the later middle ages.[134] Modern common law misdemeanors evolved from these indictable trespasses.[135] When Parliament extended the criminal law, it did so by creating new indictable trespasses.[136] This process of creating new indictable trespasses continued well into the reign of Elizabeth I.[137] The term misdemeanor began to emerge during the sixteenth century in order to make more clear the distinction between criminal and civil proceedings as both might be denominated a trespass. While these concepts were grow-

---

129.   Means II, *supra* note 24, at 343-44 argues that it is mere dictum and should carry no weight at all.

130.   2 HOLDSWORTH, *supra* note 35, at 364-65, 453-54; PLUCKNETT, *supra* note 45, at 366-67, 456-59, 465-67; 2 POLLOCK & MAITLAND, *supra* note 46, at 165-66, 510-11, 523-26, 570-71, 617-18.

131.   2 HOLDSWORTH, *supra* note 35, at 453; 2 POLLOCK & MAITLAND, *supra* note 46, at 520-21. Damages law in general seems to have evolved from these beginnings, *id.* at 520-24.

132.   2 HOLDSWORTH, *supra* note 35, at 364-65; PLUCKNETT, *supra* note 45, at 455; 2 POLLOCK & MAITLAND, *supra* note 46, at 511-17. Criminal penalties might be given in any civil case before the royal courts, since modern distinctions between crime and tort were unknown, *id.* at 517-18. Trespass soon became the usual method for combining the two forms of penalty.

133.   3 HOLDSWORTH, *supra* note 35, at 609-11.

134.   PLUCKNETT, *supra* note 45, at 456-58. Earlier studies of English legal history missed the functions of local justices in this regard, and concluded that there was a substantial gap in the criminal law as the civil aspects of suit for trespass came to predominate, 3 HOLDSWORTH, *supra* note 35, at 317-18, 370; 2 POLLOCK & MAITLAND, *supra* note 46, at 520-21.

135.   2 HOLDSWORTH, *supra* note 35, at 365; 3 HOLDSWORTH 318; 4 HOLDSWORTH 512-14; PLUCKNETT, *supra* note 45, at 456-58; 2 POLLOCK & MAITLAND, *supra* note 46, at 510-11.

136.   4 HOLDSWORTH, *supra* note 35, at 512-15.

137.   35 Eliz. 1 c.6 (1593).

ing apart, they were by no means distinct, as is shown by continuing uncertainty as to the meaning of the terms "misdemeanor," "misprision," and "trespass" well into the seventeenth century.[138] At least the Star Chamber mixed civil and lesser criminal remedies down to its abolition in 1641.[139] Apparently as late as 1601, a pronouncement by a clear majority of the court would have been binding precedent both for criminal and for civil aspects of trespass. One is still left to ponder the weight of a statement by only two of the eight justices then on the court, with the apparent acquiescence of the two additional justices then present. Even the final outcome of the case is not clear.[140] Nevertheless, Coke and other respected authorities saw the case[141] as establishing that abortion after quickening was a "great misprision," and murder if the child was born alive and thereafter died.

Sir Edward Coke played a pivotal role in transforming the law in the royal courts concerning abortion. He was Attorney-General at the time of *Sim's Case* and argued before the justices that Sims was guilty of murder.[142] The justices who thereafter spoke echoed his sentiments. Possibly Coke's later report of the principle of the case[143] merely reflected unreported views of the rest of the Bench. Others have suggested that Coke sought to represent his views as law even though they were not adopted—either through faulty memory or deliberate misstatements.[144] In any event, *Sims' Case* and the ensu-

---

138. "Misprision" had originally meant the concealment of treason or a felony, but by 1600 had acquired an extended but vague meaning, 3 HOLDSWORTH, *supra* note 35, at 389 n.1; 8 HOLDSWORTH, *supra* note 35, at 322-24.

We have already seen the confused use of the terms "misdemeanor," which was just gaining currency and "trespass," which was just losing currency in the criminal law.

139. 1 HOLDSWORTH, *supra* note 35, at 503-08; 3 HOLDSWORTH 407, 502-03; 5 HOLDSWORTH 137, 212-14; PLUCKNETT, *supra* note 45, at 459.

140. The opinion ends with the statement that "the batteror shal be arraigned of murder . . . ." which perhaps indicates which further proceedings followed, but there appears to be no record of further proceedings, 75 Eng. Rep. at 1076. *See* text accompanying notes 132-35 *supra*.

141. *See* the authorities cited at note 126 *supra*.

142. That the Attorney-General argued before the bench in itself suggests the Crown's interest in the criminal aspects of the case. *See generally* 6 HOLDSWORTH, *supra* note 35, at 457-72; PLUCKNETT, *supra* note 45, at 228-30.

143. COKE, *supra* note 126, at 50-51, does not actually cite *Sims' Case*, as the report was not published until nine years after the THIRD INSTITUTE (itself published in 1644—10 years after Coke died). The later authorities generally cited COKE rather than the report of the case. The delay in the publication of Coke's *Institutes* was caused by the opposition of King Charles, which was effective until the English Civil War, 5 HOLDSWORTH, *supra* note 35, at 454-55.

144. The Court in Roe v. Wade seems inclined toward this view, although not entirely

ing statements make it clear that the common law lawyers came to see abortion as felonious homicide if the child was born alive, and thereafter died—if the death were clearly caused by the abortion. Only Matthew Hale[145] partially rejects this development, describing an abortion after quickening when the child is born alive and dies as a great crime, but no homicide. What accounts for the broadening of the rule concerning abortions?

The most important cause of this development was the English Reformation and the emergence of the increasingly secular modern nation state. Not the least of the changes which this secularization brought about—indeed a central technique of establishing royal, and hence national, supremacy—was the replacement of ecclesiastical jurisdiction by jurisdiction in the courts of the common law. At the same time, as part of essentially the same process, the Crown itself was subjugated through attacks on the courts exercising the royal "prerogative" to the detriment of the common law courts.[146] The various courts which functioned in England during the Middle Ages had always experienced an uneasy coexistence, with frequent conflicts over jurisdiction.[147] During the seventeenth century the powers of the "prerogative" and ecclesiastical courts,[148] excepting

---

committed to it, 410 U.S. at 134-36. Means develops the theory of a deliberate misstatement of the law at length in a rather demogogic fashion, referring to it as an "outrageous attempt," or a "masterpiece of perversion." Means sees Coke's interpretation as dependent on isolated precedents, while he describes the authorities on the other side as numerous and well-established, Means II, *supra* note 24, at 343-48, 351-52. In fact, the authorities for both propositions are ambiguous and sparse—usually they are the same authorities.

145. HALE, *supra* note 126, at 433; Means II, *supra* note 24, at 349-50. *Cf.* M. DALTON, THE COUNTRY JUSTICE 213 (1618) (this last work is of little importance as the report of *Sims' Case* was not published until 1653, Means II, *supra* note 24, at 343).

146. So central was this conflict between the older royal courts and the newer prerogative courts, as well as the ecclesiastical courts, that Book IV in HOLDSWORTH is titled *The Common Law And Its Rivals.* This "Book" covers the years 1485-1700, and comprises more than one-third of the entire 17 volumes (all of volumes 4 through 9). During this period the public law of England took its modern form, and so did the basic notions of English private law. The crucible in which these forms were created was this contest for supremacy between legal systems.

147. Much of the early history of the common law also consists of devices one court invented to steal jurisdiction from another court. For early instances of intercourt rivalry, *see* 1 HOLDSWORTH, *supra* note 35, at 218-31; 2 HOLDSWORTH 251-52, 266-67, 304-07, 457-59; 5 HOLDSWORTH 412-23; 9 HOLDSWORTH 250; 4 PLUCKNETT, *supra* note 45, at 157-63, 169-73.

148. These courts existed outside the common law system to exercise directly the prerogative of the King to do justice. They were created when the common law was inadequate. Included were the Court of the Chancery, the Council (Star Chamber), the various ecclesiastical courts, the Court of Admiralty, and the Court of the Constable and the Marshall. *See generally* 1 HOLDSWORTH, *supra* note 35, at 395-525, 544-632; PLUCKNETT, *supra* note 45, at

Chancery, were dramatically captured by the common law courts—especially by the King's Bench. The struggles of these various courts were too intertwined to be wholly separated, but two particular effects of the Reformation on church courts deserve special mention:[149] the declining efficiency of church courts, and the special attraction of these courts as targets for enemies of the existing order in the state (both religious and royalist).

The lengthy controversies over orthodoxy in England led to confusion and disrespect for the established church and its ecclesiastical courts. This decline of respect led to increasing difficulty in securing convictions. An accused need only swear his innocence. The oath was taken less seriously, especially without torture to back it up. Thus there appear to have been no prosecutions before the church courts for abortion after the reign of Henry VIII, while the few reported between 1475 and Henry's death all resulted in acquittal based on the defendant's oath.[150] At the same time, as church courts became increasingly ineffective, and thus vulnerable to attacks, the growing dissension within the English Protestants (between Episcopalians, Presbyterians, Independents, and other smaller groups) made the church courts foci of attack regardless of their effectiveness.[151] At this time, control of the pulpit was particularly important as the pulpit was the only organized means of influencing a still illiterate population. Control of the pulpit could mean as much as control of mass media today.[152] Since the Tudor settle-

---

48-67, 191-98; F. WORMUTH, THE ROYAL PREROGATIVE (1939). The Star Chamber and some of the ecclesiastical courts were permanently abolished in 1641. The Court of the Constable and the Marshall largely ceased to function after 1689, although one case is reported as late as 1737, 1 HOLDSWORTH 579. The court of Admiralty existed until it merged with the High Court of Justice in 1875. There still is an Admiralty Division for this court, 1 HOLDSWORTH 638-642. Admiralty's jurisdiction was, however, severely curtailed during the sixteenth to nineteenth centuries. The court, for example, retained jurisdiction only over contracts which were both made outside the realm and to be fully performed outside the realm, G. GILMORE & C. BLACK, THE LAW OF ADMIRALTY 8-11 (2d ed. 1975); 1 HOLDSWORTH 544-59, 568-73; PLUCKNETT 657-70; D. ROBERTSON, ADMIRALTY AND FEDERALISM 35-64 (1970). Surviving ecclesiastical courts were also greatly limited in their authority. Only Chancery came through relatively unscathed.

149. *See generally* 1 HOLDSWORTH, *supra* note 35, at 588-98; 4 HOLDSWORTH 3-54, 215-17, 232, 494-510; 5 HOLDSWORTH 219-20, 273-94; PLUCKNETT, *supra* note 45, at 39-47, for discussions of the impact of the Reformation on English law, especially on church courts in England. *See also* H. TREVOR-ROPER, RELIGION, THE REFORMATION AND SOCIAL CHANGE (1967).

150. Means I, *supra* note 24, at 439 n.63; Means II, *supra* note 24, at 346-47; *compare* 6 HOLDSWORTH, *supra* note 35, at 196-203.

151. *See generally* 6 HOLDSWORTH, *supra* note 35, at 122-38.

152. 9 S. GARDINER, HISTORY OF ENGLAND 282 (1884); 6 HOLDSWORTH, *supra* note 35, at 135-36.

ment had left control of the church in royal hands, these religious issues became inextricably combined with political and economic issues of the day. Religion became the precipitating cause of the Great Rebellion (also known as the Puritan Revolution).[153]

Coke, first as Chief Justice,[154] then as leader of the parliamentary opposition to the King,[155] and finally as intellectual mentor to the Roundheads through his published *Institutes*, was the most influential individual in the process of displacing prerogative courts by the common law courts. Coke, as Chief Justice, began the successful use of writs of prohibition against rival courts.[156] These writs succeeded, however, only when the common law courts were prepared to assert jurisdiction over the controversies prohibited in the rival courts.[157] Coke's parliamentary influence was used to make certain that the opposition to the Crown believed that their triumph could only be achieved through the triumph of the common law.[158] Since the prerogative courts had been created to meet felt needs which the common law courts were not meeting, the common law could succeed only if it were to expand to meet those needs. Parliament, after all, was composed of practical men.[159] The genius of Coke was in reshaping the common law to fit their needs while

---

153. 6 HOLDSWORTH, *supra* note 35, at 133-34. 10 GARDINER, *supra* note 152, at 32, concluded that: "If no other question had been at issue than the political one there would have been no permanent division of parties, and no civil war." For a more modern analysis *see* Ashton, *The Civil War and the Class Struggle,* in THE ENGLISH CIVIL WAR AND AFTER 93-110 (R. Perry ed. 1970). Despite his heavy debt to Marxian analysis, Ashton twice in this short essay endorses Gardiner's analysis, *id.* at 96, 104. For recent studies of the causes of the English Civil War, *see* J. ALLEN, ENGLISH POLITICAL THOUGHT 1603-1660 (1938); W. HALLER, THE RISE OF PURITANISM (1938); C. HILL, PURITANISM AND REVOLUTION (1958); M. JACKSON, THE CRISIS OF THE CONSTITUTION (1949); C. WEDGWOOD, THE KING'S PEACE 1637-1641 (1955).

154. Coke was Chief Justice of the Common Pleas from 1606-1613, and of the King's Bench from 1613-1616. For a short, but detailed, study of Coke's career, *see* 5 HOLDSWORTH, *supra* note 35, at 425-56. For a recent biography *see* S. THORNE, SIR EDWARD COKE (1957). *See also* 1 J. CAMPBELL, THE LIVES OF THE CHIEF JUSTICES 245-357 (1849) [hereinafter cited as CAMPBELL, CHIEF JUSTICES]. 5 HOLDSWORTH 436 concludes that Coke, "the most offensive of attorney-generals [was] transformed into the most admired and venerated of judges."

155. 5 HOLDSWORTH, *supra* note 35, at 444-54. While in Parliament Coke wrote the Petition of Right, the next basic constitutional document in England after the Magna Carta.

156. Coke apparently invented the theory upon which these writs succeeded—that only courts of record (common law courts) could fine or imprison, *id.* at 159-60. This enabled common law courts to suppress lesser courts as well as to oppose prerogative courts. *See also id.* at 420.

157. *Id.* at 414-23. For Coke's role in this assertion of jurisdiction by the common law courts, *see id.* at 422-42, 461-78, 489-93.

158. *Id.* at 422-23.

159. D. BRUNTON & D. PENNINGTON, MEMBERS OF THE LONG PARLIAMENT (1954).

preserving intact the common law's essence.[160]

Coke's great legacies to the modern world were his *Reports* and his *Institutes*.[161] Perhaps without realizing it Coke invented modern attitudes towards the common law. Despite his heavy conservatism, leading on occasion to support for archaic points of law,[162] Coke's view that the common law solved all necessary problems compelled him to find answers even if less certain minds would not. Coke would stretch precedent not through dishonesty, but through strenuous advocacy of his convictions.[163] Nevertheless, even his sharpest opponents in his own life could find very few errors in his work[164]—except as to the political controversies, and there Parliament made him right. In short, if Coke and his contemporaries believed something deserved punishment or remedy, then Coke believed he could find the penalty or the remedy in the common law. Sometimes Parliament would make this clear by statute.[165] More often the common law courts merely took over the law of the rival courts as part of the law of England.[166] After the abolition of most of the rivals to the common law courts, some common law judges asserted that they inherited the jurisdiction and the substantive law of the eliminated rivals.[167] This process continued throughout the seventeenth century, and brought many important areas of modern law into the common law.[168] Questions of violations of morals were

---

160. 5 HOLDSWORTH, *supra* note 35, at 461-70.

161. For example, Coke invented new methods of law study still adhered to in England, *id.* at 465-66. Maitland called Coke's books "the great dividing line" between medieval and modern law, *id.* at 489.

162. *Id.* at 384, 461, 491-93.

163. *Id.* at 472-85; 1 HOLDSWORTH, *supra* note 35, at 553-54.

164. 5 HOLDSWORTH, *supra* note 35, at 476-78.

165. The process of providing penalties by statute preceded Coke. Thus sodomy and statutory rape were made felonies by statute under the Tudors, 4 HOLDSWORTH, *supra* note 35, at 504.

166. Coke himself used the law of non-common law courts, at least with regard to riot and rout, 5 HOLDSWORTH, *supra* note 35, at 198. Coke included in his reports cases from the Star Chamber, the Court of Wards, and even Chancery, apparently for citation to other courts, *id.* at 465, and reported many common law cases invading areas which had originated in other courts, *id.* at 464-65.

167. 8 HOLDSWORTH, *supra* note 35, at 406-10.

168. *See generally* 5 HOLDSWORTH, *supra* note 35, at 167-69, 183, 197-218, 291-99; 8 HOLDSWORTH 301-07, 324-417; PLUCKNETT, *supra* note 45, at 455-62, 483-502, 661. For the invention of common law libel and slander to replace the actions developed in the Star Chamber (having gotten to Star Chamber at the expense of the church courts), *see* BRANT, *supra* note 57, at 113-30, 154-73; 5 HOLDSWORTH 205-12; 8 HOLDSWORTH 333-78; PLUCKNETT 488-500. Much modern criminal law, including the punishment of attempts and conspiracies, originated in the Star Chamber, 5 HOLDSWORTH 197-205. Chancery even lost some of its

simply treated in the same way.[169] This resulted in an increasing relegation of church courts to minor matters, and the abolition of its most effective tribunal (the High Commission) in 1641.[170] These changes altered the courts in which proceedings would be brought and the authority of the crown to change the substantive law. Important as these steps were to achieving religious liberty,[171] they involved few, if any, changes in the substantive law.

The problem of the legality of abortion had long been ignored by the common law courts. Touching homicide as it did, abortion could not escape the process of transfer of jurisdiction. If Coke stretched precedents such as *Sims' Case* to capture this jurisdiction, this was no different from what he and his followers did in many other areas of law. Their victory made these captures of jurisdiction unchallengeable.[172] Means asserts that the "discovery" that abortion was a common law crime if proven to cause a death was a "masterpiece of perversion"[173] which, "while understandable in a country with a Church established by law, is for that very reason not appropriate to our country."[174] If so, then the many other innovations made in capturing ecclesiastical jurisdiction for the common law courts should also be so described.

But if jurisdiction over abortion belonged now to the common law courts, so did the problems which had confronted the church

---

jurisdiction over informal contracts at this time, 5 HOLDSWORTH 294-99, a jurisdiction which it had captured from the ecclesiastical courts, 1 HOLDSWORTH 455-57. Thus Slade's Case, 76 Eng. Rep. 1074 (K.B. 1602), facilitated the enforcement of informal contracts through an action in assumpsit, displacing both the action for debt, and the need for ecclesiastical enforcement of informal promises, 3 HOLDSWORTH 441-54.

169. 5 HOLDSWORTH, *supra* note 35, at 406-10. *Compare* 2 POLLOCK & MAITLAND, *supra* note 46, at 542-43, 554-55.

170. 16 Car. 1, c.11 (1641); 13 Car. 2, stat.1, c.12 (1661). These same acts abolished the Star Chamber and the *ex officio* oath.

171. BRANT, *supra* note 57, at 80-120; R. USHER, THE RISE AND FALL OF THE HIGH COMMISSION (1913); Means II, *supra* note 24, at 346-48.

172. Regardless of the original accuracy of his views, Coke became almost unquestionable after the triumph of Parliament, 5 HOLDSWORTH, *supra* note 35, at 471-72. His views became the basis of the modern English constitution and the common law. Hobbes' attack on Coke's views was not accepted by the legal profession, thanks largely to the work of Sir Matthew Hale, *id.* at 480-85.

173. Means II, *supra* note 24, at 359. Means asserts that Coke was deliberately misstating the law, *id.* at 360. The charge has been made by others regarding many of Coke's innovations in the law, and is carefully considered and rejected in 5 HOLDSWORTH, *supra* note 35, at 471-78. For the gist of Holdsworth's analysis, *see* text accompanying notes 161-69 *supra*. Means also terms Coke's statement an "outrageous attempt to create a new common-law misprision." Means II, *supra* note 24, at 346.

174. Means II, *supra* note 24, at 348.

courts in attempting to proscribe it. The technology involved had not changed. Chances of proving that the child was alive, and that the blow or potion had killed it, remained virtually nil—unless the child were born alive, and died in circumstances clearly traceable to the abortion. Under these circumstances, as *Sims' Case* and Coke suggested, abortion was punishable as homicide.

Only Sir Matthew Hale rejected this dictum,[175] citing the questionable authority of the *Twinslayer's Case*. Hale[176] was the next great common law lawyer after Coke, and in many respects he completed and regularized Coke's work. Hale was certainly a better historian than Coke.[177] Perhaps he was correcting Coke's misreading of the *Twinslayer's Case*. Nevertheless, his reason for his rejection of Coke on this point is that it cannot be known if the child was killed by the blow.[178] Again, the law is thwarted by the lack of the technology necessary to prove the crime, for even Hale recognizes abortion as a "great crime," if not homicide. Means would explain Hale's characterization as referring only to an ecclesiastical crime.[179] Actually Hale simply is ambiguous. He defines crimes[180] as either ecclesiastical or temporal. Although after his assertion that abortion is a great crime Hale discusses only the law of Moses,[181] in 1670 Hale himself ruled as Chief Justice that the death of the mother was murder because the potion was given to "unlawfully destroy the child within her."[182] This might be akin to felony murder, with the *mens rea* against the child linked to the *actus reus* of killing the mother to support the charge of murder.[183] This analysis faces diffi-

---

175. HALE, *supra* note 126, at 433; Means II, *supra* note 24, at 349-50.

176. *See generally* 6 HOLDSWORTH, *supra* note 35, at 574-95; PLUCKNETT, *supra* note 45, at 385. Hale was a Judge of Common Pleas (1654-1658 under Cromwell), Chief Baron of the Court of Exchequer (1660-1671 under Charles II), and Chief Justice of the King's Bench (1671-1676 under Charles II).

177. 5 HOLDSWORTH, *supra* note 35, at 483; 6 HOLDSWORTH 582-90.

178. HALE, *supra* note 126, at 433.

179. Means II, *supra* note 24, at 350, 368-69.

180. HALE, *supra* note 126, at *proemium* (unnumbered first page).

181. Perhaps Hale means abortion is a crime before ecclesiastical courts, but he clearly does not exclude possible secular criminality.

182. HALE, *supra* note 126, at 429-30; Means II, *supra* note 24, at 362. *Accord:* Margaret Tinckler's Case (1781), discussed in 1 E. EAST, A TREATISE OF THE PLEAS OF THE CROWN 354-56 (1806).

183. Byrn II, *supra* note 11, at 822. *Accord,* People v. Sessions, 58 Mich. 594, 26 N.W. 291 (1886); *Margaret Tinckler's Case, supra* note 182; 1 EAST, *supra* note 182, at 230. *Cf.* Ann v. State, 30 Tenn. (11 Hum.) 159 (1850); State v. Masilela, [1968] (2) S.A. 558 (A.D.), *noted in* 1968 RHODESIAN L.J. 15 (one who kills a "corpse"). For the status of *mens rea* in the law of England at this time see 8 HOLDSWORTH, *supra* note 35, at 433-38. The requirement of *mens*

culties since an abortion was not then a felony. An alternative analysis would be that the act was one of extreme recklessness,[184] endangering the mother's life, and, therefore, murder. Significantly, there is no precedent for the ruling by Hale. Hale's ruling also appears to have been part of the displacement of eccelesiastical law by the common law—a process in which Hale led elsewhere as well.[185]

Means satisfies himself by characterizing Hale's innovation (that the death of the mother from an abortion is murder) as an act of Restoration gallantry.[186] How one recognizes the difference between this and Coke's "masterpiece of perversion" is not explained.[187] Both were a part of the absorption of all major aspects of English law (except equity) into the common law. In the process of displacing church courts, the common law judges did not relegate important ecclesiastical crimes to private conscience.[188] In regard to abortion, one need only overcome the peculiar difficulties of proof.

Hale's doubts (if doubts they were) about the criminal nature of abortions did not prevent him from extending the protection of the law to women killed through the abortion. The difference is technological. In 1670 a jury could determine that a woman was killed by the abortion. This determination was at least as certain as for any other killing after birth. Generally one could not do so for a killing before birth—even considering this a great crime, as Hale

---

rea originated in the church courts and was taken over only later in royal courts, 2 HOLDSWORTH 258-59; 2 POLLOCK & MAITLAND, *supra* note 46, at 469-76. Hale played a major role in systemizing this idea, HALE, *supra* note 126, at 466-73. This notion of *mens rea* against one subject coupled with an *actus reus* against another subject was apparently generally accepted in England, since Parliament thought it necessary to repeal it, Homicide Act, 1957, 5 & 6 Eliz. 2, c.11, § 1.

184. Review the discussion of the technology then available for performing abortion before 1600 which does not appear to have changed during the period of Phase II, text accompanying notes 67-117 *supra*. See especially ETMULLERUS; PECHEY; SWINDELLS, *supra* note 68, for the state of the art of abortion in the eighteenth century.

185. For Hale's role in developing common law slander *see* BRANT, *supra* note 57, at 113-30, 154-73; 8 HOLDSWORTH, *supra* note 35, at 364-65; PLUCKNETT, *supra* note 45, at 496-98. The troublesome concepts of slander per se and slander per quod arose in this era as tools for seizing jurisdiction from ecclesiastical courts. *See generally* 8 HOLDSWORTH 333-78.

186. Means II, *supra* note 24, at 363.

187. *Id.* at 359. Means is, however, willing to approve of Coke's inventions when it suits him, *id.* at 374 (consent to mayhem). Means is, in fact, quite ready to contradict himself. For example, he asserts that Coke was never taken seriously in England, *id.* at 355, although Means had cited two nineteenth century English cases following Coke only four pages earlier, *id.* at 351 n.35, and notes that Hawkins, *id.* at 348, and Blackstone, *id.* at 349, followed him. Who, then, is deliberately misstating things? *Id.* at 360. *See also* note 174 *supra*.

188. Means assumes that such a relegation to private conscience did occur. Means II, *supra* note 24, at 370.

did. Other commentators recognized that proof was procurable where the child was born alive.[189] Otherwise, technological limitations effectively prevented successful prosecution. Difficulties of proof before birth did not prevent a charge of murder if the mother died because the *mens rea* would exist, or the act was reckless, regardless of the state of the foetus.

C. Phase III (1803-1967): Statutory Prohibition of Abortions

Anglo-American law regarding abortion changed again with the enactment of Lord Ellenborough's Act[190] in 1803. The Act prohibited all abortions by drugs or poisons, and provided for the death penalty if the woman was "quick with child."[191] In the United States, Connecticut enacted the first statute prohibiting abortions in 1821.[192] Gradually, other state abortion legislation followed.[193] Twenty (of thirty) states had prohibited abortion by 1850, and 26 of 36 states by the end of our Civil War. In addition, six of the then ten territories had prohibited abortions by 1865. The assertion by Justice Blackmun that such legislation did not become widespread until after the "War Between the States" is simply wrong.[194] The more populous states had enacted legislation by this time.[195] When Rhode Island prohibited abortions in 1896,[196] abortion was a crime in every

---

189. *See* sources cited *supra* note 126.

190. 43 Geo. 3, c.58 (1803).

191. For the evolution of the term "quick with child" in the nineteenth century, *see* Regina v. Wycherley, 173 Eng. Rep. 486 (N.P. 1838); *and* Byrn II, *supra* note 11, at 824-27.

192. CONN. STAT. tit. 22, § 14 (1821) (current version at CONN. GEN. STAT. ANN. §§ 53-29, 53-31a (West 1960 & West Supp. 1979)).

193. The statutes were collected in Quay, *supra* note 21, at 447-520. For cases clearly holding that abortion after quickening is a common law crime see State v. Reed, 45 Ark. 333 (1885); State v. Slagle, 83 N.C. 630 (1880); Mitchell v. Commonwealth, 78 Ky. 204 (1879); Mills v. Commonwealth, 13 Pa. 630 (1850); Commonwealth v. Parker, 50 Mass. 263, 43 Am. Dec. 396 (1845); and Commonwealth v. Bangs, 9 Mass. 387 (1812). All except *State v. Reed* were decided when there was no abortion statute in the state. In each state a statute was eventually enacted.

194. Roe v. Wade, 410 U.S. at 139.

195. Eight of the ten then most populous states had prohibited abortions by 1860. The holdouts and the dates of enactment of their first abortion statutes were: Kentucky (1910—but a common law crime from 1879); and Tennessee (1883). The ten most populous states as of the 1970 census and the dates of their first statutes are as follows: California (1850); New York (1828); Pennsylvania (1860—but common law crime in 1850); Texas (1859); Illinois (1827); Ohio (1834); Michigan (1846); New Jersey (1849); Florida (1868); and Massachusetts (1845—but common law crime from 1812). In 1850 about 75% of the United States population lived in states banning abortions, and the figure exceeded 85% by 1860. *See* Quay, *supra* note 19, at 447-520, for a thorough study of the statutory materials.

196. R.I. GEN. LAWS ch.277, § 22 (1896). The crime was also proscribed in every territory

state and the District of Columbia. Although the precise date of this phase varied somewhat in each jurisdiction, the dates for the duration of this phase in England adequately represent the time period during which these statutes won general acceptance and (until nearly the end of this period) escaped widespread criticism.

Lord Ellenborough's Act was the first comprehensive Offenses Against the Person Act in English law.[197] Prior to this time the English criminal law regarding physical injuries to persons short of homicide was unsettled. Many separate statutes had been enacted, making particular acts criminal.[198] These statutes were quite specific, and they were narrowly construed. Often these statutes prohibited acts with specific intent (*e.g.,* assault with intent to disfigure), or of peculiar danger (*e.g.,* shooting into a dwelling place). Apart from these statutes, however, great uncertainty had developed as to the criminality of even heinous mayhems.[199] To make certain of the criminality of such acts, and to systematize and generalize the relevant statutes (some of them four centuries old), Lord Ellenborough's Act was passed.[200] Abortion induced by drugs or poisons was included as a prohibited act.

Means argues that this Act for the first time made abortion a crime in England,[201] asserting that Lord Ellenborough's Act was proposed in order to change the law after some problems with the framing of an indictment.[202] Means only connects the indictment to the Act through proximity in time. His interpretation completely ignores the comprehensive nature of the Act.[203] Is one to suppose that assault with intent to commit murder was generally inoffensive prior to 1803 merely because this was the first statute to proscribe it generally? Similar questions arise as to shooting, stabbing, or cutting a person to prevent an arrest, or as to any of the other crimes

---

by 1896, except possibly New Mexico whose statute I have not been able to trace back before 1907, N.M. (Terr.) Acts, ch.36, §§ 5, 6 (1907). *See* Quay, *supra* note 19, at 447-520.

197.   11 HOLDSWORTH, *supra* note 35, at 536-37; 3 STEPHEN, *supra* note 47, at 113.

198.   For these statutes *see* 3 HOLDSWORTH, *supra* note 35, at 316-18; 4 HOLDSWORTH 512-14; 6 HOLDSWORTH 403-04; 11 HOLDSWORTH 536-37; and 3 STEPHEN, *supra* note 47, at 109-13.

199.   3 HOLDSWORTH, *supra* note 35, at 316-18 concluded that there were no common law crimes dealing with mayhem after the fourteenth century, but this is denied by PLUCKNETT, *supra* note 45, at 456-58.

200.   11 HOLDSWORTH, *supra* note 35, at 537; 3 STEPHEN, *supra* note 47, at 113.

201.   Means II, *supra* note 25 at 336, 357-59, 373.

202.   *Id.* at 355-59.

203.   Surprisingly most American commentators on abortion have failed to place this prohibition of abortions in the context of the overall act. Quay, *supra* note 19, at 431 n.40, gives its title as the Miscarriage of Women Act. *See, e.g.,* Byrn II, *supra* note 11, at 824-25.

first clearly prohibited by this statute.[204] Why should we assume that the provisions regarding abortion were considered any differently? The authorities which could be cited as to the criminality of abortion (Coke, Blackstone, etc.) were more definite than those which could be cited for some of the other offenses first clearly prohibited in Lord Ellenborough's Act.

Means also ignores the nature of Lord Ellenborough. Lord Ellenborough was probably the most conservative Chief Justice of the King's Bench ever.[205] Lord Ellenborough was exceptionally learned in the statutes, precedents, and scholarship of the common law, and quite able to develop soundly reasoned decisions where existing law allowed.[206] Nonetheless he was completely unwilling to go beyond the precedents, frequently championing archaic notions that even superficial reasoning would show to be based on outmoded social or legal factors.[207] Thus Lord Ellenborough was the first to hold that there was no action at the common law for wrongful death

---

204. For a general summary of Lord Ellenborough's Act see 13 HOLDSWORTH, supra note 35, at 390.

205. 13 HOLDSWORTH, supra note 35, at 502-04; PLUCKNETT, supra note 45, at 72. Ellenborough was Chief Justice of the King's Bench from 1802 to 1818. The only important figure in English law to approach his extreme conservatism was Lord Eldon who was Chief Justice of Common Pleas (1799-1801), and Lord Chancellor (1801-1806, 1807-1827), 13 HOLDSWORTH 181, 189, 222, 605-10; PLUCKNETT 72. For general studies of Ellenborough's career, see 4 CAMPBELL, CHIEF JUSTICES, supra note 154, at 102-254; 13 HOLDSWORTH 499-516. As to Lord Eldon's life, see 7 J. CAMPBELL, LIVES OF THE LORD CHANCELLORS 3-555 (1848); 13 HOLDSWORTH 595-638.

206. See generally 13 HOLDSWORTH, supra note 35, at 507-16; 4 CAMPBELL, supra note 154, at 164-81. Ellenborough seconded Mansfield's reception of international law, Vineash v. Becker, 3 M. & S. 284 (K.B. 1814), 13 HOLDSWORTH 508-09. Ellenborough also decided Adams v. Lindsell, 106 Eng. Rep. 250 (K.B. 1818) (acceptance by post effective when sent), 13 HOLDSWORTH 511. He even invented the rule that death is presumed on an absence of seven years based on analogous statutes, George v. Jesson, 6 East 80 (K.B. 1805); Hopewell v. De Pinna, 170 Eng. Rep. 1098 (K.B. 1810); 9 HOLDSWORTH 141.

207. Many of Lord Ellenborough's decisions were later reversed, generally by statute. For example, he held that bills payable to a fictitious payee were void, Bennett v. Farnell, 170 Eng. Rep. 902, 921 (K.B. 1807), 13 HOLDSWORTH, supra note 35, at 509-10; that a contract of life insurance was a contract of indemnity, i.e., that one could only recover provable losses caused by the death and not the face amount of the policy, Godsall v. Boldero, 103 Eng. Rep. 500 (K.B. 1807), 13 HOLDSWORTH 510; that illegitimate minors could not marry, Priestly v. Hughes, 103 Eng. Rep. 903 (K.B. 1809), 13 HOLDSWORTH 421-23, 514; and that agricultural fixtures became property of the landlord (unlike other trade fixtures because agriculture was not a mere trade), Elwes v. Maw, 102 Eng. Rep. 510 (K.B. 1803), 7 HOLDSWORTH 284-86, 13 HOLDSWORTH 514. Ellenborough in a series of cases even managed to establish himself as one of the very few champions of the Statute of Frauds the English judiciary ever had, 6 HOLDSWORTH 394-96, 13 HOLDSWORTH 511. See also 4 CAMPBELL, supra note 154, at 164-73, 176-77.

because there was no precedent for it.[208] He was quite unconcerned that the lack of precedents could be fully explained by the then only recently abolished forfeiture of a felon's goods to the crown.[209] He even approved trial by battle.[210] His position in parliamentary debates was equally unprogressive.[211] There is little possibility then that he intended anything in the Offenses Against the Person Act he authored to be an innovation, Means' conclusion to the contrary notwithstanding.

If the 1803 statutory prohibition of abortions was not an innovation, one must still ask, if abortions were technically impossible, why include their prohibition in the Offenses Against the Person Act? Other crimes were not included. Murder and manslaughter were not codified until the next general revision of the Offenses Against the Person Act in 1828.[212] This perhaps was because Ellenborough thought the law of murder and manslaughter satisfactory, without need of clarification or reemphasis. Other crimes were apparently overlooked in the consolidation.[213] The inclusion of abortion in Lord Ellenborough's Act thus itself suggests some reason for concern regarding a matter for which there had been little reason to be concerned, at least until shortly before the enactment. The conclusion that Lord Ellenborough's Act demonstrated concern about abortion when before there had been none is reinforced by the steady concern various legislatures demonstrated throughout the nineteenth century.

New provisions on abortion were enacted in England in 1828,[214]

---

208.   Baker v. Bolton, 170 Eng. Rep. 1033 (K.B. 1808), 13 HOLDSWORTH, *supra* note 35, at 513.

209.   *See* 3 HOLDSWORTH, *supra* note 35, at 328-36.

210.   Ashford v. Thornton, 106 Eng. Rep. 149 (K.B. 1818); 13 HOLDSWORTH, *supra* note 35, at 217, 405, 516, 527-28. *See also* 4 CAMPBELL, *supra* note 154, at 180-81.

211.   Ellenborough successfully opposed amelioration of the insolvent debtors' laws, 13 HOLDSWORTH, *supra* note 35, at 264-66, 503, and mitigation of the death penalty, *id.* at 279-81, 503. His own Offenses Against the Person Act, 1803, 43 Geo. 3, c.58, was described as being of "revolting severity," 4 CAMPBELL, *supra* note 154, at 241-43. This was the only bill he introduced in 18 years in Parliament. The only reform bills he favored were the abolition of the slave trade, 13 HOLDSWORTH 504, and the prohibition of cruelty to animals, although he and Eldon apparently helped to defeat the latter bill, *id.* at 266. Ellenborough even opposed reform of the fee system for judges, despite its tendency to corrupt, *id.* at 503; 4 CAMPBELL, *supra* note 154, at 164 n.1.

212.   9 Geo. 4, c. 31 (1828).

213.   The Offenses Against the Person Act of 1828, 9 Geo. 4, c.31, § 1 (1828), still found it necessary to repeal 57 statutes ranging in date from 1224 to 1762.

214.   Offenses Against the Person Act, 9 Geo. 4, c.31 (1828).

1837,[215] and 1861.[216] The general effect of these successive amendments was to gradually eliminate the various technical restrictions found in the 1803 law until all abortions, by any means, for virtually any purpose, were clearly criminal. Thus the 1828 act extended criminality to abortions by instruments, whereas the 1803 Act dealt only with abortions by drugs or potions. The 1837 Act eliminated all reference to quickening, making abortion at any stage of pregnancy (and also attempt without actual pregnancy) punishable by imprisonment for a term from 15 years to life. The 1861 Act further enlarged the scope of the law against abortion. Provision of a drug or instrument knowing that it was intended to be used in an abortion became a misdemeanor punishable by imprisonment of up to three years. The only remaining technical limitation on criminality was that a woman could not be convicted of attempting to abort herself if she were not actually pregnant. She could, however, be convicted for conspiracy to abort[217] or for aiding and abetting an attempted abortion.[218] A similar pattern of legislative activity occurred in the United States as well, resulting in a gradual increase in the restrictions on every aspect of abortion.[219]

Turning from statutory growth to reported cases one finds a parallel increase of activity at about the same time. Prior to 1670 there are no reported cases of anyone being tried at law for murder upon the death of the mother. After Hale's decision that year, one must wait 111 years before a second abortion prosecution. In England, between 1781 and 1803, two such cases are reported,[220] while in America five decisions involving abortion had been decided by 1886.[221] These American cases do not catalogue the greater number

215.　Offenses Against the Person Act, 7 Will. 4 & 1 Vict., c.85 (1837).

216.　Offenses Against the Person Act, 24 & 25 Vict., c.100, §§ 58, 59 (1861).

217.　Queen v. Whitchurch, 24 Q.B.D. 420 (1890).

218.　King v. Scokett, 72 J.P. 428 (1908).

219.　See generally Quay, supra note 19, at 435-38, 447-520. Means I, supra note 24, at 441-500 gives a lengthy study of the various reenactments in New York between 1828 and 1965 (totaling 15 enactments, id. at 453). While Means is not evenhanded, he does show the pattern, particularly in the nineteenth century, of gradually broadening prohibitions. Quickening remained as a criterion of punishment in the law of ten states in 1960, while all but two states excepted abortions to save the mother's life, or to protect her health, a position reached in England by statutory construction, King v. Bourne, [1938] 3 All E.R. 615 (K.B.). See also GRISEZ, supra note 47, at 188-94, 220-22.

220.　Margaret Tinckler's Case, supra note 182; Anonymous (1802), 3 J. CHITTY, CRIMINAL LAW 798-801 (1816), discussed in Means II, supra note 24, at 355-59.

221.　People v. Sessions, 58 Mich. 594, 26 N.W. 291 (1886); State v. Moore, 25 Iowa 128 (1868); Smith v. State, 33 Me. 48 (1851); Commonwealth v. Parker, 50 Mass. (9 Met.) 263 (1845); Commonwealth ex rel. Chauncey v. Keeper of the Prison, 2 Ashm. 227 (Pa. C.P. 1838).

of prosecutions brought without appeal, or without the death of the mother. Expressions of concern over the health of the mother also begin to appear frequently in the legal and medical literature at about this time.[222] These changes suggest the number of abortions had increased, which is not likely if abortion was still tantamount to suicide for the mother.

A new method for inducing abortion appeared in England sometime after 1750. Representing the first major technological change regarding abortions, the technique involved inserting objects into the womb to induce labor.[223] This technique was later improved by the use of surgical procedures (dilation and curettage) and in its early development was highly dangerous. These insertions opened the uterus to infection,[224] while the pain frequently induced shock.[225] The uterine wall was often punctured.[226] Dangerous and painful as these procedures were in eighteenth century England, they were not as dangerous or as immediately painful as a physical beating on the abdomen or the ingestion of a noxious potion. Although statistics with regard to illegal acts are always suspect, these new techniques appear to have quickly become the technique of choice.[227] A motivating factor in the early nineteenth century legislation was to make clear that abortion by instruments was as illegal as the more tradi-

---

222.   1 E. EAST, *supra* note 182, at 230; H. STORER, WHY NOT? A BOOK FOR EVERY WOMAN 36-37 (1865); A. TAYLOR, MANUAL OF MEDICAL JURISPRUDENCE 595 (1844); 2 LEGAL EXAMINER 10-11 (1832). *See also* State v. Murphy, 27 N.J.L. 112 (Sup. Ct. 1858). Extensive discussion of the careers of particular abortionists of this period is found in Means I, *supra* note 24, at 455-80, derived largely from New York Times accounts.

223.   The use of this abortion method was first publicly reported in *Margaret Tinckler's Case, supra* note 182, in 1781. As to the apparent late appearance of this technique, DEVEREUX, *supra* note 68, at 28, comments on the lack of inventiveness among primitives concerning abortifacients, while only a few scattered groups appear to have used insertions with mixed success, *id.* at 36-37. Only fourteen of these more than 300 societies reported such instrumentation. Primitive insertions were used in Germany, but apparently not in England or America. In Germany these techniques were successful largely through the death of the mother, BATES & ZAWADZKI, *supra* note 71, at 86-87; Breitenecker, *supra* note 71, at 219-20.

224.   BATES & ZAWADZKI, *supra* note 71, at 85-87. They describe the insertion as creating a "broad highway" to infection.

225.   *See generally* Means II, *supra* note 24, at 382-92.

226.   Puncture of the uterine wall is especially likely if a rigid object, like a screwdriver, is used. Other complications can arise when through error the bladder, rather than the uterus, is invaded. *See* BATES & ZAWADZKI, *supra* note 71, at 87.

227.   P. GEBHARD, W. POMEROY, C. MARTIN & C. CHRISTENSON, PREGNANCY, BIRTH AND ABORTION 193-96 (1958), found that over 90% of their sample had illegal abortions induced by "operative" techniques, with about 9% relying on drugs, and virtually none using "injury" techniques. *Compare* GRISEZ, *supra* note 47, at 100-02.

tional techniques of potions and beatings.[228] The legislation passed
in the early nineteenth century can be seen as a response to the
premature application of a developing technology, premature in
that the related technologies necessary to make it safe (control of
infections and shock) did not yet exist.

The enactment of statutes declaring abortion criminal accomplished several goals. These statutes clarified and settled the hitherto uncertain law governing abortion. While it was perhaps unnecessary to criminalize abortion, the statutes were nonetheless a solemn reaffirmation of social policy, warning both mothers and
would-be abortionists of the consequences of their acts. In particular, they established that abortion before quickening was at least a
misdemeanor, and under many statutes a felony. And these statutes
served to make clear that all abortions were criminal regardless of
means.

Was this increased abortion activity merely the result of changing medical technologies, or were there other social pressures leading to greater recourse to abortion in the early nineteenth century?
Little direct evidence can be adduced. Illegitimacy rates in England
appear to have been very stable over several centuries, rising only
during times of unusual prosperity.[229] Does this suggest that more
abortions are performed in bad times, or that there is less illicit sex?
One doesn't know.[230] Similarly, do the depressed living standards of
the early industrial working classes suggest a greater unwillingness
to bring children into the world? Or would parents want more children to provide additional income for the family unit? Regardless
of how we answer these questions, abortions could not have been
common if abortion were tantamount to suicide. In a very real sense
the introduction of the new technology must be seen as a necessary
precondition (a cause if you will) of the awakened awareness of
abortion as a social problem. In fact before 1800 the problem was
seen in terms of the concealment of the birth of bastards.[231]

228.　This was accomplished in England by the Offenses Against the Person Act of 1828,
9 Geo. 4, c.31 (1828). The first act in the United States to deal with abortions by instrumentation was N.Y. Rev. Stat. pt. IV. ch. I, tit. II, §§ 8, 9 (1828). *See* Quay, *supra* note 19, at 498.

229.　P. LASLETT, THE WORLD WE HAVE LOST 128-49 (1966).

230.　Perhaps the only statistical studies of "abortions" in the early modern period found
rates of 6-7% of total births, *id.* at 123. As twentieth century spontaneous abortions range
from 7½% to 11% of total births, *id.* at 266, these seventeenth century figures show few, if
any, induced abortions.

231.　Delayed marriage appears to have been the major, but often ineffective, means of
birth control at least until the nineteenth century, *id.* at 81-92, 122-23. In France abandon-

Infanticide has often been viewed as a problem closely related to abortion. In societies where abortion is technologically unfeasible, one would expect to find infanticide as a substitute procedure.[232] Infanticide, in fact, was a very common practice throughout Europe until the beginning of the nineteenth century.[233] Anglo-Saxon England apparently enforced a legal presumption that any dead child had been killed by its parents,[234] while nine centuries later reports still circulated that dead babies were a common sight on the streets of London.[235] In France, as late as the seventeenth century, some respected authorities asserted a legal right to "suppress" a new child.[236] Further evidence arises from the persistently distorted sex ratio whereby boys outnumbered girls as much as 4 to 1.[237] In fact the first crusade against infanticide was feminist in motive, representing an effort to gain equal opportunity for females simply to

---

ment appears to have been a means of population growth control. In Paris in 1772 foundlings accounted for 40% of baptisms, and 50% of these died in early childhood, Krause, *Some Implications of Recent Work of Historical Demography*, 1 COMP. STUD. IN SOC'Y AND HIST. 164, 177 (1959). See Marvick, *Nurture v. Nature: Patterns and Trends in Seventeenth Century French Child-Rearing*, in THE HISTORY OF CHILDHOOD 259, 286 (de Mause ed. 1974) [this collection is hereinafter cited as de Mause].

232. For general studies of infanticide in history, *see* D. BAKAN, SLAUGHTER OF THE INNOCENTS (1971); G. PAYNE, THE CHILD IN HUMAN PROGRESS (1916); Langer, *Infanticide: A Historical Survey*, 2 HIST. OF CHILDHOOD Q. 353 (1974) [hereinafter cited as Langer, *Infanticide*]; Langer, *Checks on Population Growth, 1750-1850*, 226 SCIENTIFIC AM. 93 (Feb. 1972); Shorter, *Infanticide in the Past*, 1 HIST. OF CHILDHOOD Q. 178 (1973).

As to the interrelation of infanticide and abortion (and the greater reliance on infanticide) in pre-Christian Greece and Rome, *see* Quay, *supra* note 19, at 406-25. For early modern Japan (at least through the nineteenth century), *see* L. LEE & A. LARSEN, POPULATION AND LAW 3-15 (1971).

Much less well known is the evidence of the frequency of infanticide or neglect to the point of death in Western Europe prior to the end of the eighteenth century. In addition to the above authorities, *see* de Mause, *supra* note 231, at 25-32, 245, 282-86, 306-11. Such practices apparently remained common in Russia late into the nineteenth century, *id.* at 393-94.

233. Langer, *Infanticide, supra* note 232, has assembled an enormous bibliography to support this conclusion, only part of which was published with the article. *See* de Mause, *The Evolution of Childhood*, in de Mause, *supra* note 231, at 63 n.140.

234. J. THRUPP, THE ANGLO-SAXON HOME 85 (1862).

235. Rolph, *A Backward Glance at the Age of "Obscenity,"* 32 ENCOUNTER 23 (June 1969). *See also* I. PINCHBECK & M. HEWITT, CHILDREN IN ENGLISH SOCIETY 302 (1969); de Mause, *supra* note 231, at 244-45.

236. Marvick, *supra* note 231, at 282.

237. De Mause, *supra* note 231, at 25-28, 284-85. This pattern was found throughout Europe well into the nineteenth century in almost every rural area. The pattern disappeared only in urban areas. The tendency to "suppress" rural girls was accentuated by the practice of rural women gaining employment as wet-nurses—at the expense of their own daughters.

live.[238] Abandonment and neglect were even more widespread than direct killing.[239] Indeed, neglect by wet-nurses was so common that one might almost characterize wet-nursing as a major population control device.[240] Finally, midwives were so commonly employed to kill the infant that in England licensed midwives were made to swear not to kill, hurt, or dismember the child.[241]

When legal action was first taken against infanticide in seventeenth century France and England, application of homicide laws to infants would appear to have been the simple solution. Infants, however, are particularly easy to kill by methods which make a later determination of the cause of death impossible. Believing undetectable murder to be particularly likely for bastards, early laws were enacted making concealment by the mother of the death of her illegitimate child punishable as murder.[242] At this time (1624) the

238. *Id.* at 285-87. The first orphanages for girls were only started in France in the seventeenth century, centuries after orphanages for boys were opened.

239. In France infanticide by abandonment of infants was so common that French monasteries, convents, and foundling homes developed a device (a *tour* or turnbox) which allowed one to leave one's child without being identified, 31 LA GRANDE ENCYCLOPEDIE 224 (1886-1902); 7 NOUVEAU LAROUSE ILLUSTRE 1069 (Ange ed. 1898-1909). Napolean made a *tour* mandatory for all foundling homes, Law of Jan. 19, 1811, [1811] BULLETIN DES LOIS (4th ser.) pt.1 at 82, but the tour device was suppressed in 1838. In discussing this experience C. FOOTE, R. LEVY & F. SANDER, CASES & MATERIALS ON FAMILY LAW 633-34 (2d ed. 1976), infer that a changing attitude toward illegitimacy was the cause of this change. Perhaps, but a more likely cause is that infanticide had become less popular given the greater feasibility of abortion. If fears of infanticide prompted the requirement of such a device, as these authors assert, only a harsh government would seek to force people back to infanticide. Little reason appears for the abhorence of infanticide by the French government to have changed in 27 years. *See also* Krause, *supra* note 231, at 177.

240. This effect of wet-nursing appears throughout Europe, de Mause, *supra* note 231, at 29-30, 282-83, 308-11, 352-55. One study confirmed 529 instances of "overlaying" (when a wet-nurse smothers the child in her sleep) from 1639-1659 for London-born children, J. RANDLE-SHORT, THE FATHER OF CHILD-CARE: LIFE OF WILLIAM CADOGAN 26 (1966). For a discussion showing that the dangers of wet-nursing were recognized at the time, *see* J. GUILLEMEAU, THE NURSING OF CHILDREN, *Preface* (1612). Some wet-nurses were expected to, or did, deliberately kill their charges. *See, e.g.,* L. ADAMIC, CRADLE OF LIFE: THE STORY OF ONE MAN'S BEGINNING 11, 45, 48 (1936).

241. The oath is quoted in Illick, *Child-Rearing in Seventeenth-Century England and America,* in de Mause, *supra* note 231, at 306: "I will not destroy the child born of woman, nor cut, nor pull off the head thereof, or otherwise dismember or hurt the same, or suffer it to be so hurt or dismembered." *See also* T. FORBES, THE MIDWIFE AND THE WITCH 144-47 (1966).

242. The statute in England was An Act to Prevent the Destroying and Murdering of Bastard Children, 21 Jac. 1, ch.27, § 3 (1623). This statute is variously reported as prohibiting the concealment of the death of, or the concealment of the birth of, a bastard. *Compare* 4 HOLDSWORTH, *supra* note 35, at 501 *and* 13 HOLDSWORTH 390 n.9. The statute prohibited concealing the death in order to conceal the birth.

criminality of abortion was still largely an academic issue. Infanticide was not.[243] Significantly the statute was enacted during a year of famine when many persons (including many children) perished.[244] Perhaps this enactment was a direct response to an upsurge of infanticide.

Even if one cannot find such a direct tie between the social conditions and the statute, the felt need to repress infanticide is clear from the creation of an irrebutable statutory presumption of murder from mere concealment. The link between abortion and this infanticide law in England becomes clear when one discovers that Lord Ellenborough's Act not only clarified and reemphasized the criminality of abortion,[245] but in the very next section also reduced the concealment penalty to a term of imprisonment.[246] However dimly Lord Ellenborough may have perceived it, this change of penalties (abortions increased to death, concealment reduced to imprisonment) corresponds directly to the change in medical technology and the change in behavior induced by the recently altered availability of abortions. Would those who would have committed infanticide prefer abortion even at some risk? Perhaps not all would have, but probably very many would, and apparently did, prefer it. Nor can this change be explained by supposing that Ellenborough was deferring to those cases where juries had nullified these infanticide laws. This remained a period of condemnation of infanticide by the articulate classes, so much so that midwifery was eventually suppressed because of its close linkage to infanticide, and its emerging linkage to abortion. Lord Ellenborough never conceded anything else to public opinion or the impracticability of a law, either as jurist or as legislator. Why should we suppose this case to be any different?

Concealment of infanticide statutes were enacted in eight of the United States prior to the first abortion laws in those states.[247] As

---

For the similar response in France, see Marvick, *supra* note 231, at 285. Compare also the response of Anglo-Saxon law, THRUPP, *supra* note 234.

243. For 30 documented cases of Elizabethan infanticide, see Tucker, *The Child as Beginning and End,* in de Mause, *supra* note 231, at 244-45.

244. LASLETT, *supra* note 229, at 113-18, 123-27.

245. 43 Geo. 3, c.58, §§ 2, 3 (1803).

246. *Id.* § 4. The term was finally reduced to a maximum of two years in 1861, Offenses Against the Person Act, 24 & 25 Vict., c.100, § 60 (1861).

247. Apparently the first concealment statute in the United States was enacted in 1696 in Massachusetts, CHARTERS & GEN'L L. OF THE COLONY & PROV. OF MASS. BAY 293 (Dane, Prescott & Story eds. 1814). For other such laws see 1801 Ky. Acts, ch.67, § 2 at 117, Act of

in England, the early American laws punished concealment as murder. The close connection between these concealment laws and abortion is shown even more clearly, since eleven states enacted prohibitions of concealments of births or deaths as part of, or, in one case, contemporaneously with, their first abortion statutes.[248] Four other states eventually included concealment statutes as part of their abortion prohibition scheme.[249] While not all of these infanticide statutes have survived various recodifications, 23 states enacted concealment or infanticide statutes at some point in their history. In 20 of these states,[250] as in England, the concealment or infanticide statutes were codified along with abortion statutes. This consistent treatment of these ostensibly separate statutes strongly reinforces the notion that infanticide and abortion legislation were seen as alternative responses to the same problem. Infanticide had been a major social problem because it was a safe (for the mother) alternative to abortion. But infanticide was made obsolete by the development of new techniques of abortion during this period. It

---

Feb. 22, 1817; 1817 La. Acts., § 3 at 182; MICH. CODE § 9 (1815), *reenacted,* 1820 Mich. (Terr.) Laws § 8; Provincial Act of 1714, 1 N.H. Original Acts 96, 1 N.H. Recorded Acts 184, 1716 N.H. Laws at 42, *reenacted* Act of Feb. 3, 1971, 1792 N.H. Laws, at 244, 1797 N.H. COMPILED LAWS, at 269; Wisc. (Terr.) Stat. § 6, at 365 (1839). Two other states also enacted statutes which declared infanticide murder and extended culpability to anyone who advised it as well as to the actual perpetrator, Del. Laws., ch.22, § 6, at 67 (1797); GA. PENAL CODE § 17 (1811). Georgia also enacted a concealment statute, GA. PENAL CODE §§ 22-24 (1816). *See* Quay, *supra* note 19, at 447-520.

For an early report of a concealment case (before any American statute was enacted), *see* 2 J. WINTHROP, HISTORY OF NEW ENGLAND 1630-1649 317-18 (Hosmer ed. 1908).

Infanticide does not seem to have been as common in the early United States as it was in contemporary Europe, Walzer, *A Period of Ambivalence: Eighteenth Century American Childhood,* in de Mause, *supra* note 231, at 351, 352-55, where infanticide appears to have been limited to bastards, Illick, *supra* note 241, at 327, 336 n.35.

248. 1887 COMPILED LAWS DAK. (Terr.), §§ 6538-40; 1868 Fla. Acts 1st Sess., ch.1637, tit. VIII, §§ 9-11; HAWAII PENAL CODE §§ 1-3 (1850); Idaho (Terr.) Laws §§ 33, 34, 42 (1863-64); ILL. REV. CODE §§ 40, 41, 46 (1827); ME. REV. STAT. ch.160, §§ 11-14 (1840); OKLA. STAT. §§ 2187-89 (1890); 1860 Pa. Laws No. 374, §§ 87-89 (1860); Wyo. (Terr.) Laws, 1st Sess., ch.3, §§ 25, 26 (1869). Minnesota enacted separate laws governing abortion and concealment during the same session, MINN. (TERR.) REV. STAT. ch.100, §§ 10, 11 (1851) & ch.107, § 7 (1851). Remember that Dakota Territory covered two states. These statutes either covered only abortion, infanticide, and other crimes against birth, or at least were grouped together in larger codes. *See* Quay, *supra* note 19, at 447-520.

249. Mo. REV. STAT. art. II, §§ 9, 10, 26, 40 (1855); Mont. Laws, Crim. Laws ch.IV, §§ 41, 42 (1871-72); NEV. REV. STAT. §§ 201.120-.150 (1959); 1845 N.Y. Laws., ch.260, §§ 1-6. *See* Quay, *supra* note 19, at 447-520.

250. Apparently only Delaware, Louisiana and Wisconsin never consolidated the infanticide, concealment, and abortion acts; all three of these states prohibited concealment or infanticide long before dealing with abortion. *See* Quay, *supra* note 19, at 447-520.

was no longer a major problem. Thus even those later states which did not enact concealment laws, or which repealed them, merely reflect this technologically-shaped reality.[251]

If the legislative and judicial activity regarding abortion which emerged in the early nineteenth century was caused by a change in the medical technology, why were activities which had become relatively safe prohibited? Other surgical procedures had comparable mortality rates from the same causes (infection and shock) but these were not banned.[252] Means nonetheless argues[253] that the purpose of this prohibition of abortion was solely to protect the health of the mother. Mortality from natural births at this time had been calculated at less than three percent.[254] One could infer from this fact that protecting the mother from her foolishness was a purpose of these statutes, if one can assume that the legislatures were aware of these facts.[255] Even the failure to enact statutes banning elective surgery generally[256] might not be fatal to such a theory, given the peculiar social pressures which a legislature might suppose were operating on a women to coerce her into dangerous surgery which others more objectively might judge unnecessary.[257] Such pressures presumably

---

251. Those who deny the "slippery slope" argument linking abortion and infanticide need not recant because of this historical linkage between the two, but they should at least explain why this linkage is no longer relevant. Most who argue along these lines seem to be rather ignorant of the historical linkage. One might even turn the "slippery slope" argument around, and assert that since many will resort to either infanticide or abortion as alternatives, abortion should be encouraged as the more humane alternative.

252. Means II, *supra* note 24, at 382-86. Few studies exist to show accurately the precise rate of mortality from lawful surgery, and no studies can pretend to measure whether abortions, had they been lawful, would have resulted in differing mortalities. Given the ease with which a uterine infection might close the cervical canal and thereby prevent drainage and healing, mortality might well have been higher than for some surgery, but no more so than for any surgery where proper dressing and draining would be difficult, *id.* at 385.

253. Means I, *supra* note 24, at 418, 453, 511-15; Means II, *supra* note 24, at 382-91.

254. Means II, *supra* note 24, at 385.

255. The earliest medical text which might arguably advance this "relative safety" test was not published until 1844 in England, A TAYLOR, MANUAL OF MEDICAL JURISPRUDENCE 595 (1844). This argument, however, related only to induced abortions in the seventh or eighth months of pregnancy. It is a justification for induced labor and caesarian sections, rather than true abortions. Taylor unequivocally condemned all true abortions, *id* at 594. *Cf.* Means II, *supra* note 24, at 394-96. By 1844 England and 12 states had effectively banned abortions.

256. In New York, the Revisors in preparing the Code of 1828 proposed a section prohibiting all surgery unless "necessary for the preservation of life," *quoted in* Means I, *supra* note 24, at 451. Why this would not have been sufficient to cover abortions if this were the only purpose served (*i.e.*, why did the Revisors include two separate abortion prohibitions as well) is not explained. In any event this ban was never enacted, a point whose significance escapes Means, *id.* at 450-53, 506; Means II, *supra* note 24, at 388-89.

257. Means I, *supra* note 24, at 506, (citing N.Y. Times, Jan. 12, 1863, at 5, col. 3).

were lacking when the question was whether to have one's leg ampu-
tated. But if these statutes were not concerned about new life, why
were they so often directly coupled with infanticide legislation? Or
are we to assume that the all-wise legislature Means assumes meant
to foster infanticide as a preferable alternative to abortion?

Evidence of a direct relation between protection of maternal
health and abortion prosecutions is ambiguous.[258] At best one can
conclude that protecting maternal health was a possible purpose of
the legal activity regarding abortions. To exclude other possible
purposes one must consider the fit of the statutes and precedents
to these other purposes.

The Court in *Roe v. Wade*[259] recognized three possible state
interests fostered by legislation prohibiting abortion: prevention of
illicit intercourse; protection of maternal health; and protection of
prenatal life. Means,[260] at least, would add a fourth interest: promotion of population growth. The first of these four reasons need not
concern us for long. No court has found prevention of illicit sex to
be a sound explanation of these cases and statutes, since in no
situation is the legitimacy of the pregnancy made a criterion even
marginally relevant to the legality of the abortion.[261] Support is
equally scant for the demographic rationale. No state has advanced
this as a goal of its action, nor has any court[262] or legislature relied

---

258. Means found only one case which expounded the purpose of nineteenth century
abortion statutes, State v. Murphy, 27 N.J.L. 112, 114-15 (1858). This case states that the
only purpose was to protect the mother. Despite Means' repeated assertions that this is the
only such case, Means I, *supra* note 24, at 507, Means II, *supra* note 24, at 389, Byrn II, *supra*
note 11, at 828 nn.137, 138, lists 9 cases explicitly adopting protection of the foetus as at least
one purpose of these statutes, five from the nineteenth century: People v. Sessions, 58 Mich.
594, 26 N.W. 291 (1886); State v. Gedicke, 43 N.J.L. 86 (1881); Dougherty v. People, 1 Colo.
514 (1872); State v. Moore, 25 Iowa 128 (1868); and State v. Howard, 32 Vt. 380 (1859). In
addition the case of State v. Crook, 16 Utah 212, 51 P. 1091 (1898), suggests a similar purpose.
The relationship between State v. Murphy and State v. Gedicke is much more complex than
Means I at 508-09 suggests.

259. 410 U.S. at 147-52.

260. Means I, *supra* note 24, at 509.

261. Roe v. Wade, 410 U.S. at 148; State v. Gedicke, 43 N.J.L. 86 (1881); Means II,
supra note 24, at 381-82.

262. Means I, *supra* note 24, at 509-10 argues that Mills v. Commonwealth, 13 Pa. 630,
632 (1850), did, but all the court said was: "It is not the murder of a living child which
constitutes the offense, but the destruction of gestation by wicked means and against nature."
Abortion is unlawful "because it interferes with and violates the mysteries of nature in that
process by which the human race is propagated and continued." *Id.* This argument seems
more metaphysical than demographic, and would appear to have become as obsolete as
arguments about the propriety of human interference with conception, or at least legal regulation thereof.

on it as a valid argument. The protection of maternal health as a basis for prohibiting abortion has already been examined. There remains only the need to examine the protection of prenatal life as a possible rationale for state legislation.

Protection of prenatal life is certainly a frequently advanced purpose for abortion laws today.[263] This reason was also advanced by courts in the nineteenth century.[264] One also finds support for this purpose in the public debates contemporaneous with the enactment of these various statutes.[265] Finally the wording of some of these early statutes itself expresses this purpose, the need to protect the unborn.[266] Was the statutory pattern consistent with this goal?

When the first statutes regulating abortion were enacted the prevalent notion of personhood was still that a foetus became a person only upon quickening.[267] During the eighteenth century scientists had engaged in strident debate over the nature of generation.[268] In particular, proponents of epigenesis[269] contested with proponents of preformation.[270] Overlaying this confusion was a long-

---

263. This purpose caused great difficulty to the Court in Roe v. Wade, 410 U.S. at 150-52, 156-64. *Cf.* the German Federal Constitutional Court Decision, Judgment of Feb. 25, 1975, 39 BVerfGE 1 *translated in* 9 J. MAR. J. PRAC. & PROC. 605-65 (1976), where unborns were held to be people which the state is under a mandatory duty to protect. This case is carefully analyzed by its translators, and other constitutional cases from other countries are noted in Gorby & Jonas, *West German Abortion Decision: A Contrast to Roe v. Wade*, 9 J. MAR. J. PRAC. & PROC. 551 (1976).

264. *See* cases cited at note 249 *supra*.

265. This support is most clearly stated by a resolution of the American Medical Association at its Twelfth Annual Meeting, 12 TRANS. A.M.A. 73-77 (1859), *quoted in* Roe v. Wade, 410 U.S. at 141-42. *See also* a resolution by the Medical Society of the State of New York, N.Y. Times, Feb. 6, 1867, at 8, cols.1-2, *reprinted in* 1867 N.Y. ASSEMBLY J. 443-44. *See also* I. T. BECK & R. BECK, ELEMENTS OF MEDICAL JURISPRUDENCE 276-77 (1823). Means I, *supra* note 24, at 459, quotes the Medical Society of the State of New York resolution, but nonetheless argues that only Catholics in the nineteenth century took such a position, *id.* at 510-11.

266. *See, e.g.,* MICH. REV. STAT. ch.153, § 32 (1846): "The willful killing of an unborn quick child by any injury to the mother of such child, which would be murder if it resulted in the death of such mother, shall be deemed manslaughter." *Cf.* Evans v. People, 49 N.Y. 86 (1872).

267. This definition was based on the assumed 40/80 day animation theory, *supra* notes 121-25. For a survey of various theories of foetal development current in the seventeenth and eighteenth centuries, *see* J. NEEDHAM, A HISTORY OF EMBRYOLOGY, 115-229 (1959). *See also* Means I, *supra* note 24, at 411-17.

268. A. MEYER, THE RISE OF EMBRYOLOGY 54-97 (1939); NEEDHAM, *supra* note 267, at 213-25.

269. The theory of epigenesis states that the parts of the embryo develop by a gradual diversification from an initially undifferentiated source. *See* MEYER, *supra* note 268, at 54-61.

270. The theory of preformation postulates that the embryo was fully preformed in

standing debate about spontaneous generation.[271] Uncertainty was compounded by the small achievement produced by a great deal of experimentation. Although van Leuwenhock discovered spermatazoa in 1677,[272] by 1800 no one had yet found any mammalian ovum.[273] It is not surprising that the predominant view was that the father generated the embryo with the mother merely providing a "home" for it. Given the great ignorance surrounding early stages of pregnancy, old ideas of "ensoulment" (or "animation") lingered on, and even scientifically sophisticated people conceded that they could not prove that a living thing had been killed before quickening.[274] Yet such proof was necessary if one were to justify punishing the abortionist with death. On the other hand, if the child were present even in a single sperm, fear that one might be killing a person might justify some penalty for abortions performed before quickening even without certainty that a living thing had been killed. This was precisely the pattern of Lord Ellenborough's Act, and of most of the early statutes in the United States, although some of these statutes omitted any mention of pre-quickening abortions. This statutory pattern, in fact, is more consistent with then prevalent theories of foetal personhood than with the protection of maternal health as the risks of infection or shock were high at all stages of pregnancy, and not just after quickening.

Early in the nineteenth century a series of scientific developments recast accepted ideas of embryology.[275] Shortly after the turn of the century the cell theory began to be applied to embryology,[276] and with it the triumph of modern theories of epigenesis was as-

---

either the sperm or the ovum, development being purely a process of growth fed by nutrition. Several explanations were advanced as to how the process of "preformation" occurred, including pangenesis, where it was theorized that the gonads assembled cells from all parts of the parent's body to make a new miniature body, or panspermatism, where the "seeds of life" floated in the air to settle in the void following coition, *id.* at 62-97. WILLIAMS, *supra* note 65, at 206-07, discusses the "box theory," *i.e.,* all persons were packed in "boxes" inside their parent's seed, boxes inside boxes all the way back to Adam and Eve. *See also* C. DARLINGTON, THE FACTS OF LIFE 32-38 (1953).

271. MEYER, *supra* note 268, at 28-53, 92-97; NEEDHAM, *supra* note 267, at 205-13.
272. MEYER, *supra* note 268, at 138-47; NEEDHAM, *supra* note 267, at 175.
273. MEYER, *supra* note 268, at 98-120.
274. The first case under Lord Ellenborough's Act, 43 Geo. 3, c.58, §§ 2, 3 (1803), was Anonymous, 170 Eng. Rep. 1310 (N.P. 1811). A directed acquittal resulted because the doctors were unable to agree "when the foetus may be stated to be quick, and to have a distinct existence." *Id.* at 1311-12. The judge then relied on the common understanding that to be quick the woman must have felt the child move, which she swore she had not.
275. *See generally* 3 HISTORY OF SCIENCE 456-69, 480-83 (R. Taton ed. 1965).
276. MEYER, *supra* note 268, at 302-19; NEEDHAM, *supra* note 267, at 223-29.

sured. In 1827 Karl Ernst von Baer accidentally discovered ova in dogs.[277] Three years earlier Prevost and Dumas had succeeded in fertilizing frogs' eggs.[278] These two discoveries alone revolutionized concepts of reproductive processes. Much work remained to be done,[279] but the basic tenets of modern embryology are rooted in these discoveries. These discoveries, linked with the theory of cellular epigenesis, provided support for the theory that a new being came into existence with the fertilization of the ovum, and that this being thereafter developed without any change of its essential substance. Within a few years medical societies,[280] and at least some major religious groups,[281] accepted the notion that a distinct human being was formed at conception. The legal pattern which emerged shortly thereafter was largely consistent with this new concept, just as the earlier laws had been consistent with the older concepts of gestation. Abortion was made uniformly criminal at any stage of pregnancy.[282] At least one court reinterpreted "quick with child" to mean any time after conception.[283] Most jurisdictions moved to make the prescribed punishment the same at any stage of pregnancy.

There were apparent exceptions to this pattern of protecting all foeti as if they were people from the moment of conception. Ten states distinguished an abortion before quickening from one per-

---

277. MEYER, *supra* note 268, at 120-31; 3 HISTORY OF SCIENCE, *supra* note 275, at 460-61.

278. 3 HISTORY OF SCIENCE, *supra* note 275, at 461. Prevost & Dumas were duplicating the earlier experiments of Spallanzini, MEYER, *supra* note 268, at 170-81. Spallanzini missed the significance of what he had done because of his preformationist convictions, *id.* at 179-80. Prevost and Dumas realized what they had done, and may even have isolated mammalian ova at this time, *id.* at 120-21.

279. *See generally* MEYER, *supra* note 268, at 182-94, 319-41; 3 HISTORY OF SCIENCE, *supra* note 275, at 461-64. One of the important discoveries yet to be made was von Bischoff's demonstration of mammalian fertilization (1838), *id.* at 461; MEYER 184-90. Also still to be worked out were the principles of genetics, 3 HISTORY OF SCIENCE 481-83.

280. *See* sources cited at note 256 *supra*.

281. For developments in the Catholic Church involving major new canonical legislation based on this new theory, *see* D. CALLAHAN, ABORTION: LAW, CHOICE AND MORALITY 410-61 (1970); GRISEZ, *supra* note 47 at 177-81; Means I, *supra* note 24, at 414-16. *See generally* Curran, *Religious Implications*, in Rosen, *supra* note 72, at 153-65.

282. This was done in England in 1837, Offenses Against the Person Act, 1837, 7 Will. 4 & 1 Vict., c.85. Illinois did so if the abortion were accomplished by the use of a noxious substance in 1827, ILL. REV. CODE § 46, at 131 (1827); the first U.S. statute making any abortion before quickening a felony was ME. REV. STAT. ch.160, §§ 13, 14 (1840). *See* Quay, *supra* note 19, at 466, 477.

283. King v. Wycherley, 173 Eng. Rep. 486 (N.P. 1838); Byrn II, *supra* note 11, at 825-26. *See also* Evans v. People, 49 N.Y. 86, 89 (1872).

formed after quickening by imposing a different punishment for each stage.[284] The penalties for abortion generally were not comparable with those established for homicide.[285] What accounts for these limitations on the principle of foetal personhood?

First of all, one might argue that there are differing treatments of unborn children and born children because foetal life is valued less highly than other forms of human life, that an unborn child is not yet considered a person.[286] Such a conclusion is not compelled by the evidence drawn from the time of the first enactment of the abortion statutes. As we have seen,[287] legislatures, courts, and the public media contained frequent assertions of foetal personhood. Secondly, despite the advances in embryology in the nineteenth century, problems of proof existed, since knowledge of gestational processes remained extremely rudimentary. Spontaneous abortions could occur without prediction. Would the child have died even without the induced abortion? If the abortion were performed by a doctor, could one be sure if the doctor asserted that he was only aiding a spontaneous abortion? Could one even be certain that the child was alive when the abortion began, since the abortion techniques then available never could have resulted in live birth? Or could one be sure that the abortion was not necessary to save the mother's life or health[288] at a time when the threat to life or health exception was interpreted to require more than good faith by the doctor?[289] The earlier the stage of the pregnancy, the greater these uncertainties became.

While uncertainties of proof could occur in any murder trial,

---

284. Grisez, *supra* note 47, at 191; Quay, *supra* note 19, at 447-520.

285. The United Kingdom, however, gave life in prison as a maximum sentence for even an attempted abortion, Offenses Against the Person Act, 24 & 25 Vict., c.100, § 58. This penalty persisted until the Abortion Act, 15 & 16 Eliz. 2, c.87 (1967).

286. Roe v. Wade, 410 U.S. at 158 n.54; Means I, *supra* note 24, at 482-83.

287. *See* notes 263-66 *supra.*

288. As recently as 1936 one could give a long list of conditions which when coupled with pregnancy would normally be treated in part by abortion, Taussig, *supra* note 71, at 277-321. By 1951 nearly all of these medical indications for abortion had disappeared, both because of improved prospects for treating the mother without abortion, and because of changed attitudes among doctors, Guttmacher, *The Shrinking Non-Psychiatric Indications for Therapeutic Abortions,* in Rosen, *supra* note 72, at 12-21; Gebhard et. al., *supra* note 227, at 196-97; Niswander, *Medical Abortion Practices in the United States,* in Abortion and the Law, *supra* note 71, at 41-45; and Quay, *supra* note 19, at 180-220; Williams, *supra* note 65, at 156-57.

289. *See* King v. Bourne, [1939] 1 K.B. 687, [1938] 3 All E.R. 615 (these two reports of the judgment are not the same); United States v. Vuitch, 402 U.S. 62 (1971).

such uncertainties were routine in abortion cases. One could rarely prove beyond a reasonable doubt that the abortion was the cause of death, even if one could prove the abortion.[290] Although there is little direct evidence of such concern over problems of proof,[291] one cannot exclude this explanation for the failure to treat abortion in all respects like other homicides. This explanation is particularly appealing because it is consistent with the frequent assertions of an intent to protect the foetus as a person,[292] whereas the alternative (that the legislators did not believe the foetus was a person) flatly contradicts those assertions. On the other hand, one cannot rule out the possibility that foetal life was considered to be a person, but not as valuable a person as one who had been born.

In summary, the nineteenth century was a period of considerable legislative activity designed to make clear that abortion by any means at any stage of pregnancy for any reason, except to preserve the life or health of the mother, was a serious crime. This was a reflection of two technological developments in the late eighteenth and throughout the nineteenth centuries, both of which created a need for strong anti-abortion laws. First, the means for inducing abortion were refined so that abortion was no longer tantamount to suicide. Abortion remained highly dangerous, however, and peculiar social pressures could be perceived which might often force a woman to undergo such risks. These pressures were lacking for other, perhaps equally dangerous, surgeries, which would justify isolating the abortion decision and prohibiting it except when strictly necessary. The second development was a gradual discovery of the nature of the gestational processes, followed by the widespread conclusion that the foetus was a person. As uncertainties of proof would prevent the straightforward application of homicide laws, special abortion laws were needed to protect the foetus without violating traditional notions of due process for the abortionist. At the same time, special treatment for infanticide became less necessary and it tended to fade in importance as abortion became more easily available. The

---

290. One could perhaps prove that the abortion was the cause of death by showing the results of careful medical examination of the foetus contemporaneously with the abortion. This would almost certainly be evidence which could only be obtained from the abortionist, however, and such self-incrimination could no longer be coerced. Even today the necessary facts, not to say the *corpi delicti,* are virtually impossible to prove sufficiently to make out a murder, Means II, *supra* note 24, at 380.

291. *But see* Anonymous, 170 Eng. Rep. 1310 (N.P. 1811); Foster v. State, 182 Wis. 298, 196 N.W. 233 (1923); Byrn II, *supra* note 11, at 832-34.

292. *See* notes 263-66 *supra.*

laws governing infanticide and abortion were well attuned to the technology of the mid-nineteenth century. If these laws reflected a new moral awareness, that moral awakening was itself the result of the very same technological developments. These laws could remain beyond dispute only so long as the underlying technologies did not change. But change they did.

D. Phase IV (1967-Present): The Legalization of Induced Abortions

Resistance to, and criticism of, the statutes prohibiting induced abortions never completely disappeared. Illegal abortions continued throughout the period discussed in Phase III,[293] although there are no reliable data presenting the number of illegal abortions at any particular time.[294] Occasional criticisms of the abortion restrictions did occur in reputable medical literature.[295] Prior to 1920, however, nearly all who commented on abortion were vehemently opposed.[296] The near unanimity of opposition to abortion began to dissolve after November 18, 1920, when the Soviets legalized abortion on demand.[297]

---

293. Anecdotal evidence abounds for this assertion. *See, e.g.*, S. DE BEAUVOIR, THE SECOND SEX 540-550 (Vintage Books ed. 1974); E. FRANKFURT, VAGINAL POLITICS 51-83 (Bantam ed. 1973); D. SCHULDER & F. KENNEDY, ABORTION RAP 44-82 (1971). For one of the few relatively careful studies of illegal abortions, *see* GEBHARD, *et. al.*, *supra* note 227, at 189-214.

294. Estimates for the United States vary from 41,000 to 700,000 per year for 1935-1940, WILLIAMS, *supra* note 65, at 191. BATES & ZAWADZKI, *supra* note 71, at 3, estimated at least 1,000,000 for 1964, but they also estimated at least 5,000 deaths, whereas the true figure for deaths is almost certainly less than 1,000. CALLAHAN, *supra* note 281, at 285, estimated 30 to 35 million abortions throughout the world each year. Much lower estimates were embraced by GRISEZ, *supra* note 47, at 35-42. Similar uncertainty as to the number of illegal abortions in other countries also exists, DE BEAUVOIR, *supra* note 293, at 135 (France); DICKENS, *supra* note 47, at 73-83 (England); GRISEZ 42-48 (general); and WILLIAMS, *supra* note 65, at 192-97 (England).

295. These criticisms are contained principally in A. TAYLOR, THE PRINCIPLES AND PRACTICE OF MEDICAL JURISPRUDENCE 790-94 (1865), in marked contrast to Taylor's earlier condemnation of abortions, TAYLOR, *supra* note 255, at 594-95. *See also* 6 H. ELLIS, STUDIES IN THE PSYCHOLOGY OF SEX 588, 601-10 (1913); C. MERCIER, CRIME AND CRIMINALS 196-97 (1918).

296. In 1919 the Eugenics Pubishing Co., Inc., of New York, published a short book to advocate family planning and sex for pleasure, H. LONG, SANE SEX LIFE AND SANE SEX LIVING (1919). In a long section on family planning, *id.* at 115-25, there occurs this statement:

On this point, let it be said that all sane and intelligent men and women agree that anything even approaching infanticide is nothing short of a crime, and that abortion, except for the purpose of saving the life of the mother, is practically murder.

But, while this is all true, to prevent the contact of two germs which, if permitted to unite, would be liable to result in a living human form, is *quite another affair*. *Id.* at 120.

297. *See generally* CALLAHAN, *supra* note 281, at 220-23; GRISEZ, *supra* note 47, at 194-

The legalization of abortion in Russia was the result of efforts by "feminists on the Left."[298] They sought to free women from enforced motherhood with its often virtual incarceration in the home. This goal fit neatly into the need for an enlarged labor force necessary to effectuate the industrialization process about to be undertaken. The decree of the Commissariats of Health and Justice also mentioned improvements of women's health as a goal.[299] The measure was also seen as a temporary expedient to be repealed as soon as safe, effective, and convenient contraceptive devices became widely available.[300]

Beginning in 1927, legalized abortion encountered social pressures favoring repeal. Propaganda against abortions became widespread in the Soviet Union. Anesthesia was denied for abortions.[301] Finally, in 1936, abortions were prohibited, except to protect the life or health of the mother, or to prevent the transmission of hereditary disease.[302] The ostensible reasons for this reversion to a restrictive approach were twofold. Unhealthy side effects of the abortion on the mother was one justification; a second reason was a drive to strengthen the family. Most western commentators have concluded, however, that the new decree was motivated by a desire to increase population for economic[303] or military reasons.[304] The earlier decree became the model which leftists and feminists in other countries emulated, and a number of Baltic countries in the late 1930's, with elected left-wing governments, adopted moderately permissive abortion statutes.[305]

In England[306] and in the United States[307] during the interwar

200; TAUSSIG, *supra* note 71, at 405-20.

298.   6 H. ELLIS, *supra* note 295, at 607-09, discusses an incipient abortion reform movement in Germany. *Cf.* CALLAHAN, *supra* note 281, at 460-68.

299.   Field, *The Re-Legalization of Abortion in Soviet Russia,* 255 NEW ENG. J. MED. 421 (Aug. 30, 1956).

300.   Margaret Sanger, of Planned Parenthood, also saw abortion as a "desperate remedy" to be made obsolete by better contraception practices, M. SANGER, MOTHERHOOD IN BONDAGE 394-96 (1928).

301.   GRISEZ, *supra* note 47, at 196; TAUSSIG, *supra* note 71, at 418-20.

302.   H. SIGERIST, MEDICINE AND HEALTH IN THE SOVIET UNION 322-33 (1947). *See also* CALLAHAN, *supra* note 281, at 223; GRISEZ, *supra* note 47, at 197-200; WILLIAMS, *supra* note 65, at 200.

303.   GRISEZ, *supra* note 47, at 198-99.

304.   CALLAHAN, *supra* note 281, at 223; WILLIAMS, *supra* note 65, at 200.

305.   CALLAHAN, *supra* note 281, at 185-217; GEBHARDT, *et. al.* *supra* note 227, at 221-32; GRISEZ, *supra* note 47, at 203-08; WILLIAMS, *supra* note 65, at 214-23.

306.   GRISEZ, *supra* note 47, at 208-20.

307.   *Id.* at 224-29. *See generally* LADER I, *supra* note 23.

period, groups of recently enfranchised feminists took up the cause of abortion reform, with varying degrees of success.[308] After World War II, however, the impetus for reform in the United States was eclipsed by the anti-left swing of opinion in the early cold war.[309] In England, with its Labor government, the reform movement continued to grow and began to move away from its leftist political origins. The last Churchill (Conservative) government twice saw unsuccessful attempts in Parliament to enact major reform legislation.[310] Finally, Glanville Williams, in the Carpentier Lectures given at Columbia University School of Law in 1956,[311] reopened the abortion debate in the United States and separated the issue from its left-leaning political sources which had temporarily beclouded the issue.[312] Professor Williams advocated limited legalization of abortions based on abhorence of the social costs of illegal abortions[313] and the rejection of foetal personhood before the 28th week of pregnancy.[314]

The social cost argument began with a rejection of foetal personhood. The contrary view was rejected as entailing an establishment of religion.[315] Williams also believed no foetal electroencephalogram was possible before the 28th week.[316] This technological

---

308. The British movement successfully sponsored Dr. Bourne in a test case which substantially liberalized the interpretation of the British abortion law, GRISEZ, *supra* note 47, at 220-24, while the American movement sponsored the highly influential studies of Dr. Frederick J. Taussig, *id.* at 226-28.

309. Abortion reform had strong left-wing ties, or at least appeared to have such ties, because of frequent (pre-1936) statements by supporters of reform like this: "Russia is the only country that has faced abortion intelligently." PALMER & GREENBERG, *supra* note 111, at 163. The movement never died out, but little public controversy occurred while the movement was divorcing itself from its leftist rhetoric, GRISEZ, *supra* note 47, at 231-32.

310. GRISEZ, *supra* note 47, at 229-31; WILLIAMS, *supra* note 65, at 201.

311. Published in book form, cited as WILLIAMS, *supra* note 65.

312. This does not mean that the abortion reform movement owed nothing to the American left thereafter, but only that the issue of abortion reform found substantial non-leftist support, and could no longer be dismissed out of hand if one rejected leftist premises. One could favor abortion reform based on a conservative, libertarian ethic. Japan provided a conservative model to be considered, CALLAHAN, *supra* note 281, at 253-77; GRISEZ, *supra* note 47, at 253-56. In short, one had to discuss the growing controversy over abortion on its merits regardless of the politics of its advocate, *See also* Guttmacher, *The Legal Status of Therapeutic Abortions,* in Rosen, *supra* note 71, at 175-86.

313. WILLIAMS, *supra* note 65, at 189-97.

314. *Id.* at 205-12. *See* Nathanson, *Deeper into Abortion,* 291 NEW ENG. J. MED. 1189 (1974), for an interesting turnabout on this point.

315. *Id.* at 177-89, 202-12. This problem is, of course, not so simple as Williams assumed, Dellapenna, *supra* note 5, at 384-409; Tribe, *supra* note 11, at 18-25, 28-32.

316. WILLIAMS, *supra* note 65, at 210.

basis of his opinion is now obsolete.[317] Williams appears primarily to adopt the 28th week as the dividing line between persons (subject to protection) and non-persons (not subject to protection) because it is convenient for the mother; *i.e.*, it justifies allowing the mother to choose abortion.[318] Having satisfied himself that foeti are not people, the social costs argument becomes simply a task of measuring the costs to women from the prohibition of abortions, against the protection afforded women by this prohibition. The social costs argument delineated by Professor Williams remains today the basic argument of those who favor permissive approaches to abortion.[319] The fact that early abortion has become safer for the mother than childbirth makes the social cost argument heavily weighted in favor of permitting abortions.[320] Put more dramatically, the argument asserts that criminal abortions take women's lives, sap their strength, and load them with guilt, for no comparable social gain.[321]

Shortly after the Williams' lectures, the A.L.I. Model Penal Code appeared. The Code's provisions on abortion[322] were closely modeled after the limited reform[323] proposed by Professor Williams.[324] Growing debate, agitation,[325] and reform legislation fol-

---

317. EEG's are now possible at least by the 8th week of pregnancy, H. LILEY, MODERN MOTHERHOOD 28 (rev. ed. 1969); Dellapenna, *supra* note 5, at 406-09; Hellegers, *Fetal Development*, 31 THEOLOGICAL STUDIES 3, 7-8 (1970); and Ramsey, *Reference Points in Deciding about Abortion*, in THE MORALITY OF ABORTION 69-79 (J. Noonan ed. 1970).

318. WILLIAMS, *supra* note 65, at 205-06, 210-12. Of course, the problem is whether to allow the choice of abortion to the mother; thus the Williams reasoning is circular at best. Williams, in a different context, gave the best possible response to this sort of approach which completely begs the question: "moral dogmatism of this kind cannot be dealt with on an intellectual level." *Id.* at 206.

319. This argument was apparently adopted by the court in Roe v. Wade, 410 U.S. at 132-36, 147-52, 162-166. *See also* COMMITTEE FOR PSYCHIATRY AND LAW, THE RIGHT TO ABORTION: A PSYCHIATRIC VIEW (1970) [hereinafter cited as RIGHT TO ABORTION].

320. This is, of course, the Means' thesis identified in text accompanying notes 26-33 *supra. See also* Roe v. Wade, 410 U.S. at 148-50, 163. There is some medical challenge to this asserted fact, Ely, *supra* note 11, at 942 n.117. Williams appeared less aware of the technological basis of his argument than Means. *See* RIGHT TO ABORTION, *supra* note 319, at 33-37, for a clear acknowledgment of this technical basis.

321. The argument is well stated in WILLIAMS, *supra* note 65, at 189-97. For individual horror stories, *see* LADER II, *supra* note 37, at 21-25; SCHULDER & KENNEDY, *supra* note 293, at 6-88.

322. MODEL PENAL CODE, § 230.3 (Proposed Official Draft 1962).

323. One of the principal drafters defended the Model Penal Code Provision, *id.*, solely on the grounds of political compromise, personally favoring complete legalization, Schwartz, *Morals Offenses and the Model Penal Code*, 63 COLO. L. REV. 669, 683-86 (1963).

324. WILLIAMS, *supra* note 65, at 212-14.

325. This debate is reported at length in LADER II, *supra* note 37. For scholarly discussion of the merits of these proposals, *see* GRISEZ, *supra* note 47, at 236-50; George, *Current*

lowed.[326] These developments culminated with the courts' declaring virtually all restrictions on abortion unconstitutional.[327] Such a dramatic reversal of the legal status of abortion in barely twenty years itself suggests that more basic processes are at work than mere coincidence of opinion, particularly in light of the world-wide scope of these changes.[328] If one seeks the cause of this dramatic change, one is brought back again to technological developments.

When modern abortion statutes were enacted, the technology of abortion had reached the point where abortions were no longer tantamount to suicide. Like any surgery, the operation entailed high risks of death from injury, infection, or shock.[329] Work to eliminate these problems continued throughout the nineteenth and twentieth centuries. This work was not directly intended to make abortions safer and more convenient for the mother. Rather, these refinements of technique occurred because of improvements in surgical procedures generally. The first important event was the development of various anesthetics which, by repressing awareness of pain, pre-

---

Abortion Law: Proposals and Movements for Reform, in ABORTION AND THE LAW, *supra* note 71, at 1-36; Leavy & Kummer, *Criminal Abortion: Human Hardship and Unyielding Laws,* 36 S. CAL. L. REV. 140, 141 (1962); Packer & Gampell, *Therapeutic Abortion: A Problem in Law and in Medicine,* 11 STAN. L. REV. 417, 450 (1959). *Cf.* CALLAHAN, *supra* note 281, 25-116.

326. The movement began with Colorado's adoption of the Model Penal Code reforms in COLO. REV. STAT. ANN. §§ 40-2-50 to 40-2-53 (Cumm. Supp. (1967)). Reform legislation moved to a new level with the virtual total repeal of restrictions on early abortions, beginning in New York in 1970, N.Y. PENAL LAW (McKinney), § 125.05 (1975). These variously reformed statutes are collected in Roe v. Wade, 410 U.S. at 140 n.37.

327. This trend began in People v. Belous, 71 Cal.2d 954, 458 P.2d 194, 80 Cal. Rptr. 354 (1969), *cert. denied,* 397 U.S. 915 (1970), and culminated in Roe v. Wade, 410 U.S. 113 (1973), and Doe v. Bolton, 410 U.S. 179 (1973). For analyses of *Roe* and *Doe, see* Dellapenna, *supra* note 5, and the studies collected in note 11 *supra.*

328. Abortion was again legalized in the Soviet Union in 1955, followed shortly thereafter by legalization in other East European countries, CALLAHAN, *supra* note 281, at 220-53; Field, *supra* note 299. For the parallel developments in England and Wales, *see* CALLAHAN 142-49; DICKENS, *supra* note 47; and GRISEZ, *supra* note 47, at 229-31, 239-40, 250-53. As to Canada, *see* A. DE VALK, MORALITY AND LAW IN CANADIAN POLITICS (1974). *See also* Veitch & Tracey, *Abortion in the Common Law World,* 22 AM. J. COMP. L. 652 (1974). *See generally* LEE & LARSON, *supra* note 232. Gorby & Jonas, *supra* note 263, at 558-62, summarized the holdings of constitutional adjudications in Austria, Canada, France, West Germany, Italy, and the United States. All these cases were decided within 2 years of each other. For a general survey of changes in the laws regarding abortion since 1966, *see* Tietze & Levit, *Legal Abortion,* 236 SCIENTIFIC AM. 21 (Jan. 1977).

329. *See* text accompanying notes 223-28 *supra.*

330. Chloroform, ethyl ether, and nitrous oxide were all experimented with in Britain and America in the 1840's, and came into general use gradually thereafter, 3 HISTORY OF SCIENCE, *supra* note 275, at 499-500.

vented shock.[330] Improved pain-killing drugs[331] had a similar effect. The introduction of antiseptics[332] after 1865 gradually reduced infection risks. Even so simple a device as surgical gloves was an important means of saving lives.[333]

These improvements in surgical technique did not at once transform abortions into safe and simple operations. The very illegality of abortions hindered both the spread of these improvements among abortionists and the refinement of abortionists' techniques. Anesthesia introduced new dangers[334] as well as eliminating the old. Nonetheless, the risks of abortion gradually decreased. One reasonable estimate[335] placed maternal deaths from skillful abortions in the early nineteenth century at 31,250 per 100,000. Today that figure, in the first trimester of pregnancy, is less than 4 per 100,000, whereas modern rates for death in childbirth range upwards from 30 per 100,000 compared with an early nineteenth century figure of 2,820 per 100,000.[336] No one can say with certainty when skillful early abortion became safer for the mother than skillful medically-assisted birth.[337] The change may not have occurred until the advent of antibiotics in the 1940's.[338] One can only be sure that this technological transition occurred between 1865 and 1955.[339]

While general improvements in surgical techniques made at least early abortion increasingly safer for the mother, doctors (and

---

331.   Morphine, for example, was first isolated in 1806, id: at 301.

332.   Lister published his findings in 1867, and antiseptic practices began to be adopted after 1884. *Id.* at 301, 394, 508-10. *See also* Means I, *supra* note 24, at 436; Means II, *supra* note 24, at 391-92.

333.   The use of surgical gloves was introduced by W. S. Halsted at Johns Hopkins University in 1899, 3 HISTORY OF SCIENCE, *supra* note 275, at 510.

334.   Pure chloroform and pure ether were soon discovered to interrupt haematosis, *id.*, and even today anesthesia poses risks far greater than most other aspects of an operation, as shown by the far higher malpractice insurance premiums charged to anesthesiologists. *See generally* J. GREENHILL, ANALGESIA AND ANESTHESIA IN OBSTETRICS (2d ed. 1962).

335.   Means II, *supra* note 24, at 384-85.

336.   The most recent study found abortions cause fewer deaths than childbirth at any time before the seventeenth week of pregnancy. This ranges from 1/3 as many deaths if performed before the twelfth week, to as little as 1/20 as many deaths before the eighth week, Tietze & Levit, *supra* note 328, at 27. *See also* CALLAHAN, *supra* note 281, at 31-43; DICKENS, *supra* note 47, at 156; GEBHARD, *et. al.,* *supra* note 227, at 215-32; GRISEZ, *supra* note 47, at 104-06; LADER I, *supra* note 23, at 17-23; LADER II, *supra* note 37, at 166; WILLIAMS, *supra* note 65, at 220-22; Means I, *supra* note 24, at 511-12; Tietze, *Mortality with Contraception and Induced Abortion,* 45 STUD. IN FAM. PLAN. 6 (1969) [hereinafter cited as Tietze, *Mortality*]; Tietze & Lehfeldt, *Legal Abortion in Eastern Europe,* 175 J.A.M.A. 1149, 1152 (April 1961).

337.   Means II, *supra* note 24, at 384 places the date between 1900 and 1933.

338.   This is suggested by Justice Blackmun in Roe v. Wade, 410 U.S. at 149.

others) gradually refined techniques for inducing abortion. Since therapeutic abortions were generally legal, such research could occur throughout this period without the researcher necessarily engaging in criminal conduct. Improvements both in surgical techniques and in specific techniques for abortion spilled over to gradually decrease the risks from criminal abortions as well. Illegality, however, probably slowed the perfection of newer abortion techniques.

Two important new techniques for performing abortions were perfected after 1960, at a time when abortions were legal in many countries. Vacuum aspiration[340] replaced dilation and curettage for abortions up to the twelfth week of pregnancy. Saline amniocentesis replaced hysterotomies for abortions after the sixteenth week of pregnancy.[341] Both methods are simpler and safer. Vacuum aspiration in particular takes only a few minutes, and causes little or no

---

339. This transition occurred between the discovery of antisepsis and the relegalization of abortion in the Soviet Union. Eastern European complication rates after 1955 are the basis of the conclusion that abortions can be safer for the mother than childbirth. Scandinavian complication rates remained considerably higher, apparently because abortions usually were performed later in the pregnancy. *See* the sources cited in note 336 *supra*. The Supreme Court apparently thinks this is so only for the first third of pregnancy, Roe v. Wade, 410 U.S. at 163. In fact, abortion today is certainly safer and less painful than childbirth at least through the second trimester as well, Means II, *supra* note 24, at 387, 401. Probably this safety factor, if not the pain advantage, remains throughout pregnancy, although the records for the third trimester are sparse as few abortions are performed then. The performance of fewer abortions at this stage presumably results more from feelings of foetal personhood than from fear for the mother. *But see* Tietze & Levit, *supra* note 328, at 26-27. *Cf.* Roe v. Wade, 410 U.S. at 149. *See generally Abortion Mortality*, 20 Morbidity and Mortality 208, 209 (July 12, 1971); Lader I, *supra* note 23, at 17-23; Liley, *supra* note 317, at 42; Parker & Nelson, *Abortion in New York City: The First Nine Months*, 3 Fam. Plan. No. 3, at 5-12 (July, 1971); Potts, *Postconception Control of Fertility*, 8 Int'l J. Gynecology & Obstetrics 957, 967 (1970); Tietze & Lehfeldt, *supra* note 336; Tietze, *Mortality*, *supra* note 336, Tietze, *United States: Therapeutic Abortions, 1963-1968*, 59 Stud. in Fam. Plan. 5, 7 (1970).

340. Lader II, *supra* note 37, at 200. In the earliest stages of pregnancy, vacuum aspiration may appear under the guise of "menstrual extraction," Byrn II, *supra* note 11, at 859. This essentially involves vacuuming the womb through a tube. For gruesome descriptions of abortion procedures, *see* Byrn I, *supra* note 9, at 31-32. The same procedures are described in abstract scientific terms in Kutner, *Due Process of Abortion*, 53 Minn. L. Rev. 1 (1968).

341. Saline amniocentesis involves injecting a saline solution into the amniotic fluid which burns the foetus, killing it, followed by labor to expel the dead or injured foetus. This process, sometimes called "salting out," can produce a badly scarred, but live foetus, to the considerable embarrassment of abortion enthusiasts, Lader II, *supra* note 37, at 164-66. A hysterotomy, essentially a caesarian section, may still be necessary for some cases. The constitutional propriety of "salting out" was upheld in Planned Parenthood v. Danforth, 428 U.S. 52, 75-79, 95-99 (1976). "Salting out" can burn the uterus as well as the foetus, and can lead to other problems as well. *See also* Colautti v. Franklin, 47 U.S.L.W. 4094, 4099-4100 (U.S. 1979).

pain to the mother.[342]

New techniques are being developed which may make abortions even safer and less painful for the mother.[343] Today, from the mother's point of view, no reason exists for the law to treat abortion any differently from any other form of minor surgery.[344] Predictably similar developments in the past have given rise to strong pressure groups who would benefit from a change in the law to permit the widespread use of the new technology. Women gained greater control over their lives, while doctors acquired a new, relatively easy source of income. Further, women as a class were emerging to new power and self-confidence and made their demands[345] felt more effectively than before.[346] On the other hand, only foeti, an inarticulate and powerless class,[347] would be hurt.

The distribution of benefits and costs from the new technology might alone explain which interest prevailed. Indeed, one might ask why the controversy has been so prolonged and difficult in the face of such obviously strong interests in changing the law. What has generated the opposition? The answer, of course, has been the conviction of many[348] that the foetus is a human being, a person, who

---

342. Vladov, *The Vacuum Aspiration Method for Interruption of Early Pregnancy*, 99 Am. J. Obstetrics & Gynecology 202 (1967). *But see* Wohl, *The Harvey Karman Controversy*, Ms., Sept., 1974, at 60, for a discussion of several problems with various types of vacuum aspiration devices invented by "Dr." Karman and now widely used by doctors and others.

343. One such procedure is the prostaglandin method discussed in Planned Parenthood v. Danforth, 428 U.S. 52, 95-99 (1976). This method involves non-caustic injections into the amniotic fluid to induce labor. This is more likely to produce a "live-birth" abortion, but is is also less likely to injure the mother seriously. *See also* Colautti v. Franklin, 47 U.S.L.W. 4094, 4099-4100 (U.S. 1979).

344. This assertion is repeatedly stressed in Doe v. Bolton, 410 U.S. at 193-94, 197-98, 199.

345. The emergence of women as an assertive and powerful class does not suggest that all women favored legalizing abortions. *See, e.g.,* M. Dienes, In Necessity and Sorrow (1976); Roiphe, *Confessions of a Female Chauvinist Sow*, 5 New York, Oct. 30, 1972, at 52.

346. For a discussion of the expression of interests as function of power, *see* J. Stone, Social Dimensions of Law and Justice 591-600 (1966).

347. A class' lack of power is sometimes seen as reason enough to fashion constitutional protections for the class, United States v. Carolene Products Co., 304 U.S. 144, 152 n.4 (1938). *See also* Ely, *supra* note 11, at 933-35. Foeti are certainly an inarticulate and powerless class if there ever was one.

348. A particularly dramatic example of this conviction is that of Dr. Bernard Nathanson, chief of obstetrics at St. Luke's Hospital in New York City, who recently publicly confessed that he was "deeply troubled by my own increasing certainty that I had in fact presided over 60,000 deaths," referring to the abortions performed at a clinic he formerly directed. Dr. Nathanson had changed from an early, militant advocate of abortion on demand, to someone searching for a middle ground which would "create a moral climate rich

is deserving of special protection by society precisely because a foetus is unable to protect itself, or even to speak for itself. And this belief is founded on technological developments.

It has already been shown that concepts of foetal personhood were fundamentally changed by the discoveries of embryology in the nineteenth century.[349] The medical sciences have continued to develop the ability to deal with foetal health problems separately from the mother.[350] This ability created a new specialty: foetology. The new skills and tools have given steadily increasing control over spontaneous miscarriages and birth defects. Not only do these developments create increased certainty that an abortion was the cause of the foetal death,[351] but they also give even greater reality to the concept of a foetus as a separate and distinct being from the mother in whom it develops.[352] As a result, foetologists, gynecologists, and obstetricians, who deal most directly with the new knowledge and are called upon to perform the abortions, are more strongly opposed to abortion than any other class of physicians.[353] This developing technology strongly reinforces the conviction of many that foeti are

---

enough to provide for abortion, but sensitive enough to life to accommodate a profound sense of loss." Nathanson, *supra* note 314.

349. *See* text accompanying notes 267-7ʊ *supra*.

350. For popular reviews of some extreme recent developments in these areas, *see* G. TAYLOR, THE BIOLOGICAL TIME BOMB (1968); A. TOFFLER, FUTURE SHOCK 197-205. *See also* Dobzhansky, *Changing Man*, 155 SCIENCE 409 (Jan. 27, 1967); Fraser, *Genetic Counseling*, HOSPITAL PRACTICF, Jan. 1971, at 49, *and* Motulsky, *Brave New World?*, 185 SCIENCE 653 (Aug. 23, 1974). For examples of technical literature from the new field of foetology, *see* ANTENATAL DIAGNOSIS (A. Dorfman ed. 1972); FETAL PHARMACOLOGY (L. Boreus ed. 1973); FOETAL AUTONOMY (G. Wolstenholme & M. O'Connon eds. 1969); G. MONIF, VIRAL INFECTIONS OF THE HUMAN FETUS (1969); PHYSIOLOGY OF THE PERINATAL PERIOD (U. Stave ed. 1970); W. WINDLE, PHYSIOLOGY OF THE FETUS (1971).

351. *Compare* text accompanying notes 289-92 *supra*.

352. Part of this reality is evidenced by ever earlier viability, as discussed in notes 9 & 10 *supra*.

353. DIENES, *supra* note 345; Byrn I, *supra* note 9, at 32; Guttmacher, *The Genesis of Legalized Abortion in New York: A Personal Insight*, in ABORTION, SOCIETY AND THE LAW 65 (1973); Mandy, *Reflections of a Gynecologist*, in Rosen, *supra* note 72, at 284; *and* TIME, Sept. 27, 1971, at 69. Psychiatrists, who of all doctors are most removed both from the new knowledge of gestation and the actual doing of abortions, are as a class most in favor. *See* RIGHT TO ABORTION, *supra* note 319; and Rosen, *Psychiatric Implications of Abortion: A Case Study in Social Hypocrisy*, in ABORTION AND THE LAW, *supra* note 71, at 72-106. Rosen's collection of essays, ABORTION IN AMERICA, *supra* note 72, at 207-243, 267-96, contains eight articles arguing for psychiatric indications for abortion, with only one, *id.* at 12-21, on the "shrinking nonpsychiatric indications." For an account of the similar experience in Soviet medicine, *see* GEBHARD, *et. al.*, *supra* note 227, at 217-18; GRISEZ, *supra* note 47, at 196-98. While none of these sources presents detailed statistics, each describes obstreticians and gynecologists as a class as being overwhelmingly hostile to, and depressed about, abortions.

people,[354] people who are even less articulate and more powerless than women may have been historically. Thus, opposition to the recent changes in abortion law also has resulted in large part directly from a developing medical technology.

III.   SOURCES AND SOLUTIONS OF THE ABORTION CONTROVERSY

The history of abortion in Anglo-American law shows a pattern of responding directly to technological developments.[355] From earliest times through 1850 two separate lines of technical development tended to point the law towards increasingly harsh attitudes, even towards abortions during early stages of pregnancy. Very slowly abortions became less likely to kill the mother, and less painful for her. These risks decreased sufficiently to result in a considerable upsurge of abortions during the eighteenth and nineteenth centuries. Nevertheless maternal mortality remained high. At the same time, there was a slow, but steady, growth in knowledge about, and health care for, conception and gestation. This development gradually provided greater certainty as to the effect of abortion on the foetus—i.e., that the foetus was neither already dead, nor that it spontaneously miscarried after the abortional act. It also had the effect of pushing back the point at which personhood was said to begin. Both of these developments supported the harsher legislation which ensued, culminating in the virtually complete prohibition of abortion in nearly the entire world beginning early in the nineteenth century.

These two lines of technological development continued to accelerate after 1850. Medical sciences continued to develop the ability to deal with foetal health problems separately from those of the mother. The emergence of these tools and knowledge has provided even greater control over spontaneous miscarriages in later stages of pregnancy, and consequently greater certainty that the abortional act was the cause of death. This technology has also clarified the certainty of foetal life and illuminated criteria by which personhood

---

354.   For a clear admission of this process, see Nathanson, supra note 314.

355.   By this statement I do not assert that the response is proven as the cause of changes in the abortion laws. The pattern is there, and is consistent through at least six centuries. At least preliminary investigation of other western countries is also consistent. Still, without cross-cultural studies, one cannot take this relationship as proven. For a thorough study of the problem of proving hypotheses in social science settings, see E. NAGEL, THE STRUCTURE OF SCIENCE 20-26, 480-605 (1961). For a brief discussion of the same problem, see A. Miller, *Corporate Gigantism and "Technological Imperatives,"* 18 J. PUB. L. 256, 262-83 (1969).

can be determined.

On the other hand, medical sciences have also developed the means to perform abortions at little risk and with little pain for the mother. Early in the pregnancy, there is now less risk to the mother in aborting than in carrying the child to full term and delivering the baby. Just as the earlier strict prohibition of abortions was made necessary by the relevant technological changes of the seventeenth and eighteenth centuries, one could predict that the relevant technological shifts of the late nineteenth and twentieth centuries would engender great pressure both to preserve, and to eliminate, the prohibition of abortions.

There is therefore a close relationship between changes in abortion law and the preceding changes in technology. A similar pattern might emerge if one were to study contraception from a technological impact perspective.[356] Less than ten years after the widespread introduction of safe, cheap, and effective means of contraception, the laws inhibiting their use began to be eliminated.[357] No major controversy lingers about these changes, in part, at least, because there is no countervailing pressure from a technology dealing with preconception cells. What controversy there is arises from questions of parent-child relations,[358] or about the safety of various devices, rather than over the rightness of contraception and family planning by persons of proper age and using safe and effective means. In short, abortion remains a focal point of controversy because many people of otherwise differing points of view, worry about the rights of a foetus. On the other hand, few people have such concerns about spermatazoa or ova. This difference appears to be based on the technology invented over the last two centuries, on the ways modern

---

356. NOONAN, *supra* note 66, for example, completely ignores this aspect. He is perhaps too ready to take contraceptive formulae at face value without asking if they worked, and if so, what their side effects were. One major difference separating our experience with contraceptives from our experience with abortion, is that contraceptives were deliberately developed, whereas the critical discoveries necessary to make abortions safe and simple for the mother, were not developed with improved abortions as a goal. *See* text accompanying notes 329-39, *supra*. This would make analogies between the two patterns somewhat less direct or certain.

357. Griswold v. Connecticut, 381 U.S. 479 (1965). *See generally*, C. T. DIENES, LAW, POLITICS, AND BIRTH CONTROL (1965). These methods (especially the IUD and the "pill") are not completely safe, but are vastly more effective than any earlier contraceptives. Of course, the vulcanization of rubber was a key breakthrough more than a century before *Griswold*, DIENES at 26, but this also produced the restrictive laws. A threat to health is sometimes argued on behalf of these early laws, *id.* at 38, but this threat remains quite unclear.

358. Eisenstadt v. Baird, 405 U.S. 438 (1972).

society has been able to assemble knowledge, skills, and tools, relating to conception and gestation, and on the resulting interpretations of these processes. While we may not be able to say that changes in abortion laws emerged inevitably from these changes in technology,[359] legal transformations at least followed predictable patterns when given the interests generated by the technologies.

A full examination of the interrelationship between law, morality, and technology is beyond the scope of this paper.[360] One could conclude that abortion, at least, is a fairly clear instance of where changes in technology have induced the perception of new interests, which have thereafter caused changes in the law. This process is, however, more complex and difficult to predict than the few references to such an analysis in the existing literature on abortion would lead one to suspect. Thus, when Robert Byrn argues that abortion reform represents an instance of "technomorality,"[361] *i.e.,* an instance where the goals of a society depend on the "know-how" of the society, he ignores half of the problem. Byrn's argument is simply that the "what" that we do is being determined by the "how" that we know to do.[362] In the context of abortion, Byrn told us, "the availability of a new technique for performing early abortions justifies a facile redefinition of the facts and law of what an abortion kills so that the technique may be used."[363]

---

359. In New York, for example, the legislature refused to place slightly less strict restrictions on general surgery in 1828 despite its similar risks at the time. *See* text accompanying notes 256-57 *supra. Cf.* MESTHENE, *supra* note 12, at 35-36.

360. See note 34 *supra.*

361. Byrn I, *supra* note 9, at 25-26. Others have also argued that morality is wholly shaped by the "objective factors" of the society wherein the decision is reached. These "objective factors" are largely technological. Consider the discussion of the origins and role of moral judgments found in GOULDNER, *supra* note 20, at 270-82, where the author asserts that arguments in terms of morality only serve to justify decisions reached on other grounds, generally self-gratification. *But see* MUMFORD, *supra* note 12, at 285-303, for the argument that technology generated nostalgia for non-technically based values. *See also* GOULDNER 73-80, 399-408; Little, *Statistical Morality, Law and Tommorrow's World,* 21 U. FLA. L. REV. 442 (1969); Moffat, *The Indispensible Role of Independent Ethical Judgment,* 21 U. FLA. L. REV. 477 (1969); Stent, *The Poverty of Scientism and the Promise of Structuralist Ethics,* 6 HASTINGS CENTER REPORT 32 (Dec. 1976); Williams, *Individual and Group Values,* ANNALS OF AAPSS 23-33 (1967). The problem of relating these theories to the non-rational factors of value judgments is reserved for later study.

362. Merton, *The Other Side of Despair,* THE CRITIC, Oct.-Nov. 1965, at 12, 15. *Cf.* Barber, *President Nixon and Richard Nixon: Character Trap,* PSYCH. TODAY Oct. 1974, at 112, 116.

363. Byrn II, *supra* note 11, at 859. This explanation of technomorality shows greater thought than Byrn's earlier comment that: "The practice of medicine changes . . . from the treatment and preservation of a beating heart and a respiring lung (the 'what') to the engi-

Certainly, no study of abortion can be made without observing the claims of autonomy made by many of the technicians. The Supreme Court itself, in *Doe v. Bolton* and *Roe v. Wade,* was deeply concerned about the physician's,[364] as well as the mother's, privacy. Some advocates of abortion reform have urged unprecedented authority for the medical profession.[365] Without denying the unavoidable impact of professional opinion on actual practice, the law has not been, and cannot be fashioned solely to accord technical autonomy. Just as teachers do not determine the constitutionality of school prayer,[366] the issues at stake in abortion are perceived as transcending mere technical competence. Despite a showing of great concern for the sensitivity of physicians,[367] the Court did not rest its decision on the privacy or special respect due to doctors. Indeed, one crucial consideration (the personhood of the foetus) appears to be left to the mother,[368] or in very limited circumstances the state.[369]

Technician autonomy is not essential for technically-based val-

---

neering of a quality life (the 'how'); and the law must not interfere in physician-patient 'privacy' when these judgments on quality are made." Byrn I, *supra* note 8, at 26. This seems to result from hasty efforts to fit abortion technology analysis into Merton's "what" and "how" dichotomy, Merton, *supra* note 362. If anything, those facts might be analyzed in reverse.

364.   *See* particularly Doe v. Bolton, where doctors were given standing as a class, 410 U.S. at 188-89, and their privacy was expressly referred to, *id.* at 192-93, 196-201. Although denying standing to a specific doctor in Roe v. Wade, 410 U.S. at 125-27, the Court repeatedly adverted to medical opinions, *id.* at 130-32, 141-46, 149-50, 159, 163, finally giving the doctor a power equal to the mother, *id.* at 153, 162-66. *See also* Wellington, *supra* note 10, at 301-02.

365.   Ziff, *Recent Abortion Law Reforms (or Much Ado About Nothing)*, 60 J. CRIM. L., CRIMINOLOGY & POLITICAL SCI. 3, 9 (1969). One reformer asserted that the issue was simply "whether a doctor should be sent to prison for performing an operation that he believes to be best for his patient?", Williams, *Euthenasia and Abortion*, 38 U. COLO. L. REV. 178, 195 (1966).

366.   This is not to deny the problem of teacher interposition or nullification, Dolbeare & Hammond, *Inertia in Midway: Supreme Court Decisions and Local Response*, 23 J. LEGAL EDUC. 106 (1970). *See also* Muir, *The Impact of Supreme Court Decisions on Moral Attitudes*, 23 J. LEGAL EDUC. 89 (1970); Reich, *Schoolhouse Religion and the Supreme Court*, 23 J. LEGAL EDUC. 123 (1970). Similarly we do not let insanity be judged by a jury of psychiatrists, Louisell, *Abortion, The Practice of Medicine and Due Process of Law*, 16 UCLA L. REV. 233, 246 (1969).

367.   *See especially* 410 U.S. at 196-97.

368.   Tribe stresses this point, *supra* note 11, at 18-41, especially at 28-29. The mother appears to control this decision in the first and second trimester, 410 U.S. at 162-63, although the Court's rule states that "the abortion decision . . . must be left to the medical judgment of the pregnant woman's attending physician," *id.* at 164. The Court reemphasized the central role of the physician in Colautti v. Franklin, 47 U.S.L.W. 4094, 4096-97 (U.S. 1979).

369.   A limited state interest in the second trimester becomes potentially controlling in the third, *id.* at 164-65, but even this must give way to the health interest of the mother.

ues to prevail. So long as technology changes the moral equation by making new choices possible, or at least much less costly, technological changes will bring about value and legal changes.[370] This thesis does not require one to conclude, as Byrn does, that the mere existence of a technology dictates that it be used.[371] Byrn's position is ultimately too simple to be valid when technology fosters fundamentally opposite values as has occurred in the case of abortion. Even if we agree with Lawrence Le Shan that "[t]echnological inventions only change a society to the degree that they bring a new idea in their wake,"[372] what do we do when new technologies bring *conflicting* ideas? The answer is difficult, and it is not made any easier by following the traditional approach of explaining legal changes in terms of unexplained alterations of attitude[373]—in short by ignoring both the sources of the change and the resistance to change. Technology is often an important source for these patterns, even if not always the only source. Law, and lawyers, in continuing to ignore deeper causes of change, risk obsolescence, if they are not already obsolete.[374]

If one approaches the judicial abrogation of laws in the United States restricting access to abortions and contraceptives from the point of view of unexplained attitude changes, one finds that there were certain basic shifts in American attitudes during the mid twen-

---

370. *Accord,* MESTHENE, *supra* note 12, at 26, 49-54. Mesthene says that technology calls society's bluff, forcing society to confront value choices it would prefer to pretend did not exist.

371. This, in essence, is the "technical axiom" espoused by Jacques Ellul, ELLUL, *supra* note 12, at 20-21, 79-82, 208-16, 335-40, 387-94. Ellul has himself developed the points made in THE TECHNOLOGICAL SOCIETY in several other books and articles, principally A CRITIQUE OF THE NEW COMMONPLACES (1968); THE MEANING OF THE CITY (1967); Ellul, *The Technological Revolution and Its Moral and Political Consequences,* in THE EVOLVING WORLD AND THEOLOGY (J. Metz ed. 1967); Ellul, *The Technological Order,* in THE TECHNOLOGICAL ORDER (C. Stover ed. 1963). A complete bibliography of Ellul's published work would run to over one hundred items, largely in French.

372. L. LE SHAN, THE MEDIUM, THE MYSTIC AND THE PHYSICIST: TOWARD A GENERAL THEORY OF THE PARANORMAL 101 (1974). MUMFORD, *supra* note 12, at 3-6, 31-54, turned the argument around, asserting that a technology only works if it follows in the wake of an idea. But the idea remains only an idea until it is realized in technology.

373. In the context of abortion, *see* Rubin, *The Abortion Cases: A Study in Law and Social Change,* 5 N.C. CENT. L.J. 215, 216-19 (1974); Comment, *Abortion: The Five Year Revolution and Its Impact,* 3 ECOLOGY L.Q. 311, 315-19 (1973) [hereinafter cited as *Five Year Revolution*].

374. Woodard, *The Limits of Legal Realism: an Historical Perspective,* 54 VA. L. REV. 689 (1968). Ellul concludes that law is already obsolete, ELLUL, *supra* note 12, at 251-52. *See also* Miller, *Science and Legal Education,* 19 CASE W. RES. L. REV. 29 (1967).

tieth century. Shifts occurred in the areas of sexual mores,[375] role expectations for women,[376] concern about overpopulation,[377] pressures created by poverty and rising illegitimacy,[378] reactions against the influence of certain religious groups,[379] and the gradual rise of a "quality of life" ethic over the traditional "sanctity of life" ethic.[380] These changes would have had little effect on the laws regarding abortion and contraception if the technical means for safe, cheap, and effective procedures had not been developed first. And these attitude changes themselves derive from technical developments.[381]

Sexual mores traditionally have been governed by what may be termed a "prudential ethic."[382] Formerly based on the triple threat of infection, detection, and conception, all three threats have been eliminated by technology: the wonder drugs, the car, and the pill, respectively.[383] Traditionally, people shunned sex through fear. Today, people tend to approach sex as autonomous individuals, making positive decisions based on an increased understanding of their sexuality. We may never fully achieve the ideal of autonomy, but it seems to define the prevalent sexual norms.

Similarly, the change in role expectations for women depended on the development of techniques for raising children outside the family, and freeing women from household chores.[384] While not yet

---

375.   *See, e.g.,* TOFFLER, *supra* note 350, at 238-59; Macklin, *Cohabitation in College: Going Very Steady,* PSYCH. TODAY, Nov. 1974, at 53.

376.   Moore, *Abortion and Public Policy: What are the Issues?,* 17 N.Y.L.F. 411 (1971); Rubin, *supra* note 373, at 216-17, 223-24; *Five Year Revolution, supra* note 373, at 318-19. *See generally* FRANKFURT, *supra* note 293.

377.   BOULDING, *supra* note 12, at 122-36.

378.   Byrn I, *supra* note 9, at 24, 29-31.

379.   Again and again Catholics are singled out as the only source of opposition, WILLIAMS, *supra* note 65, at 192-206; Byrn I, *supra* note 9, at 5; Hall, *Commentary,* in ABORTION AND THE LAW, *supra* note 71, at 224, 231; N.Y. Times, Apr. 12, 1970, § 1, at 47, col.1; *Five Year Revolution, supra* note 373, at 315-16. *See generally* LADER II, *supra* note 37. For a more balanced review of religious attitude, *see* Curran, *supra* note 281.

380.   Byrn I, *supra* note 9, at 24-31, 37-39. *See also* CALLAHAN, *supra* note 281, at 307-48 (1970).

381.   For example, fundamental changes in the way we all view the world can be traced to the invention of clear glass in thirteenth century Italy, MUMFORD, *supra* note 12, at 124-31, or the invention of mechanical clocks in medieval monasteries, *id.* at 12-17, or electronic media in the twentieth century, M. McLUHAN, UNDERSTANDING MEDIA (1974).

382.   Bloy, *The Christian Norm,* in TECHNOLOGY AND HUMAN VALUES 18-21 (J. Wilkenson ed. 1967).

383.   While this may be an oversimplification the complementing factors have also been technological. Many commentators have seen the automobile as almost solely responsible for this change, HARRINGTON, *supra* note 12, at 18-19; TOFFLER, *supra* note 350, at 437.

384.   TOFFLER, *supra* note 351, at 238-59. *See generally* B. FRIEDAN, THE FEMININE

fully developed, the impact of these technologies is already discernible.

Overpopulation is a function of death control technology without adequate use of the countervailing technology, birth control.[385] Only a sweeping general technological advance producing overall affluence in a society seems capable of overcoming resistance to birth control and solving this problem.[386] Poverty is both reduced and made persistant by technology creating the affluent skilled and the unemployable unskilled.[387] Similar analyses are possible for the other attitude shifts.

Undoubtedly, a most profound change is the triumph of the "quality of life" ethic over the traditional, "sanctity of life" ethic. The change is profound both because it sweeps into a single abstraction the pattern of changes of which abortion reform is only a part. It also portends even more sweeping changes in the near future. No longer will we be "moral morons." People will increasingly control their destinies to an extent never before possible, even if in the process they lose those qualities which before had been considered the highest expression of their humanity. People will have to choose whether to permit persons who cannot function at some minimal level, the quality of whose life is too low, to continue to drain the limited resources of the world. Wolfgang Friedman, in explaining this emergent view, also managed to show its essentially technological basis:[388] as we have the means to preserve many lives which formerly would have perished, the drain on society becomes too great. We cannot let our technical achievements blind us to the reality that nature has a way of "curing" mistakes. Whether we like it or not we must choose those who are worth preserving, or run the risk of waiting for natural processes to take over. When this "quality of life" ethic is directed at one's exercising basic choices over one's own life, the problem posed may not challenge traditional concepts of humanism. But what about choices directed at the lives of others? Abortion reform is an apparently easy first step in reordering our

MYSTIQUE (1963). As to the role of women's issues in the abortion reform movement, see text accompanying notes 298-308 supra.

385. BOULDING, supra note 12, at 125-31; A. CHASE, THE BIOLOGICAL IMPERATIVES 211-49 (1971).

386. Rising living standards seem to be the only variable which is highly correlated to adoption of birth control.

387. HARRINGTON, supra note 12, at 241-74.

388. Friedmann, Interference with Human Life: Some Jurisprudential Reflections, 70 COLUM. L. REV. 1058, 1058-59 (1970).

thinking along these lines.[389] We need only to be reminded that this version of the "quality of life" ethic was propounded by Nazi physicians[390] to become aware of its potential dangers.[391]

Usually we become aware of these dangers only when confronted by some dramatic crisis.[392] All too often this is too late. Very possibly we could find ourselves, through a succession of well-intentioned, but essentially thoughtless, acts to have abandoned any sense of reverence for life, of having become inured to seeing ourselves purely as means.[393] As Lewis Mumford asked forty-three years ago:

> What is the use of conquering nature if we fall a prey to nature in the form of unbridled men? What is the use of equipping mankind with mighty powers to move and build and communicate, if the final result of this secure food supply and this excellent organization is to enthrone the morbid impulses of a thwarted humanity?[394]

Such approaches to problems are certainly human ("hominid"), but are they humanistic? If the intention is to human-

---

389. Consider the analogous problem of terminal cases, particularly where discussed in terms of redefining death, in re Quinlan, 70 N.J. 10, 355 A.2d 647, *cert. denied sub nom.* Garger v. New Jersey, 429 U.S. 922 (1976). *See also* Bennett, *In the Shadow of Karen Quinlan,* 12 TRIAL 36 (1976); Skegg, *Irreversibly Comatose Individuals: "Alive" or "Dead"?* 33 CAMBRIDGE L.J. 130 (1974); *The Quinlan Decision: Five Commentaries,* 6 HASTINGS CENTER REPORT 23 (Feb. 1976).

390. GRISEZ, *supra* note 47 at 202-03. *See also Biomedical Ethics and the Shadow of Nazism,* 6 HASTINGS CENTER REPORTS, Special Supp. (Aug. 1976). Contrast the way in which all fears are allayed by a facile blending of the two differing ethics in CALLAHAN, *supra* note 281, at 307-346.

391. *See generally* SCIENTISM AND VALUES (H. Schoeck & J. Wiggins eds. 1960).

392. For studies of the basis of this common pattern of response, *see* GOULDNER, *supra* note 20, at 80-82; Baram, *The Social Control of Science and Technology,* 47 DEN. L.J. 567 (1970).

393. Many have argued that modern technology in general has already done so. ELLUL, *supra* note 12, at 141-46, 208-27, 319-40; GOULDNER, *supra* note 20, at 276-82; MUMFORD, *supra* note 12, at 3-6, 24-31, 41-54; Kranzburg, *supra* note 12. This process is certainly not complete, however, so long as people are valued to some extent as an end in themselves. People are so valued if their right to live is recognized quite apart from their utility. The vision of people as means, rather than as ends, originated at least as early as the first machine, for, as Mumford pointed out, before machines can replace people, the people must first be reduced to the level of machines, MUMFORD at 41-43. Consider this statement of the problem: "In attempting to seize power [over nature] man tended to reduce himself to an abstraction, or, what comes to almost the same thing, to eliminate every part of himself except that which was bent on seizing power." MUMFORD at 31. For brief discussions of the philosophic problem of distinguishing means from ends, *see* Kaplan, *Means/Ends Rationality,* 87 ETHICS 61 (1976); Nielson, *Distrusting Reason,* 87 ETHICS 49 (1976).

394. MUMFORD, *supra* note 12, at 366.

ize, as well as to "hominize,"[395] existence, one must carefully think out in advance one's acts and their consequences. Perhaps no choice exists but to substitute decisions based on the quality of life for decisions based on the sanctity of life. But is that substitution to be total? Must it be total? One must consciously define the limits if possible. For these reasons, if for no other, changes in abortion laws should not be thoughtless or merely semi-conscious acts. Abortion must be considered in context, both its technological context and moral context, as a product and as a portent.

Considering abortion from this broadened perspective, there is little to be said for the Court's approach to recent abortion cases. The Court's discussion of history is inaccurate and inconclusive,[396] and, in any event, unrelated to its later conclusions. The discussion of the moral basis for its decisions is even less helpful. The Court is unable to point to any constitutional text which appears to explicitly compel the decision. How the Court is able to imply a resolution of the problem from the Constitution is hardly mentioned.[397] In any event, an implied constitutional mandate regarding abortion must involve the Court in deriving conclusions from public mores since the constitutional text is so indefinite with regard to abortion.[398] It may well be that "moral prejudices" against abortion will have to be waived in the light of the unmitigated human misery resulting from unwanted pregnancies and unwanted children.[399] But where are these factors considered by the Court in its decision? And where is it written that this decision is the Court's to make?

Assuming, as the Court does, that "privacy" presents a meaningful basis for evaluating the constitutionality of abortion statutes, the Court gives little indication how this notion relates to interests such as whether foeti are people, which the Court disavows deciding.[400] Even disregarding these problems the Court cannot evaluate the statutes involved in any significant way because it refuses to investigate their purposes, or to tell us the weight to be given these purposes.[401] Nor does Means, so heavily relied on by the Court in

---

395.   Bloy, *supra* note 382.

396.   Roe v. Wade, 410 U.S. at 129-47.

397.   *Id.* at 152-53.

398.   As to the proper relation of morality and the constitution, *see* Dellapenna, *supra* note 5, at 389-401; Perry, *supra* note 11.

399.   BOULDING, *supra* note 12, at 129.

400.   410 U.S. at 159.

401.   Although the Court does catalogue asserted interests represented by the statutes in question, *id.* at 147-52, little discussion of these interests is given, and no effort is made to

those parts of its opinion which most closely approach the necessary analysis,[402] solve these problems.

The Means thesis[403] is that abortion laws were enacted solely to protect the health of the mother. As early abortions are now safer than childbirth for the mother, these laws are now unconstitutional because they have no rational basis.[404] There is, in fact, good evidence that restrictive abortion laws were enacted for several purposes, only one of which was to protect the health of mothers. Further, purposes can change without symbolic reenactment.[405] The values embodied in the abortion laws were the product of a much more broadly based technology than simply that necessary for performing abortion. Consequently, to argue that the law ought to cease because its technological underpinnings have ceased, one must sweep far wider in one's analysis than Means does.[406]

In the end Means and the Court may very well have been right despite their circumscribed analyses, with their distorted history and concentration on trivia. Abortion reform was a response to sweeping technological change in world culture, which in turn produced basic changes in the values relevant to the controversy. Law did not cause it, and probably could not have stopped it. Women who sought abortions were not only visible, but eventually became highly vocal. In this situation legislatures were unlikely to be an effective brake for very long. When even the Court chose to ignore possible rights for the unborn, there was no countervailing force to check the demand to use abortion technology.[407] So long as vigorous

consider the historical accuracy of these assertions. The Court's discussion of Anglo-American legal history in this regard is presented with uncertain hypotheticals, id. at 132-51, while disavowing decisions necessary to weigh these interests, id. at 159-60, and disavowing in Doe v. Bolton, 410 U.S. at 190-91, the central point of the Means thesis, without which the Court's historical summary loses its point altogether.

402. Means was cited seven times in Roe v. Wade, as is Louis Lader, who, in these respects, is Means' alter ego. See note 23.

403. Means I, supra note 24, at 418, 443, 511-15; Means II, supra note 24, at 382-84. Strictly speaking, the Court disavows this thesis in the companion case of Doe v. Bolton, 410 U.S. at 190-91, but this is only one more puzzle in this remarkable pair of opinions, for the Court apparently relies directly on this thesis in deciding Roe v. Wade, 410 U.S. at 149-52, 164-65.

404. See Kaplan, supra note 393, and Nielsen, supra note 393, for discussions of means/ends, or instrumental, rationality.

405. This fact was recognized by the Court in Doe v. Bolton, 419 U.S. at 190-91.

406. Means I, supra note 24, at 418, 443, 511-15; Means II, supra note 24, at 382-84.

407. West Germany has reached a very different result, precisely because that country's Constitutional Court chose to champion the rights of the inarticulate minority who are unborn. See Judgment of Feb. 25, 1975, 39 BVerfGE 1, translated in 9 J. MAR. J. PRAC. & PROC.

advocates of rights for the foetus are with us, however, the controversy will not die.

How then can this conflict be finally resolved? Should we merely write off foeti in early pregnancy, and hope that the peculiar nature of their personhood will prevent abortions from becoming a precedent for drastic changes in concepts of the sanctity of life generally?[408] Denying the reality of the ever broader technical changes from which the "quality of life" ethic emerges by pretending that abortion is an independent question will not make the quality of life ethic disappear. On the other hand, abortion does have its own peculiarities which would perhaps make it a worthwhile place to confront the issues raised by the "quality of life" ethic.

Abortion confronts us with possibilities for choice not yet reached in most other areas of the emerging biomedical technology. This allows us to confront the issues in a circumscribed, yet strangely complete factual context. Key issues[409] not yet fully reached in other areas of controversy thus become accessible to genuine exploration.

The abortion controversy also allows one to examine the several dimensions of the "quality of life" ethic. This ethic requires examining the effects of the abortion decision on the quality of the lives of both the foetus and the parents involved, as well as perhaps society in general in some contexts. One must also consider who is to make the decision in such cases—the foetus, its mother, some other party, or some objective decision-maker external to all direct participants. These several aspects of the problem are frequently obscured by the casting of the debate in the form of absolute prohibitions or freedoms without recognizing the genuiness of the feelings of all participants in the debate, or in the decision.

The time has come to explore these questions directly, and to seek some solution which attempts to accommodate the deeply held feelings of those forced to bear children against their will, and the likewise deeply held feelings of those who grieve at the destruction of human beings. If any solution is to be found, it probably will lie in the middle ground, where abortion may be permitted in some circumstances but even where it is permitted, it is accompanied by

---

605-84 (1976). *See* note 263 *supra.* For an American support for such an approach here, *see* Ely, *supra* note 11, at 933-35. *See also* text accompanying notes 344-48 *supra.*

408.   As was argued in Gianella, *The Difficult Quest for a Truly Human Abortion Law,* 13 VILL. L. REV. 257 (1968).

409.   Such as the nature of personhood.

a profound sense of loss.[410]

One might well ask whether any court is equipped to undertake this difficult and delicate task.[411] Perhaps not, but the court must at least act to make it possible for legislatures to begin the task of balancing and compromising the competing interests. Whether the decision ought finally to be legislative or judicial, one must take care to consider the feelings of all the various participants,[412] including the mother, the father, other family members, the doctors and other medical workers, and the other members of societies actually interested in the outcome.

A number of questions—simple to state, but difficult to resolve—must be considered, although the answer to no one of these questions can, by itself, resolve the controversy. These questions are: When does a foetus become a person?[413] What interests are legitimately affected before the stage of personhood is reached? What indications are sufficient to justify the grave step of killing if abortion is to occur after the stage of personhood is reached?[414] Are there any circumstances which justify killing the foetus when it can be removed from the mother in a viable state?[415]

---

410. Nathanson, *supra* note 314.

411. Wellington, *Common Law Rules and Constitutional Double Standards: Some Notes on Adjudication*, 83 YALE L.J. 221, 297-310 (1973), argued that only those aspects of this controversy which could be settled in a "principled" way should be settled by the court, leaving "policy" choices to the legislatures. Justice Rehnquist, of course, dissented on the grounds that none of the controversy should be decided by the court, Roe v. Wade, 410 U.S. at 171-78 (Rehnquist, J., dissenting).

412. A consideration of the interests of all participants is appallingly absent from the majority opinion in Roe v. Wade, 410 U.S. 113 (1973); Doe v. Bolton, 410 U.S. 179 (1973); Planned Parenthood v. Danforth, 428 U.S. 52 (1976); Bellotti v. Baird, 428 U.S. 132 (1976); although such balancing is perhaps made a little more likely by the decision in Singleton v. Wulff, 428 U.S. 106 (1976).

413. *See* Dellapenna, *supra* note 5, and sources cited therein for detailed analyses of this difficult question. *See also* Nathanson, *supra* note 314.

414. A similar problem is only beginning to be confronted with regard to seriously defective newborns. *See, e.g.,* L. WEBER, WHO SHALL LIVE? (1976); Campbell & Duff, *Moral and Ethical Dilemmas in the Special-Care Nursery*, 289 NEW ENG. J. MED. 890 (1973); Fletcher, *Abortion, Euthenasia, and Care of Defective Newborns*, 292 NEW ENG. J. MED. 75 (1975); Heyman & Holtz, *The Severely Defective Newborn: The Dilemma and the Decision Process*, 23 PUB. POLICY 381 (1974); Kelsey, *Which Infants Shall Live? Who Should Decide?*, 5 HASTINGS CENTER REPORT 5 (April 1975); Robertson, *Involuntary Euthanasia of Defective Newborns: A Legal Analysis*, 27 STAN. L. REV. 213 (1975); Shaw, *Dilemmas of "Informed Consent" in Children*, 289 NEW ENG. J. MED. 885 (1973). *See generally* BIOETHICS (T. Shannon ed. 1976); ETHICS OF NEWBORN INTENSIVE CARE (A. Jonsen & M. Garland eds. 1976).

415. This issue underlies the controversy over the legality of "salting out" in *Danforth*, 428 U.S. 52. The majority managed to ignore this question entirely. *See* note 341 *supra*. The issue also arises in such well publicized cases as that of Dr. Edelin in Massachusetts, Com-

These are extremely difficult questions to answer. Knowledge of the technological basis of the interests in conflict over the answers to the questions will only help in small ways to resolve them. At least such knowledge can inform us of the broader social context within which such decisions are made. Such knowledge cannot excuse us from also considering the narrow social context of the pregnant, unmarried girl, the rape victim, the woman who discovers herself pregnant with a malformed foetus, or the woman who would simply prefer not to be "tied down with a kid." Only with a full and frank consideration of both of these perspectives can we begin to resolve the abortion controversy in a way which will still debate rather than feed it. On this task we have yet to begin.

---

monwealth v. Edelin, 371 Mass. 497, 359 N.E.2d 4 (1976). Wellington, *supra* note 10 at 305-06, also raises this question. Finally, Colautti v. Franklin, 47 U.S.L.W. 4094 (U.S. 1979), presented the question directly, but the Court chose to avoid it by finding the relevant sections of the Pennsylvania statute in question to be impermissibly vague both in defining the standard of care, and in defining the point at which the standard of care would apply.

Zig-Zag Stitching and the Seamless Web: Thoughts on "Reproduction" and the Law*

Marie Ashe**

Whenever I read law relating to women and motherhood, I find myself sickened. When I read *Roe v. Wade*[1] I am filled with anger; when I read the *Baby M*[2] trial court decision, I am enraged. When I hear women referred to as "surrogates," I have the same reaction as arises when I hear women called "bitches" or "sluts." Feelings of humiliation, of indignation, of desperation, of horror, of rage. Reading *A.C.*[3], I feel something close to despair.

Often, in the last several weeks, I have set aside my notes and readings concerning motherhood and law. I leave them with a sense of hopelessness. Often I have picked up some needlework —sewing, embroidery, needlepoint, knitting — seeking respite from the feelings that overwhelm me, restoration. The rhythm of my fingers becomes a rhythm of my inner being, a peace in my breast. A dropped stitch. A gentle flutter. A minor interruption of rhythm and pattern. I pick it up easily, drawing it into the larger design. I exist in a silent space. Untroubled.

Law reaches every silent space. It invades the secrecy of women's wombs. It breaks every silence, uttering itself. Law-language, juris-diction. It defines. It commands. It forces.

Law as the seamless web we believe and die in. I cannot think of a single case involving legal regulation of motherhood without thinking of all. They constitute an interconnected network of variegated threads.

---

* © 1989 by Marie Ashe.

** Associate Professor of Law, College of Law, West Virginia University.

1. Roe v. Wade, 410 U.S. 113, *reh'g denied*, 410 U.S. 959 (1973).

2. In re Baby M, 109 N.J. 396, 537 A.2d 1227 (1988), *reversing in part*, 217 N.J. Super. 313, 525 A.2d 1128 (1987).

3. In re A.C., 533 A.2d 611 (D.C. 1987), *vacated and reh'g granted*, 539 A.2d 203 (1988).

Abortion.[4] "Surrogacy."[5] Supervision of women's pregnancies.[6] Exclusion of pregnant women from the workplace.[7] Termination of the parental rights of indigent or battered women.[8] Enforcement of the "relinquishments" for adoption executed by confused and vulnerable women.[9] Forced Caesarean sections.[10] Policings of home births.[11] Fol-

---

4. *See* Roe v. Wade, 410 U.S. 113 (1973); Doe v. Bolton, 410 U.S. 179, *reh'g denied*, 410 U.S. 959 (1973); Planned Parenthood of Central Mo. v. Danforth, 428 U.S. 52 (1976); Maher v. Roe, 432 U.S. 464 (1977); Harris v. McRae, 448 U.S. 297 (1980); Akron v. Akron Center for Reproductive Health, 462 U.S. 416 (1983); Thornburgh v. American College of Obstetricians and Gynecologists, 474 U.S. 747 (1986); and Reproductive Health Svcs. v. Webster, 851 F.2d 1071 (8th Cir.), *prob. juris. noted*, 109 S. Ct. 780 (1989).

5. *See Baby M*, 109 N.J. 396, 537 A.2d 1227.

6. *See* People v. Pointer, 151 Cal. App. 3d 1128 (1984).

7. *See* Oil, Chemical and Atomic Workers v. American Cyanimid Co., 741 F.2d 444 (D.C. Cir. 1984). For discussion of the troubling issues raised by *American Cyanimid* and related cases, *see* Becker, *From Muller v. Oregon to Fetal Vulnerability Policies*, 53 U. CHI. L. REV. 1219 (1986).

8. *See, e.g.*, West Virginia Department of Human Services v. Tammy B., No. 18217, Slip op. (1988), upholding termination of maternal rights of a battered woman.

9. *See, e.g.*, Lemley v. Barr, 343 S.E. 2d 101 (W. Va. 1986), in which the West Virginia Supreme Court of Appeals reviewed a trial court's ruling denying the claim to custody of a natural mother who, during her own minority, had relinquished her child for adoption but had sought to regain his custody five days after that relinquishment. After analysis referring to the provisions of the Uniform Child Custody Jurisdiction Act, the court determined that the trial court ought to have given full faith and credit to an Ohio court judgment that had determined the adoption of the child invalid. Nonetheless, the West Virginia Supreme Court failed to order a return of custody to the natural mother.

10. *See* Jefferson v. Griffin-Spalding Co. Hosp. Auth., 247 Ga. 86, 274 S.E. 2d 457 (1981), and related (largely unreported) cases discussed in Rhoden, *The Judge in Delivery Room: The Emergency of Court-Ordered Caesareans*, 74 CAL. L. REV. 1951 (1986). *See also* Kolder, Gallagher, & Parsons, *Court-Ordered Obstetrical Interventions*, NEW ENG. J. MED. 1192 (May 7, 1987). That article reports results of a national survey finding that court orders for Caesarean sections had been issued in 11 states, for hospital detention of pregnant women in 2 states, and for intrauterine transfusion against the desire of a pregnant woman in one state. The authors further note the class and racial implications of the policies expressed in such judicial intervention into pregnancies: "Eighty percent of the women involved were Black, Asian or Hispanic; 44 percent were unmarried; and 24 percent did not speak English as their primary language. All were treated in a teaching hospital clinic or were receiving public assistance." The survey showed strong support by medical practitioners for judicially-ordered interventions. The authors note: "Forty-six percent of the heads of fellowship programs in maternal-fetal medicine thought that women who refused medical advice and thereby endangered the life of the fetus should be detained. Forty-seven percent supported court orders for procedures such as intrauterine transfusions." *Id.* at 1192.

lowing the thread which is any one, I find it intertwined with each of the others. When I loosen a single thread, it tightens the others. Each knotted and entangled in fabrications of legal doctrine; each attached to notions of neutrality and generality.

Work on the seamless web. Writing of women, of mothers, of language and law. Rather different from passing threads through my fingers, working them into subtle or dazzling color. More like the impossible task of the miller's daughter.[12] Except — not merely to spin into golden thread a room full of straw. Beyond that, to work the threads into some recognizable shape, some better fit.

We have been weaving forever. And, apparently forever, our work has been assigned and defined by others. The work of victims: *She knows not what the curse may be/And so she weaveth steadily/ And little other care has she/The Lady of Shalott.* Work lacking inherent value: That of Penelope. Work of unfounded pride: That of Arachne. Ancillary work: That of Ariadne. Work of destruction: That of Medea.[13] Regulation and definition have always already assessed our work and our nature.

Some women have objected, of course. Our words have been moanings and screamings. And poems. *Christ, what are patterns for?*[14]

During each of the past thirty-five winters, I have — depending on the size of that winter's bed — either folded at its foot or spread over its width a counterpane worked by my maternal grandmother.[15] I never met my grandmother. She lived all her life in the West of Ireland and

---

11. *See* Bowland v. Municipal Court for Santa Cruz Judicial Dist., 18 Cal. 3d 479, 556 P.2d 1081, 134 Cal. Rptr. 630 (1976), and Smith v. State ex rel. Med. Licensing Bd., 459 N.E.2d 401 (Ind. Ct. App. 1984), both operating to proscribe the practice of lay midwifery, and Leigh v. Bd. of Registration in Nursing, 395 Mass. 670, 481 N.E.2d 1347 (1985), upholding suspension of nursing license of registered nurse who practiced midwifery and attended home births.

12. J. GRIMM, THE COMPLETE GRIMM'S FAIRY TALES (Padraic Colum, ed.) (1972).

13. A. TENNYSON, *The Lady of Shalott*, in THE COMPLETE WORKS OF ALFRED LORD TENNYSON (1893). For accounts of Penelope, Arachne, Ariadne and Medea *see* R. GRAVES, THE GREEK MYTHS (1960).

14. A. LOWELL, *Patterns*, in COMPLETE POETICAL WORKS (1955).

15. Julia O'Donnell Cahill (1882-1966).

has been dead more than half my lifetime. Besides her coverlet, I have one other gift of hers. A horn rosary. A deep moss green. I have removed the crucifix and I wear it sometimes as a necklace. Its holiness, to me, resides in her having made it a gift.

I remember the first winter when her coverlet came to me. I was, at that time of lesser sophistication, dubious about its color: a mingling of yarrow and goldenrod. Its warmth was extraordinary. Its great weight, its heaviness: transformative. Sleeping beneath it I am not merely warmed, but flattened, altered, changed in my being: I winter below the frost line.

This year I have found its yarns frayed and worn in several places. I have begun to wonder whether I will be able to repair it. I would like to give to my own daughter my grandmother's work, this text inscribing her touch and her bodily being, blessed by her eyes, recording the rhythm of breath and heartbeat, the scent of her lap.

Does the strongest of stitching come from our bodies? The mother of Snow White stained her sewing with blood.[16] What if we wrote with words from the deepest parts of our bodies, our selves. Helene Cixous and Luce Irigaray recommend, and simulate, writing with milk and with blood.[17] Which makes for a different *écriture*.[18] A writing inscribing lineaments of female bodies. Marked by our varying rhythms and cycles. Our stitches will seldom be straight.

Zig-zag stitchings and zig-zag thought. Useful (as in buttonholing) for definition; (as in edging seams) for strength; (as in embroidery) for beauty.

It has seemed to me that the major attributes of legal discourse concerning women and mothers are these: it originates in men; it defines women with certainty; it attempts to mask the operations of power; it silences other discourse.[19] I take as given: Law that silences

---

16. *See* J. GRIMM, *supra* note 12.

17. H. CIXOUS (with CATHERINE CLEMENT) THE NEWLY BORN WOMAN (1985); L. IRIGARAY, SPECULUM OF THE OTHER WOMAN (1985) and THIS SEX WHICH IS NOT ONE (1985).

18. Jones, *Writing the Body: Toward an Understanding of l'Ectriture féminine*, in THE NEW FEMINIST CRITICISM, 361-77 (E. Showalter ed. 1985).

19. For a most powerful discussion of these features of Western tradition and its figuration of the "Other" as feminine, *see* A. JARDINE, GYNESIS (1985).

any discourse is without warrant.[20]

PRIMIGRAVIDA

My first birthing happened eighteen years ago. I was a *primigravida*.[21] I had read all I could find concerning pregnancy. I was therefore able, upon hearing myself referred to as a "prima," on the morning of October 31, 1970, at Newton-Wellesley Hospital, to recognize that what was meant was *"primigravida,"* a women for the first time gravid, heavy and ripe with child. I was, however surprised to find myself so-called by someone I had not expected to meet. The doctor whom I had come to consider "my obstetrician" made no appearance that Saturday morning. I arrived at the hospital at 6:30 a.m., at which time a labor room nurse called my doctor's office and reached the physician, unfamiliar to me, who arrived at 6:50. He examined me briefly and went to the phone at the nurses' station fifteen feet from my bed. It was 7:00. I'm not sure I'll be able to make it by 9:00, he said. I'm stuck here with a *prima*. It may be a while.

I had never given birth before (I was a *prima*). I had no idea how long the process would take. I knew he was in a hurry. I knew that the *"prima"* reference was relevant to his weekend plans, that *"primas"* often take longer in labor than *"multis."*

At 7:10 I felt a change. The grinding and tearing pain abated. The nurse shouted to someone, She's ten centimeters dilated. The doctor left the nursing area. I felt a sensation of incredible pressure, without pain, and a headiness. The nurse wheeled my labor room bed through a short hallway, through the double doors of the delivery room. She positioned it alongside a narrow table. Climb across, she said. I felt utter astonishment. She spoke matter-of-factly. Did it happen that other women were able, at this stage of their labors, to climb with agility from one table to another? I don't think I can do it alone, I told her. She helped me across.

The table was extremely narrow and hard. It was like lying on an

---

20. *See* R. Barthes, Roland Barthes (1977).

21. A woman who is pregnant for the first time. Steadman's Medical Dictionary (5th ed. 1982).

ironing board. She lifted up silver stirrups for my heels, and drew loose white cotton stockings over my legs, over my thighs. There were other people in the delivery room then. I was unable to recognize them; they were robed in green, masked and gloved.

I recognized the doctor's voice as he spoke to the nurses. Push whenever you feel the urge, the nurse said to me. I felt the urge, and I pushed. Can I raise myself up on my elbows, I asked them. That won't work on this table, the nurse said. Just push again, now, it won't be long. I pushed again and uttered a long, low moan, lasting the duration of the push. There's no need for that kind of noise, he said. I felt humiliation and fury. Damn it, he said, she's not pushing hard enough. Get me a forceps.

I pushed again, my back and shoulders against the table. I liked its resistance to me. *I felt you slip down.* Stop, stop, he said. Stop pushing now, I have to numb you for the episiotomy. I tried not to push. He had a hypodermic needle between my knees and pricked it into my vagina. It hurt. I need to push, I told them. *I could feel you like a ball of fire between my thighs. I reached down to touch my own flesh, to comfort myself, to slow your passage slightly, to let you out easily.* Keep your hand away from there, he said. That's a sterile area. I needed to push again. He slit my vagina. Then he backed off. *You slipped out gently. (You were so beautiful.) I cried and I laughed. I could not take my eyes off you, Anna.* It was 7:30 a.m.

A.C. was a *prima,* too, it appears. Primigravid and, in the court's words, *in extremis.*[22] She was dying.

I think that when people are dying they call up in imagination the times of their childhood, times of having felt nurtured. I imagine that at my own death I will be less a "mother" than I am at this moment, and much more nearly a "child." My good friend Jennifer died of cancer at age 34, leaving her two young daughters. On the day of her death I visited her. She did not recognize me. Her mother was with her, and when Jennifer spoke at all, she spoke, in fragments, of her childhood. She did not speak, at that dying time, of further sacrifices that she might make for her daughters, for whom she had sacrificed

---

22. *See infra* note 44 and accompanying text.

much in her life.

As my father died, slowly, last year, I found, each time I visited him, that his thoughts and preoccupations turned, progressively, to earlier and earlier times of his life. He cared not so much about the experiences of yesterday as about the experiences of eighty years ago.

As A.C. submitted to the pain of her dying, as she passed through that deep and solitary inner experience of body and soul, she was offered — by medicine and law — not comfort but additional trial by torment. The representatives of medicine and law found it impossible to tolerate the mysterious unboundaried commingling which constituted the being of Angie Carder. What nature and her own strong desire and intent joined together, they set asunder. Finding insufficient her sharing the strength of every dying breath with her child-to-be, they violently wrenched from Angie Carder that not-ready-to-be-born being who died almost immediately thereafter. A forced abortion. The abortling passed from blissful water, through bloody fire, through hostile air. To earth with the flesh of her mother.

For Angie Carder, *primigravida*, maternity was mandatory, at the time when she was most incapable of it, at the time when she herself most needed mothering, the time of her being, *"in extremis"*. No representative of law and medicine mothered Angie Carder. Her own mother's intercession on behalf of Angie was ignored by medicine and law. Angie's own mother and Angie. The abortling and Angie. Each forcibly separated from the other. Angie's dying body cut, bled, stitched and scarred. Marked by the mutilation of a *rite de passage*. Followed by final passage. Newspaper accounts reported that Angie and the aborted being were reunited at their funeral. *Pietà manqué*. And the grandmother grieving. Pietà within pietà? Not precisely.

Did the judges understand these things? Should they have known? Could they have known? Is it a mystery in its very essence? An Eleusinian mystery? Is there something we ought to have said, or ought to begin to say, to alter legal understanding of women: our bodies, our selves.

MULTIGRAVIDA

After my first hospital birthing, I considered birthing my second child at home. In 1972, in Boston, I found a nurse who had previously attended home births, but had ceased to do so in anxiety about possible prosecution; a physician willing to attend a home birth but located two hours from my home. Unable to find anyone with medical training, within a reasonable distance, I gave birth again in the hospital. That second experience was more pleasant for me. I had learned from the first. A physician who practiced alone and committed himself to being present — in person and not by proxy — at his patients' deliveries attended my birthing. I arrived at Newton-Wellesley Hospital at 6:00 p.m. on a Saturday evening, September 9, 1972.

Calm, peaceful and in no hurry, my doctor urged me to adopt whatever posture felt most comfortable, and to do whatever felt best as I birthed my child. I did those things.As the episiotomy performed at my daughter's birth had presented the most painful aftermath of that birth, leaving me "uncomfortable," as they say, for several months, I had early specified that I wanted no episiotomy. While accomplished at abdominal massage, the doctor either did not know or was not comfortable with perineal massage. He therefore consulted me as my son's head crowned and presented itself, and told me that he felt he needed to perform an episiotomy. Deferring to his judgment, I consented to that procedure which he performed without administering anesthesia. Its execution caused me no pain, but I wondered about its necessity. (I did not stop wondering when, later, the doctor told me that he, too, had questioned the real necessity of that "very slight cut," but that he had never not performed an episiotomy at any birth he had attended. I felt that I had to do it, he said.)

Then you were born. Your blue eyes wide open. David. You looked at the world.

Settled comfortably, though for a short stay, in my hospital bed, I asked the nurses to bring you to room with me. They refused, at first, saying I needed to rest. Argument. Confusion. Then they brought you in. I kept you then in my bed, happy to be with you. Much more at rest with you close to me than when you were afar. Just as now, David.

In the morning an older nurse peeked into our room, laughed at the two of us — David warm and snug against my thigh, I sitting up crocheting a shawl. *She looked at you and you looked back at her. Your eyes followed her face and her hat as she moved above you.* He's beautiful, she said. And he's just incredibly alert. I can see that you've had a natural birth, she said, just by looking at you. I wish all women would.

The reality of multigravid-ness does not undo the singularity of each pregnancy. Pregnant in the fall of 1980, I felt for the first time the pressures of unanticipated physical problems associated with pregnancy; the related financial uncertainties — loss of wages and concern about employment security; and the workplace stresses that arise from men's ambivalences about pregnant women.

Preparing for a party at our home in the week before Christmas, at the start of my fourth month of pregnancy. House cleaning. Cooking. Feeling energetic and well after three months of exhaustion and nausea. Later that evening chatting with friends in my kitchen. Blood. On my thighs, my knees, my ankles. I leave the party. Go up to my bathroom, my bed. I weep in frustration at the bright red blood that covers my legs. At the fragments of bloody tissue. The call to the doctor. Three days in bed. A trip to the doctor's office. The urine test. Still positive. Still pregnant. Four weeks on my back in my bed while the bleeding continued, its causes unknown. Wondering whether it would abate. Wondering how long they would hold my job for me. Wondering about the mortgage payments. *Wondering what was happening to you. Your father brought me drinks, meals, kept me company. Whenever I got out of my bed, I hunched over, around you (you were a you to me, then, someone threatening to leave) to keep you within.* Then, cessation of bleeding, for reasons unknown. The ultrasound scan. *My first vision of you. Underwater. Swimming. I laughed when I saw you.*

Feeling well and strong, I returned to my work - as a public defender. Enjoying the high levels of energy that have marked the later stages of all my pregnancies. No indication of problems. Assigned to co-counsel the defense of a capital case set for trial in mid-May. Our defendant charged with the murder of his wife. We estimated a ten-day trial to end by the end of May. The trial in fact lasted four weeks — ending just a few days before the birth of my child.

— Incident with the prosecutor — I ask him to refer to me, before the jury, as "Ms." not as "Mrs." I can't understand that, he says, given your condition.

— My colleague needs an excuse for his tardiness. I hope you don't mind, he tells me, but I've told the judge we'll be late because you don't feel well. I do feel well. I feel fine. I mind his use of my pregnancy, of my being.

— At counsel table, the defendant hunches beside me. Weary, subdued. A colleague observes, several days into trial: That's a nice touch — the pregnant woman and the accused murderer sitting together. Looks good for the jury. I don't like his comment. It objectifies me. And my relationship with my client. I do like the defendant. I don't change my seat.

— Our psychiatric expert flies in from California. His national reputation: defense of marital murders. We gather for trial preparation. Start out, he tells me, by asking me if he loved her. Just ask: Did he love his wife? I consider his proposal. I've given much thought to direct examination, to tying what the expert can say to the facts and our theory. I propose a different approach. His face gets red. He stands up from the table. He addresses my colleague. He says: I *hate* macho mothers.

The confinement of pregnant women to categories. Mandated vulnerability.

HOME BIRTHS

The last three of my five birthings have occurred at home. Each time, I have been fortunate to find good and generous friends to help me through the births. Each time; I have felt it necessary to conceal with great care the identities of the women who midwifed for me, not to disclose their names to the lawyers with whom I worked or to the doctors whom I consulted, in order to protect them against the possibility of criminal prosecution.

In the city in which my third and fourth children, Tony and Michael, were born, in 1981 and 1983, a lay midwife had, only a few years before, been criminally prosecuted. She had been charged with manslaughter when a baby whose birth she had attended subsequently died. On her attorney's advise she had accepted a plea agreement that involved her pleading guilty to the criminal charge of practicing medicine without license and had been sentenced to a probation that required her leaving the state and no longer practicing midwifery. While I needed and welcomed the help of my friends, then, I feared the possibility that their understanding and generosity might have negative consequences for them.

Each birth was attended by a friend who had herself birthed at home. Each was without any formal medical training. They extended care which I had never received in a hospital. Warm herbal compresses; massage that assured both no episiotomy and no tearing as my babies were born; calm, privacy, peace. Neither of those women had had extensive experience assisting births. Each of them was extremely intelligent, very well-informed, caring, and understanding of women's needs for dignity and respect. The births were unqualifiedly joyous occasions.

The pressures against birthing at home, in the sites where our mothers and grandmothers birthed, are enormous. Friends and family so take for granted the definitions of pregnancy and birthing articulated by medicine and enforced by law that they are unable to understand the choice of home-birth except as a kind of recklessness. Beyond those pressures, both parents and birth attendants feel acutely the pressures constituted by the threat of law. Criminal prosecution looms as a possibility for lay midwives in many states, and deprivation of medical or nursing licenses threatens medically-credentialed persons who participate in home birthing. As was the experience of Vickie Smith. And of Janet Leigh.[23] That operation of law demonstrates the legal buttressing of the strictest forms of medical regulation. It precludes women's defining the degree to which we will treat our pregnancies and birthings as medical constructs. It precludes access to any middle ground — to the kind of home birthing with medical support that was successful in Great Britain for many years, for example.

Three days after the murder trial ended, on June 25, 1981, my good friend hurried from court for Tony's birthing. She changed her lawyer clothes and got out her supplies. We spread out the sterilized sheets, the sterile scissors, the sterile shoestring. After two hours of labor — with laughter and joking — Tony came forth to his family and friends. *Last night, before our friends arrived, you lettered a sign for the door. "WELLCOM," it said. Do you recall your own welcome? Your sister stole you away at once, to hold you, wrapped in your blanket, to present you to all her friends on our street. Your brother was*

---

23. *See* Smith v. State ex rel. Med. Licensing Bd., 459 N.E.2d 401 (Ind. Ct. App. 1984) and Leigh v. Bd. of Registration in Nursing, 95 Mass. 670, 481 N.E.2d 1347 (1985).

solemn. He touched you tentatively. I have never felt anything so soft, he said.

Committed to categorization, law is intolerant of porous boundaries (placentas?). It constrains and imposes the arbitrarily narrow limits within which birth attendants must operate to avoid criminal sanction, limiting not only places and conditions under which birthing women conduct our labors but imposing rigid restrictions upon the work that may be undertaken by intelligent, caring and supportive attendants.

The choice of home birthing is further pressured, not only by those constraints, but also by the reality of vindictive or violent reprisals by medical institutions. It is well-known that physicians unwilling to perform home-births frequently attempt to obtain from patients information about other professionals who may be supporting home-birth practice. Medical professionals censor and constrain one another's choices. Beyond that they punish. Retaliation? Deterrence?

*   *   *   *   *

In writing of Michael's birth and its aftermath, I noted the following:

Michael was born shortly before midnight on Sunday, December 11, 1983, after a few hours of light labor and four hours of hard labor. The midwife brought her four-week old baby and nursed him beside my bed, encouraging me all the while. My husband boiled water, prepared compresses, anticipated what I might need or desire. I kept my favorite Fra Angelico "Annunciation" by my bed to look at during the hard times. I laughed when Tim put Kay Gardner's "Emerging" onto the tape deck. The amniotic sac never broke, and Michael emerged within it. A tiny snip, a gushing of water. The sac slipped over his shoulders. Michael shrieked, enraged at his sudden transport from water to air. He knotted his fists, filled his lungs, and complained. Then he quieted. Waxy, solemn and perfect.

After the birth, we all massaged my abdomen, to encourage the passing of the placenta. I could feel that the placenta had detached from my uterine wall, that the uterus had begun to contract. The bleeding that normally follows the separation of the placenta occurred and ceased. But the placenta did not emerge spontaneously. Realizing that it would have to be removed and not wanting to attempt its removal myself, I decided to wait until morning and to visit my obstetrician at that time.

I lay awake all through the night, as is my habit following a birth. In the morning I felt splendid — though eager to be rid of the still-retained placenta. At the foot of the stairs I found the Christmas tree, decked out by Anna, David and Tony while Michael was being born.

It was very cold and the roads were icy, but we warmed the car and bundled Michael well. We drove to the clinic at which both my obstetrician and my pediatrician had offices.

Some nurses stopped while we waited in the lobby, admiring Michael. The pediatrician came out to see him. He looks great, he said. I don't want to pry at all, he said, but I wonder who was with you during the birth? I know your husband was there. But was someone else with you? I gave him no names.

The obstetrician said that it was necessary to remove the placenta immediately. I questioned the urgency, inquiring whether it might be possible to go into the hospital later in the day, where anesthesia would be available for the procedure. He assured me that the nitrous oxide he could deliver at the Clinic would be sufficient. A nurse brought in an "Informed Consent" form. I made some changes on it before signing it. A flurry of consultations. Nurses and doctor. They were angry with me.

My back on a narrow table again. The nurse. The doctor. All masked. The table was cold. The stirrups again. The nurse placed something over my mouth and nose. She told me to breathe in deeply. I did so. I lifted above the table. Like swimming in air.

My son David was reading Tolkein. *The Lord of the Rings*.[24] I read along with him. Do you like these books? he asked me. *I* really do, he said. I like them too, I told him. Except — that there are no women in them. Or hardly any. Does that matter?

Dark riders surrounded me. They were my enemies.

The nurse leaned over my head, over my face. I think it was the nurse. Her mouth and her nose were covered. I knew by her voice that she was a woman. I saw only her eyes. I wished that she would connect

---

24.   J.R.R. Tolkien, The Lord of the Rings (1974).

them to mine. But she didn't.

Last night, at the most difficult time of the labor, I said to the midwife: Please remember to keep looking directly into my eyes. Remind me to look at you. She did so.
This nurse will not look into my eyes.

When I breathe in the gas I am lifted away from the table, from what feels like a floor. They won't let me climb off the table, so I know I can't trust them. The nurse speaks soothingly. She says to relax, to breathe deeply. But I know that I should not do that. I struggle to push the mask away from my face. She holds me down, pushing it back over my mouth and nose. I struggle with her. I begin to scream.

I fear them. I think of my baby outside in his father's arms. Pain twists through me. I think of my newborn outside in his father's arms. I feel they are trying to kill me. My children will have no mother. I push the mask away again and the pain fills my ears and my throat and my eyes. The cells I never knew of. And flies out of me and I fly out of me. There is nothing I would not do to escape this pain.
I thought I had reached the farthest borders of pain last night, giving birth to my son. I had not. This pain destroys me.

If only the nurse would look at me, I would trust her, if she would just meet my eyes. I can see her eyebrows and the brown silky hair escaped from her cap and her mask. Her hair makes me soften. I recognize her. She is like me. Why won't she look at me?

The Tolkein riders pass by me again.

I scream to them then, How much longer? Just tell me how much longer, I beg them. I push his hand away. He is pressing something steel inside me. Please stop, I beg him. He doesn't answer. He drives the steel object more deeply. His face is covered like hers. Then he speaks: We have to do this. I beg him to stop. Just lie still, he says. We have to do this.

And I ask her then. How much longer. Please tell me how much longer. That will help me to bear it. But she won't answer. And I think it will never stop, till I die. I think they are killing me, slowly.

When she presses the mask against me I move into dreams. The room fills with struggle. I look for my allies. I want to trust her. I don't want to be all alone here. This is what torture is.

Someone is speaking. There is no woman here. There are no women in here. That one behind the mask is not like you. I hear horrible laughter. I push the mask away and I scream. I call them screams. But they were not screams from my throat. They were calls from every ravaged part of my body. They broke out of my breast, my heart, my lungs, my womb, my being. I could not bear to hear them. I could not bear to acknowledge who was making those sounds. Was it I?

An auger is working within me, without me, about me. It is slow and relentless. I wish I could faint. But I have to fight them.

I think I am in the earth or I am the earth and a plow is churning and ripping through me. When will it end? Her arm is thin but she's strong and she presses against me. I want them to stop. And mostly I want her to look at me. Directly. To make me believe she believes that they have to do this. But she won't look at me. She looks away. She is ashamed. Is she ashamed of me, of my howling and begging before him? Or is she ashamed of herself? How can I know. I want to think she's ashamed of me, of my weakness, of my crying in pain. I'm sorry, I say. But please stop, please, please, please stop. Please stop this.

There are no women here. And I turn my face away from her and away from him. Away from no mercy. And my cheek touches the table, still cold, and the cold is a mercy.

And they stop. He pulls out his tools and drops them onto the counter. They clang. And he rolls off his gloves. He slips the mask down. It hangs around his neck. We had to do it, he says. He turns and goes out.

She helps me to sit. She is silent. I want to leave there. I want to get out of that room. She gives me some water. I ask her, Is it always like this? Couldn't he have given me anaesthesia? Did it have to be done this way?
She shrugs.

Let me see how much you are bleeding, she says. But I won't let her touch me. Not much, I say, and I draw up my knees. I'm ready to go, I tell her. Are you sure?, she asks me. She hands me a soft cotton pad, white and clean. I press it between my thighs. It feels gentle. I get up and get dressed.

The doctor comes in. Are you ready to go?, he says. We had to do it, he says.
I feel confused. Well, I guess I'm sorry I screamed so much, I tell him.

I go out to my baby. *You were sleepy and solemn-eyed. Michael. Magical. Born in your caul. We took you home.*

My friend came to see me, a nurse. I told her about it. Why do you think he did that? she asked me. Another friend came by, a nurse also. I told her my story. He raped you, she said. I hated those words. I did not want to hear them. Or to say them. But they were true. He raped me.

*   *   *   *   *

On July 25, 1986, at 1:30 a.m., I sat in my rocker. Awaiting the midwives. I did not want to stand, to hurry the progress of my labor, before their arrival. By 2:00 a.m., all three had come in. I cannot recall ever feeling more cared-for than I was by them and my husband in the following hours.
They inspired me with their gentleness, confidence, patience and strength. Most amazingly, when, in the short intermissions between intense contractions, I thanked them, they laughed and thanked me. I never doubted their gladness in being with me.
A brief, intense labor. Encouraged by a plurality of female voices; kindness of hands that touched when I needed touching, that otherwise left me alone; understanding and courage communicated through eyes familiar with the extremities of birthing. When I stood up, in the final phases of my labor, interrupting my pushing to walk about, they laughed with me. My husband's strength supporting my back. Their bearing with me. Their confident, intelligent, patient waiting through the strenuous exertion of the end of our labor.
Their gifts of body and mind blessed me that night, and, in my memory, continue to bless me. I wish that all women, in our birthings, could feel such support and such comfort.

They delighted in you. In your scent of womb-water. Your satin.
Your color. Your plumpness. Your strength. For a week you were
nameless. I kept you beside me. I gazed at you, sleeping and waking.
Waiting for your name to disclose itself to me. Devin.

"MORTAL DECISIONS"

The "ordinary" medico-legal regulations of pregnancy and birthing (restricting time, place and manner of conducting pregnancy and of
giving birth) are so pervasive that we often fail to recognize them as in
fact regulations — particular cultural variants, perhaps, of a general
and universal regulation of female sexuality and female personhood.[25]
The "extraordinary" regulations that have recently become apparent in
abortion regulation as well as in requirements — including major surgery — imposed upon pregnant women by courts, are in fact not different in kind from the "ordinary" regulations. Nonetheless, the sudden-
ness of their introduction or the inadequacies of the theoretical
structures within which they have been discussed have disclosed their
problematic nature.

The rhetoric surrounding both discussion of abortion and discussion of recently intensified regulation of pregnancy in the name of "fetal" protection has tended to polarize into divisions about the relative
"rights" that should attach, respectively, to women and to "fetal life."
There has often seemed no common structure within which proponents
and opponents of various regulatory schemes might speak meaningfully
and understandingly with one another, with respect for our different
experiences.

One of the most striking features of "pro-life" rhetoric is its recognition of abortion as a deathly act — the extinguishment of some form
of human life — and its exposure of underlying experiences of horror
— generally transmuted into self-recrimination and moral certitude —
in the reports that pro-life women produce in recounting their abortion
experiences. I have been struck, correspondingly, by the absence from
most "pro-choice" rhetoric of a discourse of death as well as of discourses of horror or guilt. Pro-life advocates have accurately recognized
in pro-choice discourse a practice of abstraction that tends to obliterate
or to erase the realities of bloodiness and violence attached to abortion.
Women who consciously experience abortion become familiar with

---

25. Concerning the notion of a taboo relating to all sexual expression *see* G.
BATAILLE, DEATH AND SENSUALITY: A STUDY OF EROTICISM AND THE TABOO (1962).

those realities and respond variously to them; women whose anaesthetized experiences of abortion distance us from awareness of the bloody violence of abortion sometimes discover in post-abortion experiences reminders of the death-dealing power that is exercised in abortion. Both kinds of recognition — that occurring during the course of abortion and that arising later —may evoke a range of differing responses in different women.

Abortion is not merely a "moral" — but also a "mortal" decision. The failure of pro-choice discourse to so recognize it — to acknowledge the violence intrinsic to abortion — has constructed impediments to our speaking truly and deeply — and more variously — of what abortion means to us. It has discouraged our discoveries — beneath rhetoric and sloganeering, and beneath the obfuscation of medico-legal discourse — of the reality of common bodily experience underlying the various interpretations of different women.

The same failures of discourse have affected discussions of the proper legal treatment of pregnancy in general. The *A.C.* court properly characterized the judgment to be made in that case as a "mortal decision."[26] In that characterization, it hints at the questions that lie at the heart of all "reproduction"-related matters presented as legal issues: Who will be permitted to exercise the power of extinguishing certain forms of human life? May women be entrusted to exercise such power? Ought the choice of mortality by women — or the willing assumption of certain risks of death — be tolerated by law?

I ask myself: What does it mean to put to death, intentionally, a living thing?

Sheltered, like most urban people, from the realities of death-dealing that underlie daily life, I have seldom consciously accomplished the death of another being whom I have recognized as "like" me, seldom executed clearly "mortal" decisions. In the summer of 1983, during one of my pregnancies, our dog, Flash, gave birth to a litter of pups. A Monday in July. A midwestern summer afternoon. Brilliant, glaring sunlight. Oppressive heat. I watch Flash dig a deep trench alongside the foundation of our house, in the afternoon sun. She works with a kind of determined ferocity. I observe her with interest, coming, gradually, to recognize in her frenzy a preparation for her imminent birthing.

---

26. *See* In re A.C., 533 A.2d 611 (D.C. 1987), *vacated and reh'g granted*, 539 A.2d 203 (1988).

I take some soft towels and newspapers into the garage to make a nest for her, hopeful that she will come into that cool, dark place which, to me, seems more comfortable that the place she has selected. I call her into the garage and pet her. I close the door so that she won't go outside again. I leave her, to take a nap.

My son comes into my room in excitement. He sits on the edge of my bed. Flash has seven puppies, he tells me, but I think there's something wrong with one of them. . . It's not moving. In my weariness, I am not eager to go down to the dog. I tell David that I'll come soon. I rest a bit longer and then go downstairs. David meets me in the kitchen. There are eleven now, he tells me. I groan silently and go out to see Flash.

She lies on the towelling. Her eyes slightly glazed. I count eleven pups: two appear lifeless; nine squirm about. I sit on a bench and watch her deliver three more, lick them off, chew on and swallow their sacs. She looks exhausted.

I pick up the lifeless pups and wrap them in paper towelling. Put them into a shoe box. I find Flash's water bowl, fill it up, bring it to her. She drinks, lying still in her sodden nest. Using the backyard hose I fill up an old laundry tub. I then select five pups and carry them one at a time, to the tub. I drop each one into the water.

I am inexperienced at death-dealing. I don't want to watch the pups drown. I don't want my children to watch them. I drag the tub to the side of the house. I cover it with a metal lid. Cowardly, then, I leave them.

Later, in early evening, I return to uncover the tub. I lift each pup, in fascinated horror, out of the tub. I wrap each in paper towels. I am too tired and too sick to bury them. I place them, in a plastic bag, in the trash can, to be carried away in the morning.

I have never felt a continuing guilt, a profound regret, a deep misgiving about that "mortal decision." But it has remained in my memory — a grave act. I have not forgotten the weight of these small, wet, stiffened forms in my hands.

Is what I did there "right" or "wrong"? It is neither. It is only what I have done. Another women might have done differently. Even performing what appeared an identical act, she might have done differently. The farm woman drowning kittens as a matter of course may have an experience different from mine. Another woman might have felt unable to intervene in any way to cause the deaths of the helpless pups. In acting decisively I spent little or no time in reflection. What I did was what seemed to me proper, if somewhat unpleasant.

For those of us living in cities, even the care of our animals is ordinarily so medicalized — so delegated to medical practice — that in our closest contact with animal life we are generally removed from the more immediate contact with animal death that has characterized human experience in other times and places. We are seldom required to confront very directly — by our own agency or observation — the choices that present themselves to us because of the limitations of life, because of the reality of death underlying all life and encroaching upon it. We formulate moral theory in places removed from the physical realities of our death-dealing decisions. Because of our distance from those physical realities we often fail to feel — in our flesh and bones — the shudder of horror that ordinarily arises at witnessing sudden, willfully accomplished transitions from the state of individual existence to a state of undifferentiation.

Anthropologists and ethnologists report the existence of an area defined as "sacred" surrounding the intentional dealing of death — the sacrifice of animal or of human life.[27] I wonder whether those accounts have some relevance for our understanding of the processes underlying present formulations of abortion law — *Roe v. Wade*[28] as well as more restrictive state statutory schemes — and the formulations expressed in *A.C.*[29] Certainly, the medicalization of our "reproductive" processes has significantly distanced most of us — including legislators and judges — from the immediacy of the female bodily experiences of pregnancy, birth, and abortion. That distancing has obscured the horror and fear that — ethnologists theorize — arises universally in the face of female violence and that seeks to control and regulate women's "mortal decisions" for the reason that such decisions remind us of our frailties: our dependence upon the flesh and minds of our mothers; the finitude of our bodily lives; the constant imminence of a death that may swallow us up.[30] Is it possible to speak of experiences of abortion and other "mortal decisions" in a different discourse, outside the language of law and of medicine?

Many writers have theorized the powerful ambivalences about

---

27. *See* G. Bataille, *supra* note 25.
28. Roe v. Wade, 410 U.S. 113, *reh'g denied*, 410 U.S. 959 (1973).
29. In re A.C., 533 A.2d 611 (D.C. 1987).
30. *See Semiotics of Biblical Abomination*, in J. KRISTEVA, POWERS OF HORROR: AN ESSAY ON ABJECTION (1980).

death which, displaced against maternal bodies, have motivated the pan-cultural subordination of women through regulation of the broad range of our activity currently subsumed under the term "reproduction." They have noted, as a most striking attribute of discourse regulating women's activity, its unfounded confidence about the nature of "woman" and of motherhood — a confidence that purports to justify its own exercise of power.[31] Such ambivalence about maternal bodies resides in women as well as in men. Barbara Johnson,[32] in a dense and powerful discussion of the rhetoric of abortion expressed in women's poetry, has found evidence that not only medical technologists but pregnant women ourselves seem unable to speak of abortion in voices free of identification with the "fetus." She finds in the pronomic usages embodied in those texts evidence not only of the non-binary nature of the pregnancy experience but also of the reality of a recollective identification with the experience of pre-natality, of "fetal" being.

Such rhetorical and psychological analyses point to the difficulty of speaking of abortion in ways that adequately utter its subjective realities, its meanings for our personhoods. They invite deeper exploration. It seems to me that the departure point for such exploration must be women's own accounts of our experiences, uttered with a commitment of faithfulness to the truths of female bodies suppressed in the dominant discourse. To the degree that women produce such writings, we may avoid the abstraction that has characterized and limited the work of certain cautious and sensitive male commentators presently writing about female "reproductive" experiences. To the degree that we avoid essentialism we will recognize the undesirability of *any* regulation of abortion.[33]

If the purpose of contemporary feminist critique is to expose and explore profound and powerful ambivalences — most strongly ex-

---

31. *See id. See also* D. Dinnerstein, The Mermaid and the Minotaur: Sexual Arrangements and Human Malaise (1976) and N. Chodorow, The Reproduction of Mothering: Psychoanalysis of the Sociology of Gender (1978).

32. B. Johnson, *Apostrophe, Animation and Abortion,* in A World of Difference (1987).

33. *See* R. Goldstein, Mother-Love and Abortion (1987). This work confronts seriously the inadequacy of binaristic models of pregnancy that imply separate and separable existences of a pregnant woman and her "fetus". Goldstein proposes a "dyad" model to do greater justice to the reality of pregnancy which is neither unitary nor dual. A serious limitation of Goldstein's work, however, lies in his taking for granted that regulation of abortions that occur late in pregnancy does not work intolerable harm on the pregnant woman, the "representative of the dyad."

pressed in the medico-legal discourse of women — it will succeed, however temporarily, only to the degree that its own discourse departs from or ruptures through the dominant rhetoric, expressing a different knowledge. Thus, women's critiques of the prevailing discourse must be marked by a tentativeness, a newness, a preciseness, an insistent refusal to venture into abstraction unconnected to the common experiences of very different women, and a firm rejection of simplistic and violent categorizations. Our alternative discourse must be capable of responding persuasively to the question by which we must judge not only medico-legal but every discursive account of women: How do you know what you claim to know?

I have experienced a number of spontaneous abortions — miscarriages — and one intentional abortion. Of the latter experience, I am able to say with certainty that its physical and emotional aftermaths have been far more severely negative than I had been led by any medical practitioner to expect. Of the actual surgical procedure I can say virtually nothing. I was anaesthetized during the procedure, which took place quite early in my pregnancy, and therefore had no real awareness of what was done to my body. Like a woman anaesthetized in childbirth, I experience a gap between the physical trauma to my body and my waking consciousness thereof.

In the miscarriages that I have sustained, my experience has been quite other. In those situations, I have always been very much aware — and, in all those cases, distressed by — my changing body. In all those cases I have wished that the pregnancies would continue, and have grieved their endings as losses.

One of my miscarriages occurred early in the fourth month of a pregnancy. It was a slow and lengthy process, a persistent progress that exhausted and defeated me, that left me saddened for months. I remember vividly the completion of that miscarriage, which occurred during a night in the middle of November, six years ago. I had visited my doctor when the abortion first threatened and had received and followed her standard advice. She had warned me of what I might expect, as the slight bleeding indicating the possibility of miscarriage developed into more steady indications: the passage of bloody tissue about the size of an orange, accompanied by severe cramping. I felt that passage — a kind of minor birthing, accompanied by the twisting and grinding pains of childbirth, though of lesser intensity and lesser duration. That tissue, the "fetus," slid from my body — purple, quivering, silent. I caught it in a porcelain bowl from my kitchen. I touched it gently. Its appearance was stunning to me — both familiar and unfamiliar; startling. *Purple as sun-done plums, your fine remains.* I wrapped it carefully in some white linen towelling and carried it down to the living-room fireplace. I brought in some new wood and burned it there. I sat for a long time beside the fire. It seemed to me that the fire itself and the room and the house were altered — blessed, even — by that burning.

I have learned through miscarriage the bloodiness of abortion — spontaneous or induced. Every abortion involves violence and bloodiness.

Although I have grieved, sometimes at length, over every lost pregnancy, it is only my hospital abortion that has never left me alone. Why? Perhaps because it was an abortion that I really did not want. A not uncoerced election. In Gwendolyn Brooks words, *Even in my deliberateness I was not deliberate.*[34] I am sure that that reality has contributed to the degree that I am haunted by that abortion — which occurred 13 years ago. An experience of ultimate dividedness. Of rupture. Of divided will: choosing what I did not want. Of divided consciousness: not knowing in a fullness of mind the tearing of flesh and the shedding of blood that occurred in the deep reaches of my body.

There was a time when the shedding of women's blood — in childbirth, in menstruation, and, it may be, in abortion — was accompanied by elaborate ritual. Such ritual constructed and expressed the experience of the sacred generally attached to the open shedding of blood. The medicalization of abortion — like that of childbirth and pregnancy — has set women at a distance from the blood ceremonies of our bodies, placing us at the mercy of a technological priesthood that denies the sacred, detaching us from the physicality and the cultural implications of violence and bloodshed. We have become the victims, and not the agents, of bloodshed.

You, who were never "you" until you left me. You, who come to my dreams, ever silent. You, whom I recognize as my daughter. Sometimes I feel your presence before I see you. Your hair like a fiery

---

34. G. Brooks, *the mother*, in SELECTED POEMS (1963).

crown. Your dress of white linen. Your name, that I sometimes whisper, known only to you and to me. You do not break the windows and shake the walls of my house.[35] *Does that mean that you have forgiven me? But you visit me often. I am glad that you come. Except — there is so much I wish. A funeral rite that I cannot perform without feeling your flesh in my fingers, without touching our common blood. In your presence, words fail. How great is the power of flesh that binds us together. Be with me.*

The haunting words of *The Water-Lily: Ah, the waking is sad/For the tears that it brings/And she knows 'tis her dead baby's spirit that sings:/Come, mamma! Come! Quick! Follow me!/Step out on the leaves of the water-lily.*[36]

*　　*　　*　　*　　*

What I have known of abortion led me, for a long time, to generalize, to think, with Gwendolyn Brooks, that "Abortions do not let you forget. You remember the babies you got that you did not get."[37] It led me, in overgeneralization, to believe that the choice of abortion is always a difficult and troubled moral decision. However, in recent years I have come to recognize that even that generalization may be without foundation. That *my* experience is not the experience of every woman. That grief is not necessarily the prevailing emotion attached to abortion.

I have become familiar with accounts of my friends — and of other women — that express the enormous relief they have felt at bringing body into harmony with mind through abortion, at restoring their bodies to the unitary, non-pregnant states that conformed with the definitions of selfhood articulated by those women at the times when they chose abortion. Such accounts have begun to be offered to courts making abortion decisions. Consider, for example, the following:

> "Almost exactly a decade ago, I learned I was pregnant . . . I was sick in my heart and I thought I would kill myself. It was as if I had been told my body had been invaded with cancer. It seemed

---

35. *See* T. Morrison, Beloved (1987).
36. H. Lawson, *The Water-Lily*, in The Selected Works of Henry Lawson (1957).
37. G. Brooks, *supra* note 34.

that very wrong."[38]

"On the ride home from the clinic, the relief was enormous. I felt happy for the first time in weeks. I had a future again. I had my body back."[39]

Whatever our commonalities, each individual woman is a singular body. And each singular body is the site of a singular subjectivity, a unique personhood. My experience is not identical to those of my sisters. For some women, abortion is nothing other than a relief, it appears, while for others it becomes nothing other than a kind of dying — suicidal if not murderous.[40]

Different constructions of bodily experience. Different stitchings of web. When I hear varying narratives and when I recognize the various truths in different accounts, I ask whether *any* legal regulation of "reproduction" can avoid a perpetration of violence upon women. I wonder if there is any possibility of "equality" where regulation rests upon essentialist notions of gender and sexuality.[41]

A.C., AGAIN

Theorists sometimes identified as "cultural feminists" have often proposed that female experience gives rise to an ethic of "caring" that differs from the dominant ethic of "rights" constructed out of the profound alienation of men from their mothers' bodies.[42] Other femi-

---

38. Amicus Brief for the National Abortion Rights Action League, et al., Thornburgh v. American College of Obstetricians and Gynecologists, Nos. 84-498 and 84-1379 (on file at Nova Law Review). For the Supreme Court opinion *see* 476 U.S. 747 (1986).

39. *Id.*

40. *See* A. RICH, OF WOMAN BORN 272-274 (1976).

41. For feminist critiques incorporating anti-essentialist themes or perspectives, *see* Ashe, *Mind's Opportunity: Birthing a Post-Structuralist Feminist Jurisprudence*, 38 SYRACUSE L. REV. 1129 (1987); *Law-Language of Maternity: Discourse Holding Nature in Contempt*, 22 NEW ENG. L. REV. 521 (1987); Scales, *The Emergence of Feminist Jurisprudence: An Essay*, 95 YALE L.J. 1373 (1986); and Dalton, *Where We Stand: Observations on the Situation of Feminist Legal Thought*, BERKELEY WOMEN'S L.J. 1 (1988).

42. Major representatives of "cultural feminism" include Carol Gilligan, author of IN A DIFFERENT VOICE (1982) and Elizabeth Wolgast, author of EQUALITY AND THE RIGHTS OF WOMEN (1980). Such writers have pointed out the reality that certain

nist writers have critiqued the "caring" emphasis as merely a variant on rhetorics that operate to justify traditional self-victimization of women.[43] I ask: What ethic relating to "reproduction" ought to be reflected in law?

In reading of *A.C.* and of Angie Carder, I have found one clear expression marked by the attributes that, I suggested above, will characterize powerful deconstructive and reconstructive feminist critique — attributes of clarity, newness, faithfulness to bodily experience, rejection of abstraction, and refusal to be reduced or simplified to facilitate categorization. That expression comes closer to uttering what I find a persuasive feminist ethic than any other voice I have heard in discussion of *A.C.* and related cases. It is the voice of Angie Carder's mother, Nettie Stoner.

Nettie Stoner, at the time of the *A.C.* hearing, was a woman who had already known much physical suffering. She had lost both her legs in an accident that had occurred nine years before. That loss had enabled her understanding of her daughter Angie's experience of amputation two years later, incident to treatment of her cancer. So intimately did Nettie Stoner understand her daughter's experience that she recognized the recurrence of Angie's cancer during pregnancy, before that recurrence had been recognized by her diagnostic physicians. Likewise, she felt certain that the "fetus" would not survive, as a healthy child, the court-ordered surgery performed upon Angie Carder.[44]

Nettie Stoner testified at the hearing before the trial court that ordered her daughter's submission to Caesarean section. The following is an account of the testimony she gave in response to questioning by the court-appointed "lawyer for the 'fetus'."[45] It is testimony that arises out of maternal knowledge — a particular, local knowledge — that expresses an ethic characterized not by the sentimentality expected of and tolerated in mothers, but by a cold-eyed, unflinching strength, a clear recognition of the impossibility of finally avoiding

---

habits or ways of being — whether natural or culturally ingrained — tend, on the average, to distinguish women from men. They have seen the valuation and protection of such differences as the proper role of law.

43. *See Feminist Discourse, Moral Values and the Law: A Conversation*, 34 BUFFALO L. REV. 11 (1985).

44. D. Remnick, *Whose Life Is It Anyway?*", THE WASH. POST MAGAZINE, Feb. 21, 1988, at 18, 20.

45. Assumption of "fetal personhood" may be implied by the appointment of an attorney to represent the "fetus" as well as by the *A.C.* court's reference to "a patient . . . in fetal state." In re A.C., 533 A.2d 611 (D.C. 1987).

death:

> When it was time for the court to hear from Nettie, everyone leaned forward a bit to hear about Angie.
>
> "She wanted to live long enough to hold that baby," Nettie began. "She did not want me to have to take care of that baby. She told me that. She wanted to live to hold that baby."
>
> Mishkin: "This is terribly difficult for you, I know, and I'm sorry to have to ask you some questions, but I think it's important at least to get some sense of how you, as a family, would be able to cope if there were a live baby to come out of this. Do you have, for example, is there medical insurance? Is there any way that you have or are you totally stranded?"
>
> Nettie: "Nobody. Nobody would insure a baby. Nobody would insure my daughter. Nobody."
>
> Mishkin: "So there is no family insurance that would cover the baby's care?
>
> Nettie: "No. That doesn't even enter into it. I don't care about the money. It's just that I know there will be something wrong with this baby. I can't handle it. I've handled [Angie] and myself."
>
> Mishkin: "I understand."
>
> Nettie: "Nobody else can love a child like that and I know what it would be. No."
>
> Mishkin: "Would you — would you even have the resources to handle a healthy baby?"
>
> Nettie: "No."
>
> Mishkin: "If the baby was not compromised?"
>
> Nettie: "Not really. Rick, her husband, they have only been married eight months. I mean, he hasn't even had her long enough. How is he going to cope with a baby? They don't have any family, just Rick and his mom. It's me and I'm in a wheelchair. I can't put that burden on us anymore. Angela is the only one that wanted that baby to love. She said she wanted something of her very own."
>
> Mishkin: "Would you consider placing the baby for adoption?"
>
> Nettie: "Never. Never."
>
> Mishkin: "What would you do if the baby survived?"
>
> Nettie: "Who wants it?"
>
> At this point, Mishkin recalls, some of the people in the room seemed shocked at Nettie's bluntness. "I'm sure it was out of stress," Mishkin says. She pushed on.
>
> Mishkin: "I guess I'm asking you a terribly difficult question, but I'm trying to determine. . ."
>
> Nettie: "I would take care of the baby. I would never put it up for adoption. I would do the best I could, but we don't want it.

Angela wanted that baby. It was her baby. Let the baby die with
her."

Rick [Angie's husband]: "Please."

Nettie: "It's hers."

Mishkin: "I have no further questions."[46]

Nettie Stoner's voice speaks of honoring life by honoring death. It
accepts ambivalence. In discourse that "some" might find "shocking,"
that others dismiss as arising "out of stress," she honors a truth of
maternity. Nettie Stoner speaks of both the limitations and the enormous power of mother-love. She expresses the truths that "fetal life"
depends utterly upon the life and will of a pregnant woman; that sometimes "fetal" death and maternal death — human deaths — are the
best life has to offer; and that "Death is the mother of beauty."[47] I
hear in Nettie Stoner's words the enduring and insistent assertion that
legally-endorsed violations of women's bodies in the name of "life" —
hateful legal constructs that impose "love" and "self-sacrifice" upon
women as our duties — are perverse. That in its alienation from nature
law works harms far more destructive than the deaths that arise out of
nature or out of the natural limitations of women.

These words spoken by Nettie Stoner from her wheelchair echo
with power, with passion, with honest love. I honor her "mortal
decision."

When will her thought, her decision, find expression in law that
explicitly lets women be — in our limitations and in our differences,
law that leaves us alone?

The self-accounts of mothers and of all women — pregnant, birthing, aborting, suffering violations or growing in power — constitute ut-
terances closer to the reality of women's experiences than does any for-
mulation of law or of medicine. While our generalizations and
extrapolations from those experiences may be in conflict, when we attend to one another we discover truths that, rising out of our natural
and acculturated bodies, do not conflict. How to work those yarns into
the fabric of a law that calls itself "humanist"?

---

46. The preceding account of the hearing testimony is borrowed directly from D.
Remnick, *supra* note 44.

47. *Sunday Morning*, in W. STEVENS, THE COLLECTED POEMS OF WALLACE STE-
VENS (1982).

Again, I remember my grandmother. What I know of her is limited. Fragmentary. I know that she gave birth to and mothered eight children. How did she feel about her motherhood? Did her pregnancies, her birthings, her child care, tax or delight her? Did they do both? In a culture in which both church and state constrained her choices, did she feel free to state openly the full range of her feelings, her thoughts, her desires?

I know that she worked very hard to care for her children. To supplement the livelihood earned by hard labor on their small farm, she sewed, embroidered, and smocked. I recall in my own imagination my mother's memory of trying on dresses that her mother fitted and sewed for wealthier children. I know that my grandmother felt the losses my mother felt — limitations and exclusion — in a world that defined in constricting ways the scope and the value of women's work. A world in which my own beautiful, talented immigrant mother did rich people's housework. With dignity. With pride. With great self-respect. With only a trace of the raging that I express?

I wonder about the thoughts and feelings my grandmother never put into her speech. Some of them whisper to me from her coverlet. Others I cannot ever hear.

I want a law that will let us be — women. That, recognizing the violence inherent in every regulation of female "reproduction," defines an area of non-regulation, within which we will make, each of us, our own "mortal decisions."

There is a kind of embroidery called cut-work. It is executed by the careful placement of smooth satin stitch and the excision of fabric within the area outlined by that stitching.[48] The cut-work opens up spaces within the fabric. Openness itself constitutes, then, both part of the fabric and non-part. It requires both needle and scissors. Construction and deconstruction. Within — and against — patterns of sameness, it inscribes difference.

---

48. For a discussion of cut-work technique, *see* E. WILSON, ERICA WILSON'S EMBROIDERY BOOK 251 (1973).

AN AMERICAN TRAGEDY: THE SUPREME COURT ON ABORTION

ROBERT M. BYRN*

"[I]f the deliberate extinguishment of human life has any effect at all, it more likely tends to lower our respect for life and brutalize our values."[1]

"New York courts have already acknowledged that, in the contemporary medical view, the child begins a separate life from the moment of conception."[2]

I. INTRODUCTION

ON January 22, 1973, in the companion cases of *Roe v. Wade*[3] and *Doe v. Bolton*,[4] the Supreme Court of the United States declared that unborn children are not persons under section one of the fourteenth amendment. Basing its decision on a right of personal privacy to choose whether or not to abort, the Court held further that a state may not enact abortion legislation protecting unborn children for the period of gestation prior to the time the children are said to be " 'viable,' that is, potentially able to live outside the mother's womb, albeit with artificial aid. Viability is usually placed at about seven months (28 weeks) but may occur earlier, even at 24 weeks."[5]

Wade arose out of a challenge to the Texas abortion statutes.[6] Texas law incriminated all abortions except those "procured or attempted by medical advice for the purpose of saving the life of the mother."[7] In the

---

* Professor of Law, Fordham University School of Law.

1. Furman v. Georgia, 408 U.S. 238, 303 (1972) (Brennan, J., concurring).

2. Byrn v. New York City Health & Hosps. Corp., 38 App. Div. 2d 316, 324, 329 N.Y.S.2d 722, 729 (2d Dep't) (citations omitted), aff'd on other grounds, 31 N.Y.2d 194, 286 N.E.2d 887, 335 N.Y.S.2d 390 (1972), appeal dismissed, 93 S. Ct. 1414 (1973).

3. 93 S. Ct. 705 (1973).

4. 93 S. Ct. 739 (1973).

5. 93 S. Ct. at 730 (footnotes omitted). Actually, viability is now placed at twenty weeks, and it is generally recognized that the term signifies, not a qualitative characteristic of the unborn child, but the ability of technology to keep the child alive outside the womb in an artificial life support system. The child is as much alive before viability as after. See Byrn, Abortion-on-Demand: Whose Morality?, 46 Notre Dame Law. 5, 12-13 (1970) [hereinafter cited as Byrn]. Although Justices Rehnquist and White dissented in Wade and Bolton, they did not challenge the Court's holding that unborn children (even after viability) are not persons under section one of the fourteenth amendment. See 93 S. Ct. at 736 (Rehnquist, J., dissenting); Id. at 762 (White, J., dissenting).

6. Tex. Penal Code Ann. arts. 1191-96 (1961). However, art. 1195 was not challenged. 93 S. Ct. at 709 n.1.

7. Tex. Penal Code Ann. art. 1196 (1961).

district court,[8] several plaintiffs, including Roe, a pregnant woman,[9] had sought a declaration of the unconstitutionality of the Texas abortion laws and a permanent injunction against enforcement on the ground that the statutes "deprive married couples and single women of the right to choose whether to have children, a right secured by the Ninth Amendment."[10] The three-judge district court agreed,[11] and also found the statutes unconstitutionally vague.[12] However, the court refused to issue the injunction.[13] Plaintiffs appealed the denial of the injunction, and the Supreme Court determined that it had jurisdiction to deal not only with the injunction issue, but also with the merits of the plaintiffs' constitutional claims.[14]

Bolton arose out of a similar challenge to the Georgia abortion statutes.[15] Georgia law incriminated all abortions except those which, in the best clinical judgment of a duly licensed physician, were necessary because continuation of the pregnancy would endanger the life of the pregnant woman or would seriously and permanently injure her health; or the fetus would very likely be born with a grave, permanent, and irremediable mental or physical defect; or the pregnancy resulted from forcible or statutory rape.[16] In the district court,[17] numerous plaintiffs, including Doe, a pregnant woman,[18] had (as in *Wade*) sought a declaration of the unconstitutionality of the Georgia abortion laws and a permanent injunction against enforcement. Their claims were more extensive than in *Wade*. In addition to alleging vagueness and invasion of the right of privacy, the plaintiffs asserted that the statutes unconstitutionally restricted the right of physicians and others to practice their professions, and also discriminated against the poor.[19] The three-judge district court, find-

8. Roe v. Wade, 314 F. Supp. 1217 (N.D. Tex. 1970).

9. Id. at 1220.

10. Id. at 1219. There have been a number of similar challenges to state abortion laws, many of them in federal courts and some of them were cited in Wade. See 93 S. Ct. at 727-28. For the most part, discussion of these cases has been avoided in this article because obviously they did not bind the Supreme Court in Wade. The Court had to consider the merits of the various constitutional claims de novo. Its decision supersedes all others and it is that decision which is under scrutiny here.

11. 314 F. Supp. at 1221-23.

12. Id. at 1223. The Supreme Court did not reach the issue of vagueness. 93 S. Ct. at 732. But see United States v. Vuitch, 402 U.S. 62 (1971).

13. 314 F. Supp. at 1225 (1970).

14. 93 S. Ct. at 712.

15. Ga. Code Ann. §§ 26-1201 to -1203 (1972).

16. Id. § 26-1202(a). Thirteen other states have statutes similar to Georgia's and all are based on Model Penal Code § 230.3 (Proposed Official Draft 1962). See 93 S. Ct. at 720 n.37. Four states have repealed criminal sanctions on abortions during particular periods of the pregnancy. Id. The remaining states have statutes similar to the Texas law. Id. at 709 n.2.

17. Doe v. Bolton, 319 F. Supp. 1048 (N.D. Ga. 1970).

18. Id. at 1057.

19. Id. at 1051.

ing that "the concept of personal liberty embodies a right to privacy which apparently is also broad enough to include the decision to abort a pregnancy,"[20] struck down the substantive portions of the Georgia statutes; left standing certain procedural and medical standards; and refused to issue an injunction.[21] Plaintiffs appealed the last two rulings, and the Supreme Court, having passed on the substantive constitutional issues in *Wade*, restricted its opinion to a finding of the unconstitutionality of the standards. In both *Wade*[22] and *Bolton*,[23] the Court refused to reverse the denial of the injunction.[24]

The writer has long maintained that unborn children are in all respects live human beings protected by section one of the fourteenth amendment, particularly the equal protection clause.[25] In an opinion replete with error and fraught with dangerous implications, the Supreme Court in *Wade* found to the contrary. It is with these issues that this article is concerned.[26]

Roe v. Wade is in the worst tradition of a tragic judicial aberration that periodically wounds American jurisprudence and, in the process, irreparably harms untold numbers of human beings. Three generations of Americans have witnessed decisions by the United States Supreme Court which explicitly degrade fellow human beings to something less in law than "persons in the whole sense."[27] One generation was present at *Scott v. Sandford*,[28] another at *Buck v. Bell*[29] and now a third at *Roe v. Wade*. Are not three generations of error enough?

II. The Structure of the *Wade* Opinion and the Specific Holdings of the Court

Parts I through IV of the *Wade* opinion contain an analysis of the Texas anti-abortion statutes, a history of the action, a justification of the

---

20. Id. at 1055 (footnote omitted).

21. Id. at 1056-57.

22. 93 S. Ct. at 733.

23. Id. at 752.

24. It is to be noted that § 26-1202(e) of the Georgia Criminal Code contains a "conscience" clause protecting hospitals and doctors who refuse to participate in abortions. The Court in Bolton at least inferentially approved this section. 93 S. Ct. at 750.

25. See, e.g., Byrn v. New York City Health & Hosps. Corp., 31 N.Y.2d 194, 286 N.E.2d 887, 335 N.Y.S.2d 390 (1972), appeal dismissed, 93 S. Ct. 1414 (1973); Report of the Governor's Commission Appointed to Review New York State's Abortion Law, Minority Report 47, 51-56, 67-68 (1968); Byrn, Abortion in Perspective, 5 Duquesne L. Rev. 125, 126-29, 134-35 (1966).

26. Since Bolton does not deal with these issues, that decision will be referred to only in so far as it clarifies some substantive point in Wade.

27. 93 S. Ct. at 731.

28. 60 U.S. (19 How.) 393 (1857).

29. 274 U.S. 200 (1927).

Court's inquiry into the merits, and a decision on the issues of justiciability, standing and abstention.[30]

Part V sets up the basic contention of the appellants that "the Texas statutes . . . invade a right, said to be possessed by the pregnant woman, to choose to terminate her pregnancy," a right which appellants would discover "in the Fourteenth Amendment's Due Process Clause; or in personal, marital, familial, and sexual privacy said to be protected by the Bill of Rights or its penumbras . . . or among those rights reserved to the people by the Ninth Amendment . . . ."[31]

Before addressing this claim, the Court felt "it desirable briefly to survey, in several aspects, the history of abortion, for such insight as that history may afford us, and then to examine the state purposes and interests behind the criminal abortion laws."[32] The historical survey in Part VI of the opinion covers *"Ancient attitudes," "The Hippocratic Oath," "The Common Law," "The English statutory law," "The American law," "The position of the American Medical Association," "The position of the American Public Health Association,"* and *"The position of the American Bar Association."*[33]

In Part VII, the Court analyzed the three reasons usually advanced "to explain historically the enactment of criminal abortion laws in the 19th century and to justify their continued existence."[34] The first reason, not advanced by Texas and which "no court or commentator has taken . . . seriously,"[35] is to discourage illicit intercourse. The second is the protection of the pregnant woman against a hazardous medical procedure, an interest which because of "[m]odern medical techniques" has "largely disappeared," at least for the period of pregnancy "prior to the end of the first trimester," although "the State retains a definite interest in protecting the woman's own health and safety when an abortion is proposed at a late stage of pregnancy."[36] The third reason "is the State's interest—some phrase it in terms of duty—in protecting prenatal life."[37]

Parts VIII (the pregnant woman's "right of privacy" to decide whether or not to abort), IX (the absence of a compelling state interest in the

---

30. 93 S. Ct. at 709-15. Jurisdiction, justiciability, standing and abstention are outside the scope of this article.

31. Id. at 715.

32. Id.

33. Id. at 715-24. Since this article is concerned with Anglo-American law, there is no need to comment on the Court's analysis of ancient attitudes and the Hippocratic Oath.

34. Id. at 724.

35. Id. (footnote omitted).

36. Id. at 725. An inquiry as to whether abortion is truly safe in the first trimester is outside the scope of this article.

37. Id.

"fetus" as a legal person or a human life or both), and X (the residual interests of the state in safeguarding the pregnant woman against the health hazards of a late abortion and in protecting the "potentiality of life" after viability) contain the Court's decision on the merits.[38] The Court held: *first,* the "right of privacy, whether it be founded in the Fourteenth Amendment's concept of personal liberty and restrictions upon state action, as we feel it is, or, as the District Court determined, in the Ninth Amendment's reservation of rights to the people, is broad enough to encompass a woman's decision whether or not to terminate her pregnancy;"[39] *second,* "this right is not unqualified and must be considered against important state interests in regulation;"[40] *third,* the right of privacy being a "fundamental right," regulation limiting it may be justified only by a "compelling state interest," and restrictive legislation "must be narrowly drawn to express only the legitimate state interests at stake;"[41] *fourth,* Texas urges that it has a compelling state interest in protecting the fetus' right to life as guaranteed by the fourteenth amendment,[42] but "the word 'person,' as used in the Fourteenth Amendment, does not include the unborn;"[43] *fifth,* Texas urges "that, apart from the Fourteenth Amendment, life begins at conception and is present throughout pregnancy, and that, therefore, the State has a compelling interest in protecting that life from and after conception,"[44] but "[w]e need not resolve the difficult question of when life begins. When those trained in the respective disciplines of medicine, philosophy, and theology are unable to arrive at any consensus, the judiciary, at this point in the development of man's knowledge, is not in a position to speculate as to the answer,"[45] and, "the unborn have never been recognized in the law as persons in the whole sense;"[46] *sixth,* "we do not agree that, by adopting one theory of life, Texas may override the rights of the pregnant woman that are at stake;"[47] *seventh,* a state "does have an important and legitimate interest in preserving and protecting the health of the pregnant woman,"[48] however, this interest does not reach

38. Id. at 726-32.
39. Id. at 727.
40. Id.
41. Id. at 728. Justice Rehnquist in dissent objected that the compelling state interest test applies to the equal protection clause, not the due process clause. Id. at 737 (Rehnquist, J., dissenting).
42. Id. at 728.
43. Id. at 729 (footnote omitted).
44. Id. at 730.
45. Id.
46. Id. at 731.
47. Id.
48. Id.

the "compelling" point until approximately the end of the first trimester,[49] from and after which "a State may regulate the abortion procedure to the extent that the regulation reasonably relates to the preservation and protection of maternal health;"[50] but "for the period of pregnancy prior to this 'compelling' point, the attending physician, in consultation with his patient, is free to determine, without regulation by the State, that in his medical judgment the patient's pregnancy should be terminated. If that decision is reached, the judgment may be effectuated by an abortion free of interference by the State;"[51] *eighth*, a state has an important and legitimate interest in "protecting the potentiality of human life,"[52] but this interest does not reach the "compelling" point until viability,[53] and "[i]f the State is interested in protecting fetal life after viability, it may go so far as to proscribe abortion during that period except when it is necessary to preserve the life or health of the mother;"[54] *ninth*, the Texas statute "sweeps too broadly," and "cannot survive the constitutional attack made upon it here;"[55] *tenth*, no decision is made with respect to the father's rights, if any, in the abortion decision, or the rights, if any, of the parents of an unmarried pregnant minor;[56] *eleventh*, since a state "may, if it chooses," enact legislation restricting abortion within the limits set forth above,[57] it follows that the state may, if it chooses, repeal all laws restricting abortion, and allow "the potentiality of life" to be destroyed up to the moment of birth.

With respect to unborn children, the *Wade* decision means at a minimum: that an unborn child is neither a fourteenth amendment person nor a live human being at any stage of gestation; an unborn child has no right to live or to the law's protection at any stage of gestation; a state may not protect an unborn child from abortion until viability; after viability, a state may, if it chooses, protect the unborn child from abortion, but an exception must be made for an abortion necessary to preserve the life or health of the mother; and finally, health having been defined in *Doe v. Bolton* to include "all factors—physical, emotional, psychological, familial, and the woman's age—relevant to the well-being of the patient,"[58] it follows that a physician may with impunity equate the unwantedness of a

---

49. Id. at 731-32.
50. Id. at 732; see text accompanying note 36 supra.
51. 93 S. Ct. at 732.
52. Id. at 731.
53. Id. at 732.
54. Id.
55. Id.
56. Id. at 733 n.67.
57. Id. at 732-33
58. Id. at 747.

pregnancy with a danger to the pregnant woman's health—emotional, psychological or otherwise. Thus, even after viability, there is little that a state can do to protect the unborn child.

III.   THE FUNDAMENTAL ERRORS IN W*ade*: IN GENERAL

Upon analysis, it becomes evident that the structure of the Court's opinion in *Wade* is defective. The Court agreed that if the fourteenth amendment personhood of the unborn child were established, "the appellant's case, of course, collapses, for the fetus' right to life is then guaranteed specifically by the Amendment."[59] Hence, the approach of the Court should have been to decide: (a) whether the unborn child, as a matter of fact, is a live human being, (b) whether all live human beings are "persons" within the fourteenth amendment, and (c) whether, in the light of the answers to (a) and (b), the state has a compelling interest in the protection of the unborn child, or to put it another way, whether there are any other interests of the state which would justify denying to the unborn child the law's protection of his life. Instead, the Court reversed the inquiry, deciding first that the right of privacy includes a right to abort, then deciding that the unborn child is not a person within the meaning of the fourteenth amendment, and finally, refusing to resolve the factual question of whether an abortion kills a live human being. In effect, the Court raised a presumption against the constitutional personality of unborn children and then made it irrebuttable by refusing to decide the basic factual issue of prenatal humanbeingness.

The refusal to resolve the threshold question of fact at the outset is the crucial error in *Wade*. There is a " 'long course of judicial construction which establishes as a principle that the duty rests on this Court to decide for itself facts or constructions upon which federal constitutional issues rest.' "[60] This fundamental error may have been caused by the Court's misapprehension of the common law of abortion and the motivation behind early American anti-abortion statutes. This, in turn, apparently led the Court to forego researching the intent of the framers of the fourteenth amendment: to bring within the aegis of the due process and equal protection clauses every member of the human race, regardless of age, imperfection or condition of unwantedness. Left without any reliable historical basis for constitutional interpretation, the Court both failed to allude

---

59. *Id.* at 728. This statement quite clearly and correctly means that the right of personal privacy is subordinate to the fourteenth amendment right to life. Hence, the key question is whether the unborn child is a human being-cum-human person. If so, then the right of privacy does not include the right to abort.

60. Napue v. Illinois, 360 U.S. 264, 272 (1959) (footnote omitted), quoting Kern-Limerick, Inc. v. Scurlock, 347 U.S. 110, 121 (1954).

to its own prior explication of "person" under section one of the fourteenth amendment and mistook the general status in law of unborn children. Further, it adverted to a number of criteria which it erroneously interpreted as proof that the unborn child is not a person at all under the fourteenth amendment. In short, error was piled upon error.

IV. The Historical Errors

At the very beginning of its opinion in *Wade*, the Supreme Court announced:

Our task, of course, is to resolve the issue by constitutional measurement free of emotion and of predilection. We seek earnestly to do this, and, because we do, we have inquired into, and in this opinion place some emphasis upon, medical and medical-legal history and what that history reveals about man's attitudes toward the abortive procedure over the centuries.[61]

At the end of the opinion, the Court concluded that its holding was consistent "with the lessons and example of medical and legal history" and "with the lenity of the common law . . . ."[62]

It is evident that the Court's finding that unborn children are not fourteenth amendment persons was deeply influenced by its own interpretation of history, which, for all practical purposes, was dictated by an uncritical acceptance of two law review articles by abortion advocate Cyril Means.[63] Unfortunately, the Court's understanding of the Anglo-American history of the law of abortion is both distorted and incomplete. Because these errors are so significant and because they span a period beginning in the thirteenth century and extending into the twentieth, a major portion of this article must be devoted to them.

The following are the Court's key historical observations:

It is undisputed that at the common law, abortion performed *before* "quickening"—the first recognizable movement of the fetus *in utero*, appearing usually from the 16th to the 18th week of pregnancy—was not an indictable offense. . . .[64]

. . . .

. . . [I]t now appear[s] doubtful that abortion was ever firmly established as a common law crime even with respect to the destruction of a quick fetus.[65]

. . . .

---

61. 93 S. Ct. at 709.

62. Id. at 733.

63. Means, The Phoenix of Abortional Freedom: Is a Penumbral or Ninth-Amendment Right About to Arise from the Nineteenth-Century Legislative Ashes of a Fourteenth-Century Common-Law Liberty?, 17 N.Y.L.F. 335 (1971); Means, The Law of New York Concerning Abortion and the Status of the Foetus, 1664-1968: A Case of Cessation of Constitutionality, 14 N.Y.L.F. 411 (1968). The Supreme Court referred to these articles respectively as "Means II" and "Means I," and they are so cited hereinafter.

64. 93 S. Ct. at 716 (footnote omitted).

65. Id. at 718.

. . . It was not until after the War Between the States that legislation began generally to replace the common law. . . .[66]

. . . .

It is thus apparent that at common law, at the time of the adoption of our Constitution, and throughout the major portion of the 19th century, abortion was viewed with less disfavor than under most American statutes currently in effect. Phrasing it another way, a woman enjoyed a substantially broader right to terminate a pregnancy than she does in most States today. . . .[67]

. . . .

Parties challenging state abortion laws . . . claim that most state laws were designed solely to protect the woman. . . . The few state courts called upon to interpret their laws in the late 19th and early 20th centuries did focus on the State's interest in protecting the woman's health rather than in preserving the embryo and fetus.[68]

. . . .

All this, together with our observation, . . . that throughout the major portion of the 19th century prevailing legal abortion practices were far freer than they are today, persuades us that the word 'person,' as used in the Fourteenth Amendment, does not include the unborn.[69]

The historical picture painted by the Court is one of a "right" to abort, extending from the earliest common law, through most of the nineteenth century in America, until the post-Civil War enactment of abortion statutes (which, in the Court's view, were intended for the pregnant woman's protection and not that of her unborn child) and being completely unimpaired by the fourteenth amendment. At issue, therefore, is the status of abortion—or more accurately, the status of the unborn child—at common law, under nineteenth century American abortion statutes, and under the fourteenth amendment.

A. *The Common Law*

It has been claimed, alternatively, that abortion was not a crime at all at common law, but a "freedom" of the pregnant woman, or that abortion was a crime only after quickening. Ergo, the unborn child is not a fourteenth amendment person.[70] These claims obviously influenced the Court in *Wade*. The more plausible view of the common law is to the contrary; namely: (a) even the earliest common law cases do not support the proposition that abortion was regarded as a "liberty" or "freedom" or "right" of the pregnant woman or anyone else; (b) "quickening" was utilized in the later common law as a practical evidentiary test to determine whether the abortion had been an assault upon a live human being in the womb

---

66. Id. at 720.
67. Id.
68. Id. at 725-26 (footnotes omitted).
69. Id. at 729 (footnote omitted).
70. See note 63 supra.

and whether the abortional act had caused the child's death; this evidentiary test was never intended as a judgment that before quickening the child was not a live human being; and, (c) at all times, the common law disapproved of abortion as *malum in se* and sought to protect the child in the womb from the moment his living biological existence could be proved.

Anglo-Saxon law before the Norman Conquest penalized abortion civilly in the form of heavy fines, and ecclesiastically in the form of penances.[71] In the thirteenth century, abortion of a fetus "formed [or] animated, and particularly if it be animated," was condemned as homicide by Bracton[72] and, later in the same century by the anonymous legal writer, Fleta, although Fleta used the term "formed and animated."[73]

The biologists of the thirteenth century taught that a new life, biologically separate from the mother, came into being (animation) when the fetal body assumed a recognizable human form (formation), approximately forty days after conception (eighty days in the case of a female).[74] This being the science of the day, Bracton's use of the term formed *or* animated is somewhat puzzling. It is possible that he meant to leave open the question of whether animation might occur at some time before formation in deference to Christian teaching which condemned all abortion,[75] although biologically, philosophically and canonically, an abortion after formation was regarded as a much more serious offense. On the other hand, it is probably unfair to argue that Bracton incorporated into secular law a concept not supported by contemporary secular science. His use of the disjunctive "or" and the phrase "and particularly if it be animated" may have been intended only to emphasize that abortion was a crime against human life. Fleta understood Bracton to mean that formation and animation coincided ("formed and animated") and Bracton has been so translated.[76]

Biology led the way in the thirteenth century, and other disciplines, including law and ethics followed. Though Bracton was a canonist, the canon law of abortion was itself the product of current biological thought. Bracton appears to be the common law's first interdisciplinarian, using

---

71. G. Grisez, Abortion: The Myths, The Realities, and the Arguments 186-87 (1970) [hereinafter cited as Grisez].

72. Quay, Justifiable Abortion—Medical and Legal Foundations, 49 Geo. L.J. 395, 431 (1961) [hereinafter cited as Quay].

73. Id.

74. J. Noonan, Contraception 88-91, 216-17 (1966); Means I, supra note 63, at 411-12; Quay, supra note 72, at 426-31.

75. See J. Noonan, An Almost Absolute Value in History, in The Morality of Abortion: Legal and Historical Perspectives 1 (J. Noonan ed. 1970).

76. 2 H. Bracton, De Legibus et Consuetudinibus Angliae 278-79 (T. Twiss ed. 1879).

secular science as the basis for rational law, updating the disapproval of abortion that had existed even prior to the Norman Conquest.

Common law judges and lawyers from the fourteenth century onward faced a major problem: how to accommodate Bracton's substantive crime to the practical requirements of proof that the aborted woman had been pregnant, that the aborted child had been alive, and that the abortional act had killed the child.

Pro-abortion writers rely on two fourteenth century cases to "prove" that abortion was a treasured common law freedom of medieval English women.[77] One might easily question the relevance of the fourteenth century to the fourteenth amendment. Still, if one thing is certain about the two cases, it is that they do not support the pro-abortion contention.

As translated by Professor Means, the earlier case (1327) reads as follows:

> Writ issued to the Sheriff of Gloucestershire to apprehend one D. who, according to the testimony of Sir G[eoffrey] Scrop[e] [the Chief Justice of the King's Bench], is supposed to have beaten a woman in an advanced stage of pregnancy who was carrying twins, whereupon directly afterwards one twin died, and she was delivered of the other, who was baptized John by name, and two days afterwards, through the injury he had sustained, the child died: and the indictment was returned before Sir G. Scrop[e], and D. came, and pled Not Guilty, and for the reason that the Justices were unwilling to adjudge this thing a felony, the accused was released to mainpernors, and then the argument was adjourned sine die. [T]hus the writ issued, as before stated, and Sir G. Scrop[e] rehearsed the entire case, and how he [D.] came and pled.
>
> Herle: to the sheriff: Produce the body, etc. And the sheriff returned the writ to the bailiff of the franchise of such place, who said, that the same fellow was taken by the Mayor of Bristol, but of the cause of this arrest we are wholly ignorant.[78]

When the defendant originally appeared before King's Bench, and the "justices were unwilling to adjudge this thing a felony," he was released to mainpernors (akin to bail) and the argument was adjourned *sine die*. The writ was not dismissed. The report of the case, then, is not the report of the original proceedings before King's Bench but of subsequent proceedings. It is evident that the Chief Justice of King's Bench (Scrope) was reporting the prior action of King's Bench to another judicial body. Herle, who ordered the sheriff to produce the body after hearing Scrope's account of the prior proceedings, was not a member of King's Bench, but was the Chief Justice of the Common Bench. The presence and intervention of the Chief Justice of the Common Bench are explicable only if these subsequent proceedings were before the King's Council; otherwise, they are not.

---

77. See, e.g., Means II, supra note 63, at 336-41.

78. Id. at 337, 338 n.4 (footnote omitted), translating Y. B. Mich. 1 Edw. 3, f. 23, pl. 18 (1327).

The King's Council, among its other functions, served as a body of consultation and advice for justices who were experiencing legal difficulty in deciding a case.[79] The justices of the realm were *ex officio* members of the Council,[80] which operated at times either as a conference of judges,[81] or as an alternative to the King's Bench.[82] Moreover, the Council gave attention to anything that, because of the incompleteness of the law, required, in whole or in part, exceptional treatment.[83]

It is most probable that in 1327 the justices of King's Bench consulted the Council for assistance in deciding a case of first impression, as they attempted to interpret and apply Bracton and Fleta. The need to resort to the Council would explain the adjournment *sine die* and the admission of defendant to bail at the original proceedings before King's Bench.[84] However, since the arrest of the defendant on another charge precluded further proceedings, the Council's instruction was not forthcoming and no final disposition was made of the case. It is authority for nothing except the unwillingness of the court to let the abortionist go unpunished and the justices' puzzlement over how properly to deal with him. Subsequent history would suggest that the justices' dilemma was rooted in problems of proof. Had the abortionist's act really been the cause of the stillbirth? Had the two-day-old twin died from the abortion or some other cause?

The next reported abortion case was decided in 1348. Like the 1327 case, it helps the pro-abortionists not at all. As translated by Professor Means, the report reads as follows:

One was indicted for killing a child in the womb of its mother, and the opinion was that he shall not be arrested on this indictment since no baptismal name was in the indictment, and also it is difficult to know whether he killed the child or not, etc.[85]

The court did *not* dismiss the indictment on the ground that abortion was not an offense at common law. Indeed, if that were the case, there

---

79. Select Cases Before the King's Council 1243-1482, at xvii-xviii (I. Leadam & J. Baldwin eds. 1918).
80. Id. at xvi.
81. Id. at xxi-xxii.
82. Id. at xxii.
83. Id. at xxvi.
84. "Moreover a case before the justices might become a case before the council not by an appeal or change of venue, but by a postponement until the council . . . should assemble." Id. at xxi. It is to be noted that after the accession of Edward III in January, 1327, King's Bench, perhaps unsure of its authority, refused to impose criminal penalties in some cases with the result that the King called the Council to York to decide on what should be done to restore normal proceedings. Select Cases in the Court of King's Bench Under Edward II, xiv-xv (G. Sayles ed. 1957). It was while the Council (including Scrope and Herle) was at York that the proceedings in the 1327 case occurred.
85. Means II, supra note 63, at 339, translating Y.B. Mich. 22 Edw. 3 (1348).

would have been no indictment at all, or the indictment would have been dismissed expressly on that ground. Rather, the inference is that abortion was a substantive offense, but the indictment had to be dismissed for a defect in pleading (no baptismal name) and an impossibility of proof (the cause of the child's death).[86]

The 1327 case merely demonstrates the dilemma of the justices in attempting to apply Bracton's rule in a case of first impression. The inference in the 1348 case is that abortion was a crime but difficulties in pleading and proof barred prosecution and conviction.[87] Certainly there is nothing in these cases to suggest that abortion was regarded as a "freedom."

Sixteenth century writers[88] were persuaded by these difficulties to state, as a practical matter, that abortion was not a crime. Then, in the seventeenth century, a way was found to satisfy the proof requirements, at least for some abortions.

The seventeenth century, as an era of abortion law reform, began with *R. v. Sims*[89] wherein it was said that if an aborted child were born alive with marks of the abortion and then died, it was murder, but if the child were stillborn, there was no murder because it could not be known "whether the child were living at the time of the batterie or not, or if the batterie was the cause of the death . . . ."[90] The *Sims* live-birth-murder doctrine provided only a minor solution to the problems of proof which were highlighted and reiterated in the remainder of the *Sims* rule.

Later in the seventeenth century, Coke attempted to contribute a further solution:

If a woman be quick with childe, and by a Potion or otherwise killeth it in her

---

86. It is not only in abortion cases that problems of proof of causation prevented a conviction for the killing of a human being. At common law, a defendant could not be convicted of a homicide if his victim died more than a year and a day after the assault, the theory being that after that time, it was impossible, given the state of medical knowledge, to prove that the defendant's assault had been the cause of the victim's death. R. Perkins, Criminal Law 28-29 (2d ed. 1969). Of course, despite this rule, the substantive common law of homicide remained intact. So too, despite the difficulties in proof in abortion cases at common law, the clear inference from the 1348 case is that a substantive crime of abortion did exist.

87. It is probably for this reason that the canonical courts took jurisdiction of the offense. It is interesting, however, that there were apparently no abortion prosecutions in the canonical courts after the sixteenth century. Means I, supra note 63, at 439. In the seventeenth century, the common law began to find solutions to the problems of proof.

88. For example, Staundford and Lambard, two sixteenth-century writers, seem to have denied the existence of abortion as a crime. It is generally accepted that they took this position because of the historical difficulty in proving the crime, and the resulting paucity of indictments for abortion. See Davies, Child-Killing in English Law, 1 Modern L. Rev. 203 (1937).

89. 75 Eng. Rep. 1075 (K.B. 1601).

90. Id. at 1076.

wombe; or if a man beat her, whereby the childe dieth in her body, and she is delivered of a dead childe, this is a great misprison [misdemeanor], and no murder: but if the childe be born alive, and dieth of the Potion, battery, or other cause, this is murder: for in the law it is accounted a reasonable creature, in rerum natura, when it is born alive.[91]

The Supreme Court in *Wade*, in effect, accuses Coke, as attorney general in *Sims*[92] and as author of the *Third Institute*, of inventing the crime of abortion in defiance of the 1327 and 1348 cases.[93] An analysis of Coke's rules in the light of prior and contemporary law reveals that the accusation is without merit. As already pointed out, the 1327 and 1348 cases are not contrary to the substantive law propounded by Bracton and Fleta. Also, the live-birth-murder rule in *Sims*, which Coke adopted and which undisputably became fixed in English law,[94] is in accord with Bracton and Fleta. Moreover, in limiting the misdemeanor of abortion to a woman "quick with childe," Coke cited Bracton and Fleta.[95] It seems likely, therefore, that he meant to identify "quick with childe" with "formed and animated." He did, however, depart from the earlier authorities by classifying the crime as a serious misdemeanor rather than murder. The modification probably resulted from difficulties in proving that the stillbirth was the result of the abortion. Finally, Coke's statement that the child is accounted *"in rerum natura*, when it is born alive,"* is sometimes misinterpreted to mean that the common law viewed the unborn child as something less than a live human being. But when one examines the subsequent interpretation of Coke by English courts, one is led to conclude that Coke was referring only to the law of homicide where the exigencies of proof prevented labelling the intra-uterine killing a murder. For other purposes, such as inheritance, the unborn child was recognized as a person *in rerum natura* in the womb. For instance, it was held in *Wallis v. Hodson*:[96]

The principal reason I go upon in the question is, that the plaintiff was *in ventre sa mere* at the time of her brother's death, and consequently a person *in rerum natura*, so that both by the rules of the common and civil law, she was, to all intents and purposes, a child, as much as if born in the father's life-time.[97]

Wallis v. Hodson relied, *inter alia*, on *Beale v. Beale*[98] wherein Lord

91. E. Coke, Third Institute 50 (1644).
92. Coke was attorney general in 1601 and may have been the "Cook" mentioned in R. v. Sims.
93. 93 S. Ct. at 718 & n.26.
94. See R. v. West, 2 Cox Crim. Cas. 500 (1848).
95. E. Coke, Third Institute 50 (1644).
96. 26 Eng. Rep. 472 (Ch. 1740).
97. Id. at 473.
98. 24 Eng. Rep. 373 (Ch. 1713).

Chancellor Harcourt specifically cited Coke's abortion rules as authority for finding a posthumous child "to be *living at her father's death* in *ventre sa mere*."[99]

That Coke regarded the unborn child as a human being *in esse* is implicit in the live-birth-murder rule. At common law, crime was "generally constituted only from concurrence of an evil-meaning mind with an evil-doing hand . . . ."[100] The rule of concurrence means that the victim of the abortional act must have been a human being *at the time of the act*—that is, while he was intrauterine, though his subsequent death was extrauterine—or else the mind and hand of the defendant could not have concurred to produce a homicide.

Coke's abortion rules are in accord with prior law and with the contemporary status in law of the unborn child as a human being *in esse* prior to birth, at least from formation and animation. His innovations were not substantive, but evidentiary, and in this respect, it is clear that "common law doctrines are not frozen for criminal cases any more than civil cases . . . ."[101] Any inconsistency between Coke and the 1327 and 1348 cases is procedural, not substantive. However, Coke's characterization of an abortion-cum-stillbirth as a great misdemeanor, though good substantive law, did little to solve the problem of proving that the child had been alive when the abortion occurred, or even in some cases, that the woman had been pregnant.

The seventeenth century legal commentator, Sir Matthew Hale, provided another approach to the problem of proof in his posthumously published *History of the Pleas of the Crown*. Hale differed with Coke on whether abortion of a woman "quick or great with childe," resulting in a live birth and subsequent death of the child, was murder. Citing the 1327 and 1348 cases, he stated that the abortion "is not murder nor manslaughter by the law of England because [the child] is not yet in rerum natura, tho it be a great crime . . . ."[102]

The generally accepted view is that Hale took this position, as Staundford and Lambard had before him, because of the evidentiary difficulty in proving the crime.[103] On the other hand, Hale did characterize abortion as a "great crime." It has been argued that Hale was referring to an ecclesiastical crime.[104] Another plausible view, consistent with the clear inference in the 1348 case which Hale cites, is that Hale recognized

---

99. Id.

100. Morissette v. United States, 342 U.S. 246, 251 (1952).

101. United States v. Schoefield, 465 F.2d 560, 561 (D.C. Cir.), cert. denied, 93 S. Ct. 210 (1972) (footnotes omitted).

102. 1 M. Hale, History of the Pleas of the Crown 433 (1736) [hereinafter cited as Hale].

103. Davies, supra note 88, at 209 & n.23.

104. Means II, supra note 63, at 350, 368-69.

abortion as a common law crime, but was unwilling for the moment to identify it as either a felony or a misdemeanor, perhaps because of disagreement with Coke on the degree of the offense. Weight is lent to this interpretation when one considers an example of murder given elsewhere by Hale:

> But if a woman be with child, and any gives her a potion to destroy the child within her, and she takes it, and it works so strongly, that it kills her, this is murder, for it was not given to cure her of a disease, but unlawfully to destroy her child within her, and therefore he that gives a potion to this end, must take the hazard, and if it kill the mother, it is murder, and so ruled before me at the assizes at Bury in the year 1670.[105]

It has been argued that "unlawfully to destroy the child within her" refers incidentally to ecclesiastical illegality, and the case for murder rests entirely on the foreseeable danger to the woman from taking the abortifacient.[106] But this cannot be so. The abortionist "must take the hazard" specifically because "he gives a potion to this end [of destroying the child]."[107] Thus, it is the *mens rea* of intending to destroy a child and the *actus reus* of giving the potion which combine to make the death of the woman murder. The only logical conclusion is that Hale regarded abortion as a great enough secular crime to condemn the abortionist as a felony-murderer when the pregnant woman died from the abortion attempt. Further, it apparently makes no difference when, in the course of the pregnancy, the abortion takes place. While Hale had earlier used the term "quick or great with child" in connection with the death of a child, he merely specified "with child" in connection with the death of the woman. (It seems apparent that while Coke used "quick with child" to mean formed and animated, Hale employed the term to mean quickening.)

Such was the interpretation given to Hale in *People v. Sessions*:[108]

> At common law life is not only sacred but it is inalienable. To attempt to produce an abortion or miscarriage, except when necessary to save the life of the mother under advice of medical men, is an unlawful act and has always been regarded as fatal to the child and dangerous to the mother. To cause death of the mother in procuring or attempting to procure an abortion is murder at common law.[109]

Thus, at the end of the seventeenth century the law of abortion appears to have been as follows. *First*, an abortion of a woman "quick with child"

---

105. Hale, supra note 102, at 429-30; accord, R. v. Whitmarsh, 62 J.P. 1711 (1898).
106. Means II, supra note 63, at 362-63.
107. Hale, supra note 102, at 430.
108. 58 Mich. 594, 26 N.W. 291 (1886).
109. Id. at 596, 26 N.W. at 293 (citations omitted); accord, State v. Harris, 90 Kan. 807, 136 P. 264 (1913) (containing an extensive review of the abortion-homicide cases in a number of states); State v. Farnam, 82 Ore. 211, 161 P. 417 (1916).

resulting in the live birth and subsequent death of the child was either murder or "a great crime." *Second,* an abortion of a pregnant woman "quick with child" resulting in a stillbirth was a "great misprison." *Third,* an abortion of a pregnant woman, at any stage of pregnancy, which resulted in her death, was felony murder. *Fourth,* every unborn child was "a person *in rerum natura*" at common law except that problems of proof precluded such a designation in criminal abortion situations. *Fifth,* at the very least, abortion was regarded as *malum in se,* a secular wrong to the unborn child, and can hardly be said to have been considered a "freedom" of the pregnant woman. *Sixth,* the 1327 and 1348 cases are not contrary to any of these rules.

Eighteenth century legal scholars set out to solve the remaining problems of proof by identifying "quick with child" with some observable, evidentiary phenomenon in the gestational period. Hawkins agreed with Coke's statement of the crime of abortion but substituted "big with child" for quick with child.[110] Blackstone, at one point in his *Commentaries,* stated: "To kill a child in its mother's womb, is now no murder, but a great misprision: but if the child be born alive, and dieth by reason of the potion or bruises it received in the womb, it seems . . . to be murder in such as administered or gave them [citing Hawkins and Coke]."[111] In another part of the *Commentaries,* Blackstone stated:

Life is the immediate gift of God, a right inherent by nature in every individual; and it begins in contemplation of law as soon as an infant is able to stir in the mother's womb. For if a woman is quick with child, and by a potion or otherwise, killeth it in her womb; or if any one beat her, whereby the child dieth in her body, and she is delivered of a dead child; this, though not murder, was by the ancient law homicide or manslaughter [citing Bracton]. But [Sir Edward Coke] doth not look upon this offence in quite so atrocious a light but merely as a heinous misdemeanor.[112]

It is evident that Blackstone intended only to restate Coke. Coke had apparently equated "quick with child" with Bracton's "formed and animated," and, in citing both authors, Blackstone seems also to have equated the two terms. Possibly influenced by the inference of movement in "animated" and "quick," Blackstone identified the beginning of human life as the point at which the child "is able to stir in the mother's womb." The child is able to stir in the womb as early as the eighth to tenth week of gestation, but ordinarily the pregnant woman does not feel the child's movement (quickening) until the fifth month—although being purely subjective, this will vary with each woman.[113] Thus, even

110. 1 W. Hawkins, A Treatise of the Pleas of the Crown, ch. 31, § 16 (7th ed. 1795) [hereinafter cited as Hawkins].

111. 4 W. Blackstone, Commentaries *198.

112. 1 id. at *129-30.

113. See Byrn, supra note 5, at 9-10.

given Blackstone's interpretation of Coke and Bracton, it must be noted that "quick with child" is not the same as "quickening."

Of course, in the eighteenth century, the only way to prove that the child had stirred was to prove that the mother had felt him stir. Thus, the practical exigencies of proof would ultimately require that for the purposes of an abortion conviction, "quick with child" be identified with "quickening," and this may have been what Blackstone intended.

The first English abortion statute, enacted in 1803, imposed greater penalties for an abortion of a woman "quick with child" than one performed on a woman "not being, or not being proved to be, quick with child."[114] The latter crime still required proof of pregnancy,[115] and since "quick with child" probably meant "formed and animated,"[116] the statute provided the first clear abortion protection in English law for the pre-formed child.[117]

The first case decided under the statute is also the first case clearly to enunciate the quickening rule. In *Anonymous*,[118] the court held:

[The woman] . . . swore, however, that she had not felt the child move within her before taking the medicine, and that she was not then quick with child. The medical men, in their examinations, differed as to the time when the foetus may be stated to be quick, and to have a distinct existence: but they all agreed that, in common understanding, a woman is not considered to be quick with child till she has herself felt the child alive and quick within her, which happens with different women in different stages of pregnancy, although most usually about the fifteenth or sixteenth week after conception.

Lawrence, J. said, this was the interpretation that must be put upon the words quick with child in the statute; and as the woman in this case had not felt the child alive within her before taking the medicine,—he directed an acquittal.[119]

The court recognized the dichotomy between "quick with child" and "quickening," but chose quickening as the practical norm in the face of conflicting medical testimony as to "when the foetus may be stated to be quick, [alive] and to have a distinct existence . . . ."[120] If there had been

---

114. 43 Geo. 3 ch. 58, § 2 (1803).

115. R. v. Scudder, 172 Eng. Rep. 565, 566 (N.P. 1828).

116. Davies, The Law of Abortion and Necessity, 2 Modern L. Rev. 126, 134 (1938).

117. The purpose of the preformation branch of the statute is not really known. It may have been to protect the pregnant woman from the criminal abortionist, Means II, supra note 63, at 358, or it may reflect an increased sensitivity to the unborn child's right to life at all stages of gestation. It is interesting that in the very year (1803) that the statute was enacted, Thomas Percival's influential work on medical ethics appeared wherein Percival condemned all abortions except those done for theraputic reasons, insisting on the inviolatability of even "the first spark of life." Grisez, supra note 71, at 190 (citing T. Percival, Medical Ethics 134-35 (Leake ed. 1927)).

118. 170 Eng. Rep. 1310 (N.P. 1811).

119. Id. at 1311-12.

120. Id. at 1312.

available to the court uncontested medical testimony establishing the distinct, living existence of the unborn child at a stage earlier than quickening, the court obviously would have followed that evidence. Quickening was a flexible standard of proof—not a substantive judgment on the value of unborn human life.[121]

At this time, the details of human conception were still unknown. The doctrine of formation and animation remained a carryover from the ancient idea that the male inseminated the female by implanting a seed which grew within her in distinct stages. Not until formation could a new, distinct, separate life be said to exist. (Even then, in the absence of quickening, definitive proof of the separate living existence of the unborn child was lacking.) It was only when the ovum was discovered in 1827 that the true nature of conception, as co-semination instantly producing a new life, was understood.[122]

The discovery of the ovum apparently had its effect. In 1837, Parliament enacted a new abortion statute which deleted the requirement of pregnancy and imposed a common penalty for all abortional acts.[123] All problems of proof were solved and the unborn child was effectively protected from the moment of conception. In 1838, an English court[124] reinterpreted the ancient common law rule which forbade the execution of a death sentence upon a woman "quick with child." The court instructed the jury: " 'Quick with child' is having conceived. 'With quick child' is when the child has quickened."[125] The term "quick with child," which had meant formed and animated, now meant from the moment of conception.

---

121. That "quickening" was understood to have entered the law essentially as an evidentiary test is apparent from the language in Evans v. People, 49 N.Y. 86 (1872): "But until the period of quickening there is no evidence of life; and whatever may be said of the foetus, the law has fixed upon this period of gestation as the time when the child is endowed with life, and for the reason that the foetal movements are the first clearly marked and well defined evidences of life." Id. at 90 (citation omitted).

122. Andre Hellegers, M.D., quoted in Catholic News, Mar. 15, 1973, at 11, col. 3.

123. 7 Will. 4 & 1 Vict., c. 85 (1837).

124. R. v. Wycherley, 173 Eng. Rep. 486 (N.P. 1838).

125. Id. at 487. The rule of temporary reprieve of a pregnant woman from execution is of ancient origin. A pregnant woman condemned to death would, according to Coke, be granted a reprieve if she were "quick with childe . . . till she delivered, but she shall have the benefit of that but once, though she be again quick with childe." E. Coke, Third Institute 17-18 (1644). Coke distinguished "quick with childe" from pregnancy, but it must be remembered that when Coke used "quick with childe" in his abortion section, he cited Bracton and evidently meant "formed and animated." Hale, on the other hand, employs "quickening" in his version of the reprieve from execution rule. Hale, supra note 102, at 368-69. Blackstone also noted the reprieve rule and stated: "This is a mercy dictated by the law of nature, in favorem prolis . . . . execution shall be staied generally till the next session; and so from session to session, till either she is delivered, or proves by the course of nature not to have been with child at all. But if she once hath had the benefit of this reprieve,

From Bracton's time, the common law had striven to protect the unborn child against abortion from the moment science was able to establish the child's individuated, living, biological existence. The effort reached fruition in the 1830's when law and science cooperated to complete the protection of the child at every stage of gestation.

and been delivered, and afterwards becomes pregnant, she shall not be entitled to the benefit of a farther respite for that cause. For she may now be executed before the child is quick in the womb; and shall not, by her own incontinence, evade the sentence of justice." 4 Blackstone, Commentaries *395 (footnote omitted). Two things are to be noted about Blackstone's statement of the reprieve rule: first, Blackstone ameliorated Coke's statement concerning a second pregnancy after the reprive. Coke stated that the woman would be executed even though she were then quick with child. Blackstone observed that the execution would inevitably occur before the pregnancy reached that stage. Thus he showed a more mature sensitivity to the right of the child; second, whatever Blackstone may have meant by quick with child in his abortion section, in the reprieve section he seems to be referring to formed and animated, not to quickening. If quickening had occurred, there would be little doubt that the woman was with child, but Blackstone notes that the execution shall be stayed until the woman delivers "or proves by the course of nature not to have been with child at all." Id. at *395. Hence, he is referring to a stage in pregnancy earlier then quickening.

The dichotomy between "quickening" in abortion and "quick with child" in reprieve cases made sense. In an abortion case, the benefit of the doubt was with the defendant and the burden of proof on the prosecution. Quickening was thus an evidentiary sine qua non for conviction. On the other hand, in the execution cases, the benefit of doubt was with the child even to the extent that the woman might not have been pregnant at all. The distinction between the stages of gestation in the abortion and reprieve situations is made even clearer by Hawkins. For the crime of abortion, the woman must be "big with child." Hawkins, supra note 110, ch. 31, § 16. For a reprieve, she must be "quick with child." 4 id. at ch. 51, § 9. Thus, "quick with child" seems to be an earlier stage than that which will satisfy the evidentiary requirements of an abortion conviction "big with child". In Anonymous, 170 Eng. Rep. 1310 (N.P. 1811), the dichotomy is even clearer. In R. v. Wycherley, 173 Eng. Rep. 486 (N.P. 1838), the court interpreted "quick with child" as "having conceived." It appears that the only case after Wycherley that equated "quick with child" with a point in pregnancy later than conception is R. v. Webster, reported in Note, A Jury of Matrons, 9 Cent. L.J. 94 (1879). However, the case is dubious. As the note writer observed, "[t]he plea of pregnancy in arrest of execution took the learned judge by surprise, and the discussion between the bench and the bar shows that the proceeding was unusual to all concerned." Id. In Commonwealth v. Spooner, discussed in 2 P. Chandler, Amer. Crim. Trials 3 (reprint 1970), a 1778 Massachusetts case, a condemned woman claimed to be several months advanced in pregnancy, but the jury of matrons and mid-wives, after two examinations, reported that she was not "quick with child." Id. at 48-49. An autopsy after execution revealed "a perfect male foetus, of the growth of five months. . . ." Id. at 53. Chandler attributes the incident to the "prejudice, or ignorance, or malice" of the jury. Id. at 54. Peleg Chandler published his American Criminal Trials between 1841 and 1844. In the reports of the Spooner case, he cited the "having conceived" definition of "quick with child" in R. v. Wycherley as the latest (and presumably the most authoritative) English rule. Id. at 56 n.1. In State v. Arden, 1 S.C. 196, 1 Bay 487 (1795), the prisoner "pleaded pregnancy" when asked why sentence of death should not be passed upon her. A jury of matrons examined the prisoner and "found that she was not pregnant." Id. at 197, 1 Bay at 490. Perhaps the emphasis was on pregnancy rather than "quick with child," because the court had heard of, and was appalled by, the Spooner incident of 1778.

For the Supreme Court in *Wade* to conclude that at common law "a woman enjoyed a substantially broader right to terminate a pregnancy than she does in most States today"[126] is incomprehensible. A lack of criminal prosecution cannot be translated into an historic right. At common law, larceny by false promise was not a crime,[127] but few would claim a thief "enjoyed a broader right" to commit a fraudulent larceny than he does today.

For the Supreme Court in *Wade* to cite the "lenity" of the common law as a basis for holding that unborn children do not possess a fundamental right to live and to the law's protection at any time up to birth, is a perversion of Bracton, Coke, Hale, Hawkins and Blackstone. The whole history of the common law cries out against the jurisprudence of *Wade*.

B. *The American Statutes*

During the nineteenth century, several states interpreted the common law so as to render abortion criminal at all stages of pregnancy.[128] The vast majority of states, however, were in accord with the interpretation of the common law inferential in *Anonymous*,[129] that there was no practical way to prosecute an abortion prior to quickening.[130] No state held that an abortion after quickening was not a crime, and indeed, the quickening requirement seems to have been limited to the criminal law, the unborn child being regarded in other areas of the law as a human being *in esse* from the moment of conception.[131]

Almost all the then existing states enacted abortion statutes during the nineteenth century.[132] Relying on the Means articles,[133] and citing only

---

Although the New York State Legislature employed pregnant with a "quick child" in the Revised Statutes of 1829 to define the crime of manslaughter for aborting an unborn child (Law of Dec. 10, 1828, part IV, ch. 1, tit. 2, § 9, [1828] N.Y. Rev. Stat. 661), the term "quick with child" was used in the reprieve section (Law of Dec. 10, 1828, part IV, ch. 1, tit. 1 §§ 21-22, [1828] N.Y. Rev. Stat. 659). In 1872, the court of appeals affirmed that "quick with child" means having conceived. Evans v. People, 49 N.Y. 86, 89 (1872).

The whole evolution of the reprieve rule was toward the protection of the child at all stages of gestation, and the purpose of the rule is "to guard against the taking of the life of an unborn child for the crime of the mother." Union Pac. Ry. v. Botsford, 141 U.S. 250, 253 (1891).

126. 93 S. Ct. at 720.

127. See Chaplin v. United States, 157 F.2d 697, 698 (D.C. Cir. 1946).

128. See, e.g., State v. Reed, 45 Ark. 333 (1885); State v. Slagle, 83 N.C. 630 (1880); Mills v. Commonwealth, 13 Pa. 630 (1850).

129. See text accompanying notes 118-21 supra.

130. The cases are collected in Roe v. Wade, 93 S. Ct. at 718 n.27.

131. Hall v. Hancock, 32 Mass. (15 Pick.) 255, 257-58 (1834).

132. The statutes are listed in the dissenting opinion of Mr. Justice Rehnquist in Roe v. Wade, 93 S. Ct. at 738-39 nn.1 & 2. The legislative history of the state statutes is detailed in Quay, supra note 72, at 447-520.

133. 93 S. Ct. at 725 n.47.

an 1858 New Jersey case,[134] the Supreme Court in *Wade* commented: "The few state courts called upon to interpret their laws in the late 19th and early 20th centuries did focus on the State's interest in protecting the woman's health rather than in preserving the embryo and fetus."[135] The best that can be said of this statement is that it is absolutely wrong. For instance, the Supreme Court might have noted with respect to New Jersey: "This law was further extended March 26th, 1872 . . . to protect the life of the child also, and inflict the same punishment, in case of its death, as if the mother should die;"[136] and with respect to Alabama: "[D]oes not the new being, from the first day of its uterine life, acquire a legal and moral status that entitles it to the same protection as that guaranteed to human beings in extrauterine life?"[137] and with respect to Colorado, that the statute was "intended specially to protect the mother and her unborn child from operations calculated and directed to the destruction of the one and the inevitable injury of the other."[138] These decisions, rendered prior to 1918, did not involve quickening as an issue in the court's interpretation of the intent of the statute.

Had the Supreme Court in *Wade* been interested in cases decided after the early nineteenth century and before the abortion "reform" movement of the 1960's, it might have noted with respect to Idaho: "[T]he abortion statute is not designed for the protection of the woman . . . only of the unborn child and through it society . . . ;"[139] and with respect to Oklahoma: "We hold that the anti-abortion statutes in Oklahoma were enacted and designed for the protection of the unborn child and through it society;"[140] and with respect to Virginia, that the Virginia abortion statute was intended "to protect the health and lives of pregnant women and their unborn children from those who intentionally and not in good faith would thwart nature by performing or causing abortion and miscar-

---

134. State v. Murphy, 27 N.J.L. 112 (Sup. Ct. 1858).

135. 93 S. Ct. at 725-26 (footnote omitted).

136. State v. Gedicke, 43 N.J.L. 86, 90 (Sup. Ct. 1881) (citation omitted).

137. Trent v. State, 15 Ala. App. 485, 488, 73 So. 834, 836 (1916), cert. denied, 198 Ala. 695, 73 So. 1002 (1917), quoting, in the context of the purpose of the Alabama abortion statute, from Transactions Medical Association of Alabama 265-72 (1911).

138. Dougherty v. People, 1 Colo. 514, 522 (1872). In addition, for similar interpretations of the abortion statutes of other states, see the following cases: State v. Miller, 90 Kan. 230, 233, 133 P. 878, 879 (1913); State v. Tippie, 89 Ohio St. 35, 40, 105 N.E. 75, 77 (1913); State v. Ausplund, 86 Ore. 121, 132, 167 P. 1019, 1022 (1917); State v. Howard, 32 Vt. 380, 399 (1859). One might fairly add to this list Iowa and Michigan where courts, in the abortion context, termed as "sacred" and "inalienable" the lives of unborn children. See State v. Moore, 25 Iowa 128, 135-36 (1868) (discussed infra at notes 198-202); People v. Sessions, 58 Mich. 594, 596, 26 N.W. 291, 293 (1886).

139. Nash v. Meyer, 54 Idaho 283, 292, 31 P.2d 273, 276 (1934) (citation omitted).

140. Bowlan v. Lunsford, 176 Okla. 115, 117, 54 P.2d 666, 668 (1936).

riage;"[141] and with respect to Washington, that the Washington abortion statute was "designed to protect the life of the mother as well as that of her child."[142] Again, in none of these decisions was quickening a factor.

Other state courts clearly implied that their respective abortion statutes had as one of their purposes (at the very least) the protection of unborn children. As early as 1851, the Maine Supreme Court noted with approval that its statute had changed the common law by eliminating quickening: "There is a removal of the unsubstantial distinction, that it is no offence to procure an abortion, before the mother becomes sensible of the motion of the child, notwithstanding it is then capable of inheriting an estate; and immediately afterwards is a great misdemeanor."[143] In 1887, the Maryland Court of Appeals commented on the growing dissatisfaction with the common law quickening criterion which many courts were abrogating by reinterpretation of the common law, and which Maryland had changed by statute.[144] In 1907, the Nebraska Supreme Court interpreted its state abortion statute, which provided the same penalty for causing the death by abortion of the woman or the child, to apply at every stage of pregnancy,[145] thus indicating the high value the legislature placed on the life of the unborn child even prior to quickening. Indiana had a similar statute.[146]

It is regrettable, indeed, that the Court's exposition in *Wade* of nineteenth and early twentieth century judicial expressions of legislative intent did not carry it past *State v. Murphy*.[147] Perhaps the explanation is to be found in the fact that this is the only early American case (outside of New York) cited by Means.[148]

---

141. Anderson v. Commonwealth, 190 Va. 665, 673, 58 S.E.2d 72, 75 (1950).

142. State v. Cox, 197 Wash. 67, 77, 84 P.2d 357, 361 (1938).

143. Smith v. State, 33 Me. 48, 57 (1851).

144. Lamb v. State, 67 Md. 524, 532-33, 10 A. 208 (1887).

145. Edwards v. State, 79 Neb. 251, 112 N.W. 611 (1907).

146. See Montgomery v. State, 80 Ind. 338, 339 (1881). One might fairly add Utah to this list. See State v. Crook, 16 Utah 212, 51 P. 1091 (1898), wherein the court characterized abortion under the Utah statutes as "the criminal act of destroying the foetus at any time before birth . . . ." Id. at 217, 51 P. at 1093. But see Foster v. State, 182 Wis. 298, 196 N.W. 233 (1923).

147. See text accompanying note 134 supra.

148. Means I, supra note 63, at 452. Even Murphy is doubtful in its statement of legislative purpose. The New Jersey statute, with which Murphy was concerned, was enacted in 1849 after the New Jersey Supreme Court had held that abortion prior to quickening was not a common law crime. State v. Cooper, 22 N.J.L. 52 (1849). The Cooper court focused almost exclusively on the status of the unborn child. The evil to be suppressed was the killing of a human being in utero. The Wade Court might have derived greater support from State v. Carey, 76 Conn. 342, 56 A. 632 (1904), and State v. Jordon, 227 N.C. 579, 42 S.E.2d 674 (1947), both holding that their states' abortion statutes were intended to protect the pregnant woman, not the child. But see Conn. Public Act No. 1, May 1972 Spec. Sess. (1972) (Con-

Professor Means' focus is almost exclusively on New York and he argues that the early history of New York abortion statutes proves that they were intended only to protect the woman and not the child. However, an analysis of the statutes leads more logically to the conclusion that the unborn child was at least one of the intended beneficiaries of the statutes' protection.

The first New York abortion statutes were enacted as part of the Revised Statutes of 1829. Two different sections condemned abortional acts. The first section dealt with successful abortions of a quick child and the second with all other abortional acts, successful or not:

Every person who shall administer to any woman pregnant with a quick child, any medicine, drug or substance whatever, or shall use or employ any instrument or other means, with intent thereby to destroy such child, unless the same shall have been necessary to preserve the life of such mother, or shall have been advised by two physicians to be necessary for such purpose, shall, in case the death of such child or of such mother be thereby produced, be deemed guilty of manslaughter in the second degree.[149]

Every person who shall wilfully administer to any pregnant woman, any medicine, drug, substance or thing whatever, or shall use or employ any instrument or other means whatever, with intent thereby to procure the miscarriage of any such woman, unless the same shall have been necessary to preserve the life of such woman, or shall have been advised by two physicians to be necessary for that purpose; shall, upon conviction, be punished by imprisonment in a county jail not more than one year, or by a fine not exceeding five hundred dollars, or by both such fine and imprisonment.[150]

The two sections were evidently modeled after the English abortion statute of 1803.[151] The influence of *Anonymous* appears in the adoption of quickening as the key for distinguishing the provable beginning of human life.

It has been claimed that the general abortion section of the Revised Statutes (section 21) was intended solely for the protection of the pregnant woman against a dangerous medical procedure and was not for the protection of the unborn child. But there are compelling reasons for reaching a contrary conclusion.

---

necticut abortion law), the preamble of which states: "The public policy of the state and the intent of the legislature is to protect and preserve human life from the moment of conception . . . ;" State v. Slagle, 83 N.C. 630 (1880), wherein the Supreme Court of North Carolina held that abortion was a common law crime in North Carolina at all stages of gestation.

149. N.Y. Rev. Stat. (1829), pt. IV, ch. 1, tit. 2, § 9 [hereinafter referred to in the text as section 9]. The bracketed material was added by Law of Apr. 20, 1830, pt. IV, ch. 320, § 58 (1830).

150. N.Y. Rev. Stat. (1829), pt. IV, ch. 1, tit. 6, § 21 [hereinafter referred to in the text as section 21].

151. See Means I, supra note 63, at 449-50.

First, there is no question that the postquickening section (section 9), in characterizing as manslaughter the killing of a quick child by abortion, was intended to protect the life of the child. The section provided an exemption to criminal liability where the abortion "shall have been necessary to preserve the life of such woman, or shall have been advised by two physicians to be necessary for such purpose."[152] The exemption is extremely stringent. The child's life was considered so precious, that in the view of the legislature, it could not be sacrificed to a lesser value than life itself.

On the other hand, if the exemption in the general abortion section (section 21) had been designated solely to protect the mother's health, without regard to the value of the child's life, it would certainly have been phrased less stringently than the exemption in the postquickening section. Yet the two exemptions are identical. The general abortion section, like the postquickening section, places the highest value on the child's life.

Second, the less stringent exemption is found in a section proposed by the revisers and rejected by the legislature. This section was expressly intended for the preservation of health:

> Every person who shall perform any surgical operation, by which human life shall be destroyed or endangered, such as the amputation of a limb, or of the breast, trepanning, cutting for the stone, or for *hernia*, unless it appear that the same was necessary for the preservation of life, or was advised, by at least two physicians, shall be adjudged guilty of a misdemeanor.[153]

Here, indeed, one finds the more liberal exemption which he would have expected to find in the general abortion section if that section had not been intended to protect the child. There is no crime in proposed section 28 if "*it appear* that the same was necessary for the preservation of life, *or was advised, by at least two physicians* . . . ."[154] The italicized words are significantly different from the phraseology of the exemption in the abortion sections (sections 9 and 21). An abortion was non-culpable: (a) if it "shall have been necessary to preserve the life of such woman"[155]

---

152. N.Y. Rev. Stat. (1829), pt. IV, ch. 1, tit. 6, § 21.

153. Proposed section 28, pt. IV, ch. 1, tit. 6, § 28 [hereinafter referred to in the text as proposed section 28]. The Revisers' Note stated: "The rashness of many young practitioners in performing the most important surgical operations for the mere purpose of distinguishing themselves, has been a subject of much complaint, and we are advised by old and experienced surgeons, that the loss of life occasioned by the practice, is alarming. The above section furnishes the means of indemnity, by a consultation, or leaves the propriety of the operation to be determined by the testimony of competent men. This offence is not included among the mal-practices in manslaughter, because, there may be cases in which the severest punishments ought not to be inflicted. By making it a misdemeanor, and leaving the punishment discretionary, a just medium seems to be preserved."

154. Id. (emphasis added).

155. N.Y. Rev. Stat. (1829), pt. IV, ch. 1, tit. 6, § 21.

(not merely if "it appear" to have been so necessary), or, (b) if it "shall have been advised by two physicians to be necessary *for that purpose*"[156] (not merely that it "was advised, by at least two physicians").[157]

The purpose of sections 9 and 21 was manifestly different from the proposed surgical section.[158] That different purpose could only be the protection of the unborn child, or else the less stringent exemption in the surgical section would also have been written into the abortion sections. Then too, it is noteworthy that the abortion sections were enacted while the proposed surgical section was not.

Third, it is also significant that the New York State Legislature, in adopting the Revised Statutes of 1829, employed quickening ("quick child") as the key pregnancy factor in section 9, the abortion-manslaughter section, but used the term "quick with child" in the section providing for a reprieve from execution of a woman "quick with child" who was under a sentence of death.[159] In 1872, the New York Court of Appeals, relying on *R. v. Wycherley*,[160] distinguished quickening from "quick with child," defining the latter as having conceived.[161] Apparently, the intent of the legislature in 1829 was to protect the unborn child from execution with his mother at all stages of gestation. If the legislature so recognized the value of the life of the child prior to quickening in the reprieve section, must we not conclude that at least one of the purposes of the concurrently enacted abortion sections (sections 9 and 21) was the protection of the child's life against a would-be abortionist?

Fourth, prior to 1829 two significant events had occurred. The ovum had been discovered in 1827, and, for the first time, the details of human conception were well understood.[162] In 1823, the Becks, in their standard work on medical jurisprudence published in New York, had condemned the quickening doctrine for its failure to take cognizance of the fact that the unborn child is alive before he is felt to move.[163] It may be that these events also influenced the legislature to incriminate abortion prior to quickening.

In 1867, the Medical Society of New York condemned abortion at every stage of gestation, as "murder."[164] The Society's resolution was sent to

---

156. Id. (emphasis added).
157. Proposed section 28, pt. IV, ch. 1, tit. 6, § 28.
158. It is to be noted that the abortion section included both surgery and drugs.
159. N.Y. Rev. Stat. (1829), pt. IV, ch. 1, tit. 1, §§ 21-22.
160. See note 124 supra and accompanying text.
161. Evans v. People, 49 N.Y. 86, 89 (1872).
162. See text accompanying note 122 supra.
163. I.T. Beck & R. Beck, Elements of Medical Jurisprudence 276-77 (1823), cited in Grisez, supra note 71, at 191.
164. See Means I, supra note 63, at 459.

the New York State Legislature which, in 1869, amended the abortion statutes and proscribed as manslaughter an abortion of a "woman with child" which resulted in "the death of such child, or of such woman."[165] It seems as reasonable to connect the 1867 resolution with the 1869 statute as to pretend that the legislature was completely unmotivated by the Medical Society's strong condemnation of abortion as "murder."

Adverting to the common law quickening rule and its evidentiary basis, the court of appeals in 1872, in *Evans v. People*, conservatively interpreted "with child" to mean a child after quickening.[166] The legislature restored the quickening requirement in the 1881 re-codification of the Penal Law, and included a general abortion section which did not require that the woman be pregnant.[167] As a result of these enactments, the unborn child remained protected under a provision which avoided the evidentiary ruling in *Evans*.

Nothing in *Evans* can be regarded as a justification for legalizing abortion prior to quickening or as precedent for a holding that the unborn child is a non-person under section one of the fourteenth amendment. With respect to abortion, *Evans* merely reiterated a somewhat outdated rule of evidence as a basis for interpreting a statute.

On the other hand, the *Evans* court's approval of the reprieve from execution rule of *R. v. Wycherley* signifies an awareness of the fundamental rights of *all* unborn children regardless of age. In this respect, *Evans* supports the proposition that nineteenth century New York abortion legislation was intended to protect the unborn child at every stage of gestation.

Whether one chooses to concentrate only on New York or to look also to the judicial pronouncements of other states, one must conclude that the better view of nineteenth century abortion legislation is that a major purpose was the protection of unborn children without regard to age. Bolstering this view is the twentieth century abortion indictment at the Nuernberg Trials.[168] The indictment charged, *inter alia*, that "[e]astern women workers were induced or forced to undergo abortions,"[169] and hence one might conclude that the trial and judgment are irrelevant to the discussion herein. Yet the shadow of a generation of aborted children darkened Nuernberg. In addition to testifying that the abortions had all been voluntary on the part of the aborted women, one of the defendants thought it

---

165. Law of May 6, 1869, ch. 631, [1869] N.Y. Laws 92d Sess. 1502.

166. See note 121 supra.

167. See N.Y. Penal Law §§ 80, 1050 (McKinney 1944) (repealed). These were the sections enacted in 1881.

168. U.S. v. Greifelt, 4 Trials of War Criminals Before the Nuernberg Military Tribunal 608 (Government Printing Office) (1946-1949).

169. Id. at 613.

relevant to argue: "Interruption of pregnancy is or was never considered as murder, but it was considered a special violation against life. Generally this incurs considerably milder punishment than if it were murder. *Up to now nobody had the idea to see in this interruption of pregnancy a crime against humanity.*"[170]

It is possible that the defendant thought it necessary to argue that abortion is de minimis because the prosecution had introduced into evidence a captured German document (dated October 30, 1943) which commented on the "objections of a minority of reactionary Catholic physicians" to the decree on interruptions of pregnancy of female eastern workers and female Poles.[171] The doctors had many objections but the first one mentioned is: "These physicians argued that the decree was not in accordance with the moral obligation of a physician to preserve life."[172]

At Nuernberg, the prosecution and the defense joined issue on the unborn child's right to live. And the prosecutor, in addition to arguing that the abortions had been "encouraged and even forced on these women," emphasized in his closing brief:

Abortions were prohibited in Germany under Article 218 of the German Penal Code . . . . After the Nazis came to power this law was enforced with great severity. Abortions were also prohibited under the Polish Penal Code . . . , and under the Soviet Penal Code. But *protection of the law was denied to unborn children* of the Russian and Polish women in Nazi Germany. Abortions were encouraged and even forced on these women.[173]

The right of the unborn child to the law's protection was a litigated issue even though it was outside the scope of the indictment and not mentioned in the subsequent judgment. Neither prosecution nor defense could ignore the aborted children who stood as mute and invisible accusers at the trial. On behalf of the United States, an American prosecutor condemned the defendants before a court composed of American judges because "protection of the law was denied to the unborn children."[174]

On the eve of the abortion "reform" movement of the 1960's, a Michigan court could observe that American abortion statutes had been amended to delete the obsolete quickening dichotomy (which had persevered as a

---

170. Id. at 1090 (testimony of defendant Richard Hildebrandt) (emphasis added). See Roe v. Wade, 93 S. Ct. at 729 n.54: "Further, the penalty for criminal abortion specified by Art. 1195 is significantly less than the maximum penalty for murder prescribed by Art. 1257 of the Texas Penal Code. If the fetus is a person, may the penalties be different?"

171. U.S. v. Greifelt, 4 Trials of War Criminals Before the Nuernberg Military Tribunal 608, 1082 (Government Printing Office) (1946-49) (emphasis deleted).

172. Id. at 1082.

173. Id. at 1077 (emphasis added).

174. Id. But see Roe v. Wade, 93 S. Ct. 705 (1973).

norm for determining the punishment for abortion) because of the recognition of a child's legal existence while *en ventre sa mere*.[175] And even so ardent an advocate of legalized abortion as the English legal commentator, Glanville Williams, had to admit that the contemporary rationale of anti-abortion legislation was this: "The fetus is a human life to be protected by the criminal law from the moment when the ovum is fertilized."[176]

The Supreme Court in *Wade* was as wrong about the motivation behind nineteenth century abortion legislation as it was about the common law.

C. *The Fourteenth Amendment*

The early American abortion statutes were a continuum of the striving of the common law to protect human life from its very beginning. When, with the discovery of the ovum in 1827, science clearly identified conception as the beginning of life, the law began to move its protection back to the earliest stages of gestation, and penalize abortional acts prior to quickening without, in some cases, even requiring proof of pregnancy. Quickening began to disappear, first as a practical norm for initial criminality and then as a factor calling for increased punishment.[177]

The Supreme Court in *Wade* admitted that "[t]he anti-abortion mood prevalent in this country in the late 19th century was shared by the medical profession. Indeed, the attitude of the profession may have played a significant role in the enactment of stringent criminal abortion legislation during that period."[178] In 1859, an American Medical Association Committee on Criminal Abortion, appointed to investigate criminal abortion with a view to its suppression, criticized the quickening criterion of criminality and "the grave defects of our laws, both common and statute, as regards the independent and actual existence of the child before birth, as a living being."[179] On the basis of the report, the Association adopted resolutions protesting " 'against such unwarrantable destruction of human life,' calling upon state legislatures to revise their abortion laws, and requesting the cooperation of state medical societies' in pressing the subject.' "[180]

---

175. LaBlue v. Specker, 358 Mich. 558, 567, 100 N.W.2d 445, 450 (1960).

176. G. Williams, The Sanctity of Life and the Criminal Law 149 (1957).

177. Indeed, from the scientific point of view, quickening has no relevance at all today. See Byrn, supra note 5, at 9-12. See, e.g., State v. Sudol, 43 N.J. Super. 481, 129 A.2d 29, cert. denied, 25 N.J. 132, 135 A.2d 248, cert. denied, 355 U.S. 964 (1957) (stating that modern science has advanced to a point that a court is justified in taking judicial notice of the accuracy of a confirmed pregnancy test).

178. 93 S. Ct. at 721.

179. Id., quoting 12 Transactions of the Am. Med. Assn. 73-77 (1859).

180. Id., quoting 12 Transactions of the Am. Med. Assn. 28, 78 (1859).

In 1867, the Medical Society of New York condemned abortion at every stage of gestation as "murder."[181] In 1868, Francis Wharton urged the injustice of the quickening distinction in abortion statutes (as he had in earlier editions of his treatise on criminal law) and argued that unborn children should be protected regardless of gestational age.[182]

In 1871, the AMA Committee on Criminal Abortion submitted another report in which it concluded: "We had to deal with human life. In a matter of less importance we could entertain no compromise. An honest judge on the bench would call things by their proper names. We could do no less."[183]

Whatever may be said of the common law and the early nineteenth century, it is evident that in the period from 1859 to 1871, spanning a war fought to vindicate the essential dignity of every human being and the subsequent ratification of the fourteenth amendment in 1868, the anti-abortion mood prevalent in the United States can be explained only by a desire to protect live human beings in the womb from the beginning of their existence.[184] When the fourteenth amendment was ratified in 1868, the law of at least twenty-eight of the thirty-seven states of the United States incriminated abortional acts prior to quickening—two by common law,[185] and the remainder by statute.[186] In the next fifteen years, one additional state (Colorado) entered the United States and at least seven more states incriminated pre-quickening abortional acts.[187]

As previously indicated, the overwhelming weight of authority is to

---

181. See note 164 supra and accompanying text.

182. 2 F. Wharton, A Treatise on the Criminal Law of the United States 210-12 (6th ed. 1868).

183. 93 S. Ct. at 721, quoting 22 Transactions of the Am. Med. Assn. 258 (1871). But see 93 S. Ct. at 730: "We need not resolve the difficult question of when life begins. When those trained in the respective disciplines of medicine, philosophy, and theology are unable to arrive at any consensus, the judiciary, at this point in the development of man's knowledge, is not in a position to speculate as to the answer." No subsequent medical or bar association statement cited by the Court in Wade denies that abortion takes a "human life." See id. at 721-24.

184. Even in the slavery days of 1858, the legal personhood of unborn children was not unfamiliar. In Bailey v. Poindexter's Ex'r, 55 Va. (14 Gratt.) 132 (1858), counsel for the executor drew an analogy between the legal status of slaves and, inter alia, unborn children, in support of the enforceability of a choice given slaves under testator's will to choose to be sold or set free. In answer, opposing counsel argued: "[Married women] may take estates by deed or will. So may infants even in ventre sa mere, or idiots, or lunatics. They are all free persons, though under partial or temporary disabilities. To reason in favor of similar powers, rights or capacities in slaves, on the ground of analogy, is to plunge at once into a labyrinth of error." Id. at 171.

185. State v. Reed, 45 Ark. 333 (1885); State v. Slagle, 83 N.C. 630 (1880).

186. The states and statutes are collected in Quay, supra note 72, at 447-520.

187. See id.

the effect that at least one of the purposes of these statutes was the protection of unborn children at all gestational stages. The fourteenth amendment era, which finally saw the extension of the equal protection clause to aliens and corporations in the 1880's[188] and, during the same period, witnessed the expression of a new liberality in interpretation of basic constitutional guarantees,[189] was an era of solicitude for the basic right of the unborn child to live no matter what his gestational age might be, and without regard to "quickening."

Given the background of the fourteenth amendment, this solicitude should come as no surprise. The evil, for which the due process and equal protection clauses were designed as a remedy, is typified in the arguments of counsel in *Bailey v. Poindexter's Executor*,[190] wherein a provision in a will that testator's slaves could choose between emancipation and sale was held void on the ground that slaves had no legal capacity to choose. In support of the position, counsel argued:

These decisions are legal conclusions flowing . . . from the one clear, simple, fundamental idea of chattel slavery. That fundamental idea is, that, in the eye of the law, so far certainly as civil rights and relations are concerned, the slave is not a person, but a thing. The investiture of a chattel with civil rights or legal capacity is indeed a legal solecism and absurdity. The attribution of legal personality to a chattel slave,—legal conscience, legal intellect, legal freedom, or liberty and power of free choice and action, and corresponding legal obligations growing out of such qualities, faculties and action—implies a palpable contradiction in terms.[191]

The court agreed with the arguments of counsel that the slave is property and "has no civil rights or privileges,"[192] and the court, in dictum, went on to observe that the social right of "protection from injury" is limited to free persons.[193]

This, then, was the evil: human beings were degraded to the status of property, without civil rights—without even the right to the law's protection of their lives—unless the legislature, by policy decision, should grant it to them.

Slavery typified the evil, but the remedy was not limited to slaves alone. It was the intent of the framers of the fourteenth amendment that never again would *any* human being be deprived of fundamental rights by an irrational and arbitrary classification as a non-person.[194] Thus,

---

188. Yick Wo v. Hopkins, 118 U.S. 356 (1886) ; County of Santa Clara v. Southern Pac. R.R., 18 F. 385, 397-98 (C.C.D. Cal. 1883), aff'd, 118 U.S. 394 (1886).
189. See Boyd v. United States, 116 U.S. 616, 635 (1886).
190. 55 Va. (14 Gratt.) 132 (1858).
191. Id. at 142-43.
192. Id. at 191.
193. Id. at 191-92.
194. "All history shows that a particular grievance suffered by an individual or a class,

Congressman John A. Bingham, who sponsored the amendment in the House of Representatives, noted that it was "universal" and applied to "any human being."[195] Congressman Bingham's counterpart in the Senate, Senator Jacob Howard, emphasized that the amendment applied to every member of the human race:

> It establishes equality before the law, and it gives to the humblest, the poorest, the most despised of the race the same rights and the same protection before the law as it gives to the most powerful, the most wealthy, or the most haughty.[196]

The Court in *Wade* made no reference to the intent of the framers. Had it done so, in the context of a proper understanding of what had originally motivated the enactment of state abortion legislation, how could it have excluded unborn children from personhood under the due process and equal protection clauses? It was certainly less than consistent for the Court, on the one hand, to admit that the nineteenth century AMA anti-abortion statements may have played a significant role in the passage of restrictive abortion legislation, and on the other hand, to find, in effect, that the framers of the fourteenth amendment acted in defiance of both the 1859 AMA statement and state legislation, and deliberately created an unarticulated right of privacy which included the right to kill unborn children whom the framers intended to exclude from fourteenth amendment protection. If that had been the intent of the framers, one could hardly imagine three-quarters of the state legislatures ratifying the amendment while they were at the same time contemplating (or had already enacted) restrictive abortion legislation designed to protect unborn human children—especially if such legislation was the product of the AMA statements cited by the Court. Then too, what evidence is there that the framers did not share "[t]he anti-abortion mood prevalent in this country in the late 19th century . . . ?"[197]

Statutory law, common law and the prevalent mood converged in an Iowa case decided in 1868, the year in which the fourteenth amendment was ratified. *State v. Moore*[198] affirmed a conviction of murder for causing the death of a woman by an illegal abortion. The trial court had charged the jury:

> To attempt to produce a miscarriage, except when in proper professional judgment it is necessary to preserve the life of the woman, is an unlawful act. *It is known to*

---

from a defective or oppressive law, or the absence of any law, . . . is often the occasion and cause for enactments, constitutional or legislative, general in their character, designed to cover cases not merely of the same, but all cases of a similar, nature." County of Santa Clara v. Southern Pac. R.R., 18 F. 385, 397-98 (C.C.D. Cal. 1883).

195. Cong. Globe, 39th Cong., 1st Sess. 1089 (1866).
196. Id. at 2766.
197. 93 S.Ct. at 721.
198. 25 Iowa 128 (1868).

be a dangerous act, generally producing one and sometimes two deaths,—I mean the death of the unborn infant and the death of the mother. Now, the person who does this is guilty of doing an unlawful act. If the death of the woman does not ensue from it, he is liable to fine and imprisonment in the county jail . . . and, if the death of the woman does ensue from it, though there be no specific intention to take her life, he becomes guilty of the crime of murder in the second degree. The guilt has its origin in such cases in the unlawful act which the party designs to commit, and if the loss of life attend it as incident or consequence, the crime and guilt of murder will attach to the party committing such an unlawful act.[199]

In upholding the charge, the Iowa court stated: "We have quoted the court's language in order to say that it has our approval as being a correct statement of the law of the land."[200] The court went on to say:

The common law is distinguished, and is to be commended, for its all-embracing and salutary solicitude for the sacredness of human life and the personal safety of every human being. This protecting, paternal care, enveloping every individual like the air he breathes, not only extends to persons actually born, but, for some purposes, to infants in ventre sa mere.

The right to life and to personal safety is not only sacred in the estimation of the common law, but it is inalienable. It is no defense to the defendant that the abortion was procured with the consent of the deceased.

The common law stands as a general guardian holding its aegis to protect the life of all. Any theory which robs the law of this salutary power is not likely to meet with favor.[201]

Although the abortion in *State v. Moore* occurred after quickening, "no mention is made of that fact in the opinion,"[202] and the court was obviously speaking of the "sacred" and "inalienable" right to life of *all* unborn children.

In *Wade*, the Supreme Court created a new, unfettered right to deprive the unborn children of their lives. In *Yick Wo v. Hopkins*,[203] the Court declared that "the very idea that one man may be compelled to hold his life . . . at the mere will of another, seems to be intolerable in any country where freedom prevails, as being the essence of slavery itself."[204] So it is with *Wade*.

V.   THE ERRORS ON THE QUESTIONS OF HUMAN LIFE AND HUMAN-LEGAL PERSONHOOD

The *Wade* Court's historical errors were compounded by its equally erroneous holdings on the questions of whether the unborn child is a human being in fact and a human person in modern law.

---

199. Id. at 131-32 (emphasis added).
200. Id. at 132.
201. Id. at 135-36 (emphasis added) (citation omitted).
202. State v. Harris, 90 Kan. 807, 813, 136 P. 264, 266 (1913).
203. 118 U.S. 356 (1886).
204. Id. at 370.

A. *The Failure To Resolve the Crucial Question of Fact*

The framers intended that every live human being, every member of the human race, even the most unwanted, come under the aegis of the due process and equal protection clauses. History does not support the proposition that the framers intended to exclude unborn children. The Court in *Wade* observed that "[w]e need not resolve the difficult question of when life begins."[205] But the Court erred at the threshold when it failed to determine whether an individual life has already begun before an abortion takes place. That was precisely the fact, of constitutional dimension, to be resolved by the Court before it could even address itself to the rights of unborn children.[206]

The Court noted, as justification for its refusal to resolve the crucial factual issue, that "[w]hen those trained in the respective disciplines of medicine, philosophy, and theology are unable to arrive at any consensus, the judiciary, at this point in the development of man's knowledge, is not in a position to speculate as to the answer."[207] The Court then concluded that "we do not agree that, by adopting one theory of life, Texas may override the rights of the pregnant woman that are at stake."[208] But what was at stake for the unborn child was not a "theory" of life; it was the fact of life. The lack of consensus, to which the Court referred, is not a lack of consensus on the fact of existence of human life at all stages of gestation—that is established beyond cavil by medical science[209]—but on conflicting theories of the value of a human life already in existence.[210] That value judgment was made over one hundred years ago, on a constitutional level and as a matter of binding law, by the framers of the fourteenth amendment. A "consensus" is not relevant. "One's right to life . . . depend[s] on the outcome of no elections."[211]

As guardian ad litem for a class of unborn children, the writer commenced an action in New York in December, 1971 seeking, *inter alia*, a declaration of the unconstitutionality of New York's abortion-at-will law[212] as a violation of the fourteenth amendment rights of unborn chil-

---

205. 93 S. Ct. at 730.
206. See text accompanying note 60 supra.
207. 93 S. Ct. at 730.
208. Id. at 731.
209. There is no scientific basis for establishing quickening, viability, birth or any event other than conception as the beginning of human life. See Byrn, supra note 5, at 6-15.
210. See id. at 15-18. "I don't know of one biologist who would maintain that the fetus is not alive . . . . Today we are employing euphemisms to pretend that human life is not present. This stems from the fact that we are not quite ready yet to say, yes, there is human life but it has no dignity . . . .There is a consensus on the starting point of life, without any question . . . ." Andre Hellegers, M.D., quoted in The Catholic News, Mar. 15, 1973, at 1, col. 3.
211. West Virginia State Bd. of Educ. v. Barnette, 319 U.S. 624, 638 (1943).
212. Law of Apr. 11, 1970, ch. 127, [1970] N.Y. Laws 193d Sess. 852 (now N.Y. Penal

dren. In support of a motion for an injunction pendente lite, affidavits of a fetologist, a developmental biologist, a cytogeneticist and an obstetrician-gynecologist were presented to the court.[213]

The testimony of these experts was striking indeed. Relying on it, the trial court drew a composite picture of the typical victim of abortion:

Credence must, therefore, be given to the testimony, in affidavit form, submitted by plaintiff from accredited scientists that an unborn human infant has a pulsating human heart; that at that stage of development the child's brain, spinal cord and entire nervous system has been established and that, as a medical fact, the fetus is a live human being.[214]

The court then proceeded to grant the application for an injunction.

The appellate division admitted that there were "no factual issues requiring a trial and the parties so conceded on the argument of the appeal. The medical affidavits submitted by the guardian have not been factually disputed and New York courts have already acknowledged that, in the contemporary medical view, the child begins a separate life from the moment of conception . . . ."[215] However, the court dismissed the complaint on the ground that the unborn child is not a legal person.

A divided New York Court of Appeals affirmed the appellate division, but it too conceded that an unborn child "has an autonomy of development and character although it is for the period of gestation dependent upon the mother. It is human, if only because it may not be characterized as not human, and it is unquestionably alive."[216]

Needless to say, the writer disagreed with the legal conclusions of the appellate division and the court of appeals. But their factual conclusions, together with that of the trial court, are impeccable. These findings left only two questions for the appeal to the United States Supreme Court:

1. Whether the individual members of appellant's unborn class, each of whom is a "live human being," a "child [with] a separate life," a "human" who is "alive" and "has an autonomy of development and character," are human persons entitled to the protections afforded to such persons by the Constitution of the United States.

2. Whether New York's Elective Abortion Law, on its face, in its effect and as

---

Law § 125.05(3) (McKinney Supp. 1972)). The law puts no substantive restriction on abortion through the twenty-fourth week of pregnancy. Id.

213. Respectively, Leverett Lebaron de Veber, M.D.; Donald J. Procaccini, Ph.D.; James Garner, M.D., and Malcolm Hetzer, M.D. The affidavits are reproduced at pages 100a-128a of appellant's jurisdictional statement before the United States Supreme Court, filed Sept. 14, 1972 (No. 72-434) [hereinafter cited as Juris. State.].

214. Byrn v. New York City Health & Hosps. Corp., Supreme Court of the State of New York, Queens County, Index No. 13113/71, in Juris. State. 60a, 68a (unpublished opinion of Francis J. Smith, J., Jan. 4, 1972).

215. Byrn v. New York City Health & Hosps. Corp., 38 App. Div. 2d 316, 324, 329 N.Y.S.2d 722, 729 (2d Dep't 1972) (citations omitted).

216. Byrn v. New York City Health & Hosps. Corp., 31 N.Y.2d 194, 199, 286 N.E.2d 887, 888, 335 N.Y.S.2d 390, 392 (1972), noted in 41 Fordham L. Rev. 439 (1972).

applied, violates fundamental rights of the members of appellant's class, guaranteed to them by the Constitution of the United States.[217]

The Supreme Court did not address itself to these questions. Instead, it dismissed the appeal for want of a substantial federal question, citing *Wade*,[218] even though in *Wade* the Court had erred at the threshold by declining to decide the crucial question of whether an abortion kills a live human being.

Thus, paying no heed to the facts, the Supreme Court made its own value judgment, one that is contrary to the intent of the framers of the fourteenth amendment.

B. *The Failure to Allude to the Court's Own Explication of "Person" Under Section One of the Fourteenth Amendment*

Before *Wade*, the Supreme Court's explication of human "person" in section one of the fourteenth amendment had been consistent with the intent of the framers. In *Levy v. Louisiana*,[219] the Court identified the human persons protected by the equal protection clause as those who "are humans, live, and have their being."[220]

Of course, it might well be argued that *Levy* concerned the rights of afterborn illegitimate children and is inapposite to the unborn. The argument is specious unless courts and legislatures are free to draw fourteenth amendment life-or-death lines on self-serving fictions, utterly irrational by modern, secular, scientific standards. But that is precisely what they are not free to do. "To say that the test of equal protection should be the 'legal' rather than the biological relationship is to avoid the issue. For the Equal Protection Clause necessarily limits the authority of a State to draw such 'legal' lines as it chooses."[221]

Had the *Levy* standard been applied in *Wade*, the Court could not have avoided passing on the factual, "biological" question of whether unborn children are live human beings. Since, as a scientific fact, all of

---

217. This is substantially the form in which appellant presented the questions to the Supreme Court. Juris. State. 4.

218. Byrn v. New York City Health & Hosps. Corp., 93 S. Ct. 1414 (1973).

219. 391 U.S. 68 (1968).

220. Id. at 70 (footnote omitted); accord, 2 B. Schwartz, The Rights of Persons (1968): "And the language of the amendment plainly states that the guaranty of equality contained in it is to apply 'to any person.' Unless words are to be deprived of their ordinary meaning, this must include every natural human being within the jurisdiction of any state . . . ." Id. at 492.

221. Glona v. American Guarantee Co., 391 U.S. 73, 75-76 (1968); accord, B. Schwartz, The Supreme Court 265 (1957). The use of objective science in a constitutional context is far from unprecedented. The findings of modern psychology were used to update the law in Brown v. Board of Educ., 347 U.S. 483, 494-95 (1954).

them are, the Court would have been required to take the next step and find all unborn children to be human persons within section one of the fourteenth amendment. Instead, the Court omitted *Levy* completely. Indeed, having decided not to pass on the crucial question of fact, it had no choice but to ignore *Levy*.

C. *The Misunderstanding of the General Status in Law of Unborn Children*

In *Wade*, the Court stated: "In areas other than criminal abortion the law has been reluctant to endorse any theory that life, as we recognize it, begins before live birth or to accord legal rights to the unborn except in narrowly defined situations and except when the rights are contingent upon live birth."[222] In support of this statement, the Court briefly touched upon tort actions for prenatal injuries and for a stillbirth (wrongful death), as well as the property rights of the unborn child. The Court erred.

The unequivocal status of the unborn child as a legal person in these areas of the law has been analyzed at length,[223] and there is no need to reexamine it here.[224] The more startling error was the Court's failure even to advert to another area of prenatal law.

---

222. 93 S. Ct. at 731.

223. See Note, The Law and the Unborn Child: The Legal and Logical Inconsistencies, 46 Notre Dame Law. 349, 351-60 (1971).

224. Two parenthetical observations must be made. First, when the Court in Wade observed that "the traditional rule of tort law had denied recovery for prenatal injuries even though the child was born alive" (93 S. Ct. at 731 (footnote omitted)), it was speaking not of a tradition but of a relatively short-lived aberration. The common law regarded the unborn child as a human being in esse in all areas of the law except for the criminal law where the exigencies of proof gave rise to the quickening dichotomy. Hall v. Hancock, 32 Mass. (15 Pick.) 255 (1834). The prenatal injury rule was first promulgated in 1884 in Dietrich v. Inhabitants of Northampton, 138 Mass. 14 (1884). The rule has been roundly criticized for its misunderstanding of law and science in a scholarly study in 1935. Law Revision Commission, Communication to the Legislature relating to Prenatal Injuries 449, 453-54, 472-73 (1935). It was discredited in 1946, Bonbrest v. Kotz, 65 F. Supp. 138 (D.D.C. 1946), and it is now in all but complete disrepute. See Note, The Law and the Unborn Child: The Legal and Logical Inconsistencies, 46 Notre Dame Law. 349 (1971). In referring to the rule in some states which permits a wrongful death action for a stillbirth, the Court in Wade stated that "[s]uch an action, however, would appear to be one to vindicate the parents' interest and is thus consistent with the view that the fetus, at most, represents only the potentiality of life." 93 S. Ct. at 731. The statutory wrongful death action is always intended to vindicate the interests of survivors. W. Prosser, Torts 902, 903-05 (4th ed. 1971). Thus, in New York, a wrongful death action for a stillbirth is denied because the law does not consider the unborn child to have a separate juridicial existence " 'except in so far as is necessary to protect the child's own rights.' " Endresz v. Friedberg, 24 N.Y.2d 478, 485, 248 N.E.2d 901, 904, 301 N.Y.S.2d 65, 70 (1969) (citation omitted).

The recognition of the unborn child as a live human being, a legal person with fundamental human-legal rights—including the right to live and to the law's protection—is explicit in the body of law extending *parens patriae* protection to unborn children, regardless of gestational age.

At least from the time of Bracton, the King, as sovereign, was charged with a special obligation to care for those who were not able to care for themselves, particularly infants.[225] In its modern application, the *parens patriae* doctrine vests in the state, as sovereign, both the right and duty to protect a child from harm, even at the hands of his parents. The sovereign has many obligations to the child. "Chief among them is the duty to protect his right to live . . . ."[226]

Thus, parents *do not* have a right of complete dominion over their children. Most certainly, a parent does not have a right to elect whether his or her child shall live or die. As the court observed in *In re Clark:*

> No longer can parents virtually exercise the power of life or death over their children. No longer can they put their child of tender years out to work and collect his earnings. They may not abuse their child or contribute to his dependency, neglect, or delinquency. Nor may they abandon him, deny him proper parental care, neglect or refuse to provide him with proper or necessary subsistence, education, medical or surgical care, or other care necessary for his health, morals, or well-being; or neglect or refuse to provide the special care made necessary by his mental condition; or permit him to visit disreputable places or places prohibited by law, or associate with vagrant, vicious, criminal, notorious, or immoral persons; or permit him to engage in an occupation prohibited by law or one dangerous to life or limb or injurious to his health or morals. . . . And while they may, under certain circumstances, deprive him of his liberty or his property, under no circumstances, with or without due process, with or without religious sanction, may they deprive him of his *life!*[227]

It is true, of course, that *Clark* involved a post-natal child. Still, two propositions must, by common sense and common law, also be acknowledged as true: (a) the *parens patriae* doctrine protects human children precisely because they are legal persons with fundamental human-legal rights (particularly the rights to live and to the law's protection) which they are unable effectively to assert themselves because of their youth and utter dependence on others; (b) if the doctrine has been extended to unborn children, it can only mean that they too are legal persons (with the same fundamental human-legal rights) whose youth and utter dependence impose upon the state the duty to protect their respective rights to live.

In fact, the *parens patriae* doctrine has been extended to unborn children, without regard to their gestational ages, and even at the expense of

---

225. See Eyre v. Shaftsbury, 24 Eng. Rep. 659, 666 (Ch. 1722).
226. See In re Clark, 21 Ohio Op. 2d 86, 89, 185 N.E.2d 128, 132 (C.P. 1962).
227. Id. at 89, 185 N.E.2d at 131 (citation omitted).

such highly valued rights as personal (bodily) privacy, family privacy and religious freedom.[228]

In *Hoener v. Bertinato*,[229] a New Jersey court was asked to appoint a guardian for a child *in utero*, immediately prior to birth, in order that the guardian might consent to a transfusion at birth. The child's parents had refused their consent for religious reasons. In appointing the guardian, the court stated: (1) " 'This *parens patriae* jurisdiction is a right of sovereignty and imposes a duty on the sovereignty to protect the public interest and to protect such persons with disabilities who have no rightful protector;' "[230] (2) "Additionally, it is now settled that an unborn child's right to life and health is entitled to legal protection even if it is not viable;"[231] and (3) "I conclude, therefore, that the [guardianship] statute is applicable to the instant case even though the child is not yet born."[232]

An attempt might be made to distinguish *Hoener* on the grounds that the guardianship appointment was made while the unborn child was viable, and the transfusion was to be administered after birth. Consequently, it might be argued that the case applied only to born children and not to the unborn (except, possibly, if they are viable). But the plain language of the decision is to the contrary. The court applied, to a particular unborn child, who happened to be viable, the general rule that the sovereign has a *parens patriae* duty to protect *all* unborn children against the conduct of those who threaten their right to live.

Raleigh Fitkin—Paul Morgan Memorial Hospital v. Anderson[233] is a natural corollary to *Hoener*. This case arose out of a dispute over proposed blood transfusions for a pregnant woman, while the child was still in the womb. The plaintiff-hospital sought an order to administer the transfusions in the event that they would be necessary to save the life of the woman and the life of her unborn child. Such medical treatment was contrary to the religious beliefs of the woman and her husband. The court nevertheless ordered the transfusions. In its ruling, the court stated:

In *State v. Perricone*, 37 N.J. 463, 181 A.2d 751 (1962), we held that the State's concern for the welfare of an infant justified blood transfusions notwithstanding the

---

228. See Estate of Warner, No. 71 P 3681 (Cir. Ct., Cook County, Ill., May 5, 1971); Raleigh Fitkin—Paul Morgan Mem. Hosp. v. Anderson, 42 N.J. 421, 201 A.2d 537, cert. denied, 377 U.S. 985 (1964); Hoener v. Bertinato, 67 N.J. Super. 517, 171 A.2d 140 (Juv. & Dom. Rel. Ct. 1961).

229. 67 N.J. Super. 517, 171 A.2d 140 (Juv. & Dom. Rel. Ct. 1961).

230. Id. at 522, 171 A.2d at 142 (emphasis omitted), quoting Johnson v. State, 18 N.J. 422 430, 114 A.2d 1, 5 (1955).

231. 67 N.J. Super. at 524, 171 A.2d at 144 (citation omitted).

232. Id. at 525, 171 A.2d at 145.

233. 42 N.J. 421, 201 A.2d 537, cert. denied, 377 U.S. 985 (1964).

objection of its parents who were also Jehovah's Witnesses, and in *Smith v. Brennan*, 31 N.J. 353, 157 A.2d 497 (1960), we held that a child could sue for injuries negligently inflicted upon it prior to birth. *We are satisfied that the unborn child is entitled to the law's protection* and that an appropriate order should be made to insure blood transfusions to the mother in the event that they are necessary in the opinion of the physician in charge at the time.[234]

State v. Perricone involved protection of an after-born infant. *Smith v. Brennan* involved an injury to a pre-viable infant. *Raleigh Fitkin* itself involved a viable infant. Quite clearly, the *Raleigh Fitkin* court considered after-born, viable and pre-viable infants to be entitled, without distinction, to the law's protection. In allowing a cause of action for injuries sustained *in utero* by an infant while pre-viable, the *Smith* court had held that "the law recognizes that rights which he will enjoy when born can be violated before his birth."[235] It was precisely to prevent such violations of basic rights that the guardians were appointed in *Hoener* and *Raleigh Fitkin*. In neither instance was "quickening," "viability," or birth relevant. Life was the vital element.

Estate of Warner[236] leaves no doubt that *parens patriae* protection extends to all unborn children. In *Warner*, an Illinois court appointed a conservator of the "persons" of a pregnant woman and her unborn child on a doctor's petition showing that "the life of the unborn child . . . is in danger because the mother requires immediate blood transfusions in order to save the life of the unborn child,"[237] and further, that "[t]he unborn child is incapable of making any intelligent decision."[238] The operative part of the order stated: "It is further ordered that the Conservator administer or cause to be administered blood transfusions . . . *in order to save the life of the unborn child* of Katherine Warner."[239]

It is to be noted that the child was not *viable when the transfusion was ordered:*

A spokesman for Mount Sinai Hospital said the woman . . . remained in critical condition after receiving almost four pints of blood.

However, doctors said an examination showed *the 4-month old fetus* was alive "with a strong heartbeat."[240]

---

234. 42 N.J. at 423, 201 A.2d at 538 (emphasis added).

235. 31 N.J. 353, 364, 157 A.2d 497, 502 (1960).

236. No. 71 P 3681 (Cir. Ct., Cook County, Ill., May 5, 1971).

237. Id., Petition For Conservator.

238. Id., Physicians Affidavit—Conservatorship.

239. Id., Order of Adjudication of Incompetency and Appointing Conservator (emphasis added).

240. Chicago Sun-Times, May 6, 1971, at 12, col. 1 (emphasis added).

Like most cases involving emergency blood transfusions, the decision was rendered by a lower court and is unreported. Nevertheless, it remains persuasive as an inevitable application of *Hoener* and *Raleigh Fitkin* to a pre-viable child.

An attempt might be made to distinguish *Raleigh Fitkin* and *Warner* on the ground that the mothers' lives were in danger in both instances, and the transfusion orders were made solely for the women. Such an argument lacks any color of validity. In *Warner*, the "Petition For Conservator," the "Physician's Affidavit," and the "Order of Adjudication Of Incompetency and Appointing Conservator" are all framed in terms of saving the unborn child's life, with no reference to saving the life of the mother. Moreover, in *In re Estate of Brooks*,[241] the Illinois Supreme Court had ruled that a compulsory transfusion of an unwilling adult against her religious beliefs would violate the adult's first amendment rights. In *Brooks*, the adult was not pregnant. In *Warner*, the unborn child's right to live took precedence over any other right.

In *Raleigh Fitkin*, the court specifically refused to decide "the more difficult question" whether a compulsory transfusion for the pregnant woman to save her own life would be mandated, since it had already determined that the child had a right to the law's protection.[242] Thus, *Raleigh Fitkin* must have been based upon the unborn child's right to live. There was, then, no authority for a compulsory transfusion to an unwilling nonpregnant adult nor did *Raleigh Fitkin* decide that issue.

Hoener, Raleigh Fitkin and *Warner* may be viewed in three different ways, all leading to the same conclusion. First, "only those interests of the highest order and those not otherwise served can overbalance legitimate claims to the free exercise of religion."[243] The unborn child's right to life is one of those interests. At the time and under the circumstances of *Raleigh Fitkin* and *Warner*, only the right to life of a live human being, the unborn child as a legal person, could have prevailed over the pregnant woman's right of free religious exercise.

Second, "[n]o right is held more sacred, or is more carefully guarded, by the common law, than the right of every individual to the possession and control of his own person, free from all restraint or interference of others, unless by clear and unquestionable authority of law."[244] The clear

---

241. 32 Ill. 2d 361, 205 N.E.2d 435 (1965).

242. 42 N.J. at 423, 201 A.2d at 538. That issue remained undecided in New Jersey until John F. Kennedy Mem. Hosp. v. Heston, 58 N.J. 576, 279 A.2d 670 (1971), noted in 41 Fordham L. Rev. 158 (1972).

243. Wisconsin v. Yoder, 406 U.S. 205, 215 (1972).

244. Union Pac. Ry. v. Botsford, 141 U.S. 250, 251 (1891).

and unquestionable authority of law in *Raleigh Fitkin* and *Warner* can be found only in the *parens patriae* doctrine, which, in turn, extends only to legal persons who have fundamental rights to live and to the law's protection. The application of the *parens patriae* doctrine to unborn children necessarily means that every unborn child, regardless of his gestational age, is a legal person with a fundamental right to live, which the state has a basic obligation to protect.

Third, "[p]roperty does not have rights. People have rights."[245] Unborn children have rights and are, therefore, valuable people, not disposable property. A principal guarantee of the rights of people in today's society is section one of the fourteenth amendment. Of necessity, every unborn child is a legal person within that section.

The Court's error in attempting to determine the unborn child's status in law without adverting to the blood transfusion cases is obvious. In this same vein, the Court committed another error when it apparently relied on the concession by appellee in *Wade* "that no case could be cited that holds that a fetus is a person within the meaning of the Fourteenth Amendment."[246] There are two relevant observations to be made about this statement. In the first instance it may be said that the inability of appellee in *Wade* to cite a case does not mean that the case does not exist. In *Steinberg v. Brown*,[247] a federal district court stated: "Once human life has commenced, the constitutional protections found in the Fifth and Fourteenth Amendments impose upon the state the duty of safeguarding it."[248] Furthermore, the *Wade* Court might have taken note of those cases which, in the abortion context and in obvious paraphrase of the Declaration of Independence, characterize the lives of unborn children of all gestational ages as "sacred" and "inalienable."[249] The Constitution incorporates the basic guarantees of the Declaration.[250] Unless we are to assume that the framers of the fourteenth amendment intended to strip

---

245. Lynch v. Household Fin. Corp., 405 U.S. 538, 552 (1972), noted in 41 Fordham L. Rev. 431 (1972).

246. 93 S. Ct. at 728-29.

247. 321 F. Supp. 741 (N.D. Ohio 1970). Steinberg arose out of a challenge to the Ohio abortion statutes on grounds similar to those in Wade and Bolton. As indicated at the outset of this article, a discussion of these cases has been avoided. See note 10 supra. Steinberg is mentioned here only in the context of the Court's statement.

248. 321 F. Supp. at 746-47. It might be argued that this statement is dictum, not holding, but that hardly seems relevant in the context of the Court's observation.

249. See State v. Moore, 25 Iowa 128, 135-36 (1868); People v. Sessions, 58 Mich. 594, 596, 26 N.W. 291, 293 (1886); Gleitman v. Cosgrove, 49 N.J. 22, 30, 227 A.2d 689, 693 (1967).

250. Gulf, Colo. & S. Fe Ry. v. Ellis, 165 U.S. 150, 160 (1897); Monongahela Navigation Co. v. United States, 148 U.S. 312, 324 (1893).

live human beings of their sacred and inalienable right to live, these cases must be interpreted as indicating an opinion that unborn children are persons under section one of the fourteenth amendment. Finally, the blood transfusion cases discussed above[251] must be taken as decisions of fourteenth amendment significance.

Secondly, the absence of any such decision should not be influential. As was noted in still another life-or-death context, "[t]he constitutionality of death itself under the Cruel and Unusual Punishments Clause is before this Court for the first time; we cannot avoid the question by recalling past cases that never directly considered it."[252]

It is evident that the Court's errors in *Wade* are cumulative. From a distorted interpretation of the common law of abortion to a general misunderstanding of the status of the unborn in American law, the Court erected a flimsy house of cards, piling one error upon another.

D. *The Presumption Against Human Life and Legal Personhood*

Part of the reason for the Court's errors in *Wade* was its approach. By structuring the opinion to create at the outset a right of privacy which includes the right to abort, the Court shifted the burden to the State of Texas to prove that unborn children are legal persons, whereas the presumption should have been in the children's favor. Moreover, the Court guaranteed the irrebutability of the presumption by refusing to decide whether the victim of an abortion is a live human being. Having created an insurmountable barrier, the Court proceeded to decide the fourteenth amendment personhood of unborn children in a case where they were unrepresented by a guardian and wherein no comprehesive record of expert testimony on the issue of their live humanbeingness had been developed in the trial court.

---

251. See text accompanying notes 229-45 supra.

252. Furman v. Georgia, 408 U.S. 238, 285 (1972) (Brennan, J., concurring). However, the Court in Wade did just that when it claimed that it had "inferentially" held in United States v. Vuitch, 402 U.S. 62 (1971), that unborn children are not fourteenth amendment persons. 93 S. Ct. at 729. In Vuitch, the Court held that the District of Columbia abortion statute (which permits abortion only to preserve the life or health of the mother) is not unconstitutionally vague, particularly noting that "vagueness . . . is the only issue we reach here." 402 U.S. at 73 (citations omitted). Life and death issues are not decided sub silentio. "[I]llegitimate and unconstitutional practices get their first footing in that way, namely, by silent approaches . . . ." Boyd v. United States, 116 U.S. 616, 635 (1886). One might as well say the whole abortion issue was decided against the Wade and Bolton plaintiffs in Missouri ex rel. Hurwitz v. North, 271 U.S. 40 (1926), wherein the Court unanimously upheld a state statute authorizing revocation of a physician's license for unlawfully performing an abortion. Of course, the constitutional issues raised by the physician were different, but on the "inferential" approach of Wade, that should be irrelevant.

1. The Presumption

The better view of the common law, the known motivation behind nineteenth century abortion legislation, the intent of the framers, the factual humanbeingness of unborn children, the Supreme Court's own prior explication of "person" in section one of the fourteenth amendment, and the general status in law of unborn children point inexorably to a conclusion that the children are within the scope of the due process and equal protection clauses. But assuming *arguendo* that a substantial doubt still exists, unborn children are not, by virtue of that doubt, automatically excluded from the fourteenth amendment. For a number of reasons, the benefit of doubt must rest with the children, and the burden of proof with those who urge exclusion.

"[C]onstitutional provisions for the security of person and property should be liberally construed. A close and literal construction deprives them of half their efficacy, and leads to gradual depreciation of the right, as if it consisted more in sound than in substance."[253] The rule of liberal construction of constitutional rights was not meant to be thwarted by a rule of illiberal selectivity in the designation of the "person" entitled to assert those rights. Every live human being is included—*unless a specific intent to exclude particular individuals or classes can be shown.*

The rule of liberal construction places the benefit of the doubt on the side of him whose life or liberty is threatened under color of law by the state or its instrumentalities. If, as we are told by the Supreme Court in *In re Winship*,[254] the requirement of proof of guilt beyond a reasonable doubt in criminal cases is among " 'the fundamental principles that are deemed essential for the protection of life and liberty,' "[255] then how much more endangered are the rights to life and liberty when a live human being, threatened with death, has the burden of overcoming a presumption that he is legally not a person, but property, disposable at the will of his "owner" aided and abetted by government! If "[i]t is critical that the moral force of the criminal law not be diluted by a standard of proof that leaves people in doubt whether innocent men are being condemned,"[256] then how much more critical is it to the continued vitality of constitutional rights that they not be circumvented by a presumption of nonpersonhood raised against the innocent human beings who lay claim to them!

Just as "fundamental fairness"[257] requires the state to prove guilt

---

253. Boyd v. United States, 116 U.S. at 635.
254. 397 U.S. 358 (1970), noted in 39 Fordham L. Rev. 121 (1970).
255. 397 U.S. at 362, quoting Davis v. United States, 160 U.S. 469, 488 (1895).
256. 397 U.S. at 364.
257. Id. at 363.

beyond a reasonable doubt in a criminal case " 'to safeguard men from dubious and unjust convictions, with resulting forfeitures of life' "[258] so too do both fundamental fairness and an abhorrence of the forfeiture of life require that every live human being be accounted a fourteenth amendment person—*unless a specific intent to exclude particular individuals or classes can be shown.*

As heretofore noted,[259] the intent of the framers was to insure fourteenth amendment personhood not only to blacks but to every member of the human race. Slavery—the degradation in law and society of one class of live human beings to the status of property—was the occasion for a broad, remedial constitutional enactment designed to recognize the legal personhood of all classes of live human beings. All history shows that a particular grievance suffered by one class has led to remedial enactments intended to protect every class from the same fate.[260] To require any human being to hold his life at the will of others is intolerable as being of the very essence of slavery.[261] All live human beings are, by that fact alone, also fourteenth amendment persons—*unless a specific intent to exclude particular individuals or classes can be shown.*

It is submitted that had the Court in *Wade* placed the burden of proof where it belonged—on those urging exclusion of unborn live human beings from fourteenth amendment protection—the outcome, of necessity, would have been different.

2. The Lack of Representation

By ordinary standards of fairness, the *Wade* opinion should not have been considered by the Supreme Court to be decisive of the rights of unborn children.[262] They were not parties to the action, nor was there a guardian before the Court representing their interests. It might be argued, of course, that the State of Texas adequately represented the unborn children,[263] but the argument must fail.

It is true that in *Griswold v. Connecticut*[264] the Court recognized the standing of the Planned Parenthood League of Connecticut and a physician to raise the constitutional rights of married people with whom they had a professional relationship. However, *Griswold* involved a defense to

---

258. Id. at 362, quoting Brinegar v. United States, 338 U.S. 160, 174 (1949).

259. See Part IV (C) supra.

260. County of Santa Clara v. Southern Pac. R.R., 18 F. 385, 397-98 (C.C.D. Cal. 1883).

261. See Yick Wo v. Hopkins, 118 U.S. 356, 370 (1886).

262. But it was. See Byrn v. New York City Health & Hosps. Corp., 93 S. Ct. 1414 (1973).

263. In Wade, the defendant raised the fourteenth amendment personhood of the unborn child as a compelling state interest. 93 S. Ct. at 725.

264. 381 U.S. 479 (1965).

a criminal prosecution, and the Supreme Court noted that if declaratory relief had been sought, "the requirements of standing should be strict, lest the standards of 'case or controversy' in Article III of the Constitution become blurred."[265] It seems clear that a decision in *Griswold*, adverse to the constitutional rights of married people (who were not parties), would not have bound them in any pending or subsequent action.[266] Moreover, it cannot be said that the Texas Attorney General stood in substantially the same position as the class of unborn children whose rights he purported to assert. Clearly, he was not a member of the class and could not adequately represent its members.[267] As a public official, his interest was ever subject to the vagaries of legislative action and potentially in conflict with the interests of the unborn child.[268] A party possessing such potentially conflicting interests cannot represent the rights of an absent party or fairly insure their protection.[269] As the Supreme Court has said:

Some litigants—those who never appeared in a prior action—may not be collaterally estopped without litigating the issue. They have never had a chance to present their evidence and arguments on the claim. Due process prohibits estopping them despite one or more existing adjudications of the identical issue which stand squarely against their position.[270]

Not only did the Court raise a presumption against the rights of unborn children, but, in addition, it denied them a hearing.

VI. The Errors in Interpretation of Criteria Purportedly Negativing the Personhood of Unborn Children

In support of its conclusion that unborn children are not persons under section one of the fourteenth amendment and to bulwark the presumption it had raised against them, the Court in *Wade* resorted to a number of criteria of legal personhood which unborn children purportedly do not meet. None of these criteria supports the Court's conclusion.

A. *The Census Criterion*

The Court observed, "[w]e are not aware that in the taking of any census . . . a fetus has ever been counted."[271] The writer is not aware

---

265. Id. at 481.

266. See Hansberry v. Lee, 311 U.S. 32, 40 (1940).

267. Id. at 41, 43.

268. Compare Hall v. Lefkowitz, 305 F. Supp. 1030 (S.D.N.Y. 1969) (New York Attorney General defending a restrictive abortion statute) with Byrn v. New York City Health & Hosps. Corp., 31 N.Y.2d 194, 286 N.E.2d 887, 335 N.Y.S.2d 390 (1972) (New York Attorney General defending an abortion-at-will statute).

269. See Hansberry v. Lee, 311 U.S. 32, 44-45 (1940).

270. Blonder-Tongue Labs., Inc. v. University Found., 402 U.S. 313, 329 (1971).

271. 93 S. Ct. at 729 n.53.

that in the taking of any census a corporation has ever been counted either. Yet, a corporation is a legal person under the equal protection clause.[272] Obviously, the enumeration clause[273] is not exhaustive of the persons protected by section one of the fourteenth amendment. Indeed, it is too late in the evolution of human rights to label a whole class of live human beings as non-persons, while at the same time extending the equal protection of the laws to corporations, including, ironically, those which manufacture and use the abortional instruments that kill these live human beings.

B.   *The Incrimination Criterion*

The Court noted that no state forbids all abortions, and the Texas statute, in particular, contained the "typical" exception from criminality for an abortion necessary to save the life of the mother.[274] The Court then asked rhetorically: "But if the fetus is a person who is not to be deprived of life without due process of law, and if the mother's condition is the sole determinant, does not the Texas exception appear to be out of line with the Amendment's command?"[275]

No, it does not. The maternal lifesaving exception to criminal abortion is justifiable under the doctrine of "legal necessity" which also applies to postnatal human beings: "(1) the harm, to be justified, must have been committed under pressure of physical forces; (2) it must have made possible the preservation of at least an equal value; and (3) the commission of the harm must have been the only means of conserving that value."[276] The doctrine is of ancient origin and is usually cast in terms of two survivors of a shipwreck clinging to a piece of flotsam which will support only one of them.[277] Although the status of the doctrine in American law has been somewhat ambiguous,[278] the modern view is that legal necessity applies, at least in some cases, to homicide.[279] In the context of *Wade*, two features of the doctrine should be emphasized: first,

---

272. Santa Clara County v. Southern Pac. R.R., 118 U.S. 394 (1886).

273. U.S. Const. art. I, § 2, cl. 3.

274. 93 S. Ct. at 729 n.54.

275. Id.

276. J. Hall, General Principles of Criminal Law 426 (2d ed. 1960) (footnote omitted).

277. See J. Stephen, A Digest of the Criminal Law 19 (1877).

278. Compare United States v. Holmes, 26 F. Cas. 360 (No. 15,383) (C.C.E.D. Pa. 1842) with Surocco v. Geary, 3 Cal. 69, 73 (1853) (dictum). "[T]he same great principle . . . justifies the exclusive appropriation of a plank in a shipwreck, though the life of another be sacrificed . . . ." American Print Works v. Lawrence, 21 N.J.L. 248, 257-58 (Sup. Ct. 1847) (dictum).

279. See Model Penal Code § 3.02, at 5-10 (Tent. Draft No. 8, 1958).

in its application to abortion, via the maternal lifesaving exception to criminality, the doctrine was designed for the preservation of life, and typically the choice was between the loss of two lives (mother and child) or the preservation of one (the mother); second, the doctrine is applicable to both prenatal and postnatal human beings. If the availability of legal necessity as a defense to a homicide of a postnatal human being does not turn all such human beings into fourteenth amendment nonpersons, then the application of the doctrine to prenatal human beings, in the form of a maternal lifesaving exception to criminal abortion, cannot be relevant to the determination of whether these live human beings are persons under section one of the fourteenth amendment.

The issue is not whether the Supreme Court agrees with the doctrine of necessity as applied to abortion cases,[280] but whether such application is evidence of the nonpersonhood of unborn children. Clearly it is not.

C. *The Accessoryship Criterion*

The Court pointed out that "in Texas the woman is not a principal or an accomplice with respect to an abortion upon her. If the fetus is a person, why is the woman not a principal or an accomplice?"[281] The reasons appear to be historical and pragmatic and completely irrelevant to the unborn child's legal personhood. Historically, abortion was viewed as an assault upon the woman because she "was not deemed able to assent to an unlawful act against herself . . . ."[282] As a result, the woman was considered a victim rather than a perpetrator of, or an accomplice in, the abortion.[283] Pragmatically, conviction of the abortionist frequently

---

280. Apparently it does. Earlier in Wade, the Court had cited with apparent approval, The King v. Bourne, [1939] 1 K.B. 687, a controversial decision applying the necessity doctrine to abortion. 93 S. Ct. at 719. See Davies, The Law of Abortion and Necessity, 2 Modern L. Rev. 126 (1938). While the writer has elsewhere expressed his disagreement with the scope of the Bourne decision—applying the necessity doctrine to maternal health as well as life (Report of the Governor's Commission Appointed to Review New York State's Abortion Law, Minority Report 47, 68-69 (1968))—that is not the point here. The point is: how could the Supreme Court be aware of the application of the necessity doctrine to abortion in Bourne and still use the Texas maternal lifesaving exception as evidence of the nonpersonhood of unborn children without even discussing the doctrine?

281. 93 S. Ct. at 729 n.54.

282. State v. Farnam, 82 Ore. 211, 217, 161 P. 417, 419 (1916).

283. "[The woman] did not stand legally in the situation of an accomplice; for although she, no doubt, participated in the moral offence imputed to the defendant, she could not have been indicted for that offence; the law regards her rather as the victim than the perpetrator of the crime." Dunn v. People, 29 N.Y. 523, 527 (1864) (citations omitted); see Annot., 66 Am. Dec. 82, 87 (1911). There is, however, some authority that "the mother may be guilty of the murder of a child in ventre sa mere, if she takes poison with an intent to poison it,

depended upon the testimony of the aborted woman (especially if a subjective element like quickening were at issue). The woman could hardly be expected to testify if her testimony automatically incriminated her.[284] The omission to incriminate the woman is no more than a statutory grant of immunity. It has no bearing on the personhood of the child.

D.   *The Penalty Criterion*

The Court asserted that the penalty for criminal abortion in Texas is significantly less than the maximum penalty for murder. "If the fetus is a person, may the penalties be different?"[285]

The penalties may be and are different. The law recognizes "degrees of evil" and states may treat offenders accordingly.[286] Killing an unborn child may, in legislative judgment, involve less personal malice than killing a child after birth even though the result is the same—just as, for instance, a legislature may choose to categorize, as something less than murder, intentional killing under the influence of extreme emotional disturbance[287] or intentionally aiding and abetting a suicide.[288] Such legislative recognitions of degrees of malice in killing have nothing to do with the fourteenth amendment personhood of the victims.

E.   *The Citizenship Criterion*

In support of its holding that unborn children are not fourteenth amendment persons, the Court cited[289] *Montana v. Rogers*.[290] It is true that *Rogers* held that a person conceived in the United States but born elsewhere is not a citizen by birth under the citizenship clause of the fourteenth amendment,[291] but it is equally true that the term "persons" and "citizens" in the citizenship clause are not co-extensive. The clause does not relegate non-citizens to nonpersonhood. An alien is not "naturalized" but he is protected as a person by the due process and equal pro-

---

and the child is born alive, and afterwards dies of that poison." Beale v. Beale, 24 Eng. Rep. 373 (Ch. 1713) (emphasis omitted) (citations omitted) (dictum).

284. People v. Nixon, 42 Mich. App. 332, 343, 201 N.W.2d 635, 646 (1972) (concurring and dissenting opinion).

285. 93 S. Ct. at 729 n.54.

286. Skinner v. Oklahoma ex rel. Williamson, 316 U.S. 535, 540 (1942).

287. E.g., N.Y. Penal Law §§ 125.20(2), 125.25(1a) (McKinney 1967).

288. Id. §§ 125.15(3), 125.25(1b).

289. 93 S. Ct. at 729.

290. 278 F.2d 68, 72 (7th Cir. 1960), aff'd sub nom. Montana v. Kennedy, 366 U.S. 308 (1961).

291. "All persons born or naturalized in the United States, and subject to the jurisdiction thereof, are citizens of the United States and of the State wherein they reside." U.S. Const. amend. XIV, § 1.

tection clauses.[292] A corporation is not "born", but it is protected as a person by the equal protection clause.[293] The fact that an unborn child is not a citizen has no bearing on his personhood under section one of the fourteenth amendment.

F. *The Homicide Criterion*

Keeler v. Superior Court[294] and *State v. Dickinson*[295] were cited by the Court[296] as being in accord with its finding that unborn children are not fourteenth amendment persons. It is true that in these cases it was held that an unborn child, killed as a result of a crime committed upon the mother, is not a "person" within the relevant murder (*Keeler*) and vehicular homicide (*Dickinson*) statutes of the respective states. But the decisions do not pertain to the unborn's status under the fourteenth amendment.

First, an assault or a reckless driving statute, which protects a pregnant woman against wrongful injury, of necessity also protects the unborn child she carries within her. If an individual kills the baby by a deliberate assault upon the mother or by reckless driving causing harm to her, he has already committed a separate crime. The child is protected by the same law which protects the mother. On the other hand, the abortion situation is sui generis in that the child requires separate protection. *Keeler* and *Dickinson* do not deprive the child of the law's protection and cannot be said to deny his fourteenth amendment personhood.

Second, both *Keeler* and *Dickinson* correctly held that the homicide statutes under which the defendants were charged must be interpreted according to common law definitions of homicide (or else the statutes would be subject to an ex post facto objection). As pointed out earlier in this article,[297] problems of proof at common law prevented a prosecution for homicide for aborting an unborn child unless the child was born alive and then died. Statutes incorporating common law concepts of homicide must, therefore, be interpreted to exclude the unborn child.

Third, abortion statutes are the proper vehicle for protecting unborn children; such was the intent of the legislatures that enacted them.[298]

---

292. Yick Wo v. Hopkins, 118 U.S. 356 (1886).

293. Santa Clara County v. Southern Pac. R.R., 118 U.S. 394 (1886).

294. 2 Cal. 3d 619, 470 P.2d 617, 87 Cal. Rptr. 481 (1970).

295. 28 Ohio St. 2d 65, 275 N.E.2d 599 (1971).

296. 93 S. Ct. at 729.

297. See Part IV (A) supra.

298. See Part IV (B) supra. That the crime is labelled abortion instead of homicide, and the victim is called an unborn child or fetus or embryo instead of a person are not factors affecting the personhood of the unborn child under section one of the fourteenth amendment.

Keeler and *Dickinson*, like all of the criteria cited by the *Wade* Court do not support a finding that the unborn child is a fourteenth amendment nonperson.

The veneer of scholarship in the *Wade* opinion is only that and nothing more. Beneath the surface, there is little that is not error.

VII. THE DANGEROUS IMPLICATIONS IN *Wade*

Almost three years ago, the writer published an article warning of the dangerous implications of the jurisprudence of permissive abortion.[299] The article pointed out that one of the predominant characteristics of the abortion philosophy is the substitution of the quality of life for the sanctity of life; so that, under the influence of advanced technological know-how, the right to life is reserved only for those whose lives are useful, with the result that euthanasia fits as naturally into the jurisprudence of permissive abortion as does abortion itself.[300] It was also pointed out that there inhered in the quality-of-life jurisprudence the danger of compulsory abortion because any alleged right of privacy to choose whether or not to abort would be subordinated to the interests of society in maintaining a certain quality of life.[301]

Both compulsory abortion and involuntary euthanasia surfaced in *Wade*.

A. *Compulsory Abortion*

It must be remembered that the Court in *Wade* rejected any absolute right of a woman to choose whether or not to abort, and premised its holding on a limited right of privacy, subordinate to compelling state interests.[302] As one example of an appropriate state limitation on the

---

"How simple would be the tasks of constitutional adjudication and of law generally if specific problems could be solved by inspection of the labels pasted on them!" Trop v. Dulles, 356 U.S. 86, 94 (1958). "A fertile source of perversion in constitutional theory is the tyranny of labels." Snyder v. Massachusetts, 291 U.S. 97, 114 (1934). The futility of relying on labels is evident in the New York Penal Law. A " 'person,' when referring to the victim of a homicide, means a human being who has been born and is alive." N.Y. Penal Law § 125.05(1) (McKinney 1967). Yet, "[h]omicide means conduct which causes the death of . . . an unborn child with which a female has been pregnant for more than twenty-four weeks under circumstances constituting . . . abortion in the first degree or self-abortion in the first degree." N.Y. Penal Law § 125.00 (McKinney 1967). Thus, an unborn child who is not a "person" may nevertheless be the victim of a "homicide."

299. Byrn, supra note 5.
300. Id. at 24-28.
301. Id. at 28-31.
302. 93 S. Ct. at 726-27.

right of privacy, the Court cited[303] *Buck v. Bell*[304] which upheld the validity of a state statute providing for compulsory sterilization of mental defectives whose affliction is hereditary. The state "interest" in that situation was, of course, in preventing the proliferation of defectives.

It had been thought that *Buck v. Bell* died after the Nazi experience,[305] and its revival now is rather frightening. By implication in *Wade*, the Court espoused the constitutional validity of state-imposed, compulsory abortion of unborn children diagnosed intrautero as mentally defective.[306] Neither the child's constitutional rights (of which the Court could find none) nor the mother's right of privacy (which the Court, by citing *Buck*, found limited by the state's "interest" in preventing the birth of mental defectives) could, according to the theory of *Wade*, be interposed to challenge such a statute.

The spectre of compulsory abortion assumes additional substance when one reads in a concurring opinion[307] (within a page to a citation to *Buck v. Bell*) that certain situations of pregnancy make abortion "the only civilized step to take," and "[t]he 'liberty' of the mother, though rooted as it is in the Constitution, may be qualified by the State for the reasons we have stated."[308] Presumably, the state has a sufficient interest to mandate the "civilized step" of abortion in certain situations.

The social engineering overtones of the *Wade* opinion do nothing to quiet the fear of compulsory abortion. In the very beginning of its opinion, the Court asserted that "population growth, pollution, poverty, and racial overtones tend to complicate and not to simplify the problem."[309] At the end of the opinion, the Court concluded that its decision is consistent "with the demands of the profound problems of the present day."[310] Evidently, the Court, as social engineer, views abortion as a viable solution to such quality-of-life problems as pollution, poverty, population growth and race. If the state's interest in the solution of these problems can be said to be sufficiently compelling to overcome the right of individual privacy, then compulsory abortion might conceivably encompass others besides the mentally defective unborn child.

---

303. Id. at 727.

304. 274 U.S. 200 (1927).

305. See C. Rice, The Vanishing Right to Live 143-44 (1969).

306. The procedure for such diagnosis is called amniocentesis. R. Rugh & L.B. Shettles, From Conception to Birth 201 (1971). Dr. Y. Edward Hsia of Yale has suggested that amniocentesis might be made compulsory to determine whether or not a child has defects and if so abortion might also be made compulsory. Voice For Life News-Notes, Mar. 1973, at 5.

307. 93 S. Ct. at 756 (Douglas, J., concurring).

308. Id. at 760.

309. Id. at 708-09.

310. Id. at 733.

All this disquietude is compounded by the Court's apparent adoption of what the writer has called "techno-morality."[311] Because advanced technology now knows how to do something, it becomes the right thing to do and facts and law must be readjusted accordingly. Thus, in *Wade*, the Court rejected the view that life begins at conception because of, *inter alia*, "new medical techniques such as menstrual extraction."[312] In other words, the availability of a new technique for performing early abortions justifies a facile redefinition of the facts and law of what an abortion kills so that the technique may be used. What is really being redefined, of course, is the value of the human life destroyed by the abortion. Commenting on the Court's decision, a leading prenatal scientist observed: "[W]e're dealing with human beings; we're dealing with human life. . . . They have used terms like 'potential life,' trying to say that life wasn't there, when the reason for saying that life wasn't there was because they didn't attach any value to it."[313]

To find a basis for compulsory abortion in *Wade* requires no distortion of the Court's opinion. *Buck v. Bell*, judicial social engineering, and techno-morality all combine to make it a very real and very frightening prospect.

B. *Involuntary Euthanasia*

Also very real and very frightening is the prospect of involuntary euthanasia. The Court in *Wade* refused to "resolve the difficult question of when life begins [because] medicine, philosophy, and theology are unable to arrive at any consensus,"[314] even though the Court expressed its awareness of "the well-known facts of fetal development."[315] As previously pointed out,[316] the controversy to which the Court referred involves not whether abortion kills a live human being, but whether that live human being is worth keeping alive or, to put it another way, whether he may be killed with impunity. The determination is not a factual one but a value judgment on whether the life of a human being, distinguishable from other human beings only by kind and degree of dependency, is meaningful. Thus in *Wade*, the Court held: "With respect to the State's important and legitimate interest in potential life, the 'compelling' point is at viability. This is

---

311. Byrn, supra note 5, at 28.

312. 93 S. Ct. at 731. Menstrual extraction consists in suctioning out the lining of the uterus. It is performed between the fifth and seventeenth day following a missed menstrual period—before pregnancy is confirmed by a pregnancy test. Letter from William D. Walden, M.D., to the Editor, N.Y. Times, Mar. 19, 1973, at 34, col. 5.

313. Andre Hellegers, M.D., quoted in The Catholic News, Mar. 15, 1973, at 1, col. 3.

314. 93 S. Ct. at 730.

315. Id. at 728.

316. See Part V (A) supra and text accompanying note 313.

so because the fetus then presumably has the capability of *meaningful* life outside the mother's womb."[317]

The same kind of controversy might very well arise with respect to the end of life. Because of illness, age or incapacity, a live human being, indistinguishable from other live human beings except by kind and degree of dependency, might be claimed by some in the disciplines of medicine, philosophy and theology to be no longer alive in a "meaningful" way. Joseph Fletcher has argued:

> Consistency may be the virtue of merely petty minds, but I want to point out that, even though it might muddy the waters of debate, the fact is that determining whether the quality of *human* life (as distinguished from mere vitality) is present arises at both ends of the life spectrum, and therefore abortion and euthanasia are intertwined questions of ethics. A physician in North Carolina recently asked me, 'Why is it that society tell us we may terminate a life for some reasons *in utero*, but not *in terminus*?' When is the *humanum*, humanness, here and when is it gone? In our present state of knowledge I suspect this is an unanswerable question but that therefore we ought to be putting our heads together to see what criteria for being "human" we can fairly well agree upon. It's worth a try. Medical initiative is at stake in both abortion and euthanasia and the problem ethically is the same.[318]

More recently,[319] Fletcher has detailed "criteria for being 'human,'" including, among others, minimal intelligence, self-awareness, self-control, a sense of time, a sense of futurity, a sense of the past, the capability to relate to others, concern for others, communication, control of existence, curiosity, change and changeability, balance of rationality and feeling, and (as a negative criterion) that "man is not a bundle of rights."[320] In applying these criteria it must be remembered: "We reject the classical sanctity-of-life ethics and embrace the quality-of-life ethics."[321]

Given a carefully orchestrated controversy (such as that undertaken by Fletcher) and the Court's unwillingness in *Wade* to recognize the fact of life unless there is a "consensus" on its value, a state might persuasively claim that it is free to remove a live human being (*e.g.*, a senile elderly person) from the law's protection. Just as the *Wade* Court redefined the beginning of life as a "process,"[322] so too might death be viewed as a process which may be hastened by those who find that the care of a de-

---

317.   93 S. Ct. at 732 (emphasis added).

318.   Fletcher, The Ethics of Abortion, 14 Clinical Obstetrics & Gynecology 1124, 1128 (1971).

319.   Fletcher, Indicators of Humanhood: A Tentative Profile of Man, 2 Hastings Center Report, Nov. 1972, at 1-3.

320.   Id. at 3.

321.   Fletcher, The Ethics of Abortion, 14 Clinical Obstetrics & Gynecology 1124, 1129 (1971).

322.   93 S. Ct. at 731.

pendent live human being has forced upon them (as the Court said of the unwanted child in *Wade*) "a distressful life and future."[323]

The prospect of involuntary euthanasia is no mere hobgoblin. It results directly from the Court's abandonment in *Wade* of its obligation to resolve factual issues upon which constitutional rights depend.[324] The Court's refusal to decide the crucial question of the fact of life, because of the lack of a consensus on the meaningfulness or value of life, establishes a precedent that conceivably could reach as far as legalized involuntary euthanasia. An editorial in the official journal of the California Medical Association advocated a new ethic for medicine and society in these terms:

Medicine's role with respect to changing attitudes toward abortion may well be a prototype of what is to occur. . . . One may anticipate further development of these roles as the problems of birth control and birth selection are extended inevitably to death selection and death control whether by the individual or by society.[325]

Those who favor "birth selection" and "death selection" by "society" will be considerably encouraged by *Wade*.

VIII. CONCLUSION

Every decision to abort is a decision to kill a "live human being,"[326] a "child [with] a separate life,"[327] a "human"[328] who is "unquestionably alive"[329] and has "an autonomy of development and character."[330] This is the stark, overwhelming reality about abortion.

In *Wade,* the Supreme Court, with full knowledge of the mortal consequences that would ensue, removed a whole class of live human beings from the law's protection, and left their continued existence to the unfettered discretion of others.[331] But "[h]uman beings are not merely creatures of the State, and by reason of that fact, our laws should protect

---

323. Id. at 727.

324. See Part V (A) supra.

325. Editorial, A New Ethic for Medicine and Society, 113 California Medicine 67, 68 (Sept. 1970).

326. Byrn v. New York City Health & Hosps. Corp., Supreme Court of the State of New York, Queens County, Index No. 13113/71, in Juris. State. 60a, 68a (unpublished opinion of Francis J. Smith, J., Jan. 4, 1972).

327. Byrn v. New York City Health & Hosps. Corp., 38 App. Div. 2d 316, 324, 329 N.Y.S.2d 722, 729 (2d Dep't 1972) (citations omitted).

328. Byrn v. New York City Health & Hosps. Corp., 31 N.Y.2d 194, 199, 286 N.E.2d 887, 888, 335 N.Y.S.2d 390, 392 (1972).

329. Id.

330. Id.

331. But see Reitman v. Mulkey, 387 U.S. 369 (1967).

the unborn from those who would take his life for purposes of comfort, convenience, property or peace of mind rather than sanction his demise."[332]

Perhaps it is a measure of the extent to which the quality-of-life philosophy dominates our jurisprudence that a justice of the Supreme Court can write in the "environmental context" of the destruction of trees and animals, "any man's death diminishes me, because I am involved in Mankinde,"[333] while in the human context of the destruction of unborn children, he can opine, contrary to fact, that "the fetus, at most, represents only the potentiality of life;"[334] and proceed to exile the unborn beyond the pale. But unborn children are also a part of mankind and, aware of it or not, his opinion did diminish the Court and all the rest of us.

First, *Dred Scott*, then *Buck v. Bell* and now the most tragic of them all —*Roe v. Wade*. Three generations of error are three too many—and the last of them shall be called the worst.

332. Byrn v. New York City Health & Hosps. Corp., 31 N.Y.2d at 206, 286 N.E.2d at 892, 335 N.Y.S.2d at 397 (Burke, J., dissenting).
333. Sierra Club v. Morton, 405 U.S. 727, 760 n.2 (1972) (Blackmun, J., dissenting).
334. 93 S. Ct. at 731.

NEW YORK

LAW FORUM

VOLUME XIV   FALL, 1968   NUMBER 3

THE LAW OF NEW YORK CONCERNING ABORTION AND THE STATUS OF THE FOETUS, 1664-1968: A CASE OF CESSATION OF CONSTITUTIONALITY

CYRIL C. MEANS, JR.*

I. The Common Law Conception of a "Man"

An Historical Footnote

ANY discussion of the law of abortion must center upon the issue of when, if ever, during pregnancy a foetus becomes a "man," a human person, with all the rights of those already born. This philosophical puzzle has perplexed the sages down the corridors of time. During the European Middle Ages, however, there was a virtually unaminous consensus on the question by educated men of all disciplines, including theology, philosophy, medicine, and jurisprudence. All agreed that the moment of *animation,* the infusion of a rational soul into the developing foetus, occurred at some point in time between conception and birth. The theo-

* A.B., 1938, Harvard College; J.D., 1941, Wayne State University Law School; LL.M., 1948, Harvard Law School. Member, Governor's Commission Appointed to Review New York State's Abortion Law (1968); member of the Michigan and United States Supreme Court Bars.
Editor's Note. Because of the large number of Latin words and phrases in some of the footnotes of this article dealing with ecclesiastical documents, the following explanation may be helpful to readers, particularly those from disciplines other than law. The New York Law Forum follows the ordinary typographical convention, in the text, according to which foreign-language words and phrases are italicized, as are English words where emphasis is desired. In the footnotes, however, a different usage is adhered to. Foreign-language words and phrases are not italicized but are set off by double quotation marks (which do not, therefore, necessarily signify that they are being quoted from another source). English words to be emphasized in the notes are not italicized but underscored.

logians and canon lawyers fixed the moment ambivalently at forty days after conception in the case of a male foetus, and eighty days in the case of a female foetus.[1] Others, such as the jurists of the Roman Civil Law, in force in many parts of the European continent, fixed it at forty days in the case of a foetus of either sex.[2] As we shall see, the fathers of the English common law fixed it at the moment of "quickening," a phenomenon which occurs at different times in different women, and in the same woman at different times in different pregnancies, but ordinarily takes place between the sixteenth and eighteenth week.

The outlook which united the various mediaeval thinkers is more important than the details that divided them; for all were convinced that the early embryo is not yet a man, but achieves that status at a later stage of gestation. All adhered to the doctrine of *mediate animation,* which the Council of Trent treated as absolutely certain:

> Whereas no human body, when the order of nature is followed, can be informed by the soul of man except after the prescribed interval of time.[3]

Jewish thought, on the contrary, with a single aberration that was short-lived in Judaism, but of profound influence in Christianity, has always adhered to the idea that only at the moment of "birth alive" is the *nefesh,* the living soul, infused into the emerging babe.[4]

---

[1] R. Huser, The Crime of Abortion in Canon Law 55-56 (Catholic University of America Canon Law Studies No. 162, 1942). J. Noonan, Contraception: A History of Its Treatment By the Catholic Theologians and Canonists 90 (1965):

> In Aristotle, a fetus becomes human forty days after conception if the fetus is male, ninety days after conception if the fetus is female (History of Animals 7.3). A similar view may underlie the prescription in Leviticus 12:1-5 that a woman must spend forty days in becoming purified if she has given birth to a boy, eighty days if she has given birth to a girl.

Christian authors did, it is true, harmonize Aristotle and Leviticus in this fashion, but the rabbis themselves did not. Cf. Mishnah, Ahaloth 7:6; Tosefta, Yebamoth 9:4; Code of Maimonides, Murder and the Preservation of Life 1:9. These texts permit embryotomy to preserve the life of the woman in difficult labor, but forbid it once either the greater part of the infant, or its head, has emerged, for then it is considered born. According to Judaic thought, however, only birth alive confers fully human status.

[2] Noonan, supra note 1, at 217. The thirteenth century glossator Accursius maintained that the destruction of a young embryo was not homicide. He held that the penalty of exile in the Digest applied "only if the fetus in under 40 days; after 40 days the penalty for homicide applies."

[3] Catechism of the Council of Trent (1545-1563), Creed, pt. I, art. III, no. 7: "Cum servato naturae ordine nullum corpus, nisi intra praescriptum temporis spatium, hominis anima informari queat", quoted in E. Messenger, A Short History of Embryology, in Theology and Evolution 233, 236 n.1 (E. Messenger ed. 1949).

[4] Cf. I. Jakobovits, Jewish Views on Abortion, in Abortion and the Law 124, 127-28 (D. Smith ed. 1967). The Septuagint version of Exodus 21:22-23 overtranslates the Massoretic Hebrew text so as to harmonize it with Aristotelian mediate animationism. Rabbi Jakobovits attributes this eisegesis to a linguistic confusion in the minds

In the sevententh and eighteenth centuries, certain Roman Catholic physicians, encouraged by observations of advanced foetal development in what they had been led to believe were very early embryos,[5] concluded that the moment of animation was much closer to conception than had been believed, and possibly was even synchronous with conception. Until their time, it had not been the custom to baptize an abortive foetus under thirty days of age. These physicians advocated the baptism, *sub conditione*, of such foetūs. Their program long encountered dogged opposition from the Roman authorities, who ruled against them in 1658 and again in 1713.[6] They were not to win their battle

---

of the Alexandrian Jews who translated the Old Testament into Greek, id. at 128 n.7. As he points out, the Septuagint version of these verses in Exodus had no lasting effect in Judaism, but its effect upon Christian thinkers was profound and prolonged. The pre-Vulgate Old Latin versions of the Bible followed the Septuagint in regard to these verses in Exodus. P. Sabatier, Bibliorum Sacrorum Latinae Versiones Antiquae Seu Vetus Italica, tomus I, at 178 (1751). By the time Jerome's Vulgate appeared upon the scene, the acceptance by the Fathers, Greek and Latin, of Aristotelian mediate animation as mediated by the Septuagint and Old Latin Versions was virtually universal; Jerome's return to the Massoretic text came too late to influence them (including Augustine).

[5] Messenger, supra note 3, at 238-40:

Thomas Fienus, a Professor of Louvain University . . . maintained in three works published between 1620 and 1629 that a foetus was truly human when only three days of age. . . . [Paul] Zacchias, a Roman doctor . . . in 1661 published a work in which he definitely argued that the human soul is present in the embryo from the first moment . . . . Meanwhile, doctors and others continued the close and careful study of the formation of the foetus as seen in early abortions, and to discuss the interpretation of what they thought they observed. Thus Riolanus, a French contemporary of [Thomas] Harvey, said that he had studied three such foetuses. The first of these was, according to him, only one month old, but it was, he said, completely human, with all the parts and structures of a human being. . . . [O]ne of the best known writers in the discussion was Bianchi, the celebrated Professor at Turin University. He had in his Museum several aborted foetuses, and in 1724 gave a detailed description of these, with information as to their respective ages. One of these, he claimed, had come from a certain woman only 3 or 4 days from impregnation. Another, only 7 days old, had come from a most chaste and illustrious matron of Turin, one week after her nuptials. This, he asserted, could be seen from its neck and head to be sufficiently human—"satis humanus". Other foetuses similarly displayed undoubtedly human characteristics.

[6] Messenger, supra note 3, at 240-41:

It will be of interest to discuss the attitude of the [Roman] ecclesiastical authorities to these new "discoveries", and new theories based upon them. . . . In the case of baptism . . . the Mediate Animation theory seems to have been presupposed, for the Roman Ritual contained a rubric forbidding baptism in the womb, and ordering baptism only in case the head or some other member should emerge. And it does not seem to have been the custom to administer baptism to a foetus of less than 30 days. But the new embryological ideas and "discoveries" very soon attracted the attention of theologians, and in 1658 Jerome Florentinus published a work, "De hominibus dubiis sive de baptismo abortivorum." In this work the author maintained that . . . it was probable (in the theological sense [i.e., = arguable]) that the rational soul was infused into the embryo immediately after conception. Accordingly, Florentinus taught that all aborted foetuses, however small in size, and however brief the time which had elapsed since conception, ought to be baptized, under pain of mortal

for a canon commanding the baptism of every living foetus, however young, until the new Code of Canon Law in 1917. They won an earlier battle in 1869, when Pius IX erased the difference between early abor-

---

sin, and this even though no sign of life was present in the form of movement. As Cangiamila remarks ([Embryologia Sacra (1758)], p. 37), no one had previously gone so far, and the book aroused some opposition. The book was delated to Rome, and examined by the Congregation of the Index, with the result recorded in detail in a later chapter . . . .

Before passing to that, it may be proper to remark that only the custom of refusing baptism to a foetus younger than 30 days can be explained by the mediate animation principle. The rubric in the Roman ritual that forbade intrauterine baptism, and commanded baptism only if the head or another member should emerge, is reminiscent rather of the Talmudic text on embryotomy, supra note 1, and, like them, cannot be bottomed on a theory of mediate animation, but rather one of animation at birth alive. At any rate, even though the custom of not baptizing an early abortus and the rubric in the Roman ritual rest on mutually inconsistent theories, both are in turn inconsistent with the theory of immediate animation.

Returning to the attitude of the authorities at Rome to "discoveries" which these seventeenth and eighteenth century embryologists, with their poor microscopes and obvious credulity in the face of protestations of antenuptial chastity by female patients, thought they had made, H. de Dorlodot, A Vindication of the Mediate Animation Theory, in Messenger, supra note 3, at 272, 275, 278, states that:

The question was taken to the Holy See, in connection with the publication of the work "De hominimus dubiis baptizandis," published in 1658 at Lyons by a Servite, Jerome Florentine (Hieronymus Florentinus). This author maintained that, provided an aborted foetus presents characteristics which enable one to distinguish it from a shapeless mass (mola), one cannot affirm with certitude that it is not a human being, and hence one ought to baptize it "sub conditione," whatever may be the time elapsed since conception. The book was delated to the Congregation of the Index, which decided that there was no need for a formal condemnation, but that publication of a second edition would be authorized only on the following conditions: (1) The author was to put at the front of the work a declaration protesting that he had no intention of defining anything, but only of setting forth the question "per modum problematis," and that he had no intention in the present matter of maintaining that there existed in practice an obligation [to baptize an early abortus, sub conditione] under pain of mortal sin, but only of setting forth speculative reasons, leaving undecided the question itself, and that he had no idea of introducing a new ceremony. (2) The author was to make it quite clear in the proper place in the book "se de iis loqui abortivis qui omnino sensibiles essent ac prima saltem ostenderent humani corporis lineamenta" ["that he is speaking of abortive foetūs which are entirely capable of sensation and also display at least the rudimentary lineaments of the human body] (author's translation from the Latin).

. . . .

The work was reprinted at Lucca, with the required corrections, and on the first of April, 1666, the Sacred Congregation of the Index issued the following decree: "Disputatio de Hominibus dubiis non permittitur nisi correcta, juxta impressionem Luccae ex typographia Hyacinthi Pacii [The Disputation concerning Doubtful Men is not permitted to be published except as corrected, in accordance with the edition at Lucca from the press of Hyacinth Paci]" . . . . [A] decree of the Holy Office of [April 5] 1713, confirmed the doctrine of the Congregation of the Index. Here is the text, as found in the "Collectanea de Prop[aganda] Fide," ed. 2a, no. 282:

"In the cases put (namely, of baptism of an abortive foetus), if there be at hand a rational basis for questioning whether that foetus be animated by a rational soul, then it can and ought to be baptized "sub conditione"; if, however, no reasonable basis exists for such a doubt, then it cannot be baptized at all. Moreover, for ascertaining whether there be a reasonable basis for such a

tion and abortion after "the prescribed interval of time" for the purpose of applying one of the canonical penalties for this offense (automatic excommunication). In 1917, the new Code erased it for the other (irregularity).[7]

This new theory of immediate animation provided a rationale for these nineteenth century innovations in the canonical legislation of the Roman Catholic Church, but that Church has never defined this theory as dogmatically true. Apologetic considerations may underlie this curious ambivalence.[8]

---

doubt, physicans and theologians are to be consulted as to contingencies of fact, or in individual cases" (author's translation from the Latin). . . . But on the other hand, the new [1917] Code of Canon Law [Canon 747] seems to have [modified] the preceding decrees.

[7] Canon 747 of the 1917 Code of Canon Law provides, for the first time in ecclesiastical history, for the absolute baptism of all abortive foetūs however young. Baptism "sub conditione" is restricted to cases where there is doubt that the abortive foetus is alive.

Care is to be taken that all abortive foetūs, whenever brought forth, if they certainly be living, be absolutely baptized; if there be doubt as to whether they be living, then "sub conditione" (author's translation from the Latin).

In other words, the pre-1917 condition, "si animatus es", may no longer be pronounced: the only permissible condition since 1917 is: "si vivis." While it seems fairly clear that the authors of this new canon were immediate animationists, a canon does not serve as dogmatic definition.

Huser, supra note 1, at 75-76 discusses the erasure of the animation distinction by Piux IX's "Apostolicae Sedis" (Oct. 12, 1869) in regard to the censure of automatic excommunication, and, at 94-95, the same erasure by the 1917 Code in respect of irregularity.

[8] From her first receipt of the Dominical command, "Go ye, therefore, and teach all nations, baptizing them in the name of the Father, and of the Son, and of the Holy Ghost" (Matthew 28:19), until the decree of the Holy Office of April 5, 1713, the Church had not baptized abortive foetūs of less than 30 days. From that decree until the new Code of 1917, the baptism of such an early foetus was permitted if the doctors and theologians consulted entertained a reasonable doubt as to whether it had yet received a rational soul. Since 1917, such a foetus must be baptized, and that baptism is absolute in form.

If, therefore, a Pope today were to pronounce a dogmatic definition in favor of immediate animation, he would thereby accuse the Church of having, before 1713, withheld baptism from millions of creatures now recognized to have been "men," and, between 1713 and 1917, of having left the question of their baptism to the uninstructed vagaries of reasonable doubts entertained by individual physicians and theologians consulted in particular cases. If, on the other hand, a Pope were now to define mediate animation as true, he would thereby accuse the Church, since 1917, of commanding the absolute baptism, and, between 1713 and 1917, of having allowed the conditional baptism of millions of creatures now recognized as not having yet been "men." Similar difficulties would arise from either definition in regard to the old rubric in the Roman ritual forbidding intrauterine baptism.

The legislative activity of the Popes in 1869 and 1917 in erasing the animation distinction for all practical purposes of canon law clearly betrays a personal belief on their part in immediate animation since 1869. They have not reinforced their legislative changes by pronouncing a dogmatic definition, though in various pronouncements of a less magisterial character they have edged as close to such a definition as they

It has come to pass, in our modern pluralistic society, that the mediaeval consensus in favor of mediate animation, in which the English common law was born and bred, has disappeared. Mediate animation survives, and has its advocates, but it is no longer the sole school of thought. It has been joined by two others, immediate animation on the right, and animation at birth on the left, each with ardent advocates of its own.

In a pluralistic society, the secular law, where possible, should abstain from metaphysical controversies. Unfortunately, this is an area where such abstention is impossible. Problems of life, presented to the courts, often compel decisions which cannot avoid answering metaphysical questions underlying legal disputes. It does not "desectarianize" the controversy to alter terminology from the "animationism" of traditional theology, grounded in a soul-body distinction, to humanistic vocabulary of "person" or Scriptual simplicity of "man." These are mere semantic shifts, and do not disguise from the discerning eye the fact that the underlying reality remains the same. What is sought

---

could without falling into the history-set traps above mapped out. That they have avoided such a definition is, under the circumstances, not so remarkable as it seems at first glance, and those who expect them to pronounce one are destined, I think, to wait for it until the Greek Kalends.

Very distinguished priests and laymen continue to advocate, within the Church, the doctrine of mediate animation. See Donceel, Abortion: Mediate v. Immediate Animation, 5 Continuum 167 (1967); O'Mahoney & Potts, Abortion and the Soul, 224 The Month Nos. 1199-1200, at 45-50 (1967); Springer, Abortion and the Law, 28 Theological Studies 308, 330-35 (1967). Father Springer poses some intriguing questions in his article, id. at 333:

> When does animation occur? When is a fetus a person? The perennial question is still with us without conclusive answer. . . .
> There are new biological data but they concern the time when animation is not present. . . . [R]esearch scientists in reproduction maintain that the occurrence of identical twins may take place several days after fertilization. . . . This requires that we reexamine our traditional [sic] Catholic view of the probable presence of human life from the moment of conception. How can a person, matter and spirit, be divided into two or more unique incommunicable beings?

If the word "modern" were substituted for "traditional," Father Springer's passage could not be faulted.

More than 26 years ago, the following eminently cogent and astute observation was made by Father Huser, supra note 1, at 106-07:

> It need not be concluded that through the medium of the new [i.e., 1869 and 1917] canons dealing with penalties for abortion the Church has given a doctrinal solution to the question, "At what moment is the rational soul infused into the human body?" At least, the Church says in effect that whatever may be the speculative and academic merit of the theory of retarded animation, it can have no practical application in regard to the [canonical] crime of abortion, or in the matter of conferring baptism upon an aborted fetus.
> There is, of course, no true homicide unless a rational being is killed. But in the present day law of the Church her legislation concerning the procuring of an abortion may well be considered a separate juridical institute; it is a crime in its own right, independently of the crime of homicide.

is a legally precise definition of the initial contours of the human person. Any such definition must, in the present state of scientific knowledge, lack real scientific sanction, and rest, now, as in the middle ages, on a philosophical interpretation of such scientific data as are available. Our principal difficulty is that now we have not one such interpretation, but three: immediate animation; mediate animation; and the birth-alive criterion.

Immediate animationists commonly oppose all but the most grudging and minuscule of abortion law reform. Mediate animationists today[9] are open to degrees of abortion law reform ranging from the conservative Model Penal Code (1959) proposals of the American Law Institute[10] to abortion at will as advocated by the American Civil Liberties Union.[11] They only require that the operation be performed while the foetus is still in the pre-human (the Civil Liberties Union says "pre-viable") stage. Those who believe that only birth alive produces a human person see no metaphysical reason for placing legal limitations on the stage in pregnancy at which an otherwise legal termination may take place, though they are alive to possible medical contraindications of an abortion late in pregnancy. In their views of desirable reform they, too, range from abortion at will at one extreme to no change at all at the other, as in the case of Orthodox Jews whose opposition to broadening the indications for legal abortion are bottomed not on metaphysical but on moral considerations.[12]

Out of this bewildering welter of latter-day confusion, twentieth century parliaments and legislatures must thread their way, seeking solutions which, if they cannot command the unanimous consensus that the common law enjoyed in its mediaeval heyday, will at least strike as even a balance among the conflicting views as now can be achieved. Before embarking upon reform of the legal structure of our abortion law, we shall do well to try to understand it. To that end, an historical conspectus is submitted.

---

[9] Immediate animationists today pray in aid the fact that the mediate animationists of the past all opposed abortion even in early pregnancy. This is true, but it proves nothing, because, like everyone else at that time, they also opposed contraception. Only in the twentieth century have significant numbers of Jews and Christians adopted an attitude of moral approval of contraception. The Anglican Communion, for example, took this step at its Lambeth Conference of 1930.

Once contraception is accepted as morally licit, the question of the morality of abortion in early pregnancy must in its turn be faced. The answer turns, in large part, though not wholly, upon the solution one adopts to the question of mediate versus immediate animation.

[10] Model Penal Code § 207.11 (Tent. Draft No. 9, 1959); Model Penal Code § 230.3 (Proposed Official Draft, 1962).

[11] N.Y. Times, March 25, 1968, at 35, col. 1.

[12] See Jakobovits, supra note 4, at 134-43.

We need not be surprised if we find that the old solution of the philosophical question, so long embedded in our common and our statute law, serves better than either of the newer alternatives to ground the currently required compromise between polarized extremes. As we shall see, our criminal law attaches nearly human value only to the quickened foetus, but even its life is not equated with its mother's. The pre-quickened foetus is not now, and has never been, itself an object of protection by our criminal law; the common assumption that it is will be dispelled by a study of legislative history, herein revealed for the first time. The object of our statutes making destruction of the unquickened foetus an offense was not its *own* protection, but the preservation of the health and life of the *pregnant woman*, under the surgical conditions of 140 years ago, when not only all abortions, but all other surgical operations, even in hospitals, were often fatal. We shall see, too, that in the law of property and torts, a foetus, whatever its stage of development, has no rights if stillborn. Only by birth alive can a child assert rights in these areas prenatally acquired by what the courts expressly recognize as a legal fiction, adopted as such fictions are to accomplish equity. It is thus curious but true that in these non-criminal areas of our law the Jewish emphasis upon birth alive provides a better metaphysique of the legal results than either of the two Christian theories (mediate and immediate animationism). Mediate animationism, however, still serves to explain the rules of our criminal law. The only one of the three theories that explains absolutely nothing in our legal system is immediate animationism.

New York's law of abortion, and other aspects of the status of the foetus, has a rich history. It has contributed original ideas copied by many other States and countries in their legislation. No intelligent attempt to summarize it can be made without first investigating its three centuries of history, in an endeavor to understand what it has been and what it is. As was said long ago by Sir Edward Coke, "Out of the ould fields shall come and growe the new corn."

The English Common Law

Roman-Dutch law was in force in the Province of New Netherland for forty years (1624-64) but, as no trace of it has survived, no attempt has been made to ascertain its provisions concerning abortion and the status of the foetus.

With the English conquest on September 8, 1664, the common law of England was introduced into the Province, renamed New York, and has remained the basis of law in the State of New York until the present day.

On the subject of abortion, English common law remained in force in the mother country until 1803,[13] and was the law of New York for over 165 years, until January 1, 1830, when those sections of the Revised Statutes of 1829 took effect which, for the first time, made abortion a statutory offense in this State. What, then, was the common law of abortion from 1664 through 1829?

The Concept of Quickening in the Criminal Law in England

Two thirteenth century treatises, the earlier by Henry de Bracton, chancellor of Exeter Cathedral and a justice of the court soon to be known as the Court of King's Bench, the second by his commentator, Fleta, point to the fact that the common law of England reflected the Roman canon law of that time. Bracton wrote:

> If there be anyone who strikes a pregnant woman or gives her a poison whereby he causes an abortion, if the foetus be already formed or animated, and especially if it be animated, he commits homicide.[14]

Every other mediaeval writer I have read has equated (physical) formation with (rational) animation. Bracton is unique in suggesting that animation may follow formation by an interval of time. Fleta, for example, loses his master's insight and apparently reverts to the common equation of his contemporaries (physical formation = rational animation):

> One is rightly a homicide who has pressed on a pregnant woman or has given her a poison or struck her to produce an abortion . . . if the foetus was already formed and ensouled . . . .[15]

---

13 In England, the common law was superseded by Lord Ellenborough's Act, 43 Geo. III, ch. 58 (1803). That was the first statute on the subject in any English-speaking country.

14 H. de Bracton, The Laws and Customs of England, III, ii, 4, quoted in original Latin in D. Davis, The Law of Abortion and Necessity, 2 Modern L. Rev. 126, 133 (1938) (author's translation).

15 Noonan, supra note 1, at 216 (translating Fleta, I, 23).

Bracton's quirk is really a profound insight, a magnificent anticipation of the principle to which modern zoologists and embryologists adhere, viz.: that form precedes function. There are instances when the performance of the function commences almost immediately after the physical development of the form. In the case of other functions, the form is complete for some time before the corresponding function starts. If reason be accepted as the defining note of man, the physical form of reason is not virtually complete and human in relative dimensions and configuration until the end of the second trimester of pregnancy, in the shape of the human cerebral cortex. But the function of reason does not become manifest until some time after birth—perhaps when the child first uses the word "true."

At some point between the thirteenth and seventeenth centuries, English common law developed along the line suggested by Bracton's distinction between formation and animation. In so doing, it postulated the latter event as occurring at the time of quickening (*i.e.*, toward the end of the fourth or the beginning of the fifth month of pregnancy), as witnessed by the statement of Sir Edward Coke:

> If a woman be quick with childe, and by a potion or otherwise killeth it in her wombe, or if a man beat her, whereby the childe dyeth in her body, and she is delivered of a dead childe, this is a great misprision, and no murder; but if the childe be born alive and dyeth of the potion, battery, or other cause, this is murder; for in law it is accounted a reasonable creature, *in rerum natura*, when it is born alive.[16]

Both the early and the mature manifestations of the English common law distinguish between abortion in early pregnancy and abortion later in pregnancy. The latter was regarded as murder by the early common law, as it was by canon law. By Coke's time, the common law regarded abortion as murder only if the foetus is (1) quickened, (2) born alive, (3) lives for a brief interval, and (4) then dies. If, however, a *quickened* foetus is killed *in* the womb and then stillborn, the offense was "a great misprision."[17] American courts usually convert Coke's "misprision" into "misdemeanor" in articulating the degree of the offense of abortion *after quickening*. The quickening criterion established at common law was more liberal than the eighty-days norm, the more liberal of the two norms of the canon law.

As Coke's language indicates, and as decisions afterwards made clear, an abortion *before* quickening, with the woman's consent, whether killing the foetus while still within the womb, or causing its death after birth alive was not, at common law, an indictable offense, either in her or in the abortionist. It was not a crime at all. Such an abortion after quickening, on the other hand, was a misprision or misdemeanor on the part of the abortionist, and perhaps of the woman as well, whether she consented or not, if foetal death occurred *in utero*; if the injured baby died after live birth, it was murder.

---

[16] 3 Coke, Institutes *50 (1648).

[17] 3 Holdsworth, History of English Law 389 n.1 (3d ed. 1923):
[I]n Coke's day an element of confusion had arisen in that the term "misprision" had got an extended meaning; to use Coke's words, it was not merely a "crimen omissionis," consisting in the concealment of treason or felony, it was also "crimen commissionis," as in committing some heinous offence under the degree of felony; in this latter sense it was a vague offence which covered many various contempts.
Cf. id. at *36, *139.

In addition, the common law rigorously adhered to the quickening criterion with reference to the procedural rule of reprieve. In the event that a woman was convicted of a capital offense, she was granted a reprieve only if she was found to be quick with child. It was not enough that she be merely pregnant.[18]

While both substantive (abortion and murder) and procedural (reprieve) criminal law adhered to the criterion of quickening, the common law, when confronted with problems in the civil sphere, such as bastardy and inheritance, ignored this criterion. For example, if a landowner died, survived by a widow, the widow was not her husband's heir. If the landowner died without issue his brother was deemed his heir presumptive. If, however, the widow truthfully claimed to be pregnant by her late husband, the offspring, upon birth, would take precedence over the decedent's brother. The brother could have protected himself by bringing a writ *de ventre inspiciendo* to have the widow inspected to determine pregnancy.[19] If the woman was found not to be pregnant, the presumptive heir would inherit, but would subsequently lose the inheritance if a child was born within forty weeks from the death of the husband. The 40-week period was also applied in cases arising under the Rule against Perpetuities.[20]

---

[18] 4 Blackstone, Commentaries on the Laws of England *394-95 (1769):
Reprieves may also be "ex necessitate legis" (from legal necessity); as where a woman is capitally convicted and pleads her pregnancy; though this is no cause to stay the judgment, yet it is to respite the execution till she be delivered. This is a mercy dictated by the law of nature, "in favorem prolis" (in favor of the offspring); and therefore no part of the bloody proceedings in the reign of Queen Mary [I] hath been more justly detested than the cruelty that was exercised in the Island of Guernsey of burning a woman big with child, and when, through the violence of the flames, the infant sprang forth at the stake and was preserved by the bystanders, after some deliberations of the priests who assisted at the sacrifice, they cast it again into the fire as a young heretic,— a barbarity which they never learned from the laws of ancient Rome, which direct, with the same humanity as our own, "quod praegnantis mulieris damnatae poena differatur, quoad pariat (that the punishment of a pregnant woman condemned shall be deferred till after her delivery)"; which doctrine has also prevailed in England as early as the first memorials of our law will reach [citing Fleta, Book I, c. 38]. In case this plea is made in stay of execution, the judge must direct a jury of twelve matrons or discreet women to inquire the fact, and if they bring in their verdict "quick with child" (for barely, "with child," unless it be alive in the womb, is not sufficient), execution shall be stayed generally till the next session, and so from session to session, till either she is delivered or proves by the course of nature not to have been with child at all. But if she once hath had the benefit of this reprieve and been delivered, and afterwards becomes pregnant again, she shall not be entitled to the benefit of a further respite for that cause. For she may now be executed before the child is quick in the womb, and shall not, by her own incontinence, evade the sentence of justice.
[19] 1 Blackstone, id. at *456 (1765), citing Britton, ch. 66, at 166 (circa 1290):
If the widow be upon due examination found not pregnant, the presumptive heir shall be admitted to the inheritance, though liable to lose it again, on the birth of a child within 40 weeks from the death of the husband.
[20] The multifarious citations to the various reports and stages of the case of Gore

In a New York case decided in 1802, a testator devised land in Islip, with a series of limitations of estates for life designed to create the equivalent of an estate in tail male. One remainderman died, leaving his wife *enceinte*; twenty weeks and three days later she bore her deceased husband's posthumous son. Had this son been born before his father's death, he would have been the next remainderman. The father's younger brother would have been the next remainderman after the son. The question was whether the fact that the son was not born when his father died caused him to be passed over in favor of his uncle. This question had been decided in England in 1695 by the House of Lords in favor of such posthumous son.[21] The New York Court held the House of Lords decision declaratory of the common law of New York, Chancellor Kent writing one of the two opinions, both unanimous, which reached this result.[22]

Classical common law, therefore, was ambivalent. For civil law purposes, it traced the prenatal existence of the foetus back, forty weeks if necessary, to conception. For criminal law purposes, it refused to recognize the prenatal period of the foetus at any point earlier than quickening.

The Common Law Definition of a Person for Civil Purposes

At this point, an excursion into prenatal injuries must be made. In 1884, Justice Oliver Wendell Holmes, Jr., then of the Supreme Judicial Court of Massachusetts, wrote the opinion of the court in a case involving a pregnant woman who slipped and fell on a defective pavement, and whose four to five month old foetus, which the opinion assumed had quickened, but which, of course, was not yet viable, had been miscarried in consequence of the mother's fall, and survived this premature expulsion for ten to fifteen minutes. Letters of adminstration

---

v. Gore, 2 P. Wms. 28 (1722), and a full discussion, may be found in J. Gray, The Rule Against Perpetuities § 174 (4th ed. 1942). In Gore v. Gore, a testator [T] had left land by will for a term of years to A, after which term it was to go to the first and other sons of B. B was T's son, and, at the date of T's death, B was still a bachelor. The validity, under the Rule Against Perpetuities, of the executory devise to B's first son, who might be posthumous, was the question which perplexed the Lord Chancellor. At his request, in 1722, the Court of King's Bench certified that the executory devise to B's first son was invalid "because it is not to take place within that compass of time which the law allows," this being so "because it might subsist 40 weeks after the death of [B], and they [the judges] were not for going a day farther than a life in being." On a second referral in 1734, however, the court reversed itself in this case, certifying that this devise was good, and the Chancellor decreed accordingly.

[21] Reeve v. Long, 83 Eng. Rep. 754 (H.L. 1695), rev'g 91 Eng. Rep. 202 (K.B. 1694) (the King's Bench having affirmed the Common Pleas). This reversal by the House of Lords was "against the opinion of all the Judges, who were much dissatisfied with the reversal. . . ."

[22] Stedfast v. Nicoll, 3 Johns. Cas. 18 (N.Y. 1802).

were taken out on the footing that the child was a "person" within the meaning of the Massachusetts wrongful death statute, under which the administrator sued the town for the infant's wrongful death. Plaintiff's counsel placed a heavy reliance on Coke's statement that, if an abortion be attempted causing the child to be born alive, and it then dies of injuries, this constitutes murder. Justice Holmes held that the Massachusetts abortion statute did not produce the result called for by Coke's statement, and even doubted whether Coke's statement was valid at common law.[23] Holmes pointed out that if a civil action for prenatal injuries were allowed, such right to recover

> [W]ould not be affected by the degree of maturity reached by the embryo at the moment of the organic lesion or wrongful act. Whereas Lord Coke's rule requires that the woman be quick with child, which, as this court has decided, means more than pregnant, and requires that the child shall have reached some degree of quasi independent life at the moment of the act. . . . For the same reason, this limitation of criminal liability is equally inconsistent with any argument drawn from the rule as to devisees . . . which is laid down without any such limitations . . . .[24]

Justice Holmes then went on to deny recovery in all such cases of prenatal injuries, thereby reaching a result inconsistent with both the quickening criterion of the common law as applied to the criminal matters of murder, abortion and reprieve, and the conception criterion of the common law as to civil matters.

From 1884 to 1946, all American decisions followed Holmes, including a New York Court of Appeals decision in 1921.[25] However, since 1946, the trend has been in the other direction. In 1951, the New York Court of Appeals, in *Woods v. Lancet,* joined this movement and overruled its prior decision by establishing the criterion of viability—that time when the child, if delivered, can survive to adulthood apart from its mother.[26]

---

23 Dietrich v. Inhabitants of Northampton, 138 Mass. 14, 15 (1884).

24 Id. at 16.

25 Drobner v. Peters, 232 N.Y. 220, 133 N.E. 567 (1921).

26 Woods v. Lancet, 303 N.Y. 349, 356-57, 102 N.E.2d 691, 694-95 (1951):
    The other objection to recovery here is the purely theoretical one that a foetus "in utero" has no existence of its own separate from that of its mother, that is, that it is not "a being in esse." We do not deal here with so large a subject. It is to be remembered that we are passing on the sufficiency of a complaint which alleges that this injury occurred during the ninth month of the mother's pregnancy, in other words, to a viable foetus, later born. Therefore, we confine our holding in this case to prepartum injuries to such viable children. Of course such a child, still in the womb is, in one sense, a part of its mother, but no one seems to claim that the mother, in her own name and for herself, could get damages for the injuries to her infant. To hold, as matter of law, that no viable

While the *Woods* decision is the latest pronouncement by New York's highest court, in 1953, a lower New York appellate court allowed recovery to a child born alive for prenatal injuries inflicted during the third month of gestation, long before both quickening and viability. It is noteworthy that these two events are entirely distinct in time and can be separated by as much as twelve weeks. A passage in the opinion of the lower court seems to have confused the two,[27] possibly having been misled by a curiously worded passage in the 1884 opinion of Justice Holmes, who, never having had the personal experience of fatherhood, may have had the two ideas confused in his mind.[28] However, the Appellate Division was on firm ground in pointing out that, in other areas of noncriminal law, "no distinction between viability [and] non-viability was . . . drawn in determining the point of vestiture of a legal right. Conception and vestiture [coincided]. . . ."[29] At common law, of course, there were only the three criteria: conception, quickening, and birth alive. Viability was never mentioned by common-law judges or treatise writers. Since viability almost invariably occurs later than quickening, the Court of Appeals, in *Woods v. Lancet*, may have used it a fortiori.

Whether the courts ultimately decide to use a conception criterion, thereby assimilating prenatal injury cases to other civil matters, or a quickening criterion, thereby assimilating them to criminal matters, or a viability criterion, thus treating them as *sui generis*, is really of little

---

foetus has any separate existence which the law will recognize is for the law to deny a simple and easily demonstrable fact. This child, when injured, was in fact, alive and capable of being delivered and of remaining alive, separate from its mother.

[27] Kelly v. Gregory, 282 App. Div. 542, 543, 125 N.Y.S.2d 696, 697 (3d Dep't 1953): "[T]he point at which the foetus becomes viable has been of usefulness in drawing some legal distinctions . . . ." One wonders just what legal distinctions (apart from post-1946 prenatal injuries cases) Mr. Justice Bergan had in mind. Probably, as stated in the text, he was thinking of quickening, not viability.

[28] Dietrich v. Inhabitants of Northampton, supra note 23, at 16:
[L]ord Coke's rule requires that the woman be quick with child, which, as this court has decided, means more than pregnant, and requires that the child shall have reached some degree of quasi independent life at the moment of the act.

Probably Holmes meant no more by "quasi independent life" than that the foetus was stirring and the mother could feel it stir, in other words, quickening, which is of course what Coke had meant and had said. Holmes's language is however, strongly suggestive of the medical notion of viability (which he could have picked up from his physician father). Viability normally occurs at 28 weeks, but there is a single recorded case in medical history of a premature infant with a foetal life of only 20 weeks who survived and lived into adulthood. Quickening usually occurs between the 16th and the 18th week. A nonfather is unlikely to keep these two concepts firmly distinguished in his mind. Even if Holmes himself was perfectly clear about the distinction, this language of his blurred it for others. Many of the decisions in the post-1946 line of prenatal injuries cases seem to have read Holmes's language as referring to viability, when in fact he was talking about quickening.

[29] Supra note 27, at 545, 125 N.Y.S.2d at 696, 698.

importance in settling the metaphysical question of how early in pregnancy the foetus is a "man" or a "person," for neither in the prenatal injury cases, nor in any other civil case, has recovery been allowed where a foetus was stillborn.[30] Only plaintiffs already born alive have thus far succeeded in New York.

The best recent exposition of the law on this subject is found in the unaminous opinion of the Court of Appeals in the 1959 case of *Matter of Peabody*.[31] In that case, a woman had created a trust, with various named beneficiaries, but after doing so changed her mind, and desired to revoke it. In such a case, section twenty-three of the Personal Property Law required that every "person beneficially interested" consent to such revocation.[32] The woman who had created the trust eventually succeeded in obtaining the consent of all the beneficiaries who had been born alive. By that time, however, she was herself eight months pregnant, and the Chase bank, as trustee, raised the question as to whether the near-term foetus, who, if born, would, as the settlor's issue, under the terms of the trust indenture, clearly have been a "person beneficially interested," was already a *person* whose consent would, therefore, be necessary. The Supreme Court, the Appellate Division, and the Court of Appeals, all held unanimously that this foetus was not such a "person." The unsuccessful appellant was the guardian ad litem appointed to protect the infant's interests after birth. Judge Fuld, speaking for the court, refused to apply the analogy of a child conceived prior to the death of his father, but born posthumously, who is allowed to take through the father. Recognizing that the fiction deeming the unborn child a living person was a result of the policy of the common law to supply an heir to every feudal estate, the court held this fiction no longer necessary in consequence of a statutory provision protecting the posthumous child's interest. Likewise, the court refused to draw an analogy from the cases permitting recovery from prenatal injuries:

---

[30] The New York courts are firmly in the camp of those which deny wrongful death recovery for the intrauterine death of a stillborn foetus. See Matter of Peabody, 5 N.Y.2d 541, 158 N.E.2d 841, 186 N.Y.S.2d 265 (1959); Endresz v. Friedberg, 52 Misc. 2d 693, 276 N.Y.S.2d 469 (Sup. Ct., Onondaga Cty 1966); Matter of Bradley, 50 Misc. 2d 72, 269 N.Y.S.2d 657 (Sur. Ct., Nassau Cty 1966); Matter of Irizarry, 21 Misc. 2d 1099, 198 N.Y.S.2d 673 (Sur. Ct., N.Y. Cty 1960); Matter of Logan, 4 Misc. 2d 283, 156 N.Y.S.2d 49 (Sur. Ct., N.Y. Cty), aff'd mem., 2 App. Div. 2d 842, 156 N.Y.S.2d 152 (1st Dep't 1956); Matter of Scanelli, 208 Misc. 804, 142 N.Y.S.2d 411 (Sur. Ct., Nassau Cty 1955). The courts in other states are divided on this question; see Annot., 15 A.L.R. 3d 992 (1967).

[31] Matter of Peabody, supra note 30.

[32] N.Y. Per. Prop. Law § 23 has been repealed and its subject matter is now covered by N.Y. E.P.T.L. § 7-1.9 (McKinney 1967) which provides that "upon the written consent . . . of all persons beneficially interested in a trust of property . . . the creator of such trust may revoke . . . ."

Nor do the cases which permit a child to recover for injuries negligently or intentionally inflicted upon it before birth (see Woods v. Lancet. 303 N.Y. 349 (1951)), assist the appellant. Reflecting a rule of equity requiring a wrongdoer to compensate a child for the damages which he caused, those decisions do not justify the conclusion that a foetus is a "person" before its birth. On the contrary, this court held just the opposite when it refused to allow the "parent" of a stillborn child to sue for its wrongful death. (See Matter of Logan, 3 N.Y.2d 800 (1957)). In short, just as in the cases involving succession to property, a child *en ventre sa mere* is not regarded as a person until it sees the light of day.[33]

Before leaving our comparison of the common law quickening criterion in criminal matters with the common law conception criterion in civil matters, we should emphasize the further point that the common law superimposed a birth-alive criterion on both the former criteria. Thus, the common law of crimes held that if a quickened foetus were aborted, and survived the expulsion, though only for a moment, the abortionist was guilty of murder, whereas if the quickened foetus had been killed within the womb the offense was only a misprision or misdemeanor. In regard to non-criminal matters, as we have seen, the common law required the foetus to be born alive in order to derive any benefit.

Thus the interlacing of these three criteria—conception, quickening, and birth alive—in the criminal and civil domains of the common law, forms a coherent and well articulated pattern, the whole of which must be understood before one can properly evaluate any part of it.

Quickening Applied in the United States

In England, Coke's statement was never challenged. No law officer of the Crown ever brought criminal proceedings, at common law, against anyone for aborting a willing woman before quickening. In the United States, it was otherwise. The courts of seven states were compelled to decide this question under the common law, unmodified by any statute.

The courts of five states, Massachusetts, New Jersey, Iowa, Alabama and Kentucky, followed Coke and held that no one could be indicted for aborting a willing woman before quickening.[34] Two states,

---

[33] Matter of Peabody, supra note 30, at 547, 158 N.E.2d at 844, 186 N.Y.S.2d at 270.

[34] Smith v. Gaffard, 31 Ala. 45, 51 (1857) (slander of unmarried female plaintiff that she had aborted herself, without specifying whether before or after quickening: demurrer sustained; in Alabama, common law still applied to the pregnant woman herself.

Pennsylvania and North Carolina, held contra, but admitted that the weight of authority was against them.[35] In dicta, courts of eleven other jurisdictions aligned themselves with Coke as to what had been their pre-statutory common law.[36]

"At common law, the production of a miscarriage was a punishable offense, provided the mother was at the time 'quick with child' "); Commonwealth v. Parker, 50 Mass. (9 Met.) 263, 265-66 (1845) ("at common law, no indictment will lie, for attempts to procure abortion with the consent of the mother, until she is quick with child"); Commonwealth v. Bangs, 9 Mass. 387, 388 (1812) ("if an abortion had been alleged and proved to have ensued, the averment that the woman was quick with child at the time is a necessary part of the indictment"); In re Vince, 2 N.J. 443, 449-50, 67 A.2d 141, 143-44 (1949) (woman aborted when ten weeks pregnant, i.e., when "the child had not yet quickened," was asked before a grand jury to identify the abortionists: she refused on the basis of the New Jersey statute against self-incrimination. New Jersey's Supreme Court held that she must answer, because the New Jersey abortion statute does not cover the pregnant woman herself, but only the abortionist; consequently, she is still subject to the common law. "The common law crime of abortion is not committed unless the mother be quick with child"; here, quickening had not yet occurred); State v. Cooper, 22 N.J.L. 52, 58 (Sup. Ct. 1849) ("the procuring of an abortion by the mother, or by another with her assent, unless the mother be quick with child, is not an indictable offense at the common law"). Abrams v. Foshee, 3 Iowa 274, 278 (1856) ("And certainly, independent of statute, it [abortion] is not a punishable offence, when the child is not quick in the womb"); Mitchell v. Commonwealth, 78 Ky. 204, 210 (1879) ("it never was a punishable offense at common law to produce, with the consent of the mother, an abortion prior to the time when the mother became quick with child").

35 State v. Slagle, 83 N.C. 630 (1880); Mills v. Commonwealth, 13 Pa. 631 (1850).

36 Hunter v. Wheate, 53 App. D.C. 206, 209 (D.C. Cir. 1923) ("it never was an indictable offense at common law to commit abortion before the woman had become quick with child"); Eggart v. Florida, 40 Fla. 527, 532, 25 So. 144, 146 (1898) ("it is argued that at the common law it was no crime to procure the miscarriage of a woman with her consent, unless she was in that advanced state of pregnancy technically known as being 'quick with child.' Such undoubtedly was the common law"); State v. Alcorn, 7 Idaho 599, 606, 64 P. 1014, 1016 (1901) ("At the common law an abortion could not be committed prior to the quickening of the foetus"); Smith v. State, 33 Me. 48, 55 (1851):

> At common law, it was no offense to perform an operation upon a pregnant woman by her consent, for the purpose of procuring an abortion, and thereby succeed in the intention, unless the woman was "quick with child." . . . If, before the mother had become sensible of its motion in the womb, it was not a crime. . . .

Lamb v. Maryland, 67 Md. 524, 533, 10 A. 298, 300 (1887):

> But as the life of an infant was not supposed to begin until it stirred in the mother's womb, it was not regarded as a criminal offence to commit an abortion in the early stages of pregnancy [at common law]. . . .

Edwards v. State, 79 Neb. 251, 252, 112 N.W. 611, 612 (1907) ("At common law . . . a person could not be guilty of abortion unless the pregnant woman was quick with child."); State v. Tippie, 89 Ohio St. 35, 39 (1913):

> [homicide]: [T]he statute does not now require, as formerly and at common law, that the drug shall have been administered to a woman . . . "pregnant with a quick child" . . . .

State v. Ousplund, 86 Ore. 121, 131 (1917) (abortional manslaughter), rehearing denied, 87 Ore. 649 (1918), writ of error dismissed by stipulation, 251 U.S. 563 (1919) ("at common law the procuring of a miscarriage before quickening of the foetus is not punishable"); Gray v. State, 77 Tex. Crim. 221, 224 (1915) ("at common law an abortion could not be performed upon a woman, unless and until the child was 'quick' within her

Thus, the common law rule was settled that no indictment would lie for aborting a consenting woman before quickening, but would lie for such an act after quickening. This rule applied to everyone other than the woman herself. Did it also apply to her if she submitted to an abortion at the hands of another, or if she performed an abortion upon herself?

It is undisputed that the woman herself was not indictable for submitting to abortion, or for aborting herself, before quickening. What, then, was the position if she did so after quickening? There are no decisions directly in point, but dicta exist in four states and they are equally divided.[37]

The Role of the Husband at the Common Law

What was the rule at the common law if the woman desiring the abortion was married? Did her consent alone suffice to make the act noncriminal, or was her spouse's consent necessary as well?

The author has found no decision or dictum that specifically speaks to this question. Only a few of the reported cases make mention

---

womb"); State v. Dickinson, 41 Wis. 299, 309 (1877) ("[T]he procuring or attempting to procure a miscarriage or abortion was not an offense at common law, if the pregnant woman was not quick with child and consented to the act."). Miller v. Bennett, 190 Va. 162, 169, 56 S.E.2d 217, 221 (1949) ("It was not an indictable offense at common law to procure an abortion before the woman had become quick with child.").

[37] Smith v. State, supra note 36, at 55:

> [T]he acts may be those of the mother herself and they are criminal only as they are intended to affect injuriously, and do so affect the unborn child. If before the mother had become sensible of its motion in the womb, it was not a crime; if afterwards, when it was considered by the common law, that the child had a separate and independent existence, it was held highly criminal . . . .

In re Vince, supra note 34, at 450, 67 A.2d at 144:

> The statute and construction thereof make it plain that [it does not apply to the pregnant woman, and that the common law, which does, provides that] a woman who performs an abortion upon herself or consents to its performance upon her by others is chargeable criminally only if the child were quick, a factor lacking in the instant case.

Contra, State v. Carey, 76 Conn. 342, 351 (1904) ("At common law an operation on the body of a woman quick with child, with intent thereby to cause her miscarriage, was an indictable offense, but it was not an offense in her to so treat her own body, or to assent to such treatment from another"); In re Vickers, 371 Mich. 114, 118 (1963) ("At common law she was not guilty of a crime even though she performed the aborting act upon herself or assented thereto"). It is to be noted that the Michigan dictum does not use the expression "quick with child" and that the Connecticut court's use of that expression may have been inaccurate, and really have intended no more than "with child." If these conjectures are justified, then the support of these dicta for the noncriminality of the self-aborter or the assenter-to-abortion after quickening disappears: hence the adverb "apparently" in the text.

The American Law Institute has expressed the opinion that "[a]t common law it was a misdemeanor for the mother to destroy her fetus after quickening." Model Penal Code, Comment on § 207.11, at 158 (Tent. Draft. No. 9, 1959).

of the abortee's marital status. Of those that do, after one eliminates those that describe her as single, widowed, or divorced, there remain only three in which she is described as married.[38] The most meaningful thing that can be said of these cases is that there is no mention of the husband's consent. In fact, in one case, it was held that a wife who had decided, after separating from her husband, and evidently without his consent or even knowledge, to submit to an abortion before quickening, had not violated the New Jersey common law (which still applies to the woman herself).[39]

The silence of these three courts, in decisions that span nearly a century, leaves one with the strong impression that the common law of abortion was a stranger to any requirement of consent on the part of the abortee's husband, an impression that is strengthened when one considers the absence of such a requirement from the provisions for legal abortion either in the "old" abortion statutes (those enacted between 1803 and 1966) or in the "new" (those enacted in Mississippi in 1966, in Colorado, North Carolina, California, and the United Kingdom in 1967, and in Georgia and Maryland in 1968). Of the seven new abortion statutes, only two, Colorado's and North Carolina's, mention husband's consent at all. Colorado only requires such where the woman is under eighteen.[40] North Carolina requires consent where she is under twenty-one or incompetent.[41] The others ignore the husband in all instances.

Since the "old" abortion statutes make abortion legal in most

---

[38] Abrams v. Foshee, supra note 34; Commonwealth v. Parker, supra note 34; In re Vince, supra note 34.

[39] In re Vince, supra note 34; cf. Statement of Facts in Brief for Lillian Del Gobbo Vince at 1 (petitioner "had been compelled to separate from her husband [and] was then pregnant with his child"). If, at common law, a husband's consent to an abortion before quickening of a foetus begotten by him were a necessary element to make such an act noncriminal, then failure to obtain such consent would have placed Mrs. Vince in jeopardy of self-incrimination upon her being compelled to identify the abortionists; yet neither counsel nor court adverted to any such possible requirement, nonfulfillment of which would have entitled Mrs. Vince to remain silent.

[40] Colo. Laws ch. 190, § 1 (1967) adding Colo. Rev. Stat. § 40-2-50(4) (a) I (Cum. Supp. 1967) requires:

> [T]he request of said woman or if said woman is under the age of 18 years, then . . . the request of said woman and her then living parent or guardian, or if the woman is married and living with her husband . . . the request of said woman and her husband.

[41] N.C. Laws ch. 367, § 2 (1967) adding N.C. Gen. Stat. 14-45.1 (Cum. Supp. 1967), unnumbered paragraph 5, which provides that a justifiable abortion may be performed:

> [O]nly after the said woman has given her written consent for said abortion to be performed, and if the said woman shall be a minor or incompetent as adjudicated by any court of competent jurisdiction then only after permission is given in writing by the parents, or, if married, her husband, guardian or person or persons standing in loco parentis to said minor or incompetent.

states only to save the woman's life, and in a few, to preserve her health, and the "new" statutes add a variety of causes, they all, to the extent that they do legalize abortion before quickening, merely preserve or restore the common law freedom to abort, once enjoyed by all women. If the common law had required the husband's consent, it is reasonable to assume that these many statutes would have preserved and codified such a requirement. Once more, the *argumentum ex silentio* is deafening.

There is no reported case of a husband's having brought suit to prevent an abortion justified under any one of the "old" statutes. The author has found only one such action brought under the "new" statutes, in which suit was brought to enjoin the operation claiming that the new California statute was unconstitutional since it deprived the father, without due process, of the right to have his child born.[42] After losing in both the Superior Court of Santa Clara County and the California Court of Appeal for the First District, plaintiff appealed to the California Supreme Court, which affirmed the denial in a one word decision.[43]

The California case, of course, is a civil decision, but if the California statute had required a husband's consent, so that an operation without it would have been illegal, the three California courts would clearly have granted the civil relief sought.

Damage suits by husbands against abortionists, where the wife had consented to the abortion but the husband had not, are rare. There are only two such reported cases in New York; both were brought against physicians.

In the earlier case, *Philippi v. Wolff*,[44] plaintiff's wife had died in consequence of an abortion performed upon her in 1869. Her death was not, however, instantaneous; she survived the abortifacient act for six days. Defendant demurred on the ground that the common law did not give the husband a cause of action in such a case. At general term, the Supreme Court, New York County, overruled the demurrer. While the common law allowed a husband no cause of action if the wife's death was instantaneous, it was held to create in him a cause of action for the loss of her society and services during any

---

[42] Letter from the Hon. George H. Barnett, Presiding Judge, Superior Court for the County of Santa Clara, San Jose, Calif., to Mrs. Sylvia Bloom, Administrative Assistant, Association for the Study of Abortion, Inc., Dec. 22, 1967.

[43] O'Beirne v. Superior Court, 1 Civ. 25174 (Sup. Ct. of Cal., Dec. 6, 1967); Los Angeles Herald-Examiner, Dec. 7, 1967, at B-4, col. 1; Los Angeles Herald-Examiner, Dec. 8, 1967, at A-20, cols. 1-3.

[44] Philippi v. Wolff, 14 Abb. Pr. (n.s.) 196 (Sup. Ct., N.Y. Cty 1873).

period, however brief, during which she survived the tortious, death-causing act.

The complaint alleged that the defendant "unlawfully procured an abortion on plaintiff's said wife and treated [her] in so negligent and unskilful a manner as a Physician that he caused her death."[45] The principal contention urged in support of the demurrer was that plaintiff's wife's consent to the abortion would have barred a suit by her: therefore her husband's suit was also barred. The court did not question that an effective consent by the wife would have barred a suit both by her and by her husband, but ruled:

> The consent of the wife to the treatment was not a consent to be ignorantly or negligently treated, nor would it deprive the husband of his claim for damages occasioned thereby.[46]

The later case, *Herko v. Uviller*,[47] was decided in 1952 at a special term of the Supreme Court, Kings County [Brooklyn]. This time plaintiff's wife had neither been killed nor injured by the operation, which had been performed by a licensed physician—either her uncle (defendant) or another (unknown to plaintiff) to whom he had referred her. The Herkos had been married and had had a son in 1948.[48] The complaint alleged that in May or June of 1950 they were still living together as man and wife, and Mrs. Herko was again pregnant. She consulted her physician-uncle (defendant) about an abortion. Before it was performed, Mr. Herko learned of his wife's intention, whereupon he "instructed both his wife and the defendant that he was unalterably opposed to any abortion," notwithstanding which declaration defendant "contrary to law and in opposition to the direct wishes of the plaintiff herein, performed, or caused to be performed, an abortion on the plaintiff's wife," which was an "illegal tortious act."[49]

Mr. Justice Keogh held that "[t]he charge that defendant's acts were illegal and tortious is merely conclusory and unsupported by any

---

[45] Philippi v. Wolff, papers filed Nov. 20, 1872, No. P-1 (Sup. Ct., N.Y. Cty) (complaint sworn to October 5, 1869, folios 12-13).

[46] Supra note 44, at 199.

[47] Herko v. Uviller, 203 Misc. 108, 114 N.Y.S.2d 618 (Sup. Ct., Kings Cty 1952).

[48] A separation suit, Herko v. Herko, complaint filed Oct. 18, 1951, No. 15,572 (Sup. Ct., Kings Cty). This being a matrimonial cause, the papers were not available for inspection by the author, but he was informed by an assistant county clerk for Kings County, who did examine them, that the papers on file disclosed that the parties had been married on January 1, 1948, in New York City and that the only issue of the marriage was Michael J. Herko, born October 4, 1948. This separation suit was filed over a year after the abortion alleged in the tort suit.

[49] Herko v. Uviller, supra note 47, complaint filed Apr. 30, 1952, No. 7048.

facts."[50] He thus treated the case as one of a presumably legal abortion. Turning then to the question whether Mrs. Herko's consent barred not only any suit by her but the present suit by her husband, Justice Keogh held that her consent barred them both. *Herko v. Uviller* thus squarely holds that, where husband and wife are living together, hers is the only consent required for a legal abortion. If the spouses are living apart, the same result should be reached a fortiori, but there is no decision on this specific case.

Philippi v. Wolff thus establishes the proposition that an illegal operation, negligently performed, gives rise to an action based on malpractice either by the wife or the husband; neither will be barred by the wife's consent. One is entitled to assume that the same would be true of a legal abortion if negligently performed. *Herko v. Uviller* holds that a legal operation, carefully performed, gives rise to no action by either wife or husband; her consent will bar them both. What about an illegal operation, carefully performed? There is no case on this question in New York where the husband was plaintiff, but, in a case decided on similar principles, in which the parents of a female patient in a State mental institution, who had been aborted by the staff physicians, without the parents' consent, were plaintiffs, the Appellate Division stated, by way of dictum, "that consent will foreclose recovery even if the act be criminal,"[51] the consent alluded to being that which

---

[50] Supra note 47. In Mr. Herko's complaint, he alleged that the operation deprived him of "further offspring." Just what he meant by this allegation is unclear. As the couple already had one child, he may have meant by this expression only the foetus which was killed in the abortion upon which he based his cause of action. Counsel for defendant, however, in their memorandum of law, cited a line of New York cases (Butler v. Manhattan Ry., 143 N.Y. 417, 420, 38 N.E. 454, 454-55 [1894]; Devine v. Brooklyn Heights R.R., 131 App. Div. 142, 115 N.Y.S. 263 [2d Dep't 1909], rev'd, 198 N.Y. 630, 92 N.E. 1083 [1910]; Lennox v. Interurban St. Ry., 104 App. Div. 110, 93 N.Y.S. 230 [2d Dep't 1905]; Witrack v. Nassau Elec. R. R., 52 App. Div. 234, 65 N.Y.S. 257 [2d Dep't 1900]) which held that where a negligent tortfeasor causes a pregnant woman to miscarry, and she loses not only that foetus but, through the injury, becomes incapable of bringing to term foetūs subsequently conceived, no recovery, either by the husband or by the wife, is permitted for such loss of future offspring, since permitting juries to fix damages in such cases would be too speculative. Probably all that counsel for defendant intended by citing these cases was to show that even if the operation had rendered Mrs. Herko incapable of bringing future foetūs to term plaintiff could not recover. The likelihood that such foetūs would ever be begotten was slight, since by the time the tort suit was brought (1952), the parties had already separated (1951). In any case, the citation of this line of cases is the only note in the case which, by any interpretation, could be thought to imply, even hypothetically, that negligence or malpractice had been present at the 1950 abortion of Mrs. Herko. From the opinion, it is clear that the court treated the case as not raising any issue of malpractice or negligence.

[51] McCandless v. New York, 3 App. Div. 2d 600, 605, 162 N.Y.S. 570, 574 (3d Dep't 1957), aff'd mem., 4 N.Y.2d 797, 149 N.E.2d 530, 173 N.Y.S.2d 30 (1958). The contrary was held in Touriel v. Benveniste, Civil No. 766,790 (Super. Ct., Los Angeles

should have been obtained from the parents, the abortee herself having been mentally incapable of giving it. One is justified in concluding, therefore, that a case such as *Herko v. Uviller* would be decided the same way today, even if the abortion were illegal.

The author has been informed that in those hospitals in the State of New York which have established therapeutic abortion committees, it is the common practice of such committees to require, in every case where the applicant is known to be a married woman, that the written consent of her husband be obtained, before they will approve performance of an abortion, even if he is not living with her, and even if he is not the father of the foetus! *Herko v. Uviller* illustrates how unjustified such a requirement is in every case. But the fact that it was decided only by a court of first instance has doubtless led counsel for hospitals and their malpractice insurers to insist, *ex maiore cautela*, that the husband's consent be obtained in every instance. It would doubtless require an affirmation by the Court of Appeals that *Herko v. Uviller* is indeed the law, or a legislative enactment to that effect, to dispel the anxiety of counsel underlying this practice.

Since, in New York, a married abortee's consent to an abortion, certainly to a legal abortion and probably to an illegal one also, bars a civil suit by her nonconsenting husband (in the absence of negligence amounting to malpractice), it seems virtually certain that a husband's consent has never been prerequisite to the legality, as a matter of criminal law, of an otherwise legal abortion in this State.

At this point it is worth noting that the proposed Dominick-Blumenthal bill requires the consent of the husband,[52] but also provides that if his refusal is arbitrary, capricious or unreasonable, the court may dispense with such consent.[53] Presumably, this enables

---

Cty, Oct. 20, 1961), noted in Recent Developments, 14 Stan. L. Rev. 901 (1962) and Recent Cases, 110 U. Pa. L. Rev. 908 (1962). Doctors Touriel and Benveniste were both physicians and had been personal friends. Plaintiff did not learn of his wife's abortion until after the fact, nor of defendant's identity as the abortionist until long afterwards. The abortion was illegal. The court held that the husband had a cause of action, notwithstanding his wife's consent. This decision has been characterized as creating, in California, a new species of tort.

Larocque v. Conheim, 42 Misc. 613, 616-17, 87 N.Y.S. 625, 626-27 (Sup. Ct., Oneida Cty 1904), supports the McCandless dictum. Mr. Larocque's daughter had been seduced and impregnated by Conheim, who had induced her to undergo an illegal abortion, which had caused her death. The father sued both for the seduction and the illegal abortion. Insofar as the suit was based on the illegal abortion, the court held that the father was barred by the deceased daughter's consent. Miss Larocque's age at death was 19.

52 Dominick-Blumenthal Bill (in N.Y. Legislature), S. 529, A. 761, prefiled January 3, 1968, § 3, adding to the New York Public Health Law a new section (§ 2591), of which subsection (b)(iii) provides that where "the pregnant woman is married, the consent of her husband shall be necessary" (p. 5, lines 7-8).

53 Id., § 3, adding to the N.Y. Public Health Law a new section (§ 2593) contain-

the court to dispense with the consent of a husband who withholds consent out of spite or as a weapon in the course of marital discord. However, how can a court cope with the case of a couple, where the husband has conscientious scruples against all abortions while the wife does not? Since the Dominick-Blumenthal bill elsewhere quite properly provides a "conscience" clause enabling any doctor or hospital employee to opt out of participating in abortions,[54] a court could hardly characterize such a husband's refusal of consent as "arbitrary, capricious or unreasonable." One wonders if such a statutory scheme would survive constitutional attack as an infringement of the First Amendment. Since a state cannot constitutionally command a woman to obey her own religion, a fortiori, it cannot constitutionally compel her to obey her husband's. Furthermore, a serious question of equal protection is presented, for the statute would divide all wives into two categories: those whose husbands' consciences permitted abortion; and those whose husbands' consciences did not. Is this reasonable classification? Is it related to any legislative objective?

Such questions have never arisen before, simply because to date no legislature has ever required the husband's consent in the case of an adult, mentally competent, married woman. Neither did the common law, a remarkable fact when one remembers that, prior to the enactment, in the nineteenth century, of the Married Women's Acts, the common law could scarcely be suspected of a pro-feminist bias, at least in regard to married women.

Policy of the Common Law

The question may at this point fairly be asked: What policy did the common law reflect in the matter of abortion? Did it actually encourage abortions of consenting women before quickening? The answer is decidedly not. This is made crystal clear in the following

---

ing the language, "If the [supreme] court shall find that . . . the failure or refusal of a husband . . . to consent to the performance thereof [i.e., of a justifiable abortion], is arbitrary, capricious or unreasonable . . . the court shall authorize the performance of the abortion" (p. 7, lines 7-16).

[54] Supra note 52, § 3, adding to the N.Y. Public Health Law a new section (§ 2595), of which (b) and (c) provide: "(b) No hospital employee or member of a hospital medical staff shall be required to participate in a procedure authorized by this title who shall inform the hospital of his or her election not to participate hereunder. (c) No physician shall be required to give advice with respect to, or participate in, any procedure authorized by this title who shall inform a patient that the failure or refusal to do so is based on his or her election not to give such advice or to participate in any such procedure" (p. 8, lines 14-22).

exerpts from opinions of the Supreme Judicial Courts of Massachusetts and Maine in cases decided in 1845 and 1851:

> The use of violence upon a woman with an intent to procure
> her miscarriage, without her consent, is an assault highly
> aggravated by such wicked purpose, and would be indict-
> able at common law. So where, upon a similar attempt by
> drug or instruments, the death of the mother ensues, the
> party making such an attempt, with or without the consent
> of the woman, is guilty of the murder of the mother, *on the
> ground that it is an act done without lawful purpose,
> dangerous to life*, and that the consent of the woman can-
> not take away the imputation of malice, any more than in
> the case of a duel, where, in like manner, there is the consent
> of the parties. (Emphasis added.)[55]
>
> If medicine is given to a female to procure an abortion,
> which kills her, the party administering, will be guilty of
> her murder. . . . This is upon the ground that the party mak-
> ing such an attempt with or without the consent of the female,
> is guilty of murder, *the act being done without lawful pur-
> pose and dangerous to life, and malice will be imputed.*
> (Emphasis added.)[56]

The key phrases in these passages are "act done without lawful
purpose" and "dangerous to life." Let us consider the second phrase
first. What does it mean? Dangerous to *whose* life, the pregnant
woman's or that of the foetus?

Here we need scarcely pause to answer. The common law protected the life of the foetus from destruction at its mother's will only
after quickening. The formula we are considering, "dangerous to
life," occurs in passages which deal with abortions commited at *any
stage* of pregnancy. Clearly, then, the person whose life the common
law deemed any abortional act dangerous toward was the pregnant
woman, *not* the foetus.[57] Why were *all* abortions, even those performed

---

[55] Commonwealth v. Parker, supra note 34.

[56] Smith v. State, supra note 37, at 54-55 (1851). The earliest authority for this
proposition cited by the Supreme Judicial Court of Maine is a posthumously published
(1736) treatise by Sir Matthew Hale (1609-1676).

[57] In his well-reasoned dissenting opinion in the case of Gleitman v. Cosgrove, 49
N.J. 22, 52, 227 A.2d 689, 705 (1967), Mr. Justice Jacobs observed:
> [T]he termination of pregnancy before any quickening was . . . not . . . a
> criminal offense at common law . . . . But at that time in history [i.e., in 1849],
> all abortions were considered medically dangerous, and the design of the [New
> Jersey] statute [of 1849], according to contemporaneous judicial expressions,
> "was not to prevent the procuring of abortions, so much as to guard the health
> and life of the mother against the consequences of such attempts."

by licensed physicians in hospitals, considered medically dangerous during the nineteenth century?

It was not until 1857 that Louis Pasteur discovered that minute invisible organisms cause fermentation of liquids, nor until 1864 that he established the presence of such organisms in the atmosphere. Lord Lister saw the applicability of Pasteur's discoveries to surgery and, in 1865, revolutionized surgical practice by using carbolic acid to exclude atmospheric germs, thus inaugurating aseptic surgery.[58]

Until 1867, therefore, not only abortions, but *all* forms of surgery were inherently dangerous to the life of the patient, since surgeons did not know what caused infection or how to prevent it.

When the common law made the judgment that all abortions were dangerous to life, one wonders just how dangerous it really was. Prior to the inauguration of antiseptic surgery it is likely that the maternal death rate from abortions remained at a constant figure, declining thereafter gradually, as a result of the spread of that technique, and more recently with the aid of sulfa drugs and antibiotics, to a figure perhaps one fiftieth of what it had been before Lister.[59]

---

[58] Lister published his findings in The Lancet in 1867.

[59] No statistics for the incidence of maternal mortality due to abortion before and after Lister are available. The statement made in the text is inferential, and based on a probable parallelism between the incidences of maternal mortality due to childbirth and maternal mortality due to abortion. Statistics do exist for a significantly large universe of Europeans in respect to maternal mortality due to childbirth since 1500, in the study by S. Peller, Birth and Death among Europe's Ruling Families since 1500, in D. Glass & D. Eversley, Population in History 87-100 (1965). Peller illustrates that from 1500 to 1850 maternal mortality due to childbirth among European queens and princesses hovered around twenty per thousand, and fell to about fifteen per thousand in the second half of the nineteenth century. His figures do not go beyond 1900, but we know that the present rate of maternal mortality in advanced countries is about .2 per thousand, i.e., about one-hundredth of the royal rate from 1500 to 1850. It stands to reason that whatever the rate of maternal mortality due to abortion was before Lister, it has suffered a parallel decline since. Because we are speaking of maternal mortality due to all abortions, the overwhelming majority of which are illegal, and therefore performed under substandard conditions (in contrast to childbirths), it seems safe to assume that the present rate is still one-fiftieth of the pre-Lister rate, instead of only one-hundredth, as in the case of childbirth.

To Christopher Tietze, M.D., Associate Director, Bio-Medical Division of the Population Council, and Lecturer in Obstetrics and Gynecology, Columbia University College of Physicians and Surgeons, and my colleague on The Governor's Commission to Review New York State's Abortion Law, I am indebted for the references in this note and for the reasoning upon which it is based. The reader will understand, of course, that the unsatisfactory state of the data renders it impossible to get any closer to the truth than comparative orders of magnitude. Even these, however, show that the medical fact of life reflected in the common law's judgment, "dangerous to life," has virtually ceased to exist.

In Hatch v. Mutual Life Ins. Co., 120 Mass. 550, 551 (1876), the Supreme Judicial Court noted a finding of fact that had been made by the trial judge to the effect that

What of the phrase, "without lawful purpose"? This implies that an abortional act might be done for a lawful purpose.[60] But, what that lawful purpose would be can be detected by inversion of the phrase following, "dangerous to life." Before the late 1860's, all abortions were dangerous to life; therefore, the only purpose that could justify such a procedure was the same as that which justified any surgical procedure equally dangerous to life (*i.e.*, the preservation of the patient's life). If the danger from the abortion was outweighed by the danger of allowing the pregnancy to continue, then the operation would be *with* lawful purpose, in which case, even if the patient died, the physician would not be guilty of any offense, let alone murder.

The therapeutic exception thus was already present in the common law, not in the domain of pre-quickening abortion, for all such abortions were noncriminal, provided the patient consented, and survived, but rather in the domain of murder as imputed to the abortionist whose patient died. When Parliament and the state legislatures began making abortion before quickening an offense, the therapeutic exception was either written into such statutes by the legislators or read into them by the courts.

The common law exibited an ambivalence in the matter of abortion that underlines its native respect for the two great values of liberty and life. So fond was it of liberty, that it allowed the pregnant woman to run the risk of death on the operating table, at a time when this risk was real and substantial, if she chose to rid herself of the foetus before quickening; yet so fond was it also of life that, if she did not survive the operation or its aftermath, he who had performed it was hanged. Thus, the abortionist was, in law, made an insurer of the success of the procedure, on the penalty of his life, at a time when every abortion was a serious gamble. This being so, few physicians, at common law, could have ever performed anything but thera-

---

"the evidence offered in this case shows that not more than about one per cent of such operations [i.e., illegal abortions] result in causing the death of the woman." The report of the case on appeal does not disclose the evidence upon which the trial judge based this finding. In State v. Gedicke, 43 N.J.L. 86, 96 (Sup. Ct. 1881), the court observed that abortion "in almost every case endangers the life and health of the woman."

60 This phrase reminds one of the word "unlawfully" in § 58 of the Offences Against the Person Act, 1861, 24 & 25 Vict., ch. 100, as construed by Mr. Justice Macnaghten in his charge to the jury in The King v. Bourne, [1939] 1 K.B. 687, 691 (C.C.C. 1938):

> In my opinion the word "unlawfully" is not, in that section, a meaningless word. I think it imports the meaning expressed by the proviso in § 1, sub-§ 1, of the Infant Life (Preservation) Act, 1929 (19 & 20 Geo. V, c. 34), i.e., "Provided that no person shall be found guilty of an offence under this section unless it is proved that the act which caused the death of the child was not done in good faith for the purpose only of preserving the life of the mother."

peutic abortions. Thus, the abortion-seeking woman had two problems. Firstly, to find someone willing to perform the abortion who was as well qualified as possible; and, secondly, to survive the procedure. Today, she still has the first problem, but thanks to medical progress the second has atrophied.

It will also be noted that not a single New York case has been cited to establish what the common law was in New York during this period (1664-1829). In 1872, however, a generation after the complete replacement of the common law by statute, the Court of Appeals in New York decided *Evans v. People*,[61] which summarized, in dictum, the common law rule:

> At common law, an unsuccessful attempt to effect the destruction of an infant "quick" in its mother's womb, appears to have been treated as a misdemeanor, and an actual destruction of such infant as a high crime.[62]

While this dictum deals only with the offense after quickening, it cites and relies on the two Massachusetts cases which held that defendants had to be set free because their offenses had not been proved to have occurred after quickening. Thus, it stands to reason that, in 1872, the New York Court of Appeals would have followed the Supreme Judicial Court of Massachusetts as to what had been the common-law rule governing abortion before quickening.

Comparisons have occasionally been made between the permissiveness of the common law toward abortion early in pregnancy and the similar attitude of modern Japanese (since 1948) and Eastern European (since 1955) legislation. However, there is a subtle difference. The common law *tolerated* abortion on request *before* quickening; the modern legislation *legalizes early abortion*. An important consequence is derived from this distinction. The imputability of murder, at common law, to the abortionist whose patient died, finds no echo in the modern legislation. But, the medical fact remained that the operation was dangerous to life at the common law; whereas, in the latter half of the twentieth century, it no longer is. A simple return to our ancestral common law, though sentimentally attractive, is out of the question. The medical facts of life on which it was predicated *no longer exist*. Abortion is no longer "dangerous to life." On the other hand, we gain an insight into the treasured value which our forebears placed on personal liberty when we reflect that, though abortion was "dangerous to life," they allowed women to risk it before quickening,

---

[61] 49 N.Y. 86 (1872).
[62] Id. at 88.

without paternalistic interference from the State. They were liberals when liberalism cost something.

This permissiveness in regard to abortion before quickening is not an isolated or exceptional feature of the Mediaeval English law, which knew only two sexual offenses: rape and abortion after quickening. All others, such as incest, adultery, fornication, sodomy, etc., were exclusively cognizable in ecclesiastical courts. The most recent prosecutions of abortionists before the English ecclesiastical courts that the author has discovered, occurred in the reigns of Henry VII and Henry VIII.[63] Thereafter, the prosecution of this canonical crime seems to have fallen into desuetude, though jurisdiction remained in the courts of the Church of England until Lord Ellenborough's Act (1803).[64]

---

[63] The Venerable William Hale Hale, Archdeacon of London, A Series of Precedents and Proceedings in Criminal Causes Extending from the Year 1475 to 1640, extracted from Act-Books of Ecclesiastical Courts in the Diocese of London, Illustrative of the Discipline of the Church of England 34 (No. 128), 105 (No. 331) (London 1847) (known among Anglican canonists as "Hale's Precedents"). The texts relating to these two cases, both of which were before the Commissary of London, are as follows (my translation from the Latin):

Pag. 34, No. 128. Parish of Saint Nicholas in Masselyn.
John Russell struck Alice Wanten and by reason of the blow of the aforesaid Robert [sic], the said Alice had been delivered of a dead existing child ("puero existente mortuo"). On February 15 [1493] he appeared and denied the article, purging himself by oath. f. 58 b.
Pag. 105, No. 331. Parish of Hampton.
December 7 [1527], at the home of the Lord Commissary.
Margaret Sawnders was cited for killing with potions a little infant ("infantulum") in the womb of Joan Byrde: she appeared and the Lord Commissary put her and Joan Byrde under oath faithfully to answer the articles to be charged against them by him, and Joan Byrde denied the article charged. f. 102 b.
In both these cases the foetus destroyed seems to have been past quickening, from the language used.

[64] Abortion: An Ethical Discussion 13-14 (Published for the Church [of England] Assembly Board for Social Responsibility, by the Church [of England] Information Office, Church House, Westminster, S.W. 1 [1965]) (a pamphlet whose collective author was a committee of Anglican canonists, moral theologians, physicians and lawyers of high standing):

It was not, in fact, until 1803 that the procuring of an abortion became a statutory crime at all. This does not mean, however, that before that date the act was not unlawful: the preamble to the Statute of 1803 (Lord Ellenborough's Act [43 Geo. III, c. 58]) asserted that the Act was necessary because "no adequate means have hitherto been provided for the prevention and punishment of such offences." They were "offences" before the enactment of the statute, for they had formerly been offences punishable in the ecclesiastical courts under the canon law—for the enforcement of which, however, the King's law afforded the final sanction: a lay person, excommunicate in the ecclesiastical court, and refusing for forty days to submit to penance, i.e., to the penalty of a fine, or humiliation, or whipping, could be arrested and imprisoned by the sheriff on a supplication from the bishop to the King's judges. The decline of the ecclesiastical jurisdiction over what were once extensive areas of social life left the nation without adequate sanction against these and other offences. The re-definition

While the American colonies were under the spiritual oversight of the Bishops of London, the latter never established ecclesiastical courts here; instead it was customary for Kings to include in the letters patent appointing the Royal Governors, a clause making them the surrogates of the Bishops of London for the trial of all causes of ecclesiastical jurisdiction. From 1664 to 1776, therefore, there doubtless existed, as an academic possibility, a dormant jurisdiction on

---

of them as secular crimes by means of statute was, therefore, a logical step in filling the gaps left in the power and authority of the law. But there was no doubt in the interim of the legal status of abortion: Blackstone, in the mid-eighteenth century, could echo Coke, from the early seventeenth, that abortion is "a great misprision," "a heinous offence." In English law the offence is certainly older than the first statutory definition of it.

There is another point of significance in the law's cognizance of abortion before it was defined by statute. The common law lawyers took over from the canon law the distinction between the "animate" and the "inanimate" foetus, determined at the point of "quickening." So Blackstone: "Life begins in contemplation of law as soon as an infant is able to stir in the mother's womb." So abortion is illegal "if a woman is quick with child." Coke too affirmed that, in his day, abortion before quickening was, on the Continent, less punishable than after quickening, and in England not punishable at all. The same point appears in Blackstone's interpretation of the old common law prohibition of the hanging of a pregnant woman: to be saved thus from the gallows the woman must be "quick with child—for barely with child, unless he be alive in the womb, is not sufficient."

The distinction persisted in the first two relevant statutes: in Lord Ellenborough's Act of 1803 and Lord Landsdowne's Act of 1828 (9 Geo. IV, c. 31), the offence was capital if the woman was quick with child; if not, the penalty was imprisonment, transportation or whipping. The next Act, passed in 1837 (7 Will. IV and 1 Vic., c. 85), abolished both the distinction and the death penalty; and neither has reappeared subsequently. The Offences Against the Person Act of 1861 (24 and 25 Vic., c. 100)—the Act still in force [this was written in 1965]—made the attempt to procure a miscarriage an offence, if performed by the woman herself "being with child," or by other persons whether the woman were or were not with child; the distinction between a quickened and an unquickened foetus was evidently not in contemplation. And a verdict of 1879 determined that common law abortion was punishable only after quickening, and so it would continue to be except where statute had determined the illegality from the beginning of the pregnancy—a point of significance now only in common law countries overseas, because in England there had been this statutory determination.

The foregoing precis of the history of English canon and common law in regard to abortion is admirable for its thoroughness and concision, but in spots it may mislead the unwary. Before Lord Ellenborough's Act, abortion after quickening was an offence at common law, as well as at canon law: there was therefore concurrent jurisdiction in the courts of the Church and in the King's courts to proceed against it. Abortion before quickening was not an offense at common law at all (unless the patient died). Was it an offense at canon law, in England? I do not know. One would have to know whether the ecclesiastical courts in England, either during the papal paramountcy, or since the establishment of royal supremacy, ever actually tried cases of abortion before quickening. The research in old manuscripts that would be required to answer this question can be done only in England: it would be a project worthy of the attention of the scholars of the Selden Society. Only if it were established that English ecclesiastical courts, before Lord Ellenborough's Act, actually did try cases of abortion before quickening, could I subscribe to the thesis here advanced by this Church of England Committee that, before 1803, abortion before quickening was even a canonical offense. The thesis may be true, but it has not been proved.

the part of the Governors of the Province of New York to try abortionists pursuant to the rules of the canon law, but the lack of any activity of this kind in the ecclesiastical courts in the mother country suggests that there was similar inactivity on this side of the Atlantic. In any event, even as a remote possibility, this jurisdiction ended with the British evacuation of New York City on November 25, 1783.

From that date until January 1, 1830, a period of over forty-six years, women in New York were absolutely free to have abortions before quickening without fear of prosecution from any court. During that period the common law, and only the common law, applied to the subject of abortion in New York.

II. NEW YORK STATUTORY LAW, JANUARY 1, 1830-SEPTEMBER 1, 1967

Execution and Reprieve of Pregnant Felons

The common-law rule, both as to the execution of pregnant female felons and as to abortion, remained in force until January 1, 1830, the effective date of most of the Revised Statutes of 1829. The Revisers and the Legislature of 1828 dealt with both these subjects,[65] although the two subjects were dealt with differently. Pre-statutory rules as to the execution of pregnant female felons were altered only in a minor procedural way,[66] whereas the offense of abortion was expanded to include abortions prior to quickening. Furthermore, abortion after quickening was elevated from misprision (misdemeanor) to manslaughter (a felony).

The common-law rule regarding reprieves for female convicts was not changed by the 1829 statutes; it still applied only to a female convict who was quick with child.[67] Therefore, reprieve would

---

[65] Report of the Commissioners Appointed to Revise the Statute Laws of this State made to the Legislature, Oct. 15, 1828, 6 The Original Reports of the Different Chapters Composing the Revised Statutes; As Presented to the Legislature By The Revisers, ad Part IV, ch. 1, tit. 1, § 21 (1828) [hereinafter cited as 6 Revisers' Notes (1828)] (this section was renumbered § 20 when enacted). Part IV, Chapter 1, of the Revised Statutes of 1829 is divided into several Titles, e.g., the execution of pregnant female felons is dealt with in Title 1 while abortion is dealt with in Titles 2 and 6.

[66] The statutory rules as to execution of pregnant convicts under sentence of death are contained in Revised Statutes 1829, Pt. IV, ch. 1, tit. 1, § 20-22.

[67] Id. §§ 21-22:

§ 21. If by such inquisition it appears that such female convict is quick with child, the sheriff shall in like manner suspend the execution of her sentence; and shall transmit the inquisition to the governor.

§ 22. Whenever the governor shall be satisfied that such female convict is no longer quick with child, he shall issue his warrant, appointing a day for her execution pursuant to her sentence; or he may in his discretion commute her punishment to perpetual imprisonment in the state prison.

not be granted if the female convict were no more than pregnant. The contrast between "pregnant" and "quick with child" is thus of decisive significance. With only immaterial changes, the pertinent sections of the 1829 statutes were carried forward into the Code of Criminal Procedure of 1881.[68]

In 1872, in *Evans v. People*, the New York Court of Appeals held that, before quickening, "although there may be embryo life in the foetus, there is no living child."[69] Evidently the New York Legislatures of 1828, 1881, and 1910 felt the same way; otherwise they would not have, by statute, perpetuated the common-law rule making mandatory the destruction of the unquickened foetus in the womb of the female convict through her execution. And although the New York Legislature of 1965, in enacting the Revised Penal Law, transferred the dividing line between simple abortion (now called abortion in the second degree) and manslaughter (now called abortion in the first degree) from the moment of quickening to the end of the twenty-fourth week of pregnancy, thus placing the dividing line at least six weeks farther from conception than before, and although the Legislature in 1967 passed an Act[70] amending the Code of Criminal Procedure to make it conform with the Revised Penal Law, it made no such conforming amendments to the reprieve sections, which stand

---

[68] The Laws of 1881, ch. 442, §§ 500-02 [1881] N.Y. Code Crim. Proc. included these changes. These sections were amended in 1910 to eliminate a previous requirement of attendance by the district attorney and to substitute the "warden of the state prison" for "sheriff." Laws of 1910, ch. 338, §§ 5-7. These changes undoubtedly reflected the centralization of executions in the state prison; nevertheless, the key words "pregnant" and "quick with child" were unaffected. Judge Pound's statement in Drobner v. Peters, supra note 25, at 222-23, 133 N.E. at 567 is the sole comment on these provisions by the New York courts:

> By the criminal law, such being the solicitude of the state to protect life before birth, it is a great crime to kill the child after it is able to stir in the mother's womb by any injury inflicted upon the person of the mother . . . and it may be murder if the child is born alive and dies of prenatal injuries. . . . If the mother with the intent to produce her own miscarriage, produces the death of the quick child whereof she is pregnant, she may be guilty of manslaughter. . . . If the child is not quick, it may be felony to produce a miscarriage. . . . If a female convict under sentence of death is quick with child she may not be executed. . . .

The bill which became the Act of 1910 was introduced on April 20, 1910 by Senator Bayne (S. Int. No. 973, Pr. No. 1159). On May 12, 1910, the Senate passed it, 45:0. On May 19, 1910, the Assembly passed it, 98:0. 1910 N.Y. Senate J. 819, 1475-76, 1734; 1910 N.Y. Assembly J. 3154. The Governor who signed it on May 21, 1910 was Charles Evans Hughes, a future Chief Justice of the United States. Judging by these votes, there was not a single defender of the immediate animation theory in the New York Legislature of 1910. This shows how recent an innovation in American public life the immediate animation theory is.

[69] Evans v. People, supra note 61, at 90.

[70] Code Crim. Proc. §§ 69-c, -d, -e (McKinney Supp. 1968) (Law of April 27, 1967, ch. 68, § 78).

today, as they have since last amended in 1910, and as their predecessors have since 1830, with the expression "quick with child" embedded therein. In regard to the law concerning the execution of pregnant women sentenced to death, therefore, there has been no substantive change in the law of New York from 1664 to the present day: such women may be executed if they are merely "with child" or simply "pregnant" but not if they are "quick with child."

It would, it is submitted, be hard to come by clearer proof that whatever may be the merits of the philosophical speculation that an embryo before quickening is a "man," and that such a foetus has "a right to be born," neither the Legislature of 1828, nor those of 1881, 1910, and 1967, have concurred therewith. The sovereign State of New York does not authorize the slaughter of an innocent *child* after birth because of its mother's crime, and it likewise spares the quickened foetus before birth, by reprieving its sentenced mother, but it executes both her and her foetus before the latter's quickening without hesitation, not because the unquickened foetus is not innocent, but because, not being a human person it is incapable of guilt or innocence. While the 1965 legislation has severely restricted the type of murder for which the death penalty can be imposed, it has not been abolished in New York. And so the quickening distinction remains a part of the living law of the State in this sphere.

Criminal Abortion: New York Revised Statutes of 1829

In regard to the criminal law of abortion, the Revised Statutes of 1829 defined three distinct offenses, of which the following is the first:

> § 8: The wilful killing of an unborn quick child, by any injury to the mother of such child, which would be murder if it resulted in the death of such mother, shall be deemed manslaughter in the first degree.[71]

In the text of this section, as submitted by the Revisers, before the word "mother" appeared the word "pregnant," which the legislators of 1828 struck out on the obvious ground of redundancy. The Revisers' note accompanying section 8 reads:

> The killing of an unborn quick child, by striking the mother is now only a misdemeanor. . . . see note to section 10.[72]

---

[71] Revised Statutes 1829, Pt. IV, ch. 1, tit. 2, § 8.
[72] 6 Revisers' Notes 12 (1828) to Revised Statutes 1829, Pt. IV, ch. 1, tit. 2, § 8.

This cross-reference to section 10 is important, although the Legislature declined to enact that section, because, in the Revisers' scheme, section 10 was complementary to, and therefore helpful in defining the scope of section 8. The never-enacted section 10, and the Revisers' note accompanying it, read as follows:

> § 10: The involuntary killing of an unborn quick child, by an injury to the mother pregnant with such child, shall be manslaughter in the same cases, and in the same degree, as if such mother had been killed by such injury.
>
> (Revisers' Note) A child not born, is considered as not being in *rerum natura,* and therefore not the subject of murder, so that the [sic] killing such a child is not murder or manslaughter.[73]

At this point an instructive regression may be made to the prenatal injury cases already discussed.[74] In each of those cases, injury was inflicted upon the foetus through injury to the pregnant woman, not through malice, but by negligence. That is also the factual presupposition of unenacted section 10. There is, however, a salient difference between the two. In the prenatal injury cases, the foetus is afterwards born alive, still suffering from the prenatally inflicted injury, for which, after birth, the infant brings suit. In the case presupposed by unenacted section 10, a quickened foetus is killed while still inside the womb and is thereafter stillborn.

In *Matter of Logan,*[75] as expounded by *Matter of Peabody,*[76] an attempt was made to bring a wrongful death action on behalf of a prenatally killed, stillborn foetus, but the Court of Appeals refused to allow such a proceeding on the very ground that "a child *en ventre sa mere* is not regarded as a person until it sees the light of day." The refusal by the Legislature of 1828 to enact criminal penalties for such an intrauterine killing, even where the foetus was already quick, constitutes a formidable argument (by way of analogy from the criminal law) against allowance of any such tort action.

A comparison of the texts of sections 8 and 10 discloses that section 8 presupposes no malice toward the pregnant woman (which is made clear by the Revisers' Note to section 8, which refers to abortion by blows, a technique formerly much favored by ignorant midwives),

---

[73] 6 Revisers' Notes 13 (1828) to Revised Statutes 1829, Pt. IV, ch. 1, tit. 2, § 10.

[74] Drobner v. Peters, supra note 25; Woods v. Lancet, supra note 26; Kelly v. Gregory, supra note 27.

[75] Matter of Logan, supra note 30.

[76] Matter of Peabody, supra note 30, at 547, 158 N.E.2d at 845, 186 N.Y.S.2d at 270.

whereas section 10 presupposes no malice either toward the pregnant woman or toward the quickened foetus. Commentators, however, have been misled into thinking that section 8 presupposes malice toward the pregnant woman, but not toward the quickened foetus.

Had the Legislature of 1828 enacted section 10 as well as section 8, a visual comparison of the two sections would have enabled commentators to avoid this error. Without section 10 to compare, and with no therapeutic exception in section 8 in striking contrast with the presence of such an exception in two other sections (9 and 21, presently to be considered) which define other abortion-causing offenses in which the intent is clearly to destroy the foetus, it is easy to see how commentators have been misled.

Thus, Professor B. James George, Jr., of the Law School of the University of Michigan, has found statutory provisions in seven states[77] similar to this section of the New York Revised Statutes of 1829, which, being the earliest, served as model for the others. Of these eight states he writes:

> Eight states make it a separate offense wilfully to kill an unborn quick child under circumstances in which, if the mother and not the fetus had been killed, it would have been murder. The aim of these statutes is not entirely clear from either the language or the interpreting cases, but their target is probably the person who intends to cause a pregnant woman to abort *without her consent* and who uses physical violence against her body to achieve the purpose. Conceptually these statutes accord independent personality to the fetus, for the killing of the fetus under these circumstances is called manslaughter, and the sections themselves are usually found with the other homicide sections.[78]

The Revisers' Note to section 8 did not limit the offense to cases where the blow-striker was trying to abort a woman against her will, a very uncommon case. The language of both the section and Note doubtless includes such a case, but also the more typical case of the abortion of a willing woman by striking her.[79] The key to a

---

[77] 4 Ark. Stat. Ann. § 41-2223 (1964); 22 Fla. Stat. Ann. § 782.09 (1965); 2 Kan. Stat. Ann. § 21-409 (1964); 25 Mich. Stat. Ann. § 28.554 (1954); 2A Miss. Code Ann. § 2222 (1942); 2 N.D. Century Code § 12-25-03 (1960); Okla. Stat. Ann., tit. 21, § 713 (1958).

[78] B. George, Jr., Current Abortion Laws: Proposals and Movements for Reform, in Abortion and the Law 1, 11 (D. Smith ed. 1967).

[79] For an actual precedent of such a case in the ecclesiastical court of the Diocese of London in the 15th century see Hale, *supra* note 63, at 34, No. 128 (1493) (abortion by blows).

proper understanding of this section is to be found in the words, "which would be murder if it resulted in the death of such mother." This is a clear allusion to the common-law principle, according to which an abortionist was guilty of murder if the patient died, whether she had consented or not, and whatever the stage of pregnancy at which the abortional act had been performed.

It stands to reason that section 8 is as broad as the common-law principle to which it alludes, *i.e.*, that it covers abortions of willing as well as of unwilling females. The supposed difficulty arising from the fact that section 8 contains no therapeutic exception, whereas the other two sections on abortion do, dissolves when one considers the phrasing of the exception in those other sections: "unless the same shall have been necessary to preserve the life of such mother, or shall have been advised by two physicians to be necessary for such purpose."[80] No physician in 1828 would have advised blows as an acceptable technique of therapeutic abortion.

Section 8 slept tranquilly upon the books until the revision of the criminal law that became the Penal Code of 1881. Section 190 of the Penal Code read:

> The wilful killing of an unborn quick child, by any injury committed upon the person of the mother of such child was manslaughter in the first degree.[81]

What had happened is clear. The Revisers of 1881, in looking at the language of the Revisers of 1828, "which would be murder if it resulted in the death of such mother," did not realize that this was allusive language, pointing to the common-law rule abovementioned, but thought that it was unduly restrictive and therefore they deleted it. In fact, the common-law principle alluded to was anything but restrictive.

In this same form section 190 was consolidated into the Penal Code Law of 1909 as the second unnumbered paragraph of subdivision 2 of section 1050. As Professor George observes, it was "not carried as such into the Revised Penal Law."[82] Probably, the Revisers of 1961-65 felt that their language in other sections was broad enough to embrace this offense.

The second offense of an abortional character defined in the Revised Statutes of 1829 appears in the very next section, as follows:

---

[80] This was incorporated in sections nine and twenty-one of the Revised Statutes 1829.

[81] Laws of 1881, ch. 676, § 190 [1881] N.Y. Penal Code.

[82] B. George, Jr., *supra* note 78, at 11 n.58.

> Every person who shall administer to any woman preg-
> nant with a quick child, any medicine, drug or substance
> whatever, or shall use or employ any instrument or other
> means, with intent thereby to destroy such child, unless the
> same shall have been necessary to preserve the life of such
> mother, or shall have been advised by two physicians to be
> necessary for such purpose, shall be deemed guilty of man-
> slaughter in the second degree.[83]

This section is also complementary to the preceding one but in a
different way. Whereas section 8 dealt with ignorant midwives who
battered the bellies of abortion-seeking women, and made them guilty
of manslaughter in the first degree, section 9 has in view the physician,
licensed or quack, who uses drugs, dilators, and curettes. They are
guilty of manslaughter also, but only in the second degree.

On its face, however, section 9, as enacted, is an astounding text.
It makes the actor guilty of manslaughter for an act that may not
destroy the life of any living being, mother or foetus. This obviously
was an inadvertence; less than four months after the Revised Statutes
entered into effect the Legislature of 1830 amended this section by
inserting, after the word "shall," and before the words "be deemed
guilty of manslaughter in the second degree," the qualification: "in
case the death of such child or of such mother be thereby produced."[84]

While this added language made it clear that the statutory manslaughter defined by the section was committed only if either the
mother or a quickened foetus was killed, a lacuna was left in the
statute which the new words did not fill and which resulted from an
infelicity in the original draftsmanship of the section. This section
brought under a single umbrella two completely different abortional
offenses known to the common law: (1) homicide of the pregnant
woman, which the common law made the felony of murder, if it resulted from an abortifacient act (except to save her life) performed
at *any* stage of pregnancy; and (2) foeticide *in utero*, which the
common law rated only at misprision, high crime, or misdemeanor,
if it resulted from an abortifacient act (except one done to save the
woman's life), provided such act was performed *after* quickening.
This section, by commencing with the words, "Every person who shall
administer to any woman pregnant with a quick child," imposed on
both offenses the requirement that the foetus be quick, whereas the
common law had imposed it only on the offense of foeticide *in utero*.

---

83 N.Y. Rev. Stat. (1829), Pt. IV, ch. 1, tit. 2, § 9.
84 Law of April 20, 1830, ch. 320, § 58 [1830] Laws of New York.

The section also equalized the two offenses by making them both statutory manslaughter.

The question thus arises: Suppose a pregnant woman died as the result of an abortifacient act done *before* quickening? Prior to the statute, this had been murder. What was it now? By its terms, the statute failed to cover this case; so it could be argued that, in respect of it, the common law remained in force. Such an interpretation, however, would produce the incongruous result that the death of an abortee before quickening would still be common-law murder whereas the death of an abortee after quickening would be reduced to statutory manslaughter. So bizarre a result could scarcely have been intended by the legislature. If not, however, the courts had but one alternative: to hold that this section had been intended as a complete replacement of both common-law offenses. This interpretation made the death of an abortee before quickening impune. It had ceased to be a crime. The legislature could hardly have intended this result either.

Faced with a choice between two constructions of a statute, each of which led to a result the legislature had not intended, the courts, bearing in mind that the text they were construing was a penal statute, would choose the one favorable to the accused. As we shall presently see, though there is no reported decision, there is some evidence that this is exactly what the courts in New York City did as long as this lacuna remained in the statute.

No Revisers' Note accompanies this section in the Revisers' Report, a perfectly astounding fact when one realizes that this section wrought no fewer than three significant changes in the common law, *viz.*, a characterization of both the offenses described in the section as manslaughter; a reduction from murder in the event it was the pregnant woman who was killed; and, an elevation from misdeameanor (misprision or high crime) in case it was the quickened foetus that was killed. One cannot help wondering whether there may not have been the missing qualification clause (that had to be inserted in 1830), together with a proper explanatory Revisers' Note, in the manuscript copy which the Revisers should have sent to the printer, but that the wrong manuscript was sent; so that we have been irretrievably deprived of the Revisers' comments on this section.[85]

As has been mentioned, Professor George found statutes in seven sister states modeled after section 8.[86] Of these, five have also patterned

---

[85] See note 90, *infra*, accompanying text, and the two paragraphs following.
[86] *Supra* note 77.

statutes after section 9.[87] And in the case of statutes modeled on both these sections, we must agree with Professor George that,

> [C]onceptually these statutes clearly accord independent personality to the [quickened] foetus, for the killing of the foetus under these circumstances is called manslaughter, and the sections themselves are usually found with the other homicide sections.[88]

Both §§ 8 and 9 deal only with a quickened foetus. We now pass from Title 2 to Title 6, section 21, which deals with abortion of the unquickened foetus:

> Every person who shall wilfully administer to any pregnant woman, any medicine, drug, substance or thing whatever, or shall use or employ any instrument or other means whatever, with intent thereby to procure the miscarriage of any such woman, unless the same shall have been necessary to preserve the life of such woman, or shall have been advised by two physicians to be necessary for that purpose; shall, upon conviction, be punished by imprisonment in a county jail not more than one year, or by a fine not exceeding five hundred dollars, or by both such fine and imprisonment.[89]

This section is modeled rather closely on section 9, but section 9's "pregnant with a quick child" has been replaced by "any pregnant woman." The Revisers' Note to this section reads:

> The last section is founded upon an English statute . . . but with a qualification which is deemed just and necessary. See a note on this subject, to § 9, in Title 3, of this Chapter.[90]

The English statute is, of course, Lord Ellenborough's Act, 1803. The "qualification which is deemed just and necessary" is the therapeutic exception inserted in an *abortion statute* in an English-speaking country for the first time, by the New York Revisers.

The cross-reference to "a note on this subject, to section 9, in Title 3, of this Chapter" is erroneous. None of the Revisers' Notes of any of the sections could be the object of this cross-reference. This tends to confirm the author's conjecture, ventured above, that section

---

[87] 4 Ark. Stat. Ann. § 41-2224 (1964); 22 Fla. Stat. Ann. § 782.10 (1965); 25 Mich. Stat. Ann. § 28.555 (1954); 2 N.D. Century Code 12-25-02 (1960); Okla. Stat. Ann. tit. 21, § 714 (1958).

[88] B. George, Jr., supra note 78.

[89] N.Y. Revised Statutes, Pt. IV, ch. 1, tit. 6, § 21.

[90] 6 Revisers' Notes, Pt. IV, ch. 1, tit. 6, § 24, at 74 (1828) (in enacting this section the legislature renumbered it § 21).

9 of Title 2 did have a Revisers' Note, which failed to be printed. That note would also have referred to Lord Ellenborough's Act and to the therapeutic exception. The error in the cross-reference, if this hypothesis be well founded, is a simple misprint, *i.e.*, Title 3 should be Title 2.

Lord Ellenborough's Act was the first in the common-law world to make abortion of a willing woman before quickening a crime, and also the first to elevate abortion of a quickened foetus from misprison, high crime, or misdemeanor to felony. The Illinois Revised Code of 1827 contained the second enactment making abortion, even before quickening, a crime, but the New York Revisers' Note does not betray any awareness on their part of the Illinois legislation of only a year before.[91] Neither the English nor the Illinois statutes contained, *expressis verbis*, a therapeutic exception. However, nearly all statutes enacted after New York's inauguration of the therapeutic exception as a statutory clause have followed suit. In the few cases where the legislatures neglected to do this, the courts have read such an exception into the statutes.

The therapeutic exception as embodied in sections 9 and 21 contained two alternative branches: to preserve the life of the mother, or, upon advice by two physicians, a statement that an abortion was necessary for such purpose.[92] If, therefore, the abortionist, whether a physician or not, acted without the advice of two physicians, he ran the risk of a prosecution, in the course of which, the question whether he had acted to preserve the abortee's life would be in issue. If, however, the advice of two physicians that the abortion was necessary to preserve the patient's life preceded the abortion, this advice concluded the question of necessity, and prevented any prosecution.

This therapeutic exception by the New York Revisers and Legislature of 1828 is their unique contribution to the corpus of statutory abortion law in English-speaking countries. Have we any contemporary clue as to just what they meant by it? Fortunately, we do. Even more fortunate is the fact that this piece of contemporary evidence (herein disclosed for the first time) also reveals the true reason for the Revisers' proposing, and the 1828 Legislature's passing of the abortion statutes themselves.

---

[91] Ill. Rev. Code § 46 (1827). In contrast to the English and New York statutes, the Illinois legislation prohibited only potional abortion before quickening until 1867.

[92] In N.Y. Rev. Stat. (1829), Pt. IV, ch. 1, tit. 6, § 21: the two exceptions read: . . . unless the same shall have been necessary to preserve the life of such woman, or shall have been advised by two physicians to be necessary for that purpose . . . .

The clue alluded to consists of yet another section which the Revisers proposed, but which the Legislature declined to enact. Proposed section 28 of Title 6 and the accompanying Revisers' Note read:

> Every person who shall perform any surgical operation, by which human life shall be destroyed or endangered, such as the amputation of a limb, or of the breast, trepanning, cutting for the stone, or for *hernia*, unless it appear that the same was necessary for the preservation of life, or was advised, by at least two physicians, shall be adjudged guilty of a misdemeanor.

> Revisers' Note: The rashness of many young practitioners in performing the most important surgical operations for the mere purpose of distinguishing themselves, has been a subject of much complaint, and we are advised by old and experienced surgeons, that the loss of life occasioned by the practice, is alarming. The above section furnishes the means of indemnity [impunity], by a consultation, or leaves the propriety of the operation to be determined by the testimony of competent men. This offence is not included among the mal-practices in manslaughter, because, there may be cases in which the severest punishments ought not to be inflicted. By making it a misdemeanor, and leaving the punishment discretionary, a just medium seems to be preserved.[93]

From this remarkable disquisition it becomes clear that, in 1828, it was not only by abortions, but by *"any* surgical operation" (emphasis added) of a major character that the patient's life might be, and often was, "destroyed or endangered." We now know, as these New Yorkers of 140 years ago did not, the scientific reasons for the severe danger to the patient's life of either an abortion or any other major surgical operation. The first was infection, not to be reduced until after the publication in 1867 of Lister's *Lancet* article.[94] The second was shock. The first public demonstration of the use of ether to produce insensibility to pain during a surgical operation was made on October 16, 1846, at the Massachusetts General Hospital, by dental surgeon William T. G. Morton.

Although the therapeutic exception in proposed section 28 ("was necessary for the preservation of life, or was advised, by at least two physicians") appears to be a cruder, and therefore probably an earlier, version of the more smoothly phrased therapeutic exception in sections

---

[93] 6 Revisers' Notes, Pt. IV, ch. 1, tit. 6, § 28, at 75 (1828).
[94] Supra note 58.

9 and 21 defining abortional offenses, there is no difference in meaning between the two formulations. Therefore, the second sentence of the Revisers' Note to proposed section 28 is applicable to interpret the same exception as enacted in sections 9 and 21.

The *purpose* of the exception, both in unenacted section 28 and in enacted sections 9 and 21, was to preserve for the patient, within the restricted confines of the exception, *i.e.*, for the sole purpose of preserving the patient's life, the liberty which one had enjoyed, without restriction, at common law to risk one's life in general surgery (or abortion before quickening). If one's life would be endangered if the operation were not performed, it was only reasonable to allow the patient to gamble on surviving the operation.

The content of the exception points unerringly to the purpose of the general prohibition of such surgery, whether of operations in general, as in proposed section 28, or of abortions in particular, as in enacted sections 9 and 21, *viz.*, to prevent a "loss of life occasioned by the practice" which "old and experienced surgeons" had advised the Revisers to be "alarming." Or, as the old Supreme Court of New Jersey put it in 1858, in commenting on that State's first abortion statute enacted in 1849, the purpose of that statute "was not to prevent the procuring of abortions, so much as to guard the health and life of the mother against the consequences of such attempts."[95] Until now, this observation, in *State v. Murphy*,[96] had been the sole piece of contemporary evidence as to why the legislatures enacted these statutes abridging the liberty to abort before quickening, a right which women enjoyed at common law for centuries. It remains the sole *judicial* exposition of such a statute contemporary with its enactment. Now it is joined by this long forgotten proposed section 28, and accompanying Revisers' Note as an authentic indication, from the legislative *travaux préparatoires*, of the only full-scale revision of the laws of the State of New York that has ever been accomplished, of the reasoning behind the enactment of the second oldest, and the most widely imitated, of American state abortion statutes. It is even more contemporaneous with the statute it expounds than *State v. Murphy*, which it preceded by thirty years. More importantly, sections 9 and 21 and *State v. Murphy* are in complete accord.[97] Neither has a word to say about promoting population, promoting public morals, or enshrining any new metaphysical speculation as to the beginning of the

---

[95] State v. Murphy, 27 N.J.L. 112, 114 (Sup. Ct. 1858).

[96] Id.

[97] Not only with each other but with the Revisers' rationale for the proposed but unenacted section 28.

life of a human person. With regard to the latter, both were content with the quickening criterion of the common law.

It is also interesting to note that neither abortion before quickening (section 21) nor surgical operations in general (proposed section 28) are "included among the mal-practices in manslaughter"; both are merely made misdemeanors. Abortion after quickening (section 9), on the other hand, *is* "included among the mal-practices in manslaughter."

Medicine and Constitutionality

Morton, Semmelweiss, Pasteur, Lister, and a host of others have, in the past 140 years, made abortion into one of the safest, instead of one of the most dangerous, operations. *Cessante ratione legis cessat et ipsa lex* is a maxim of jurisprudence as old as Justinian in the Roman law, and as Coke in the English. As will be seen, New York Legislatures have amended and reenacted the work of the Legislature of 1828 on fourteen different occasions (1830, 1845, 1846, 1868, 1869, 1872, 1875, 1880, 1881, 1909, 1942, 1944, 1953, 1965). Thus, it is obvious that the legislature has not been conscious that the sole purpose for which this statute was originally enacted has long since vanished. Since that purpose (the protection of the patient's health and life) is the only one adverted to either in the 1828 Revisers' Notes or, as will be seen, in the 1965 Commission Staff Notes, and as these are the only indicia of legislative purpose in the entire period of 140 years, it is a matter for serious consideration whether the invocation of this recognized chief purpose of the police power of the State (citizens' health and life) and no other (*e.g.*, morals, population promotion, etc.) renders the abortion statutes today, insofar as they apply to abortion before quickening, vulnerable to constitutional attack. Women have been deprived of an ancient common-law liberty in the name of health. The deprivation was justifiable under the surgical facts of life then existing. The radical alteration in the state of surgical art in the seven score years since obviates any reasonable basis for the exercise of this particular police power, and none other has ever been invoked. *Ergo*, statutory restrictions on abortion before quickening have become, and now are, unconstitutional. It is a formidable argument.

It could be contested by a licensed surgeon performing an abortion under hospital or hospital-equivalent conditions, who would be willing to challenge the district attorney to prosecute, as Alec Bourne did, in London, in 1938. Only an abortion performed by a physician under such conditions would qualify as not dangerous to life today.

Whatever the merits of this constitutional contention, only the courts can decide them, in a proper case. Meanwhile, we must return to the statutory record in New York.

Act of 1845 and Those Which Followed

In 1845, the Legislature enacted a statute of six sections intended to deal comprehensively with abortion and related offenses.[98] Section 6 repealed sections 9 and 21 of the Revised Statutes, which were replaced, respectively, by sections 1 and 2 of the new Act. These two sections added prescribing, and advising or procuring a woman to take, any medicine, drug or substance whatever, to administering such medicine, drug or substance, in defining their respective offenses. There were, however, two major oversights. The draftsmen of section 1 (manslaughter of quick child) apparently had before them the text of section 9 as originally enacted in the Revised Statutes. They were unaware of the 1830 corrective legislation[99] which the Legislature of 1846, therefore, had to and did imitate (thus perpetuating the lacuna where an abortee died before the foetus had quickened).[100] Secondly, the therapeutic exception was included only in section 1.

The therapeutic exception in section 1 was truncated by lopping off the second branch, "or shall have been advised by two physicians to be necessary for such purpose," and leaving only the first branch, "unless the same shall have been necessary to preserve the life of such mother." If the bill had been more carefully drafted in other respects, one might conclude that the elimination of the physicians' advice was intentional, and reflected legislative distrust of the medical profession, but, as we have seen, the 1845 act was drafted so poorly that the omission may have been merely inadvertent. Inadvertent or not, it was destined to be permanent, thereby effectively transferring the question of medical necessity from the hands of professional doctors to those of medically illiterate courts, lawyers, and juries.

The real innovation of the Act of 1845, however, came in section 3, which for the first time brought the abortee herself under the criminal sanctions of the statute.[101] This section, it must be noted,

---

98 Law of May 13, 1845, ch. 260 [1845] Laws of N.Y.

99 Law of April 20, 1830, ch. 320, § 58 [1830] Laws of N.Y.

100 Law of March 4, 1846, ch. 22, § 1 [1846] Laws of N.Y.

101 Law of May 13, 1845, ch. 260, § 3 [1845] Laws of N.Y.:

Every woman who shall solicit of any person any medicine, drug, or substance or thing whatever, and shall take the same, or shall submit to any operation, or other means whatever, with intent thereby to procure a miscarriage, shall be deemed guilty of a misdemeanor, and shall, upon conviction, be punished by imprisonment in the county jail, not less than three months nor more than one year, or by a fine not exceeding one thousand dollars, or by both such fine and imprisonment.

puts the self-aborter and the submitter, irrespective of the stage of pregnancy, in the same predicament (guilt of misdemeanor) as the common law placed such a woman if the act were done after quickening. From 1845 to 1881 this inconsistency was to remain in New York law: the woman herself was guilty of the same offense whether her act or submission occurred before or after quickening, while the abortionist's crime was much greater if committed after quickening. After 1881, the same gradation of offenses based on the quickening criterion was introduced for the woman as well.

From 1846 to 1869, a period of 23 years, the legislature passed no amendments to the abortion statutes. This was the longest period of legislative inactivity in this sphere between the passage of the earliest abortion statute in 1828 and the enactment of the Penal Code of 1881. The Sixties and the early Seventies, however, were to be marked by a spurt of sensational reports in the metropolitan press of abortional homicides, the like of which had never been seen before, nor was ever to recur. One of these cases eventually made its way to a landmark decision by the Court of Appeals in 1872. The entire series of cases led to the Acts of 1869 and 1872, each of which will be examined in due course. Meanwhile their antecedents will be traced.

The most celebrated abortionist in the history of New York, known as Madame Restell, pursued a career that spanned more than four decades (1836-1878), and was brought to a close only by her suicide, following an arrest engineered by Anthony Comstock, in the latter year. She lived and worked in a palatial mansion she had built at No. 1, East Fifty-second Street. Though she spent a fortune during her long career, her estate at death, derived solely from her earnings as an abortionist, exceeded three quarters of a million dollars.[102] Before her nemesis appeared in the shape of Comstock (who pretended

---

[102] The biographical sketch, "Mrs. Lohman's History," in N.Y. Times, Apr. 2, 1878, at 2, col. 1, states:

Madame Restell was originally Ann Trow. She was born in Paineswick, Gloucestershire, England, in 1812 . . . . [She came to New York City with her first husband, who died here.] . . . She met Charles R. Lohman, a printer . . . and married him. Soon after their marriage, in 1836, she announced herself as a physician who could cure a certain class of diseases. At this time she assumed the title of Mme. Restell, while her husband was known as "Dr." Mauriceau. . . . Man and wife made money rapidly. . . . Her husband . . . died on January 5, 1877. Early in January last [1878] Mr. Anthony Comstock, agent of the Society for the Suppression of Vice paid two visits to her house . . . .

The story of her arrest as the result of Comstock's ruse—he pretended to be the husband of a poor woman with several children who could afford no more—is told in the following issues of the N.Y. Times; she committed suicide the morning (April 1, 1878) she was to go to trial: Feb. 12, 1878, at 8, col. 1; Feb. 14, 1878, at 8, cols. 3-4; Feb. 15, 1878, at 2, col. 2; Feb. 16, 1878, at 3, col. 1; Feb. 24, 1878, at 5, col. 3; Feb. 28, 1878, at 2, col. 7; Mar. 2, 1878, at 8, col. 1; Mar. 6, 1878, at 8, col. 2; Mar. 8, 1878, at 2, col. 5; Mar. 13, 1878, at 3, cols. 4-5; Mar. 30, 1878, at 3, cols. 2-3; Apr. 2,

to be a poor father of many children who could afford no more, and begged her to sell him an abortifacient for his wife), she had been arrested only once. That case had gone to the Court of Appeals, and involved a technical question of pleading: the conformity of the indictment to the two sections of the legislation of 1845-46.[103] Between the decisions of her case (both adverse to her) in the Supreme Court and in the Court of Appeals, a bill was introduced in the Legislature of 1848, which passed the Assembly, 73:5, only five days before adjournment and died in the Senate.[104] Though the bill is no longer extant, it seems a fair guess that it was inspired by the Restell litigation: its title shows that it would have amended the Act of 1845.

The first judicial intimation that there might be difficulty in securing convictions under the more severe (felony) section 1 of the Act of 1846 came in a dictum in *Cobel v. People*,[105] decided in the Supreme Court, New York County, in 1862. Though the indictment was dismissed on a different ground, Presiding Justice Ingraham noted that the court had not examined "the question whether, under an indictment for using instruments upon a female with the intent to destroy a quick child, of which such female was pregnant [*i.e.*, in violation of section 1 of the Act of 1846], the prisoner could be convicted of a misdemeanor in using such instruments upon the same female with intent to procure a miscarriage [*i.e.*, in possible violation of section 2 of the Act of 1845]"—a form of language which, however guarded, inevitably cast doubt upon an affirmative answer to the question. It requires little imagination to perceive variance which, as Justice Ingraham's language insinuates, the court had discerned, between an indictment under section 1 (1846) and a conviction under section 2 (1845). The former called for a quick child as the intended victim; the latter did not. In section 2, the victim is *not* the not-yet-quickened foetus, since this is not yet a person; it is the pregnant woman herself. It is this switching of victims, from the quickened foetus to the pregnant woman herself, which constituted the variance.

Cobel v. People is the earlier of the only two reported cases in

---

1878, at 1, col. 7, at 2, cols. 1-2; Apr. 4, 1878, at 8, col. 3; Apr. 5, 1878, at 8, col. 4. In an editorial on Apr. 2, 1878, at 4, col. 6, the Times exclaimed:

> The death of "Mme. Restell" by her own hand is a fit ending to an odious career. The fact that such a woman should have amassed property to the value of three-quarters of a million dollars is a sufficiently conclusive proof of the magnitude of the ghastly traffic of which she was the most notorious agent.

[103] People v. Ann Lohman, alias Madam Restell, 2 Barb. 216, 450 (Sup. Ct., N.Y. Cty 1848), aff'd., Ann Lohman, alias Madame Restell v. People, 1 N.Y. 379 (1848).

[104] 1848 N.Y. Assembly J. 692, 926-27, 957, 971-72, 1177-78 (Mar. 14, 28, 29, 30, Apr. 7). The Legislature of 1848 adjourned on April 12.

[105] Cobel v. People, 5 Parker's Crim. Rpts. 348, 350 (Sup. Ct., N.Y. Cty 1862).

which a prosecution has been mounted in New York for the abortional homicide of a foetus. Since the jury found Cobel not guilty of manslaughter, but guilty only of the misdemeanor, the People must have failed to prove that the foetus had quickened.

On January 12, 1863, *The New York Times* ran a story which inaugurated its campaign for more stringent laws against abortion. The article related the tragic death of Mrs. Elizabeth Huntington at the hands of Dr. McGonegal.[106] The story went on with details of the case. The Coroner empanelled his jury in the dying woman's home, so that she could make her deathbed declaration before them. She testified that Dr. McGonegal had performed the operation with an instrument on December 29, 1862, for a fee of $8, at which time she "was about two months gone in pregnancy."

At that stage of gestation, of course, the foetus would not yet be quick. Assuming Mrs. Huntington died, could Dr. McGonegal have been indicted under section 1 of the Act of 1846? His case would have fallen within the lacuna in that statute which, as we have seen, requires the existence of a quickened foetus, whether it is foeticide or maternal homicide that the abortion causes. It should not surprise us, therefore, that there is no report of further proceedings against Dr. McGonegal. Only nine days later the *Times* ran another story. This time the patient had already died by press time.[107]

It was no doubt owing to these sensational newspaper reports that a bill was introduced in the Senate, referred, and reported by the judiciary committee favorably to passage, which would have amended (doubtless in the direction of greater stringency) the Act of 1846, but,

---

[106] N.Y. Times, Jan. 12, 1863, at 5 col. 3:

HORRIBLE CASE OF ABORTION

A woman [Mrs. Elizabeth Huntington], the Mother of Five Children, Dying from the Effects of Malpractice

Statement of the Victim

The Doctor [McGonegal] Arrested—Verdict of the [Coroner's] Jury

    Within the past few months, cases of malpractice, from which death has ensued, have become alarmingly frequent.

    It is high time that the attention of the public be directed to the scoundrels who, under pretence of giving relief, entail direct misery upon thoughtless women, and at times hurry rash mortals into an undesirable eternity.

[107] N.Y. Times, Jan. 21, 1863, at 3, col. 1:

ANOTHER CASE OF ABORTION

A Williamsburgh Physician Suspected—The Wife of a Soldier of the Seventh Regiment, New York Volunteers [Mrs. Rosa Abner], the Victim—Post-Mortem Examination Made by the Deputy Coroner

After recounting the details, the story concluded:

    It is stated that not less than ten cases of this nature—some of them of a very aggravated character—have been brought to light in this vicinity within the last three months.

having been introduced no earlier than mid-March (1863), it proceeded no further.[108]

No fewer than eight more cases of abortion, five of which had resulted in the death of the patients by press time, were reported by the *Times* in the quadrennium 1865-1869. In the five fatal cases, two pointed to a famous abortionist of the era, Dr. Henry D. Grindle of No. 6, Amity Place, but the coroner's jury found that the evidence was insufficient to hold him on both occasions.[109] In a third case, an unknown physician was the guilty party.[110] In a fourth, a midwife was arrested.[111] In the fifth, Dr. Gabriel Wolff, of whom we shall hear more, was arrested but the grand jury found no true bill against him.[112] In the three non-fatal cases, one physician was arrested for aborting a foetus of four months,[113] another physician was arrested for aborting a foetus of six months,[114] and in the third case a midwife was arrested.[115]

---

[108] 1863 N.Y. Senate J. 250, 253 (Mar. 12, 13).

[109] N.Y. Times, Sept. 28, 1865, at 5, col. 4; Sept. 29, 1865, at 8, col. 1 (victim: Miss Lucinda Sagendorf); Aug. 29, 1868, at 8, col. 4; Aug. 30, 1868, at 8, col. 1; Sept. 4, 1868, at 2, cols. 1-3; Sept. 9, 1868, at 2, cols. 2-3 (victim: Miss Susannah Lattin).

[110] N.Y. Times, May 5, 1867, at 6, col. 4 (victim: Mrs. Mary Catherine Throop).

[111] N.Y. Times, Nov. 24, 1867, at 5, col. 5 (victim: a Mrs. Morehouse; abortionist: Mrs. Jacobine Eckhardt).

[112] N.Y. Times, Mar. 19, 1869, at 8, col. 3; Mar. 24, 1869, at 11, col. 7; Mar. 25, 1869, at 2, col. 2. This account of Dr. Gabriel Wolff's case ends with the statement: "Coroner Rollins committed the accused for trial, refusing to receive bail for his appearance," which tells us, of course, that the committal was for the felony of manslaughter in the second degree under § 1 of the Act of 1846, not for the misdemeanor. defined by § 2 of the Act of 1845. The Times did not further report the proceedings, though both criminal and civil suits were brought against him. From his answer to the civil suit brought by decedent's husband, however, the author has ascertained "That thereafter such proceedings were had that the Grand Jury duly empanelled in the City of New York upon the evidence as then and there presented found that there was no evidence against this defendant." Answer of defendant Gabriel J. Wolff, sworn to November 25, 1869, ¶ Fourth, in Philippi v. Wolff, supra note 45.

At the autopsy performed on Magdalena Philippi, "it appeared that the uterus had been impregnated, and the woman delivered of a child [i.e., a foetus] from four to five months old." N.Y. Times, Mar. 19, 1869, at 8, col. 3. As Mrs. Philippi was no longer alive, she was not available to testify as to whether the foetus had quickened before the abortion had been performed. If it had not, Dr. Wolff's case fell within the lacuna in § 1 of the Act of 1846. This was probably the lack of evidence which led to the grand jury's failure to indict him.

[113] N.Y. Times, May 28, 1867, at 5, col. 4 (abortee: Mrs. Ella Dalbello; abortionist: Dr. Peter J. Harrison) (stillbirth).

[114] N.Y. Times, Aug. 26, 1867, at 8, col. 5 (abortee: Mrs. Delia Bell; abortionist: Dr. Henry S. Crosby). In this case the six-month-old foetus was ejected alive. It lived for about 30 minutes and then died. Under Coke's rule, at common law, this would have been a clear case of murder.

[115] N.Y. Times, Aug. 25, 1867, at 8, col. 1 (abortee: Mrs. Ameila Hartzog; abortionist: Mrs. Johanna Weite).

The ten abortion cases reported by the *Times* between 1863 and 1869 involved seven married and three unmarried women, a ratio that many authorities believe to be typical today.

It was toward the end of this cacophony of sensational and usually fatal abortion cases, as reported in the daily press, that the Medical Society of the State of New York met in Albany on February 5, 1867,[116] and adopted the following preamble and resolutions and transmitted them to the two houses of the State Legislature, then in session:

[Preamble]

Whereas, from the first moment of conception, there is a living creature in process of development to full maturity; and whereas, any sufficient interruption to this living process always results in the destruction of life; and whereas, the intentional arrest of this living process, eventuating in the destruction of life (being an act with intention to kill), is consequently murder; therefore,

[Resolutions]

Resolved, That this society do express their abhorrence, and deprecate, in a most emphatic manner, the growing increase of that demoralizing aid given and practice rendered in procuring criminal or unnecessary abortion.

Resolved, That this society will hail with gratitude and pleasure, the adoption of any measures or influences that will, in part or entirely, arrest this flagrant corruption of morality among women, who ought to be and unquestionably are the conservators of morals and of virtue.

Resolved, That the publication in newspapers, and by secret circulars, of ostensible remedies for female diseases, that suggest abortion, are highly detrimental to public health and morals; and that the Legislature ought, by enactment of a suitable law, to forbid such publications.

Resolved, That a copy of this preamble and resolutions be transmitted to both branches of the Legislature now in session.[117]

In the Assembly, this document was referred to the committee on public health and medical colleges and societies.

The preamble to these resolutions must be one of the most re-

---

[116] N.Y. Times, Feb. 6, 1867, at 8, cols. 1-2.

[117] The text of this preamble and these resolutions, together with the letter transmitting them (dated Albany, Feb. 27, 1867, and signed by William H. Bailey, secretary to the Medical Society of the State of New York), is printed in 1867 N.Y. Assembly J. 443-44 (Feb. 28, 1867).

markable communications ever sent by a medical society to a parliamentary body. While nobody could take exception to anything in the preamble up to the last three words, "is consequently murder," that conclusion is not only a theological, philosophical, and juridical *non sequitur* to what precedes it, but, since it states a nonmedical conclusion which pertains to three disciplines, theology, philosophy, and jurisprudence, in respect of which medical men, as such, are not and do not claim to be experts, it is surely among the most overweening exhibitions of extradisciplinary omniscience in the annals of professional bodies. It is not even good journalism. The *Times*, in its opening story in 1863, had propounded no such metaphysical anthroposis of the foetus, but had appealed directly and pragmatically to the "direct misery" and "death" inflicted by abortionists upon "thoughtless women . . . rash mortals," not upon unborn foetūs.[118]

After the doctors' *démarche*, which came too late in the 1867 session to be acted upon, there were two legislative responses, in 1868 and 1869. In 1868 a blunderbuss act[119] was passed, including a provision aimed at contraceptives, abortifacients, and the spreading of information as to "where, how, or of whom, or by what means" they might be obtained. This met the doctors' third resolution.

In 1869 the Legislature turned to the doctors' second resolution, amending the abortion statutes directly.[120] In section 4, the Act of

---

118 Supra note 106.

119 Law of Apr. 28, 1868, ch. 430, [1868] N.Y. Laws. Also, a bill was introduced by Senator Francis W. Thayer "to amend the Revised Statutes in relation to criminal abortions;" it was read twice and referred to the committee on the judiciary, where it died. 1868 N.Y. Senate J. 334 (Mar. 23, 1868). As the Acts of 1845 and 1846 had repealed two of the three sections in the Revised Statutes on abortion, one can only speculate as to what the purport of Senator Thayer's bill would have been.

120 Law of May 6, 1869, ch. 631, [1868] N.Y. Laws. The journals tell us practically nothing. The Senator who introduced the bill, on Mar. 17, 1869, was the bearer of a very distinguished name in legal history: Matthew Hale! 1869 N.Y. Senate J. 290, 345, 530-31, 564, 585, 1046 (Mar. 17, 25, Apr. 9, 12, 14, May 6, 1869); 1869 N.Y. Assembly J. 1153, 1190, 1407, 1900 (Apr. 14, 16, 22, May 5, 1869). The noncontroversial character of the measure is attested by the unanimous votes by which it was passed both in the Senate (20:0) and in the Assembly (85:0).

Section 1 of the Act of 1869 will be set out in the text. In addition, there are two other sections of interest.

Section 2 created a new offense, which for the first time made it possible to be guilty even if the woman was not actually pregnant. It reads:

> Whoever shall unlawfully supply or procure any medicine, drug, substance or thing whatever, knowing that the same is intended to be unlawfully used or employed with intent to procure the miscarriage of any woman, whether she be or be not pregnant, shall be deemed guilty of a misdemeanor, and shall upon conviction, be punished by imprisonment in the county jail not less than three months nor more than one year, or by a fine not exceeding one thousand dollars, or by both such fine and imprisonment.

1869 repealed both section 1 of the Act of 1846, and section 2 of the Act of 1845; section 1 of the 1869 Act took their place.

How the Legislature accomplished this can best be illustrated by a tricolumnar synoptic comparison:

Act of 1845, § 2	Act of 1846, § 1	Act of 1869, § 1
Every	Every	Any
person who shall administer to any	person who shall administer to any	person who shall administer to any
pregnant woman,	woman pregnant with a quick child,	woman with child,
or prescribe for any such woman, or advise or procure	or prescribe for any such woman, or advise or procure	or prescribe for any such woman, or advise or procure
any such woman	any such woman	her
to take any medicine, drug,	to take any medicine, drug, or	to take any medicine, drug,
substance or thing whatever,	substance whatever	substance or thing whatever,
	or shall use or employ any instrument or other means,	or shall use or employ any instrument or other means whatever,
with intent thereby to	with intent thereby to	with intent thereby to
procure the miscarriage of any such woman,	destroy such child,	procure the miscarriage of any such woman,
	unless the same shall have been neccessary to preserve the life of such mother,	unless the same shall have been neccessary to preserve her life,
shall, upon conviction,	shall, in case the death of such child, or of such mother be thereby produced,	shall, in case the death of such child, or of such woman be thereby produced,
be punished by imprisonment in the county jail, not less than three months nor more than one year.	be deemed guilty of manslaughter in the second degree.	be deemed guilty of manslaughter in the second degree.

A comparison of these texts brings into relief several features of importance. It should be noted that section 2 (1845), which alone ap-

This section seems aimed at druggists and at unlicensed vendors of abortifacients. The next section contains the first immunity provision to find its way into the abortion law:

§ 3. Every person offending against either of the provisions of this act, shall be a competent witness against any other person so offending, and may be compelled to appear and give evidence before any magistrate or grand jury, or in any court, in the same manner as other persons; but the testimony so given shall not be used in any prosecution or proceeding, civil or criminal, against the person so testifying.

plies to an unquickened foetus, forbids potional but not surgical abortion, whereas section 1 (1846), which applies only to a quickened foetus, prohibits both surgical and potional abortion. From 1830 to 1845, the careful draftsmanship of Spencer and Butler had prohibited both surgical and potional abortion of both an unquickened and a quickened foetus. It seems, therefore, that the Legislatures of 1845 and 1846 relegalized, or restored to noncriminal status as at common law, the surgical abortion of an unquickened foetus. Possibly this explains why the therapeutic exception was inserted only in section 1 (1846), and was omitted from section 2 (1845), although it had been in both the sections of the Revised Statutes which had been repealed and replaced by the 1845-1846 Acts. In section 1 (1846), the Legislature was thinking about surgeons, since it forbade surgical abortion in that section. Nineteenth century physicians did not prescribe potions for abortion: that was the specialty of ignorant midwives and quacks. In section 2 (1845), the Legislature had only the latter in mind, since there it forbade only potions, not surgery. The therapeutic exception was legislatively designed for the use of doctors, not of midwives and quacks.

Now we can understand more fully the meaning behind Justice Ingraham's words in *Cobel v. People,* mooting

> [T]he question whether, under an indictment for using *instruments* upon a female with the intent to destroy a quick child, of which such female was pregnant [in violation of section 1 (1846)], the prisoner could be convicted of a misdemeanor in using such *instruments* upon the same female with intent to procure a miscarriage. . . .[121] (emphasis added)

Section 2 (1845) did not forbid the use of *instruments* at all!

Can we conclude from this that the Legislatures of 1845 and 1846 intended to restore to New York women their common-law liberty to procure surgical abortions before quickening? No; for section 3 (1845), which for the first time brought the woman herself under the New York abortion statute, makes such a conclusion impossible. That section punishes a woman who solicits potions, or who "shall submit to any operation," to induce a miscarriage, whatever her stage of pregnancy. The upshot is that the Legislatures of 1845 and 1846 created an anomaly: a woman who submitted to a surgical abortion before quickening was made guilty of a new statutory misdemeanor, whereas the surgeon who performed it was guiltless of any crime, having been put

---

[121] Supra note 105.

out of the statute and back under the common law! Can so bizarre a result have been within the conscious intention of the legislators of 1845-46? It seems unlikely; yet, as Justice Ingraham intimated, this is the consequence which the words they used produced.

Now taking into view all three sections [section 2 (1845); section 1 (1846); section 1 (1869)], we note that the Act of 1869 recriminalized surgical abortion before quickening by adopting the "instrument" clause of section 1 (1846). Indeed, inspection of the three columns reveals that the 1869 Act follows the 1846 Act not only in this, but in every material respect, with two exceptions: (1) 1869's "woman with child" in meaning coincides with the all-inclusive scope of 1845's "pregnant woman," and is not restricted to 1846's "woman pregnant with a quick child;" and (2) 1869's intent, like 1845's is merely to "procure the miscarriage of any such woman," it not being necessary to show, as under 1846, intent to "destroy such [quick] child." The 1869 legislative intent, which one would gather from this comparison of texts, is simple and might be expressed as follows: abortion, whatever the means used to induce it and whatever the stage of gestation at which it is induced and whether the pregnant woman is killed or not, is to be treated and punished indiscriminately as manslaughter in the second degree.

Does this mean that the Legislature of 1869 had hearkened to the metaphysical romanticism of the Medical Society of the State of New York in its preamble of 1867, and was enacting that a foetus, even before quickening, was a "man," who could be the subject of "manslaughter"? It could be argued that this was the Legislature's design, but a more common view among contemporary lawyers was doubtless the one expressed by Algernon S. Sullivan, Assistant District Attorney for New York County, in his Brief for the People in *Evans v. People,* filed in the Court of Appeals in 1872, namely "that the statute of 1869 used the term *'manslaughter'* as . . . an *arbitrary title* for the offense defined in the statute, and to indicate the degree of punishment therefor," and not as "something more" than that.[122]

A review of the cases, both those officially reported and those mentioned only in the daily press, give us further clues as to the quite practical, non-metaphysical considerations the Legislature had in mind. So far as abortional homicide of the pregnant woman was concerned, the Legislature of 1869, by abolishing the requirement that she be "pregnant with a quick child," filled the lacuna which had existed in

---

[122] Brief for the People at 9, Evans v. People, 49 N.Y. 86 (1872). Emphasis as in the original.

the statutory enactments ever since the Revised Statutes. What if the woman was pregnant, but the foetus was not yet quick, or could not be proved to have been quick? Mrs. Huntington's foetus had clearly not been quick in 1863, for it was only two months old; consequently Dr. McGonegal could not be prosecuted for her manslaughter. Mrs. Philippi's foetus in 1869 may have been quick, as it was from four to five months old, but she was dead, and there was no way of proving it to have been quick; so Dr. Wolff could not be prosecuted for her manslaughter.[123] Yet both these ladies were dead, and, had the common law still applied, Drs. McGonegal and Wolff could have been prosecuted for their murders. Such cases, in future, would be covered, as statutory second degree manslaughter, by the Act of 1869. Turning from abortional homicide of the pregnant woman to foeticide, the Legislature of 1869, by merging the separate sections of the 1845 and 1846 statutes, and abolishing the quickening distinction, simplified the problem of proof for the prosecutor. By prohibiting surgical as well as potional abortion at all stages of gestation, the 1869 Act eliminated the possibility of the variance adumbrated in *Cobel v. People.*

---

[123] It is uncertain whether the abortional homicide case of Magdalena Philippi at the hands of Dr. Gabriel Wolff itself influenced the Legislature in its consideration of the bill that became the Act of 1869. Mrs. Philippi died in New York City on March 16, 1869. The bill was introduced in Albany the very next day by Senator Matthew Hale. But the first publication of the case, in the N.Y. Times, at least, did not occur until Mar. 19, 1869, at 8, col. 3. That story, which contained the autopsy finding that the foetus had been "from four to five months old", together with the second story (N.Y. Times, Mar. 24, 1869, at 11, col. 7) reporting the first day of the hearing before the coroner's jury, preceded—and thus could have affected—the Senate judiciary committee's report of the bill, which favored passage, but with amendments, on Mar. 25, 1869. Only on the latter date was the third and final story, including the verdict of the coroner's jury and the coroner's committal of the accused to trial, without bail, published (Mar. 25, 1869, at 2, col. 2). It must have been shortly thereafter, probably during the March 1869 Term of the Grand Jury in the Court of General Sessions, that that body found that there was insufficient evidence to warrant an indictment of Dr. Wolff. The subsequent steps in the bill's course through the Senate (April 9, 12, 14, 1869) and the Assembly (April 14, 16, 22, May 5, 1869), and again the Senate (May 6, 1869), could thus have been influenced by the legislators' knowledge that it had been impossible to indict Dr. Wolff under § 1 of the Act of 1846. See 1869 N.Y. Senate J. 290, 345, 530-31, 564, 585, 1046, and 1869 N.Y. Assembly J. 1153, 1190, 1407, 1900. Were the successive versions of the bill at these various dates available, a more confident assessment of the influence, if any, of the Philippi-Wolff case on the provisions of the bill could be made.

Even if that particular contemporary case had no influence, the 1863 case of Elizabeth Huntington for whose death Dr. McGonegal seems never to have been indicted, doubtless because of the lacuna in § 1 of the Act of 1846, would have had its influence. So would other cases which were not individually reported in the press, but which were referred to as "alarmingly frequent" (N.Y. Times, Jan. 12, 1863, at 5, col. 3) and as numbering "not less than ten cases [of abortional homicide] . . . within the last three months" (N.Y. Times, Jan. 21, 1863, at 3, col. 1). The legislators must have been aware of all these cases, from information available through the various county coroner's offices.

The year 1871 was marked by intense activity among the proponents of a more stringent abortion law, prompted by a new series of
sensationally reported abortional homicide cases. Oddly enough, however, it was not one of the abortional homicide cases themselves, but a
simple foeticide case to which one of the abortional homicide cases led
the police, *Evans v. People*, which established the controlling precedent,
and became the leading case, on the law of abortion in New York.

The facts of the *Evans* case occurred in 1870. The *dramatis per-
sonae* were an unmarried pregnant woman originally from New Jersey
known as Ann O'Neill, whose real name was Ann Drew,[124] and an
abortionist whose real name was Thomas Lookup, to which he had
added the name Evans.[125] He claimed to have been graduated from
the University of Edinburgh and the Royal College of Surgeons in
London, to have studied under Sir James Simpson, and to have practiced medicine for thirty years.[126] He could not produce his diploma,
claiming to have lost it during his travels.[127]

At the trial, which was held May 12-18, 1871, in the Court of
General Sessions, presided over by Judge Gunning S. Bedford (of
whom we shall hear more), the evidence for the People was substantially as follows: On August 10, 1870, Dr. Evans performed an operation on Ann O'Neill, by inserting a long instrument into her womb,[128]
which failed to produce an abortion at that time.[129] He considered her,
at a previous examination shortly before the date of the operation, to
have been "from three to four months pregnant."[130] After the failure
of this attempt, she decided against further surgery, and to go ahead
and bear the child.[131] In the latter part of September 1870, she returned to Dr. Evans's house, at 94 Chatham Street, and engaged board
there,[132] remaining five weeks,[133] when another pregnant boarder, Mary
Gereaty, died in the house,[134] whereupon Dr. Evans was arrested by
the Coroner's order, on November 2, 1870,[135] the house was broken
up,[136] and Ann O'Neill was sent, as a prisoner, by the Coroner's

---

[124] Error Book at 29, Evans v. People, supra note 122.
[125] Id., at 108.
[126] Id., at 103-04.
[127] Id., at 110.
[128] Id., at 19.
[129] Id., at 34.
[130] Id., at 16, 44.
[131] Id., at 34-35.
[132] Id., at 22.
[133] Id., at 23.
[134] Id., at 25, 73, 96.
[135] Id., at 50.
[136] Id., at 25.

order,[137] to Bellevue Hospital where, on November 5, 1870, she gave birth to premature[138] twins[139] of whom one died the following day, the other on November 9, 1870.[140] Both twins were very small and delicate; one had a black spot on the abdomen.[141]

The cases of Mary Gereaty and Ann O'Neill were the converse of each other: Mary had died but her child survived,[142] while Ann survived but her twins had died. Some months seem to have been spent in proceedings against Dr. Evans for Mary Gereaty's death, but these did not succeed,[143] whereupon the authorities took up the case against him in regard to the short-lived twins born to Ann O'Neill.

On March 6, 1871, the grand jury returned an indictment of Evans on two counts: (1) assault with intent to commit manslaughter in the second degree, and (2) actual manslaughter in the second degree by reason of "the miscarriage and premature and forcible delivery" which allegedly caused the twins' deaths soon after their births. In his charge, Judge Bedford told the jury as a matter of law that the evidence would not support a conviction of manslaughter in the second degree.[144] He left it to them to decide whether the prisoner was guilty of assault with intent to commit that offense. Since 87 days had elapsed between the operation on August 10 and the births on November 5, 1870, the Assistant District Attorney's contention that the operation had "ultimated in the[ir] premature delivery"[145] was dubious on its face, and rendered extremely problematic by one of the People's own witnesses, Dr. William Shine, who had been Deputy Coroner until December 31, 1870 and had examined the bodies of the twins,[146] who testified that any causal connection between the operation and the premature births was "possible" but "not probable."[147]

---

137 Id., at 34.
138 Id., at 49.
139 Id., at 25.
140 Id., at 26.
141 Id., at 40, 43.
142 Id., at 96.
143 Id., at 119: "Mary Gereaty, a woman who died of fits when three other doctors could not save her in two days—I, who never prescribed for her, they tried to throw the blame on me, but I was acquitted . . . this time it is for the jury to say," expostulated Dr. Evans on the witness stand. His use of the word "acquitted," if technically accurate, would imply a trial, but probably no more than a grand jury's failure to indict is meant: a conclusion the more likely in view of the contrast he underscores between the disposition of the Gereaty case and his present trial on the O'Neill case: "this time it is for the jury to say" (emphasis added).
144 Id., at 137.
145 Id., at 52.
146 Id., at 54-55.
147 Id., at 59.

Another medical witness for the People, Dr. Walter Judson, house physician at Bellevue, gave testimony that agreed with Dr. Shine's as to improbability of causation.[148] In addition, Dr. Judson gave the following testimony, whose rationale was destined to influence New York legislation on the scope of abortion and of the threapeutic exception for 95 years (from 1872 to 1967):

Q. The artificial destruction of the foetus is a definition of abortion?
A. Perhaps the foetus might live.
Q. Can there be an abortion without destruction?
A. Yes, within the medical meaning of the term.[149]

It is not at all clear just what Dr. Judson meant by this. Was he referring to (1) the occasional expulsion of a nonviable foetus which lives for some time after birth but then necessarily dies in infancy? Or to (2) the premature delivery of a viable foetus which lives to adulthood? Or to (3) both? Only (1) conforms to the Sixtine definition (1588) of abortion ("foetus *immaturi* . . . ejectionem"),[150] which has been followed by the canonists ever since, and which reflected the mainstream of medical usage both then and now. There seems, however, to have been an aberrant usage in some medical circles in New York in 1871 which expanded the scope of the term abortion to include the expulsion of a viable as well as a nonviable foetus.[151] The 1872 Legislature adopted this variant usage which was copied by some other states[152] and endured in New York legislation for nearly a century.

The jury found it nearly impossible to digest the legislative *fiat* of 1869 which had elevated the simple abortion of an unquickened foetus into something called "manslaughter in the second degree." After an hour's deliberation, they returned with a verdict of "Guilty of an attempt at abortion,"[153] which reflected the jury's common sense,

---

[148] Id., at 46, 47.

[149] Id., at 50.

[150] Sixtus V, Constitution, Effraenatam, Oct. 29, 1588, § 1, quoted in full, G. Pennacchi, De Abortu Et Embryotomia 5-9 (1884).

[151] See the first legislative recommendation in the Report on Criminal Abortion of a Committee of the Medico-Legal Society of New York, Dec. 14, 1871, in Papers Read Before The Medico-Legal Society of New York From its Organization (Second Series) 14, 23 (rev. ed. 1882) (hereinafter cited as Committee Report, Papers). This will be discussed infra.

[152] B. George, Jr., Current Abortion Laws: Proposals and Movements for Reform, in Abortion and the Law, 9 n.43 (D. Smith ed. 1967), lists six States other than New York which have this bicephalic form of therapeutic exception. Presumably these were all originally copied from the New York Act of 1872.

[153] Error Book, at 143, Evans v. People, supra note 122.

if not the fulmination of the 1869 statute. Judge Bedford told the jury that such a verdict was impossible. Under the Act of 1869 they had only two alternatives: acquittal or conviction of "an assault on Ann O'Neill with intent to commit manslaughter in the second degree."[154] Counsel for defendant asked: "With intent to kill the child?" Judge Bedford ignored this question.

After a desultory colloquy, the Foreman asked:

> *Foreman.* We should like to have the stenographer refer to the evidence at the time that the operation was said to have been made, as to whether the child was then quick.
> *Counsel* [for defendant]. There is no proof on that subject.
> *The Court.* It is immaterial, as a matter of law, if you find that she was pregnant.[155]

This was the instruction which the Court of Appeals would hold reversible error, almost a year afterward. The jurors' recollection that there had been testimony on the question of quickening was accurate, but counsel for the prisoner was correct in stating that it had not amounted to "proof on that subject." The testimony given by Dr. Shine on cross-examination by defendant's counsel was as follows:

> A. If you qualify your question and state [at] what period of pregnancy the operation was done.
> Q. We will say four months?
> A. A four months' child has no life then.
> Q. Are not children sometimes quick in four months?
> A. Yes, sir; a child is not considered viable though then.
> Q. In four months the woman will feel it quickening?
> A. A child is not viable till the end of the six months, according to all authors.[156]

Dr. Shine's unaccountable declaration that a foetus of four months "has no life then" obviously did not mean that such a foetus was not yet alive, but rather that (as his subsequent testimony makes clear), if born, such a foetus has no chance of extended life. It was counsel for the prisoner who asked about quickening. Dr. Shine answered affirmatively a question whether a four months' foetus was "sometimes quick," but the remainder of his answers show that he was talking about viability, not quickening. Counsel and witness were talking at cross purposes: the former wanted to know about quickening, the

---

154 Id.
155 Id., at 143-44.
156 Id., at 60.

latter wanted to speak about viability. This non-responsive cacophany clearly did not constitute proof on the subject of quickening. Ann O'Neill, the principal witness for the People, could have been asked whether her twins had quickened by August 10, 1870, but no one had asked her.

The foreman also put a question that was troubling one of the jurors: whether Dr. Evans could be guilty of an *assault* "inasmuch as it was done by Ann O'Neill's consent." He had to put this question five separate times, slightly rephrasing it each time, before Judge Bedford gave a responsive answer. Finally, the judge defined "an assault in law [as] any unlawful touching" and stated that it made "no difference at all, whether she consented or not."[157]

This instruction was, of course, correct. Yet the question to which it was responsive, as well as the entire jury's question about quickening, betray a remarkable popular conversance with, and loyalty to, the ancient common-law principle that the act of foeticide before quickening, with the pregnant woman's consent, is no crime at all: a conversance and a loyalty which, be it noted, had survived the advent of a contrary statutory scheme in New York for 41 years.

After being kept together overnight, the jury rendered a verdict of guilty of assault with intent to commit manslaughter in the second degree.[158]

The New York Times bracketed the proceedings against Evans with two editorials, the first published the day after his arrest in connection with the death of Mary Gereaty, the second the day after Judge Bedford sentenced him to 3½ years' imprisonment at the close of the trial growing out of the deaths of Ann O'Neill's twins. The earlier editorial, captioned "The Least of These Little Ones"—a plausible sounding but actually spurious[159] quotation from the Gospels—referred metonymously to Madame Restell and Dr. Evans by their respective addresses:

> [T]he hideous traffic . . . flaunts in open day, and finds a location in every quarter of this great City. From a "palatial mansion" in Fifth Avenue, down to wretched chambers in the slums of Chatham-street, there is accomodation for the perpetration of infant murder suited to every rank and condition of life . . . .

---

[157] Id., at 144-46.

[158] Id., at 146.

[159] "[L]east of these" occurs in Matthew 25:40, 45; "little ones" in Matthew 10:42, 18:6, 10, 14; Mark 9:42; and Luke 17:2. In the Gospels, these two expressions are never combined.

The "offence is rank and smells to heaven."[160] Why is
there no hint of its punishment? Are the Police under the
delusion that they are appointed merely for the purpose of
dealing with open and public offenses? . . .[161]

In the later editorial the *Times* jubilated over the sentence and the
"stinging rebuke" meted out by Judge Bedford to Evans and the
"abominable fraternity" of "professional miscreants of whom Evans
is a sample," and then observed:

The case of Ann O'Neill can be matched any week in this
City. Every grade of social position has its corresponding
professors of the art of murder and its perpetual roll of consenting victims.[162]

In these lines there lurks an irreconcilable confusion of thought.
In speaking of the "art of murder" the editorialist plainly means the
art of foeticide: indeed, in the earlier editorial he had expressly referred to "infant murder." He is not discussing abortional homicide of
the pregnant woman; for the cases he says he has in mind "matched"
Ann O'Neill's, and she survivied though her twins did not. In the
O'Neill type case, the victim is not the woman who consents to and
survives the operation, but, presumably, the foetus, and the foetus
neither does nor can consent. The editorial writer is here caught in an
anomaly produced by the inconsistency and conflict of two completely
different rationalia for the new abortion statutes: (1) the historic and
authentic rationale which the *Times* itself in its 1863 newsstory about
Dr. McGonegal had identified as the protection of desperate women
from "the scoundrels who, under the pretence of giving relief, entail
direct misery upon . . . and at times hurry . . . into an undesirable
eternity" such women;[163] and (2) the new metaphysical rationale,
utterly devoid of any historic basis, contrived by the Medical Society
of the State of New York in 1867 to the effect that foeticide is
"murder;" so that the foetus rather than the woman is thought of as
the victim. The influence of the personalities of the owners and editors
of the *Times* on the paper's attitude to abortion, as reflected in news-

---

[160] Cladius: "Oh my offense is ranke, it smels to heaven" (Hamlet, Act III,
Scene iii). As we shall see, the author of this editorial was Louis John Jennings, who
had married a leading lady of Wallack's Theatre, Madeleine Louise Henriques. If she
is responsible for this quotation from Shakespeare, she was a more reliable source than
Jennings's own memory when he cited Scripture.

[161] N.Y. Times, Nov. 3, 1870, at 4, col. 4.

[162] N.Y. Times, May 19, 1871, at 4, col. 6.

[163] N.Y. Times, Jan. 12, 1863, at 5, col. 3.

stories and editorials during this period, makes a fascinating study of its own.[164]

---

[164] Henry Jarvis Raymond (1820-1869), an orthodox but not a fanatical Presbyterian, who had been one of the founders of the New York Times in 1851, was its managing proprietor and Editor-in-Chief until the day of his death (See N.Y. Times, June 19, 1869, at 4 passim [Henry Jarvis Raymond's biography]; June 22, 1869, at 1, col. 1 [his funeral in the University Place Presbyterian Church]; June 28, 1869, at 8, col. 1 [eulogy of his life and character by the Reverend Dr. Northrup]. For modification of his earlier Presbyterian orthodoxy, see F. Brown, Raymond of the Times 330 [1951]). The philosophy expressed in the 1863 McGonegal news story probably reflected his thinking. It certainly was attuned to the historically authentic rationale of the abortion statutes. On Raymond's death, the proprietorship and business management of the paper became vested in one of his co-founders, George Jones (1811-1891), until the latter's death, while a succession of Editors-in-Chief handled that side of the paper. From late 1869 until 1876, the Editor-in-Chief was an Englishman, Louis John Jennings (1836-1893). Jennings was the author of the two editorials just discussed.

It was Jones and Jennings who, in 1870-71, pitted the Times almost single-handedly against the mighty ring of organized municipal corruption headed by William Marcy Tweed (1823-1878), and, against everybody's expectations, succeeded in bringing about its downfall. The Tweed Ring proffered Jones a $5 million bribe to drop the campaign; in refusing it, Jones wistfully remarked that he thought that never again would the Devil offer him so high a price.

Jones and Jennings found many targets for their moral indignation, among them New York's teeming fraternity of abortionists. Both men were Anglicans. (Concerning Louis John Jennings who, at death, was the Conservative M.P. for Stockport, see The Times, London, Feb. 10, 1893, at 5, col. 6 [obituary]; Feb. 15, 1893, at 10, col. 3 [his Church of England funeral at St. Jude's, South Kensington]; N.Y. Times, Feb. 10, 1893, at 5, col. 3 [obituary]; Apr. 28, 1893, at 3, col. 4 [interesting account of Jennings's breach, once more on a point of principle, with Lord Randolph Churchill, in 1890]. Concerning George Jones, see N.Y. Times, Aug. 13, 1891, at 2, cols. 1-2; cols. 5-7; at 2, cols. 1-2; Aug. 14, 1891, at 4, col. 2; Aug. 15, 1891, at 4, cols. 5-6 [Episcopalian funeral at All Souls' Church conducted by the Reverend Dr. R. Heber Newton]; Aug. 16, 1891, at 4, cols. 3-4; Oct. 9, 1891, at 4, col. 2; Nov. 2, 1891, at 4, col. 2; see also at 8, cols. 1-3 [eulogy on All Saints' Day at All Souls' Church by Dr. Newton].) In a eulogy delivered after Jones's death, he was praised by his rector for having always refused to print abortionists' ill-disguised advertisements in the Times, though other respectable papers did print them (see e.g., Reverend Dr. R. Heber Newton's All Saints Day eulogy of George Jones at All Souls Church, in the N.Y. Times, Nov. 2, 1891, at 8, cols. 1-3):

> Hosts of papers throughout the land were in the habit of allowing such advertisements as he rejected, the so-called religious papers not excepted. Hosts of papers throughout the land still draw large revenues from the advertisements of evils unnamable here.

One such respectable paper that did accept such advertisements was the New York Herald of James Gordon Bennett, Sr. (1795-1872), a Roman Catholic. (In his youth in Scotland, Bennett had studied at an Aberdeen seminary for the Roman Catholic priesthood, but he had never proceeded to Holy Orders. His funeral was conducted by the Vicar General of the Archdiocese of New York. Interestingly, one of his pall-bearers was Judge Bedford, his son's "intimate friend." See N.Y. Times, June 14, 1872, at 5, col. 3.)

The Herald's readiness to accept advertisements from abortionists was a recurring theme of Jennings's editorials. In one, he announced that "[i]n the Herald of yesterday" he had counted "some fifty-eight lines of so-called 'medical' advertisements, devoted to

In the Evans case the persistent juror had been shrewd enough
to put his finger on the same fallacy in asking how Evans could be
guilty of an "assault" on the person of Ann O'Neill when he had done
to her precisely what she had asked him to do, neither more nor less.
Had the draftsmen of the indictment been more sensitive to the spirit,
or even the letter, of the Act of 1869, they would have worded it to
sound in assault on the person, not of Ann O'Neill, but of the two
foetūs in her womb, and would thus have spared this perceptive juror
many a qualm.

---

the service of fourteen practitioners about whose character there can be but one opinion."
(N.Y. Times, Aug. 30, 1871, at 4, cols. 2-3 ['Advertising Facilities for Murder'].)

A contemporary source confirms the prevalence of such advertising (See E. Van de
Warker, M.D., The Criminal Use of Proprietary or Advertised Nostrums, June 13, 1872,
Papers 77, 78-79 [rev. ed. 1882]):

> It is not uncommon to find their [abortionists' and abortifacient-mongers'] notices
> published in the advertising department of what are regarded as first-class maga-
> zines. And, to the shame of the religious community be it written, it is very
> common to find these advertisements occupying prominent places in the so-called
> religious journals. Every school-girl knows the meaning and intent of these
> advertisements. . . .
> . . . .
>
> In view of the extent of this trade, I am forced to believe that in relation
> to this crime [abortion] there exists a moral obliquity in all ranks of native-
> born society. . . .

Evidently Victorian moralism was found too dear by many Victorian journalists
when its price was the loss of advertising revenues. This comes as something of a shock
to Anglo-Saxons who have always thought that venality was a vice of the press only in
France.

The fact that, in his later years, Raymond carried on an extra-marital dalliance with
Rose Eytinge, a leading lady at Wallack's Theatre, doubtless resulted in a more temperate
treatment of sexual mores by the Times during his life. (For Raymond's relationship to the
"dark-eyed Rose Eytinge," see F. Brown, Raymond of the Times 288, 323, 331 [1951].)
No such inhibition palsied the pen of Jennings, who had married another leading lady at
Wallack's, Madeleine Louise Henriques. No breath of scandal ever clouded his bright
crusader's shield or that of his chief, George Jones. Indeed, Jennings had won his
editorship-in-chief through a display of righteous zeal in the domain of sexual morality. In November 1869 a sensational murder had been committed in the office of the
Tribune, then owned and edited by Horace Greeley (1811-1872). The victim was a
leading shareholder in the Tribune; the assassin was a hubsand he had cuckolded.
Though George Shepard was Editor-in-Chief of the Times and Jennings then only first
assistant, the latter "succeeded in getting into The Times" editorials concerning this
affair which drew the moral that little else was to be expected of a journal owned by
a Universalist and one-time advocate of Fourier's socialism (i.e., Greeley)! These violent
pieces provoked a furious counter-offensive, which drove Shepard to ask Jones to let
Jennings "fight his own battles." Jones did so, by retiring Shepard to the ranks and
promoting the dauntless Jennings to the editorship-in-chief. (See E. Davis, History of
the New York Times, 1851-1921, 85, 86 [1921].)

Jones and Jennings were zealots, it is true; but men whose moral mettle could
not be melted by a $5 million bribe, and who did not quail before the threats of
William Marcy Tweed, may merit forgiveness if righteous fervor betrayed them into
metaphysical pitfalls in a different part of the moral forest, where the issues were hardly
hued in such vivid blacks and whites.

Evans was indicted on March 6, and arraigned on March 11, 1871, in regard to the deaths of Ann O'Neill's twins. On March 14, 1871, Senator Norton, the *Times* reported, introduced a bill that

> [M]akes a most radical change in the laws relating to the procuring of abortions, and the selling of the medicines and instruments used for such purposes. The first section provides that any person who shall administer any medicine, or in any other way procure an abortion upon any woman, shall be guilty of manslaughter in the second degree. And if a plea of necessity to save the life of the woman is put in, proof of this necessity shall devolve upon the accused. Any person supplying or procuring a drug, knowing that it is to be used for such a purpose, shall be guilty of a misdemeanor, and be imprisoned for one year or pay a fine of $1,000. Any person publishing any advertisement that shall, in any way, tend to produce the knowledge that any drug or medicine will produce abortion, shall be guilty of a misdemeanor. Any person offending against this act, shall be a competent witness against any other person so offending, and may be compelled to appear and give evidence. The section providing for the calling of any person guilty of the offense, to testify against any other person, is qualified by the clause that the testimony so elicited shall not be used against the witness in any criminal or civil proceeding. The feeling is so strong in favor of a stringent law upon the subject that this bill will probably pass without much opposition.[165]

The Norton measure was not enacted, probably because of its late introduction in the session, and its section 1 did not go beyond the Act of 1869. Its other sections did go considerably further. Some but not all of them were to find their way into later versions of the New York abortion statutes.

In the midst of the trunk mystery hullabaloo,[166] the *Times* pub-

---

[165] N.Y. Times, Mar. 15, 1871, at 1, col. 5.

[166] In August 1871, Jennings assigned a Times reporter, Augustus St. Clair, to perform the mission of visiting the well-known abortionists of New York City, accompanied by a lady, for the purpose of soliciting their services in terminating her falsely asserted or implied pregnancy. The object was to gather materials for an article in depth on the abortionists' qualifications, practices, and fees. The ruse was successful. St. Clair published a three-columned exposé which remains to this day the best study ever printed of the real world of abortion in New York City. He captioned his piece "The Evil of the Age." An excerpt from this article follows (N.Y. Times, Aug. 23, 1871, at 6, cols. 1-3 [unsigned]. St. Clair identified himself as the author of "The Evil of the Age" in an interesting signed sequel, prompted by the "Trunk Mystery," N.Y. Times, Aug. 30, 1871, at 8, cols. 2-3):

> The enormous amount of medical malpractice [a common Nineteenth Century euphemism for surgical abortion] that exists and flourishes, almost un-

lished an editorial, "Advertising Facilities for Murder," in which it excoriated the *Herald* for accepting abortionists' advertisements, and reverted to the authentic rationale for the abortion statutes:

> [In many newspapers'] "medical" columns . . . the consequences of shame are promised to be averted by means still more shameful, and through which the victim finds a shattered constitution or an early grave. . . .
>
> In the *Herald* of yesterday there are some fifty-eight lines of so-called "medical" advertisements, devoted to the service of fourteen practitioners about whose character there can be but one opinion.[167]

Early in September 1871 Judge Bedford's charge to the grand jury in the Court of General Sessions was reported as follows by a vigorously assenting *Times*:

> I have reference, gentlemen to that mysterious trunk which, but a few days ago, was discovered in this City, containing the lifeless body of a . . . most unfortunate girl. [S]he gave herself up, and was robbed of her existence, by the murderous hand of the abortionist. . . . [O]f late we have been living, as it were, in an atmosphere of abortion. . . .
>
> And now, gentlemen, in conclusion, let me express the earnest hope (shared in, as I feel confident it will be, by you and all other right-minded citizens) that the Legislature, at its next session, will so amend the Statute Book so that "any person who shall administer to any woman with child,

---

checked, in the City of New York, is a theme for most serious consideration. Thousands of human beings are thus murdered before they have seen the light of this world, and thousands upon thousands more of adults are irremediably robbed in constitution, health, and happiness. . . .

It is interesting to note the contrast between St. Clair's repeated references to the historically authentic rationale of the statutes against abortion ("adults are irremediably ruined in constitution, health, and happiness . . . methods in vogue . . . are all . . . extremely perilous . . . operations . . . are always hazardous, and not unfrequently fatal") and his isolated instance of lip service to the newly current metaphysical speculation ("human beings are murdered before they have seen the light of this world").

As if to justify Jennings's preoccupation with the subject, the most sensational abortional homicide story in the history of New York broke only four days after the publication of St. Clair's article: the celebrated "trunk mystery." (N.Y. Times, Aug. 27, 1871, at 1, col. 4.) The nude body of a beautiful young blonde girl, concealed inside a trunk, was discovered in a railway station baggage room. The autopsy showed that her death had been caused by an abortion. Exciting detective work through a trail of clues led to the arrest of Dr. Jacob Rosenzweig, whose trial and appeals were to provide grist for the Times's mills for several years to come. There is no room here for the details of this case, but its pendency and publicity galvanized the Legislature of 1872 into amending the abortion law in the direction of severer repression—the goal toward which Jennings and his fellow crusaders were so vigorously pressing.

[167] N.Y. Times, Aug. 30, 1871, at 4, cols. 2-3.

or prescribe for any such woman, or advise or procure her to take any medicine, drug, substance or thing whatever, or shall use or employ any instrument or other means whatever, with intent thereby to procure the miscarriage of any such woman, unless the same shall have been necessary to preserve her life, shall, in case the death of such child, or of such woman be thereby produced, be deemed guilty of manslaughter in the second degree," (commonly known as the crime of abortion,) shall be declared to be murder in the first degree, and punishable as such with death, instead of, as now, but manslaughter in the second degree, punishable by imprisonment not exceeding seven years.

At the conclusion of this address there was loud applause in Court.[168]

It will be noted that Judge Bedford quoted section 1 of the Act of 1869 in full, and proposed only one change in it: the elevation of the description of the crime from manslaughter in the second degree to murder in the first, with a consequent substitution of the death penalty for a maximum term of seven years in prison. To the author's knowledge, this is the only serious proposal ever made to the Legislature of New York to carry to its logical consequence the metaphysical theory that from conception onward an embryo is as much a man as if it had been already born. Judge Bedford himself, though a staunch Roman Catholic, soon receded from the full extremity of this proposal, "explain[ing] that his advocacy of this view was only intended for its effect on 'professional' abortionists."[169]

Judge Bedford was a member by invitation of a committee on criminal abortion of the Medico-Legal Society of New York. His colleagues on that committee, while expressing sympathy with his view that all abortion "should be made a capital felony" as "intrinsically just," considered that

[A]ny serious attempt to carry it into practice at the present time would probably result in lessening the chances for a conviction in any case. This is evident from the recent trial of Rosenzweig in the New York General Sessions, when two jurors united in a recommendation to mercy, thus showing a disinclination to convict even of a felony, though the prisoner did not attempt to justify his conduct, but rested his defense upon his alleged innocence of the whole matter.[170]

---

[168] N.Y. Times, Sept. 7, 1871, at 8, col. 2.
[169] Committee Report, Papers at 24.
[170] Id., at 24-25.

A passage like this tells volumes about the real state of public opinion, even in that heyday of Victorian moralism. Jurors were hard to mobilize to convict a physician who had done exactly what the patient had asked him to do, even where her death had ensued, even where no more than seven years' imprisonment could be imposed. Jurors were undoubtedly as aware as physicians of the danger to a woman's health and life of such operations, under contemporary conditions of surgery, but they were less optimistic than their professional betters about the efficacy of legislative repression of a practice to which so many women resorted in conscious violation of the law. In this regard the populace was shrewder than these doctrinaires of the professional elite.

The Medico-Legal Society of New York had been organized in 1867 by physicians attached to the Coroner's office. Eventually lawyers were brought in who shared their medical colleagues' interest in medical jurisprudence. The reading before the Society, on December 14, 1871, of the Report of its Committee on Criminal Abortion was reported with satisfaction by the *Times:*

> It was very clearly read by Jas. O'Dea, the President of the Committee, and its gist was to recommend a change in the law of '69, whereby it should be simply a felony without any specific denomination, and its penalty should be imprisonment for not less than four years. This would give the Judge the power in aggravated cases, such as those of professional abortionists like Rosenzweig, to sentence the criminals to imprisonment for life. The report was unanimously adopted, and a committee was appointed consisting of Dr. S[tephen] Rogers, the President [of the Society]; W. A. Hammond, Judge Bedford and Dr. O'Dea to wait on the Governor, and through him present it to the Legislature. There was a very numerous attendance among whom were many ladies.[171]

In its Report, the Committee stated its position in regard to the metaphysical question in this way:

> Among those who are competent to pronounce on this question of *"quickening"*, there is, however, but one opinion, and to it your committee ask the undivided attention of the community. *The foetus is alive from conception, and all intentional killing of it is murder.* The world is free to discuss the transcendental problem concerning the stage of

---

[171] N.Y. Times, Dec. 15, 1871, at 1, col. 5.

development at which the foetus becomes endowed with a soul. Some may believe, with Plato, that this event is deferred till birth. Others may hold, with Aristotle, that it occurs at the fortieth day for boys and the eightieth for girls! Only, let such opinions have their due place and weight. Whatever may be their value as evidences of intellectual activity, they have no bearing whatever on the great practical question of child-murder. If there were never such an existence as a soul, if men perished utterly when they died, laws against murder would still hold good, because laws against murder were enacted not for the soul's sake, but to preserve the peace and even the existence of society. Opinions such as these now indicated are harmless enough if jealously confined to the field of abstract speculation. It is only when suffered to influence conduct toward the foetus that they become delusive and pernicious errors. Too great, unfortunately, has been their power in this respect; hence the necessity of combating them and of exhibiting them to the public in their true light, as evils which have long waged war against the dearest interests of society. All such speculations cannot be too strictly excluded from the sphere of practical morals; and furthermore, the public should be taught that the significance attached to *"quickening"* is unfounded, that the current deductions therefrom, already indicated, are utterly erroneous and immoral, and warned that the community, whose regard for foetal life is influenced by either, is courting a terrible retribution. Herein is ample work for the two great educators of a nation, its pulpit and its press.[172]

The committee sadly conceded, however, in regard to the contrary view, namely, that "[a]bortions . . . caused before [quickening] were suffered to pass unnoticed" and were not "branded as serious crimes":

> How effectually it influences the opinion and practice of our own time, how completely it has permeated all, but more particluarly the higher ranks of contemporary society, needs not to be insisted upon here.[173]

In reviewing New York's legislation before 1869, the committee characterized the term *quick* as "obnoxious;" it noted with satisfaction that the legislature of 1869 had omitted it, "thereby relieving

---

[172] Committee Report, Papers at 19.
[173] Id., at 18-19.

the prosecution from the necessity of proving a fact almost impossible," and had "altered the *intent* to the production of the miscarriage of the woman, instead of to the destruction of the child."[174]

After adverting to the unwillingness of jurors to convict abortionists of manslaughter in the second degree, let alone murder in the first, where the patients survived, the committee, while it "hoped the time will soon arrive for [foeticide's] punishment as [murder],"[175] and while it believed that "[a] statutory enactment punishing the crime [of abortion] with death would be the most effectual preventive if it were practicable,"[176] concluded that it was not; so it chose what it "believe[d] to be a more practical course," *i.e.*, "to make the offense a felony without specific name, and to fix the *minimum* of punishment at not less than four years, leaving the *maximum* to . . . the discretion of the court."[177]

Judge Bedford doubtless told his colleagues on the committee what a struggle he had had in getting the Evans jury to swallow the legislative *fiat* of 1869 that the abortion of an unquickened foetus was to be called manslaughter. If the felony were nameless, this type of jury resistance would be eliminated. But the proposed enactment would enable a judge to give a sentence of as much as life imprisonment. This would help to educate public opinion toward the glorious day when these Nineteenth Century fanatics could secure legislative recognition of the truth so clear to them but so obscure to the generality of mankind, that foeticide is literally murder, and to be punished by death.

While the committee's paper is almost entirely devoted to arguments for its metaphysical belief that foeticide is murder, and that it should be punished as severely as juries could be inveigled into digesting, it does make one fleeting reference to the historically authentic reason for the passage of the abortion statutes when it mentions that, "as too often happens, [the patient] succumbs to the operation or its consequences."[178] One is encouraged to learn that these medical crusaders had not, in their zeal for the foetus, wholly forgotten the pregnant woman.

Turning its attention to the therapeutic exception, the committee pointed out that section 1 of the Act of 1869

---

[174] Id., at 21.
[175] Id., at 24.
[176] Id., at 25.
[177] Id.
[178] Id., at 24.

[D]oes not justify the procurement of a miscarriage, *except* when necessary to save the life *of the mother.* Cases may, however, occur where, in the judgment of an experienced medical man, premature labor should be induced, and be absolutely necessary to save the life *of the child.* Hence, the statute ought properly to comprehend either contingency.[179]

This recommendation shows that this committee believed that the medical and legal meaning of the word "miscarriage" covered a viable as well as a previable foetus, a belief more remarkable in view of the fact that the committee itself, in a footnote[180] of its Report, quoted the earliest statutory definition of abortion in European public law, that of Pope Sixtus V in his bull *Effraenatam* (1558): "foetūs immaturi . . . ejectionem." The word *immaturi*, of course, means previable. The Sixtine restriction of the material object of abortion to the previable foetus reflected the prevailing medical usage not only of the Sixteenth Century, but of all subsequent periods. All subsequent statutes using merely the term "abortion" or "miscarriage" have generally been supposed to incorporate, tacitly, the Sixtine restriction. The Medico-Legal Society of New York in 1871 was thus originating a novel and aberrant concept of the scope of the term "abortion;" since the Legislatures of New York and a few other States adopted it, the statutes which they passed must be interpreted in conformity with this unusual usage, which remained in the New York statutes from 1872 to 1967.

The committee then proposed a text to replace section 1 of the Act of 1869, which the Legislature of 1872 did, in fact, use as a basis for section 1 of the Act of 1872. The committee's proposed text and the Legislature's enactment will be compared presently.

The committee mentioned that the community had been "grievously shocked . . . by the terrible deeds of certain abortionists lately exposed"[181] and Chairman O'Dea made this allusion explicit by citing the abortional homicides committed by Dr. Rosenzweig and a Dr. Wolff[182] and the unconsummated foeticide attempted by the unhappy

---

179 Id., at 23.

180 Id., at 18, asterisked footnote.

181 Id., at 25.

182 This defendant was Dr. Michael A. A. Wolff, not to be confused with the Dr. Gabriel J. Wolff who had not been indicted for the abortional homicide in 1869 of Magdalena Philippi. The name of Dr. Michael A. A. Wolff's victim, who died on June 12, 1870, was never mentioned in the otherwise very full report of his trial before Judge Bedford at the General Sessions in January 1871. This exceptional departure

Dr. Evans.[183] He quoted resolutions of the New York Academy of Medicine of May 18 and September 21, 1871, supporting and commending Judge Bedford.[184] These 1871 resolutions of the New York Academy of Medicine called abortion a "pervading" and "widespread crime," and a "pestilence," but refrained from calling it "murder" as had the Medical Society of the State of New York in 1867 and as did this committee of the Medico-Legal Society of New York in 1871.

On January 9, 1872, the Medico-Legal Society's proposed one-section bill was introduced by Assemblyman George H. Mackay of New York County,[185] a lawyer who had served on the staff of Coroner Wildey, and had accompanied him on his investigation of a gruesome abortional homicide case, that of Lucinda Sagendorf supposedly at the hands of Dr. Grindle of 6 Amity Place, in 1865.[186]

---

from the Times's usual explicitness in regard to the decedent's name suggests that she was of a socially prominent family: not all the news was all that fit to print.

A special interest was displayed in the case . . . on account of the extreme rarity of trials for abortion in this City—an offense which is known to be very common. . . . The indictment charge[d] [Dr. Michael A. A. Wolff] with manslaughter in the second degree [under the Act of 1869]. . . . Assistant District Attorney Fellows . . . referred to the prevalence of the crime of scientific abortion. . . .

N.Y. Times, Jan. 26, 1871, at 3, cols. 2-3. This defendant's methods do not seem, by today's standards, to have been all that scientific; for he had used potions as well as an instrument. The next day the Times concluded its report of the trial:

The verdict [Guilty] and the sentence [7 years' imprisonment] created a lively feeling of gratification on account of the terrible warning which they gave to professional abortionists, whose hideous vice, which is nothing less than ante-natal murder, has hitherto escaped punishment. They have openly carried on their infamous practice in this City to a frightful extent, and have laughed at the defeat of respectable citizens who have vainly attempted to prosecute them . . . .

[The Deputy Coroner, Dr. Beach, who had performed the post mortem, testified that the foetus] must have been between five and six months old at the time of the abortion.

(N.Y. Times, Jan. 27, 1871, at 3, col. 1.) The advanced somatic age of this abortus would raise a presumption that quickening had occurred in the minds of most medical men, but not a legal presumption in a court of law. The foregoing facts, in the absence of express testimony that quickening had occurred, would not have sufficed for a conviction under § 1 of the Act of 1846. By Judge Bedford's interpretation of the Act of 1869, it had dispensed with the necessity of showing that quickening had occurred; for the first time, therefore, in most of these abortional homicide cases, convictions had become possible.

Even so, the jury in this case recommended mercy, but was brow-beaten by the prosecutor into withdrawing the recommendation. In pronouncing the maximum sentence the law allowed, Judge Bedford said: "In one word, the authorities have declared war to the bitter end against the fraternity which you, today, so guiltily represent." Id.

1871 was marked by a series of three spectacular trials of two abortional homicides and one attempted foeticide; of the three, Dr. Wolff's trial was first; Dr. Evans's second; Dr. Rosenzweig's third.

183 Committee Report, Papers at 15.
184 Id.
185 N.Y. Times, Jan. 10, 1872, at 1, col. 6; 1872 N.Y. Assembly J. 60.
186 N.Y. Times, Sept. 28, 1865, at 5, col. 4; Sept. 29, 1865, at 8, col. 1.

Encouraged by these allies and their efforts, Jennings penned the following leader in the *Times:*

It is only too notorious that an abominable crime, much advertised in one or two daily and several weekly papers, is made a trade of in this city. For this crime "Look-up Evans" and a rascal named Wolff, were sent to prison, we believe, for seven years, by Judge Bedford. More recently, Rosenzweig was sentenced for the same term by Recorder Hackett. These two Judges have done all that lies within their power to suppress this infamous traffic, and have thus added to the many services they have rendered to the public. . . .

But the best of Judges cannot suppress an evil practice unless the law enables them to do so. In regard to this particular crime the law is defective—no matter how great may have been the crimes committed by a male or female Rosenzweig, the Judge has very little discretion left to him with regard to the term of imprisonment inflicted. Hence it is that great mansions on grand avenues are occupied by disgusting "practitioners", who continue to escape prosecution because the law is not strong enough to reach them.

Among the social reforms which are needed, there is no direction in which reform is more necessary than this. The New York Medico-Legal Society has drawn up a bill which would answer the purpose, and which, we are happy to say, has already been presented to the Legislature. It is very short, and was drawn up by several eminent medical gentlemen with the assistance of Judge Bedford. It is far-reaching enough to catch hold of all who assist, directly or indirectly, in the destruction of infant life; it constitutes the crime a felony, and it imposes an imprisonment of not less than four years on any person found guilty. No one can possibly find an objection to the bill except the rogues, male and female, who carry on their hideous trade. The bill has been presented by Assemblyman Mackay—let him have due credit for it.

May we not hope that Assemblymen and Senators will see to it that this bill is made law without unnecessary delay? There is no doubtful question involved in it. Our best City Magistrates ask for it—the people demand it. Is there any man in either House who will refuse to vote for it? We hope not.[187]

---

[187] N.Y. Times, Jan. 12, 1872, at 4, col. 4,

In declaring that none but the abortionists could "possibly find an objection to the bill" crusader Jennings seems to have forgotten the scores of thousands of New York women who, as the abortionists' customers, kept them in business. In that day, however, *their* objections could not be voiced, and thus could be treated as non-existent. Jennings's rhetorical question, "Is there any man in either House who will refuse to vote for it?", was to receive an unexpected answer.

The Legislature of 1872 enacted every word of the Medico-Legal Society's proposed text, but altered it in several particulars by adding fifteen new words of its own. The section is here set forth, with the legislative additions in italics:

> Any person who shall *hereafter wilfully* administer to any woman *with child, or prescribe for any such woman,* or advise or procure her to take any medicine, drug, substance or thing whatever, or shall use or employ, or advise or procure her to submit to the use or employment of any instrument or other means whatever, with intent thereby to produce the miscarriage of any such woman, unless the same shall have been necessary to preserve her life, or that of such child, shall, in case the death of such child or such woman be thereby produced, be deemed guilty of a felony, and upon conviction shall be punished by imprisonment in a State prison for a term not less than four years *or more than twenty years.*[188]

The five words added at the end were a bitter blow for the cru-

---

[188] The text of the Medico-Legal Society's proposed bill was printed at the end of the Committee Report, Papers at 26-27. The text of Law of App. 6, 1872, ch. 181, [1872] N.Y. Laws, is printed not only in the Session Laws of 1872 but also after the end of the Committee's Report. Id. at 27-29.

In addition to § 1, there were three more sections in the Act of 1872. Sections 2 and 3 are worth quoting here; they will be discussed in the text, infra:

Any woman pregnant with child who shall take any medicine, drug, substance or thing whatever, or shall use or employ, or suffer any other person to use or employ, or submit to the use or employment of any instrument or other means whatever, with the intent thereby to produce the miscarriage of the child of which she is so pregnant, unless the same shall have been necessary to preserve her life or that of such child, shall, in case the death of such child be thereby produced, be deemed guilty of a felony, and upon conviction shall be punished by imprisonment in the State prison for a term not less than four years or more than ten years.

Every person who shall administer to any pregnant woman, or prescribe for any such woman, or advise or procure any such woman to take any medicine, drug, substance or thing whatever . . . or shall use or employ any instrument or other means whatever, with intent thereby to procure the miscarriage of any such woman, shall upon conviction be punished, by imprisonment in a county jail, or in a State prison, not less than one nor more than three years, in the discretion of the court.

Section 4 of the Act of 1872 virtually copies § 2 (1869), which was aimed primarily at druggists and nonlicensed vendors of abortifacients. The only change is that "advice" is added to abortifacients that may be unlawfully supplied or procured.

saders, who had wanted the option of imposing a life sentence left to the discretion of the judge. Had the Legislature granted them that wish, the metaphysicians among the crusaders could have argued that there had been at least a tacit legislative recognition that foetal life was equivalent to adult life, since an adult abortionist could lose his liberty for life in punishment for having destroyed the pre-natal life of a foetus. At a time when the average expectancy of life in America was not much in excess of 40 years, the legislative limitation to 20 years of the maximum sentence of imprisonment that could be imposed meant that the Legislature was willing to go no further with the crusaders than to equate one foetal life with one-half of an adult life.

The President of the Medico-Legal Society of New York, speaking just six months after the passage of the Act of 1872, stated that the opposition to the Society's proposal had come from "Senators Lewis, Bowen and Chatfield."[189]

A close reading of the legislative journals tends to substantiate Dr. Rogers's accusation.[190] The Senate, after receiving the bill (ap-

---

[189] S. Rogers, M.D., The True Object of Medical Legislation, 1872, Papers at 105, 112.

[190] The intermediate appeal of Evans v. People was argued at General Term of the Supreme Court, New York County, on December 6, 1871. Just over a month later, Assemblyman Mackay introduced his bill, on January 9, 1872; it was read twice and referred to the Assembly committee on public health. 1872 N.Y. Assembly J. 60. On January 17, 1872, Assemblyman Loughran from that committee reported the bill, with amendments, recommending passage. The report was agreed to and the bill was referred to committee of the whole. Id., 97. On January 20, 1872, the Assembly considered the bill in committee of the whole. After the Speaker resumed the chair, Assemblyman Alvord from the committee of the whole reported in favor of passage, which was agreed to. The bill was engrossed for third reading. Id., 116. On January 22, 1872, Assemblyman A. L. Van Dusen from the committee on engrossed bills reported the bill as correctly engrossed. Id., 121. In the Senate, on February 2, 1872, Senator J. Wood, from the Senate Judiciary Committee, to which the bill as passed by the Assembly had been referred, reported it in favor of passage; it was referred to the Senate in committee of the whole. 1872 N.Y. Senate J. 153. On February 2, 1872, the Senate considered the bill in committee of the whole. After the President resumed the chair, Senator McGowan from the committee of the whole reported progress on the bill, and asked leave to sit again. Senator Benedict moved recommittal to the Senate Judiciary Committee, which motion passed in the affirmative. Id., 159.

On February 10, 1872, the Supreme Court at General Term, in an unpublished opinion of eight lines by Justice Barnard, affirmed the conviction of Dr. Evans. N.Y. Times, Feb. 11, 1872, at 3, col. 7. For the text of Justice Barnard's opinion, see Error Book, at 154, Evans v. People, supra note 122. On March 1, 1872, the case was orally argued in the Court of Appeals. The Error Book and the Briefs for Prisoner and People were, therefore, printed and filed in Albany in the Court of Appeals between February 11 and 28, 1872. As soon as they were filed, the Senate Judiciary Committee, to which the bill was recommitted during that period, would have had access to them.

On March 2, 1872, Senator J. Wood, from the Senate Committee on the Judiciary, reported the bill again, with amendments, in favor of passage; it was referred to the

parently the one-section text proposed by the Medico-Legal Society, with some amendments) as passed by the Assembly, and after considering it in committee, recommitted it to the Senate committee on the judiciary on February 2, 1872. The reason for the recommittal was not stated in the Senate Journal, but the date is significant. *Evans v. People* was argued in the Court of Appeals on March 1,

---

Senate in committee of the whole. 1872 N.Y. Senate J. 293-94. On March 9, 1872, the Senate again considered the bill in committee of the whole. After the President resumed the chair, Senator Brown, from the committee of the whole, reported progress, and asked and obtained leave to sit again. Senator Benedict moved that the bill, as amended, be printed; this motion passed in the affirmative. Id., 342. On March 11, 1872, the Senate further considered the bill in committee of the whole. After the President resumed the chair, Senator J. Wood from the committee of the whole reported in favor of passage, with amendments. The report was agreed to, and the bill was ordered to a third reading. Id., 344. On March 15, 1872, the Senate passed the bill, on third reading, unanimously, 21:0. Id., 388. Among the 21 senators recorded as voting for the bill at this stage were two of the three named by Dr. Rogers as having opposed the Medico-Legal Society's objective (George Bowen and Thomas I. Chatfield); the third (Loren L. Lewis) apparently was absent. They had doubtless accomplished the frustration of the Medico-Legal Society's objective of facultative life imprisonment by an amendment while the bill was in committee of the whole.

Back in the Assembly, on March 19, 1872, the bill came from the Senate "with a message that they had passed the same, with the following amendments: Strike out all after the enacting clause, and insert the following: . . ." At this point the full text of six sections, in virtually the form finally adopted, is printed. The Assembly concurred in the Senate amendments, 81:0. The bill was ordered returned to the Senate with a message informing them of the Assembly's concurrence in their amendments. 1872 N.Y. Assembly J. 689-91. On March 21, 1872, the Senate received this message from the Assembly, and ordered the bill returned to the Assembly as the House of its origin. 1872 N.Y. Senate J. 436. Meanwhile, on March 20, 1872, the Assembly ordered that its Clerk deliver the bill to the Governor.

At this point an extremely unusual parliamentary procedure took place. On March 23, 1872, Assemblyman Mackay offered a resolution that a respectful message be sent to His Excellency the Governor, requesting him to return to the Assembly, for further amendment, Assembly Bill No. 10; it passed in the affirmative. 1872 N.Y. Assembly J. 787. The Senate concurred in the Mackay resolution the same day, and the Assembly ordered its Clerk to deliver the resolution to the Governor. 1872 N.Y. Senate J. 453; 1872 N.Y. Assembly J. 788. On March 26, 1872, Governor John T. Hoffman returned Assembly Bill No. 10 to the Assembly. Assemblyman Mackay moved reconsideration, which passed in the affirmative, 90:0. On Assemblyman Mackay's motion, and by unanimous consent, a technical amendment as to the form of § 1 was passed, and also the word "hereafter" was inserted after the words "who shall," thus making § 1 expressly purely prospective in operation. These amendments, on third reading, passed in the affirmative, 85:0, and the bill as amended was sent to the Senate. 1872 N.Y. Assembly J. 805-06. On April 2, 1872, the Senate voted to reconsider, 21:0, and to pass as amended by the Assembly, 20:0, and returned the bill to the originating House. 1872 N.Y. Senate J. 556. It was received by the Assembly that same day. 1872 N.Y. Assembly J. 981.

And also on that same day, April 2, 1872, the Court of Appeals handed down its opinion in Evans v. People, supra note 122.

On April 3, 1872, the Assembly noted correct re-engrossment, and on April 4, 1872, ordered its Clerk to deliver the bill to the Governor. 1872 N.Y. Assembly J. 1002, 1014.

Governor Hoffman signed Assembly Bill No. 10 in its final version on April 6, 1872.

1872, but the printed Briefs of counsel were doubtless filed some weeks before the oral argument, and they were, of course, available to the Senate judiciary committee as soon as they were filed.

The Brief for the Prisoner argued:

> The only "attempt" or "intent" which the evidence would at the worst authorize the jury in finding, was an attempt to procure a miscarriage. Yet to procure a miscarriage is neither at common law [n]or by statute manslaughter in the second or any other degree.
>
> 1. And that the instruction covered the case of a miscarriage of any foetus though not *"quick"* and therefore the subject of "death" is expressly shown on the top of page 144 (fol. 518).
>
> 2. That at common law, the procuring of a miscarriage of a child "not quick" was not a crime of any sort, not even an assault, if the woman consented is settled.
>
> . . . .
>
> 3. That no statute now in existence in this state since 1869, makes the mere procuring a miscarriage without loss of life, even a misdemeanor is quite clear. The statute making it misdemeanor has been expressly repealed by the act of 1869.
>
> 4. The attempt therefore merely to procure a miscarriage cannot be an attempt to commit even a misdemeanor, much less to commit manslaughter. The necessary element to make it manslaughter must be the death of a woman or child. The mere procuring of a miscarriage is not enough and, hence the attempt to procure a miscarriage cannot be punished as an attempt to commit manslaughter.[191]

This line of argument was destined to be adopted, in large measure, by the Court of Appeals in its opinion in *Evans v. People* on April 2, 1872. While the Senate judiciary committee could not have known in advance how the Court of Appeals would decide the case, it must have been sufficiently impressed with the cogency of the Prisoner's Brief to conclude that something more elaborate was needed than the single-section proposal of the Medico-Legal Society.

Accordingly, on March 2, 1872 (the day after *Evans v. People* was orally argued in the Court of Appeals), the Senate judiciary committee reported the bill "with amendments," and the Senate in committee of the whole agreed to them. As thus amended, the Sen-

---

[191] Brief for the Plaintiff in Error [Dr. Evans], pp. 13-14, Evans v. People, supra note 122.

ate, on March 15, 1872, passed the bill, 21:0, the affirmative votes including those of Senators Bowen and Chatfield, but not that of Senator Lewis, who was absent. The text of the bill as thus amended and passed by the Senate is printed in the Assembly Journal. The Senate's amendments consisted of striking the whole of the Assembly bill (apparently still basically the one-section Medico-Legal Society proposal) and inserting six sections, in virtually the form in which they finally appeared in the Act of 1872.[192] With additional changes of no material consequence, the bill was finally agreed upon by both Houses, and was sent to Governor Hoffman for his approval on April 2, 1872, the very day on which the Court of Appeals handed down its decision in *Evans v. People*. He approved and signed it four days later.

It is thus evident that it was not the court's opinion itself that influenced the legislators in passing the Act of 1872, but rather those legislators' remarkable ability to read the handwriting on the wall as to what that opinion would contain, between the lines of the Prisoner's Brief.

In *Evans v. People*, the Court of Appeals held:

> It was error to charge that the death of a child could be caused or produced before it had given evidence of life, had become "quick" in the womb, and that the crime of manslaughter under the statute could be predicated of the destruction of the foetus before that period.
>
> For this error of the court the judgment of the Supreme Court and of the Sessions should be reversed and a new trial granted.[193]

Addressing itself to the metaphysical question, the Court gave the immemorial answer of Anglo-American law: "There is a period during gestation when, although there may be embryo life in the foetus, there is no living child."[194]

Our study of the Act of 1869 led us to the conclusion that the Legislature in that year had intended to punish abortion at any stage of pregnancy as statutory manslaughter in the second degree, using the latter term merely as an "arbitrary title" or piece of "nomenclature," as Assistant District Attorney Sullivan unsuccessfully argued in the Court of Appeals.[195] The court, however, rejected this

---

[192] 1872 N.Y. Assembly J. 689-90 [March 19] prints in full the six sections substituted by the Senate for the shorter bill the Assembly had passed. It is rare for the legislative journals to print the texts of amendments. When, as here, it is done, it is always helpful in recapturing the legislative history.

[193] Supra note 122, at 91.

[194] Supra note 122, at 90.

[195] Brief for the People, at 3, 9, Evans v. People, supra note 122.

nominalist or semanticist approach, apparently on the ground that the particle "man" in the word "manslaughter" required at least a "living child," and that, before a foetus had quickened, it simply was not a "living child."

In his solitary dissent, Judge Grover pointed out that the court's opinion (written by Judge Allen) so construed the Act of 1869 as to make it wholly inapplicable to abortion of an unquickened foetus, which was therefore restored to its noncriminal status at common law. This disturbed Judge Grover, but not his colleagues. Apparently they realized that from 1845 to 1869 *surgical* abortion before quickening had been outside the statute and therefore not a crime at common law, and what Dr. Evans had done was to attempt a surgical abortion. That the Legislature of 1869 had not succeeded in bringing surgical abortion before quickening back under the statute (as it had been from 1830 to 1845), even though perhaps it had intended to do so, did not strike the majority as either surprising or calamitous.

The Legislature of 1872 was more concerned about this possibility, though it was clearly not so excited as the zealots. We have noted the amendments it made, by way of additions, to the text proposed by the Medico-Legal Society of New York. By adding (after the words "any woman") the words "with child," the Legislature of 1872 meant to restrict the highly punitive provisions of this felony (section 1) to cases where the woman actually was pregnant. Probably the 1872 Legislature meant (at least consciously) to do no more than this when it added the words "with child." On the other hand, section 1 of the 1872 Act corresponds to section 1 of the 1869 Act. The words "with child" occur at the same place in this section in both Acts. It is a familiar principle that when a legislature enacts a provision from an earlier act, it is presumed that the language it reenacts has the same meaning as the courts either have held, or may hereafter hold, to apply to the earlier statute. Now, in this case, the Court of Appeals was on the verge of holding that the words "with child" in the Act of 1869 really meant "with a *quick* child;" so, by reenacting them in the Act of 1872, the Legislature must be deemed to have taken them with this (only slightly future) gloss.

There is another reason, however, for supposing that the Legislature of 1872 was prescient that its phrase "with child" added to the felony section (1) would be held to mean "with a *quick* child," namely, the fact that it added another section (3) which prohibited both potional and surgical abortion of "any pregnant woman" as a misdemeanor. Obviously, section 3 was not intended to be redundant. If it covers something that section 1 does not, that something must be abortion before quickening, which shows that section 1 is restricted to abortion after quickening. This section 3 (1872) was modeled after section 2 (1845), but went beyond the earlier section, which prohibited only potional abortion before quickening, by prohibiting surgical abortion before quickening as well. Both section 2 (1845) and section 3 (1872) lack a therapeutic exception. This omission was rational in the earlier section, which dealt not with surgeons but only with midwives and quacks. In the later section, which deals with surgeons as well, its omission was doubtless an inadvertence.

In section 2 (1872) the Legislature used as a model section 3 (1845) which for the first time had brought the woman herself within the statute, and which had never been repealed. 1845's "Every woman" became 1872's "Any woman pregnant with child." 1845's "with intent thereby to procure a miscarriage" became 1872's "with intent thereby to produce the miscarriage of the child of which she is so pregnant." Just what, if anything, section 2's (1872) "pregnant with child" may add to or subtract from section 1's (1872) "with child" or section 3's (1872) "pregnant," we have no way of knowing, because the section bringing the woman within the ambit of the statute is and always has been a dead letter. In section 2 (1872), the therapeutic exception is rendered in the bicephalic form recommended by the Medico-Legal Society of New York in 1871 ("to preserve her life or that of such child").

The Act of 1872[196] was enlarged in 1875 by the addition of a new section 6 making admissible in evidence "the dying declarations of the woman whose death is produced" by violation of the Act, "subject to the same restrictions as in cases of homicide" in all prosecutions under the Act.[197] One thinks at once of Elizabeth Huntington's dying declaration against Dr. McGonegal before the Coroner's Jury in 1863. Clearly abortions, particularly illegal ones, had not ceased to be "dangerous to [maternal] life" by 1875.

In 1880 the Legislature amended section 3 (1872) to add advising or procuring the woman's submission to an operation; but still no therapeutic exception was added.[198]

Thus matters stood on the eve of the adoption of the Penal

---

196 Law of April 6, 1872, ch. 181, N.Y. Laws.
197 Law of May 15, 1875, ch. 352, [1875] N.Y. Laws.
198 Law of May 13, 1880, ch. 283, [1880] N.Y. Laws.

Code of 1881. The Revisers who framed that Code consecrated the opinion of the Court of Appeals in *Evans v. People* by restoring the word "quick" to the statute, the word which the Medico-Legal Society had found so "obnoxious," and which the Legislatures of 1869 and 1872 had omitted. These framers of the Code of 1881 also extended the quickening distinction for the first time to the woman's offense, dividing it into two grades accordingly.

There was no conflict in 1872 between the Court of Appeals and the Legislature over quickening. Anti-quickening crusaders in medicine and journalism brought enormous pressure in 1871-1872. The response of the Court of Appeals was a flat negation. With greater diplomacy, the Legislature gave the Medico-Legal Society every word it asked for, but by adding other words and even other sections, denied the Society the prize it strove so hard to win. Dr. Rogers's own subsequent statement shows that this legislative half-loaf was not what they had crusaded for.

By 1881, even the half-loaf disappeared from the statutes, and in its place the doctrine of the Court of Appeals in *Evans v. People* became the *lex scripta* of the State. The Penal Code of 1881 thus ended, hopefully forever,[199] the campaign of these Nineteenth Cen-

---

[199] So far as the author knows, there has been only one effort in this direction, in New York, since the 1881 burial of the crusade of 1871-72. On August 30, 1967, at the New York State Constitutional Convention then in session at Albany, one of the delegates proposed that the equal protection clause in the bill of rights be altered by the addition, after the word "person", of the words "from the moment of conception". The proponent was Charles E. Rice, a Roman Catholic layman, professor of Constitutional Law at Fordham University, and one of the state vice chairmen of the Conservative Party of New York. According to its reported purpose, this proposal, if adopted, "would have prohibited all abortions, even those now permitted by law. [It was] defeated by a voice vote." N.Y. Times, Aug. 31, 1967, at 26, col. 4 (datelined Albany, August 30, 1967, by-lined Sidney Schanberg).

Although the Transcript of Proceedings of the New York State Constitutional Convention has not yet been published, the author has been informed that delegate Bartlett reported that Professor Rice's proposal had been considered by the appropriate sub-committee, which had recommended unanimously against its adoption. Professor Rice contended that medical and embryological science recognizes that a "child" is in existence from the moment of conception. Presiding Justice Botein, who was also a delegate, enlivened the proceedings by asking whether, if the scientific evidence were as irresistible as Professor Rice contended, persons from the moment of conception would not be covered by the equal protection clause as it stands, without the proposed amendment!

If Professor Rice's proposal really did intend to do away with the therapeutic abortion exception, it went far beyond the object of the crusaders of 1871-72. Even the Roman Catholics among them, like Judge Bedford, recognized the morality of an abortion done to save the pregnant woman's life. Judge Bedford's father, Dr. Gunning S. Bedford, was one of New York City's most distinguished professors of gynaecology until his death in 1870. In his Principles And Practice of Obstetrics 679 (4th ed., 1868), Dr. Bedford justified therapeutic abortion when "without the operation two lives would certainly be sacrificed, while, with it, it is more than probable that one would be saved."

tury doctrinaires to innovate a legislative recognition of their meta-physical notion that an hour-old zygote is a "living child" and therefore a "man."

The Penal Code of 1881

The Penal Code of 1881[200] organized the pre-existing statutes into a systematic and symmetrical scheme. Sections 190, 191, and 194 dealt with a quickened foetus. Sections 190 and 191 provided that its violators (anyone wilfully causing the death of a child by injury to its mother or by administering drugs to her) would be guilty of manslaughter in the first degree.[201] Section 194 provided

---

This is the precise proposition which the Holy Office would condemn on July 24, 1895, with the personal approbation of Leo XIII the following day. Acta Sanctae Sedis, vol. 28, pp. 383-84. From that day onward, Roman Catholic gynaecologists desiring to conform to their Church's official teaching have had to allow both to die rather than kill either to save the other. The 1895 decree is the first official condemnation of therapeutic abortion in the history of the Roman Catholic Church; before it was pronounced many moral theologians taught the same as Dr. Bedford. As their obituary notices show, Dr. Bedford was a college classmate and lifelong friend of two Archbishops of New York (Hughes and McCloskey), and his son ex-Judge Bedford was a personal friend of a third, Archbishop Corrigan, who pronounced the benediction at his requiem Mass in St. Patrick's Cathedral; so their view that a therapeutic abortion was morally justifiable can scarcely have been considered heretical in their lifetimes. N.Y. Times, Sept. 6, 1870, at 2, col. 7 (Dr. Gunning S. Bedford's obituary); Oct. 30, 1893, at 5, col. 5 (ex-Judge Gunning S. Bedford's obituary); Nov. 1, 1893, at 8, col. 6 (his requiem Mass). Professor Rice would seem to be the first post-1895 Roman Catholic who has proposed to bring the secular law of New York into conformity with the decree of the Holy Office of Leo XIII.

Apropos of Judge Bedford, the ecumenical honeymoon between him and Jones and Jennings of the Times in their common crusade against the City's abortionists foundered in an early divorce, because of the Judge's behavior at a trial for murder where his conduct showed "that Bedford is the tool of the Jesuits." Bedford's nomination for reelection was the doing of "the Herald and its interior friends the Jesuits and the Tammany Convention flattened like a field of grain to the wind, and Bedford went in [i.e., was renominated] by acclamation. . . ." The Times warned its readers that Bedford's reelection would mean "a triumph of the Jesuits toward their avowed object of making our City Roman Catholic entirely." N.Y. Times, Oct. 29, 1872, at 5, col. 6. The outcome of the election delighted the Times. N.Y. Times, Nov. 6, 1872, at 4, cols. 3-4; Nov. 7, 1872, at 4, col. 1 ("Bedford is literally nowhere in the race"); Nov. 8, 1872, at 4, col. 3 (Judge Sutherland hailed as the victor over "the present incompetent and untrustworthy occupant of the Bench of the City Court"); at 8, col. 2 (by a vote of 78,649:52,609). Bedford never held elective office again.

200 Law of July 26, 1881, ch. 676, [1881] Laws of N.Y. (repealed 1909).
201 Law of July 26, 1881, ch. 676, § 190, [1881] Laws of N.Y. (repealed 1909): "The willful killing of an unborn quick child, by any injury committed upon the person of the mother of such child, is manslaughter in the first degree." Law of July 26, 1881, ch. 676, § 191, [1881] Laws of N.Y. (repealed 1909):

A person who provides, supplies, or administers to a woman, whether pregnant or not, or who prescribes for, or advises or procures a woman to take any medicine, drug, or substance, or who uses or employs, or causes to be used or employed, any instrument or other means with intent thereby to procure the miscarriage of a woman, unless the same is necessary to preserve her life, in case the death of the woman or of any quick child of which she is pregnant, is thereby produced, is guilty of manslaughter in the first degree.

for the guilt of a woman (manslaughter in the second degree) who submitted to an abortion.[202]

Sections 294 and 295 provided for punishment whether the abortion was performed before or after quickening.[203] Finally, section 297 provided for punishment for manufacturers, suppliers or vendors of abortifacients.[204]

It must be admitted that the framers of the Penal Code of 1881 did an excellent job of eliminating redundancies and inconsistencies in the pre-Code statutory materials. So far as this author can detect, they introduced only one inconsistency of their own. Sections 191, 194, 294 and 295 all mention the therapeutic exception, but, whereas last three sections included both branches, *i.e.*, to preserve either the pregnant woman's life, or that of the child whereof she is pregnant, section 191 speaks of preserving the life of the pregnant woman only. The alternative of preserving the life of a quickened foetus (omitted in section 191, mentioned in 194) makes sense if premature induction of labor is intended. The presence of such an alternative in sections 294 and 295 is sensible only if one remembers that those offenses, while they may be committed before quickening, may also be committed after quickening. The prosecutor thus has an election whether to proceed under section 191 *or* 294, or under section 194 *or* 295, if the foetus has already quickened.

In the consolidation of the Penal Code of 1881 into the Penal

---

[202] Law of July 26, 1881, ch. 676, § 194, [1881] Laws of N.Y. (repealed 1909):

A woman quick with child, who takes or uses, or submits to the use of any drug, medicine, or substance, or any instrument or other means with intent to produce her own miscarriage, unless the same is necessary to preserve her own life, or that of the child whereof she is pregnant, if the death of such child is thereby produced, is guilty of manslaughter in the second degree.

[203] Law of July 26, 1881, ch. 676, § 294, [1881] Laws of N.Y. (repealed 1909):

A person who, with intent thereby to procure the miscarriage of a woman, unless the same is necessary to preserve the life of the woman, or of the child with which she is pregnant, either

1. Prescribes, supplies, or administers to a woman, whether pregnant or not, or advises or causes a woman to take any medicine, drug, or substance; or

2. Uses, or causes to be used, any instrument or other means;

Is guilty of abortion, and is punishable by imprisonment in a state prison for not more than four years, or in a county jail for not more than one year. Law of July 26, 1881, ch. 676, § 295, [1881] Laws of N.Y. (repealed 1909):

A pregnant woman, who takes any medicine, drug, or substance, or uses or submits to the use of any instrument or other means, with intent thereby to produce her own miscarriage, unless the same is necessary to preserve her life, or that of the child whereof she is pregnant, is punishable by imprisonment for not less than one year, nor more than four years.

[204] Law of July 26, 1881, ch. 676 § 297, [1881] Laws of N.Y. (repealed 1909):

A person who manufactures, gives or sells an instrument, a medicine or drug, or any other substance, with intent that the same may be unlawfully used in procuring the miscarriage of a woman, is guilty of a felony.

Law of 1909 [205] no changes were made in the language of the foregoing sections, but they were re-arranged and re-numbered.[206] The only change made in this legislation until September 1, 1967 was the addition in 1942[207] of a new section, numbered 81-a. It concerned witnesses' immunity and was amended in 1944[208] and 1953;[209] as amended it provided for the grant of immunity to a female who has violated the Act.[210]

New York is in the minority of American states whose statutes go through the solemn mockery of proclaiming the woman guilty of crime if she either aborts herself or submits to an abortion, although everyone knows that no such woman ever has been, or is ever likely to be, prosecuted. The reason these statutes are dead letters is simple. Convictions require unanimous jury verdicts, and it would be very difficult to empanel a jury today, at least one or two of whose members did not, if male, have a close female relative who had undergone an illegal abortion, or who, if female, had not undergone one herself. Prosecutors know very well which laws merely serve the ends of social hypocrisy, but, under which juries simply will not convict, and they do not put their reputations for securing convictions in jeopardy by initiating prosecutions where their chances of success are virtually nil.

Nevertheless, the very existence of these dead letters, theoreti-

---

[205] Law of Mar. 12, 1909, ch. 88, [1909] Laws of N.Y. (repealed 1965).

[206] N.Y. Penal Code (1881)

N.Y. Penal Code (1881)	N.Y. Penal Law (1909)
§ 190	§ 1050, penultimate paragraph
§ 191	§ 1050, last paragraph
§ 194	§ 1052, paragraph captioned "Woman producing miscarriage"
§ 294	§ 80
§ 295	§ 81
§ 297	§ 82

[207] Law of May 11, 1942, ch. 791, § 1, [1942] Laws of N.Y. (repealed 1944).

[208] Law of Mar. 4, 1944, ch. 104, § 1, [1944] Laws of N.Y. (repealed 1953).

[209] Law of July 2, 1953, ch. 891, § 1 (adding a new § 2447 to the Penal Law) and § 2 (amending Penal Law § 81-a) [1953] Laws of N.Y. (repealed 1967). These provisions were superseded in 1967 by additions to the Code of Criminal Procedure, but the superseding clauses do not effect any major changes, N.Y. Code Crim. Proc. §§ 619-c, -d(2)(c), -e (McKinney 1967) (Law of Apr. 27, 1967, ch. 681, § 78).

[210] Law of July 2, 1953, ch. 891, § 2, (old Penal Law § 81-a) [1953] Laws of N.Y. (repealed 1967):

§ 81-a Witnesses' Immunity: In any criminal proceeding before any court, magistrate or grand jury for or relating to a violation of sections eighty, eighty-one, eighty-two, ten hundred and fifty, or eleven hundred and forty-two of this chapter, the court, magistrate or grand jury may confer immunity upon a female who has violated section eighty-one of this article or who has committed an attempt to violate such section in accordance with the provisions of section two thousand four hundred and forty-seven of this chapter.

cally making the woman as criminally liable as the abortionist, as Professor George shrewdly points out,

> [M]eans that the woman may claim privilege [against self-incrimination] when she is summoned to testify for the state. However, because of the importance, in many instances, of the woman's testimony in establishing the abortionist's guilt, legislatures have had to provide . . . that immunity against prosecution is conferred upon the woman when she testifies for the state. This brings the matter around full circle to about where it would be if the woman were not considered a criminal in the first place.[211]

Apart from the immunity section, the Penal Code of 1881 was just over eighty-six years old when it was superseded by the Revised Penal Law. This is why journalists keep referring to New York's "86-year-old" abortion law. As we have seen, the Penal Code of 1881 was merely a codification of past abortion laws. It introduced no new principles or ideas. New York has had a statutory law on abortion since January 1, 1830; so it would be correct to refer to New York's "138-year-old" abortion law. Or, if one wishes to focus attention on the statute now in force, the Revised Penal Law of 1965, effective September 1, 1967, one should refer to New York's year-old abortion law, to which latter creation we shall presently turn.

Before doing so, however, we must pause to examine the earliest attempt to liberalize the New York abortion law, a bill introduced in both Senate and Assembly, in identical texts, in 1944. Senator Walter J. Mahoney, of Buffalo, who served in the Senate from 1937 to 1964, and was majority leader from 1954 to 1964, sponsored the Senate bill, which he introduced on February 7, 1944.[212] Assemblyman Harry D. Suitor, of Niagara Falls, who served in the Assembly from 1934 until his death in 1945, sponsored the Assembly bill, which he introduced on February 23, 1944.[213]

As originally introduced, the Mahoney-Suitor bill added the mother's physical and mental health to her life as values which abortion could legally protect. It also required that legal abortions be performed in hospitals.[214] However, before passage, the Senate amen-

---

[211] B. George, Jr., supra note 78, at 13-14.

[212] S. Introductory No. 657, Print No. 710 (1944).

[213] Assembly Introductory No. 1537, Print No. 1713 (1944). Both men were Republicans, graduates of the University of Buffalo Law School, and members of the Bar of New York. Assemblyman Suitor was a Baptist; former Senator Mahoney, who now practices law in Buffalo, is a Roman Catholic.

[214] The Committee on Public Health of the New York Academy of Medicine "drafted the proposed amendment" in 1943, 41 N.Y. Acad. Med. Bull. (n.s.) 406, 407-08

ded the bill.[215] It was then sent to Governor Dewey, who vetoed it without message on April 14, 1944.

The foregoing is the bare legislative record. Two men, otherwise very well informed on this subject, have been misled by an examination of this sparse record. Without scrutiny of the texts of the bills as introduced and as amended by the Senate, they misconstrued Governor Dewey's veto as indicative of opposition to abortion law reform.[216]

(1965); quoting the language of the Committee's proposal, from which the Mahoney-Suitor Bill was copied. See address by A. Chace, The New York Academy of Medicine, Annual Meeting, Jan. 1944, noted in N.Y. Times, Jan. 7, 1944, at 19, col. 1.

[215] In the upper house Senator Mahoney's bill was read twice, printed, and committed to the Committee on Codes. The committee was discharged of the bill, which the Senate amended on March 6, 1944. The bill was reprinted as amended, and recommitted to the Committee on Codes and no further action was taken in respect of it. In the Assembly, Mr. Suitor's bill was read twice, printed, and committed to the Committee on Codes, which reported it on March 1, 1944. It was read a third time on March 2, 1944, and passed by the Assembly on March 8, 1944, and sent to the Senate, where it was referred to the Senate Committee on Codes March 9, 1944. That committee was discharged of the bill, which the Senate then amended on March 10, 1944 (in exactly the same way as that in which it had amended Senator Mahoney's bill four days earlier). The Suitor bill, as thus amended by the Senate, was reprinted, and recommitted to the Committee on Codes of the Senate, on March 10, 1944. On March 15, 1944 the committee reported it to the Senate, and it was read a third time. On March 16, 1944, the Senate passed the amended bill, but reconsidered the vote and restored the bill to a third reading. On March 18, 1944, it was repassed by the Senate, and sent to the Assembly, which concurred in the Senate's amendments. 1944 N.Y. Assembly J. 731, 1019, 1178, 1221, 1278, 1464 (Suitor bill, Feb. 23, Mar. 1, 2, 3, 6, 8, 1944); 1944 N.Y. Senate J. 930, 999, 1254, 1452-53, 1615-16, 1696 (Suitor bill, Mar. 9, 10, 15, 16, 18, 1944); 1944 N.Y. Assembly J. 2365-66, 2388, 2525, 2656 (Suitor bill, Mar. 18, 1944). See also 1944 N.Y. Senate J. 192, 754 (Mahoney bill, Feb. 7, Mar. 6, 1944). All recorded votes in both houses were unanimous. The Suitor bill was A. Int. No. 1537, A. Pr. No. 1713 (Feb. 23, 1944), S. Rec. No. 382, S. Repr. No. 2017 (Mar. 10, 1944) (as amended by the Senate). As amended by the Senate, it is also printed in 1944 N.Y. Assembly J. 2365-66 (Mar. 18, 1944). The Mahoney bill was S. Int. No. 657, S. Pr. No. 710 (Feb. 7, 1944), S. Pr. No. 1891 (Mar. 6, 1944) (as amended by the Senate). The Senator who moved that the Committee on Codes be discharged of consideration of the original Suitor bill, and that that bill be amended, reprinted, and recommitted to that committee, was Benjamin F. Feinberg. 1944 N.Y. Senate J. 999 (Mar. 10, 1944).

[216] Thus the Hon. Percy E. Sutton, then as Assemblyman (now President of the Borough of Manhattan), testifying in behalf of a bill he had introduced patterned on the Model Penal Code of the American Law Institute, before the Assembly's Committee on Health, on March 7, 1966 (Minutes of the Proceedings of a Public Hearing of the Assembly Health Committee on Abortion, Assembly Introductory No. 3844, Print No. 3931 (1966); S. Introductory No. 2003, Print No. 2056, at 81 (1966)), stated:

> [M]any of us are mindful that just 22 years ago this Legislature here in Albany, both the Senate and the Assembly, passed a bill which would permit therapeutic abortions under circumstances not too dissimilar to the circumstances here urged. . . . This bill did not become law because it was vetoed by Governor Dewey in the year 1944.

The distinguished author, Lawrence Lader, in his major work on abortion, L. Lader, Abortion 145 (1966), wrote:

> [A] reform bill passed by both houses of the New York State legislature, was vetoed by Governor Thomas E. Dewey.

A comparison of the texts of the bill passed by the two houses discloses that the Senate amendments on March 6 and 10, 1944, in effect substituted a new bill for the original Mahoney-Suitor bill, a new bill in which the new indications, the pregnant woman's physical and mental health, had been eliminated, and the sole indication left was her life, exactly as in existing law. The new bill also required abortions to be performed in hospitals (which existing law does not require) except in emergencies. It was the new bill produced by these emasculating amendments that Governor Dewey vetoed. This bill could not in any sense be called a reform bill, or a liberalizing bill. The bill as amended by the Senate would have substituted a legislative command to the medical profession as to how to practice medicine for the custom of modern medical practice, which is to perform abortions in hospitals, except in emergencies, where the abortions are legal. Governor Dewey is therefore to be commended for vetoing a reactionary measure rather than criticized for vetoing a liberal one.[217]

Errors like this are self-perpetuating. In a background memorandum circulated to the members of the Governor's Commission to Review New York State's Abortion Law, under cover of a letter dated January 29, 1968, Assemblyman Albert H. Blumenthal wrote:

> In 1944 the Legislature passed a bill calling for the establishment of procedures to determine when such abortions may be performed. Governor Thomas E. Dewey vetoed the bill.

Here the error is not only perpetuated; it is compounded. The Mahoney-Suitor bill said not one word about such procedures.

217 All this becomes quite clear when the texts of the bill passed by the Assembly and of the bill as amended by the Senate are placed in parallel columns, for easier comparison:

The Suitor Bill as Introduced and as Passed (Mar. 8, 1944) by the Assembly (A. Int. No. 1537, A. Pr. No. 1713 [Feb. 23, 1944]):

The Suitor Bill as Amended (Mar. 10, 1944) by the Senate (S. Rec. No. 382, S. Repr. No. 2017 [Mar. 10, 1944]):

Section 1. Section eighty of the penal law is hereby repealed.

Section 2. The penal law is hereby amended by inserting therein a new section to be known as section eighty, to read as follows:

Section 1. The penal law is hereby amended by inserting therein a new section, to be known as section eighty-a, to read as follows:

Section 80. Definition of abortion and therapeutic abortion, and punishment of one who performs a nontherapeutic abortion.

Section 80-a. Definition of therapeutic abortion. Conditions under which it may be performed.

1. An abortion is the interruption of intra-uterine pregnancy before the period of viability (up to 28 weeks of gestation) is reached.

Original Bill (February 1944)	Amended Bill (March 1944)
2. A therapeutic abortion is the artificial interruption of an intra-uterine pregnancy before the period of viability (up to 28 weeks of gestation) is reached	1. A therapeutic abortion is the artificial interruption of pregnancy before the period of viability
where the continuance of such pregnancy would jeopardize the life of the woman	when such interruption is necessary to preserve the life of the woman.
or so aggravate the physical or mental disease from which she suffers as seriously to impair her health or threaten her life.	
It may be performed only by a physician duly licensed in the State of New York and only in a hospital recognized by the department of social welfare of New York state or the department of health of New York state or approved by the American College of Surgeons and/or the American Medical Association,	A therapeutic abortion may be performed only by a duly licensed physician and only in a hospital recognized by the department of social welfare of the state of New York or by the department of health of the state of New York or approved by the American College of Surgeons or by the American Medical Association
after written opinions as to its necessity have been obtained from two competent, qualified and recognized consultants in the respective specialties involved, which said written opinions shall be incorporated in the records of the hospital.	after written opinions as to the necessity for such therapeutic abortion have first been obtained from two qualified and recognized consultants in the specialities involved, which said opinions shall be incorporated in the records of the hospital.
	2. In case of an emergency in localities where such recognized or approved hospital is not available, the therapeutic abortion may be performed in such place as the physician performing it may select and without the written opinions of two consultants, if their services are not promptly obtainable. In such emergency cases as defined in this subdivision the physician performing the therapeutic abortion shall within forty-eight hours after performing such therapeutic abortion made [sic] a written report to the local district health officer in such form as the state department of health shall prescribe.
3. A person who prescribes, supplies, or administers to a woman or advises or causes a woman to take any medicine, drug, or substance, or uses or causes to be used any instrument or other means with the intent of producing an abortion other than a therapeutic abortion as above defined, is guilty of a felony punishable by imprisonment in the state prison for not more than four years.	3. A person who, in any manner or by any means, performs or advises or assists in the performance of therapeutic abortion in violation of the provisions of this section shall be guilty of a misdemeanor.
4. A person who as a consultant willfully makes a false or misleading certificate is guilty of a misdemeanor punishable by imprisonment for a term not to exceed one year and a fine not to exceed five hundred dollars or both for the first offense, and for	

In both its original and the amended versions, this bill would have confined the offense of abortion to the period prior to viability; for this reason the preservation of the *child's* life, first introduced as an alternative to the preservation of the mother's life in the therapeutic exception (section 1 of the Act of 1872), is omitted in both versions of the 1944 bill. This reform was eventually accomplished in the Revised Penal Law of 1965, effective September 1, 1967.

In its original version, the Mahoney-Suitor bill, in defining abortion, excluded the termination of ectopic pregnancies by requiring the pregnancy terminated to be intrauterine; the amended version abandons this nicety but continues the immunity of the terminator of an ectopic pregnancy under the life-preservation exception. It must be admitted that the amended version reduces the penalty and grade of the offense from felony to misdemeanor. Only in this sense could the amended version be described as more liberal than the original. In deleting the physical and mental health indications, however, the amended version stripped the original bill of the real advances it had designed to graft upon the existing law.

The Senate bill as amended, when it reached Governor Dewey's desk, contained a paternalistic command by the legislature as to how

---

a second and subsequent offense, such person shall be guilty of a felony punishable by imprisonment in a state prison for a term of not more than three years or a fine not to exceed one thousand dollars or both.

Section 2. Subdivision two of section twelve hundred sixty-four of chapter twenty-one of the laws of nineteen hundred nine entitled "An act relating to education, constituting chapter sixteen of the consolidated laws," as amended by chapter one hundred forty of the laws of nineteen hundred ten, such section having been added by chapter eighty-five of the laws of nineteen hundred twenty-seven, and such subdivision having been last amended by chapter seven hundred twelve of the laws of nineteen hundred forty-two, is hereby amended by adding thereto a new subdivision (f), to read as follows:

(f) That a physician, in any manner or by any ways or means whatsoever, did perform or agree to perform or advise or assist in the performance of a therapeutic abortion in violation of section eighty-a of the penal law.

§ 3. This act shall take effect September first, nineteen hundred forty-four.

§ 3. This act shall take effect September first, nineteen hundred forty-four.

the medical fraternity should practice their profession (legal abortions only in hospitals, except in emergencies, plus paper work—none of these being required by existing law). The Governor's veto, under such circumstances, is scarcely patent of an anti-liberal interpretation. Probably it meant no more than that he thought doctors were better equipped to practice medicine than were legislators.

III. The Revised Penal Law of 1965

The Revised Penal Law of 1965 represents the latest development of the New York abortion law.[218] Article 125 of the Revised Penal Law, captioned "Homicide, Abortion and Related Offenses," serves as both a mirror of the past and as an up-dating and codification of the underlying rationale of abortion law.

Initially, it should be stated that the 1965 legislation specifically makes provisions for the therapeutic exception, classifying such as a "justifiable abortional act."[219] In accord with classical standards, a woman is justified in aborting a foetus upon the advice of a duly licensed physician that such is necessary to preserve her life.[220] The remaining provisions deal with cases where the act is not thus "justified."

With regard to a woman who commits or submits to an abortional act during the first 24 weeks of pregnancy, this conduct has been reduced to self-abortion in the second degree, a class B misdemeanor.[221] The 24-week period can be considered as parallel to the common law concept of quickening. If, however, such an act is committed after

---

[218] N.Y. Penal Law §§ 125.00 et seq. (McKinney 1967) (Law of July 20, 1965 ch. 1030).

[219] N.Y. Penal Law § 125.05(3) (McKinney 1967): "'Justifiable abortional act.' An abortional act is justifiable when committed upon a female by a duly licensed physician acting under a reasonable belief that such is necessary to preserve the life of such female. . . ." The 1872-1967 alternative to preserve the life of the "child" (i.e., viable foetus) was dropped without explanation by the revisers of 1961-65 and the Legislature of 1965. (It was still in revisers' 1964 study bill).

[220] Id.:

"Justifiable abortional act." . . A pregnant female's commission of an abortional act upon herself is justifiable when she acts upon the advice of a duly licensed physician that such is necessary to preserve her life. The submission by a female to an abortional act is justifiable when she believes that it is being committed by a duly licensed physician, and when she acts upon the advice of a duly licensed physician that such is necessary to preserve her life.

A physician today would never advise a pregnant woman to commit an abortional act upon herself, except under extraordinary circumstances (e.g., if she were injured and trapped in a mine, and he were in telephonic communication with her). Even a woman gynaecologist cannot perform an auto-abortion with safety. Perhaps the Legislature of 1965 was looking forward to the advent of effective abortifacient pills; even now such pills are yet to be perfected.

[221] N.Y. Penal Law § 125.50 (McKinney 1967).

the 24-week period (quickening) the woman is guilty of self-abortion in the first degree, a class A misdemeanor.[222]

Speaking to the abortionists, where death does not follow, the legislature again discriminates on the basis of the 24-week criterion. One who commits an abortional act resulting in miscarriage, during the first 24 weeks of gestation, is guilty of abortion in the second degree, a class E felony.[223] Whereas, such an act committed after 24 weeks is considered abortion in the first degree, a class D felony.[224]

Finally, where the abortional act results in the death of the woman the abortionist is guilty of varying grades of manslaughter, again depending upon when the act is committed. If the act is performed during the first 24 weeks of gestation, manslaughter in the second degree, a class C felony, has been committed; while the same act done after the first 24 weeks of gestation constitutes manslaughter in the first degree, a class B felony.[225]

---

[222] N.Y. Penal Law § 125.55 (McKinney 1967).

[223] N.Y. Penal Law § 125.40 (McKinney 1967).

[224] N.Y. Penal Law § 125.45 (McKinney 1967).

In notes 179 and 180, supra, and accompanying text, it was noted that the 1872 addition of the preservation of the life of the viable foetus to that of the pregnant woman as an alternative object of the therapeutic exception (1) was due to the aberrant medical usage foisted upon the Legislature by the Medico-Legal Society of New York, and (2) extended the coverage of the New York statute from viability to the term of pregnancy. In note 219, supra, it has been observed that the 1872 alternative in favor of the viable foetus was removed, without explanation, from the New York legislation in 1967. Does this removal signify that the New York statute since September 1, 1967 (just as it did from 1830 to 1872) applies only to a previable foetus?

An affirmative answer seems improbable. By moving the dividing line between simple abortion and abortional homicide of the foetus from quickening (usually between the 16th and 18th week) to the end of the 24th week of pregnancy, the Legislature of 1965 appears to have been reaching for a viability criterion.

Classical medicine declared that viability occurred in the 28th week, and this is undoubtedly true of the vast majority of foetūs today as well. There has, however, been a single foetus in medical history which, delivered at the amazingly early somatic age of 20 weeks, survived to adulthood. That foetus, therefore, was individually viable at 20 weeks. This phenomenon has led at least one international gynaecological congress to define viability as occurring at 20 weeks. The 1965 Legislature's choice of 24 weeks appears possibly to have been an averaging of the 28 weeks of classical medicine and the innovative figure of 20 weeks. If that was the legislative intention, then clearly foeticide of a viable [i.e., older than 24 weeks] foetus is covered by the present New York statute all the way from the end of the 24th week to term.

It is possible, of course, that the 1965 Legislature did not intend to create its own definition of viability at 24 weeks, but simply to name that figure as an arbitrary criterion resting on pure legislative fiat. In that case, one could argue that foeticide between the end of the 24th and the end of the 28th week is now abortional homicide, whereas foeticide between the end of the 28th week and term (usually the end of the 40th) is no offense at all. It seems bizarre, however, to attribute such an inexplicable result to deliberate legislative intent.

The better interpretation would appear to be that since September 1, 1967, as indeed since 1872, the New York legislation has covered foeticide all the way to term.

[225] N.Y. Penal Law §§ 125.15(2), 125.20(3) (McKinney 1967).

The New York statute makes no mention of the consent of the woman's husband, and it appears that the common law rule that such consent is not required continues.

IV. The Argument for Unconstitutionality

In regard to reprieve or non-reprieve of death-sentenced pregnant felons, the critical moment in gestation is the same today as it was 304 years ago, when the common law of England was first introduced into New York. That moment is quickening. Before quickening, the Province and the State of New York for more the three centuries has solemnly declared that the pregnant felon *cum foetu* symbiosis constitutes but one human being. That single human being is the pregnant felon. Her guilt and sentence justifies her execution, which *incidentally* also destroys a genetically distinct organism, the unquickened foetus. The latter is neither innocent nor guilty of the crime of her who carries it, or indeed of any crime, because, not yet being a human person, it cannot be the subject of guilt or innocence. Once the foetus has quickened, the felon *cum foetu* complex constitutes two distinct human beings. One of them, the quickened foetus, is innocent not only of the other's crime, but of any crime, and therefore must be spared her fate.

Is it objected that the foregoing is unwarranted eisegesis, that the rules do not say all this in so many words? To this there is a short and adequate reply: Of what other explanation are these rules capable?

It is now advisable to scrutinize the seven common-law rules on abortion, both in their original state and as modified by statute.[226] They exhibit two consistent themes.

---

[226] The seven common law rules and their statutory modifications are indicated below:

CONCERNING THE WOMAN

Common Law (1664-1845), Rule 1:
   It was not an offense on her part to abort herself, or to submit to abortion by another, before quickening.
Statutory Modifications (1845-1968):
   Her conduct was first made a misdemeanor (1845-1872), then raised to a felony (1872-1967), and has now been reduced to self-abortion in the second degree, a class B misdemeanor (1967-present). The period of gestation during which this (and no higher) offense is committed was at first the whole period of pregnancy (1845-1881), then only before quickening (1881-1967), and has now been enlarged to the first 24 weeks of pregnancy (1967-present).
Common Law (1664-1845), Rule 2:
   Such behavior after quickening may or may not have been an offense on her part; there are only [four non-New York] dicta on this point, and they are equally divided.
Statutory Modifications (1845-1968):
   Her [post-quickening] conduct was first made a misdemeanor (1845-1872), then raised to a felony (1872-1881), then raised to manslaughter in the second degree (1881-1967), and has now been reduced to self-abortion in the first degree,

First, there is the perennial importance of the quickening criterion. During the common-law period, it divided non-crime from crime.

a class A misdemeanor, which is no longer included in "manslaughter" but is still labelled "homicide" (1967-present). The period of gestation during which this offense is committed was at first the whole period of pregnancy (1845-1881), then only after quickening (1881-1967), and has now been reduced to the period after the first 24 weeks of pregnancy (1967-present).

CONCERNING THE ABORTIONIST

Common Law (1664-1830, 1869-1872), Rule 3:
It was not an offense on his part to abort a willing woman before quickening, provided the patient lived.
Statutory Modifications (1830-1869, 1872-1968):
His [pre-quickening] conduct was first made a misdemeanor (1830-1869), reduced to a non-crime by a revivor of the common law (1845-1872 in regard to surgical abortion; 1869-1872 in regard to nonsurgical), then made a felony (1872-1967), and has now been made abortion in the second degree, a class E felony (1967-present). The period of gestation during which this (and no higher) offense is committed was only before quickening (1830-1869, 1872-1967), and has now been enlarged to the first 24 weeks of pregnancy (1967-present).
Common Law (1664-1830, 1869-1872), Rule 4:
If she died in consequence of the procedure, he was guilty of murder, unless he had acted to preserve her life.
Statutory Modifications (1830-1869, 1872-1968):
His conduct was reduced from murder to manslaughter in the second degree (1830-1845, in regard to all types of abortion; 1845-1869, in regard to nonsurgical abortion; 1869-1872, in regard to all types), changed to a felony (with maximum imprisonment of 20 years) (1872-1881), raised to manslaughter in the first degree (1881-1967), and has now been reduced to manslaughter in the second degree (1967-present). The period of gestation during which this offense is committed was the whole period of pregnancy (1830-1967), but has now been restricted to the first 24 weeks of pregnancy (1967-present).
Common Law (1664-1830), Rule 5:
It was a misdemeanor [misprision] on his part to abort a willing woman after quickening, provided the patient lived.
Statutory Modifications (1830-1968):
His offense was raised to manslaughter in the second degree (1830-1872), changed to a felony (with maximum imprisonment of 20 years) (1872-1881), raised to manslaughter in the first degree (1881-1967), and has now been reduced to abortion in the first degree, a class D felony, which is no longer included in manslaughter but is still labelled homicide (1967-present). The period of gestation during which this offense is committed was the period after quickening (1830-1967), and has now been reduced to the period after 24 weeks (1967-present).
Common Law (1664-1830), Rule 6:
If she died in consequence of the [post-quickening] procedure, he was guilty of murder, unless he had acted to preserve her life.
Statutory Modifications (1830-1968):
His offense was reduced from murder to manslaughter in the second degree (1830-1872), changed to "a felony" (with maximum imprisonment of 20 years) (1872-1881), and then raised to manslaughter in the first degree (1881-1967), where it still remains (1967-present). The period of gestation during which this offense is committed was the whole period of pregnancy (1830-1967), but has now been restricted to the period after the first 24 weeks of pregnancy (1967-present).

CONCERNING THE WOMAN'S HUSBAND

Common Law (1664-1830), Rule 7:
His consent was not required.
Statutory Modifications (1830-1968):
None.

During the statutory period (until September 1, 1967) it divided simple abortion from abortional homicide of the foetus. The legislature made two attempts to abandon it, both short-lived. One succeeded for a time: from 1845 to 1881 the newly created and never prosecuted offense of the woman herself was the same whether committed before or after quickening. The other failed almost at once: the attempt by the Legislature of 1869 to erase the quickening distinction in regard to the abortionist's offense was frustrated by the Court of Appeals in 1872. Apart from these two aberrations, therefore, quickening remained, from 1830 to 1967, as vital an element of New York statutory law as it had been of New York common law from 1664 through 1829.

Secondly, the therapeutic exception, which existed only in the case of abortional homicide of the patient at common law (by which it was murder), was extended to the statutory offenses of simple abortion and abortional homicide of the foetus.

It is a curious fact that, during the 1830-1967 portion of the statutory period, the quickening criterion was not used to aggravate the offense of abortional homicide of the patient. Since 1967, the new criterion of 24 weeks of pregnancy, which has replaced quickening, *has* been used to aggravate the offense of abortional homicide of the patient (dividing manslaughter in the second from manslaughter in the first degree).

Could one argue from this last-mentioned innovation that the Legislature of 1965 recognized that two lives, and not merely one, are destroyed in this case if the foetus is over 24 weeks old? Such an argument finds no support in the Commission Staff Note, which merely affirms that "[g]reater liability is predicated in this situation because an abortion at this stage is considerably more dangerous."[227] Now, obviously it is no more dangerous to the *foetus* by reason of being performed after rather than before the end of the 24th week of pregnancy: it is, therefore, the greater danger to the patient, *and only to her*, that inspires this new distinction. Compare the similar Commission Staff Note on abortion in the first degree: "The aggravating factor is the pregnancy of more than 24 weeks duration, rendering the operation more dangerous than at an earlier stage."[228]

Why was the period of 24 weeks substituted for quickening? Often the only witness who can testify as to whether quickening has yet taken place is the woman herself; a fixed period of weeks is thus less vulnerable to testimonial prevarication. The 1964 study bill pro-

---

[227] Commission Staff Note to N.Y. Penal Law § 125.20(3) (McKinney 1967).
[228] Commission Staff Note to N.Y. Penal Law § 125.45 (McKinney 1967).

posed that this period be 26 weeks, but the 1965 bill, which became law, reduced it to 24.[229] The revisers of 1961-65 evidently thought that they were hewing rather closely to the quickening line, for they refer to pregnancy's " 'quick' or 'unborn child' stage—twenty-four weeks under this code [*i.e.*, the Revised Penal Law]."[230]

This indicates that the 1961-65 revisers were not conscious of making any major innovation. It may plausibly be argued, therefore, that they adopted *sub silentio* the reasoning behind the quickening distinction of their common-law and statutory predecessors, *viz.*: that after quickening [now after 24 weeks] the mature foetus has achieved the status of a second human being in the pregnant woman *cum foetu* symbiosis, and its life deserves distinct, though not equal protection. The fact that they retained the "homicide" label for the first degree offenses of abortion and self-abortion, though demoting them from "manslaughter," corroborates this argument.[231] On the other hand, the only explicit reason they give for using the distinction is the greater danger of the operation to the *woman* if it is performed after 24 weeks.

It is thus curious but true that both the Revisers of 1828 and the revisers of 1961-65 give one and the same reason, and no other, for their respective proposals to the legislature: danger to the woman. There is one salient difference, however. In 1828, all pre-quickening abortions were, if nonfatal, non-criminal; but all were dangerous, even those performed in hospitals by licensed surgeons. In 1965, *e contrario*, all but a few pre-quickening abortions were criminal, while any such abortions performed in hospitals by licensed surgeons were extremely safe.

Thus the 1828 Revisers' reference to the dangerousness of such operations was a legislative allusion to a surgical fact created, not by any law, but by the existing state of the surgical art. The 1961-65 revisers' references to the dangerousness of such operations, though verbally identical, must be interpreted against a very different background of surgical practice. This 1965 reference to danger is a reference to a fact, but it points to the danger of such operations when performed outside hospitals and by others than licensed surgeons, *i.e.*, criminal abortion. That criminal abortions are dangerous is a fact, and was in 1965 when thus alluded to, but it is a fact created *not by the*

---

[229] Commission Staff Note ¶ 7 to N.Y. Penal Law § 125.15 (McKinney 1967).

[230] Commission Staff Note to N.Y. Penal Law § 125.15(2) (McKinney 1967).

[231] N.Y. Penal Law § 125.00, Commission Staff Note ¶ 2 to N.Y. Penal Law § 125.15(2), Commission Staff Note to N.Y. Penal Law § 125.45, Commission Staff Note ¶ 2 to N.Y. Penal Law § 125.55 (McKinney 1967).

state of contemporary surgical art but by the abortion statutes themselves.

For constitutional purposes, this distinction may make a vital difference. The 1828 reference to a non-law-created surgical fact gave warrant for an exercise at that time—and as long thereafter as that state of surgical fact continued—of the police power of the State of New York to protect the health and lives of its female citizens. By 1965, however, this reference was circular: Criminal abortions are dangerous because they are criminal—hence hospitals are unavailable for their performance and so, generally, are licensed surgeons. But this hardly defines the same kind of danger to health and life as existed in 1828. By 1965, it was the law itself, alone, not only apart from, but as it were in headlong collision with, vastly different conditions of surgical fact, that created the danger. But an enactment cannot create the very basis for the exercise of the constitutional power to enact it; like horsemen, statutes have yet to learn how to hoist themselves by their own bootstraps.

This constitutional animadversion applies only to so much of the existing legislation as prohibits abortion before quickening. The common law itself prohibited abortion after quickening and hanging a pregnant felon after quickening, because the life of a second human being would thereby be taken, although it did not call the offense murder or manslaughter. As the common law was in effect when both our federal and state constitutions and bills of rights were adopted, the validity of prohibition of abortion after quickening is *not* open to constitutional challenge. But that same common law also tolerated abortion before quickening, punishing only if the patient died.

If, therefore, the abortion statutes, insofar as they purport to prohibit abortion before quickening have quietly, while no one was looking, as it were, become unconstitutional by erosion of their surgical-factual basis, then has there been a revivor of the common law in regard to such abortions?

Where would such a revivor of the common law leave us? In the first place it would make every abortion before quickening, where the patient survives, noncriminal. This would cover all but an infinitesimal percentage of cases in which patients die. What would the position be in such rare cases?

Theoretically, a revivor of the common law would make a surgeon whose patient died in one of these rare cases guilty of murder. One may well ask, however, if the revivor of *this* branch of the common law would be constitutional. Common-law rules, like statutory ones, may become unconstitutional if their factual basis disappears. The factual basis of this common-law rule, making pre-quickening abortion murder if the patient died, was the same as was the factual basis of the later statutory prohibition of abortion before quickening: the danger of surgery (even in hospitals) at that time. By hypothesis, we are considering a case in which a court in the 1970s had already declared the statutory prohibition unconstitutional because its factual basis had disappeared, and was now asked, in a very rare case in which the patient had died, to enforce the common law rule as to murder, which rested on the very same factual basis. It seems clear that such a court would hold that the common law rule, too, had lost its factual basis. So, with the theoretically revived common-law rule: *cessante ratione legis, cessat et ipsa lex.*

In New York however, since 1881, "[t]here is no longer any common-law crime."[232] Consequently, the effect of a judicial decision declaring unconstitutional the New York statute as applied to abortions before quickening would be to totally decriminalize such abortions, and not revive the common law concerning abortion in any of its aspects.

In liberal circles the contention is current that the statutes forbidding abortion violate the Federal Constitution on a variety of grounds. The most scholarly presentation of this catena of arguments has been made in a recent law review article by Roy Lucas.[233]

The difficulty which courts are likely to sense in weighing these arguments is that every one of them, if valid today, was just as valid in 1828, when the earliest American statute (New York's) forbidding surgical[234] as well as all other types of abortion before quickening was passed. The New York Constitution of 1821, in force at that time, contained the very same due process clause[235] that has been in the

---

[232] People ex rel. Blumke v. Foster, 300 N.Y. 431, 433, 91 N.E.2d 875, 876 (1950): "In this State, no act or omission is a crime unless some statute of the State makes it so." (Law of Mar. 12, 1909, ch. 88, § 22, [1909] N.Y. Laws.). See also, People v. Knapp, 206 N.Y. 373, 380, 99 N.E. 841, 844 (1912):

> According to the Penal Law no act or omission is a crime except as prescribed by statute. (Penal Law [1909], § 22; Penal Code [1881], § 2). There is no longer any common-law crime in this state.

[233] Lucas, Federal Constitutional Limitations on the Enforcement and Administration of State Abortion Laws, 46 N.C. L. Rev. 730 (1968).

[234] Quay, Justifiable Abortion, II, 49 Geo. L.J. 395, 435 (1961), correctly points out that though Illinois's earliest abortion statute was passed in 1827 and therefore a year earlier than New York's, the Illinois act prohibited potional, but not surgical abortion; not until 1867 did the Illinois statute prohibit all kinds of abortion before quickening. See id., 466-67. But Mr. Quay errs in thinking that Lord Ellenborough's Act (1803) prohibited only nonsurgical abortion, and that it was not until Lord Lansdowne's Act (1828) that the use of instruments was forbidden by statute in England. See id., 432; cf. 43 Geo. III, c. 58, § 2 (Royal assent, June 24, 1803; in effect, July 1, 1803).

[235] N.Y. Const. 1821, Art. VII, § 7.

Fifth Amendment to the Federal Constitution since 1791 and in the Fourteenth since 1868. Judges may understandably feel uneasy if urged to declare, or even to imply, that these statutes have been patently unconstitutional on a dozen or more grounds for 140 years under the State Constitution and for a full century under the Federal, and that five generations of American Constitutional lawyers have been too dim of eye to descry these grounds, which had to wait until 1968 to be perceived by a new "Daniel come to judgement, yea a Daniel."[236]

There is no need to lay such "heavy burdens and grievous to be borne"[237] upon the conscience of the courts. History teaches the contrary.

There are only two contemporary authentic texts which expound, in the very words of men responsible for their passage,[238] the reason for the enactment of any of the new Nineteenth Century statutes forbidding abortion before quickening.

The earliest was the New York Revisers' Report of 1828, which has already been considered, but now may profitably be reviewed. The Legislature adopted the Revisers' first proposal, to prohibit nontherapeutic abortion, but not their second proposal, to prohibit other types of nontherapeutic surgery. Why not? Not because the Legislature disagreed with the Revisers' stated reasons for their second proposal; in 1828 no sensible man could have disagreed with those. The difference in legislative reaction to the two proposals was doubtless due to the following consideration. In respect of every operation except abortion, a combination of patient's caution and practitioner's professional conscience sufficed to prevent unnecessary surgery. As *The New York Times* observed in 1863, however, it was different with surgical abortion. In regard to *that* operation extreme social and economic pressures were operative, which, in the *Times's* words, drove "thoughtless women . . . rash mortals into an undesirable eternity."[239] In the case of abortion alone, therefore, did the legislators of 1828 deem necessary a new provision in the penal law.

The English Act of 1803 and the New York legislation of 1828 forbidding surgical abortion before quickening broke the ground.

---

236 Shylock to Portia, in The Merchant of Venice, Act IV, Sc. 1: "A Daniel come to judgement, yea a Daniel. O wise young Judge, how do I honour thee."

237 Matthew 23:4.

238 John Canfield Spencer (1788-1855) was not only one of the two New York Revisers responsible for Part IV of the Revised Statutes and the accompanying Revisers' Report; he was also a State Senator (1825-1828) and actively sheperded his and his Reviser-colleague's work through debates in that house of the Legislature during the 1828 session. And the role of Governor Daniel Haines in approving New Jersey's original statute of 1849, and nine years later, as a Justice of the New Jersey Supreme Court, in construing it, will be commented on in the text.

239 N.Y. Times, Jan. 12, 1863, at 5, col. 3.

Before 1850, eleven more American States had followed suit.[240] Only one of these Nineteenth Century statutes, the New Jersey Act of March 1, 1849,[241] ever received a judicial construction by a contemporary court explaining why it had been passed. In 1858, in *State v. Murphy*, the old Supreme Court of New Jersey, in a unaminous Opinion written by one of America's greatest judges,[242] Chief Justice Henry Woodhull Green, declared:

> The design of the statute was not to prevent the procuring of abortions, so much as to guard the health and life of the mother against the consequences of such attempts.[243]

Of the three Associate Justices who joined their Chief in this opinion, one was Daniel Haines, who had been the Governor of New Jersey who, on March 1, 1849, had approved and signed the very statute which this opinion, nine years later, construed.[244]

The New York Revisers' Report of 1828 and the New Jersey decision of 1858 in *State v. Murphy* are literally the only known contemporary authoritative texts explaining the reason for the enactment of any of these novel prohibitions of abortion before quickening. Both point to the life and health of the pregnant woman as the *sole*[245] objective in legislative view.

---

[240] Ohio (1834), Indiana and Missouri (1835), Maine (1840), Alabama (1840-41), Massachusetts (1845), Michigan and Vermont (1846), New Hampshire and Virginia (1848), and New Jersey (1849). For citations and texts consult the monumental collection of American statutory materials on abortion in Appendix I of Quay, supra note 234, at 447-520. Every subsequent scholar in the abortion field must acknowledge a keen debt of gratitude to Mr. Quay for this meticulously researched and clearly presented compendium, which is the nearest thing that now exists to a complete collection of the American statutes.

[241] N.J. Laws 1849, at 266.

[242] When Roger Brooke Taney died in 1864, President Lincoln offered the post of Chief Justice of the United States to Chancellor Green. Ill health compelled him to decline it. H. Knott, Henry Woodhull Green, 7 Dict. Am. Biog. 546 (1931).

[243] State v. Murphy, 27 N.J.L. 112, 114-15 (Sup. Ct. 1858).

[244] 1849 N.J. Assembly Minutes 1057-59 (Governor Daniel Haines's message of March 1, 1849, to the Speaker of the House of Assembly).

[245] Francis, J., concurring, in Gleitman v. Cosgrove, 49 N.J. 22, 41 (1967), stated, as his individual opinion (in which none of his colleagues joined), that if the 1858 court in State v. Murphy had "meant to suggest that the only purpose of the 1849 act was to protect the life and health of the mother, I disagree." A careful reading of the entire opinion in State v. Murphy confirms, however, that the 1858 court did not merely suggest, it decided, that the sole purpose of the 1849 Act was to protect the life and health of the pregnant woman. If a confrontation between the four Justices of 1858 and their 1967 critic were possible, one can easily picture ex-Governor Justice Haines addressing Justice Francis in the same fashion as that in which in the Common Pleas almost seven centuries ago Chief Justice Hengham dressed down Serjeant Malmesthorpe, in Aumeye v. Anon., Y.B. 33 & 35 Edw. I (Rolls Ser.), 78-82 (C.P. 1305), translated in T. Plucknett, Statutes and Their Interpretation in the Fourteenth Century 183, 184 (1922):

Do not gloss the statute; we understand it better than you, for we made it. . . .

The common law protected the quickened (but not the unquickened) foetus as a being with its own right to life, immune to destruction at maternal will. By prohibiting surgical as well as nonsurgical destruction of an unquickened foetus, the new statutes, beginning in 1803 and 1828, could easily be mistaken as intended to confer a similar right and immunity upon the early foetus. That this was not the legislative intention, however, is demonstrated by the fact that the statutes of New York enacted at the same time, and still in force today, permit the execution of a pregnant woman under sentence of death and authorize her reprieve only if the foetus has quickened.[246]

The new statutes were inspired by reverence for life, to be sure; but the life they revered was the pregnant woman's, not that of the unquickened foetus. In contrast, the common law had revered the life of the foetus itself, after quickening.[247] To read into these new enactments, as does Professor Glanville Williams, a "pronouncement . . . metaphysical," is an eisegesis at war with all the contemporary evidence that exists.[248]

It is instructive to note that the old Supreme Court of New Jersey in 1881, 23 years after *State v. Murphy* (1858), with not a single Justice of the 1858 Court still on the bench, reiterated the earlier decision's *rationale* of the 1849 act, but with the addition of a significant gloss, which is italicized in the following passage:

> The design of the statute was not so much to prevent the procuring of abortions, *however offensive these may be to morals and decency*, as to guard the health and life of the female against the consequences of such attempts. (Emphasis added.)[249]

This express judicial disclaimer, in *State v. Gedicke* (1881), of "morals" and "decency" as motives for the passage of this legislation is of paramount significance, having been uttered in the heyday of Victorian moralism and American "Comstockery."

The 1881 court proceeded to observe that abortion "in almost every case endangers the life and health of the woman."[250] If this was still true in 1881 in New Jersey, fourteen years after *The Lancet* had

---

[246] See notes 64-67, supra. The earliest version of these statutes was enacted on the same date (December 10, 1828) as the earliest statutes against abortion before quickening, and with them formed part of Part IV of the Revised Statutes of 1829.

[247] See Weintraub, C.J., dissenting in part, in Gleitman v. Cosgrove, supra note 245, at 60-61, for an excellent discussion of this contrast in objectives as between the common law and the statute.

[248] G. Williams, The Sanctity of Life and the Criminal Law 227 (1957).

[249] State v. Gedicke, supra note 59, at 89.

[250] Id., at 96.

published Lord Lister's discovery of antiseptic surgery, it was likewise still true across the Hudson in that same year, in which the New York Penal Code of 1881 was enacted.

This observation (that abortion "in almost every case endangers the life and health of the woman") was stated by the 1881 court in *State v. Gedicke* as the very reason, and no other was mentioned or implied, for its holding that the penalties imposed on abortionsts by the statute were "a reasonable punishment . . . not cruel or unusual,"[251] and hence not violative of the interdiction of "cruel and unusual punishments" by the New Jersey Constitution of 1844.[252]

While the New York Revisers' Report of 1828 and the New Jersey Supreme Court decision of 1858 (reiterated in 1881) are the only contemporary authentic texts stating the reason for passage of the *legislative* acts prohibiting abortion before quickening, it will be remembered that the Supreme Courts of two states *judicially* legislated against it, Pennsylvania in 1850 (*Mills v. Commonwealth*[253]) and North Carolina in 1880 (*State v. Slagle*[254]). The North Carolina Court merely quoted from the earlier Pennsylvania decision deeming unnecessary any "further discussion" of its own.[255] Thus we need consider only the Pennsylvania Court's opinion.

In that opinion Justice Richard Coulter stated flatly that "[i]t is not the murder of a living child which constitutes the offence, but the destruction of gestation by wicked means and against nature;" it is a crime "[b]ecause it interferes with and violates the mysteries of nature in that process by which the human race is propagated and continued."[256] The mysteries of nature in regard to human reproduction are much less considerable in 1968 than they were in 1850; at that time the first microscopic observation of a spermatozoon entering an ovum (Keber, 1853) and the first such observation of the union of the nuclei of the two gametes in the zygote (Hertwig, 1875) were still in the future. But the Pennsylvania Court's appeal to the mysteriousness of the reproductive process seems to have been a makeweight argument, even in 1850: the real thrust is a demographic one—the propagation and continuance of the human race.

Propagation and continuance of the human species was in 1850, and remains today, beyond all cavil, a perfectly legitimate object, constitutionally speaking, of legislative oversight and protection. But what

---

251 Id.
252 N.J. Const. 1844, Art. I, ¶ 15.
253 13 Pa. St. 631 (1850).
254 83 N.C. 630 (1880).
255 Id., at 632.
256 13 Pa. St. 631, 633 (1850).

is needed now is different from what was needed then. In the middle of the Nineteenth Century, the death rate was very high. Every additional child that could possibly be begotten and born was needed to counterbalance, and, with luck, ever so slightly to exceed, the death rate. Had the men of 1850 not bred their kind as close as possible to the biological maximum, many of us would not be here today to discuss these problems. Today, however, medical science has so drastically reduced the death rate that, to continue to reproduce the human species at the same rate that was necessary and proper in 1850 would mean an overpopulated planet in two generations. It is curious that only the judicial legislators of the prohibition of abortion before quickening concerned themselves with mysteries of nature and human propagation and continuance. The *legislative* legislators concerned themselves solely with the life and health of the pregnant woman. But then, the law itself is less mysterious to those who manufacture it every day in State capitols than to those black-robed mystics of the Bench who dare alchemize new law only now and then.

Professor Williams's misreading of history—

> When, in 1803, the English Parliament extended the law of abortion to cover the embryo before quickening, it made not merely a legal pronouncement but an ethical or metaphysical one, namely that human life has a value from the moment of impregnation—[257]

is proved erroneous by both kinds of Nineteenth Century legislators. The real ones, as we have seen, were deafeningly silent about metaphysics, while the judicial ones expressly excluded it: "It is *not* the murder of a living child which constitutes the offence" (emphasis added).

Professor Williams favors liberalization of the abortion statutes. Another legal scholar, Mr. Eugene Quay, of the Illinois and District of Columbia Bars, opposes liberalization. Mr. Quay, from the opposite end of the jousting field, flirts with the same misreading of history, in another form. Quay finds it "strange to hear charges that our laws against abortion are due to pressure from the [Roman] Catholic population;" he refutes these charges by pointing out that Lord Ellenborough's Act (1803) was passed by a Parliament to which, until 1829, Roman Catholics were by law ineligible; that New Hampshire's Act of 1848 was enacted by a Legislature to which, until 1877, the State Constitution forbade the election of any but Protestants; and that the other early (*i.e.*, pre-1850) "American laws against abortion were en-

---

[257] Williams, supra note 248, at 227.

acted by States in which, at the time, [Roman] Catholics were an object of curiosity rather than a political force."[258] It is, indeed, a fact that the two New York Revisers who authored the Report to the Legislature of 1828 were a Presbyterian (Benjamin F. Butler) and an Episcopalian (John Canfield Spencer), and that the four Justices (Green, C.J., and Elmer, Potts, and [ex-Governor] Haines, JJ.) who decided *State v. Murphy* in New Jersey in 1858 were all Presbyterians.[259]

These facts may be cheerfully admitted, but, as presented, they have been construed to imply too much, as will be readily perceived if this tacit implication is articulated: a passel of Protestants in Nineteenth Century Parliament and Legislatures were eagerly embracing the latest metaphysical speculations concerning immediate animation then becoming current in the schools of moral theology of contemporary Rome. Anyone who can believe that, can believe anything. In fairness to Mr. Quay, he has not himself, so far as the author knows, ever said this, but numerous less astute debaters on his side of the abortion law liberalization controversy have relied on this passage in his article to support contentions of this kind.

Our Protestant forebears, of course, did not intend to enact anybody's metaphysics (not even their own) into their penal codes. They did intend—and this was all they intended—to protect the health and lives of women with unwanted pregnancies from damage and destruction by abortion, an operation which, in their day, even when performed in hospital on a healthy patient, "in almost every case endangers the life and health of the woman." It produced greater maternal mortality than childbirth. This was inevitably so because, unlike normal delivery at term, every surgical abortion requires the introduction of instruments into the womb. In an age when surgeons did not sterilize their instruments one needs little imagination to picture the consequences.

Thanks to Lord Lister and many others of his profession, both

---

[258] Quay, supra note 234.

[259] Benjamin F. Butler died in Paris in 1858; "[h]is body was brought back to New York and buried from the Mercer Street Presbyterian Church of which he had been a devoted member." 3 Dict. Am. Biog. 356 (1929).

John Canfield Spencer "served as a Vestryman from 1845 to 1851 and as a Warden in 1852" of old St. Peter's [Episcopal] Church, Albany, according to a letter dated February 15, 1968, to the author from the present Rector, the Reverend Laman H. Bruner, Jr., Ph.D. John C. Spencer's father, Chief Justice Ambrose Spencer, was buried from old St. Peter's, Albany, in 1848. 1 J. Munsell, Annals of Albany 167 (1850).

Chief Justice Henry Woodhull Green was a Presbyterian. L. Elmer, The Constitution and Government of the Province and State of New Jersey, With . . . Reminiscences of the Bench and Bar During More than Half a Century 400 (1872). So was Justice Stacy G. Potts. Id., at 359-60. So was Daniel Haines, who was both a Governor and a Justice. Id., 262. (Interestingly, Haines and Green were college classmates. Id., at 256). And so was Lucius Quintius Cincinnatus Elmer. 6 Dict. Am. Biog. 117, 118 (1931).

the abortient and the parturient rates of maternal mortality have
now sunk to infinitesimal fractions of what they were 140 years ago.
But this reduction in their absolute values is not the only change.
There has also been a reversal in their relative magnitudes. That
which was higher—the rate of maternal mortality suffered by healthy
women in consequence of hospital abortions—now is lower. Today it
is safer for a healthy woman to have a hospital abortion early in pregnancy than to bear a child in the same hospital.

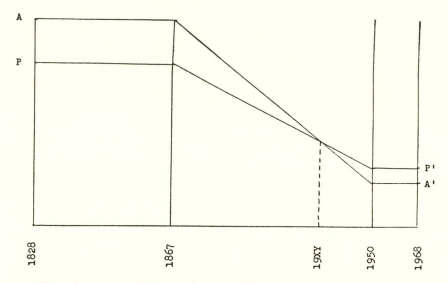

The above graph is a schematic[260] diagram in which curve PP'
represents the parturient rate of maternal mortality during the past
140 years, and curve AA' represents the abortient rate of maternal

---

[260] The eminent medical statistician, Christopher Tietze, M.D., who is also a gynaecologist, has advised the author that statistical data exist which support the general shape
of the curve PP' for the entire period of 140 years, and that portion of the AA' curve
since 1950. Before 1950, there simply are no statistical data in series large enough to
produce statistically significant rates. Speaking not as a statistician but as a gynaecologist,
however, Dr. Tietze agrees that the AA' curve undoubtedly was higher than the PP' curve
before 1867, and that at some subsequent time before 1950 it must have intersected it
in the fashion depicted in Figure No. 1. Without statistical data wherewith to plot AA'
before 1950, it is impossible to do anything but guess as to the year in which the intersection occurred.

Furthermore, it must be remembered that AA' is herein defined as the curve representing the maternal mortality of healthy women aborted in hospitals. There can have
been few of these until the widespread practice in recent times of accepting psychiatric
indication (suicidal tendency) as legal justification for hospital abortion. Before that, the
AA' curve is really almost theoretical. All the same, it represents a medical, if not a
statistical, reality: If a healthy woman had been aborted in hospital in 1828, her chances
of survival would have been less than if she had gone ahead and borne the child.

mortality ([as used herein] the rate of maternal mortality of healthy women aborted in hospitals). Both curves begin to descend after Lister's inauguration of antiseptic surgery (1867). At some point before 1950, when the first statistically significant universes of maternal mortality data on healthy women aborted in hospitals became available (*i.e.*, from Japan and Eastern Europe), the more rapidly descending curve AA' intersected curve PP', passing below it, and remaining below it. The date of this intersection is represented by the expression 19xy. 19xy is thus a critical date: it marks a constitutional watershed in regard to these Nineteenth Century abortion statutes which, called by a more descriptive name, are compulsory gestation statutes.

Before 19xy, the continued enforcement of these statutes continued to effectuate their original purpose: to compel women to choose the safer of two alternatives—childbirth rather than an abortion, even in a hospital. After 19xy, continued enforcement of these laws according to their letter not only did not serve their original purpose: thenceforth it frustrated their original purpose, by compelling women to choose the less safe of the two alternatives (childbirth). This is the effect of continued enforcement of these statutes, even when such enforcement is successful and the statutes are obeyed.[261]

---

[261] The author wishes gratefully to acknowledge his indebtedness to Judge Charles W. Froessel, Chairman of the Governor's Commission, for the basic idea that prompted the present analysis. It was Judge Froessel who, among the Members of the Commission, noticed the words "that the continuance of the pregnancy would involve risk to the life of the pregnant woman . . . greater than if the pregnancy were terminated" in the British Abortion Act, Eliz. II, 1967, c. 87, § 1(1)(a), and interpreted them as follows: "Potentially, the more radical concept in the [new] British statute is its allowance of an abortion whenever continuance of the pregnancy would involve greater risk to the mother than termination. Since carrying a baby full term causes greater risk than an early abortion under hospital conditions, this language, if liberally construed, could amount to virtually unrestricted abortion." State of New York, Report of the Governor's Commission Appointed to Review New York State's Abortion Law 11 (March 1968). Judge Froessel's interpretation of this clause in the new British Act is, of course, an exercise in statutory interpretation, not Constitutional analysis, and is probably focussed solely on the peculiar wording of the new British Act.

What struck the author was that the wording of this clause in the 1967 British Act may be peculiar as a matter of language, but as a matter of meaning it uncannily recaptures the real intentions of all the British and American legislators on this subject in the nineteenth century. They expected physicians to do exactly what the new British Act states they should do, viz.: to weigh the patient's chance of surviving a surgical abortion against her chances of surviving continuance of pregnancy. In the case of most women— all healthy women and many unhealthy ones—in their day, childbirth was the safer alternative; so abortion was forbidden. But in the case of an unhealthy woman whose condition combined with pregnancy could be dangerous, abortion might be the safer alternative; if it was, then the doctor was to go ahead and abort her, under the therapeutic exception. Nowadays, however, early abortion in hospital is safer than childbirth in hospital in the case of all healthy women. The new British clause would not have looked

Not only common-law rules, but prohibitory statutes[262] and even prohibitions embedded in state constitutions[263] have been struck down by courts which applied the Roman legal maxim, *Cessante ratione legis, cessat et ipsa lex.* If ever a statute deserved that fate, it is the just dessert of each of these now obsolete compulsory gestation laws.

The courts which used this Roman legal maxim to declare obsolete prohibitory statutes and state constitutional provisions applied it as a norm of statutory construction rather than as a criterion of continued constitutionality. No decision that has used it as a touchstone for the latter purpose, at least none that has done so explicitly, comes to mind.[264]

"radical" at all to the nineteenth century parliamentarians and legislators. It looks radical now only because it has so widely been forgotten what the real purpose of the abortion statutes was.

If the new British clause constitutes, as the author believes, the correct interpretation of all the prior British and American statutes, then, as a matter of statutory construction, even under the existing statutes, virtually every woman is entitled to "abortion on demand." But however the courts decide this question of statutory construction, there is an independent question, in America, of constitutionality to be faced.

May the legislatures command a woman to run the greater risk of childbirth rather than let her choose the lesser risk of an abortion in hospital? Presumably, since both risks are so low, the legislature could command women to assume the greater risk if there were a demographic need for increased population (e.g., if the country's population had just been decimated by a nuclear holocaust). But, under demographic conditions as they now exist, it is unthinkable that any legislature would embark upon a program of promoting population growth, or that any court would attribute such irrational motives to a contemporary Legislature.

[262] State v. Passaic Turnpike Co., 27 N.J.L. 217, 220 (Sup. Ct. 1858), deciding that § 7 of An Act to Incorporate the Passaic Turnpike Company, passed February 2, 1833 (N.J. Laws 1832-33, at 51), had ceased because its object had ceased, thus acquitting the company of a charge of criminal trespass. This case was decided by the same court that decided State v. Murphy; again the court's opinion was unanimous, and written by Chief Justice Green.

[263] People v. Stephens, 13 Hun. 17, 23 (N.Y. Sup. Ct., 3d Dep't 1878) (deciding that N.Y. Const. 1846, Art. VII, § 6, had ceased because its object had ceased, thereby disabling the state to proceed in a civil suit to vacate letters patent issued by the governor).

[264] Nevertheless, though the Latin maxim itself has not been quoted, its rationale has been applied, on the numerous occasions when the United States Supreme Court has declared statutes, both federal and state, including some that the Court had in earlier decisions held constitutional, to have become unconstitutional through changed circumstances. E.g., Nashville, Chattanooga & St. Louis Ry. v. Walters, 294 U.S. 405, 415 (1935) ("A statute valid when enacted may become invalid by change in the conditions to which it is applied." Brandeis, J. Quoted with approval by Clark, J., concurring, in Baker v. Carr, 369 U.S. 186, 254, n. 6 [1962].); Abie State Bank v. Bryan, 282 U.S. 765, 772 (1931) (In 1911 Nebraska's 1909 "Bank Guaranty Law was sustained by this Court as a police regulation", but "a police regulation, although valid when made, may become, by reason of later events, arbitrary and confiscatory in operation." Hughes, C.J.); Chastleton Corp. v. Sinclair, 264 U.S. 543, 547-48 (1924) ("A law depending upon the existence of [a] . . . certain state of facts to uphold it may cease to operate if . . . the facts change even though [the law was] valid when passed." Holmes, J.). In this line of cases none has been found overturning a penal statute, but a dictum

One ventures to think, however, that responsible and responsive courts could be persuaded to do so where, as here, penal statutes passed to shield pregnant women from danger to health and life now, *when obeyed*, endanger their health and life. *Cessante ratione constitutionalitatis, cessat et ipsa constitutionalitas.*

---

in Perrin v. United States, 232 U.S. 478, 487 (1914), a prosecution for violation of an 1894 Act of Congress prohibiting sale of liquor to a tribe of Indians on a reservation, in which the statute was held still constitutional, conceded that "the conditions may become so changed in the future as to render the prohibition inoperative" (Van Devanter, J.).

The New York Court of Appeals has likewise declared that four statutes (at least two of which were penal) had become unconstitutional by reason of changed circumstances. Landes v. Town of North Hempstead, 20 N.Y.2d 417, 419, 231 N.E.2d 120, 121, 284 N.Y.S.2d 441, 443 (1967) (holding that, by 1967, a statute imposing local real estate ownership as a qualification for the post of town councilman [Town Law §§ 23, 23-a], which, in successive recensions, had been on the books since 1830 [N.Y. Revised Statutes 1829, Pt. I, ch. 11, tit. 3, §§ 11, 12] and which the Court of Appeals had held constitutional only thirty years before [Becraft v. Strobel, 274 N.Y. 577, 10 N.E.2d 560 (1937)], had become unconstitutional. "Recent developments in constitutional law, as well as changes in the pattern of town and suburban living, call for a reconsideration of our 1937 decision in Becraft . . . and of the constitutionality of the statutes here involved." Fuld, C.J.); Defiance Milk Prods. Co. v. Du Mond, 309 N.Y. 537, 541, 132 N.E.2d 829, 830 (1956) (holding that, by 1951, a statute [Agriculture & Markets Law § 64(2)] passed in 1922 [Law of March 30, 1922, ch. 365, § 1 [1922] N.Y. Laws], which in effect prohibited the retail sale of evaporated skimmed milk, and violation of which was a misdemeanor [Agriculture & Markets Law § 41], had become unconstitutional: "even though a police power enactment may have been or may have seemed to be valid when made, later events or later-discovered facts may show it to be arbitrary and confiscatory", Desmond, J.); Vernon Park Realty, Inc. v. City of Mount Vernon, 307 N.Y. 493, 499, 121 N.E.2d 517, 519 (1954) (holding that, by 1952, a municipal zoning ordinance originally adopted in 1927, varied in 1932, and amended as recently as 1952, had become unconstitutional: "an ordinance valid when adopted will nevertheless be stricken down as invalid when, at a later time, its operation under changed conditions proves confiscatory", Dye, J.); Municipal Gas Co. v. Pub. Serv. Comm'n, 225 N.Y. 89, 95-96, 121 N.E. 772, 774 (1919) (holding that, by 1918, a public utility rate regulation act [Law of April 26, 1907, ch. 227 [1907] N.Y. Laws] section three of which punished every violation of the act by a forfeiture "to the people of the state" of $1,000 "for each offense", had become unconstitutional. "But the argument is that a statute is either valid or invalid at the moment of its making, and from that premise the conclusion is supposed to follow that there is a remedy for present confiscation, but not for confiscation that results from changed conditions. We do not view so narrowly the great immunities of the Constitution, or our own power to enforce them. A statute prescribing rates is one of continuing operation. It is an attempt by the legislature to predict for future years the charges that will yield a fair return. The prediction must square with the facts or be cast aside as worthless. . . . It must square with them in one year as in another, at the beginning but equally at the end. In all such legislation, from the hour of its enactment, there thus inheres the seed of an infirmity which the future may develop. It is the infirmity that always waits upon prophecy; the coming years must tell whether the prophecy is true or false." Cardozo, J.).

NEW YORK
LAW FORUM

| VOLUME XVII | NUMBER 2 | 1971 |

THE PHOENIX OF ABORTIONAL FREEDOM: IS A PENUMBRAL OR NINTH-AMENDMENT RIGHT ABOUT TO ARISE FROM THE NINETEENTH-CENTURY LEGISLATIVE ASHES OF A FOURTEENTH-CENTURY COMMON-LAW LIBERTY?

CYRIL C. MEANS, JR. **

In ancient Eastern folklore, the phoenix was a fabulous bird, said to live for five hundred years in the Arabian desert, then to build its own funeral pyre, on which it would burn itself to ashes, out of which it would then arise young again. Is it the destiny of elective abortion to recapitulate the career of the phoenix?

Readers of this journal will recall an article published three years ago,[1] in which I described the nineteenth-century legislative funeral

---

* A.B., 1938, Harvard College; J.D., 1941, Wayne State University Law School; LL.M., 1948, Harvard Law School. Member, Governor Rockefeller's Commission Appointed to Review New York State's Abortion Law (1968). Associate Professor of Law, New York Law School. Member of the Michigan and United States Supreme Court Bars.

** For invaluable aid in the task of historical research which had to be done to prepare this article, I make grateful acknowledgment to Dr. Edith Henderson, Curator of the Rare Book Room of the Library of the Harvard Law School (and Secretary for the United States of America of The Selden Society), and to Mr. Anthony Grech, Librarian of The Association of the Bar of the City of New York. For first editions, I normally had to go to Cambridge, but Mr. Grech's library contains nearly everything I needed in second and later editions, including a magnificent "vulgate" edition of the Year Books that was once owned by President Martin Van Buren. I also wish to express gratitude to Professor Samuel Thorne, of the Harvard Law School faculty, for time he has generously spent with me discussing the various problems presented by this paper, and to my colleague, Professor Joel Lee, of the New York Law School faculty, for some invaluable leads in clearing up the long-mooted question as to how soon after the accession of Edward III Sir Geoffrey Scrope resumed his place as Chief Justice of the King's Bench. For any errors of emphasis or content, however, I take full responsibility.

[1] Means, *The Law of New York Concerning Abortion and the Status of the Foetus, 1664-1968: A Case of Cessation of Constitutionality,* 14 N.Y.L.F. 411 (1968).

pyre on which English and American women's common-law liberty
of abortion at will was reduced to ashes. The original contribution of
that article was the revelation of a truth that had been long forgotten:
that the sole historically demonstrable legislative purpose behind these
statutes was the protection of pregnant women from the danger to
their lives imposed by surgical or potional abortion, under medical
conditions then obtaining, that was several times as great as the risk
to their lives posed by childbirth at term, and that concern for the life
of the conceptus was foreign to the secular thinking of the Protestant
legislators who passed these laws. Novel as this thesis was at the time,
it has since received approbation by distinguished judges, and is no
longer seriously challenged.

The present article makes a different contribution to the history
of this subject, probing the true position of abortion at common law,
prior to the nineteenth century. It reveals the story, untold now for
nearly a century, of the long period during which English and American women enjoyed a common-law liberty to terminate at will an
unwanted pregnancy, from the reign of Edward III to that of George
III. This common-law liberty endured, in England, from 1327 to
1803; in America, from 1607 to 1830. Thus its life-span closely ap-
proximated the semimillenium of the phoenix.

The United States Supreme Court will soon hear argument, both
on jurisdiction and on the merits, of two cases[2] in which the constitutionality of state abortion laws is drawn in question. Should the merits be reached in either case, counsel and the Court may find the
present conspectus of the Anglo-American legal history of abortion
of assistance; for, only if in 1791 elective abortion was a common-
law liberty, can it be a ninth-amendment right today.

I. Did an Expectant Mother and Her Abortionist Have a Common-Law Liberty of Abortion at Every Stage of Gestation?

Surprisingly enough, the correct answer to this question is

---

[2] Doe v. Bolton, 319 F. Supp. 1048 (N.D. Ga. 1970), *jurisdiction postponed to argument
on the merits*, 402 U.S. 941 (1971); Roe v. Wade, 314 F. Supp. 1217 (N.D. Tex. 1970),
jurisdiction postponed to argument on the merits, 402 U.S. 941 (1971).

These are both direct appeals from decisions of three-judge courts. In *Roe v. Wade*, the
Texas statute (Penal Code of Tex. Ann. tit. 15, ch. 9, art. 1191 (Vernon 1961)) is being
challenged. In *Doe v. Bolton*, the attack is upon Georgia's new statute (Code of Ga. Ann. tit.
26, § 1201 (rev. 1970)), based on the American Law Institute's Model Penal Code.

"Yes." The primary case which establishes this liberty was decided in the Court of King's Bench at the very beginning of the long reign of Edward III (1327-77). Like most Year Book cases it is anonymous; so, for convenience of reference I have given it a name, *The Twinslayer's Case:*[3]

> Writ issued to the Sheriff of Gloucestershire to apprehend one D. who, according to the testimony of Sir G[eoffrey] Scrop[e] [the Chief Justice of the King's Bench], is supposed to have beaten a woman in an advanced stage of pregnancy who was carrying twins, whereupon directly afterwards one twin died, and she was delivered of the other, who was baptized John by name, and two days afterwards, through the injury he had sustained, the child died: and the indictment was returned before Sir G. Scrop[e], and D. came, and pled Not Guilty, and for the reason that the Justices were unwilling to adjudge this thing a felony, the accused was released to mainpernors, and then the argument was adjourned sine die.[4]

---

[3] Y.B. Mich. 1 Edw. 3, f. 23, pl. 18 (1327); *also reported in*, Livre des Assises, 3 Edw. 3, f. 4, pl. 2 (1679) and in Fitzherbert, Graunde Abridgement, tit. *Enditement*, f. 327, pl. 4, & tit. *Corone*, f. 264, pl. 146 (1st ed. 1516) f. 251, pl. 146 (3d ed. 1565). I cite folio numbers to both the first and the third editions of the Graunde Abridgement, but have copied the text from the third edition, which has fewer contractions.

[4] The full text of *The Twinslayer's Case, id.*, as reported in the Year Book, is as follows:

Brief issist al viĉ de Glouĉ de prendr̄ un D. q̄ p' tesmoigñ de Sir G. Scrop, duist aver batu un feme grosse enseint de deux enfãts, issint q̄ maintenant apres, lun enfant morust, & fuit del alter deliver, q̄ fuit baptise John p' nosme, & deux jours apres, p' le male, q̄ lenfãt avoit, il morust; & le indictmēt fuit returne devãt Sir G. Scrop, & D. veigñ, & pled' de rien culp̄, & p̄ ceo q̄ les Justices ne fuerent my en volũte de ajudge cest chose felonie, lendictee fuit lesse a mainprise, & puis la parol demurra sans jour, issint q̄ brief issist come devãt, & dit q̄ Sir G. Scrop rehersa tout le case, & coment il venit & pled'.

Herle, au viĉ, faits vener son corps &c. & le viĉ returne le br̄e al bailie de la franchise de tiel lieu, q̄ disoyent, q̄ mesme celuy fuist pris p' le Major de Brist. mes la cause de la prisel penitus ignoramus &c.

I have taken this quotation from the Tottell edition of 1562, the Yetsweirt edition of 1596 and the "vulgate" edition of 1679. Most American lawyers today will find readier access to it as reprinted in a footnote to Rex v. Enoch, 5 Carrington & Payne 539, 541, 172 Eng. Rep. 1089, 1090 (Worcester Assizes 1833), just as their forebears after 1834 found it easier to read it reprinted in the same footnote to the same case in 24 Eng. Common L. Rep. 446, 447 (T. Sergeant ed. 1834).

The fact that American lawyers after 1834 had ready access to the law French text of *The Twinslayer's Case* in 24 Eng. Common L. Rep. at 447, however, does not mean that all of them could read and interpret it accurately. Thus, the Massachusetts Criminal Law Commissioners

The singular importance of this case is obvious. It establishes beyond all cavil that an abortion, whether resulting in the intrauterine death of the twin who died at once, or in the death after birth alive of the other, was not a felony at all at common law.

In the middle of the same reign another case was decided which is not in the Year Books, but which Sir Anthony Fitzherbert (1470-1538) reported in his *Graunde Abridgement*[5] as having been decided

---

in their Report of the Penal Code of Massachusetts in their chapter on *Homicide* at 20 n. (y) (1844) paraphrased this case as follows:

> There the defendant had beaten a woman pregnant with two children. One of them was dead born; the other was born alive and baptized, but died two days after the injury, in consequence (as was charged) of the beating of its mother before its birth.
> The judges held that the defendant was not guilty of a felony, (murder or any homicide,) but of a misdemeanor only.

Now the entire paraphrase is quite accurate down to the last five words ("but of a misdemeanor only"), which are pure nonsense. There is not one word in any of the reports of *The Twinslayer's Case* hinting that any act of defendant, either in respect of the stillborn foetus, or of the liveborn infant, was even a misdemeanor. That lawyers of the eminence of Willard Phillips and Samuel B. Walcott (the two commissioners who signed this report) thought they discerned such a holding in *The Twinslayer's Case* is not so much proof of their own imagination as of the mesmeric hold which Sir Edward Coke had at that time on the thinking of Anglo-American lawyers.

In Michaelmas Term, 1327, the Chief Justice of the Court of King's Bench was Sir Geoffrey Scrope, and the Puisne Justices were Robert of Mablethorp, Walter of Friskney, and Robert Baynard. In that term the Court met at York, whither the King had gone because of an impending threat of invasion by the Scots. The Common Bench, whose Chief Justice was William Herle, also was transferred to York, much to the indignation of the citizens of London, whose deputation and protest were rebuffed by the King on the ground that the more people had to come to York, the more there would be to defend the north. *See* 74 Selden Society, Select Cases in the Court of King's Bench under Edward II, vol. 4, at xlii n. 2, lxxxvii, xci, cii (G.O. Sayles ed. 1957).

The unconstitutional presence of the Common Bench in York at Michaelmas Term, 1327 explains how the intervention of the Chief Justice of that Court (Herle) in this King's Bench case, as reported in the second paragraph of the Year Book report (but it is not mentioned in the Liber Assisarum or in Fitzherbert), was physically possible, but it does not explain what business Herle had in doing this. I have consulted Professor Samuel Thorne, of the Harvard Law School, about this, and he is as mystified as I am.

In order to leave the text of this article uncomplicated by this tangential mystery, I omitted the last few lines of the first paragraph, and the whole of the second paragraph, from the translation printed above, but translate them here for completeness:

> [T]hus the writ issued, as before stated, and Sir G. Scrop[e] rehearsed the entire case, and how he [D.] came and pled.
> Herle: to the sheriff: Produce the body, etc. And the sheriff returned the writ to the bailiff of the franchise of such place, who said, that the same fellow was taken by the Mayor of Bristol, but of the cause of this arrest we are wholly ignorant.

[5] Fitzherbert, Graunde Abridgement, tit. *Corone*, f. 268, pl. 263 (1st ed. 1516), f. 255, pl. 263 (3d ed. 1565) (Y.B. Mich. 22 Edw. 3 (1348)). While the court is not specified, doubtless it was the King's Bench.

in 1348. For convenience I have named it simply *The Abortionist's Case*:

One was indicted for killing a child in the womb of its mother, and the opinion was that he shall not be arrested on this indictment since no baptismal name was in the indictment, and also it is difficult to know whether he killed the child or not, etc.[6]

The definitive analysis of these two cases is given by Sir William Stanford (1509-58), whose work, *Les Plees del Coron*[7] is the first systematic treatise on English criminal law. Here follows my transla-

---

[6] The following is a copy of the original text:

Un fuit endite de ce que il tua enf. en le ventř sa mer, & lopinion que il ne serř arr sur ce eo que nul nosm̃ de baptime fuit en lenditement, et auxi est duř de conustř sil luy occist ou non &c.

Fitzherbert, *id.*

At Michaelmas Term 1348, the Chief Justice of the King's Bench was William Thorp, and there were but two Puisne Justices, Roger of Bakewell and William Basset; thus there had been a complete change of judicial personnel of this tribunal between 1327 and 1348. *See* 82 Selden Society, Select Cases in the Court of King's Bench under Edward III, vol. 6, at lii (G.O. Sayles ed. 1965).

Curiously, the Massachusetts Criminal Law Commissioners in 1844 seem to have been unaware of *The Abortionist's Case*; for they wrote: "There are no cases in the American, and but two have been found in the English books upon this subject." Report of the Penal Code of Massachusetts, ch. *Homicide*, at 20 n. (y) (1844). The two English cases they proceed to discuss are *The Twinslayer's Case* (K.B. 1327) and *Sims's Case*, Gouldsborough 176, pl. 110, 75 Eng. Rep. 1075 (K.B 1601). However, both those cases involve at least one liveborn infant who afterwards died of prenatal blows, which was the subject-matter of § 33 of the commissioners' proposed chapter on homicide, whereas *The Abortionist's Case* (K.B. 1348) dealt only with a stillborn foetus; so perhaps the 1844 commissioners knew of it but did not mention it for that reason.

[7] W. Stanford, Les Plees del Coron (1557). In 5 E. Foss, The Judges of England 390-91 (1857), we learn that:

[O]n October 19, 1553, three months after the accession of Mary [Tudor], whose [Roman Catholic] religion he professed, he [Stanford] was made one of the queen's serjeants . . . [In] 1554, Staunford was raised to the [common] bench. . . . The new judge was knighted by King Philip on January 27, 1555, and retained his seat in the Common Pleas during the rest of his life, which terminated on August 28, 1558, three months before the demise of Queen Mary. . . . He was a great and learned lawyer . . . the author of . . . a Treatise on the Pleas of the Crown . . . which is still [*i.e.*, in 1857] of great authority. . . .

Since Stanford is the primary authority for the proposition that, at common law, abortion after quickening is not even a misprision, it is well to note that he professed what he would have called the 'Old Religion', what its contemporary opponents would have called Popery, and what today would be called Roman Catholicism; thus this proposition cannot be suspected of being

tion of Book I, c. 13 (What Things are Required to Constitute Homicide)[8] of Serjeant Stanford's treatise:

> It is required that the thing killed be *in rerum natura*. And for this reason if a man killed a child in the womb of its mother: this is not a felony, neither shall he forfeit anything, and this is so for two reasons: First, because the thing killed has no bapitsmal name; Second, because it is difficult to judge whether he killed it or not, that is, whether the child died of this battery of its mother or through another cause. Thus it appears in the [*Abortionist's Case* (1348). And see *The Twinslayer's Case* (1327)] a stronger case: if a man beats a woman in an advanced stage of pregnancy who was carrying twins, so that afterwards one of the children died at once and the other was born and given a name in baptism, and two days afterward through the injury he had received he died, and the opinion was, as previously stated, that this was not a felony, etc. [Stanford here gives an alternative citation to *The Twinslayer's Case*, and then reverts to *The Abortionist's Case*.] But it seems that this reason, that he had no baptismal name, is of no force, for you shall see [here, Stanford cites an infanticide case decided in 1314-15][9] that there was a presentment 'That a certain woman whilst walking opposite a chapel gave birth to a son, and immediately she cut his throat and threw him in a pond of stagnant water and fled: on that account she shall be summoned by writ of *exigent* and shall be outlawed'; for this was homicide inasmuch as the thing was *in rerum natura* before being killed: thus this [infanticide] case is in no wise like those above mentioned where the child is killed in the womb of its mother, etc. Which case Bracton affirmed as law in his division of homicide, above mentioned [in a previous

---

an invention of the Reformation.

King Philip (the husband of Queen Mary I) was not a king regnant, but only a king consort, in England; thus he could not have conferred an English peerage. But, as Coke explained in another place, the honour of knighthood is universal throughout Christendom, and can be conferred by any Christian prince, and Philip was, after all, a king regnant of Spain. Thus Stanford's knighthood was valid as an English knighthood, though conferred, in England, by a King of Spain, who was merely husband of the Queen of England.

[8] The original title of this chapter is *Queux choses sont requisites a faire homicide.*

[9] Fitzherbert, Graunde Abridgement, tit. *Corone*, f. 237, pl. 418 (1st ed. 1516), f. 259, pl. 418 (3d ed. 1565) (writ found in the Chancery dated 8 Edw. II [1314-15]).

chapter in Stanford's treatise] saying as follows: 'If there be anyone who strikes a pregnant woman or gives her a poison whereby he causes an abortion, if the foetus be already formed or animated, and especially if it be animated, he commits homicide.' But the contrary of this seems to be the law as above stated.[10]

Stanford's masterly analysis of the mediaeval texts and cases has never been improved upon. He clarifies one point that they left obscure, at least to a modern reader. *The Twinslayer's Case* and *The Abortionist's Case* made it crystal clear that abortion was not a felony of any kind, even when committed late in pregnancy, but one asks whether it may not have been what we now call a misdemeanor, and was then called a misprision. In effect Stanford says that it was not even a misprision, for he not only declares that "this is not a felony" but, he immediately adds, "neither shall he forfeit anything." Now, in the same treatise, Book I, c. 39 (Misprisions), Stanford wrote:

And in all these cases of misprision he shall forfeit only these chattels and as to them he shall forfeit them only during his life.[11]

---

[10] The following is a copy (from the 1568 edition, which has fewer contractions than the first edition of 1557) of W. Stanford's original text:

Est requisit que le chose occise: soit *in rerum natura*. Et pur c si home tua enfant in le venter sa mier: c̄ nest felonye, ne il forfetera ascū chose, & ceo pur deux causes. Lū: pur c̄ q̄ la chos occise nauer nosme de baptisme, lauter q̄ il est difficil daiuger sil luy occist ou non. s. si lenfaunt murrust de cel baterie de sa mier ou p' auter encheson. Vt patet titulo coron in fits P. 263. Et vide la P. 146. pluis fort cas. s. home batist auter fēe grosemt enseint de deux infants, issint que ap̄s maintenant vn de les enfants murrust, & lauter fuist nee et baptise p' nosme, et ii. ioures ap̄s pur le male que el auer resceu: el murrust, et loppinion cōe deuāt q̄ c̄ ne fuist feloñ &c. Et vide m̄ le cas in fits titulo inditemēt: P. 4. Sed sēble q̄ cel reason q̄ il nad asc̄ nosme de baptisme nest dascun force, car veires titulo coron deuant P. 418. que p̄sent fuist. *Quod quedam mulier eundo versus capellam, peperit filium, et statim abscidit gulam, et proiecit in stagnum, et fugit, ideo exigatur & vtlagetur,* car ceo fuist homicide eo que le chos fuist *in rerum natura* auāt le tuer, issint nient semble a les cases deuāt s. ou lenfant est tue in le venter sa mier &c. Le q̄l cas Bracton affirma pur ley in sa diuisiō dhomicide deuat disant in c̄e mañ. *Si sit aliquis qui mulierem p̄gnantē p'cusserit, vel ei venenū dederit, p' quod fecerit abortiuuū, si puerperiū iā formatum vel animatū fuerit, & maxime si animatum, facit homicidiū.* Mes le contrarie de ceo semble ley cōe deuāt. *Id.* f. 21c.

[11] The following is the original text from W. Stanford, *supra* note 7, at Book 1, c. 39 (Misprisions), f.38a:

Stanford thus negatives not only the felonious, but even the criminal, character of abortion at common law. It simply was not an offense of any kind, no matter at what stage of gestation it was performed.

In 1581, William Lambarde (1536-1601) published the first edition of his *Eirenarcha, or of The Office of the Justices of Peace*. In that edition, he wrote:

> If the mother destroy hir childe newely borne, this is Felonie of the death of a man, though the childe have no name, nor be baptized. [Citing the infanticide case of 1314-15.] And the Justice of Peace may deale accordingly. But if a childe be destroyed in the mothers belly, is no manslayer nor Felone to be imprisoned upon this Statute [*i.e.*, the statute empowering J.P.s to bind over persons accused of crime].[12]

In the second edition (1582), Lambarde modernized the English of the final sentence to make it read:

> But if the child be destroied in the mothers belly, the destroier is no manslayer, nor Felone.[13]

Thus the text remained in the third edition (1583).[14] In the fourth edition (1588), Lambarde expands the passage to read as follows:

> Moreover, to hurt a woman great with child, whereby the child either dieth within her body, or shortly after that she is delivered of it: or to strike any person so, as he dieth not thereof, till the yeare and day be fully past: will not wrap a man within the daunger of these Felonious manslaughters . . . For in the former case, the child is not reckoned to be *In rerum natura*, untill it bee borne, though M. Bracton (Fol. 121) taketh it to be Homicide if the blow be given *Postquam*

Et in touts ceux cases de misprisiõ, il ne forfetera forsq' ces bñs & c quãt a cestres il eux forfetera forsq' durãt sa vie.

[12] W. Lambarde, Eirenarcha, or Of the Office of the Justices of Peace, at 217-18 (1st ed. 1581).

[13] W. Lambarde, Eirenarcha, or Of the Office of the Justices of Peace, at 217-18 (2d ed. 1582).

[14] W. Lambarde, Eirnarcha, or Of the Office of the Justices of Peace, at 217-18 (3d ed. 1583).

puerperium animatum fuerit [*i.e.*, after the foetus shall have
been ensouled] And in the latter case, it cannot reasonably be
alleaged, that the man died of that blow, which he received a
whole yeare before.[15]

This final revised version then persisted through six succeeding editions,[16] Lambarde gives the same citations of *The Twinslayer's Case*
and *The Abortionist's Case* in this revised version as he had in his
earlier versions, but he does add the note that Master Bracton "tak-
eth" the law to have been different in his day.

The third case which treats of this question is *Sims's Case*,
mooted in the Queen's Bench in 1601. The following is the report in
Gouldsborough:

> Trespasse and assault was brought against one *Sims* by
> the Husband and the Wife for beating of the woman, *Cook*,
> the case is such, as appears by examination, A man beats a
> woman which is great with child, and after the child is born
> living, but hath signes, and bruises in his body, received by the
> said batterie, and after dyed thereof, I say that this is murder.
> *Fenner & Popham, absentibus caeteris*, clearly of the same
> opinion, and the difference is where the child is born dead, and
> where it is born living, for if it be dead born it is no murder,
> for *non constat*, whether the child were living at the time of
> the batterie or not, or if the batterie was the cause of the death,
> but when it is born living, and the wounds appear in his body,
> and then he dye, the Batteror shall be arraigned of murder,
> for now it may be proved whether these wounds were the cause
> of the death or not, and for that if it be found, he shall be
> condemned.[17]

It is difficult to ascertain whether this was a decision or not. Coke
was Attorney General at the time, and was expressing his opinion
from the Bar, not from the Bench. The Court consisted of four justi-

---

[15] W. Lambarde, Eirenarcha, or Of the Office of the Justices of Peace, at 235 (4th ed.
1588).

[16] W. Lambarde, Eirenarcha, or Of the Office of the Justices of Peace, at 235 (5th ed.
1591), 226-27 (6th ed. 1592), 229 (7th ed. 1594), 229 (8th ed. 1599), 236 (9th ed. 1602), 227
(10th ed. 1614).

[17] Sims's Case, *supra* note 6 (full text).

ces—Sir John Popham, Chief Justice, and three Puisne Justices, Edward Fenner, Francis Gawdy, and John Clench. Only half the justices were present. Furthermore, the case appears to be a civil action for trespass, not an indictment for murder; so what the two justices said appears to be dictum. To add to the ambiguity, it is not clear whether the woman consented to the beating or not. If she consented to it, it is hard to see how either she or her husband could bring a civil trespass suit against the batteror. If she did not consent, then there was early mediaeval authority, though by no means unanimous, that she might have an appeal of homicide for the destruction of her foetus.[18]

If one assumes that this was a case of voluntary abortion, then the opinion of the justices shows that their understanding of *The Twinslayer's Case* and *The Abortionist's Case* was that the difficulty-of-proof reason given in the latter of those two cases was the only rationale that explained both of them. The difficulty-of-proof reason is sufficient to explain the result in *The Abortionist's Case*, where there was only one foetus, and it was stillborn. It would have been sufficient to explain the result in respect of the stillborn twin in *The Twinslayer's Case* also, but, of course, it could not explain the result in that case in regard to the liveborn, but afterwards dying twin. So, were Popham and Fenner undertaking to overrule, by their dictum in *Sims's Case*, so much of *The Twinslayer's Case* as held nonfelonious the death of the liveborn twin? If so, they were not very explicit about it.

Even if that was the intention of Popham and Fenner, they carefully left intact the portion of *The Twinslayer's Case* that related to the stillborn twin, and the whole of *The Abortionist's Case*, by pointing out that *"non constat"*—it cannot be established—whether a stillborn foetus "were living at the time of the batterie or not." In penning his *Third Institute*, in retirement some three decades later,

---

[18] In an opinion written early in his career as a Justice of the Supreme Judicial Court of Massachusetts, Oliver Wendell Holmes, Jr., surely the most distinguished legal historian ever to grace an American bench, collected these early but discordant authorities. Dietrich v. Inhabitants of Northampton, 138 Mass. 14, 15 (1884) (following the sentence: "Some ancient books seem to have allowed the mother an appeal for the loss of her child by a trespass upon her person . . . Which again others denied.") The very discordance of these early mediaeval cases where the abortion was against the expectant mother's will suggests how impossible it was for the common law to see any crime at all when the abortion had been performed at the expectant mother's own behest.

Coke was to forget this salutary wisdom of Chief Justice Popham and Justice Fenner.

As Gouldsborough's Reports were not published until 1653, this case, for whatever it is worth, was not citable until after the publication of Coke's *Third Institute* in 1644. Coke's own motive for not citing it is obvious, and it has rarely been cited by others.[19]

Stanford's total negation of the criminal character of abortion was repeated in virtually the same words by Michael Dalton (*ob. ca.* 1648) in *The Countrey Justice, Conteyning the Practice of the Justices of the Peace*:[20]

> Note also in murder, or other homicide, the party killed must be in *Esse, sc. in rerum natura*, For if a man kill an infant in his mothers wombe, by our law, this is no felony: neither shall he forfeit anything for such offence: and whether (upon a blow or hurt given to a woman with child) the child die within her body, or shortly after her deliverie, it maketh no difference.[21]

Thus the common law stood in 1618, after the first colonization of this country, and thus the common law would have remained, but for—and actually did remain, in spite of—a tendentious passage written by Sir Edward Coke (1552-1634), in his posthumously published *Third Institute*:[22]

> If a woman be quick with childe, and by a Potion or otherwise killeth it in her wombe; or if a man beat her, whereby the childe dieth in her body, and she is delivered of a dead childe, this is a great misprision, and no murder: but if the childe be born alive, and dieth of the Potion, battery, or other cause, this is murder: for in law it is accounted a reasonable creature, in rerum natura, when it is born alive. And the Book in 1 E. 3 was never holden for law. And 3 Ass. p. 2. is

---

[19] The Massachusetts Criminal Law Commissioners quoted from *Sims's Case* in their Report of the Penal Code of Massachusetts, ch. *Homicide*, at 20 n.(y) (1844). I do not recall seeing it cited elsewhere.

[20] M. Dalton, The Countrey Justice, Conteyning the Practice of the Justices of the Peace (1618).

[21] M. Dalton, *id.* at 213.

[22] E. Coke, Third Institute (1644).

but a repetition of that case. And so horrible an offence should not go unpunished. And so was the law holden in Bractons time, *Si aliquis qui mulierem praegnantem percusserit, vel ei venenum dederit, per quod fecerit abortivum, si puerperium jam formatum fuerit; & maxime si fuerit animatum, facit homicidium.* And herewith agreeth Fleta: and herein the law is grounded upon the law of God, which saith, *Quicumque effuderit humanum sanguinem, fundetur sanguis illius, ad imaginem quippe Dei creatus est homo.* If a man counsell a woman to kill the childe within her wombe, when it shall be born, and after she is delivered of the childe, she killeth it; the counsellor is an accessory to the murder, and yet at the time of the commandement, or counsell, no murder could be committed of the childe in utero matris: the reason of which case proveth well the other case.[23]

Coke thus resurrects Bracton's dictum, which Serjeant Stanford had so thoroughly discredited, quotes Genesis ix. 6, and cites a distinguishable precedent from the Cambridge gaol delivery of 1560,[24] all in an effort to show that the nonsense he has written is correct. In the margin he cites both *The Twinslayer's Case* and *The Abortionist's Case*, and Stanford into the bargain! Such candor—or was it simply gall?—enables the reader who looks up the marginal citations to evaluate this impassioned outburst at its true worth.

In saying that abortion after quickening is "no murder", Coke is perfectly correct. It is only his calling it a "misprision", let alone a great one, which is pure invention. The reader who wishes further evidence that this is so may turn with profit to Coke's chapter 65 in the same book, devoted to "Misprisions divers and severall."[25] Here Coke enumerates the miscellaneous offenses below the degree of felony which the common law recognized at the time. His treatment is exhaustive, yet there is not a single reference to abortion after quickening.

Coke had a politico-religious motive for this outrageous attempt to create a new common-law misprision. One of the reasons for his dismissal from the bench had been his stedfast opposition to the

---

[23] E. Coke, *id.* at *50-51.

[24] Parker's Case, 2 Dyer 186a, 73 Eng. Rep. 410 (Cambridge Gaol Delivery 1560).

[25] E. Coke, *supra* note 22, at *139-142.

jurisdiction, claimed by the Court of High Commission, a new tribunal among the ecclesiastical courts, to fine and imprison laymen for offenses cognizable at canon law. Abortion had always been an offense within the exclusive jurisdiction of the canonical courts.[26] Coke obviously felt strongly about abortion after quickening ("so horrible an offence should not go unpunished"), and in the privacy of his study he faced a painful dilemma.

If he acknowledged the ancient and exclusive ecclesiastical jurisdiction to try and punish laymen for this offense, then, according to his well-known view, those courts could impose only spiritual penalties (*pro salute animae*) for such offense, such as penances and the ultimate threat of excommunication. Coke knew perfectly well that the laypeople of his time, who had seen so much religious upheaval, were no longer cowed, as their mediaeval ancestors had been, by the threat of purely spiritual penalties. Those who were bent on having abortions after quickening would go ahead and procure them, and thumb their noses at such threats. For Coke to affirm the traditional ecclesiastical jurisdiction, within its traditional bounds, over this offense, would, in effect, be to let it "go unpunished."

If Coke had held that the ecclesiastical courts retained jurisdiction of the offense, but that they could impose really effective punishment for it (fine and imprisonment), his concession would have contradicted those numerous writs of prohibition he had issued, whilst still a sitting judge, to ecclesiastical courts where they had tried to fine and imprison laypeople.

If, on the other hand, he denied the existence of the ecclesiastical jurisdiction over abortion after quickening, such as had always existed, he either had to let it go unpunished, even by spiritual penalties, or assert a common-law jurisdiction over this offense. He chose the latter expedient.[27]

While most Americans will sympathize with Coke's objective, to exempt laypeople from the innovative compulsory jurisdiction of ec-

---

[26] Even before the Conquest; as Sir James Fitzjames Stephen remarked, "Procuring abortion seems to have been regarded as an ecclesiastical offence only" among the Anglo-Saxons. 1 J. Stephen, History of the Ciminal Law of England 54 (1883). *See* 1 Commissioners on the Public Records of the Kingdom, Ancient Laws and Institutes of England 574 (1840). At the Conquest, as is well known, the Norman Kings divided the ecclesiastical from the secular jurisdiction much more sharply than had been the case in Anglo-Saxon times.

[27] For full treatment of this fascinating struggle between Coke and the High Commission, in English politico-religious history, see the magisterial work, R. Usher, The Rise and Fall of the High Commission (1913).

clesiastical courts to fine and imprison them, in this country we have achieved that goal by a better expedient than the only one that was available to Coke as an author, namely, the clause in the first amendment prohibiting an establishment of religion. The expedient he resorted to, while understandable in a country with a Church established by law, is for that very reason not appropriate to our country.

In this connection, it is instructive to note that the Plantagenet justices who had consistently affirmed the noncriminality of abortion at every stage of pregnancy in the reign of Edward III were each and every one of them in full communion with the See of Rome, as was their sovereign, and as were all other Christian Englishmen of their time. They knew perfectly well that the mediaeval Church, through its ecclesiastical courts, punished abortion, whenever committed during pregnancy, as a purely spiritual offense, by purely spiritual penalties. They had no jurisdiction over that; that was the Church's business, not theirs. Theirs was the task of defining secular crimes at common law. In performing that task, they maintained a practical separation of Church from State, from which Coke, for the special reasons above rehearsed, departed, but to which American judges in the twentieth century could do no better than to return. Those king's justices of six and a half centuries ago had no establishment clause, nor even a written constitution, to guide them in their work, but with unerring instinct they pointed the way toward those great achievements then still in the womb of time.

Had our early bench and bar known why Coke wrote this inventive passage, they would have rejected it as wholly unsuited to our conditions. But they did not. By 1716, when Serjeant Hawkins (1673-1746) published his *Treatise of the Pleas of the Crown*, he treated this subject as follows:

> And it was anciently holden, That the causing of an Abortion by giving a Potion to, or striking, a Woman big with Child, was Murder: But at this Day, it is said to be a great Misprision only, and not Murder . . . .[28]

Hawkins cites all the authorities, but it is Coke who mesmerizes him into repeating the discredited dictum of Bracton, and adopting Coke's brand new misprision.

---

[28] W. Hawkins, Treatise of the Pleas of the Crown, Book 1, ch. 31, § 16, at 80 (1716).

By the time of Sir William Blackstone (1723-80), uncritical acceptance of Coke was at its apogee. In his *Commentaries*, Blackstone faithfully resurrects Bracton, and then says: "But [Sir Edward Coke] doth not look upon this offence [abortion after quickening] in quite so atrocious a light [as Bracton], but merely as a heinous misdemeanor."[29] We are now in a position to appreciate the irony of this statement. Coke, the archrestricter of the real common-law liberty of abortion, is now paraded as the liberalizer of a rigorous Bractonian common law that had never existed! Blackstone repeats the same thought in another passage: "To kill a child in its mother's womb is now no murder, but a great misprision. . . ."[30] After Blackstone, the course of judicial dicta was predictable. The earliest American case to deal with abortion, and the only one decided before the New York Legislature of 1828 enacted this state's first statute on the subject, was *Commonwealth v. Bangs.*[31] There, defendant had got a girl with child and gave her a potion to abort it. The indictment did not aver that she was "quick with child at the time" she drank the potion; this defect the Massachusetts Supreme Judicial Court held fatal.

The only remaining English legal commentator whose thinking on this subject remains to be considered is Sir Matthew Hale (1609-76). In his posthumously published *History of the Pleas of the Crown*, he wrote:

> If a woman be quick or great with child, if she take, or another give her any potion to make an abortion, or if a man strike her, whereby the child within her is kild, it is not murder nor manslaughter by the law of *England*, because it is not yet *in rerum natura*, tho it be a great crime, and by the judicial law of Moses [Exodus xxi. 22] was punishable with death, nor can it legally be known, whether it were kild or not, 22 E. 3. Coron. 263 [*The Abortionist's Case*]. [S]o it is, if after such child were born alive, and baptized, and after die of the stroke given to the mother, this is not homicide. 1 E. 3. 23.b. Coron. 146 [*The Twinslayer's Case*].
>
> But if a man procure a woman with child to destroy her

---

[29] 1 W. Blackstone, Commentaries *129-130 (1765).

[30] 4 W. Blackstone, Commentaries *198 (1769).

[31] 9 Mass. 387 (1812). This decision is summarized in 6 N. Dane, General Abridgment and Digest of American Law 734 (1823).

infant, when born, and the child is born, and the woman in pursuance of that procurement kill the infant, this is murder in the mother, and the procurer is accessary to murder, if absent, and this whether the child were baptized or not. 7 Co. Rep. 9. Dyer 186 [*Parker's Case*].[32]

The modern reader, who is used to employing the word "crime" to mean an offense exclusively against the secular state, may easily be misled by Hale's clause, "tho it be a great crime," into thinking that here, a generation after Coke, is confirmation of his nonsense about abortion after quickening being a great misprision. But one need only turn to the very first page of the author's *Proemium* to this book, to see what Hale himself meant by the word "crime":

> Crimes that are punishable by the laws of *England* are for their matter of two kinds.
>   1. *Ecclesiastical.*
>   2. *Temporal.*[33]

Now, in Hale's day, and from time immemorial until 1803, abortion was and always had been, in England, a crime at canon law, of purely ecclesiastical cognizance. So Hale's calling it a great crime merely meant that it was a great ecclesiastical crime. Coke's calling it a great misprision was a very different matter, for "misprision" was a term used only at the secular law, like "felony", and such a statement asserted that the secular courts in England had jurisdiction of it. Hale never said that.

The remainder of Hale's passage shows how completely he understood and accepted the authority of the mediaeval decisions, and thus how baseless was Coke's assertion that *The Twinslayer's Case* "was never holden for law." It was never holden for anything else but law, both before and after Coke, and this passage in Sir Matthew Hale, surely one of the most scholarly judges who has ever graced the English bench, proves it.

In looking back over this tortuous path of the English law on abortion, one is struck with the fact that the justices in 1327 were content merely to hold that abortion was not felony. They felt it

---

[32] M. Hale, History of the Pleas of the Crown 433 (1736).

[33] M. Hale, *id.* at *Proemium* (unnumbered first page) (1736).

unnecessary to give reasons. This must be because the reason was so obvious that it did not need to be mentioned. It was not a felony because it was a purely ecclesiastical offense, and always had been, even in Anglo-Saxon times.

In 1348, on the other hand, the justices began to speculate as to reasons for their reluctance to hold abortion a crime. The baptismal-name argument was pure make-weight; after all, Turks and Jews were perfectly proper victims of murder, and they were never baptized.[34] The difficulty-of-proof argument, on the other hand, had and has about it the solid ring of truth.

In fairness to Coke, perhaps it should be acknowledged that his criticism of that part of *The Twinslayer's Case* which let D. off in respect of the twin who was born alive and then died, insofar as that acquittal may be thought to have been based on the difficulty-of-proof argument, is plausible. So far as the intrauterinely killed twin was concerned, however, how can anyone ever know that it did not die shortly before the blows were struck? The difficulty-of-proof ground stands firm against convicting D. of killing the stillborn twin. But the twin who was born alive obviously had not died just before the abortifacient blows. In regard to his death, therefore, the difficulty-of-proof argument is not really available. Interestingly enough, in the nineteenth century, the English courts finally decided, at common law, that Coke had been right about the twin who was born alive and then died.[35] They never reached such a decision about the stillborn twin.

But the true reason for the decision in *The Twinslayer's Case* is not the difficulty-of-proof argument of the justices in *The Abortionist's Case* in 1348, but the simple negation of secular criminality (and hence the implied recognition of purely ecclesiastical criminality) which the justices of the King's Bench had made 21 years earlier in *The Twinslayer's Case* itself. Coke's attack never damaged that ground, and it is as sound in 1971 as it was in 1327.

Of course, quite apart from abortion, there were various heads of jurisdiction over which the ecclesiastical courts had exclusive cognizance in the middle ages which American legislatures have under-

---

[34] In his Third Institute, Coke tells us that "Reasonable creature, in rerum natura" includes "Christian, Jew, Heathen, Turk, or other Infidell, being under the Kings peace." E. Coke, *supra* note 22, at *50. In the margin he cites mediaeval authorities that so held.

[35] Rex v. Senior, 1 Moody 346, 168 Eng. Rep. 1298 (Cr. Cas. Res. 1832). *See also* Regina v. West, 2 Cox's Cases in Crim. L. 500 (Nottingham Spring Assizes 1848) (Maule, J.).

taken to vest in secular tribunals. One thinks of such matters as matrimonial causes, probate of wills, the crime of incest, and the like. In these instances, however, American states have been exerting their police power in pursuit of strong secular objectives, which are still as compelling as they were when they first passed those secularizing laws. In the case of statutes against abortion, there was such a compelling secular state interest when these laws were first passed, and it lasted for some decades, but then passed into medical history. Abortion at will is not a woman's ninth-amendment right today simply because it was her ancestress's common-law liberty in fourteenth-century England, but the fact that it was, helps. Common-law liberties may be abridged, though protected by the ninth amendment, but only when the state in abridging them originally had, and still continues to have, a compelling secular state interest. It is this hurdle which no American state today can surmount if it tries to go on enforcing the nineteenth-century abortion laws.

I have covered the English common law history thoroughly for several reasons:

1.	No modern American scholar has shown any awareness of it.[36]

2.	It has been presented only to two of the many courts that recently have considered the constitutionality of abortion statutes.[37]

---

[36] Justice Holmes seems to have been the last American legal historian to mention these mediaeval authorities:

> We shall not consider how far Lord Coke's authority should be followed in this Commonwealth [Massachusetts], if the matter were left to the common law, beyond observing that it was opposed to [The Twinslayer's Case]; which seems not to have been doubted by Fitzherbert or Brooke, and which was afterwards cited as law by Lord Hale.

Dietrich v. Inhabitants of Northampton, *supra* note 18, at 15.

It is worth remembering, as a needed antidote to the hyperdulia of Coke, that Sir Heneage Finch called Chief Justice Hale:

> [S]o absolutely a master of the science of the law, and even of the most abstruse and hidden parts of it, that one may truly say of his [Hale's] knowledge in the law, what St. Austin [Augustine] said of St. Hierome [Jerome]'s knowledge in divinity—"Quod Hieronymus nescivit, nullus mortalium unquam scivit' [What Jerome did not know, no mortal ever knew]."

[37] On June 1, 1971, I argued much of this material before the United States Court of Appeals for the Second Circuit, in United States *ex rel.* Williams v. Zelker, 445 F.2d 451 (2d Cir. 1971) (panel consisting of retired Justice Tom C. Clark, Circuit Judge Smith, and Senior District Judge Zavatt). On October 15, 1971, I again used most of this material in arguing a motion for new trial in DeLand, Florida, before the Felony Court of Record of Volusia County, in State v. Wheeler, No. 1400 (Uriel Blount, Jr., J.).

3. In my 1968 article, *The Law of New York Concerning Abortion and the Status of the Foetus, 1664-1968: A Case of Cessation of Constitutionality*,[38] I gave it only cursory attention, and therefore made the same error that all other modern authors have made in this field, *i.e.*, I assumed that Bracton and Fleta described the real common law of their century, and that Coke described the real common law of his. The bulk of my 1968 article, which dealt with the history of the New York statutes from 1828 onward, remains perfectly sound. It is only the preface treating the English common-law background that I now perceive to have been inadequate. As the legal historian on Governor Rockefeller's Commission to Review New York State's Abortion Law (1968), I wrote the original version of that paper as a monograph on New York's legislative history of abortion, simply for the information of my fellow commissioners.[39] So immersed did I become in what New York revisers of 1828 believed the common law to be, that I took their evidence at face value as representing what the common law was. For example, I quoted[40] the following two revisers' notes:

> The killing of an unborn quick child, by striking the mother is now only a misdemeanor. . . .
> A child not born, is considered as not being *in rerum natura*, and therefore not the subject of murder, so that the killing such a child is not murder or manslaughter.[41]

The second of these revisers' notes is correct. The first states Coke correctly, but Coke, as we have seen, did not state the common law correctly. As Stanford and Dalton had made perfectly clear, at common law, abortion, even after quickening, was not even a misprision.

4. The 1830-1970 New York abortion legislation, and that of the forty or more other states which copied it, as I maintained in my article and maintain herein, was constitutional when first passed and so remained for many years, because of medical conditions then

---

[38] Means, *supra* note 1.

[39] The Commission decided so submit my monograph as an annexure to its Report to the Governor. At the suggestion of the Chairman, the Honorable Charles W. Froessel, an enlarged and revised version was published in the New York Law Forum. *See* Means, *supra* note 1.

[40] Means, *supra* note 1, at 443, 444.

[41] 6 Revisers' Notes 12, 13 (1828) io N.Y. Rev. Stat. pt. IV, ch. 1, tit. 2, §§ 8, 10 (1829).

prevailing. But, with the change in those medical conditions, it became unconstitutional and has been unconstitutional now for many years. The question thus arises as to what is the scope of the common-law liberty in respect of abortion to which the cessation of constitutionality of the former statutes restored the women and physicians of New York and other states? Was it the restrictive liberty allowed by Coke (abortion before quickening), or the unlimited liberty allowed by the justices of Edward III and by Serjeant Stanford? If historically valid content is to be given to the "fundamental right to an abortion" that so many federal judges have perceived, through the constitutional lenses of the penumbral zone and the ninth amendment, it is important to know.

Prior to the present article, all historical treatments of the English law of abortion had mentioned the *loci classici* in Bracton (and his pupil, Fleta) and in Coke, leaving the 400 years of legal history between Bracton and Coke a giant void. I plead guilty to having done this myself in my 1968 article.[42] I have here tried to make amends for following the other authors down this false path. Curiously, a distinguished member of the Supreme Court of California was not deceived by Bracton. Writing for the court in *Keeler v. Superior Court of Amador County*,[43] Mr. Justice Mosk observed: "There seem to be no reported cases supporting Bracton's view, and it need not further detain us."[44] The sagacity of this insight was confirmed for me by the leading living authority on Bracton, Professor Samuel Thorne, of the

---

[42] Means, *supra* note 1, at 419-20 (1968).

In 1939 the British Ministry of Health and Home Office published the report of the[ir] Inter-Departmental Committee on Abortion, which contains the following:

The great authorities on the history of English criminal law are remarkably silent upon the matter [of abortion]. From Bracton, who wrote in the early part of the thirteenth century, and was the first of the writers to attempt a general survey of the existing criminal law, down to the 'Institutes' of Coke some 350 years later, the specific references to abortion are few in number. The reason for this comparative silence seems to be that the offence of procuring abortion was regarded as an offence to be dealt with by the ecclesiastical courts, and the writers on criminal law were only concerned to deal with it as it affected [the secular] criminal law, as in the case of homicide.

British Ministry of Health and Home Office, Report of the Inter-Departmental Committee on Abortion ¶ 66, at 26-27 (1939). Of the fifteen members of that Inter-Departmental Committee on Abortion, several were lawyers, of whom the most distinguished was W. Norman Birkett, K.C., but it is clear from the foregoing that all had lost touch with the mediaeval authorities on this subject.

[43] 2 Cal. 3d 619, 470 P.2d 617, 87 Cal. Rptr. 481 (1970).

[44] *Id.* at 625 n.4, 470 P.2d at 620 n.4, 87 Cal. Rptr. at 484 n.4.

Harvard Law School, who remarked, when I drew Justice Mosk's statement to his attention: "When Bracton had cases to support his view, he cited them."

It now occurs to me that Justice Mosk's remark about Bracton applies with equal force to Coke's passage. There are plenty of dicta supporting Coke's statement that abortion after quickening is a common-law misdemeanor (misprision), but no decisions, certainly none holding the abortee herself guilty of such an offense.[45] Faced with the treatises of Stanford, Lambarde, and Dalton, justices of the peace were not about to bind women, or their abortionists, over for an offense which those authors had held not to exist, whatever the opinions of the far more eminent commentator, Sir Edward Coke, may have been. Coke has never been taken all that seriously on his own side of the Atlantic.

Bernard M. Dickens, a barrister of the Inner Temple, has written a recent treatise on *Abortion and the Law*, in which he concludes his section dealing with "The Position at Common Law" by pointing out a single instance of an indictment,[46] of an abortionist who had given a pregnant woman pills to cause an abortion. This is the same indictment that was discussed in 1845 in *Commonwealth v. Parker*,[47] by Chief Justice Lemuel Shaw, one of the greatest common-law judges Massachusetts ever produced. That was a prosecution at common law for an abortion with no averment or proof of quickening. In ruling the indictment invalid, Chief Justice Shaw wrote:

> The only authority, adduced in support of the prosecution, was a precedent in 3 Chit. Crim. Law, 798, which is an indictment at common law, in which it is not alleged that the woman was quick with child. It does not appear that any judgment was rendered on this indictment, which was found shortly before the passing of the act of 43 Geo. 3; but as it is inserted, as a precedent, in a work of good authority, it was probably deemed good evidence of the law. But, upon a careful consideration of this precedent, it will not be found incon-

---

[45] *See* the dicta discussed in Means, *supra* note 1, at 428 n.37.

[46] This indictment is printed in 3 J. Chitty, Criminal Law 798-801 (1816). Taken from the Crown Office, Mich. 42 Geo. 3 (1802)—*i.e.*, just before the passage of Lord Ellenborough's Act, 43 Geo. 3, c. 58 (1803), since which abortion has been an exclusively statutory offense in England.

[47] 50 Mass. (9 Met.) 263 (1845).

sistent with what we take to be the rule of the common law. The indictment contains several counts, and they all charge an assault upon the woman; and there is no intimation that the applications were made with her consent, but the conclusion, from the averments, is otherwise. It is then the case of an assault at common law, with aggravations. But what is more material is, that, although the woman was not alleged to be quick with child, yet it is averred that she was pregnant and big with child, and that the act was done by the defendant wilfully, and with intent feloniously, wilfully, and of his malice aforethought, to kill and murder the child with which she was so big and pregnant. And in other counts, it is laid that drugs were administered to her, she being pregnant with another child, and with intent to cause and procure her to miscarry and bring forth said child dead, &c. The whole proceeds on the averment, that she was then pregnant with a child, then so far advanced as to be regarded in law as having a separate existence, a life capable of being destroyed; which is equivalent to the averment that she was quick with child.[48]

When one reads the whole of the indictment as set forth in Chitty,[49] one discovers that there were five counts, of which the fifth need not detain us, as it was only for common assault. Counts I, II, and III all refer to one pregnancy, which defendant terminated by a combination of blows and pills, in 1799. Count IV refers to a second pregnancy, apparently at a later date, which Chitty conceals under an "on, etc.", which defendant attempted to terminate by a combination of blows and the insertion of "a certain instrument called a rule . . . into the womb and body of the said Anne." Count IV does not aver that defendant succeeded in terminating the second pregnancy. Count I does aver that he succeeded in terminating the first pregnancy, the child being "born alive." Counts II and III merely offer varying dates and types of pills administered in successive efforts to terminate the first pregnancy.

Count I states that both mother and the live-born child "became and w[ere] rendered weak, sick, diseased, and distempered in body" as a result of the prenatal abortifacient acts, and further that the

---

[48] *Id.* at 267.
[49] 3 J. Chitty, *supra* note 46.

mother "underwent and suffered great and excruciating pains, anguish and torture both of body and mind", and that this lasted for "the space of six months then next following." Similar averments occur in Counts II, III, and IV in regard to the mother's suffering.

In view of these allegations in Count I, the only count which, as quoted by Chitty, tells us whether the child was stillborn or born alive, we see that this abortus not only survived the operation, but, in the interval of time between February 1799, when the first abortion was accomplished and his live birth resulted, and September or October (Michaelmas Term) 1802, when the grand jury found the indictment, this child remained alive—a period of over three years, since, if the child had died, the indictment would surely have recounted that macabre fact. What Count I is charging, therefore, is the performance of an abortifacient act, after quickening, which resulted in the birth alive of an infant which, had it died within a year and a day after birth, would have been the victim, according to Coke, of murder, but which survived though "rendered weak, sick, diseased, and distempered in body." Count I (and the variant Counts II and III) is thus charging, so far as the infant is concerned, an offense short of murder that would, according to Coke, have been murder, had the infant died after birth within the year and a day. It is thus evidence that the law officers in the Crown Office thought—in seeking such an indictment from a grand jury—that Coke was right about abortion after quickening being murder if the foetus were live-born and then died. They were merely extending this principle to the lesser offense of assault with intent to murder.

Although as we know, Oliver Wendell Holmes, Jr., in speaking for a unanimous Supreme Judicial Court in 1884, doubted that even this half of Coke's text (calling abortion after quickening murder if the abortus is born alive and then dies) had ever become the common law of Massachusetts,[50] the English courts did accept this half of Coke's passage in a later nineteenth-century case.[51]

What Counts I-III do not establish is that the law officers in the Crown Office in 1802 believed that abortion after quickening resulting in a stillbirth was a crime at common law. True, they did include Count IV, but apparently they felt it necessary to strengthen it by adding the averment that the procedure had caused the said Anne to

---

[50] *See supra* note 36.
[51] *See* cases, *supra* note 35.

become, continue and remain "weak, sick, sore, lame, diseased and disordered in body . . . for the space of six months then next following", and they do not tell us whether the abortion was a success or not. This indicates a belief on the part of the law officers in the Crown Office in 1802 that an abortion after quickening which resulted in severe illness or morbidity in the abortee was some kind of offense, but it falls far short of indicating that they were confident that an abortion after quickening, resulting in a stillbirth, which did not make the patient seriously unwell, was an offense at common law.

Thus the various counts in the 1802 indictment set forth in Chitty, even if, notwithstanding Chief Justice Shaw's words, any judgment was rendered on this indictment, would not establish a precedent that abortion after quickening resulting in a stillbirth was an offense of any kind at common law, unless serious morbidity to the abortee herself resulted. The endemic, inveterate concern of the common law with the life and health of the expectant mother, rather than with those of the foetus, is once again underscored.

In fact, however, there is nothing to show that there ever was any prosecution under any of the counts of this indictment. In view of the fact that Lord Ellenborough's bill was introduced into Parliament a very short time after the return of this indictment, one would probably be closer to the truth in assuming that the law officers in the Crown Office decided that Coke was just plain wrong, in the face of the mediaeval authorities, and that nothing but a statute could change them. What we are probably looking at in this 1802 indictment in Chitty is the reason for the passage of Lord Ellenborough's Act.

While I have never been able to find strictly contemporaneous evidence (apart from this indictment) for the passage of Lord Ellenborough's Act, it is a fact that an unsigned article in an 1832 issue of the London *Legal Examiner* states flatly: "The reason assigned for the punishment of abortion is not that, thereby an embryo human being is destroyed, but that it rarely or never can be affected by drugs without the sacrifice of the mother's life."[52] The writer also mentions a certain claim made in his day to the effect that there had become available by 1832 "an operation by which, even in an advanced stage

---

[52] 2 Legal Examiner 10-11 (1832) (unsigned article on trial of William Russell at the Huntingdon Assizes, March 1832). The new and relatively safe operation which the writer goes on to mention is undoubtedly induction of premature labor in the third trimester, a technique now little employed.

of gestation, abortion may be effected with trifling danger", and recorded his "doubts of the assertion", as well he might, since Lister's regime of antiseptic surgery was still 35 years in the future as to its discovery, and half a century in the future as to its adoption, in 1832. The 1802 indictment and the 1832 *Legal Examiner* piece thus unite in pointing to the life of the mother, as the reason for the passage of Lord Ellenborough's Act, from which all American statutes on the subject are derived.

In view of the probable reluctance of the law officers in the Crown Office to prosecute the 1802 indictment (or its probable dismissal by the English court if they did prosecute), one can understand why Mr. Dickens concludes his passage thus: "However, references to the procuring of abortion as a crime at Common Law before it became a statutory offense in 1803 are not numerous, and are fairly late in date."[53] The references are, of course, found in works of authors, not in decisions, or even dicta, of courts.

It is thus no accident that the Attorneys General of Texas and Georgia have not produced a single English common-law decision, prior to 1776 or 1840, the dates as of which Georgia and Texas, respectively, adopted the English common law, or prior to 1791—the date on which the ninth amendment became a part of the Constitution, nor any American colonial or early state decision holding that abortion either before or after quickening was any offense at all at common law. The earliest such dictum is in *Commonwealth v. Bangs*,[54] and that case was decided in 1812.

There remains only an ironic footnote to Coke's masterpiece of perversion of the common law of abortion. In 1970 the Harvard University Press published a book, under the general editorship of Professor John T. Noonan, Jr., of the Boalt Hall Faculty of Law, called *The Morality of Abortion*. The chapters are by different authors, but the final one, captioned "Constitutional Balance", is a joint production of Professor David W. Louisell, also of Boalt Hall, and Noonan. The section of this chapter titled, "The Fetus in the Criminal Law", purports to give the history of the subject at common law, in which these eminent authors quote the *locus classicus* in Coke's *Third Institute* about abortion after quickening, but misquote Coke as calling it "a great misprision and so murder." For Coke's

---

[53] B. Dickens, Abortion and the Law 23 (1966).
[54] 9 Mass. 387 (1812). *See also supra* note 31.

"no" Louisell and Noonan have substituted "so". Since a misprision is always under the grade of felony, and murder is always a felony, the sentence as altered by Louisell and Noonan makes no sense to anyone who knows the meaning of the word *misprision*. Nevertheless, at the argument before the Supreme Court of the United States on January 12, 1971, of *United States v. Vuitch*,[55] I saw and heard Assistant Solicitor General Samuel Huntington (in all innocence, of course) cite this very page of the Noonan book, containing this very corruption of Coke's text, as the Government's idea of the true history of the common law on abortion! Fortunately, the Court was not misled, as in that case it did not reach the constitutional issue which would have required it to review this history.

One can only say that, after Coke's savaging of the truth about the common law on this subject in his *Third Institute*, in the interest of punishing "so horrible an offence" as abortion after quickening, he has now, more than three centuries later, received poetic justice at the hands of two law professors who, wittingly or unwittingly, have corrupted his text as violently as he, clearly knowingly, misstated the mediaeval decisions. One is reminded of the lines sung by the Mikado in the Gilbert and Sullivan operetta of that name:

> My object all sublime
> I shall achieve in time—
> To let the punishment fit the crime—
> The punishment fit the crime . . . .

This punishment must be all the more odious to the shade of the doughty Sir Edward, seeing that it has been administered by the two most distinguished legal spokesmen in this country on this question of that very Papacy which he so strongly opposed throughout his career.

But the tale does not end here. There is a footnote to the footnote. A group of three Washington, D.C., lawyers, and one Washington, D.C., law firm, one New Jersey lawyer, and Professor Robert M. Bryn, of the Fordham University Law School (a colleague of mine on Governor Rockefeller's 1968 New York State Abortion Law Review Commission), filed an *amicus curiae* brief dated October 8,

---

[55] 402 U.S. 62 (1971).

1971, in the United States Supreme Court, for The National Right to Life Committee. A passage appears on page 25 of that brief which makes interesting comparative reading when set beside the passage on page 223 of the 1970 Louisell-Noonan effort:

Louisell-Noonan: Ryan-Gartlan-Scanlan-Flynn-
                                     Byrn-Shea & Gardner:

This [Bracton's] language was   Early in the 17th Century, Lord
repeated early in the seven-   Coke repeats what Bracton said
teenth century by Coke in a   in a passage which begins "If a
passage which begins, "If a   woman be quick with child . . . .
woman be quick with child . . .   this is a great misprision and so
this a great misprision and so   murder."[57]
murder."[56]

    I must congratulate these seven attorneys for The National Right to Life Committee for correcting the Louisell-Noonan misquotation of Coke by inserting the word "is", which is in Coke, but is missing from Louisell-Noonan. This must have required somebody to look up the original. What a pity that he did not look five words further on and see Coke's "no" and substitute it for Louisell-Noonan's "so", at the same time!

    After such persistence in misquoting Coke as having said "so" where he did say "no", I am beginning to wonder whether these gentlemen really believe that Coke and Bracton said the same thing. Quite evidently they intend others to believe it. After all, how else can one explain that they say that Coke "repeated" (Louisell-Noonan) or "repeats" (Byrn et al.) Bracton's dictum? Repetition implies that Coke accepted and adopted Bracton's dictum, whereas in fact, of course, he merely quoted it. Yet, by changing Coke's "no" to "so", both these groups of lawyers for the foetus have made Coke adopt Bracton the whole way, while all that Coke did was to quote him, and to attempt to pervert the English law halfway toward Bracton, by calling abortion after quickening a misprision, but not the homicide which Bracton had dubbed it.

---

    [56] D.W. Louisell & J.T. Noonan, *Constitutional Balance*, in The Morality of Abortion: Legal and Historical Perspectives 223 (Noonan ed. 1970).

    [57] Brief for The National Right to Life Committee as Amicus Curiae at 25, Roe v. Wade and Doe v. Bolton, *supra* note 2.

After all this, one can only conclude that Clio has many clients, and some of them are clowns.[58]

II. THE TWILIGHT OF THE COMMON LAW AND THE DAWN OF THE NINTH AMENDMENT

There remains a significant strand of the tangled skein of the common law of abortion prior to 1791 still to be unravelled. What if the abortionist's act resulted in his patient's death—an event that must have occurred in three cases out of eight.[59]

The mediaeval law was silent on this question. One can surmise from this that it was content to let the risk fall where nature had laid it: on the woman. She had gambled, and lost. That was all.

In 1670, however, Sir Matthew Hale, sitting at the Assizes at Bury St. Edmunds, decided such a case, which is reported only in his *Treatise of the History of Pleas of the Crown*,[60] where he wrote:

> But if a woman be with child, and any gives her a potion to destroy the child within her, and she take it, and it works so strongly, that it kills her, this is murder, for it was not given to cure her of a disease, but unlawfully to destroy the child within her, and therefore he, that gives a potion to this end, must take the hazard, and if it kill the mother, it is murder, and so ruled before me at the assizes at *Bury* in the year 1670.[61]

Advocates of Coke's *Third Institute* position would doubtless pray in aid Hale's adverb "unlawfully" in this passage, but Hale

---

[58] If this judgment seems hard on these latter-day zealots, let them take comfort in the company of that giant of time gone by, Sir Edward Coke. Was it not he who had obtained the agreement of the other Chief Justice, and of the Chief Baron of the Exchequer, "that the King by his proclamation cannot create any offence which was not an offence before, for then he may alter the law of the land by his proclamation in a high point; for if he may create an offence where none is, upon that ensues fine and imprisonment." Procalamations, 12 Co. Rep. 74, 76, 77 Eng. Rep. 1352, 1354 (1610). Yet twenty years later we find him in his study at Stoke Pogis, devoting the final quinquennium of his life to the preparation of his *Institutes* for publication, and, in the course of this labor, doing the very thing by stealth that he had denied King James I the power to do by open proclamation. Of such ironies is history woven. *See also* Cope, *Sir Edward Coke and Proclamations, 1610*, 15 Am. J. of Legal Hist. 215 (1971).

[59] *See* text pp. 384-86, *infra*.

[60] M. Hale, *supra* note 32.

[61] M. Hale, *supra* note 36, at 429-30.

himself doubtless meant no more by it than that such a purpose contravened the King's ecclesiastical law. Hale cites no earlier precedent for his nisi prius decision in 1670; had any existed, he surely would have known of it, and cited it. One thus perceives the nature of the innovation the Lord Chief Justice made at Bury three centuries ago. Theretofore the common law, following nature, had let the *woman* "take the hazard." With Restoration gallantry, Sir Matthew imposed a new legal risk upon her abortionist. He did not merely shift a legal risk from her shoulders to the abortionist; for there is no evidence that the common law had ever treated an abortee who died as *felo de se*. It had simply closed its eyes to her fate. Sir Matthew Hale opened its eyes, but even he did not call her *felo de se*, though he did condemn her abortionist as a murderer, if she died.

I have found only one other case prior to 1791 in which an abortee died, and her abortionist was held guilty of her murder. This was *Margaret Tinckler's Case*, tried to a jury at the Durham Assizes (Crown Side) in 1781, before Sir George Nares (1716-86), a Puisne Justice of the Common Pleas. Like Hale's case in 1670, this one also is reported only in a treatise, written, however, not by the justice who decided it, but by Sir Edward Hyde East 22 years after the decision.[62] East's report of the case follows:

> Margaret Tinckler was indicted for the murder of Jane Parkinson, by inserting pieces of wood into her womb. A second count charged her as accessary before the fact. It was proved by several witnesses, that from the first time of the deceased taking to her bed, which was on the 12th of July, she thought that she must die, making use of different expressions, as, *that she was going; that she was working out her last*; and exclaiming, *Oh! that Peggy Tinckler has killed me*. She lin-

---

[62] 2 E. East, A Treatise of the Pleas of the Crown (1803). This work was published in the same year in which Lord Ellenborough's Act, 43 Geo. 3, c. 58 (1803), was passed. East's preface is dated May, 1803. Lord Ellenborough's Act received the royal assent on June 24, 1803, though its first reading in Commons had occurred on March 28, 1803. 36 Parl. Hist. cols. 1245-47 (1803). In any event, East makes no reference to the bill or the statute. His discussion is based entirely on the position at common law. He treats *Margaret Tinckler's Case* twice in the first volume of his treatise: in a comment of his own at 230, and in a full report at 354-56. The report, according to marginal notes, is based principally on a manuscript of Henry Gould (cir. 1700-94), a Puisne Justice of the Common Pleas, and on the Manuscripts of Crown Cases Reserved, but also in part on a manuscript of Francis Buller (1746-1800), a Puisne Justice of the King's Bench.

gered till the 23d, when she died. She never was up but once during that time, when on telling a friend who attended her that she thought herself better, she advised her to get up, which the deceased did, and walked as far as the passage going out of the room, but was forced to return and go to bed again. It appeared by the testimony of several witnesses, that from the moment of her taking to her bed till the time of her death she had declared, *that Tinckler had killed her and dear child,* (stating the particular means used, which agreed with the charge in the indictment.) And during the same period she had declared more particularly, 'that she was with child by one P. a married man, who, being fearful lest his wife should hear of it if she were brought to bed, advised her to go to the prisoner, a midwife, to take her advice how she should get rid of the child, being then five or six months gone.' 'That the prisoner gave her the advice' in question, which she followed accordingly. It was proved by the testimony of a witness, that three days before the delivery, which was on the 10th July, she saw the deceased in the prisoner's bed-chamber, when the prisoner took her round the waist and shook her in a very violent manner six different times, and tossed her up and down: and that she was afterwards delivered at the prisoner's house. The deceased also declared during her illness, that after her delivery the prisoner gave her the child to take home; and bid her go to bed that night and sleep, and get up in the morning and go about her business, and nobody would know anything of the matter; but that appearing very ill the next day at a relation's house, they had ordered her to go home and go to bed, which she did. The child was born alive, but died instantly; and the surgeons, who were examined, proved that it was perfect. There was no doubt but that the deceased had died by the acceleration of the birth of the child: and upon opening her womb it appeared that there were two holes caused by the skewers, one of which was mortified, and the other only enflamed; and other symptoms of injury appeared. A short time before her death she was asked whether the account she had from time to time given of the occasion of her death, and the prisoner's treatment of her were true; and she declared it was. It was objected that the above evidence of the deceased's declarations ought not to be admitted, as she

herself was particeps criminis, and likewise as it appeared at
the time of her declarations she was better, or thought herself
so. But Nares J. was of opinion, that however this objection
might hold with respect to the second count, in which the
prisoner was charged as an accessary with the deceased, yet
the deceased was not willingly or knowingly an accessary to
her own death; and therefore it was like the common case of
any other murder. And as to the objection that she once
thought herself better, and tried to get up, yet the same declarations she then made had been made repeatedly before to
persons whom in confidence she told that she never should
survive, when she first took to her bed; and she had repeated
the same declarations the day before she died, and within a
few hours of her death. And as to the fact itself, he was clearly
of opinion it was murder, on the authority of Lord Hale.
[Marginal citation: 1 Hale, 429.] The jury found the prisoner
guilty on the first count, charging her as a principal in the
murder, and execution being respited to take the opinion of
the judges on the whole case, they all met to consider of it
[Marginal note: First day of Mich. term 1781, at Serjeant's
Inn.]: and were unanimously of opinion that these declarations of the deceased were legal evidence: for though at one
time the deceased thought herself better, yet the declarations
before and after and home to her death were uniform and to
the same effect. And as to her being particeps criminis, they
answered, that if two persons be guilty of murder, and one be
indicted and the other not, the party not indicted is a witness
for the crown. And though the practice be not to convict on
such proof uncorroborated, yet the evidence is admissible; and
here it was supported by the proof of the prisoner tossing the
deceased in her arms in the manner stated. Most of the judges
indeed held that the declarations of the deceased were alone
sufficient evidence to convict the prisoner; for they were not
to be considered in the light of evidence coming from a particeps criminis; as she considered herself to be dying at the time,
and had no view or intent to serve in excusing herself, or fixing
the charge unjustly on others. But others of the judges thought
that her declarations were to be so considered; and therefore
required the aid of the confirmatory evidence.[63]

---

[63] 1 E. East, *id.* at 354-56.

Though not officially reported, this case is of high authority, having commanded the concurrence of the Twelve Judges of England. It is of great interest, not only for the authority it does cite (Hale), but for the authority it ignores (Coke). After all, since Jane Parkinson's bastard "was born alive, but died instantly", this was the very case which Coke had held murder of the infant, but which *The Twinslayer's Case* in 1327, and Hale writing his treatise between 1670 and 1676, had held was not murder of the infant. If the law officers of the Crown in 1781 had thought that Coke was a more satisfactory authority on this point than *The Twinslayer's Case* and Sir Matthew Hale, why was Margaret Tinckler not also indicted for the murder of Jane Parkinson's live-born child? The very same evidence that was held competent and sufficient to convict her of the murder of Jane Parkinson would equally have served to convict her of the murder of the child. Also, it must have been psychologically much easier, in 1781 as in more recent times, to persuade a jury to send a midwife to the gallows for the murder of a nonconsenting babe than for that of the woman who has asked to be aborted.

In the light of these reflections, one perceives how far astray Sir Edward Hyde East, writing 22 years later, went when, in commenting on *Margaret Tinckler's Case*, he declared:

> *Homicide from a particular Malice to one, which falls by Mistake or Accident upon another.*
>
> In these cases the act done follows the nature of the act intended to be done. Therefore if the latter were founded in malice, and the stroke from whence death ensued fell by mistake or accident upon a person for whom it was not intended, yet the motive being malicious, the act amounts to murder. . . .
>
> Thus A. having malice against B., strikes at and misses him, but kills C.; this is murder in A.: and if it had been without malice, but with an instrument or in a manner calculated to create danger, though not likely to kill, it would have been manslaughter. Again, A. having malice against B., assaults him, and kills C. the servant of B., who had come to the aid of his master; this is murder in A.; for C. was justified in attacking A. in defence of his master, who was thus assaulted. So if A. give a poisoned apple to B., intending to poison her, and B. ignorant of it give it to a child, who takes

it and dies; this is murder in A., but no offence in B.; and this, though A. who was present at the time endeavored to dissuade B. from giving it to the child.

Hither also may be referred the case of one who gives medicine to a woman; and that of another who put skewers in her womb, with a view in each case to procure an abortion; whereby the women were killed. Such acts are clearly murder; though the original intent, had it succeeded, would not have been so, but only a great misdemeanor: for the acts were in their nature malicious and deliberate, and necessarily attended with great danger to the person on whom they were practiced.[64]

East's words, "the original intent, had it succeeded, would not have been [murder], but only a great misdemeanor", present an exegetic dilemma so ambiguous as almost to defy solution. Two mutually inconsistent solutions may be considered, but each is beset with perplexity.

First Solution: East is referring to Coke's "great misprision and no murder." If so, why does East cite in the margin not Coke but Hale?[65] Nor does East explain why, if indeed he was accepting the authority of Coke's *Third Institute* passage for the proposition that an abortion followed by stillbirth is a great misprision, he did not also accept the other teaching in the same passage that abortion followed by live birth and then the infant's death is murder. That East did not accept the latter teaching seems clear enough; for, if he had, he would have had a shorter leap to transfer the malice toward the murdered infant to the infant's mother, than from the misdemeanor aimed at producing a stillbirth to the mother's death. It would have been a simpler case of two murders, as where A shoots B, killing him, and the bullet passes through B's body into that of C, whom A did not intend to harm, killing C: here, A is clearly guilty of the murders of both B and C. Yet, East does not discuss *Margaret Tinckler's Case* as one of two murders, as Coke surely would have done. East discusses it on the footing of a failed but intended abortion followed by stillbirth, and a consummated but unintended murder of the expectant mother.

---

[64] 1 E. East, *id.* at 230.
[65] 1 E. East, *id.* at 355. His marginal citation is precise: "(1 Hale, 429.)."

Second Solution: East is relying on Hale, and not at all upon Coke, but East misunderstood Hale's "great crime" and "unlawfully" as meaning, in the one case, a common-law misdemeanor (abortion resulting in stillbirth), and, in the other, as done contrary to the common law. This solution has the obvious advantage over the one previously considered of explaining why East did not perceive two murders—the infant's as well as Jane Parkinson's—but only one (Jane's). Coke would have perceived two murders, but Hale would have discerned only one; for Hale had expressly held that "if after such child were born alive, and baptized, and after die of the stroke given to the mother, this is not homicide [citing *The Twinslayer's Case*]."[66] If, therefore, East consciously rejected Coke but endeavored to follow Hale (which seems to be what in 1781 the law officers of the Crown and the Twelve Judges of England did) then he perceived but one murder (Jane Parkinson's), and that not intended, and one misdemeanor (*i.e.*, Hale's "a great crime", as interpreted by East), and that intended. If East interpreted Hale's "a great crime" to mean "a great misdemeanor", then it must be committed by producing the abortion, whether the abortion results in a stillbirth or in a live birth followed by the infant's death.

There are, however, two difficulties with such an interpretation of Hale's "a great crime" as equivalent to East's "a great misdemeanor."

The first difficulty is linguistic. On the page of his treatise preceding the one on which Hale calls abortion "not murder nor manslaughter by the law of England . . . tho it be a great crime",[67] Hale discusses another case in almost, but not quite, the same language (the difference being nice, but significant), *viz.*:

> A man infected with the plague, having a plague sore running upon him, goes abroad. '[W]hat if such person goes abroad to the intent to infect another, and another is thereby infected and dies? whether this be not murder by the common law might be a question, but if no such intention evidently appear, tho *de facto* by his conversation another be infected, it is no felony by the common law, tho it be a great misdemeanor. . . .[68]

---

[66] M. Hale, *supra* note 32, at 433.
[67] M. Hale, *supra* note 32, at 433.
[68] M. Hale, *supra* note 32, at 432.

Now, this case of the nonintending infectant Hale characterizes as "a great misdemeanor"—a precise common-law expression which excludes ecclesiastical, and affirms an exclusively common-law jurisdiction of the offense. In the case of the abortionist, a page later, Hale alludes to his offense as "a great crime", which neither excludes ecclesiastical nor necessarily affirms a common-law jurisdiction, on its face, and, against the historic background that abortion had immemorially, in England, belonged exclusively to the ecclesiastical jurisdiction, Hale's ambivalent "a great crime" must be referred to canon law.

The second difficulty inheres in the varying extents of the two reasons given by Hale for his conclusions in regard to abortion. Hale gives one reason which is common to both the case where abortion produces a stillbirth and the case where it produces a live birth followed by the infant's death. This reason is that the foetus is, at the moment the stroke is given, "not yet *in rerum natura*"—an expression which sounds philosophical and even metaphysical but which, as used by the mediaeval common-law lawyers might best be translated: "in the world of secular reality." Hale gives another reason that applies to a stillborn abortus, but not to one that is born alive and then dies. That reason is: "nor can it legally be known, whether it were kild or not [citing *The Abortionist's Case*]."[69] Since the reason that the foetus "is not yet *in rerum natura*" applies to both cases, it is more significant in coming at the real reationale which compels Hale to reach the same result in both cases.

In regard to an abortus that is born alive but dies soon afterward, the "not yet *in rerum natura*" ground suggests two similar cases which Hale describes five pages earlier in his treatise:

> If a mortal stroke be given on the high sea, and the party comes to land in England and die, the admiral shall not have jurisdiction in this case to try the felon, because the death, that consummated the felony, happened upon the land, nor the common law shall not try him, because the stroke, that made the offense, was not *infra corpus comitatus* [within the body of the county] [citing several cases].

---

[69] M. Hale, *supra* note 32, at 433.

At common law, if a man had been stricken in one county and died in another, it was doubtful whether he were indictable or triable in either, but the more common opinion was, that he might be indicted where the stroke was given, for the death is but a consequent, and might be found tho in another county.[70]

The modern mind has no difficulty in approving the greater common sense exhibited by "the more common opinion" in the two-counties case, in contrast to the fiasco of falling between two stools in the high sea-dry land case. The solution achieved in the two-counties case parallels the one which Hale (if one interprets his "a great crime" correctly, *i.e.*, as referring to a canonical crime) arrives at in the case of an abortion resulting in a live birth followed by the neonate's death. In this case, too, the stroke is given while the victim is in one jurisdiction ("not yet *in rerum natura*", *i.e.*, in the ecclesiastical jurisdiction), while the death occurs after the victim has crossed into another jurisdiction (through live birth, *in rerum natura, i.e.*, in the common-law jurisdiction). Yet the courts that had exclusive jurisdiction of the stroke (the abortifacient act)—the ecclesiastical courts—remain exclusively competent to try the postnatal death as well. The analogy to the jurisdiction of the courts of the first county in the two-counties case is perfect.

From an American constitutional point of view, of course, the proper line of demaraction between the jurisdiction of secular courts and ecclesiastical courts is of far greater significance than it was for Hale in Restoration England. To Hale, both the common law and the ecclesiastical law were emanations of the same sovereign. To us, with the first amendment's disestablishment clause, the sphere of jurisdiction properly belonging to the English ecclesiastical courts is relegated to the domain of private conscience.

The full report of *Tinckler's Case* in East contains not one word inconsistent with this understanding of Hale, the only authority relied on by the trial justice and, one assumes, the Twelve Judges of England. Only East's effort to analyze the case, and to fit it into a theoretical pattern along with other cases, made in a different part of his (East's) treatise nearly a quarter of a century after the decision, created perplexities. In his report of the case, East merely copied and

---

[70] M. Hale, *supra* note 32, at 426.

collated the manuscripts left by the judges who decided the case; in his analysis, East tried his own hand at explanation.

In his treatise, Sir William Oldnall Russell, writing 16 years after East, and 38 years after the decision, did considerably greater justice to Hale—and to the judges of 1781—than East had done. Russell wrote that, "though the death of the women was not intended, the acts were of a nature deliberate and malicious, and necessarily attended with great danger to the persons on whom they were practiced."[71]

This is the reasoning followed by the Supreme Judicial Courts of Massachusetts and of Maine, in 1845 and 1851, respectively, in the first two American cases to adhere to Sir Matthew Hale's 1670 decision at Bury St. Edmunds:

> The use of violence upon a woman, with an intent to procure her miscarriage, without her consent, is an assault highly aggravated by such wicked purpose, and would be indictable at common law. So where, upon a similar attempt by drugs or instruments, the death of the mother ensues, the party making such an attempt, with or without the consent of

---

[71] 1 W.O. Russell, A Treatise on Crimes and Misdemeanors 659-60 (1819).

Russell is less successful, however, in dealing with Coke's second invention in this *Third Institute* passage. Russell says:

> Where a child, having been born alive, afterwards died by reason of any potions or bruises it received in the womb, it seems always to have been the better opinion that it was murder in such as administered or gave them.

Id. at 618. Russell then cites Coke, Hawkins, Blackstone, and East, in favor of this view, and cites as holding the contrary view Stanford and Hale, explaining:

> [B]ut the reasons on which the opinions of the two last writers seem to be founded, namely, the difficulty of ascertaining the fact, cannot be considered as satisfactory, unless it be supposed that such fact never can be clearly established.

Id. at n.(b). Russell here misreads Stanford and Hale, who urged the difficulty-of-proof argument only in regard to a stillborn abortus, never in regard to a live-born but afterward dying abortus. In regard to a stillborn abortus "such fact never can be clearly established" (to borrow Russell's phrase), if the fact sought to be proved is that the foetus was alive just before the abortifacient act.

Stanford and Hale held both the live-born but afterwards dying abortus, and the stillborn abortus, nonvictims of murder or manslaughter, on the very different ground that, at the moment of the stroke—the abortifacient act—neither was "yet *in rerum natura*".

That is what in effect the Justices of the King's Bench had done in 1327 in deciding *The Twinslayer's Case*, which involved both a stillborn and a live-born but afterwards dying abortus. In 1348, in *The Abortionist's Case*, different justices of the same court had been confronted with only one abortus, and that stillborn. In that case, they originated the difficulty-of-proof argument, which is applicable, of course, only to a stillborn abortus. Stanford and Hale followed the 1327 and 1348 precedents faithfully. Russell seems not to have been aware of them.

the woman, is guilty of murder of the mother, on the ground that it is an act done without lawful purpose, dangerous to life, and that the consent of the woman cannot take away the imputation of malice, any more than in the case of a duel, where, in like manner, there is the consent of the parties.[72]

If medicine is given to a female to procure an abortion, which kills her, the party administering will be guilty of her murder. . . . This is upon the ground that the party making such an attempt with or without the consent of the female, is guilty of murder, the act being done without lawful purpose and dangerous to life, and malice will be imputed.[73]

There is a slight but significant change made in Hale's language by Chief Justice Shaw of Massachusetts in the 1845 case (which was followed by the 1851 Maine case). Whereas Hale had said "unlawfully", Shaw said "without lawful purpose." Hale was writing (in 1670-76) in a country with an established Church, canon law, and ecclesiastical courts. An abortifacient act and purpose contravened the canon law publicly recognized by the English secular state, though it did not contravene the same country's common law. Shaw, on the other hand, was writing in 1845 in Massachusetts, a Commonwealth that had no established Church, canon law, or ecclesiastical courts, but only a secular common law (and, as yet, not even a statute on abortion). In Massachusetts when Shaw wrote, therefore, it would have been false to say that an abortifacient act was done "unlawfully"; it merely lacked "lawful purpose." In its own way, this seemingly slight change of wording by Chief Justice Shaw shows that he was perfectly well aware that Hale's "a great crime" meant a great crime at canon law.

Unlike her foetus, the expectant mother met Hale's "*in rerum natura*" test both at the moment of the stroke (the abortifacient act) and at the hour of her death; so, in asserting a common-law jurisdiction over her death as murder, Hale, although he was innovating, nevertheless, was not trespassing on the already established and exclusive jurisdiction of the ecclesiastical courts, which had never concerned themselves with the fate of abortees who died.

In 1661—only nine years before Hale's decision at Bury—the

---

[72] Commonwealth v. Parker, *supra* note 47, at 265-66.
[73] Smith v. State, 33 Me. 48, 54-55 (1851).

Restoration Parliament, in re-establishing all the traditional ecclesiastical courts (but not the High Commission), at last abolished forever the *ex officio* oath in ecclesiastical trials, thereby extending to the canonical tribunals the common-law privilege against self-incrimination.[74] From 1661 to the present day, therefore, it has been impossible for any tribunal of the Church of England to compel even a religiously observant woman to testify against herself by giving evidence of foetal life prior to an abortifacient act, and, without such evidence, conviction of such a canonical crime, though still theoretically possible, has become a practical impossibility. The statutory abolition of the *ex officio* oath in ecclesiastical trials thus appears to have been the beginning of the right of privacy in regard to abortion thenceforward enjoyed by English and American women—in England for 140 years (1661-1803) and in America for a quarter of a century more. During the late seventeenth, the whole of the eighteenth, and early nineteenth centuries, English and American women were totally free from all restraints, ecclesiastical as well as secular, in regard to the termination of unwanted pregnancies, at any time during gestation. During virtually the same period (*i.e.*, starting with Hale's decision in 1670), however, the common law had imposed a new risk on the woman's abortionist: he became the insurer of her survival. What the common law said to the woman was: If you undergo an abortion, you may die or you may survive. Whichever your fate, you will have committed no crime. To the woman's abortionist, the same law said: If your patient die, you will hang for her murder. If she survive, you will have committed no offense.

During the oral argument in the United States Supreme Court of *United States v. Vuitch*,[75] Mr. Justice Blackmun asked one of defendant's counsel, Professor Norman Dorsen, a noted constitutional law expert and a general counsel of the American Civil Liberties Union, whether, if the Court were to accept the principle he was asserting—that a woman has the right to control her own body and that this right includes elective abortion—it would then have to hold unconstitutional state laws against (1) suicide, and (2) auto-mayhem (*i.e.*, either inflicted on oneself, or consentingly undergone at the hands of another). Professor Dorsen stated that he had given considerable thought to (1), albeit not to (2), and had been unable to reach

---

[74] 13 Car. 2, Stat. 1, c. 12, § 4 (1661).
[75] 402 U.S. 62 (1971). This case was argued on January 12, 1971.

a conclusion. Chief Justice Burger pursued the question as to auto-mayhem. He asked whether a patient, man or woman, who wanted his arm lopped off, under sanitary conditions, without risk of infection and with anaesthesia, did not have a constitutional right to the aid of a physician in performing such an operation. Again Professor Dorsen stated that he had not yet made up his mind as to the answer to such a question.

The shrewdness of this question is obvious. It accepts the premise of the vast majority of advocates of abortion liberalization—that the foetus is simply a "part" of the woman's body which she has a right to discard under a more general right to control her body—and then asks if this asserted right applies to other parts of the body as well. What both the Chief Justice and Justice Blackmun were searching for were the outer limits, if any, which could be put on such an asserted right to control one's body.

This is one of those questions in regard to which Holmes's wise saying, that a page of history is worth a volume of logic, is especially helpful. Throughout its long history the common law has always set its face against suicide; its doctrine of *felo de se* is too well known to require supporting citations. Less well known, perhaps, but equally certain, is the common law's antagonism to auto-mayhem. There appear to have been only two decisions holding auto-mayhem a crime in the course of Anglo-American legal history. One was decided by Sir Edward Coke on circuit in Leicestershire in 1613-14,[76] the other by the Supreme Court of North Carolina in 1961.[77] Both held that at common law the crime existed and that the maimee's consent was nugatory. So, in 1791, when the ninth amendment was adopted, there existed no common-law liberty of suicide, and there also existed no common-law liberty of auto-mayhem. Consequently, no such liberties were among the nonenumerated rights "retained by the people" under that amendment, or under the penumbral zone surrounding it and various other amendments in the Bill of Rights.

E contrario, in 1791 English and American women did enjoy a common-law liberty to undergo abortion at any stage of pregnancy, whether fatal or not to themselves, and their abortionists enjoyed a common-law liberty to perform nonfatal abortions on their patients. What more is being sought today? If one limits the constitutional

---

[76] Rex v. Wright, reported in Co. Litt. § 194, at 127-28 (1628).
[77] State v. Bass, 255 N.C. 42, 120 S.E.2d 580 (1961).

claim in 1971 to the common-law liberty enjoyed in 1791, one has no difficulty in answering close questions put by shrewd justices.

III. THE ADOPTION BY GEORGIA AND TEXAS OF THE ENGLISH COMMON LAW

In his brief for appellees[78] in *Doe v. Bolton*, the Attorney General of Georgia has gone to considerable pains to establish that, since the passage of an Act of February 25, 1784, the common law of England which was in force and binding on the inhabitants of Georgia on May 14, 1776, has been incorporated into the law of Georgia. He did this excellent piece of historical research, of course, because he believed that the common law of England on May 14, 1776 prohibited abortion after quickening as a misdemeanor; his belief is based, as his citations show, on Coke, Hale, Hawkins and Blackstone. As we have seen, Hale does not support his belief at all, and insofar as Hawkins and Blackstone do, their statements are based on Coke, whose witness as to what the common law was on this point is self-demonstrably false.

The Attorney General of Georgia has, in fact, though unwittingly, established that Georgia women, prior to the earliest Georgia abortion statute (passed in 1876), had an unfettered liberty of abortion, at every stage of pregnancy, since that is what, in reality, the English common law accorded them on May 14, 1776.

The Attorney General of Texas, in his brief for appelles in *Roe v. Wade*, has not gone into this question in regard to his state. It appears, however, that an Act of Congress of the Republic of Texas of January 20, 1840, adopted, as of that date, the common law of England as the rule of decision in the courts of Texas.[79]

In 1913 the Supreme Court of Texas had to construe the 1840 Texas common-law adoption statute in a case raising the question whether common-law marriage was valid in Texas. The court noted that, in 1823, Parliament had abrogated common-law marriage in England, so that, in 1840, it no longer existed in that country. The Texas Supreme Court held that it was the prestatutory (*i.e.*, prior to 1823) common law of England, as it still existed in the several states

---

[78] Brief for Appellees at 43-53, Doe v. Bolton, *supra* note 2.

[79] Great S. Life Ins. Co. v. City of Austin, 112 Tex. 1, 9, 243 S.W. 778, 780 (1922).

of the Union in 1840, which the Texan Congress had adopted in 1840; so that common-law marriage was valid in Texas.[80]

Similarly, though in 1803 Lord Ellenborough's Act had abrogated, in England, the pre-existing common-law liberty of abortion at will, the overwhelming majority (all but eight) of the American states still enjoyed this common-law liberty in 1840; so it was adopted in that year by the Texan Act of Congress. The only judicial decision by an American state court prior to 1840 expounding the common law as to abortion was *Commonwealth v. Bangs*,[81] in 1812. It had *held* only that abortion before quickening was not a common-law crime, but in dictum it had *said* that abortion after quickening would be one. It would thus appear that the common-law of England, as still existing in the states of the Union which had not abrogated it by statute on January 20, 1840, continued to vouchsafe pregnant women and their abortionists the liberty they had had since the fourteenth century; so that in Texas, until that state's first abortion statute was passed in 1859, this common-law liberty remained, just as in Georgia it had lasted until that State's first abortion statute in 1876.

This is not only of historic interest; it is of constitutional significance. If every Georgia woman before 1876, and every Texas woman before 1859, who desired an abortion was at liberty to undergo, and her abortionist at liberty to perform, such a procedure according to the English and American common law, and if all American women (and their abortionists) enjoyed such liberty on September 25, 1789, when the ninth amendment was proposed by the First Congress (in New York City), and on December 15, 1791, when it was adopted, then there is sound ground for holding that such liberty is preserved by that amendment today (subject to abridgment only to promote a compelling secular state interest). Such is the clear implication of *Griswold v. Connecticut*.[82] It is a nonenumerated right among the "others retained by the people" which the ninth amendment protects.

IV. HAVE AMERICAN STATE LEGISLATURES EVER PROTECTED AN UNQUICKENED FOETUS FOR ITS OWN SAKE?

The short answer to this question is "Never," at least by means

---

[80] Grigsby v. Reib, 105 Tex. 597, 153 S.W. 1124 (1913).
[81] *Supra* note 31.
[82] 381 U.S. 479 (1965).

of abortion laws. In New York, for example, the legislatures of 1828, 1881, and 1910 authorized the killing, by public authority, of certain unquickened foetūs.[83] The 1910 Act, presently in effect, was approved by Governor Charles Evans Hughes. The legislature of 1970 directed that these provisions be transferred, as of September 1, 1971, from the Code of Criminal Procedure to the Correction Law, where they now appear without change.[84]

Georgia, in her Penal Code of 1833,[85] followed these provisions of the New York Revised Statutes of 1829, and these statutory rules remain in force in Georgia.[86]

The statutory provisions just mentioned merely re-enact, with procedural improvements in the method of ascertaining the facts, an ancient rule of the common law, according to which an expectant mother under sentence of death was examined by a jury of matrons. If their verdict was that her foetus was not yet quick, she was hanged forthwith; if they found that quickening had already taken place, she was reprieved until after delivery, and then hanged. Until the passage of the Sentence of Death (Expectant Mothers) Act,[87] this had been the rule in England from at least as early as 1349.[88]

---

[83] Ch. 442, [1881] N.Y. Laws 76; ch. 338, §§ 5-7, [1910] N.Y. Laws 601.

[84] N.Y. Correction Law §§ 658-60 (McKinney 1972).

[85] O.H. Prince, Digest of the Laws of the State of Georgia 663, 664 (2d ed. 1837) (§§ 38, 40 of Ga. Penal Code of 1833).

[86] Ga. Code Ann. ch. 26, § 26-9920a (1970).

[87] 21 & 22 Geo. 5, c. 24 (1931).

[88] In the Livre dis *Assisas* Pasch. 22 Edw. 3, f. 101a, pl. 71 (K.B. 1349) Chief Justice Thorp "commanda a's Marschals de met? la feme en un chambre, & faire veñ femes a proῦ' & examiñ, si el' fuit enseint oue vife enfant ou nient . . . ." commanded the marshal to place the [sentenced] woman in a room and cause matrons to come and prove and examine her, whether she was pregnant of a quick child or not. Their verdict was negative, and she was hanged. This case is also reported by Fitzherbert, Graunde Abridgment, tit. *Corone* f. 226, pl. 180 (1st ed. 1516), f. 252, pl. 180 (3d ed. 1565). Serjeant Staford informs us:

> Si feme soit arraigne de felonie, nest ple pur luy adire que el est enseint, eins doit pleder al felonie, et quãt el est troue culpable, el peut dire que el est enseint, et sur ceo il serra commaunde al Marshal ou viscont de mitter la feme in vn chamber, & a faire venir femes a trier & examiner si el soit enseint de viue enfant ou nient, et si troue soit que cy: donsques el demurrera donec peperit, &c. & si non: donsque serra el pendus maintenant. Mes le quel el soit enseint ou nient enseint, vnquore iugement ne serra per ceo delay, mes solement lexecucion del iugement. Auxi si apres tiel respiter de luy, el soit deliuere de enfant &c puis nouelment enseint, quel el obiecta auterfoitz pur sa vie prolonger: le Iuge sauns inquerer de ceo, doet commaunder execucion maintenant destre fait, eo que el nauera le benefit de son venter forsque vn

foitz. Mes si le luge inquira de ceo, il serra a nul auter intent forsque amitter fine sur le Marshal ou viscont, qui auer luy garde cy remissement: que el ad ewe le companie dhome. Et de ceux matters, vide titulo Coron in fitz. P. 180. P. 240. P. 130. P. 188. & P. 168. Issint per ceux liures, apieroit que priuement enseint: ne doit seruir pur obiection, eo que les liures sont, que el doit estre enseint de viue enfant.

W. Stanford, *supra* note 7, at ff. 197-98.

Which, being translated, reads:

If a woman be arraigned for felony, it is no plea for her to say that she is pregnant, but she must plead to the felony, and if she be found guilty, she can say that she is pregnant, and thereupon the marshal or sheriff will be ordered to place the woman in a room, and cause matrons to come to try and examine whether she be pregnant of a quick child or not, and if it be found that she is: then she shall remain until she shall have given birth, etc. and if not then she shall be hanged forthwith. But whether she be pregnant or not pregnant still judgement shall not be delayed thereby, but only the execution of the judgement. Also if after such respiting of her, she be delivered of child and then [become] pregnant afresh which [new pregnancy] she again objects in order to prolong her life: the judge without inquiring thereof, must order that execution proceed forthwith and that she shall not have the benefit of her womb except one time. But if the judge inquire thereof he shall do so for no other purpose than to impose a fine upon the marshal or the sheriff who had with such laxity imprisoned her that she had had the company of a man. And concerning these matters, *see* Fitz[herbert, Graunde Abridgement, citing the Liber Assisarum case of 1349 and others]. Thus from these books it appears that *privily pregnant* may not serve as objection, in that the books are that she must be *pregnant with a quick child.*

Coke informs us:

And when a woman commits High Treason and is quick with childe, she cannot upon her arraignment plead it, but she must either pleade not guilty or confesse it: and if upon her plea she be found guilty, or confesse it, she cannot alleage it in arrest of judgement, but judgement shall be given against her: and if it be found by an inquest of matrons that she is quick with childe, (for *priviment ensent* will not serve) it shall arrest, and respite execution till she be delivered, but she shall have the benefit of that but once, though she be again quick with childe: so as this respite of execution for this cause is not to be granted, only in case of felony, whereof Justice Stanford speaketh, but in case of High Treason, and Petit Treason also.

E. Coke, *supra* note 22, n.16, at *17-18.

Blackstone echoes the earlier authorities, declaring that the matrons' verdict must be "*quick with child* (for barely, *with child*, unless it be alive in the womb, is not sufficient)". 4 W. Blackstone, *supra* note 30, n.24, at *395.

The only instance I have been able to discover of the hanging of an American feloness whom the jury of matrons had found pregnant but not quick occurred in Massachusetts in 1778. Commonwealth v. Bathsheba Spooner, 2 Am. Crim. Trials 1 (1844). Mrs. Spooner's trial, for the murder of her husband, was presided over by Chief Justice Cushing of the Supreme Judicial Court of the Commonwealth. *See also* the following notes of the jury of matrons: 48 Am. L. Rev. 280 (1914); 9 Cent. L.J. 94 (1879); 3 Harv. L. Rev. 44 (1889).

It is worthy of note that the earliest *Jury of Matrons Case* in the Liber Assisarum in 1349, before the Court of King's Bench, was decided by the same Court before which *The Abortionist's Case* had been decided the year before. In both years, the Chief Justice was William Thorp, and William Basset was a Puisne Justice. Roger of Bakewell was a Puisne Justice in 1348, but he had left the Court before the decision of the earliest *Jury of Matrons Case* in 1349, so that at the latter time there were only two sitting justices. *See* 82 Selden Society, *supra* note 6, at li, lii. Chief Justice Thorp and Justice Basset obviously perceived a difference between the act of a

In his *Travels Over England*[89] M. Misson described the way the rule really worked:

> The Women or Wenches that are condemn'd to Death, never fail to plead they are with Child, (if they are old enough) in order to stop Execution till they are delivered. Upon this they are order'd to be visited by Matrons; if the Matrons do not find them Quick, they are sure to swing next Execution-Day; but very often they declare they are with Child, and often too the poor Criminals are so indeed; for tho' they came never so good Virgins into the Prison, they are a Sett of Wags there that take Care of these Matters. No Doubt they are diligent to inform them the very Moment they come in, that if they are not with Child already, they must go to work immediately to be so; that in case they have the Misfortune to be condemn'd, they may get Time, and so perhaps save their Lives. Who would not hearken to such wholesome Advice?[90]

Nor is this a rule of which the New York Legislature has not been reminded in recent times. Assemblyman Blumenthal, after reading about these statutes in my 1968 article,[91] quoted those sections to his colleagues during the floor debate on the abortion liberalization bill which failed to pass in 1969.

Massachusetts, whose 1845 statute prohibiting abortion is still on the books, has also enacted into statute the common-law reprieve rule in regard to expectant mothers sentenced to death.[92]

---

private subject causing an abortion, and the act of the King in authorizing execution of a feloness; for they applied the quickening distinction in the latter case but not in the former.

In the entire history of Anglo-American law there appears to be only one reported case in which the judge misunderstood the meaning of the expression "quick with child" in the verdict the jury of matrons were required to render. This is *Regina v. Wycherly*, 8 Carrington & Payne, 262, 263, 173 Eng. Rep. 486, 487 (Stafford Assizes Crown Side 1838) (Baron Gurney). By the time this case was decided, the execution of felonesses had doubtless become a rarity in England, and Baron Gurney's error was doubtless due to his unfamiliarity with the older practice. As could have been expected, the mistaken definition of Baron Gurney in this isolated case is quoted as representing the entire tradition of English law on this question in the *amicus* brief filed by The National Right to Life Committee, *supra* note 57, at 26.

[89] It appears that this book was written in 1698, but was translated from the French by Ozell and published in 1719.

[90] Quoted in L. Radzinowicz, A History of English Criminal Law and Its Administration from 1750: The Movement for Reform 1750-1833, at 12 n.35 (1948).

[91] Means, *supra* note 1, at 441-42 & nn.66-68 (1968).

[92] Ch. 166, [1876] Mass. Sess. Laws; Mass. Gen. Laws Ann. ch. 279, § 47 (1959).

It may legitimately be asked why the justices of Edward III were not guilty of inconsistency in, on the one hand, holding noncriminal the private foeticide of even a quickened foetus, whilst, on the other, staying the execution of a condemned feloness if her foetus had quickened. Was not Coke merely harmonizing the two rules, by applying the quickening distinction both to private and to State conduct?

Of course, Coke was harmonizing the two rules, but the Edwardine justices had good reason for keeping them distinct and different. In the one case, the conduct of private subjects was drawn in question, whereas, in the other, the conscience of a Christian King (by whose authority the feloness would be hanged) was implicated. Even today, we expect the State to abide by stricter norms than are imposed upon the populace, particularly by the sanctions of criminal law.

On a deeper analysis, however, the supposed inconsistency between the two rules disappears. The sound ground given in 1348 for the noncriminality of abortion by blows was that it could not be known whether the batterer had killed the foetus or not. On reflection, a twentieth-century reader will discover how profound an insight this was. We know now, and evidently the justices suspected then, that a very large fraction of all foetūs conceived die *in utero*, and are aborted spontaneously. In regard to any particular foetus which is intentionally aborted, it is simply impossible to know whether or not it died *in utero* a short time before the abortifacient intervention, whatever its form, took place. Even the most skilled pathologist could not exclude this possibility, even today. The only way one could be sure would be if the testimony of the woman herself were forthcoming, and it were to the effect that she had perceived a foetal movement just before the abortifacient act. Only rarely would this be the fact; rarer still would be the abortion-seeking woman who would admit it.

In disclaiming jurisdiction of such an unprovable offense on behalf of the common-law courts, the King's justices relegated such cases to the ecclesiastical courts, which had never felt deterred by such difficulties of proof, and anyway, through the *ex officio* oath, could force a religiously observant woman to testify against herself, there being no privilege against self-incrimination at canon law. This was contrary to the genius of the common-law courts in many ways. How could it ever be said that it had been proved beyond a reasonable doubt—or at all—that the foetus aborted (if stillborn) had been still alive just before the allegedly fatal blow was struck? How could the requirements of *corpus delicti* be satisfied? True, these two rules, so familiar to us now, had not been crystallized in the fourteenth-century, but these cases are, I submit, harbingers of both of them.

In disregarding the wisdom that lay behind the decisions in *The Twinslayer's Case* and *The Abortionist's Case*, Coke allowed his visceral hatred of abortion after quickening to darken his otherwise luminous perception of the true genius of the common law.

In regard to the reprieve rule, on the other hand, the Edwardine justices were not faced with any such insoluble question of proof. Once the jury of matrons find that the condemned woman's foetus has quickened, she is spared until it is born. So no risk is run. If the matrons find her merely pregnant, she is hanged, but then, every Mediaeval knew that an early foetus was not a "man", or as we should now say, a "person."[93]

The vice which the justices in 1348 would have found in statutes punishing abortion "in case the death of such child or of such mother be thereby produced", would have inhered in this very phrase. Of this they would have said, "The cases of the mother and the foetus are different. The mother herself has already been born; so she is visible, right up to the moment of her death. Witnesses can observe her living before the abortifacient act, languishing after and dying because of it. With the foetus, it is invisible. Even after quickening, it often does not move. So, often the mother, herself, will not know if it was still alive when the abortive act was done. If she does know, she is not likely to tell us that it was, if she procured the doing of the abortion." Such an analysis was unassailable in 1348, and is still unassailable today, 623 years later.

V. WERE THE NINETEENTH-CENTURY ABORTION LAWS PASSED TO DISCOURAGE SEXUAL PROMISCUITY?

Many think they were, but they were not. Note the judicial disclaimer in 1881 of nineteenth-century "morals and decency" as a

---

[93] As I pointed out in my 1968 article, the Council of Trent had summed up the philosophy of the Middle Ages on this question in the following passage in its Catechism:

[N]o [human] body, when the order of nature is followed, can be informed by the soul of man except after the prescribed interval of time (servato naturae ordine nullum corpus, nisi intra praescriptum temporis spatium, hominis anima informari queat).

Means, *supra* note 1, at 412. To this day, the Roman Catholic Church has never dogmatically repudiated this passage in the Tridentine Catechism.

reason for the passage of the New Jersey abortion act of 1849 in *State v. Gedicke.*[94]

A woman who becomes pregnant through marital intercourse, or because of rape, has transgressed no norm of Judaeo-Christian morality. Yet all the nineteenth-century abortion statutes forbade her recourse to abortion just as stringently as they did her erring sister whose pregnancy resulted from fornication, adultery, or incest. If the legislators' sole purpose in passing the old abortion laws had been to discourage sexual promiscuity, they would have exempted married women and rape victims. If such moral zeal had been only one of their purposes, they would have made the penalties lighter for married women and rape victims. They never did. No legislature has ever treated the termination of pregnancy differently according to the moral quality of the act that caused it.

Neither, for that matter, did the common law, which allowed all women, married or unmarried, moral or immoral, to terminate their pregnancies at will.

The most recent reiteration of the obvious answer to this perennial question is found in the specially concurring opinion of Justices Ervin and Adkins in *Walsingham v. State*:

> The [Florida] statute also does not show a compelling state interest in prohibiting premarital sexual intercourse (the prelude to unwed mothers) since it draws no distinction between married and unmarried women.[95]

VI. THE REAL, PURELY MEDICAL, AND PERFECTLY CONSTITUTIONAL REASON FOR THE PASSAGE OF THE NINETEENTH-CENTURY ABORTION LAWS

Having disposed of the contentions that our nineteenth-century abortion laws were passed either to protect unquickened foetūs for their own sake or to discourage sexual promiscuity, we now reach the true reason for their enactment. This reason was wholly secular and, at the time, admirable. As late as 1884 in New York, as we shall see, an abortion, even when performed early in pregnancy by a physician, was from ten to fifteen times as dangerous to the patient's life as was

---

[94] 43 N.J.L. 86, 89 (Sup. Ct. 1881).
[95] 250 So. 2d 857, 863 (Fla. 1971).

childbirth at full term. This remained true until the last decade-and-a-half of the nineteenth century, when New York surgeons began to adopt the antiseptic techniques first published by Lister in *The Lancet* in 1867. Their adoption elsewhere in the country followed gradually.

Thereupon two notable phenomena occurred. Hitherto the curves representing patient mortality in the two procedures (physician-performed abortion and childbirth) had been parallel, horizontal straight lines. Now both began to plunge sharply, and ended at levels minuscule by comparison with their former heights. Second, the physician-performed-abortion mortality curve, for the first time in medical history, ended up well below the childbirth morality curve. This happened because the physician-performed-abortion mortality curve plunged more rapidly than, and therefore intersected, afterwards falling and remaining below, the childbirth mortality curve.

This intersection of the two curves is not only of medico-historical importance. It is also of constitutionally critical significance. Before this intersection, the legislature's command, *Thou shalt not abort*, if obeyed, compelled a woman to adopt the *less* dangerous of the two procedures (at that time, childbirth). Once this point of intersection has been passed, however, continued enforcement of the same legislative command, even when obeyed, compels a woman to adopt the *more* dangerous of the two procedures (now, childbirth). Thus the nineteenth-century abortion laws, in recent decades, have not only no longer effectuated their original purpose, they have positively frustrated it. And they have done this, not because they are disobeyed, but even when they are obeyed. These laws have always been massively disobeyed, but massive disobedience does not make a law unconstitutional. But where a law abridges an immemorial common-law liberty for a reason within the police power of the state (the protection of pregnant women's lives), and then the facts of surgery so change that continued enforcement of the law as written not only no longer protects the lives of pregnant women, even when they obey the law, but affirmatively endangers them, the law then ceases to be constitutional, on the age-old principle, *cessante ratione legis cessat et ipsa lex*. In many cases the United States Supreme Court has recognized and applied this principle to the constitutionality of statutes.[96] The

---

[96] *See* cases collected in Means, *supra* note 1, at 514-15 n.264. A more recent example than any I there cited is, of course, Baker v. Carr, 369 U.S. 186 (1962), where the Court held that a Tennessee statute which had obviously been constitutional when enacted in 1901, had, because of intervening shifts of population, become unconstitutional by 1961.

relevant data and conclusions in support of the statements made on
the two preceding pages, so far as I had explored them through 1968,
are set forth in my 1968 article.[97]

During my oral argument on a motion for a three-judge court
in *Lyons v. Lefkowitz*,[98] Judge Weinfeld asked me to specify the year
in which the two curves, representing parturitional and (physician-
performed) abortional patient mortality and identified in a diagram
in my 1968 article[99] as AA′ and PP′, had intersected. In my 1968
article I had designated this year as 19xy. After the three-judge court
was convened, I took the deposition of Christopher Tietze, M.D.,
Associate Director, Bio-Medical Division, The Population Council,
who had been my colleague on Governor Rockefeller's 1968 Commission to Review New York State's Abortion Law. Dr. Tietze is both
a distinguished gynaecologist and the leading bio-medical statistician
in the demographic field. He testified "emphatically" that the cross-
over point of AA′ and PP′ must have occurred prior to the year
1933 and may have occurred as early as 1900.[100] Thus:

$$1900 < 19xy < 1933,$$

is the best answer I was able to obtain to Judge Weinfeld's question.

In *Lyons v. Lefkowitz* I also took the deposition of William B.
Ober, M.D., pathologist and historian, who had studied the New
York Hospital's registers (1) of surgery performed during 1808-33
and (2) of the lying-in ward during 1809-25. He testified that in the
operations which today would be classified as "major peripheral surgery", 37½ per cent of the patients died, 31 per cent of them from
sepsis.[101] During this period no case of surgical abortion is recorded
in the surgical register of the New York Hospital, 1808-33;[102] if any
had been, Dr. Ober testified that it would have been classified as

---

[97] Means, *supra* note 1, at 434-39 (especially 436 n.59), 450-54, 502-04, 506-09, 511-15 (especially the diagram on 512 and accompanying n.260).

[98] 305 F. Supp. 1030 (S.D.N.Y. 1969). The motion was granted and a three-judge court convened, consisting of Circuit Judge Friendly and District Judges Weinfeld and Tyler, but the case became moot on July 1, 1970, upon the entry into force of ch. 127, [1970] N.Y. Sess. Laws 852, which substantially repealed New York's 1830-1970 abortion legislation.

[99] Means, *supra* note 1, at 512. AA' stands for patient mortality in physician-performed abortion; PP' for patient mortality in parturition.

[100] Deposition of Christopher Tietze, M.D., Dec. 22, 1969, at 42-44, Lyons v. Lefkowitz, *supra* note 98.

[101] Deposition of William B. Ober, M.D., Dec. 22, 1969, at 12, 17, 18, Lyons v. Lefkowitz, *supra* note 98.

[102] *Id.* at 13.

"major surgery", and would be so designated now.[103] He testified that "then as now every surgical abortion would require the introduction of an instrument into the womb."[104] When asked whether, if such instrument "were not sterilized, the danger from sepsis would be similar to that of an incisive instrument in another form of operation," Dr. Ober replied:

> Possibly even more so, because of the poor drainage from an infected uterus.
>
> The uterus essentially is a semi-closed organ, with a very, very narrow canal.
>
> Under ordinary circumstances, if you introduce an unsterilized instrument into the uterus and create a small infection, which might heal were it an exposed surface, the swelling of the uterus would effectively close—might effectively close up the cervical canal and create a large pocket of pus.
>
> The risk might even be higher than from just an ordinary superficial wound which could be dressed, because, after all, this is internal.[105]

From this Dr. Ober drew the obvious inference that the death rate due to sepsis from abortional surgery, even when performed in hospital, was at least as high as 31 ¼ per cent when New York's first abortion statute was passed in 1828.[106]

Turning to the register of the lying-in ward patients at the New York Hospital, 1809-25, Dr. Ober computed a maternal mortality rate of 2.82 per cent.[107]

When asked whether "the rate of mortality that a woman could anticipate as a result of subjecting herself to an abortion under hospital conditions at this period would be of the order of magnitude of at least ten to fifteen times as high as the rate of mortality to which she would subject herself by bringing the child to term", Dr. Ober thought that "that would be a fair approximation."[108]

I have been unable to find any such statistics compiled and pub-

---

[103] *Id.* at 17.
[104] *Id.* at 19.
[105] *Id.* at 20.
[106] *Id.* at 23.
[107] *Id.* at 22.
[108] *Id.* at 23.

lished during the nineteenth century, but the facts which the foregoing statistics quantify were common knowledge, not only among doctors, but of laymen as well, during that century.

In a work entitled *Why Not? A Book for Every Woman*, for which he was awarded a gold medal by the American Medical Association, Horatio Robinson Storer, M.D., of Boston, warned:

> A larger proportion of women die during or in consequence of an abortion, than during or in consequence of childbed at the full term of pregnancy.[109]

Dr. Storer made it clear that he was referring not merely to criminal abortions not performed by physicians, but to legal, physician-performed abortions as well, in the following passage:

> The results of abortion from natural causes . . . are much worse than those of the average of labors at the full period. If the abortion be from accident, from external violence, mental shock, great constitutional disturbance from disease or poison, *or even necessarily induced by the skilful physician in early pregnancy*, the risks are worse.[110]

Let us now contrast these sombre nineteenth-century facts with data from the present day. The First fourteen months (July 1, 1970-August 31, 1971) since the entering into effect of the new New York State abortion law,[111] have seen 205,614 legal abortions performed in New York City.[112] During the same period there have been nine deaths of patients who have undergone legal abortions in New York City.[113] This works out at a patient mortality rate of 4.4 per 100,000. Legal abortions in New York may be done through the 24th week of pregnancy. Comparing 4.4 per 100,000, the 1970-71 mortality rate for physician-performed abortions in New York City, with Dr. Ober's figure of 31 ¼ per cent (or 31,250 per 100,000, to use today's denomi-

---

[109] H.R. Storer, Why Not? A Book For Every Woman, at 36-37 (1865).

[110] *Id.* at 46-47 (emphasis added).

[111] Ch. 127, [1970] N.Y. Sess. Laws 852.

[112] New York City Department of Health, Health Services Administration, Bulletin on Abortion Program, at 5.1 (Aug. 31, 1971).

[113] New York City Department of Health, Health Services Administration, Bulletin on Abortion Program, End of First Year Report, at 8 (June 30, 1971); Bulletin on Abortion Program, *supra* note 112, at 8.

nator) from sepsis alone in comparable surgery performed at the New York Hospital in 1808-33, one sees that physician-performed abortions in New York City are now only 1/7102 as dangerous to patients' lives as they were a century and a half ago. Put the other way round, legal physician-performed abortions today are more than 7000 times as safe as when the pre-Lister abortion laws were enacted.

Not only is that true, but the relative safety of physician-performed abortion and childbirth has been reversed. From Dr. Tietze I have obtained the following:

Maternal Mortality in New York City
(Excluding Death Due to Abortion)
Per 100,000 Live Births[114]

1951-53	47
1954-56	39
1957-59	35
1960-62	42
1963-65	36
1966-67	35

Using 35 per 100,000—which is not only the most recent (1966-67) available but is also the lowest (1957-59 and 1966-67) New York City maternal mortality (excluding abortion) rate ever obtained—as undoubtedly close to the 1970-71 rate, which is not yet available, and comparing it with the 4.4 per 100,000 legal physician-performed abortional mortality rate actually achieved by New York City during the first fourteen months in 1970-71 under the new New York law, we must conclude that, in 1970-71, physician-performed legal abortion was only ⅛ or 12 per cent as dangerous to a pregnant woman's life (if performed at any time within the first 24 weeks of pregnancy) as childbirth. Put the other way, any American state which, in 1970-71, obstinately continued to enforce the prohibition of abortion laid down by a nineteenth-century statute thereby endeavored to compel women with unwanted pregnancies to put their lives at eight times the risk they would have run had legal abortion been available to them and they had chosen that procedure.

---

[114] These figures are taken from An Unpublished Table Prepared by the New York City Department of Health, Bureau of Records and Statistics, Maternal Mortality in New York City (excluding death due to abortion) per 100,000 live births (mimeographed June 1969), and from J. Pakter & F. Nelson, *Abortion in New York City: The First Nine Months*, 3 Family Planning No. 3, at 5-12 (July 1971).

There is here an unbelievable historical irony. A statute was passed more than a century ago for the purpose of imposing on women the duty of protecting their lives from destruction through wanted but dangerous abortional surgery. Now that the danger has all but disappeared, the State's obstinate persistence in enforcing the law's letter, but not its purpose, denies its intended beneficiaries (pregnant women) the very right to protect their lives from death which the law originally imposed on them as a duty! Compare the famous statement of Mr. Justice Johnson, on circuit, in *Elkison v. Deliesseline*:

"[C]ertainly that law cannot be pronounced necessary which may defeat its own ends; much less when other provisions of unexceptionable legality [*i.e.*, constitutionality] might be resorted to, which would operate solely to the end proposed. . . ."[115]

A woman's right to protect her life is fundamental, in the abortion context as well as in any other. The Supreme Court of California has reminded us that "[t]he woman's right to life is involved because childbirth involves risks of death."[116] As Mr. Justice Holmes observed, "We have seen more than once that the public welfare may call upon the best citizens for their lives"[117] in military service, but only the country's compelling interest in its own security and defense suffices to subordinate the male conscript's right to life. Likewise, a state must show some compelling interest of comparable magnitude to require a woman to risk her life by continuing an unwanted pregnancy. No American state has shown such an interest; the only secular one that could be put forward—a need for a larger population— would be so absurd under present conditions as to be laughed out of court.[118]

The clue to the true reason both for the passage of the 1828 New

---

[115] 8 F. Cas. 493, 496 (No. 4,366) (C.C.D.S.C. 1823).

[116] People v. Belous, 71 Cal. 2d 954, 963, 458 P.2d 194, 199, 80 Cal. Rptr. 354, 359 (1969), *cert. denied*, 397 U.S. 915 (1970).

[117] Buck v. Bell, 274 U.S. 200, 207 (1927).

[118] The Attorney General of Georgia cites an 1892 edition of Bishop's *New Criminal Law* for the proposition that, at common law, abortion was "one of the leading offenses against population", but he does not suggest that this is a currently valid reason for such laws. Brief for Appellees at 52, Doe v. Bolton, *supra* note 2.

York statutes against abortion and to the meaning of the therapeutic exception included in those statutes is provided by another section which the revisers proposed, but which the legislature did not enact, which contained virtually the same therapeutic exception. The proposed but unenacted section would, if passed, have forbidden:

> any surgical operation, *by which human life shall be destroyed or endangered,* such as the amputation of a limb, or of the breast, trepanning, cutting for the stone, or for hernia, *unless it appear that the same was necessary for the preservation of life* . . . .[119] (emphasis added)

In their note accompanying this proposed section, the revisers stated that "the loss of life occasioned by" the performance of such operations "is alarming."[120] Just as only necessity for the preservation of life would, in 1828, have justified performance of any of the operations enumerated in this proposed but unenacted section; so only the very same necessity would, at that time, have justified the performance of an abortion.

The legislature accepted the revisers' recommendation and enacted their proposed section against nontherapeutic abortion before quickening, but rejected this section forbidding the performance of these other operations when not "necessary for the preservation of life." This difference in treatment of the two proposed sections doubtless reflects a legislative judgment that only in the case of abortion were both patient and surgeon under strong extramedical pressures to undergo the risks of the operation. In other types of surgery, professional conscience and patients' caution could be relied upon to prevent unnecessary operations[121] without the aid of a new penal law. It can scarcely be said that such a legislative differentiation between abortion and other equally dangerous types of surgery was, in 1828, unreasonable.

The only contemporaneous judicial explanation for the enactment of any of the pre-Lister abortion statutes—a decision of 1858 construing New Jersey's first such statute passed in 1849—contains the following:

---

[119] The full text of this section is quoted in Means, *supra* note 1, at 451.

[120] The full text of this revisers' note is quoted in Means, *supra* note 1, at 451.

[121] *See* Means, *supra* note 1, at 506.

The design of the statute was not to prevent the procuring
of abortions, so much as to guard the health and life of the
mother against the consequences of such attempts.[122]

The author of that unanimous opinion was Chief Justice Henry
Woodhull Green, afterwards Chancellor of New Jersey, to whom,
after the death in 1864 of Roger Brooke Taney, President Lincoln
offered the Chief Justiceship of the United States, which Chancellor
Green declined for reasons of health. One of the Associate Justices
joining in the opinion was the man who as Governor of New Jersey
had approved the act of 1849.[123]

In none of the various re-enactments of the 1828 New York
legislation, prior to 1965, was there ever any manifestation of a legislative purpose different from the one revealed by the 1828 revisers'
notes. The New York Revised Penal Law was enacted in 1965, but it
did not take effect until September 1, 1967. Nevertheless, the Commission Staff Notes to the 1965 law's sections reveal a contemporary
purpose which, significantly enough, was identical with the purpose
of the revisers and legislators of 1828. Thus, the Commission Staff
Note to Revised Penal Law § 125.45 adverts to the new dividing line
at 24 weeks of pregnancy (in substitution for the former dividing line
at quickening) between first and second degree abortion and explains
the choice of this new dividing line as follows:

"The aggravating factor is the pregnancy of more than 24
weeks duration, rendering the operation more dangerous than
at an earlier stage."[124]

A Commission Staff Note of similar tenor accompanies another section, § 125.20(3), of the New York Revised Penal Law of 1965. Now
a termination of pregnancy after 24 weeks is *less* dangerous to the
foetus than one before, because more and more foetus become viable
as and after that point is passed. So when the Commission Staff Note
characterizes the late operation as "more dangerous" than the earlier, it obviously means more dangerous to the *pregnant woman*. Thus
it is beyond cavil that the New York Legislature of 1965, like that of

---

[122] State v. Murphy, 27 N.J.L. 112, 114 (Sup. Ct. 1858).
[123] *See* Means, *supra* note 1, at 507-08.
[124] Means, *supra* note 1, at 502.

1828, was thinking solely in terms of danger to the expectant mother.[125]

The protection of the life of the pregnant woman is therefore the only reason ever advanced for the passage of the New York statutes in 1828 or for their reënactment in revised form in 1965. In all the long history of the New York legislation of 1830-1970, no other reason was ever put forward. It was a valid and validating reason so long as it lasted. The intervening change in the relative safety of physician-performed abortion and childbirth rendered continued enforcement of that body of legislation according to its letter frustrative of its original purpose; before that change a woman who obeyed the law was rewarded by less risk to her life than one who disobeyed it; since that change the reward of obedience has been greater risk to the woman's life. The one reason ever put forward for its passage was sufficient to sustain its constitutionality so long as it lasted. When that reason disappeared, the 1830-1970 New York legislation became unconstitutional.

Since the abortion laws of so many other states were copied from the New York legislation of 1830-1970, the New York legislative intent came to those other states with the statutory texts they borrowed.

VII.　When Did New York Surgeons Finally Adopt the Antiseptic Methods First Recommended by Lister in 1867?

Not until 1884. Throughout the world, surgeons were very slow to accept new antiseptic surgical techniques, although Lister had first published them in *The Lancet* in 1867. Not until a memorable debate at the New-York Academy of Medicine in 1884 did the majority of physicians and surgeons in New York City accept them.[126]

In 1895 Dr. Howard A. Kelly, professor of gynaecology and obstetrics at Johns Hopkins, in his introduction to Dr. Hunter Robb's *Aseptic Surgical Techniques with Especial Reference to Gynaecological Operations* described "the past ten years" as the decade which had seen "changes wrought in our surgical techniques . . . unparalleled [in] any previous century of medical or surgical progress."[127]

---

[125] Means, *supra* note 1, at 502 & nn.227, 228.

[126] C. Haagensen & W. Lloyd, A Hundred Years of Medicine 291-93 (1943) [hereinafter cited as Haagensen & Lloyd].

[127] H. Robb, Aseptic Surgical Techniques with Especial Reference to Gynaecological Operations, at xv-xvi (1895).

The pre-antiseptic surgeons "dared not invade the great cavities of the body" lest they infect their patients. "Operation therefore was generally only undertaken with the object of saving life. . . . Many of the greatest [of the pre-antiseptic] surgeons were fully of the opinion that the knife should be used only as a last resort."[128] Drs. Eugene H. Pool and Frank J. McGowan in their book, *Surgery at the New York Hospital One Hundred Years Ago,* disclose a rule adopted by the board of governors "that *no* operation should be undertaken except after consultation by *all* the physicians and surgeons. We find evidence in the notebook that this rule was scrupulously observed."[129]

Though the pre-antiseptic surgeons knew the danger of sepsis, they did not know its cause:

> None realized that, in general, it was they themselves who were unconsciously poisoning their patients every time they used the probe or the knife. The probe . . . was never sterilized . . . . Who could devise a better means of carrying infection? And these conditions continued until late in the 19th century.[130]

Is it any wonder that today the medical profession is so forgetful of this unhappy phase of its long history? Men dedicated to curing the ills of their fellow man unconsciously shrink from the realization that less than a hundred years ago the best of their surgical predecessors killed almost as many patients as they cured.

The earliest Texas and former Georgia abortion statutes, like those of nearly all their sister states, were enacted prior to the 1884 debate at the New-York Academy of Medicine. It was only after that debate that the acceptance of Lister's surgical techniques spread throughout the country.

VIII. The Realtive Safety Test

In recent decades surgeons have commonly complained that they cannot understand what is meant by words such as "necessary to preserve [her] life" in the text of *abortion* statutes. They understand

---

[128] Haagensen & Lloyd, at 19.

[129] H. Pool & F. McGowan, Surgery at the New York Hospital One Hundred Years Ago, at 4 (1930).

[130] Haagensen & Lloyd, at 24.

perfectly well what those words mean in other operations of a dangerous character, but, of course, those words do not appear in any statute
in regard to other operations, but only in the common understanding
of the profession as to when to resort to dangerous surgery. Since
abortion now is not dangerous, surgeons cannot make head or tail of
these words in a statute relating to abortions.

The doctors' dilemma reminds one of the words of Judge Water-
man, speaking for the United States Court of Appeals for the Second
Circuit, in *Eck v. United Arab Airlines, Inc.:*

> [I]nquiry may lead the court to conclude . . . that when the
> words were first chosen the language accurately reflected the
> provision's purpose but that today the same words imper-
> fectly reflect this purpose because conditions have changed in
> the area to which the words of the provision refer . . . .[131]

In *People v. Belous,*[132] the Supreme Court of California discussed
the relative safety test that had first been suggested in my 1968 article[133] as follows:

> There is one suggested test which is based on a policy
> underlying the statute and which would serve to make the
> statute certain. The test is probably in accord with the legisla-
> tive intent at the time the statute was adopted. The Legislature
> may have intended in adopting the statute that abortion was
> permitted when the risk of death due to the abortion was less
> than the risk of death in childbirth and that otherwise abor-
> tion should be denied. As we have seen, at the time of the
> adoption of the statute [1850 in California] abortion was a
> highly dangerous procedure, and under the relative safety test
> abortion would be permissible only where childbirth would be
> even more dangerous. In the light of the test and the then
> existing medical practice, the question whether abortion
> should be limited to protect the embryo or fetus may have
> been immaterial because any such interest would be effec-
> tuated by limiting abortions to the rare cases where they were

---

[131] 360 F.2d 804, 812 (2d Cir. 1966).
[132] *Supra* note 116.
[133] Means, *supra* note 1, at 513-14 n.261.

safer than childbirth.

   . . . .

> Although the suggested construction . . . making abortion lawful where it is safer than childbirth and unlawful where abortion is more dangerous, may have been in accord with legislative intent, the statute may not be upheld against a claim of vagueness on the basis of such a construction. The language of the statute, 'unless the same is necessary to preserve her life,' does not suggest a relative safety test, and no case interpreting the statute has suggested that the statute be so construed. . . . In the circumstances, we are satisfied that the statute may not be construed to adopt the relative safety test as against a claim of vagueness, because the language does not suggest that test and because of the practical evidence before us that men of 'common' intelligence, indeed of uncommon intelligence, have not guessed at this meaning.[134]

It is, of course, true that in recent decades no one had guessed at this meaning until the publication of my 1968 article. But the real inquiry is not whether men of common or uncommon intelligence today are able, under today's conditions, to guess at this meaning, but whether men of common intelligence at the time the statute was first passed understood perfectly well what its words meant. That they did understand it, and understood it to mean a relative safety test, can be historically demonstrated.

Alfred Swaine Taylor, M.D., F.R.S. (1806-80), was the most respected author on medical jurisprudence writing in English during the nineteenth century. His treatise on this subject was published in a shorter version, called the *Manual of Medical Jurisprudence* (which went through ten editions in London and eight in Philadelphia during the author's lifetime), and in a longer version, called *Principles and Practice of Medical Jurisprudence* (which went through two editions during the author's lifetime, in 1865 and 1873, and has gone through six more since his death). An extensive chapter on criminal abortion, containing a significant passage on the relative safety test, appeared in every edition of both books, commencing with the earliest of the

---

[134] People v. Belous, *supra* note 116, at 970-72, 458 P.2d at 204, 205, 80 Cal. Rptr. at 364, 365.

Manual (London 1844).[135] The passage on the relative safety test as it appeared in the last edition of *Principles and Practice* to be published in Dr. Taylor's lifetime reads as follows:

> Hence a cautious selection should be made, 'because the operation is necessarily attended with some risk . . . . All that we can say is, that, according to general professional experience, it places her in a better position than she would be in if the case were left to itself. It appears to me that before a practitioner resolves upon performing an operation of this kind he should hold a consultation with others; and, before it is performed, he should feel assured that *natural delivery cannot take place without greater risk to the life of the woman than the operation would itself create.*[136]

While at this particular point Dr. Taylor was discussing the relative safety test as applied to the induction of labor in the seventh or eighth month (a technique now almost totally abandoned), and while he preferred that technique to abortion early in gestation, it is quite obvious that, if he had confronted a case where early abortion was indicated rather than a late induction of labor, he would have applied the same relative safety test to early abortion. Indeed, the relative safety test is one which surgeons resort to even today in regard to operations that still are dangerous to the patient's life. They weigh the danger to be apprehended from the operation itself against the danger of doing nothing. It is simple common sense.

In speaking of abortion early in gestation, Dr. Taylor notes that "the life of the woman would be seriously endangered", but adds that abortion, especially in the United States, "is resorted to by medical men in the interest of the mother alone at the expense of the life of the child."[137]

It is very interesting to note that in the second posthumous edition of Taylor's *Principles and Practice*[138] the new editor made only one change in Taylor's text of this passage. Whereas Taylor had said,

---

[135] A. Taylor, Manual of Medical Jurisprudence, 595 (1844).

[136] 2 A. Taylor, Principles and Practice of Medical Jurisprudence, 202 (2d ed. 1873).

[137] *Id.* at 201.

[138] 2 A. Taylor, Principles and Practice of Medical Jurisprudence, 209 (4th ed., T. Stevenson 1894).

in 1873, that "the life of the woman would be seriously endangered" by an abortion early in pregnancy, Stevenson, in 1894, deleted the adverb "seriously." The adoption of Lister's technique of antiseptic surgery, in England, took place between these two dates.

If the *Belous* court had had before it this passage in Taylor, it might very well have concluded that the relative safety test not merely "probably", but certainly, was "in accord with the legislative intent at the time the statute was adopted."

The same may be said of the following passage in the opinion of Mr. Justice Adkins, speaking for a majority of five of the seven justices of the Supreme Court of Florida in *Walsingham v. State*:

> Protection of the mother from unsafe surgical procedures may well have been in the legislators' minds when they enacted the [Florida] abortion statutes in 1868. Modern-day medicine, whoever [sic] makes induced miscarriage in the first trimester of pregnancy a safer procedure than delivery at full term. See *People v. Belous,* 71 Cal. 2d 954, 80 Cal. Rptr. 354, 360, 458 P.2d 194, 200. At the time of the adoption of these statutes, the State, to protect the interest of its citizens, could reasonably restrict the availability of abortion to those women who faced an equally serious risk of death if the operation were not performed.[139]

The difficulty remains, however, that the administrators of these laws—physicians and surgeons—have, in recent decades, forgotten why they were passed, and therefore are no longer able to guess at their meaning. The laws have become vague through obsolescence; the profession has lost touch with their meaning through obliviscence.

Were the American medical profession now suddenly to remember the reason for the passage of these laws, they would grant an abortion to every woman in the first or second trimester who requested one; for, today, abortion is always safer than childbirth, as the New York figures now show, not only during the first trimester, but during the first 24 weeks of pregnancy.

---

[139] 250 So. 2d 857, 861 (Fla. 1971).

IX. RECENT DECISIONS ON THE CHALLENGED CONSTITUTIONALITY
OF STATE ABORTION LAWS

The earliest and still the best of this line of cases is *People v. Belous*.[140] Since that decision, ten federal district courts have considered the constitutionality of state abortion statutes, at the challenge of women and/or physicians. Eight of the ten have reached the merits, whereas two abstained out of federal deference to state courts.[141]

Of the eight federal district courts which have ruled on the merits of the constitutional challenge to the abortion statutes based on a woman's fundamental right to terminate an unwanted pregnancy, and to the aid of a physician in doing so, four have held them unconstitutional,[142] while four have upheld them.[143] These eight courts were all three-judge courts. Thus, a total of fourteen federal judges have ruled in favor of this fundamental right and so have held the abortion statutes unconstitutional. Ten have upheld them. The circuit judges were evenly divided on this constitutional question, 4:4, while the district judges voted in favor of the right and against the statutes, 10:6.

The successive judicial formulations of the woman's fundamental right to an abortion are of interest:

(1) *People v. Belous:*

The fundamental right of the woman to choose whether to bear children follows from the [United States] Supreme Court's and this court's repeated acknowledgement of a 'right

---

[140] *Supra* note 116.

[141] Doe v. Randall, 314 F. Supp. 32 (D. Minn. 1970), *aff'd sub nom.*, Hodgson v. Randall, 402 U.S. 967 (1971); Rodgers v. Danforth, Civil No. 18360-2 (W.D. Mo., filed Sept. 10, 1970), *appeal filed*, 39 U.S.L.W. 3390 (U.S. Feb. 8, 1971) (No. 70-89).

[142] Doe v. Scott, 321 F. Supp. 1385 (N.D. Ill. 1970) (2:1), *appeals filed sub nom.*, 39 U.S.L.W. 3438 (U.S. Mar. 29, 1971) (Nos. 70-105, 70-106); Doe v. Bolton, *supra* note 2; Roe v. Wade, *supra* note 2; Babbitz v. McCann, 310 F. Supp. 293 (E.D. Wis. 1970), *appeal dismissed for want of grant or denial of injunction*, 400 U.S. 1 (1970), *injunction granted by three-judge court*, 320 F. Supp. 219 (E.D. Wis. 1970), *writ of prohibition to three-judge court denied sub nom.* McCann v. Kerner, 436 F.2d 1342 (7th Cir. 1971), *injunction (but not the declaratory judgment) vacated sub nom.* McCann v. Babbitz, 402 U.S. 903 (1971).

[143] Doe v. Rampton, No. C-234-70 (D. Utah, filed Sept. 8, 1971) (2:1); Corkey v. Edwards, 322 F. Supp. 1248 (W.D.N.C. 1971), *appeal filed*, 40 U.S.L.W. 3098 (U.S. July 17, 1971) (No. 71-92); Rosen v. Louisiana State Bd. of Med. Examiners, 318 F. Supp. 1217 (E.D. La. 1970) (2:1), *appeal filed*, 39 U.S.L.W. 3302 (U.S. Nov. 27, 1970) (No. 70-42); Steinberg v. Brown, 321 F. Supp. 741 (N.D. Ohio 1970) (2:1).

of privacy' in matters related to marriage, family, and sex. . . . That such a right is not enumerated in either the United States or California Constitution is no impediment to the existence of the right. . . . It is not surprising that none of the parties who have filed briefs in this case have disputed the existence of this fundamental right.[144]

(2) *United States v. Vuitch*:

[A]s a secular matter a woman's liberty . . . may well include the right to remove an unwanted child at least in the early stages of pregnancy. . . .[145]

(3) *Babbitz v. McCann*:

The police power of the state does not entitle . . . it to deny to a woman the basic right reserved to her under the ninth amendment to decide whether she should carry or reject an embryo which has not yet quickened. . . .[146]

(4) *Roe v. Wade*:

[The court recognized a woman's] Ninth Amendment right to choose to have an abortion. . . .[147]

---

[144] *Supra* note 116, at 963-64, 458 P.2d at 199-200, 80 Cal. Rptr. at 359-60.

[145] 305 F. Supp. 1032, 1035 (D.D.C. 1969). In this case, District Judge Gesell held the District of Columbia abortion statute unconstitutionally vague, but included this half-hearted dictum about a woman's fundamental right in his opinion. The Supreme Court reversed on the vagueness point, but held that:

Although there was some reference to [the claim that a woman has a fundamental right to an abortion] in the opinion of the court below, we read it as holding simply that the statute was void for vagueness . . . . Since that question of vagueness was the only issue passed upon by the District Court it is the only issue we reach here.

United States v. Vuitch, *supra* note 49, at 55.

Two state courts, in recent decisions, seem to have over-interpreted this refusal of the United States Supreme Court to reach the question of the woman's fundamental right. One characterized it as "judicial reticence." People v. Pettegrew, 18 Cal. App. 3d 677, 680, 96 Cal. Rptr. 189, 190 (2d Dist. 1971). Another stated that the Supreme Court had "noted that the arguments based on Griswold v. Connecticut . . . did not control." Thompson v. State, No. 44,071 (Tex. Crim. App., Nov. 2, 1971). They did not control the decision in the *Vuitch* case only because the district court had not squarely ruled on them; in another case, in which the lower court had done so, they might well control.

[146] *Supra* note 142, at 302 (Kerner, Reynolds & Gordon, JJ.).

[147] *Supra* note 2, at 1223 (Goldberg, Hughes & Taylor, JJ.).

(5) *Doe v. Bolton*:

For whichever reason [penumbral zone or ninth amendment]
personal liberty . . . is . . . broad enough to include the decision to abort a pregnancy. . . .

. . . .

[T]he Court does not postulate the existence of a new being
with federal constitutional rights at any time during gestation. . . .[148]

(6) *Doe v. Scott*:

[W]omen have a fundamental interest in choosing whether to
terminate pregnancies [hence, the state may not prohibit] the
performance of abortions during the first trimester of pregnancy by licensed physicians in a licensed hospital or other
licensed medical facility.[149]

(7) *Rosen v. Louisiana State Board of Medical Examiners*
(dissenting opinion):

[I]n some ways the right to have an abortion is more compelling than the rights involved in *Griswold* . . . . At least two
fundamental human rights are . . . involved: The mother's
autonomy over her own body, and her right to choose whether
to bring a child into the world.[150]

(8) *Steinberg v. Brown dissenting opinion)*:

[A] woman has . . . the fundamental right to choose
whether to bear children.[151]

(9) *Doe v. Rampton* (dissenting opinion):

The flaw in the Utah abortion statute is that it . . . invades

---

[148] *Supra* note 2, at 1055 & n.3 (Morgan, Smith & Henderson, JJ.).
[149] *Supra* note 142, at 1390 (Swygert & Robson, JJ.).
[150] *Supra* note 143, at 1235 (Cassibry, J., dissenting).
[151] *Supra* note 143, at 759 (Green, J., dissenting).

the plaintiff's right of privacy with no showing of a *compelling* state interest.[152]

(10)	*People v. Barksdale*:

[A] woman has a constitutional right to terminate her pregnancy, subject only to reasonably imposed state restrictions designed to safeguard the health of the woman, and to protect the advanced fetus.[153]

The shrewdest historical insight, among all these federal court opinions, occurs in the following excerpts from the dissenting opinion of District Judge Ben C. Green, in *Steinberg v. Brown*:

[W]hen the abortion statutes were enacted the surgical procedure required in an abortion presented a substantial risk of death to the woman involved. [T]his situation no longer exists with today's medical advances. Protection of the mother from unsafe surgical procedures may well have been in the legislators' minds when they enacted the Ohio statute in 1834. Modern day medicine, however, makes induced miscarriage in the first trimester of pregnancy a safer procedure than delivery at full term. See, *People v. Belous, supra,* [71 Cal. 2d 964-65,] 80 Cal. Rptr. 360-361, 458 P. 2d 200-201. In many areas the mortality rate from therapeutic abortion is less than that occasioned by childbirth. . . .

Viewed in its historical perspective, the Ohio statute could well have been considered as a reasonable measure when it was adopted 136 years ago. At that time the risk of death on the operating table for any surgical procedure was extremely serious, and the state, to protect the interests of its citizens, could reasonably restrict the availability of abortion

---

[152] *Supra* note 143 (Ritter, J., dissenting) (emphasis in original).

[153] 18 Cal. App. 3d 813, 825, 96 Cal. Rptr. 265, 272 (1st Dist. 1971). In another recent state court case, the Texas Court of Criminal Appeals stated: "Without determining whether or not seeking an abortion is operating within a constitutionally protected zone of privacy, we do hold that the State of Texas has a compelling interest to protect fetal life." Thompson v. State, *supra* note 6. This is, of course, a formula which enables the Texas court to say that it is not necessarily denying the woman's fundamental right while actually denying it. It is interesting that even a court bent on denying the woman's fundamental right, as this one was, feels it necessary to conceal what it is doing under such a disclaimer.

to those women who faced an equally serious risk of death if the operation was not performed.[154]

Since the memorable delineation of the comparative safety test in *People v. Belous*,[155] this has been the second articulate judicial recognition of the true original meaning of the words "necessary to preserve [the patient's] life."

On July 12, 1971, the Supreme Court of Florida handed down its decision in *Walsingham v. State* which contains the third express recognition of the relative safety test.[156] The statement in this and other judicial opinions rendered since the *Belous* case was decided on September 5, 1969, rely on the opinion in that case for the statement that abortion is safer than childbirth if performed in the first trimester by a physician. At the time the *Belous* case was argued and decided, there were not yet available any massive statistics on legal abortions from any American state; so the limitation of the comparison of safety as between childbirth and abortion was expressed, in those days, by cautious medical writers, as limited to abortion performed in the first trimester. So the *Belous* court similarly limited the comparison in its opinion, and, following it, so has Florida's Supreme Court in the *Walsingham* case. Today, however, massive statistics concerning legal abortion are available from New York, for more than an entire year under the new New York law, which permits unfettered abortion till the end of the twenty-fourth week—or for eleven of the thirteen weeks of the second trimester of pregnancy. These data show that abortion performed by a physician during the first twenty-four weeks of pregnancy is now safer than childbirth. The limitation of this comparison to the first trimester is therefore already obsolete.

X.   DOES A FOETUS POSSESS FEDERAL CONSTITUTIONAL RIGHTS?

The only one of the cases which have recently passed on the question of the constitutionality of the state abortion laws which has had a direct statement in it on this question is *Doe v. Bolton*. A footnote in that opinion declares that "the Court does not postulate the existence of a new being with federal constitutional rights at any time

---

[154] *Supra* note 143, at 750-51 (dissenting opinion).

[155] *Supra* note 116, at 970-72, 458 P.2d at 204-05, 80 Cal. Rptr. at 364-65.

[156] 250 So. 2d 857, 861 (Fla. 1971). *See* text *supra*, p. 396.

during gestation . . . ."[157] This cautious but quite correct statement was made in response to one of the persistent attempts to intervene in these litigations by religiously interested parties who apply for appointment as guardians *ad litem* for unborn children.

When such a person presents himself to a court and in effect says, "The unborn children I wish to represent are entitled to life and I am here to represent them since, obviously, their expectant mothers are bent on murdering them," the court then must face the preliminary question whether or not such foetūs are or are not *persons* entitled to a right to life. Though the three-judge court in Georgia decided they were not, a single judge in the federal court in the northern district of Illinois granted one Dr. Bart Heffernan the guardianship *ad litem* of all unborn children in Illinois.[158] What is the problem, legally speaking, a court must face when it has to consider the merits of a contention of this kind? I think the wording of the Georgia federal court significant: Is this a being that has federal constitutional rights?

In order to determine that, a court must ascertain what the word "person" means in the Federal Constitution, in which this word is used many times both in the original instrument and in the Bill of Rights in the fourth, and the fifth, amendments. The word "persons" is also quite significantly used in the enumeration clause in the original Constitution.[159] That is the clause which commands the taking of a census every ten years. There, the mandate is laid down that once every decade the "whole Number of . . . Persons" in each state must be counted.

From the first census of 1790 to the latest one in 1970, no census-taker has ever counted a foetus. A sufficient reason why no foetus has ever been counted is that from the 1790 census onward, Congress has by statute prescribed a certain form that the census-taker must fill out. This is divided into columns, and there is a sexual breakdown. He is required to list all male persons and all female

---

[157] *Supra* note 2, at 1055 n.3.

[158] Senior District Judge Campbell, a Roman Catholic, signed such an order on April 10, 1970, *non pro tunc* [sic: *nunc pro tunc*] as of March 11, 1970." Afterwards a three-judge court was convened. Judge Campbell, as initiating judge, was a member of the panel. The three-judge court held (2:1) that the Illinois abortion statute is unconstitutional, with Judge Campbell dissenting. Curiously, however, the majority did not revoke the order appointing Dr. Heffernan. *Doe v. Scott, supra* note 142.

[159] U.S. Const. art. I, § 2, cl.3.

persons.[160] A census-taker confronted with a foetus whose expectant parents asked him to count it would find it impossible to decide in which column to put it, unarmed with the very recent and still expensive technique by which a doctor now can antenatally determine foetal sex.

One derives from this the obvious intention of the very First Congress, which met in New York City, and in which many members sat who had served in the Philadelphia Convention which had framed the original Constitution, and all of whose members—that is to say, of the First Congress—helped to frame the Bill of Rights, that they did not think that a foetus was a person. Since a foetus is not a person within the meaning of the enumeration clause of the Constitution, one would have to have affirmative evidence that those passing the amendments forming the Bill of Rights intended to give it any other meaning. There is no such evidence.

If one goes beyond the constitutional text to determine what may well have been the intention of the framers of the original Constitution and of the Bill of Rights on this subject, one could do no better than to consult the first treatise on medical jurisprudence that was ever published in the English language. It was a work by Samuel Farr called *Elements of Jurisprudence,* published in London in 1787, the year in which the Philadelphia Convention sat, and it contains the following passage:

> The first rudiments or germen of the human body is not a human creature, if it be even a living one; it is a foundation only upon which the human superstructure is raised. This is evident to anatomical observation. Were a child to be born in the shape which it presents in the first stages of pregnancy, it would be a monster indeed, as great as any which was ever brought to light.[161]

The refreshing simplicity of this eighteenth-century text encourages one to hope that when this question finally is argued before the Supreme Court of the United States, this clear echo of the Age of

---

[160] The act of the First Congress which mandated the taking of the first census expressly enjoined "distinguishing the sexes" of the persons counted. Act of March 1, 1790, ch. 2, 1 Stat. 101.

[161] I have had access to this work only as reprinted in T. Cooper, Tracts on Medical Jurisprudence (1819), where the passage quoted appears at 12.

Reason will outweigh the sentimental romanticism that has been spawned in recent years about little human beings in the early stages of pregnancy.

Whatever one or more of the several states of the United States may choose to do, either with their legal rules or with their legal nomenclature, is of no federal constitutional significance, because the word "person" in the Federal Constitution must, of course, have a nationwide uniform federal interpretation.

There is an interesting precedent on this subject. It is the famous case of *Dred Scott v. Sanford*,[162] the case decided by the United States Supreme Court in 1857 in which the question that the Court preliminarily had to reach was whether or not the words "Citizens of different States" in the diversity of citizenship clause[163] in Article III of the original Constitution did or did not include a Negro who originally had been a slave, but who had moved to free soil and under the law there enforced became free.

One of the points decided by the Court in that case was that the word "Citizens" in Article III had to have a uniform nationwide federal meaning which an individual state could not vary. That part of the decision (although not the rest of it, obviously, for the remainder has been reversed by history) is still good law. So no matter what a state could elect to do on the subject, by way of declaring a foetus to be a "person" for some state law purposes, it could not bind either federal or state courts in interpreting the word "person" in the Federal Constitution.

In New York, the 1967 State Constitutional Convention, alas, proved abortive, since the voters decided to reject the Convention's efforts. Nevertheless, at the Constitutional Convention in 1967, a specific proposal was made by Professor Charles Rice of the Fordham University Law School to add to the State Constitution's equal protection clause, after the word "person", the words "from the moment of conception." His obvious purpose, which he supported in a debate covering about three printed pages, was to prevent all abortions. He felt that even the law that was in force in New York from 1830 to 1970 was too liberal and that abortion should be prohibited in every instance. The committee of the Constitutional Convention to which this proposal was referred recommended unanimously against

---

[162] 60 U.S. (19 How.) 393 (1857).
[163] U.S. Const. art. III, § 2, cl. 1.

its adoption, and it was defeated by an overwhelming voice vote on August 30, 1967, on the floor of the convention.[164]

Suppose, however, that Professor Rice's proposal had passed. Could that have made any difference from the federal constitutional point of view? Of course not. The only instance that I can cite by way of precedent for that is Wisconsin. Wisconsin is the only state in the Union which, albeit not in its state constitution, but in one of its statutes relating to abortion, has put the very words after the word "person" Professor Rice wanted to insert—"from the moment of conception."[165] Notwithstanding this text, the federal three-judge court in Wisconsin in the case of Dr. Babbitz gave it absolutely no effect and did not recognize it as conferring any federal constitutional rights on the foetus.[166]

The Attorney General of Texas, in his brief in *Roe v. Wade,* has:

> most seriously argued that the "life" protected by the Due Process of Law Clause of the Fifth Amendment includes the life of the unborn child. Further, it would be a denial of equal protection of the law not to accord protection of the life of a person who had not yet been born but still in the womb of its mother. If it is a denial of equal protection for a statute to distinguish between a thief and an embezzler under a statute providing for the sterilization of the one and not the other, then it is surely a denial of equal protection for either the state or federal government to distinguish between a person who has been born and one living in the womb of its mother.[167]

Of course, the Attorney General of Texas is here alluding not to the fifth amendment, but to the fourteenth. What he says is astonishing. Unwittingly, it seems, he has just condemned as unconstitutional all the abortion laws of Texas throughout its history, since none of them has punished the killing of "one living in the womb of its moth-

---

[164] 3 Proceedings of the Constitutional Convention of the State of New York, April fourth to September twenty-sixth 1967, at 400-03 (1967).

[165] This unique Wisconsin statute speaks of the "time" of conception rather than of Professor Rice's "moment", which sets the stage for a nice metaphysical debate about how much time there is in a moment. The statute reads: "In this section 'unborn child' means a human being from the time of conception until it is born alive." Wis. Stat. Ann. tit. XLV, ch. 940, § 940.04(6) (1958) (added by ch. 696, § 1, [1955] Wis. Laws).

[166] Babbitz v. McCann, *supra* note 142, at 301.

[167] Brief for Appellee at 56, Roe v. Wade, *supra* note 2.

er" as severely as the killing of "a person who has been born." Does not the equal protection clause demand that this inequity be levelled, either by making all abortionists guilty of murder, or reducing the penalty for murder to that which is imposed on abortionists? Furthermore, the law against murder in Texas does not, presumably, contain a therapeutic exception, permitting the act to be done to preserve somebody else's life simply because that somebody else requests it. Does not that deny equal protection? As astounding as these consequences of the Texas Attorney General's *ipse dixit* are, it will surprise nobody who has read the preceding two dozen pages of his brief, which he has copied nearly *verbatim* from the *amici curiae* brief of Certain Physicians, Professors, and Fellows of the American College of Obstetrics and Gynecology[168] (*i.e.,* those who dissent from the pro-abortion stand taken by ACOG as an organization, in the *amicus curiae* brief it filed in these cases). That brief devotes six pages to argument that the word "person" in the due process clauses of the fifth and fourteenth amendments and in the equal protection clause of the fourteenth includes a foetus. Needless to say, this argument also cites no single authority for this proposition, and rests fairly and squarely on the *ipsi dixerunt* of the Certain Physicians, Professors, and Fellows, and their counsel, who apparently have not yet discovered the enumeration clause in the Constitution of 1787.

The Attorney General of Georgia, in *Doe v. Bolton,* did not embark upon the slippery slope down which the Attorney General of Texas has so awkwardly slid. In his case, the 1968 Georgia statute, which he is defending, being an American Law Institute Model-Penal-Code-patterned statute, not only differentiates between foetūs and persons already born, but even between various classes of foetūs. If that is equal protection, some foetūs must be more equal than others.

In his brief for appellee in *Roe v. Wade,* the Attorney General of Texas filled many pages with a verbatim copy of the embryological section of the *amicus* brief filed in both cases on behalf of certain dissenting Physicians, Professors and Fellows of the American College of Obstetrics and Gynecology (ACOG). In the embryological section of the ACOG dissenters' *amicus* brief, an earnest effort is

---

[168] Brief for Certain Physicians, Professors and Fellows of the American College of Obstetricians and Gynaecologists as Amicus Curiae at 58-63, Roe v. Wade and Doe v. Bolton, *supra* note 2. A similar assertion appears in Brief for The National Right to Life Committee as Amicus Curiae at 44, Roe v. Wade, *supra* note 2.

made to recount in week-by-week detail the progressive intrauterine evolution of the human foetus. Virtually all these details have been known to embryologists for some time, and no criticism of the data as data could be made. It is only the philosophical inferences that the ACOG dissenters endeavor to draw from the data that are not a little suspect. For example, at one point appears the following sentence in italics, the only sentence chosen for that degree of emphasis in the entire two dozen printed pages of this embryological extravaganza:

> Dr. Still has noted that electroencephalographic waves have been obtained in forty-three to forty-five day old fetuses, and so conscious experience is possible after this date.[169]

Such an assertion is meant to imply, if it does not quite say, that after the forty-fifth day of gestation the foetus already has a type of consciousness similar to that which adult human beings possess. Such an idea is sheer nonsense. It is common knowledge among embryologists that cortical tissue has been removed from the brain and kept alive for days, during which period such tissue continues to emit waves which are picked up on an electroencephalograph. That this indicates the presence of consciousness is scarcely to be affirmed, unless one defines consciousness much more broadly than the rational human consciousness of adult life.

What the ACOG dissenters are trying to establish, by their electroencephalograms-at-45-days-of-gestation argument, is that what theologians call a human soul is already present in the foetus. They eschew using the word "soul", because they are afraid of the first amendment; so they substitute the word "consciousness." Changing labels does not alter substance, however; so I shall use both words, with an equality sign between them. The mediaeval theologians felt that a foetus had not just one soul (= consciousness), but, successively, three souls (= consciousnesses): first, a vegetable soul (= vegetable consciousness), second, an (irrational) animal soul (= animal consciousness), and third, a human or rational soul (= human consciousness). In other words, the Mediaevals were aware, as the ACOG dissenters are not, that consciousness itself undergoes intrauterine

---

[169] Brief for Certain Physicians, Professors and Fellows of the American College of Obstetrics and Gynecology as Amicus Curiae at 23, Roe v. Wade and Doe v. Bolton, *supra* note 2, repeated verbatim (but without italics), in Brief for Appellee at 52, Roe v. Wade, *supra* note 2.

evolution, from an extremely primitive, pre-human form, to one which became (in the mediaeval belief) fully human. The ACOG dissenters are trying to prove that fully human consciousness occurs as early as the forty-fifth day of gestation, but the scientific data on which they rely simply do not demonstrate this.

All philosophers and theologians agree that man is a rational animal, but the "reason" to which they refer must be either a form or a function. For our purposes (the question as to what the law should protect from destruction at the whim of another) we must necessarily be concerned with form, rather than function; otherwise, the law would not protect persons asleep, or madmen, or the unconscious. In biology, form always precedes function, sometimes by many years. Thus the gonads appear at the foetal stage, but are not used until puberty. Likewise, the human cerebral cortex appears at the foetal stage, but the function of human reason, which is its distictive role, is not exercised until about the third year of postnatal life—at the time when, in the words of my friend Joseph Donceel, S.J., a professor of philosophy at Fordham—the child first uses such words as "true" or "false."

If, therefore, we are to resort to embryological data to determine the "moment" when a human foetus acquires the form of reason, we shall find that the organization of the human cerebral cortex is not finished before birth. In the words of Percival Bailey, Professor of Neurology and Neurosurgery at the University of Illinois Medical School, "The greater part of the cortex . . . completes its structural organization some time after birth."[170]

Two articles in the recently published *Evolution of the Forebrain: Phylogenesis and Ontogenesis of the Forebrain,*[171] make it quite clear that the formation of the human cerebral cortex is not completed until after birth. Thus, Th. Rabinowicz declares:

> In the cerebral cortex of the premature infant of the 8th month, a great number of nerve cells are still not quite clearly differentiated.[172]

---

[170] P. Bailey, Cortex and Mind, in Mid-Century Psychiatry: An Overview 11 (R. Grinker ed. 1953).

[171] Evolution of the Forebrain: Phylogenesis and Ontogenesis of the Forebrain (R. Hassler & H. Stephan eds. 1967).

[172] Th. Rabinowicz, *The Cerebral Cortex of the Premature Infant of the 8th Month,* in Evolution of the Forebrain: Phylogenesis and Ontogenesis of the Forebrain 40 (R. Hassler & H. Stephan eds. 1967).

And, speaking of certain synapses which he designated " 'counter' contact structures in the shape of appendages ('thorns')", G.I. Poliakov states:

> In the human cerebral cortex such appendages on the dendrites begin to develop in the seventh month of intrauterine life. Before birth they are observed only in the biggest neurons . . . after birth they greatly spread and densely cover the dendrite ramifications of many efferent neurons of the cortex. . . .
>
> Main elements of the cortical organization, typical of the brain of an adult, reach definite degree of development at the time of birth. . . .[173]

Thus the scorn affected by the ACOG dissenters in their assertion, "There is no magic in birth",[174] appears unwarranted. Birth does, according to *relevant* embryological data, mark approximately the stage at which the human cerebral cortex—the form of reason, and therefore the defining note of man—reaches its "definite degree of development." So, perhaps our ancestors, including those who wrote the enumeration clause and the ninth amendment, were not such fools after all, when they thought that "person" does not include a foetus, but does include the newborn babe.

The question is not, as the ACOG dissenters put it, whether or not "The Unborn Offspring of Human Parents is an Autonomous Human Being." Of course it is. It is "human", since it was produced by human parents, and it is a "being", since it exists. And it is "autonomous", if nothing more is meant by that adjective than that it possesses a unique genetic organization. The question is whether, prior to birth, the offspring of human parents is a human *person*. Only *persons* are the subjects of legal rights, whether constitutional or other.[175]

---

[173] G.I. Poliakov, *Embryonal and Postembryonal Development of Neurons of the Human Cerebral Cortex*, in Evolution of the Forebrain: Phylogenesis and Ontogenesis of the Forebrain 254, 257 (R. Hassler & H. Stephan eds. 1967).

[174] Brief for Certain Physicians, Professors and Fellows of the American College of Obstetrics and Gynecology as Amicus Curiae at 30, Roe v. Wade and Doe v. Bolton, *supra* note 2, repeated verbatim in Brief for Appellee at 53, Roe v. Wade, *supra* note 2.

[175] Thus Sir Frederick Pollock declared: "The person is the legal subject or substance of which rights and duties are attributes. An individual human being, considered as having such attributes, is what lawyers call a *natural person*." F. Pollock, A First Book of Jurisprudence

A useful analogy can be drawn from the other end of the life-span, from the agreed ethical norms governing heart transplants. It is now universally agreed that the donor of a heart must have suffered such massive brain damage that it can be stated categorically by the attending physicians that mental activity will never again be possible. A flat electroencephalogram for a stated period is required. Only then can the donor's heart be removed and transplanted into the cardial cavity of the donee. But the heart at removal is not dead. If it were, it would not do the donee any good. The life that is still in the heart is the same as the life that is still in the rest of the donor's body, and has been there all along. It is not because human life has departed, that the donor's body can be used for the benefit of the donee. It is because there is no longer present in that still living body the human *person* who has been present in it since birth. Since that human person is no longer present, his consent can no longer be asked. Whose consent is asked? The next of kin of the departed, just as if this still living body were already a cadaver. In other words, it is possible for a human body to be alive but no longer to contain a human person.

If that can happen at the *terminus ad quem* of the life span, why can it not happen at the *terminus a quo*? Prior to birth, human life is of course present in the foetus, but a human person is not. For the removal of the foetus, whose consent must be asked? As there is as yet no human person in the foetus, then by the analogy of the heart transplant cases, we must ask the consent of the next of kin. It is harder to imagine a nearer kin than the pregnant woman who is carrying the foetus. That is what the common law required for abortion at will—the will or consent of the expectant mother. Why should more be required now?

---

111 (3d ed. 1911) (emphasis in original). One need only read the words of the Federal Constitution, including its amendments, to realize that their framers penned these texts with this same notion in mind. The fifth and fourteenth amendments do not confer rights upon human life; they treat life as the object, not as the subject, of rights. They forbid governments to deprive a *person* of his life, without due process of law. If the phenomenon of human life can exist apart from a human person, it is not protected by the fifth or fourteenth amendment. The crucial question, therefore, is whether a human person is present in the life which is asserted to be inviolable. It is not human life, as such, but the human person, as such, that is sacred.

JUDITH JARVIS THOMSON   A Defense of Abortion[1]

Most opposition to abortion relies on the premise that the fetus is a human being, a person, from the moment of conception. The premise is argued for, but, as I think, not well. Take, for example, the most common argument. We are asked to notice that the development of a human being from conception through birth into childhood is continuous; then it is said that to draw a line, to choose a point in this development and say "before this point the thing is not a person, after this point it is a person" is to make an arbitrary choice, a choice for which in the nature of things no good reason can be given. It is concluded that the fetus is, or anyway that we had better say it is, a person from the moment of conception. But this conclusion does not follow. Similar things might be said about the development of an acorn into an oak tree, and it does not follow that acorns are oak trees, or that we had better say they are. Arguments of this form are sometimes called "slippery slope arguments"—the phrase is perhaps self-explanatory—and it is dismaying that opponents of abortion rely on them so heavily and uncritically.

I am inclined to agree, however, that the prospects for "drawing a line" in the development of the fetus look dim. I am inclined to think also that we shall probably have to agree that the fetus has already become a human person well before birth. Indeed, it comes as a surprise when one first learns how early in its life it begins to acquire human characteristics. By the tenth week, for example, it already has

1. I am very much indebted to James Thomson for discussion, criticism, and many helpful suggestions.

a face, arms and legs, fingers and toes; it has internal organs, and brain activity is detectable.[2] On the other hand, I think that the premise is false, that the fetus is not a person from the moment of conception. A newly fertilized ovum, a newly implanted clump of cells, is no more a person than an acorn is an oak tree. But I shall not discuss any of this. For it seems to me to be of great interest to ask what happens if, for the sake of argument, we allow the premise. How, precisely, are we supposed to get from there to the conclusion that abortion is morally impermissible? Opponents of abortion commonly spend most of their time establishing that the fetus is a person, and hardly any time explaining the step from there to the impermissibility of abortion. Perhaps they think the step too simple and obvious to require much comment. Or perhaps instead they are simply being economical in argument. Many of those who defend abortion rely on the premise that the fetus is not a person, but only a bit of tissue that will become a person at birth; and why pay out more arguments than you have to? Whatever the explanation, I suggest that the step they take is neither easy nor obvious, that it calls for closer examination than it is commonly given, and that when we do give it this closer examination we shall feel inclined to reject it.

I propose, then, that we grant that the fetus is a person from the moment of conception. How does the argument go from here? Something like this, I take it. Every person has a right to life. So the fetus has a right to life. No doubt the mother has a right to decide what shall happen in and to her body; everyone would grant that. But surely a person's right to life is stronger and more stringent than the mother's right to decide what happens in and to her body, and so outweighs it. So the fetus may not be killed; an abortion may not be performed.

It sounds plausible. But now let me ask you to imagine this. You wake up in the morning and find yourself back to back in bed with an unconscious violinist. A famous unconscious violinist. He has been found to have a fatal kidney ailment, and the Society of Music Lovers

2. Daniel Callahan, *Abortion: Law, Choice and Morality* (New York, 1970), p. 373. This book gives a fascinating survey of the available information on abortion. The Jewish tradition is surveyed in David M. Feldman, *Birth Control in Jewish Law* (New York, 1968), Part 5, the Catholic tradition in John T. Noonan, Jr., "An Almost Absolute Value in History," in *The Morality of Abortion*, ed. John T. Noonan, Jr. (Cambridge, Mass., 1970).

has canvassed all the available medical records and found that you alone have the right blood type to help. They have therefore kidnapped you, and last night the violinist's circulatory system was plugged into yours, so that your kidneys can be used to extract poisons from his blood as well as your own. The director of the hospital now tells you, "Look, we're sorry the Society of Music Lovers did this to you—we would never have permitted it if we had known. But still, they did it, and the violinist now is plugged into you. To unplug you would be to kill him. But never mind, it's only for nine months. By then he will have recovered from his ailment, and can safely be unplugged from you." Is it morally incumbent on you to accede to this situation? No doubt it would be very nice of you if you did, a great kindness. But do you *have* to accede to it? What if it were not nine months, but nine years? Or longer still? What if the director of the hospital says, "Tough luck, I agree, but you've now got to stay in bed, with the violinist plugged into you, for the rest of your life. Because remember this. All persons have a right to life, and violinists are persons. Granted you have a right to decide what happens in and to your body, but a person's right to life outweighs your right to decide what happens in and to your body. So you cannot ever be unplugged from him." I imagine you would regard this as outrageous, which suggests that something really is wrong with that plausible-sounding argument I mentioned a moment ago.

In this case, of course, you were kidnapped; you didn't volunteer for the operation that plugged the violinist into your kidneys. Can those who oppose abortion on the ground I mentioned make an exception for a pregnancy due to rape? Certainly. They can say that persons have a right to life only if they didn't come into existence because of rape; or they can say that all persons have a right to life, but that some have less of a right to life than others, in particular, that those who came into existence because of rape have less. But these statements have a rather unpleasant sound. Surely the question of whether you have a right to life at all, or how much of it you have, shouldn't turn on the question of whether or not you are the product of a rape. And in fact the people who oppose abortion on the ground I mentioned do not make this distinction, and hence do not make an exception in case of rape.

Nor do they make an exception for a case in which the mother has to spend the nine months of her pregnancy in bed. They would agree that would be a great pity, and hard on the mother; but all the same, all persons have a right to life, the fetus is a person, and so on. I suspect, in fact, that they would not make an exception for a case in which, miraculously enough, the pregnancy went on for nine years, or even the rest of the mother's life.

Some won't even make an exception for a case in which continuation of the pregnancy is likely to shorten the mother's life; they regard abortion as impermissible even to save the mother's life. Such cases are nowadays very rare, and many opponents of abortion do not accept this extreme view. All the same, it is a good place to begin: a number of points of interest come out in respect to it.

1. Let us call the view that abortion is impermissible even to save the mother's life "the extreme view." I want to suggest first that it does not issue from the argument I mentioned earlier without the addition of some fairly powerful premises. Suppose a woman has become pregnant, and now learns that she has a cardiac condition such that she will die if she carries the baby to term. What may be done for her? The fetus, being a person, has a right to life, but as the mother is a person too, so has she a right to life. Presumably they have an equal right to life. How is it supposed to come out that an abortion may not be performed? If mother and child have an equal right to life, shouldn't we perhaps flip a coin? Or should we add to the mother's right to life her right to decide what happens in and to her body, which everybody seems to be ready to grant—the sum of her rights now outweighing the fetus' right to life?

The most familiar argument here is the following. We are told that performing the abortion would be directly killing[3] the child, whereas doing nothing would not be killing the mother, but only letting her die. Moreover, in killing the child, one would be killing an innocent person, for the child has committed no crime, and is not aiming at his mother's death. And then there are a variety of ways in which this

---

3. The term "direct" in the arguments I refer to is a technical one. Roughly, what is meant by "direct killing" is either killing as an end in itself, or killing as a means to some end, for example, the end of saving someone else's life. See note 6, below, for an example of its use.

might be continued. (1) But as directly killing an innocent person is always and absolutely impermissible, an abortion may not be performed. Or, (2) as directly killing an innocent person is murder, and murder is always and absolutely impermissible, an abortion may not be performed.[4] Or, (3) as one's duty to refrain from directly killing an innocent person is more stringent than one's duty to keep a person from dying, an abortion may not be performed. Or, (4) if one's only options are directly killing an innocent person or letting a person die, one must prefer letting the person die, and thus an abortion may not be performed.[5]

Some people seem to have thought that these are not further premises which must be added if the conclusion is to be reached, but that they follow from the very fact that an innocent person has a right to life.[6] But this seems to me to be a mistake, and perhaps the simplest way to show this is to bring out that while we must certainly grant that innocent persons have a right to life, the theses in (1) through (4) are all false. Take (2), for example. If directly killing an innocent person is murder, and thus is impermissible, then the mother's directly killing the innocent person inside her is murder, and thus is

4. Cf. *Encyclical Letter of Pope Pius XI on Christian Marriage*, St. Paul Editions (Boston, n.d.), p. 32: "however much we may pity the mother whose health and even life is gravely imperiled in the performance of the duty allotted to her by nature, nevertheless what could ever be a sufficient reason for excusing in any way the direct murder of the innocent? This is precisely what we are dealing with here." Noonan (*The Morality of Abortion*, p. 43) reads this as follows: "What cause can ever avail to excuse in any way the direct killing of the innocent? For it is a question of that."

5. The thesis in (4) is in an interesting way weaker than those in (1), (2), and (3): they rule out abortion even in cases in which both mother *and* child will die if the abortion is not performed. By contrast, one who held the view expressed in (4) could consistently say that one needn't prefer letting two persons die to killing one.

6. Cf. the following passage from Pius XII, *Address to the Italian Catholic Society of Midwives*: "The baby in the maternal breast has the right to life immediately from God.—Hence there is no man, no human authority, no science, no medical, eugenic, social, economic or moral 'indication' which can establish or grant a valid juridical ground for a direct deliberate disposition of an innocent human life, that is a disposition which looks to its destruction either as an end or as a means to another end perhaps in itself not illicit.—The baby, still not born, is a man in the same degree and for the same reason as the mother" (quoted in Noonan, *The Morality of Abortion*, p. 45).

impermissible. But it cannot seriously be thought to be murder if the mother performs an abortion on herself to save her life. It cannot seriously be said that she *must* refrain, that she *must* sit passively by and wait for her death. Let us look again at the case of you and the violinist. There you are, in bed with the violinist, and the director of the hospital says to you, "It's all most distressing, and I deeply sympathize, but you see this is putting an additional strain on your kidneys, and you'll be dead within the month. But you *have* to stay where you are all the same. Because unplugging you would be directly killing an innocent violinist, and that's murder, and that's impermissible." If anything in the world is true, it is that you do not commit murder, you do not do what is impermissible, if you reach around to your back and unplug yourself from that violinist to save your life.

The main focus of attention in writings on abortion has been on what a third party may or may not do in answer to a request from a woman for an abortion. This is in a way understandable. Things being as they are, there isn't much a woman can safely do to abort herself. So the question asked is what a third party may do, and what the mother may do, if it is mentioned at all, is deduced, almost as an afterthought, from what it is concluded that third parties may do. But it seems to me that to treat the matter in this way is to refuse to grant to the mother that very status of person which is so firmly insisted on for the fetus. For we cannot simply read off what a person may do from what a third party may do. Suppose you find yourself trapped in a tiny house with a growing child. I mean a very tiny house, and a rapidly growing child—you are already up against the wall of the house and in a few minutes you'll be crushed to death. The child on the other hand won't be crushed to death; if nothing is done to stop him from growing he'll be hurt, but in the end he'll simply burst open the house and walk out a free man. Now I could well understand it if a bystander were to say, "There's nothing we can do for you. We cannot choose between your life and his, we cannot be the ones to decide who is to live, we cannot intervene." But it cannot be concluded that you too can do nothing, that you cannot attack it to save your life. However innocent the child may be, you do not have to wait passively while it crushes you to death. Perhaps a pregnant woman is vaguely felt to have the status of house, to which we don't allow the right of self-defense. But if the woman houses the child, it should be remembered that she is a person who houses it.

I should perhaps stop to say explicitly that I am not claiming that people have a right to do anything whatever to save their lives. I think, rather, that there are drastic limits to the right of self-defense. If someone threatens you with death unless you torture someone else to death, I think you have not the right, even to save your life, to do so. But the case under consideration here is very different. In our case there are only two people involved, one whose life is threatened, and one who threatens it. Both are innocent: the one who is threatened is not threatened because of any fault, the one who threatens does not threaten because of any fault. For this reason we may feel that we bystanders cannot intervene. But the person threatened can.

In sum, a woman surely can defend her life against the threat to it posed by the unborn child, even if doing so involves its death. And this shows not merely that the theses in (1) through (4) are false; it shows also that the extreme view of abortion is false, and so we need not canvass any other possible ways of arriving at it from the argument I mentioned at the outset.

2. The extreme view could of course be weakened to say that while abortion is permissible to save the mother's life, it may not be performed by a third party, but only by the mother herself. But this cannot be right either. For what we have to keep in mind is that the mother and the unborn child are not like two tenants in a small house which has, by an unfortunate mistake, been rented to both: the mother *owns* the house. The fact that she does adds to the offensiveness of deducing that the mother can do nothing from the supposition that third parties can do nothing. But it does more than this: it casts a bright light on the supposition that third parties can do nothing. Certainly it lets us see that a third party who says "I cannot choose between you" is fooling himself if he thinks this is impartiality. If Jones has found and fastened on a certain coat, which he needs to keep him from freezing, but which Smith also needs to keep him from freezing, then it is not impartiality that says "I cannot choose between you" when Smith owns the coat. Women have said again and again "This body is *my* body!" and they have reason to feel angry, reason to feel that it has been like shouting into the wind. Smith, after all, is

hardly likely to bless us if we say to him, "Of course it's your coat, anybody would grant that it is. But no one may choose between you and Jones who is to have it."

We should really ask what it is that says "no one may choose" in the face of the fact that the body that houses the child is the mother's body. It may be simply a failure to appreciate this fact. But it may be something more interesting, namely the sense that one has a right to refuse to lay hands on people, even where it would be just and fair to do so, even where justice seems to require that somebody do so. Thus justice might call for somebody to get Smith's coat back from Jones, and yet you have a right to refuse to be the one to lay hands on Jones, a right to refuse to do physical violence to him. This, I think, must be granted. But then what should be said is not "no one may choose," but only "*I* cannot choose," and indeed not even this, but "*I* will not *act*," leaving it open that somebody else can or should, and in particular that anyone in a position of authority, with the job of securing people's rights, both can and should. So this is no difficulty. I have not been arguing that any given third party must accede to the mother's request that he perform an abortion to save her life, but only that he may.

I suppose that in some views of human life the mother's body is only on loan to her, the loan not being one which gives her any prior claim to it. One who held this view might well think it impartiality to say "I cannot choose." But I shall simply ignore this possibility. My own view is that if a human being has any just, prior claim to anything at all, he has a just, prior claim to his own body. And perhaps this needn't be argued for here anyway, since, as I mentioned, the arguments against abortion we are looking at do grant that the woman has a right to decide what happens in and to her body.

But although they do grant it, I have tried to show that they do not take seriously what is done in granting it. I suggest the same thing will reappear even more clearly when we turn away from cases in which the mother's life is at stake, and attend, as I propose we now do, to the vastly more common cases in which a woman wants an abortion for some less weighty reason than preserving her own life.

3. Where the mother's life is not at stake, the argument I mentioned at the outset seems to have a much stronger pull. "Everyone

has a right to life, so the unborn person has a right to life." And isn't the child's right to life weightier than anything other than the mother's own right to life, which she might put forward as ground for an abortion?

This argument treats the right to life as if it were unproblematic. It is not, and this seems to me to be precisely the source of the mistake.

For we should now, at long last, ask what it comes to, to have a right to life. In some views having a right to life includes having a right to be given at least the bare minimum one needs for continued life. But suppose that what in fact *is* the bare minimum a man needs for continued life is something he has no right at all to be given? If I am sick unto death, and the only thing that will save my life is the touch of Henry Fonda's cool hand on my fevered brow, then all the same, I have no right to be given the touch of Henry Fonda's cool hand on my fevered brow. It would be frightfully nice of him to fly in from the West Coast to provide it. It would be less nice, though no doubt well meant, if my friends flew out to the West Coast and carried Henry Fonda back with them. But I have no right at all against anybody that he should do this for me. Or again, to return to the story I told earlier, the fact that for continued life that violinist needs the continued use of your kidneys does not establish that he has a right to be given the continued use of your kidneys. He certainly has no right against you that *you* should give him continued use of your kidneys. For nobody has any right to use your kidneys unless you give him such a right; and nobody has the right against you that you shall give him this right—if you do allow him to go on using your kidneys, this is a kindness on your part, and not something he can claim from you as his due. Nor has he any right against anybody else that *they* should give him continued use of your kidneys. Certainly he had no right against the Society of Music Lovers that they should plug him into you in the first place. And if you now start to unplug yourself, having learned that you will otherwise have to spend nine years in bed with him, there is nobody in the world who must try to prevent you, in order to see to it that he is given something he has a right to be given.

Some people are rather stricter about the right to life. In their view, it does not include the right to be given anything, but amounts to, and only to, the right not to be killed by anybody. But here a related difficulty arises. If everybody is to refrain from killing that violinist, then everybody must refrain from doing a great many different sorts of things. Everybody must refrain from slitting his throat, everybody must refrain from shooting him—and everybody must refrain from unplugging you from him. But does he have a right against everybody that they shall refrain from unplugging you from him? To refrain from doing this is to allow him to continue to use your kidneys. It could be argued that he has a right against us that *we* should allow him to continue to use your kidneys. That is, while he had no right against us that we should give him the use of your kidneys, it might be argued that he anyway has a right against us that we shall not now intervene and deprive him of the use of your kidneys. I shall come back to third-party interventions later. But certainly the violinist has no right against you that *you* shall allow him to continue to use your kidneys. As I said, if you do allow him to use them, it is a kindness on your part, and not something you owe him.

The difficulty I point to here is not peculiar to the right to life. It reappears in connection with all the other natural rights; and it is something which an adequate account of rights must deal with. For present purposes it is enough just to draw attention to it. But I would stress that I am not arguing that people do not have a right to life— quite to the contrary, it seems to me that the primary control we must place on the acceptability of an account of rights is that it should turn out in that account to be a truth that all persons have a right to life. I am arguing only that having a right to life does not guarantee having either a right to be given the use of or a right to be allowed continued use of another person's body—even if one needs it for life itself. So the right to life will not serve the opponents of abortion in the very simple and clear way in which they seem to have thought it would.

4. There is another way to bring out the difficulty. In the most ordinary sort of case, to deprive someone of what he has a right to is to treat him unjustly. Suppose a boy and his small brother are jointly given a box of chocolates for Christmas. If the older boy takes the box and refuses to give his brother any of the chocolates, he is unjust to him, for the brother has been given a right to half of them. But

suppose that, having learned that otherwise it means nine years in bed with that violinist, you unplug yourself from him. You surely are not being unjust to him, for you gave him no right to use your kidneys, and no one else can have given him any such right. But we have to notice that in unplugging yourself, you are killing him; and violinists, like everybody else, have a right to life, and thus in the view we were considering just now, the right not to be killed. So here you do what he supposedly has a right you shall not do, but you do not act unjustly to him in doing it.

The emendation which may be made at this point is this: the right to life consists not in the right not to be killed, but rather in the right not to be killed unjustly. This runs a risk of circularity, but never mind: it would enable us to square the fact that the violinist has a right to life with the fact that you do not act unjustly toward him in unplugging yourself, thereby killing him. For if you do not kill him unjustly, you do not violate his right to life, and so it is no wonder you do him no injustice.

But if this emendation is accepted, the gap in the argument against abortion stares us plainly in the face: it is by no means enough to show that the fetus is a person, and to remind us that all persons have a right to life—we need to be shown also that killing the fetus violates its right to life, i.e., that abortion is unjust killing. And is it?

I suppose we may take it as a datum that in a case of pregnancy due to rape the mother has not given the unborn person a right to the use of her body for food and shelter. Indeed, in what pregnancy could it be supposed that the mother has given the unborn person such a right? It is not as if there were unborn persons drifting about the world, to whom a woman who wants a child says "I invite you in."

But it might be argued that there are other ways one can have acquired a right to the use of another person's body than by having been invited to use it by that person. Suppose a woman voluntarily indulges in intercourse, knowing of the chance it will issue in pregnancy, and then she does become pregnant; is she not in part responsible for the presence, in fact the very existence, of the unborn person inside her? No doubt she did not invite it in. But doesn't her partial responsibility for its being there itself give it a right to the use of her body?[7] If so, then her aborting it would be more like the boy's taking away the chocolates, and less like your unplugging yourself from the violinist—doing so would be depriving it of what it does have a right to, and thus would be doing it an injustice.

And then, too, it might be asked whether or not she can kill it even to save her own life: If she voluntarily called it into existence, how can she now kill it, even in self-defense?

The first thing to be said about this is that it is something new. Opponents of abortion have been so concerned to make out the independence of the fetus, in order to establish that it has a right to life, just as its mother does, that they have tended to overlook the possible support they might gain from making out that the fetus is *dependent* on the mother, in order to establish that she has a special kind· of responsibility for it, a responsibility that gives it rights against her which are not possessed by any independent person—such as an ailing violinist who is a stranger to her.

On the other hand, this argument would give the unborn person a right to its mother's body only if her pregnancy resulted from a voluntary act, undertaken in full knowledge of the chance a pregnancy might result from it. It would leave out entirely the unborn person whose existence is due to rape. Pending the availability of some further argument, then, we would be left with the conclusion that unborn persons whose existence is due to rape have no right to the use of their mothers' bodies, and thus that aborting them is not depriving them of anything they have a right to and hence is not unjust killing.

And we should also notice that it is not at all plain that this argument really does go even as far as it purports to. For there are cases and cases, and the details make' a difference. If the room is stuffy, and I therefore open a window to air it, and a burglar climbs in, it would be absurd to say,"Ah, now he can stay, she's given him a right to the use of her house—for she is partially responsible for his presence there, having voluntarily done what enabled him to get in, in full knowledge that there are such things as burglars, and that burglars

7. The need for a discussion of this argument was brought home to me by members of the Society for Ethical and Legal Philosophy, to whom this paper was originally presented.

burgle." It would be still more absurd to say this if I had had bars installed outside my windows, precisely to prevent burglars from getting in, and a burglar got in only because of a defect in the bars. It remains equally absurd if we imagine it is not a burglar who climbs in, but an innocent person who blunders or falls in. Again, suppose it were like this: people-seeds drift about in the air like pollen, and if you open your windows, one may drift in and take root in your carpets or upholstery. You don't want children, so you fix up your windows with fine mesh screens, the very best you can buy. As can happen, however, and on very, very rare occasions does happen, one of the screens is defective; and a seed drifts in and takes root. Does the person-plant who now develops have a right to the use of your house? Surely not—despite the fact that you voluntarily opened your windows, you knowingly kept carpets and upholstered furniture, and you knew that screens were sometimes defective. Someone may argue that you are responsible for its rooting, that it does have a right to your house, because after all you *could* have lived out your life with bare floors and furniture, or with sealed windows and doors. But this won't do—for by the same token anyone can avoid a pregnancy due to rape by having a hysterectomy, or anyway by never leaving home without a (reliable!) army.

It seems to me that the argument we are looking at can establish at most that there are *some* cases in which the unborn person has a right to the use of its mother's body, and therefore *some* cases in which abortion is unjust killing. There is room for much discussion and argument as to precisely which, if any. But I think we should sidestep this issue and leave it open, for at any rate the argument certainly does not establish that all abortion is unjust killing.

5. There is room for yet another argument here, however. We surely must all grant that there may be cases in which it would be morally indecent to detach a person from your body at the cost of his life. Suppose you learn that what the violinist needs is not nine years of your life, but only one hour: all you need do to save his life is to spend one hour in that bed with him. Suppose also that letting him use your kidneys for that one hour would not affect your health in the slightest. Admittedly you were kidnapped. Admittedly you did not give

anyone permission to plug him into you. Nevertheless it seems to me plain you *ought* to allow him to use your kidneys for that hour—it would be indecent to refuse.

Again, suppose pregnancy lasted only an hour, and constituted no threat to life or health. And suppose that a woman becomes pregnant as a result of rape. Admittedly she did not voluntarily do anything to bring about the existence of a child. Admittedly she did nothing at all which would give the unborn person a right to the use of her body. All the same it might well be said, as in the newly emended violinist story, that she *ought* to allow it to remain for that hour—that it would be indecent in her to refuse.

Now some people are inclined to use the term "right" in such a way that it follows from the fact that you ought to allow a person to use your body for the hour he needs, that he has a right to use your body for the hour he needs, even though he has not been given that right by any person or act. They may say that it follows also that if you refuse, you act unjustly toward him. This use of the term is perhaps so common that it cannot be called wrong; nevertheless it seems to me to be an unfortunate loosening of what we would do better to keep a tight rein on. Suppose that box of chocolates I mentioned earlier had not been given to both boys jointly, but was given only to the older boy. There he sits, stolidly eating his way through the box, his small brother watching enviously. Here we are likely to say "You ought not to be so mean. You ought to give your brother some of those chocolates." My own view is that it just does not follow from the truth of this that the brother has any right to any of the chocolates. If the boy refuses to give his brother any, he is greedy, stingy, callous—but not unjust. I suppose that the people I have in mind will say it does follow that the brother has a right to some of the chocolates, and thus that the boy does act unjustly if he refuses to give his brother any. But the effect of saying this is to obscure what we should keep distinct, namely the difference between the boy's refusal in this case and the boy's refusal in the earlier case, in which the box was given to both boys jointly, and in which the small brother thus had what was from any point of view clear title to half.

A further objection to so using the term "right" that from the fact that A ought to do a thing for B, it follows that B has a right against A that A do it for him, is that it is going to make the question of whether or not a man has a right to a thing turn on how easy it is to provide him with it; and this seems not merely unfortunate, but morally unacceptable. Take the case of Henry Fonda again. I said earlier that I had no right to the touch of his cool hand on my fevered brow, even though I needed it to save my life. I said it would be frightfully nice of him to fly in from the West Coast to provide me with it, but that I had no right against him that he should do so. But suppose he isn't on the West Coast. Suppose he has only to walk across the room, place a hand briefly on my brow—and lo, my life is saved. Then surely he ought to do it, it would be indecent to refuse. Is it to be said "Ah, well, it follows that in this case she has a right to the touch of his hand on her brow, and so it would be an injustice in him to refuse"? So that I have a right to it when it is easy for him to provide it, though no right when it's hard? It's rather a shocking idea that anyone's rights should fade away and disappear as it gets harder and harder to accord them to him.

So my own view is that even though you ought to let the violinist use your kidneys for the one hour he needs, we should not conclude that he has a right to do so—we should say that if you refuse, you are, like the boy who owns all the chocolates and will give none away, self-centered and callous, indecent in fact, but not unjust. And similarly, that even supposing a case in which a woman pregnant due to rape ought to allow the unborn person to use her body for the hour he needs, we should not conclude that he has a right to do so; we should conclude that she is self-centered, callous, indecent, but not unjust, if she refuses. The complaints are no less grave; they are just different. However, there is no need to insist on this point. If anyone does wish to deduce "he has a right" from "you ought," then all the same he must surely grant that there are cases in which it is not morally required of you that you allow that violinist to use your kidneys, and in which he does not have a right to use them, and in which you do not do him an injustice if you refuse. And so also for mother and unborn child. Except in such cases as the unborn person has a right to demand it—and we were leaving open the possibility that there may be such cases—nobody is morally *required* to make large sacrifices, of health, of all other interests and concerns, of all other duties and commitments, for nine years, or even for nine months, in order to keep another person alive.

6. We have in fact to distinguish between two kinds of Samaritan: the Good Samaritan and what we might call the Minimally Decent Samaritan. The story of the Good Samaritan, you will remember, goes like this:

> A certain man went down from Jerusalem to Jericho, and fell among thieves, which stripped him of his raiment, and wounded him, and departed, leaving him half dead.
>
> And by chance there came down a certain priest that way; and when he saw him, he passed by on the other side.
>
> And likewise a Levite, when he was at the place, came and looked on him, and passed by on the other side.
>
> But a certain Samaritan, as he journeyed, came where he was; and when he saw him he had compassion on him.
>
> And went to him, and bound up his wounds, pouring in oil and wine, and set him on his own beast, and brought him to an inn, and took care of him.
>
> And on the morrow, when he departed, he took out two pence, and gave them to the host, and said unto him, "Take care of him; and whatsoever thou spendest more, when I come again, I will repay thee."   (Luke 10:30-35)

The Good Samaritan went out of his way, at some cost to himself, to help one in need of it. We are not told what the options were, that is, whether or not the priest and the Levite could have helped by doing less than the Good Samaritan did, but assuming they could have, then the fact they did nothing at all shows they were not even Minimally Decent Samaritans, not because they were not Samaritans, but because they were not even minimally decent.

These things are a matter of degree, of course, but there is a difference, and it comes out perhaps most clearly in the story of Kitty Genovese, who, as you will remember, was murdered while thirty-eight people watched or listened, and did nothing at all to help her. A Good Samaritan would have rushed out to give direct assistance against the murderer. Or perhaps we had better allow that it would have been a Splendid Samaritan who did this, on the ground that it would have involved a risk of death for himself. But the thirty-eight not only did not do this, they did not even trouble to pick up a phone to call the police. Minimally Decent Samaritanism would call for doing at least that, and their not having done it was monstrous.

After telling the story of the Good Samaritan, Jesus said "Go, and do thou likewise." Perhaps he meant that we are morally required to act as the Good Samaritan did. Perhaps he was urging people to do more than is morally required of them. At all events it seems plain that it was not morally required of any of the thirty-eight that he rush out to give direct assistance at the risk of his own life, and that it is not morally required of anyone that he give long stretches of his life—nine years or nine months—to sustaining the life of a person who has no special right (we were leaving open the possibility of this) to demand it.

Indeed, with one rather striking class of exceptions, no one in any country in the world is *legally* required to do anywhere near as much as this for anyone else. The class of exceptions is obvious. My main concern here is not the state of the law in respect to abortion, but it is worth drawing attention to the fact that in no state in this country is any man compelled by law to be even a Minimally Decent Samaritan to any person; there is no law under which charges could be brought against the thirty-eight who stood by while Kitty Genovese died. By contrast, in most states in this country women are compelled by law to be not merely Minimally Decent Samaritans, but Good Samaritans to unborn persons inside them. This doesn't by itself settle anything one way or the other, because it may well be argued that there should be laws in this country—as there are in many European countries—compelling at least Minimally Decent Samaritanism.[8] But it does show that there is a gross injustice in the existing state of the law. And it shows also that the groups currently working against liberalization of abortion laws, in fact working toward having it declared unconstitu-

8. For a discussion of the difficulties involved, and a survey of the European experience with such laws, see *The Good Samaritan and the Law*, ed. James M. Ratcliffe (New York, 1966).

tional for a state to permit abortion, had better start working for the adoption of Good Samaritan laws generally, or earn the charge that they are acting in bad faith.

I should think, myself, that Minimally Decent Samaritan laws would be one thing, Good Samaritan laws quite another, and in fact highly improper. But we are not here concerned with the law. What we should ask is not whether anybody should be compelled by law to be a Good Samaritan, but whether we must accede to a situation in which somebody is being compelled—by nature, perhaps—to be a Good Samaritan. We have, in other words, to look now at third-party interventions. I have been arguing that no person is morally required to make large sacrifices to sustain the life of another who has no right to demand them, and this even where the sacrifices do not include life itself; we are not morally required to be Good Samaritans or anyway Very Good Samaritans to one another. But what if a man cannot extricate himself from such a situation? What if he appeals to us to extricate him? It seems to me plain that there are cases in which we can, cases in which a Good Samaritan would extricate him. There you are, you were kidnapped, and nine years in bed with that violinist lie ahead of you. You have your own life to lead. You are sorry, but you simply cannot see giving up so much of your life to the sustaining of his. You cannot extricate yourself, and ask us to do so. I should have thought that—in light of his having no right to the use of your body—it was obvious that we do not have to accede to your being forced to give up so much. We can do what you ask. There is no injustice to the violinist in our doing so.

7. Following the lead of the opponents of abortion, I have throughout been speaking of the fetus merely as a person, and what I have been asking is whether or not the argument we began with, which proceeds only from the fetus' being a person, really does establish its conclusion. I have argued that it does not.

But of course there are arguments and arguments, and it may be said that I have simply fastened on the wrong one. It may be said that what is important is not merely the fact that the fetus is a person, but that it is a person for whom the woman has a special kind of responsibility issuing from the fact that she is its mother. And it might be argued that all my analogies are therefore irrelevant—for you do not have that special kind of responsibility for that violinist, Henry Fonda does not have that special kind of responsibility for me. And our attention might be drawn to the fact that men and women both *are* compelled by law to provide support for their children.

I have in effect dealt (briefly) with this argument in section 4 above; but a (still briefer) recapitulation now may be in order. Surely we do not have any such "special responsibility" for a person unless we have assumed it, explicitly or implicitly. If a set of parents do not try to prevent pregnancy, do not obtain an abortion, and then at the time of birth of the child do not put it out for adoption, but rather take it home with them, then they have assumed responsibility for it, they have given it rights, and they cannot *now* withdraw support from it at the cost of its life because they now find it difficult to go on providing for it. But if they have taken all reasonable precautions against having a child, they do not simply by virtue of their biological relationship to the child who comes into existence have a special responsibility for it. They may wish to assume responsibility for it, or they may not wish to. And I am suggesting that if assuming responsibility for it would require large sacrifices, then they may refuse. A Good Samaritan would not refuse—or anyway, a Splendid Samaritan, if the sacrifices that had to be made were enormous. But then so would a Good Samaritan assume responsibility for that violinist; so would Henry Fonda, if he is a Good Samaritan, fly in from the West Coast and assume responsibility for me.

8. My argument will be found unsatisfactory on two counts by many of those who want to regard abortion as morally permissible. First, while I do argue that abortion is not impermissible, I do not argue that it is always permissible. There may well be cases in which carrying the child to term requires only Minimally Decent Samaritanism of the mother, and this is a standard we must not fall below. I am inclined to think it a merit of my account precisely that it does *not* give a general yes or a general no. It allows for and supports our sense that, for example, a sick and desperately frightened fourteen-year-old schoolgirl, pregnant due to rape, may *of course* choose abortion, and that any law which rules this out is an insane law. And it also allows for and supports our sense that in other cases resort to abortion is even positively indecent. It would be indecent in the woman to request an

abortion, and indecent in a doctor to perform it, if she is in her seventh month, and wants the abortion just to avoid the nuisance of postponing a trip abroad. The very fact that the arguments I have been drawing attention to treat all cases of abortion, or even all cases of abortion in which the mother's life is not at stake, as morally on a par ought to have made them suspect at the outset.

Secondly, while I am arguing for the permissibility of abortion in some cases, I am not arguing for the right to secure the death of the unborn child. It is easy to confuse these two things in that up to a certain point in the life of the fetus it is not able to survive outside the mother's body; hence removing it from her body guarantees its death. But they are importantly different. I have argued that you are not morally required to spend nine months in bed, sustaining the life of that violinist; but to say this is by no means to say that if, when you unplug yourself, there is a miracle and he survives, you then have a right to turn round and slit his throat. You may detach yourself even if this costs him his life; you have no right to be guaranteed his death, by some other means, if unplugging yourself does not kill him. There are some people who will feel dissatisfied by this feature of my argument. A woman may be utterly devastated by the thought of a child, a bit of herself, put out for adoption and never seen or heard of again. She may therefore want not merely that the child be detached from her, but more, that it die. Some opponents of abortion are inclined to regard this as beneath contempt—thereby showing insensitivity to what is surely a powerful source of despair. All the same, I agree that the desire for the child's death is not one which anybody may gratify, should it turn out to be possible to detach the child alive.

At this place, however, it should be remembered that we have only been pretending throughout that the fetus is a human being from the moment of conception. A very early abortion is surely not the killing of a person, and so is not dealt with by anything I have said here.

Legal Reasoning From the Top Down and From the Bottom Up: The Question of Unenumerated Constitutional Rights

Richard A. Posner†

I. Top-Down and Bottom-Up Reasoning

I want to approach the subject of my debate with Professor Dworkin—unenumerated constitutional rights—by distinguishing two types of legal reasoning: what I shall call reasoning from the top down and reasoning from the bottom up. In top-down reasoning, the judge or other legal analyst invents or adopts a theory about an area of law—perhaps about all law—and uses it to organize, criticize, accept or reject, explain or explain away, distinguish or amplify the existing decisions to make them conform to the theory and generate an outcome in each new case as it arises that will be consistent with the theory and with the canonical cases, that is, the cases accepted as authoritative within the theory. The theory need not be, perhaps never can be, drawn "from" law; it surely need not be articulated in lawyers' jargon. In bottom-up reasoning, which encompasses such familiar lawyers' techniques as "plain meaning" and "reasoning by analogy," one starts with the words of a statute or other enactment, or with a case or a mass of cases, and moves from there—but doesn't move far, as we shall see. The top-downer and the bottom-upper do not meet.

I am associated with several top-down theories. One, which is primarily positive (descriptive), is that the common law is best understood on the "as if" assumption that judges try to maximize the wealth of society. Another, primarily normative, is that judges should interpret the antitrust statutes to make them conform to the dictates of wealth maximization. In the development of the lat-

---

† Judge, United States Court of Appeals for the Seventh Circuit; Senior Lecturer, The University of Chicago Law School. This is a slightly expanded text of my talk at *The Bill of Rights in the Welfare State: A Bicentennial Symposium*, held at The University of Chicago Law School on October 25-26, 1991. The reader should bear in mind that it was prepared for oral delivery. I thank Ronald Dworkin, Frank Easterbrook, Lawrence Lessig, Andrew Schapiro, and Cass Sunstein for many helpful comments.

ter theory, Robert Bork—Dworkin's *bête noire*[1]—was a pioneer. Bork called his theory "consumer welfare maximization,"[2] but that is just a reassuring term for wealth maximization. He divided the Supreme Court's antitrust cases into a main tradition informed by the principles of wealth maximization and a deviant branch of that tradition, and he argued for lopping off the branch.[3]

Dworkin himself is prominently associated with a theory of constitutional law that makes such law the expression of liberalism, weighted with egalitarianism.[4] Richard Epstein has a broadly similar view of constitutional law but he weights his liberalism not with egalitarianism but with economic freedom.[5] John Hart Ely has a different but equally ambitious theory of constitutional law, one that yokes the various clauses together to draw the plow called promoting the values of a representative democracy.[6] Bruce Ackerman has still another.[7] A famous common-law top-downer from an earlier generation was Christopher Columbus Langdell.[8] And before him Hobbes.

Yet legal reasoning from the bottom up is the more familiar, even the more hallowed, type.[9] The endlessly repeated refrain of modern judicial opinions that in interpreting a statute the judge must start with its words is in this tradition. And we all remember our first day in law school, when we were asked to read for each course not an overview or theoretical treatment of the field but a case—a case, moreover, lying in the middle rather than at the historical or logical beginning of the field. Those of us who are judges also remember our first day in that job, when we were handed a

---

[1] See the following works by Ronald Dworkin: *Reagan's Justice*, NY Rev Books 27 (Nov 8, 1984); *The Bork Nomination*, NY Rev Books 3 (Aug 13, 1987); *From Bork to Kennedy*, NY Rev Books 36 (Dec 17, 1987); and *Bork's Jurisprudence*, 57 U Chi L Rev 657 (1990).

[2] Robert H. Bork, *The Antitrust Paradox: A Policy at War With Itself* 7 (Basic, 1978) ("the only legitimate goal of antitrust is the maximization of consumer welfare").

[3] See Robert H. Bork, *The Rule of Reason and the Per Se Concept: Price Fixing and Market Division (Part I)*, 74 Yale L J 775 (1965); Robert H. Bork, *The Rule of Reason and the Per Se Concept: Price Fixing and Market Division (Part II)*, 75 Yale L J 375 (1966).

[4] See, for example, Ronald Dworkin, *Taking Rights Seriously* (Harvard, 1977).

[5] See, for example, Richard A. Epstein, *Property, Speech and the Politics of Distrust*, 59 U Chi L Rev 41 (1992).

[6] See John Hart Ely, *Democracy and Distrust: A Theory of Judicial Review* (Harvard, 1980).

[7] See, for example, Bruce Ackerman, *We the People: Foundations* (Belknap, 1991).

[8] See, for example, Christopher Columbus Langdell, *A Selection of Cases on the Law of Contracts* (Little Brown, 1871) (preface).

[9] For a classic statement, see Edward H. Levi, *An Introduction to Legal Reasoning* (Chicago, 1949).

sheaf of briefs in cases from fields we may have known nothing about and told that in a few days we would be hearing oral argument and would then take our tentative vote.

There is a question whether legal reasoning from the bottom up amounts to much. Dworkin thinks not. His extensive writings evince little interest in the words of the Constitution, or in its structure (that is, in how its various parts—the articles, sections, clauses, and amendments—work together), in the texture and details of the complex statutes that his works discuss, such as Title VII of the Civil Rights Act of 1964,[10] or in any extended body of case law, let alone in the details of particular cases. His implicit legal universe consists of a handful of general principles embodied in a handful of exemplary, often rather bodiless, cases.

I do not myself see the law in quite that way but I agree there isn't much to bottom-up reasoning.[11] We don't ever really "start" from a mass of cases or from a statute or from a clause of the Constitution. To read a case, to read a statute, a rule, or a constitutional clause presupposes a vast linguistic, cultural, and conceptual apparatus. And more: You don't see judicial opinions that say, for example, "On page 532 of Title 29 of the U.S. Code appears the following sentence . . . ." The opinion invariably gives you the name of the statute ("The Sherman Act provides . . ." or "ERISA provides . . .") and immediately you are primed to react to the words in a particular way. And if, as is so common, the case or statute or other enactment is unclear, and maybe even when it seems quite clear, the reader, to extract or more precisely to impute its meaning, must *interpret* it; and interpretation, we now know, is as much creation as discovery.

Nor is it clear what it means to reason "from" one case to another, the heart of bottom-up reasoning in law. It sounds like induction, which from Hume to Popper has taken hard knocks from philosophers. Actually, most reasoning by analogy in law is an oblique form of logical reasoning. Cases are used as sources of interesting facts and ideas, and hence as materials for the creation of a theory that can be applied deductively to a new case. But not as the *exclusive* materials for the creation of the theory; that would unjustifiably exclude whole worlds of other learning and insight.

Reasoning by analogy also has an empirical function. If case A is canonical within your theory, and along comes case B, and the theory implies that the outcome of B should be different from A,

---

[10] Ronald Dworkin, *A Matter of Principle* 316-31 (Harvard, 1985).
[11] See Richard A. Posner, *The Problems of Jurisprudence* ch 2 (Harvard, 1990).

you had better be sure that the two outcomes are logically consistent; otherwise you have a problem with the theory. So cases accepted within a theory provide testing instances for its further application. But there must be a theory. You can't just go from case to case, not responsibly anyway. You can't say: I have no theory of privacy or due process or anything else, but, given *Griswold*,[12] *Roe*[13] follows. You have to be able to say what in *Griswold* dictates *Roe*. *Griswold* doesn't tell you how broadly or narrowly to read *Griswold*.

II. Unenumerated Rights and the Two Methods of Reasoning

All this may be too compressed to carry conviction. But I'm not centrally interested here in showing the limitations of bottom-up reasoning. I am more interested in reminding you of its established place in our legal tradition and in relating it to the issue of unenumerated rights. The relation is this. The issue of unenumerated rights looks quite different when you approach it bottom up than when you approach it from the top down.

Start with top-down. If we wanted to take a top-down approach to the Constitution we might proceed as have Dworkin, and Epstein, and Ely, and many others, each in his own way, by creating from a variety of sources—the text, history, and background of the Constitution (with the text given no particular primacy, because people who are sophisticated about interpretation know that text doesn't come first in any illuminating sense), the decisions interpreting the Constitution, and sundry political, moral, and institutional values and insights—a comprehensive theory of the rights that the Constitution should be deemed to recognize. Armed with such a theory one can select a main tradition of cases and discard or downplay the outliers and thus decide new cases in a way that will be consistent both with the theory and with the (duly pruned) precedents.

If I were to attempt such a project I might come out a good deal closer to Professor Dworkin than many in this audience would think possible. I consider myself a liberal, albeit in the classical tradition, the tradition of John Stuart Mill, Herbert Spencer, and Milton Friedman, rather than in the newer, welfarist or redistributive sense pioneered by John Rawls; and if I weight economic free-

---

[12] *Griswold v Connecticut*, 381 US 479 (1965).
[13] *Roe v Wade*, 410 US 113 (1973).

dom more and equality less than Dworkin, and perhaps, owing to a different temperament, to different experiences in the law, or whatever, would be more timid than he about assertions of judicial power and more inclined than he to give the states room for experimentation, the practical differences might be small, especially in the areas of personal rights such as freedom of speech, religious freedom, and sexual and reproductive liberty. And then indeed, as Dworkin says in the very interesting article that he has prepared for this debate, the right to use contraceptives and the right to burn the American flag (provided you own the flag you burn) would be seen to stand on the same plane as far as the distinction between enumerated and unenumerated rights is concerned.[14]

The distinction has no significance to a comprehensive constitutional theory. The theory may use the text as one of its jumping-off points (*one of*, not *the*), but it goes beyond and eventually submerges textual distinctions, because, on the approach I am describing, specific constitutional rights such as the right to burn flags or to use contraceptives come out of the theory rather than (directly) out of the text.

The situation is different if you follow a bottom-up approach. For then you start by paging through the Constitution and you will find nothing that seems related to contraception, sex, reproduction, or the family. You will find no mention of the flag either but you will find a reference to freedom of speech, and it is easy to move analogically from literal speech to flag burning, as in the following interior Socratic dialogue:

> "I see nothing here about flags or about the use of fire. Speech is verbal. Flag-burning is not a verbal act."
>
> "Well, to begin, must speech be oral? Is sign language speech? If so, doesn't this show that speech goes beyond words, to include gestures? And what about communicating with semaphores? Semaphores *are* flags, as a matter of fact."
>
> "I fully agree that sign language and semaphores are speech, but they are merely different methods from spoken language of encoding words—as is Morse code, or writing itself."
>
> "Since we're talking about the flag-*burning* issue, what about the chain of fires that in Aeschylus's great play *Aga-*

---

[14] Ronald Dworkin, *Unenumerated Rights: How and Whether* Roe *Should be Overruled*, 59 U Chi L Rev 381, 388-89 (1992).

memnon are used to signal the fall of Troy to Clytemnestra hundreds of miles away?"

"Well, that's not quite speech because the fires don't encode a particular form of words, but they do communicate a simple message."

"Is the essence of constitutionally protected speech, then, the communication of a message?"

"Yes."

"So the signal fires would be protected (provided there were no safety concerns, etc.)?"

"Surely."

"But doesn't flag-burning, when employed as an element of a protest or a demonstration rather than as a method of discarding a piece of worn-out cloth or starting a (literal) conflagration, communicate a message?"

"Well, I suppose so, but it involves the destruction of property and that's different."

"People are allowed to destroy their own property, aren't they? And this isn't wanton destruction; it's consumption; it's just like the destruction of a forest to produce the Sunday *New York Times*. Isn't it?"

"I guess you're right."

This method of "proof" may well be spurious. It shows that there is a sense of "speech" that embraces flag burning—just as there is a sense of the word that embraces a right of association and a right not to be forced to express support for a cause one disfavors.[15] But it doesn't furnish a reason for adopting that sense rather than a narrower one. For that, one must range wider and consider the differences, not just the similarities, between burning a flag and engaging in the other forms of communication that the courts have held to be constitutionally protected. One must, in fact, develop or adopt a theory of free speech and then apply it to the case at hand. The development of such a theory was Bork's project in his famous 1971 *Indiana Law Journal* piece,[16] which he later retracted in part.[17]

---

[15] See *NAACP v Alabama*, 357 US 449, 460 (1958); *West Virginia State Board of Education v Barnette*, 319 US 624, 633 (1943).

[16] Robert H. Bork, *Neutral Principles and Some First Amendment Problems*, 47 Ind L J 1 (1971).

[17] Nomination of Robert H. Bork to be Associate Justice of the Supreme Court of the United States, Hearings Before the Senate Committee on the Judiciary, 100th Cong, 1st Sess 269-71 (Sep 16, 1987).

III. The Scope of the Theory: Holistic or Clause-by-Clause?

But even after we acknowledge that bottom-up reasoning is not reasoning but is at best preparatory to reasoning and that legal reasoning worthy of the name inescapably involves the creation of theories to guide decision, we are left with the question of the appropriate scope of such theories. Must they embrace entire fields of law, such as federal constitutional law or the common law? Must they, perhaps, embrace all of law? Or can they be limited to narrower slices of legal experience, such as particular clauses of the Constitution, or particular statutes, or clusters of related statutes? Can they be so limited even if this results in theories that are not consistent with one another, so that you have clauses sometimes pulling in different directions?

Professor Dworkin answers the last two questions "no." An interpretation of individual clauses that fails to achieve consistency of principle across clauses is illegitimate. A theory of constitutional law must take in the whole Constitution, or at least the whole of the Bill of Rights plus the Fourteenth Amendment—must to that extent be coherent, holistic.[18] For his basic criticism of Bork is that Bork has no constitutional philosophy.[19] But as Dworkin well knows, Bork is famous for his theory of free speech, and for his theory of antitrust as well.[20] And these are very much top-down theories. Bork doesn't go case to case. He derives an overarching principle which he then applies to the cases, discarding many. But his theories are tied to specific provisions; they lack the political and moral generality and ambition that Dworkin prizes. Bork's

---

[18] [T]he Supreme Court has a duty to find some conception of protected liberties, some statement defining which freedoms must be preserved, that is defensible both as a political principle and as consistent with the general form of government established by the Constitution.

Dworkin, *Reagan's Justice*, NY Rev Books at 30 (cited in note 1). Or, as he has put it elsewhere, "[t]he system of [constitutional] rights must be interpreted, so far as possible, as expressing a coherent vision of justice." Ronald Dworkin, *Law's Empire* 368 (Belknap, 1986). The qualification "so far as possible" enables Dworkin to make room for some pragmatic compromises. See, for example, id at 380-81.

[19] "[I] am interested . . . in a different issue: not whether Bork has a persuasive or plausible constitutional philosophy, but whether he has any constitutional philosophy at all." Dworkin, *The Bork Nomination*, NY Rev Books at 3 (cited in note 1). Bork's "constitutional philosophy is empty: not just impoverished and unattractive but no philosophy at all." Id at 10. "[H]e believes he has no responsibility to treat the Constitution as an integrated structure of moral and political principles . . . ." Id. "[H]e has no theory at all, no conservative jurisprudence, but only right-wing dogma to guide his decisions." Id.

[20] The first sentence of Bork's 1971 *Indiana Law Journal* article begins: "A persistently disturbing aspect of constitutional law is its lack of theory . . . ." Bork, 47 Ind L J at 1 (cited in note 16).

only *general* theory of constitutional law is—*distrust* of general theory.

The question of the proper scope of a constitutional theory connects with a topic discussed in the preceding debate, about what level of generality of the Framers' intentions should guide judges in interpreting the Constitution.[21] If you ask what is the intention behind the Equal Protection Clause, you find that it was both to benefit blacks in some ways but not others and to promote an ideal of equality that may be inconsistent with aspects of the more specific intention (for example, that the blacks were entitled only to political, and not to social, equality with whites). The choice of which intention to honor determines for example whether the Supreme Court was correct to outlaw racial segregation in public schools. But it is a question about the level of generality of intention behind a single clause. To pass beyond that to intentions concerning the Constitution as a whole, a sheaf of documents written at different times and covering a variety of discrete topics, is to enter cloudcuckooland. This is not to disparage the holistic approach but to distinguish it from an approach that depends on the Framers' intentions, whether broadly or narrowly construed. Yet it will be a demerit of the holistic approach, in the eyes of many legal professionals, that it cuts free from the Framers' intentions.

IV. Implications for *Roe v Wade*

The issue of holistic versus clause-by-clause is not merely aesthetic or methodological. Despite the efforts that Dworkin makes to ground *Roe v Wade* in a particular clause of the Constitution, he cannot have great confidence that the rights he especially cherishes can be generated by theories limited to individual clauses, such as the Due Process Clause, *Roe*'s original home. The substantive construal of that clause stinks in the nostrils of modern liberals and modern conservatives alike, because of its association with Dred Scott's case[22] (though in fact it played only a small role in that decision) and with *Lochner*[23] and the other freedom of contract cases, because of its formlessness, because of its being rather buried in the Fifth Amendment (making one wonder whether it can be all that important—though, granted, it is featured more

---

[21] A topic to which Dworkin has made important contributions. See, for example, Dworkin, *Taking Rights Seriously* at 134-37 (cited in note 4); Dworkin, *A Matter of Principle* at 48-50 (cited in note 10); Dworkin, 57 U Chi L Rev at 663-74 (cited in note 1).

[22] *Scott v Sandford*, 60 US (19 How) 393 (1857).

[23] *Lochner v New York*, 198 US 45 (1905).

prominently in the Fourteenth Amendment), and because it makes a poor match with the right to notice and hearing that is the procedural content of the clause. If we must go clause by clause in constructing our constitutional theory (actually theor*ies*, on this approach), we are conceding, Dworkin must believe, too much rhetorical ammunition to the enemies of the sexual liberty cases.

Could the Ninth Amendment dissolve the tension between the clause-by-clause and holistic approaches? It is a chunk of the text, after all. It says, "The enumeration in the Constitution, of certain rights, shall not be construed to deny or disparage others retained by the people." Could this be a warrant for judges to recognize new rights, both against the federal government and against the states? There is an extensive literature on this question,[24] but it has had little impact because, with rare exceptions, neither the clause-by-clausers nor the holists are happy with basing decisions on the Ninth Amendment. The reason is that the amendment does not identify any of the retained rights, or specify a methodology for identifying them. If it gives the courts anything, it gives them a blank check. Neither the judges nor their academic critics and defenders want judicial review to operate *avowedly* free of any external criteria. Even "due process" and "equal protection" seem directive compared to the Ninth Amendment—or to "privileges and immunities," another constitutional orphan. So, not only is there not enough textual support for unenumerated constitutional rights, there is too much textual support for them.

The tension between the clause-by-clause approach and the holistic approach is stark in Dworkin's discussion of *Roe v Wade*. Despite the many insightful and even moving observations that he offers about the abortion problem,[25] he is not able to find a clause in which the right to an abortion can be made to fit comfortably, though he tries very hard to find one. In his account, as in that of his predecessors in the effort to rationalize the decision, *Roe v Wade* is the Wandering Jew of constitutional law. It started life in

---

[24] See, for example, Randy E. Barnett, ed, *The Rights Retained by the People: The History and Meaning of the Ninth Amendment* (George Mason, 1989).

[25] Not all of which I agree with, however. (For the reasons, see my book *Sex and Reason* ch 10 (Harvard, 1992).) For example, that "a great many abortions took place, before *Roe v Wade*, in states that prohibited abortion." Dworkin, 59 U Chi L Rev at 411 (cited in note 14); that Catholicism "could not comprehensively change its views about abortion without becoming a significantly different faith," id at 413; or that illegal abortions are "dangerous," id at 411. And I don't understand why the Constitution must be interpreted to give *conclusive* weight to a woman's desire that her fetus die rather than that it be carried to term and turned over "to others to raise and love." Id at 411.

the Due Process Clause, but that made it a substantive due process case and invited a rain of arrows. Laurence Tribe first moved it to the Establishment Clause of the First Amendment, then recanted.[26] Dworkin now picks up the torch but moves the case into the Free Exercise Clause, where he finds a right of autonomy over essentially religious decisions.[27] Feminists have tried to squeeze *Roe v Wade* into the Equal Protection Clause.[28] Others have tried to move it inside the Ninth Amendment (of course—but if I am right it has no "inside"); still others (including Tribe) inside the Thirteenth Amendment.[29] I await the day when someone shovels it into the Takings Clause, or the Republican Form of Government Clause (out of which an adventurous judge could excogitate the entire Bill of Rights and the Fourteenth Amendment), or the Privileges and Immunities Clause. It is not, as Dworkin suggests, a matter of the more the merrier; it is a desperate search for an adequate textual home, and it has failed. I cannot adequately explain the reasons for this conclusion here,[30] but I will give the flavor of them by glancing briefly at the equal protection argument, which Catharine MacKinnon,[31] Sylvia Law,[32] Cass Sunstein,[33] and others have pressed.

The argument begins by noting that a law forbidding abortions weighs more heavily on women than on men. Granted. But a difference in treatment does not violate the Equal Protection Clause if it is justifiable, and this particular difference in treatment seems, at first glance anyway, justified by the fact that men and women are, by virtue of their biology, differently situated in relation to fetal life. To show that the difference is not substantially related to an important governmental interest, and is therefore unconstitutional under the prevailing standard for reviewing sex dis-

---

[26] See Laurence H. Tribe, *American Constitutional Law* 1349-50 & nn 87-88 (Foundation, 2d ed 1988) (acknowledging "shift in the author's thinking" between 1973 and 1978).

[27] Dworkin, 59 U Chi L Rev at 419 (cited in note 14).

[28] See notes 31-33 and accompanying text.

[29] Laurence H. Tribe, *The Abortion Funding Conundrum: Inalienable Rights, Affirmative Duties, and the Dilemma of Dependence*, 99 Harv L Rev 330, 337 (1985); Andrew Koppelman, *Forced Labor: A Thirteenth Amendment Defense of Abortion*, 84 Nw U L Rev 480 (1990).

[30] For a fuller discussion, see chapter 12 of my book, *Sex and Reason* (cited in note 25).

[31] See Catharine MacKinnon, *Toward a Feminist Theory of the State* 184-94 (Harvard, 1989); Catharine A. MacKinnon, *Feminism Unmodified: Discourses on Life and Law* 93-102 (Harvard, 1987); Catharine MacKinnon, *Reflections on Sex Equality Under Law*, 100 Yale L J 1281, 1309-28 (1991).

[32] Sylvia A. Law, *Rethinking Sex and the Constitution*, 132 U Pa L Rev 955 (1984).

[33] Cass R. Sunstein, *Neutrality in Constitutional Law (With Special Reference to Pornography, Abortion, and Surrogacy)*, 92 Colum L Rev 1 (1992).

crimination challenged under the Fourteenth Amendment, requires consideration of the benefits to the fetus and the costs to others, an intractable inquiry or at least one that the proponents of *Roe v Wade* do not wish to undertake.

The door to that inquiry cannot be slammed shut by arguing that, whatever justifications *might* be offered for laws forbidding abortion, the support for those laws *in fact* comes from people who want to keep women down; and an invidious purpose can condemn a law. Realistically, an invidious purpose can condemn only a trivial law, such as a law imposing a poll tax or requiring a literacy test for prospective voters; courts are not going to deprive the people of essential legal protection just because some of the supporters of such laws (laws criminalizing rape, for example) had bad motives. The principal support for anti-abortion laws, moreover, comes not from misogynists or from "macho" men (Don Juan would favor abortion on demand because it would reduce the cost of sex), but from men and women who, whether or not Roman Catholic (many of them of course are Roman Catholic), believe on religious grounds in the sanctity of fetal life. That is not a sexist or otherwise discriminatory or invidious belief, even though it is positively correlated with a belief in the traditional role of women, a role that feminists, with much support in history, consider subordinate. No doubt for many opponents of abortion, opposition to abortion is commingled with opposition to a broader set of practices and values—call it feminism. But for many supporters, abortion on demand is the very symbol of feminism. Should the courts take sides in this clash of symbols?

Behind symbols, ideology, even religious belief may lie concrete interests. The debate over abortion, and over the sexual and reproductive freedom of women more broadly, is in part a debate between women who lose and women who gain from that freedom. The sexually freer that women are, the less interest men have in marriage, and women specialized in household rather than market production are therefore harmed. This is a clash of interests, and in a democratic system legislatures rather than courts are generally considered the proper arenas for resolving such clashes.

Dworkin takes a different tack. He considers a person's view of the sanctity of life a religious view even if the person is an atheist; and he says that the government cannot, without violating the Free Exercise Clause, make a person act on one religious view rather than another. Well, fine, but if "religion" is to be understood so broadly, then we must allow for a religion of free markets (economic freedom *is* a religion to Murray Rothbard, Milton and

David Friedman, Friedrich Hayek, Ayn Rand, Richard Epstein, and perhaps even Robert Nozick, whom, by the way, Dworkin has acknowledged as a fellow liberal[34]), a religion of animal rights, of environmentalism, of art, and so on. An ordinance that forbade an aesthete to alter the exterior of his landmark house would thus be an infringement of religious freedom. Dworkin's expansive notion of religion actually dissolves the distinction he wants to draw between restrictions on abortion and other restrictions on personal freedom.

Dworkin is able to make abortion a matter of the varying opinions that Americans hold about the sanctity of life, rather than an issue of life or death, only because he will not allow states to define the fetus as a person and therefore abortion as murder. (If he did allow this, he would not be able to distinguish abortion from infanticide.) Yet the states are allowed to decide what is property and (in the case of prisoners for example) what is liberty, for purposes of the Due Process Clause; why not what is a person? Can't a state decide that death means brain death rather than a stopped heart? And if it can decide when life ends why can't it decide when life begins? Here by the way is an illustration of one of the modest functions I assigned earlier to bottom-up reasoning, that of testing the consistency of our thought.

An Illinois statute makes abortion murder,[35] and on the civil side wrongful death.[36] The Supremacy Clause prevents its application to abortions privileged by *Roe v Wade*, but with that qualification the constitutionality of the statute cannot be doubted. It shows that the states are already in the business of defining human life. They can, thus, classify a fetus as a human being, and the question is then—because I do not think the state's declaration of personhood should be conclusive (what if it declared a meat loaf a person?)—the strength of the state's interest in protecting that newly recognized human being against various menaces to it.

Quite apart from the specific objections that can be made to Dworkin's attempt to ground a right of abortion in the Free Exercise Clause, it blurs his holistic approach. There is no actual inconsistency, because his interpretation of the Free Exercise Clause draws on values derived from his reflections on other provisions in the Constitution, consistent with his insistence on the integrity of

---

[34] See Bryan Magee, *Three Concepts of Liberalism: A Conversation with Ronald Dworkin*, New Republic 41, 47 (Apr 14, 1979).

[35] Homicide of an Unborn Child, Ill Rev Stat ch 38, ¶ 9-1.2 (1989).

[36] Wrongful Death Act, id at ch 70, ¶ 2.2.

the document as a whole. But his position would be clearer, and I think more persuasive, if he were content to derive a right of abortion from his general theory of constitutional law, in which the clauses merge and lose their distinctness and the issue of the right of abortion becomes the place of such a right in the liberal theory of the state—and I agree that it has the place in that theory that Dworkin assigns to it. *Griswold*, the first of the sexual liberty cases, actually started down this road. For we recall how Justice Douglas, albeit in his usual slipshod way, tried to extract a general (or at least generalizable) principle of sexual liberty from a collection of seemingly unrelated constitutional clauses.[37] But no judge has picked up this particular spear and tried to throw it farther.

V. A ROLE FOR CONSCIENCE; A BASIS IN FACT

The arguments against the holistic approach are familiar. The basic one is that it gives judges in a democracy (perhaps in any polity) too much discretion. When you think of all those constitutional theories jostling one another—Epstein's that would repeal the New Deal, Ackerman's and Sunstein's that would constitutionalize it, Michelman's that would constitutionalize the platform of the Democratic Party, Tushnet's that would make the Constitution a charter of socialism, Ely's that would resurrect Earl Warren, and some that would mold constitutional law to the Thomists' version of natural law—you see the range of choice that the approach legitimizes and, as a result, the instability of constitutional doctrine that it portends. It is no good saying that Epstein is wrong, or Michelman is wrong, or St. Thomas is wrong; the intellectual tools do not exist for administering a death blow to these theories (to *all* of them, at any rate). Logic, science, statistical inquiry, the lessons of history, shared intuitions—none of these techniques of either exact or practical reasoning can slay them, or even wound them seriously in the eyes of those drawn to them for reasons of temperament or personal experience. If the only constraints on constitutional decisionmaking are good arguments, the embarrassment is the number and strength of good arguments on both sides—on many sides—of the hot issues.

Heat is important here. If you're indifferent to the outcome of a dispute, you'll weigh up the arguments on both sides and give the nod to the side that has the stronger arguments, even if the weaker side has good arguments too. But if you have a strong emotional

---

[37] *Griswold*, 381 US at 484-86.

commitment to one side or another, it would be not only unnatural, but imprudent, to abandon your commitment on the basis of a slight, or even a not so slight, preponderance of arguments against your side. Our deepest commitments are not so weakly held. Hence there can be practical indeterminacy about an issue even if a disinterested observer would not think the competing arguments evenly balanced.[38]

A comprehensive theory of constitutional law is apt to step on the toes of many deeply held commitments without being supportable by decisive arguments. That is why the situation with respect to constitutional theory is one of practical indeterminacy, driving the cautious jurist back into the clause-by-clause approach. It is much easier to impute a purpose to a particular clause and then use that purpose both to generate and circumscribe the meaning of the clause—which is all I meant in speaking of Bork's "theories" of free speech and of antitrust—than to impute a purpose to the Constitution as a whole. The problem with the modest approach is that it opens up large gaps in constitutional protection. As the eighteenth century recedes, and the original text becomes a palimpsest overlaid with the amendments of two centuries, not only the vision but the very identity of the Founders blurs and by going clause by clause one could end up with a document that gave answers only to questions that no one was asking any longer. Americans like to think that the Constitution protects them even against political enormities that don't fit comfortably into one clause or another. This is the practical appeal of an approach that makes of the Constitution a tire that seals up automatically when it is punctured or gashed. In 1791 such an approach might well have been otiose; the modest top-down, the ambitious top-down, the bottom-up approaches might all have coincided. No more. They diverge further with every passing year, and the ambitious top-down approach becomes more attractive with every passing year. It is not just academic fashion that has made constitutional theorizing a bigger activity today than a century ago.

I would abandon, however, as too ambitious, too risky, too contentious, the task of fashioning a comprehensive theory of constitutional law, an "immodest" top-down theory intended to guide judges.[39] At the same time I would allow judges to stretch clauses—even such questionable candidates as the Due Process

---

[38] See Posner, *The Problems of Jurisprudence* at 124-25 (cited in note 11).

[39] The qualification "theory intended to guide judges" is vital. Academic theories have academic value, and can moreover point to or highlight facts that can alter judges' thinking,

Clause—when there is a compelling practical case for intervention. This was Holmes's approach, and later that of Cardozo, Frankfurter, and the second Harlan. Holmes said (privately, to be sure) that a law was constitutional unless it made him want to "puke."[40] If we follow this approach we must be careful not to appoint judges whose stomachs are too weak. Of course he was not speaking literally; nor am I. The point is only that our deepest values (Holmes's "can't helps"[41]) live below thought and provide warrants for action even when we cannot give those values a compelling or perhaps any rational justification. This point holds even for judicial action—although I may think this only because it makes a judge happier in his job. He knows that he won't have to ratify a law or other official act or practice that he deeply feels to be terribly unjust, even if the conventional legal materials seem not quite up to the job of constitutional condemnation. He preserves a role for conscience.

It is easy for legal professionals and intellectuals of every stripe to ridicule this approach—which, by the way, transcends both top-down and bottom-up reasoning by locating a ground for judicial action in instinct rather than in analysis. They can ridicule it for its shapelessness (shades of substantive due process!), its subjectivity, its noncognitivism, its relativism, its foundationlessness, its undemocratic character unredeemed by pedigree or principle. But the alternatives are unpalatable (to continue the digestive metaphor); and maybe what was good enough for Holmes should be good enough for us. And it need not, perhaps—this alternative approach that I am discussing—be quite as shapeless, as subjective, as visceral as I have implied. Certainly it need not be inarticulate (in this respect the digestive metaphor is inapt); Holmes was the most eloquent judge in the history of this country, perhaps of any country. And it can be—it should be—informed through empirical inquiry more searching than is normal in judicial opinions. Simple prudence dictates that before you react strongly to some-

---

just as economic theory can help us interpret the recent events in eastern Europe and the Soviet Union as a refutation of socialism.

[40] See Philippa Strum, *Louis D. Brandeis: Justice for the People* 361 (Harvard, 1984) ("[Justice Brandeis] told [his law clerks] that Justice Holmes employed a simple rule of thumb for judging the constitutionality of statutes, summed up in Holmes's question, 'Does it make you puke?' ").

[41] See Letter of Oliver Wendell Holmes, Jr., to Harold J. Laski (Jan 11, 1929), in Mark DeWolfe Howe, ed, 2 *Holmes-Laski Letters* 1124 (Harvard, 1953) ("when I say that a thing is true I only mean that I can't help believing it—but I have no grounds for assuming that my can't helps are cosmic can't helps").

thing you try to obtain as clear an idea as possible of what that something is.

The *Griswold* case, for example, in part because of the excellent brief of the lawyers for the birth control clinic (one of whom was Thomas Emerson of the Yale Law School faculty), provided an opportunity—which the Court didn't take—to deploy pertinent data in support of a professionally more respectable precedent than what emerged from Douglas's majority opinion and the concurrences. The brief highlights some striking facts which subsequent research[42] has confirmed. One is that statutes forbidding contraceptives had been passed in a wave in the late nineteenth century but had been repealed in all but two states, Connecticut and Massachusetts, in both of which repeal, though repeatedly attempted, had been blocked by the vigorous lobbying of the Catholic Church working on the large Catholic population in both states. But while the statute had remained on the books, the only efforts to enforce it—and they were entirely successful—were directed against birth control clinics, whose clientele was dominated by the poor and the uneducated; middle-class women preferred to go to their private gynecologist for contraceptive advice and devices. So the clinics were closed down and of course abortion was illegal at the time, making the sexual and reproductive dilemmas of poor women acute, while middle-class women had unrestricted access to contraceptives, and probably to safe illegal abortions as well if contraception failed, but it was less likely to fail for them.

And remember that the law made no distinction between married and unmarried persons; it could be thought therefore to burden marriage—specifically marriage by the poor and the working class—and to do so arbitrarily. The law had been founded on Protestant (indeed, such are the ironies of history, on anti-Catholic) concern with fornication, adultery, and prostitution, and with the immorality of immigrants and of the lower class generally, though it may actually have discouraged marriage—and fostered immorality—among the poor; and its survival owed everything to a belief, by 1965 limited essentially to Catholics and by no means shared by all of them, that it is sinful to impede the procreative outcome of an act of sexual intercourse.

The law, in sum, was sectarian in motive and rationale, capriciously enforced, out of step with dominant public opinion in the country, genuinely oppressive, and, I think it fair to say, a national

---

[42] See my discussion in chapters 7 and 12 of *Sex and Reason* (cited in note 25).

embarrassment—as would be a law forbidding remarriage, or limiting the number of children a married couple may have, or requiring the sterilization of persons having genetic defects, or denying the mothers of illegitimate children parental rights, or forbidding homosexuals to practice medicine, or forbidding abortion even when necessary to spare a woman from a crippling or debilitating illness, or requiring the tattooing of people who carry the AIDS virus, or—coming closest to *Griswold* itself—requiring married couples to have a minimum number of children unless they prove they're infertile. It is not the worst thing in the world to have judges who are willing to strike down such laws in the name of the Constitution. The sequelae to *Griswold* show that the risks in this approach are enormous too, but smaller I think than the risks that would be entailed by the totalizing approach that Professor Dworkin defends with such elegant tenacity.

Dworkin believes that only his approach can prevent constitutional doctrine from changing with every change in the composition of the Court. This exaggerates both the possibility of cogent theorizing at the high level of abstraction implied by the holistic approach and the fidelity of judges, especially Supreme Court Justices, whose decisions are unreviewable, to the doctrines (as distinct from narrow holdings) of their predecessors. Nothing but *force majeure* can prevent judges from giving vent to their political and personal values, if that is what they want to do.

I remind you, in support of my suggested approach, that judicial decision precedes articulate theory—because the duty to resolve the dispute at hand is primary—that few judges (few anybody) are equipped to create or even evaluate comprehensive political theories, that our judges are generally not appointed on the basis of their intellectual merit, and that instinct can be a surer guide to action than half-baked intellectualizing. I know that I seem to be indulging in paradox in proposing an approach that accepts the role of personal values in adjudication and asks only that they be yoked to empirical data. This may seem a strange match indeed. But personal values, while influenced by temperament and upbringing, are not independent of adult personal experience; and research—into facts, not into what judges have said in the past—can be a substitute for experience, can bring home to a judge the realities of a law against contraception or against abortion or against sodomy. That at least has been my own experience. It may not be typical. Yet I think it is apparent that most judges can handle facts better than they can handle theories. Of course that is what bottom-up reasoners say in defense of their approach.

Bottom-up reasoning *pretends*, however, to be—reasoning. I ask you to join with me in abandoning that pretense.

In doing so we will make room for the greatest judge in the history of our law, and probably the greatest scholar. I refer of course to Holmes—who also had the finest *philosophical* mind in the history of judging. His most famous judicial opinion is his dissent in *Lochner*.[43] But, judged by the usual principles of legal reasoning, it is a flop, because it illustrates Holmes's inveterate tendency "to substitute epigrams for analysis: instead of taking *Lochner* as the opportunity to show what the due process clause was all about, Holmes contented himself with the smug assertion that the clause did not 'enact Mr. Herbert Spencer's Social Statics.' "[44] I agree: "It is not, in short, a good judicial opinion. It is merely the greatest judicial opinion of the last hundred years."[45] There is something wrong with the conventional principles of legal reasoning. They miss the vital essence of legal growth and insight.

I remind you finally that I am speaking primarily of areas of constitutional law in which constitutional history and text give out. In an area such as freedom of speech, where we have a text and a history and a long case experience, the materials are at hand for the creation of a theory, albeit clause-bound, that will guide future decisions; and so, perhaps, with such questions as whether and what types of sex discrimination fall under the ban of the Equal Protection Clause.[46] In areas to which the constitutional text and history and a long decisional tradition cannot fairly be made to speak, such as that of sexual rights, we must either renounce a judicial role or suffer the judges to fall back on their personal values enlightened so far as they may be by a careful study of the pertinent social phenomena. Neither top-down nor bottom-up legal reasoning can finesse this painful choice.

---

[43] 198 US at 74.

[44] David P. Currie, *The Constitution in the Supreme Court: The Second Century: 1888-1986* 82 (Chicago, 1990). See also id at 81-82, 130.

[45] Richard A. Posner, *Law and Literature: A Misunderstood Relation* 285 (Harvard, 1988).

[46] There are, of course, many areas outside of constitutional law where field-specific theories are entirely feasible: torts, contracts, and antitrust are examples.

THE CONCEPT OF UNENUMERATED RIGHTS

Unenumerated Rights: Whether and How *Roe* Should be Overruled

Ronald Dworkin†

Judge Posner and I have been asked to debate the subject of unenumerated rights. I am at a disadvantage, because I think that the distinction between enumerated and unenumerated constitutional rights, a distinction presupposed by our assignment, is bogus. I shall explain why, but it would be unfair to end my contribution to the expected debate with that explanation. The topic "unenumerated rights" on a conference menu leads the audience to expect some discussion of abortion, the most violently debated constitutional issue of our era. So I shall try to explain how that constitutional issue should be resolved once the distinction between enumerated and unenumerated rights is safely shut up with other legal concepts dishonorably discharged for bad philosophy.

I. The Real Bill of Rights

We are celebrating the Bill of Rights, which we take to include the Civil War Amendments. I begin by asking you, in your imagination, to *read* that part of the Constitution. Some parts of the

† Professor of Law, New York University, and Professor of Jurisprudence and Fellow of University College, Oxford University. ©1992 by Ronald Dworkin. This Article is based on a much expanded version of remarks at *The Bill of Rights in the Welfare State: A Bicentennial Symposium*, held at The University of Chicago Law School on October 25-26, 1991. I would like to thank Arnand Agneshwar, Alice Hofheimer, Sharon Perley, and Richard Posner for very helpful information, comments and advice, and also to thank the Filomen D'Agostino and Max E. Greenberg Research Fund of New York University Law School.

Bill of Rights are very concrete, like the Third Amendment's prohibition against quartering troops in peacetime. Others are of medium abstraction, like the First Amendment's guarantees of freedom of speech, press, and religion. But key clauses are drafted in the most abstract possible terms of political morality. The Fourteenth Amendment, for example, commands "equal" protection of the laws, and also commands that neither life nor liberty nor property be taken without "due" process of law. That language might, in some contexts, seem wholly concerned with procedure—in no way restricting the laws government might enact and enforce, but only stipulating how it must enact and enforce whatever laws it does adopt. Legal history has rejected that narrow interpretation, however, and once we understand the constitutional provisions to be substantive as well as procedural, their scope is breathtaking. For then the Bill of Rights orders nothing less than that government treat everyone subject to its dominion with equal concern and respect, and that it not infringe their most basic freedoms, those liberties essential, as one prominent jurist put it, to the very idea of "ordered liberty."[1]

II. The Natural Reading of the Bill of Rights

On its most natural reading, then, the Bill of Rights sets out a network of principles, some extremely concrete, others more abstract, and some of near limitless abstraction. Taken together, these principles define a political ideal: they construct the constitutional skeleton of a society of citizens both equal and free. Notice three features of that striking architecture. First, this system of principle is comprehensive, because it commands both equal concern and basic liberty. In our political culture these are the two major sources of claims of individual right. It therefore seems unlikely that anyone who believes that free and equal citizens would be guaranteed a particular individual right will not also think that our Constitution already contains that right, unless constitutional history has decisively rejected it. That is an important fact about constitutional adjudication and argument, to which I shall return.

Second, since liberty and equality overlap in large part, each of the two major abstract articles of the Bill of Rights is *itself* comprehensive in that same way. Particular constitutional rights that follow from the best interpretation of the Equal Protection Clause, for example, will very likely also follow from the best interpreta-

---

[1] Justice Cardozo in *Palko v Connecticut*, 302 US 319, 325 (1937).

tion of the Due Process Clause. So (as Justice Stevens reminded us in the address which opened this conference)[2] the Supreme Court had no difficulty in finding that, although the Equal Protection Clause does not apply to the District of Columbia, racial school segregation in the District was nevertheless unconstitutional under the Due Process Clause of the Fifth Amendment, which does apply to it. Indeed, it is very likely that, even if there had been no First Amendment, American courts would long ago have found the freedoms of speech, press, and religion in the Fifth and Fourteenth Amendments' guarantees of basic liberty.

Third, the Bill of Rights therefore seems to give judges almost incredible power. Our legal culture insists that judges—and finally the justices of the Supreme Court—have the last word about the proper interpretation of the Constitution. Since the great clauses command simply that government show equal concern and respect for the basic liberties—without specifying in further detail what that means and requires—it falls to judges to declare what equal concern really does require and what the basic liberties really are. But that means that judges must answer intractable, controversial, and profound questions of political morality that philosophers, statesmen, and citizens have debated for many centuries, with no prospect of agreement. It means that the rest of us must accept the deliverances of a majority of the justices, whose insight into these great issues is not spectacularly special. That seems unfair, even frightening. Many people think that judges with that kind of power will impose liberal convictions on less-liberal majorities. But they are equally likely to impose conservative convictions on less-conservative majorities, as the Supreme Court did in *Lochner*, and is now doing again in, for example, its affirmative action decisions. The resentment most people feel about unelected judges having that kind of power is bipartisan.

III. Constitutional Revisionism

In any case, many academic constitutional theorists have for a long time thought that their main job is to demonstrate to themselves, the legal profession, and the public at large that the Constitution does not mean what it says—that it does not, properly understood, actually assign that extraordinary and apparently unfair power to judges. The revisionist strategy is a simple one. It denies

---

[2] Justice John Paul Stevens, *The Bill of Rights: A Century of Progress*, 59 U Chi L Rev 13, 20 (1992).

that the Bill of Rights has the structure I said was its natural interpretation. It aims to picture it differently, not as defining the skeleton of an overall conception of justice, but as only an antique list of the particular demands that a relatively few people long ago happened to think important. It hopes to turn the Bill of Rights from a constitutional charter into a document with the texture and tone of an insurance policy or a standard form commercial lease.

In one way this collective revisionist effort has been remarkably successful. It has achieved the Orwellian triumph, the political huckster's dream, of painting its opponents with its own shames and vices. It has persuaded almost everyone that turning the Constitution into an out-of-date list is really *protecting* that document, and that those who stubbornly read the Constitution to mean what it says are the actual inventors and usurpers. Even judges who accept the broad responsibility the Constitution imposes on them still adopt the misleading names their revisionist opponents assign them. They call themselves "activists," or "noninterpretivists," or champions of "unenumerated rights," who wish to go "outside" the "four corners" of the Constitution to decide cases on a "natural law" basis.

In that important political way, the massive effort to revise and narrow the Bill of Rights has been successful. But in every substantive way, it has failed—not because it has constructed coherent alternative interpretations with unattractive consequences, but because it has failed to construct any coherent alternative interpretations at all.

Part of the revisionist effort has not even attempted an alternative *interpretation*. I refer to what I call the "external" revisionist strategy, which does not propose an account of what the Constitution itself actually means, but rewrites it to make it more congenial to what the revisionists consider the best theory of democracy. In its rewritten version, the Constitution leaves as much power to government as is possible, consistent with genuine majority rule and with what the text of the Constitution uncontroversially forbids. Learned Hand held a version of this theory,[3] and John Hart Ely has provided its most elaborate form.[4] The external revisionist strategy plainly begs the question. "Democracy" is itself the name of an abstraction: there are many different conceptions of democracy, and political philosophers debate which is the most

---

[3] See, for example, Learned Hand, *The Bill of Rights* (Harvard, 1958).
[4] See John Hart Ely, *Democracy and Distrust: A Theory of Judicial Review* (Harvard, 1980).

attractive. The American conception of democracy is whatever form of government the Constitution, according to the best interpretation of that document, establishes. So it begs the question to hold that the Constitution should be amended to bring it closer to some supposedly purer form of democracy.[5]

For the most part, however, the revisionists have indeed tried to disguise their revisionism as only "better" interpretations of the actual Constitution. They argue that the natural interpretation I described—that the Constitution guarantees the rights required by the best conceptions of the political ideals of equal concern and basic liberty—is not in fact the most accurate interpretation. They say that that natural interpretation neglects some crucial *semantic* fact, some property of language or communication or linguistic interpretation which, once we grasp it, shows us that the abstract language of the great clauses does not mean what it seems to mean. Constitutional scholars have ransacked the cupboard of linguistic philosophy to find semantic constraints of that character and power. They found in that cupboard, for example, the important idea that what philosophers call the "speaker's meaning" of an utterance may differ from the meaning an audience would likely assign the utterance if it were ignorant of any special information about the speaker.

Some constitutional lawyers try to transform that point into a so-called "framers' intention" theory of constitutional interpretation. They argue that the great constitutional clauses should be understood, not to declare abstract moral requirements, as they do if read acontextually, but in the supposedly different and much less expansive sense which some presumed set of "framers" supposedly "intended."

That suggestion is self-destructive, however, as Robert Bork's unsuccessful attempt to defend it (largely by abandoning it) in his recent book shows.[6] We must take care to make a distinction on which the philosophical idea of speaker's meaning crucially depends: the distinction between what someone means to say and what he hopes or expects or believes will be the consequence for the law of his saying it. Many of the framers undoubtedly had dif-

---

[5] See Ronald Dworkin, *A Matter of Principle* ch 2 (Harvard, 1985); Ronald Dworkin, *Law's Empire* ch 10 (Harvard, 1986); and Ronald Dworkin, *Equality, Democracy and the Constitution: We the People in Court*, 28 Alberta L Rev 324 (1990).

[6] See Robert H. Bork, *The Tempting of America: The Political Seduction of the Law* (Free Press, 1990) (especially chapters 7, 8, and 13). See also Ronald Dworkin, *Bork's Jurisprudence*, 57 U Chi L Rev 657, 663-74 (1990), for my review of Bork's book.

ferent beliefs from mine about what equality or due process requires, just as my beliefs about that differ from yours. They
thought that their abstract commands about equality and due process had different legal implications for concrete cases from the
implications you or I think those abstract commands have. But it
does not follow that they meant to *say* anything different from
what you or I would mean to say if we used the same words they
did. We would normally use those words to say, not that government is forbidden to act contrary to the speakers' own conceptions
of equality and justice, but that it is forbidden to act contrary to
the soundest conception of those virtues. All the evidence (and
common sense) suggests that that is what they meant to say as
well: they meant to use abstract words in their normal abstract
sense. If so, then strict attention to speakers' meaning only reinforces the broad judicial responsibility that the revisionists hope to
curtail.

IV. Enumerated and Unenumerated Rights

The distinction I am supposed to be discussing, between enumerated and unenumerated rights, is only another misunderstood
semantic device. Constitutional lawyers use "unenumerated rights"
as a collective name for a particular set of recognized or controversial constitutional rights, including the right of travel; the right of
association; and the right to privacy from which the right to an
abortion, if there is such a right, derives. They regard this classification as marking an important structural distinction, as the terms
"enumerated" and "unenumerated" obviously suggest. If the Bill
of Rights only enumerates *some* of the rights necessary to a society
of equal concern and basic liberty, and leaves other such rights un-
mentioned, then judges arguably have only the power to enforce
the rights actually enumerated.

Some lawyers accept the distinction, but deny the inference
about judicial power. They say that judges *do* have the power to
enforce unenumerated rights, and claim that the Court has often
done so in the past. But lawyers who argue in this way have conceded a very great deal to their opponents who deny that judges
should have this kind of power. Their opponents are then able to
say that judges have no *authority* to add to the enumerated. If we
allow judges to roam at will beyond the "four corners" of the Constitution, they add, we abandon all hope of limiting judicial power.
That is the argument made by Justice White in *Bowers v Hard-
wick*, for example, to explain why the Court should not recognize a

right of homosexual sodomy.[7] He said that judge-made constitutional law was particularly suspect when it had "little or no cognizable roots in the language or design of the Constitution";[8] and he presumably had in mind the putative right of abortion, as well as that of homosexual sodomy.

So the distinction between enumerated and unenumerated rights is widely understood to pose an important constitutional issue: the question whether and when courts have authority to enforce rights not actually enumerated in the Constitution as genuine constitutional rights. I find the question unintelligible, however, as I said at the outset, because the presumed distinction makes no sense. The distinction between what is on some list and what is not is of course genuine and often very important. An ordinance might declare, for example, that it is forbidden to take guns, knives, or explosives in hand luggage on an airplane. Suppose airport officials interpreted that ordinance to exclude canisters of tear gas as well, on the ground that the general structure of the ordinance, and the obvious intention behind it, prohibits all weapons that might be taken aboard and used in hijacks or terrorism. We would be right to say that gas was not on the list of what was banned, and that it is a legitimate question whether officials are entitled to add "unenumerated" weapons to the list. But the distinction between officials excluding pistols, switch-blades and hand-grenades on the one hand, and tear gas on the other, depends upon a semantic assumption: that tear gas falls within what philosophers call the *reference* of neither "guns" nor "knives" nor "explosives."

No comparable assumption can explain the supposed distinction between enumerated and unenumerated constitutional rights. The Bill of Rights, as I said, consists of broad and abstract principles of political morality, which together encompass, in exceptionally abstract form, all the dimensions of political morality that in our political culture can ground an individual constitutional right. The key issue in applying these abstract principles to particular political controversies is not one of reference but of *interpretation*, which is very different.

Consider the following three constitutional arguments, each of which is very controversial. The first argues that the Equal Protection Clause creates a right of equal concern and respect, from which it follows that women have a right against gender-based discriminations unless such discriminations are required by important

---

[7] 478 US 186 (1986).
[8] Id at 193-94.

state interests. The second argues that the First Amendment grants a right of symbolic protest, from which it follows that individuals have a right to burn the American flag. The third argues that the Due Process Clause protects the basic freedoms central to the very concept of "ordered liberty," including the right of privacy, from which it follows that women have a constitutional right to abortion. By convention, the first two are arguments (good or bad) for enumerated rights: each claims that some right—the right against gender discrimination or the right to burn the flag—is an instance of some more general right set out, in suitably abstract form, in the text of the Constitution. The third argument, on the other hand, is thought to be different and more suspect, because it is thought to be an argument for an unenumerated right. The right it claims—the right to an abortion—is thought to bear a more tenuous or distant relationship to the language of the Constitution. It is said to be at best implied by, rather than stated in, that language.

But the distinction cannot be sustained. Each of the three arguments is interpretive in a way that excludes the kind of semantic constraints the distinction assumes. No one thinks that it follows just from the meaning of the words "freedom of speech" either that people are free to burn flags, or that they are not. No one thinks it follows just from the meaning of the words "equal protection" that laws excluding women from certain jobs are unconstitutional, or that they are not. In neither case does the result follow from the meanings of words in the way it follows from the meaning of "gun" that it refers to pistols but not to canisters of gas. Nor are the three arguments different in how they are interpretive. Each conclusion (if sound) follows, not from some historical hope or belief or intention of a "framer," but because the political principle that supports that conclusion best accounts for the general structure and history of constitutional law. Someone who thinks that this manner of constitutional argument is inappropriate—who thinks, for example, that framers' expectations should play a more decisive role than this view of constitutional argument allows—will have that reservation about all three arguments, not distinctly about the third. If he thinks that the third argument is wrong, because he abhors, for example, the idea of substantive due process, then he will reject it, but because it is wrong, not because the right it claims would be an unenumerated one.

In his reply to my remarks, Judge Posner constructs a Socratic dialogue in which the straight man is brought to see that "speech" in the First Amendment includes flag burning, though Posner concedes that the argument might have gone the other way.[9] He does not construct a parallel dialogue in which another dupe is made to agree that gender is a suspect category under the Equal Protection Clause, though it is easy to see how that second dialogue might go. And it would be equally easy to construct a third dialogue ending with a straight man's startled recognition that abortion is, after all, a basic liberty protected by the Due Process Clause. Posner does suggest that this argument might take us "further" from the text. But the metaphor of distance is wholly opaque in this context: it means or suggests nothing. Posner cannot mean, for example, that a right to abortion is further away from the Constitution's language than a right against gender-discrimination is, in the sense that "tear gas" is further from the meaning of "gun" than "pistol" is. "Pistol" is closer because "gun" refers to a pistol and does not refer to tear gas. But since neither a right to abortion nor a right against gender-discrimination follow from the meanings of textual words, neither can be closer to or further from the text than the other in that sense.

It is sometimes said that the Constitution does not "mention" a right of travel, or of association, or of privacy, as if that fact explained why these rights are usefully classified as unenumerated. But the Constitution does not "mention" flag burning or gender discrimination either. The right to burn a flag and the right against gender-discrimination are supported by the best interpretation of a more general or abstract right that is "mentioned." It is true that the phrase "right to privacy" is itself more abstract than the phrase "right to burn a flag as protest," and that the former phrase therefore figures more in the conversation and writing of constitutional scholars than the latter. But these facts reflect accidents (or highly contingent features) of usage. Scholars have found it useful to develop a name of middling abstraction—the right of privacy—to describe a stage in the derivation of particular concrete rights from the even more abstract rights named in the constitutional text. But it hardly follows that those concrete rights—including the right to abortion—are more remote from their textual beginnings than are concrete rights—such as the right to burn a flag—that are derived by arguments that do not employ names for rights of middling abstraction. Constitutional lawyers might well have adopted the middling terms "right of symbolic protest" or "right of gender equality" in the way they have

---

[9] Richard A. Posner, *Legal Reasoning From the Top Down and From the Bottom Up: The Question of Unenumerated Constitutional Rights*, 59 U Chi L Rev 433, 437-38 (1992).

adopted "right of privacy." It is hardly a deep fact of constitutional structure that they have not.

I must be clear. I am not arguing that the Supreme Court should enforce unenumerated as well as enumerated constitutional rights, any more than I meant to argue, in my remarks about speaker's meaning, that the Court is right to ignore or modify what the framers said. I mean that the distinction between enumerated and unenumerated rights, as it is commonly used in constitutional theory, makes no sense, because it confuses reference with interpretation.

I should say—to complete this exercise in provocation—that I take much the same view of a variety of other distinctions popular among constitutional lawyers, including those Posner discusses in his reply. He distinguishes between what he calls a "top-down" and a "bottom-up" method of legal reasoning, and also between a "clause-by-clause" and a "holistic" approach. He apparently regards the second of these distinctions as more important than the first. Though he says he agrees with me that "there isn't much to bottom-up reasoning,"[10] he thinks that I am wrong to criticize Bork's "clause-by-clause" approach,[11] and also that I would do better to make my own arguments about abortion more explicitly "holistic."[12]

Neither of the two distinctions makes any sense, however. We cannot understand a particular precedent, for example, except by construing that decision as part of a more general enterprise, and any such constructive interpretation must, as I argued at length in *Law's Empire*, engage the kind of theoretical hypothesis characteristic of what Posner calls top-down reasoning.[13] So bottom-up reasoning is automatically top-down reasoning as well. The same point also erodes the distinction between clause-by-clause and holistic constitutional interpretation. Legal interpretation is *inherently* holistic, even when the apparent target of interpretation is a

---

[10] Id at 435.

[11] Id at 439-40. Posner objects to my claim that Bork has no coherent constitutional philosophy, that Bork has theories of particular clauses, but not of the Constitution as a whole. But Bork does not, as Posner says he does, distrust general theory. On the contrary, Bork claims a perfectly general, comprehensive, constitutional theory. He claims that all of the Constitution, not just particular clauses, are exhausted by the intentions of the Framers, and he argues for that global theory by appealing to a single, global theory of democracy and a single, global account of what law, by its very nature, is like. Bork does not have a coherent constitutional philosophy, as I argued in *Bork's Jurisprudence*, 57 U Chi L Rev 657 (cited in note 6). But that is not because he does not claim one.

[12] Posner, 59 U Chi L Rev at 444-45 (cited in note 9).

[13] Dworkin, *Law's Empire* (cited in note 5). See particularly id at 65-68.

single sentence or even a single clause rather than a document. Any interpreter must accept interpretive constraints—assumptions about what makes one interpretation better than another—and any plausible set of constraints includes a requirement of coherence. An interpretation of the Bill of Rights which claims that a moral principle embedded in one clause is actually rejected by another is an example not of pragmatist flexibility, but of hypocrisy.

V. Law's Integrity

Where do we stand? The most natural interpretation of the Bill of Rights seems, as I said, to give judges great and frightening power. It is understandable that constitutional lawyers and teachers should strive to tame the Bill of Rights, to read it in a less frightening way, to change it from a systematic abstract conception of justice to a list of discrete clauses related to one another through pedigree rather than principle. These efforts fail, however, and are bound to fail, because the text and history of the Bill of Rights will not accept that transformation. They are bound to fail, moreover, in a paradoxical and disastrous way. Because the semantic distinctions on which the efforts are based have no sense as they are used, they are powerless themselves to define any particular set of constitutional rights. As the recent history of the Court amply demonstrates, a judge who claims to rely on speaker's meaning, "enumeration," or a preference for clause-by-clause interpretation must actually choose which constitutional rights to enforce on grounds that have nothing to do with these semantic devices, but which are hidden from view by his appeal to them. The search for limits on judicial power ends by allowing judges the undisciplined power of the arbitrary.

Posner's reply acknowledges that fact, with typical candor. He says that the semantic devices beloved of conservative lawyers "could end up with a document that gave answers only to questions that no one was asking any longer,"[14] and that judges who say they are constrained by those useless devices will necessarily decide according to their own "personal values,"[15]—according, he says, to what makes them "puke."[16] His own personal values en-

---

[14] Posner, 59 U Chi L Rev at 446 (cited in note 9).

[15] Id at 449.

[16] Id at 447. Posner takes this phrase—which gives new meaning to the old realist thesis that the law is only what the judge had for breakfast—from Holmes. I should say that though I understand Posner's hagiographic admiration for that jurist, I do not share it. Holmes wrote like a dream. His personal conversion from the view that the First Amend-

dorse "stretching" the Due Process Clause to yield *Griswold*, and, if I read correctly between the lines, *Roe v Wade* as well. But he knows that other judges have stronger stomachs about society dictating sexual morality: their puke tests will flunk affirmative action programs instead.[17] The idea that the Constitution cannot mean what it says ends in the unwelcome conclusion that it means nothing at all.

What is to be done? We can finally, after the 200 years we celebrate in this symposium, grow up and begin to take our actual Constitution seriously, as those many nations now hoping to imitate us have already done. We can accept that our Constitution commands, as a matter of fundamental law, that our judges do their best collectively to construct, re-inspect and revise, generation by generation, the skeleton of liberal equal concern that the great clauses, in their majestic abstraction, demand. We will then abandon the pointless search for mechanical or semantic constraints, and seek genuine constraints in the only place where they can actually be found: in good argument. We will accept that honest lawyers and judges and scholars will inevitably disagree, sometimes profoundly, about what equal concern requires, and about which rights are central and which only peripheral to liberty.

We will then acknowledge, in the political process of nomination and confirmation of federal judges, what is already evident to anyone who looks: that constitutional adjudicators cannot be neutral about these great questions, and that the Senate must decline to confirm nominees whose convictions are too idiosyncratic, or who refuse honestly to disclose what their convictions are. The second stage of the Thomas confirmation hearings was, as most people now agree, physically revolting. But the first stage was intellectually revolting, because candidate and senators conspired to pretend that philosophy had nothing to do with judging, that a nominee who said he had abandoned convictions the way a runner sheds clothing was fit for the office he sought.[18]

---

ment must be limited to a Blackstonian condemnation of prior restraint to the radically different view that it must be understood as a much more abstract and general principle, was an epochal event in American constitutional history. But most of his gorgeous epigrams were the vivid skins of only very lazy thoughts, and his philosophical pretensions, almost entirely in service of an unsophisticated, deeply cynical form of skepticism, were embarrassing—as I believe the metaphysical observations Posner includes in his own new collection of Holmes's writings demonstrate. See Richard A. Posner, *Introduction,* in Richard A. Posner, ed. *The Essential Holmes* xvii–xx (Chicago, 1992).

[17] I discuss Posner's own recommendations in note 22.

[18] Ronald Dworkin, *Justice for Clarence Thomas,* NY Rev Books 41 (Nov 7, 1991).

The constitutional process of nomination and confirmation is an important part of the system of checks through which the actual Constitution disciplines the striking judicial power it declares. The main engines of discipline are intellectual rather than political, however, and the academic branch of the profession has a responsibility to protect that intellectual discipline, which is now threatened from several directions. Of course, we cannot find a formula which will guarantee that judges will all reach the same answer in complex or novel or crucial constitutional cases. No formula can protect us from a *Lochner*, which Posner tells us stinks, or from a *Bowers*. The stench of those cases does not lie in any jurisdictional vice or judicial overreaching. After a near century of treating *Lochner* as a whipping-boy, no one has produced a sound mechanical test that it fails. The vice of bad decisions is bad argument and bad conviction; all we can do about those bad decisions is to point out how and where the arguments are bad. Nor should we waste any more time on the silly indulgence of American legal academic life: the philosophically juvenile claim that, since no such formula exists, no one conception of constitutional equality and liberty is any better than another, and adjudication is only power or visceral response.[19] We must insist, instead, on a principle of genuine power: the idea, instinct in the concept of law itself, that whatever their views of justice and fairness, judges must also accept an independent and superior constraint of *integrity*.[20]

Integrity in law has several dimensions. First, it insists that judicial decision be a matter of principle, not compromise or strategy or political accommodation. That apparent banality is often ignored: The Supreme Court's present position on the politically sensitive issue of affirmative action, for example, cannot be justified on any coherent set of principles, however conservative or unappealing.[21] Second, integrity holds vertically: a judge who claims a particular right of liberty as fundamental must show that his claim is consistent with the bulk of precedent, and with the

---

[19] See Ronald Dworkin, *Pragmatism, Right Answers and True Banality*, in Michael Brint, ed, *Pragmatism and Law* (forthcoming 1992). See Posner, 59 U Chi L Rev at 447 (cited in note 9).

[20] I discuss integrity at considerable length in *Law's Empire* at ch 7 (cited in note 5).

[21] I believe that Professor Fried unwittingly demonstrated this incoherence in defending the position in his recent book. See Charles Fried, *Order and Law: Arguing the Reagan Revolution—A Firsthand Account* (Simon & Schuster, 1991), and my review of this book in Ronald Dworkin, *The Reagan Revolution and the Supreme Court*, NY Rev Books 23 (Jul 18, 1991). See also Fried's letter to the editor and my letter in reply, in NY Rev Books 65 (Aug 15, 1991).

main structures of our constitutional arrangement. Third, integrity holds horizontally: a judge who adopts a principle must give full weight to that principle in other cases he decides or endorses.

Of course, not even the most scrupulous attention to integrity, by all our judges in all our courts, will produce uniform judicial decisions, or guarantee decisions you approve of, or protect you from those you hate. Nothing can do that. The point of integrity is principle, not uniformity: We are governed not by a list but by an ideal, and controversy is therefore at the heart of our story. We are envied for our constitutional adventure, and increasingly imitated, throughout the democratic world: in Delhi and Strasbourg and Ottawa, even, perhaps, in the Palace of Westminster, and perhaps tomorrow or the day after, in Moscow and Johannesburg. In all those places people seem ready to accept the risk and high promise of government by ideal, a form of government we created in the document we celebrate. We have never fully trusted that form of government. But unless we abandon it altogether, which we will not do, we should stop pretending that it is not the form of government we have. The energy of our best academic lawyers would be better spent in making, testing, and evaluating different conceptions of liberal equality, to see which conception best fits our own history and practice. They should try to guide and constrain our judges by criticism, argument, and example. That is the only way to honor our great constitutional creation, to help it prosper.[22]

---

[22] Posner describes my account of integrity-based constitutional reasoning as "holistic" and "top-down." He says it is "too ambitious, too risky, too contentious." Posner, 59 U Chi L Rev at 446 (cited in note 9). He says that when judges are called upon to interpret the great abstract moral clauses of the Constitution they should react as their "conscience" demands: they should cite the abstract moral language of these clauses to strike down only what they instinctively find "terribly unjust." Id at 447. He would not require a judge to provide much, if anything, by way of a principled explanation of how or why he believes a law unjust, or to aim at consistency of principle even himself, from one day to the next, let alone with decisions other judges have made on other days. His views, as always, are striking and powerful. But how can he think that advice less "risky," or less likely to produce "contentious" decisions, than the more familiar advice that judges should at least do their best, as their time and talent allows, to discipline their initial reactions by accepting those responsibilities?

Is Posner right, at least, that his proposals are less "ambitious" because less "holistic?" He says judges should declare statutes unconstitutional, on moral grounds, only when there is a "compelling practical case" for doing so. Id at 447. The word "practical" is a familiar obscuring device in pragmatist philosophy: it is meant somehow to suggest, with no further argument, that moral decisions can be based not on "reason" but on more hard-headed sounding "experience" in the shape of obvious social needs. But Posner's extended discussion of *Griswold* shows that Connecticut's ban on contraceptives was not impractical but unjust. That will be true in almost every case in which a Posnerian judge's "can't helps" are in play: his decision will engage his moral convictions, not his practical good sense. Posner

VI. Abortion: What is the Argument About?

In the discussion of abortion that I promised, I shall try to illustrate the role that integrity should play in legal argument. I begin by briefly summarizing claims about the constitutional status of that issue that I have argued elsewhere,[23] and will argue in much more detail in a book about abortion and euthanasia now in manuscript.[24] A woman, I assume, has a constitutionally protected right to control the use of her own body. (I shall later consider the constitutional source of that right.) Therefore a pregnant woman has a right to an abortion unless her state's government has some legitimate and important reason for prohibiting it. Many people think governments do have such a reason, and would have no difficulty in saying what it is.

A state must make abortion a crime, they say, in order to protect human life. That is indeed what many state officials have said, in preambles to regulatory statutes, in legal briefs and in political rhetoric. That is, moreover, what the Supreme Court justices who dissented in *Roe v Wade*, or who later announced their view that it is wrong, say a state's reason for forbidding abortion is. And even justices and lawyers who support that decision say something similar. In his opinion for the Court in *Roe v Wade*, Blackmun recognized that a state had an interest in protecting what he called "fetal life."[25] He said that a state's interest in protecting life did not

---

insists, however, that his moral convictions are discrete "instincts," not the product of some comprehensive theory of the entire Constitution. But the distinction is mysterious in this context, because any judge's opinions about whether a ban on contraception is profoundly unjust, or maximum-hours legislation deeply unfair, or affirmative action an insult to the very idea of equal citizenship, will reflect and be drawn from much more general opinions and attitudes that will also fix his reactions to other legislation he tests "viscerally" against other clauses, at least if he is acting in moral good faith on any of these occasions. If any judge's immediate reaction really was one off—if it really was just a response to one set of facts with no implications for others—it would not be a response of *conscience* at all, but only a whim or a tic.

So Posner's contrast between clause-by-clause and holistic adjudication seems wildly overdrawn. He uses the reason-passion vocabulary of eighteenth-century philosophical psychology. But he has in mind, not an epistemological distinction between different mental faculties judges might use, but a contrast between two views of judicial responsibility. He rejects integrity, which insists that judges do the best they can to exhibit a principled basis for their decisions, in favor of a different standard that encourages them to keep that basis dark. I do not claim, in the discussion of abortion that follows, that integrity produces only one plausible view, or that it can end controversy. But I shall claim, at several points, that integrity rules out some accommodations that politics or weariness or even laziness might recommend, accommodations I fear Posner's unbuttoned license would guarantee.

[23] See Ronald Dworkin, *The Great Abortion Case*, NY Rev Books 49 (Jun 29, 1989).
[24] This book, to be published by Alfred Knopf in 1993, is not yet titled.
[25] 410 US 113, 163 (1973).

give it a compelling reason for prohibiting abortion until the third trimester, but he conceded that it did have that interest throughout pregnancy.[26] The premise on which so many people rely is, however, dangerously ambiguous, because there are two very different aims or purposes a state might have, each of which might be described as protecting human life. A good part of the confusion that surrounds both the legal and the moral argument about abortion is the result of ignoring that ambiguity. Consider the difference between two kinds of reasons a government might have for prohibiting murder within its territory. First, government has a responsibility to protect the rights and interests of its citizens, and chief among these, for most people, is an interest in staying alive and a right not to be killed. I shall call this a derivative reason for prohibiting murder, because it presupposes and derives from individual rights and interests. Government sometimes claims, second, a very different kind of reason for prohibiting murder. It sometimes claims a responsibility not just to protect the interests and rights of its citizens, but to protect human life as an objective or intrinsic good, a value in itself, quite apart from its value to the person whose life it is or to anyone else. I shall call this responsibility a detached one, because it is independent of, rather than a derivative of, particular people's rights and interests.

If government does have a detached responsibility to protect the objective, intrinsic value of life, then its laws against murder serve both its derivative and detached responsibility at once. They protect the rights and interests of particular victims, and they also recognize and respect the intrinsic value of human life. In some cases, however, the two supposed responsibilities might conflict: when someone wishes to kill himself because he is in terrible pain that doctors cannot relieve, for example, or when relatives wish to terminate the mechanical life support of someone who is permanently unconscious. In such cases, suicide or terminating life support might be in the best interests of the person whose life ends, as he or his relatives think it is. These acts nevertheless seem wrong to many people, because they think that any deliberate killing, or ever allowing someone to die who might be kept alive longer, is an insult to the intrinsic value of human life. It makes a great difference, in such cases, whether a government's legitimate reasons for protecting human life are limited to its derivative concern, or whether they include a detached concern as well. If the latter, then

---

[26] Id at 162-64.

government is entitled to forbid people from ending their lives, even when they rightly think they would be better off dead.

We have identified two different claims a state that proposes to forbid abortion in order to protect human life might be making: a derivative claim and a detached claim. The derivative claim presupposes that a fetus already has rights and interests. The detached claim does not, though it does presuppose that the intrinsic value of human life is already at stake in a fetus's life. You will notice that I did not describe either of these claims as claims about when human life begins, or about whether a fetus is a "person," because those runic phrases perpetuate rather than dissolve the ambiguity I described.

Though scientists disagree about exactly when the life of any animal begins, it seems undeniable that in the ordinary case a fetus is a single living creature by the time it has become implanted in a womb, and that it is human in the sense that it is a member of the animal species *homo sapiens*. It is, in that sense, a human organism whose life has begun. It does not follow that it also has rights and interests of the kind that government might have a derivative responsibility to protect. Nor that it already embodies the intrinsic value of a human life that a government might claim a detached responsibility to guard. But when people say that a fetus is already a living human being, they often mean to make either or both of these further claims.

"Person" is an even more ambiguous term. We sometimes use it just as a description (in which use it is more or less synonymous with human being) and sometimes as a term of moral classification, to suggest that the creatures so described have a special moral standing or importance that marks them out from other species. So someone who said that a just-conceived fetus is already a person might simply mean that it is a member of the human—rather than some other animal—species. Or he might mean, not just that a fetus is alive and human, but that it already has that special kind of moral importance. But even the latter claim is ambiguous in the way I described. It might mean that a fetus is already a creature with the interests and moral rights we take persons, as distinct from other creatures, to have. Or it might mean that a fetus is already a creature whose life has the intrinsic moral significance the life of any person has. So the clarity of the public debate is not improved by the prominence of the questions "Is a fetus a person?" or "When does human life begin?" We do better to avoid that language so far as we can. I suggest that we consider, instead, whether states can justify anti-abortion legislation on one of the two grounds—derivative or detached—that I described.

Most people think that the great constitutional debate about abortion in America is obviously and entirely about a state's derivative grounds. They think the argument is about whether a fetus is a person in the sense in which that means having a right to life. That is why one side claims, and the other denies, that abortion is murder. (Some might add that the detached ground I described is too mysterious or metaphysical even to make sense, let alone to provide a plausible ground for anti-abortion legislation.) Not just the political argument, but the legal and academic discussion as well, seems to assume that view of the controversy. Lawyers and philosophers discuss whether a fetus is a person with rights. They speculate about whether abortion is morally permissible even if a fetus does have a right to life. But they almost all assume that if it does not, then there is no moral objection even to consider.

In the following two sections I shall assess the constitutional argument understood in that familiar and popular way. I shall interpret the claim that states have a responsibility to protect life to mean that they have a derivative responsibility to protect the right to life of a fetus. I shall argue, however, that if we do understand the dispute that way, then the constitutional argument is a relatively simple one. On that basis, *Roe* was not only correct but obviously correct, and its many critics are obviously wrong. I conclude that the constitutional debate about abortion is actually *not* about whether a fetus has rights and interests. It must be understood, if at all, as about the different claim I just conceded some people may find mysterious: that a state can legitimately claim a detached responsibility to protect the intrinsic value of human life.

VII. Is a Fetus a Constitutional Person?

The national Constitution defines what we might call the constitutional population. It stipulates who has constitutional rights that government must respect and enforce, and therefore whose rights government must take into account in curtailing or limiting the scope of other people's constitutional rights in cases of conflict. States would of course have a derivative reason for forbidding abortion if the Constitution designated a fetus as a constitutional person, that is, as a creature with constitutional rights competitive with those of a pregnant woman. Our analysis must therefore begin with a crucial threshold question. Is a fetus a constitutional person? In *Roe v Wade*, the Supreme Court answered that question in the only way it could: in the negative. If a fetus is a constitutional person, then states not only *may* forbid abortion but, at least in some circumstances, *must* do so. No justice or prominent politician has even advanced that claim.

It is true, as a number of legal scholars have pointed out, that the law does not generally require people to make any sacrifice at all to save the life of another person who needs their aid. A person ordinarily has no legal duty to save a stranger from drowning even if he can do so at no risk to himself and with minimal effort.[27] But abortion normally requires a physical attack on a fetus, not just a failure to come to its aid. And in any case parents are invariably made an exception to the general doctrine. Parents have a legal duty to care for their children; if a fetus is a person from conception, a state would discriminate between infants and fetuses without any justification if it allowed abortion but did not permit killing infants or abandoning them in circumstances when they would inevitably die.[28] The physical and emotional and economic burdens of pregnancy are intense, but so are the parallel burdens of parenthood.

We may safely assume, then, that the national Constitution does not declare a fetus to be a constitutional person whose rights may be competitive with the constitutional rights of a pregnant woman. Does this leave a state free to decide that a fetus shall have that status within its borders? If so, then *Roe v Wade* could safely be reversed without the politically impossible implication that states were required to prohibit abortion. The Supreme Court could then say that while some states have chosen to declare fe-

---

[27] These scholars argue that for that reason anti-abortion laws are unconstitutional even if a fetus is considered a person, and they would certainly reject my much stronger claim that in that event many laws permitting abortion would be unconstitutional. The legal arguments rely on a famous and influential article about the morality of abortion by Judith Jarvis Thompson: *A Defense of Abortion*, 1 Phil & Pub Aff 47 (1971). The legal arguments applying Thompson's views to constitutional law are best and most persuasively presented in Donald H. Regan, *Rewriting* Roe v. Wade, 77 Mich L Rev 1569 (1979). Thompson does not argue that every pregnant woman has a right to an abortion, even if a fetus is a person, but only that some do, and she recognizes that a woman who voluntarily risks pregnancy may not have such a right. In any case, her arguments assume that a pregnant woman has no more moral obligations to a fetus she is carrying, even if that fetus is a person with rights and therefore her son or daughter, than anyone has to a stranger—to a famous violinist a woman might find herself connected to for nine months because he needs the use of her kidneys for that period in order to live, for example.

[28] In the article cited in the preceding note, Regan questions the analogy between abortion and infanticide on the ground that parents have the option of arranging an adoption for their child. Regan, 77 Mich L Rev at 1597 (cited in note 27). But that is not inevitably true: minority infants, in particular, may not be able to find adoptive homes, and their parents are not permitted to kill them, or abandon them in circumstances that will inevitably lead to their death, whenever they can in fact make no alternative arrangement.

tuses persons within their jurisdiction, other states need not make the same decision.

There is no doubt that a state can protect the life of a fetus in a variety of ways. A state can make it murder for a third-party intentionally to kill a fetus, as Illinois has done, for example, or "feticide" for anyone willfully to kill a quickened fetus by an injury that would be murder if it resulted in the death of the mother, as Georgia has. These laws violate no constitutional rights, because no one has a constitutional right to injure with impunity.[29] Laws designed to protect fetuses may be drafted in language declaring or suggesting that a fetus is a person, or that human life begins at conception. The Illinois abortion statute begins, for example, by declaring that a fetus is a person from the moment of conception.[30] There can be no constitutional objection to such language, so long as the law does not purport to curtail constitutional rights. The Illinois statute makes plain, for example, that it does not intend to challenge or modify *Roe v Wade* so long as that decision remains in force.[31]

So qualified, a declaration that a fetus is a person raises no more constitutional difficulties than states raise when they declare, as every state has, that corporations are legal persons and enjoy many of the rights real people do, including the right to own property and the right to sue. States declare that corporations are persons as a shorthand way of describing a complex network of rights and duties that it would be impossible to describe in any other way, not as a means of curtailing or diminishing constitutional rights that real people would otherwise have.

The suggestion that states are free to declare a fetus a person, and thereby justify outlawing abortion, is a very different matter, however. That suggestion assumes that a state can curtail some persons' constitutional rights by adding new persons to the constitutional population. The constitutional rights of one citizen are of course very much affected by who or what else also has constitutional rights, because the rights of others may compete or conflict with his. So any power to increase the constitutional population by

---

[29] It is a separate question whether a state would violate the Eighth Amendment if it punished feticide with the death penalty. Though Illinois does use the death penalty, the statute making the killing of a fetus murder rules out that penalty for that crime. Homicide of an Unborn Child, Ill Rev Stat ch 38, ¶ 9-1.2(d) (1989).

[30] Abortion Law of 1975, id at ch 38, ¶ 81-21(1).

[31] Id.

unilateral decision would be, in effect, a power to decrease rights the national Constitution grants to others.

If a state could not only create corporations as legal persons, but endow each of those corporations with a vote, it could impair the constitutional right of ordinary people to vote, because the corporations' votes would dilute theirs. If a state could declare trees to be persons with a constitutional right to life, it could prohibit publishing newspapers or books in spite of the First Amendment's guarantee of free speech, which could not be understood as a license to kill. If a state could declare the higher apes to be persons whose rights were competitive with the constitutional rights of others, it could prohibit its citizens from taking life-saving medicines first tested on those animals. Once we understand that the suggestion we are considering has that implication, we must reject it. If a fetus is not part of the constitutional population, under the national constitutional arrangement, then states have no power to overrule that national arrangement by themselves declaring that fetuses have rights competitive with the constitutional rights of pregnant women.

I am uncertain how far Posner disagrees with that conclusion. He says that states can indeed create new persons. But he adds that it remains an open question how far they can treat these new persons' interests as if they were the interests of real people. This leaves mysterious what he thinks creating a new person amounts to. Perhaps he means only to agree with me that though a state can create persons for a variety of purposes, it cannot thereby acquire a power to abridge constitutional rights that it would not otherwise have had.

That position would be consistent with the examples he offers. He says, for example, that states can create property and liberty in ways that affect people's procedural rights under the Due Process Clause.[32] These are not, however, powers to decrease constitutional rights by adding competing rights-holders to the constitutional scheme. They are powers to create new rights under state law that, once created, satisfy standing conditions for constitutional protection without decreasing the constitutional rights of others. He also says that states can decide whether "death means brain death" or "a stopped heart"[33] and that it follows that they can "decide when life begins."[34] A state can certainly decide when life begins and

---

[32] Posner, 59 U Chi L Rev at 444 (cited in note 9).

[33] Id.

[34] Id.

ends for any number of reasons, as I said a moment ago. It can fix the moment of death for purposes of the law of inheritance, for example, just as it can declare that life begins before birth in order to allow people to inherit through a fetus. But it cannot change constitutional rights by its decisions about when life begins or death happens. It cannot escape its constitutional responsibilities to death-row prisoners by declaring them already dead, or improve its congressional representation by declaring deceased citizens still alive for that purpose. I cannot think of any significant constitutional rights that would be curtailed by treating someone as dead when his brain was dead, however. So none of Posner's examples suggest that he really accepts the position I reject.

Nor, I dare say, do many of even the strongest opponents of *Roe v Wade* really accept it, because it is inconsistent with other views they hold. Chief Justice Rehnquist, who dissented in that case, had "little doubt" that a state could not constitutionally forbid an abortion that was necessary to save a pregnant woman's life.[35] Of course, if a state could declare a fetus a constitutional person, it could prohibit abortion even when the pregnancy threatens the mother's life, just as it normally forbids killing one innocent person to save the life of another.

VIII. Do Fetuses Have Interests?

Consider this argument, however. "Even if a fetus is not a constitutional person, and states have no power to make it one, a state can nevertheless legislate to protect a fetus's interests, just as it can legislate to protect the interests of dogs, who are not constitutional persons either." States can protect the interests of non-persons. But it is extremely doubtful whether a state can appeal to such interests to justify a significant abridgement of an important constitutional right, such as a pregnant woman's right to control her own body. It can do that only in deference to the rights of other constitutional persons, or for some other "compelling" reason.

But it is important to see that this argument fails for another reason as well: a fetus has no interests before the third trimester. Not everything that can be destroyed has an interest in not being destroyed. Smashing a beautiful sculpture would be a terrible insult to the intrinsic value that great works of art embody, and also very much against the interests of people who take pleasure in see-

---

[35] 410 US at 173 (Rehnquist dissenting).

ing or studying it. But a sculpture has no interests of its own; a savage act of vandalism is not unfair to *it*. Nor is it enough, for something to have interests, that it be alive and in the process of developing into something more mature. It is not against the interests of a baby carrot that it be picked early and brought to table as a delicacy. Nor even that it is something that will naturally develop into something different or more marvelous. A butterfly is much more beautiful than a caterpillar; but it is not better for the caterpillar to become one. Nor is it enough, for something to have interests, even that it is something *en route* to becoming a human being. Imagine that, just as Dr. Frankenstein reached for the lever that would bring life to the assemblage of body parts on the table before him, someone appalled at the experiment smashed the apparatus. That act, whatever we think of it, would not have been harmful to the assemblage, or against its interests, or unfair to it.

These examples suggest that nothing has interests unless it has or has had some form of consciousness—some mental as well as physical life.[36] Creatures that can feel pain of course have an interest in avoiding it. It is very much against the interests of animals to subject them to pain, in trapping them or experimenting on them, for example. Causing a fetus pain would be against its interests too. But a fetus cannot feel pain until late in pregnancy, because its brain is not sufficiently developed before then. Even conservative scientists deny that a fetal brain is sufficiently developed to feel pain until approximately the twenty-sixth week.[37]

---

[36] Catholic doctrine, it is true, now holds that a fetus is endowed with an eternal soul at conception, and has interests for that reason. (Earlier in its history the Church held that God ensouled a fetus at some point after conception: at forty days for a male and eighty for a female, and that abortion before that point, though wrong because it violated the intrinsic value of God's creation, was not murder. Laurence H. Tribe, *Abortion: The Clash of Absolutes* 31 (Norton, 1990).) That argument offers a counter-example to my claim that nothing can have interests without a brain, though not to my more general claim that nothing can have interests without some form of consciousness, because I assume that a soul, which can suffer, is itself a special form of consciousness. If someone accepts this argument, then he does have a reason for insisting that a fetus (or more accurately the soul it contains) has an interest in continuing to live. But states are not entitled to act on reasons of theological dogma.

[37] See Clifford Grobstein, *Science and the Unborn: Choosing Human Futures* 130 (Basic, 1988):

To provide a safe margin against intrusion into possible primitive sentience, the cortical maturation beginning at about thirty weeks is a reasonable landmark until more precise information becomes available.

Therefore, since we should use extreme caution in respecting and protecting possible sentience, a provisional boundary at about twenty-six weeks should provide safety against reasonable concerns. This time is coincident with the present definition of viability . . . .

Of course many things that are against people's interests cause them no physical pain. Someone acts against my interests when he chooses someone else for a job I want, or sues me, or smashes into my car, or writes a bad review of my work, or brings out a better mousetrap and prices it lower than mine, even when these things cause me no physical pain, and, indeed, even when I am unaware that they have happened. In these cases my interests are in play not because of my capacity to feel pain but because of a different and more complex set of capacities: to enjoy or fail to enjoy, to form affections and emotions, to hope and expect, to suffer disappointment and frustration. I do not know when these capacities begin to develop, in primitive or trace or shadowy form, in animals including humans. Infants may have them in at least primitive form, and therefore so may late-stage fetuses, whose brains have been fully formed. But of course such capacities are not possible before sentience, and therefore, on conservative estimates, not before the twenty-sixth week.

We must beware the familiar but fallacious argument that abortion must be against the interests of a fetus, because it would have been against the interests of almost anyone now alive to have been aborted. Once a creature develops interests, then it becomes true, in retrospect, that certain events would have been against those interests if they had happened in the past. It obviously does not follow that these events were therefore against interests some-one had *when* they happened. Suppose we assume that it was good for me that my father was not sent on a long business trip the night before my parents conceived me, rather than, as in fact hap-pened, two days later. It does not follow that it would have been bad for anyone, in the same way, had he left on the earlier date. There never would have been anyone for whom it could have been bad.

Of course, when a fetus is aborted, there is something for whom someone might think this bad, a candidate, as it were. But the fetus's existence makes no difference to the logical point. If the fact that I would not now exist had my father left early does not entail that there was some creature for whom it would have been bad if he had, as it plainly does not, then the fact that I would not exist if I had been aborted doesn't entail that either. Whether abortion is against the interests of a fetus must depend on whether the fetus itself has interests, not on whether interests will develop if no abortion takes place.

This distinction may help explain what some observers have found puzzling. Many people who believe that abortion is morally permissible nevertheless think it wrong for pregnant women to smoke or drink or otherwise to behave in ways injurious to a child they intend to bear. Critics say that this combination of views is contradictory: since killing something is worse than injuring it, it cannot be wrong to smoke and yet not wrong to abort. But if a woman smokes during pregnancy, someone will later exist whose interests will have been seriously damaged by her behavior. If she aborts, no one will exist against whose interests that will ever have been.

IX. The Real Issue in *Roe v Wade*

An important conclusion follows from my argument so far: If the only issue at stake in the constitutional debate was whether states could treat a fetus as a person whose rights are competitive with those of a pregnant woman, then *Roe v Wade* would plainly be right. But that is not the only issue at stake, and (though this is widely misunderstood) that is not even the central issue in the underlying national debate about the *morality* of abortion. Most people, it is true, say that both the moral and the legal debate turns on some question about the moral personality, or rights, or interests of a fetus. They say that it turns, for example, on whether a fetus is a metaphysical or moral person, or whether a fetus has interests of its own, or how its interests should rank in importance with those of a pregnant woman, or some other question of that sort. In fact, however, most people's actual views about the morality of abortion in different circumstances make no sense if we try to understand these views as flowing from a set of consistent answers they give to questions about fetal personhood or rights or interests.

Most people think, for example, that abortion is always morally problematic, and must never be undertaken except for very good reason, but that it is nevertheless sometimes justified. Some think it justified only to save the life of the mother. Other overlapping but non-identical groups think it justified in other circumstances as well: to protect the mother from non-life threatening physical impairment, for example, or in cases of rape and incest, or in cases of serious fetal deformity. Some people who think abortion always morally problematic also think it justified when childbirth would severely cripple a mother's chances for a successful life herself. Many people also think that a pregnant woman should be free to decide about abortion for herself, even when she chooses abortion in circumstances in which they believe it morally impermissible. None of these complex positions flows from a consistent answer to the question whether a fetus is a moral person, or how its interests compare in importance to other people's interests.

Most people's views about abortion can only be understood as responses to a very different set of issues. They assume that human life is *intrinsically* valuable, and worthy of a kind of awe, just because it is human life. They think that once a human life begins, it is a very bad thing—a kind of sacrilege—that it end prematurely, particularly through someone's deliberate act. That assumption does not presuppose that the creature whose life is in question is a person with rights or interests, because it does not suppose that death is bad *for* the creature whose life ends. On the contrary, the assumption explains why some people think suicide morally wrong even in circumstances in which they believe suicide would be best for the person who dies. Most people take a parallel view about the destruction of other things they treat as sacrosanct, which plainly involve no moral personhood: works of art, for example, and particular animal species. Our attitude toward the destruction of human life has the same structure, though it is, understandably, much more intense.

Though most people accept that human life is sacrosanct, and must be respected as such, the American community is divided about what that respect actually requires in the kinds of circumstances I just described: rape, incest, fetal deformity, and cases in which motherhood would have a serious and detrimental impact on the potential mother's own life. Some Americans think that respect for life forbids abortion in some or all of these circumstances; others think that respect for life recommends and even requires abortion in some or all of them.[38] As I argue in the forthcoming book I mentioned, these differences reflect profound differences in people's views about the relative importance of divine, natural and human contributions to the overall intrinsic value of a human life. They also reflect, as Kristin Luker has argued, different convictions about the appropriate lives for women to lead in our society.[39] The public is deeply divided about these matters. It is divided, however, not into two bitterly opposed groups—one of which affirms and the other of which denies that a fetus is a person—but in a much more complex way, because judgments about whether abortion dishonors or respects the intrinsic value of life in different circumstances involve a large variety of separate issues.

---

[38] *McRae v Califano*, 491 F Supp 630, 727-28 (E D NY), rev'd as *Harris v McRae*, 448 US 297 (1980).

[39] Kristin Luker, *Abortion and the Politics of Motherhood* ch 8 (California, 1984).

So what I take to be the uncontroversial propositions that a fetus is not a constitutional person, and that a state may not enlarge the category of constitutional persons, do not, after all, entail that *Roe v Wade* was right. Neither paintings nor animal species nor future human beings are constitutional persons. But no one doubts that government can treat art and culture as having intrinsic value, or that government can and should act to protect the environment, endangered animal species, and the quality of life of future generations of people. The majority in a community can levy taxes that will be used to support museums. It can forbid people to destroy their own buildings if it deems these to be of historical or architectural value. It can prohibit building or manufacturing that threatens endangered species or that will injure future generations. Why should a majority not have the power to enforce a much more passionate conviction—that abortion is a desecration of the inherent value that attaches to every human life?

So the most difficult constitutional issue in the abortion controversy is whether states can legitimately claim a detached interest in protecting the intrinsic value, or sanctity, of human life. Does our Constitution allow states to decide not only what rights and interests people have and how these should be enforced and protected, but also whether human life is inherently valuable, why it is so, and how that inherent value should be respected? We cannot dispose of that question in the quick way some liberals might prefer: we cannot say that an individual woman's decision whether or not to have an abortion affects only herself (or only herself and the fetus's father) and that it is therefore none of the community's business which decision she makes. Individual decisions inevitably affect shared collective values. Part of the sense of the sacred is a sense of taboo, a shared sense of horror at desecration, and it is surely harder to maintain a sense of taboo about abortion in a community in which others not only reject the taboo but violate it openly, especially if they receive official financial or moral support. It is plainly more difficult for a parent to raise his or her children to share the conviction that abortion is always a desecration in such a community than in one in which abortion is branded a crime.

The constitutional question I describe therefore lies at the intersection of two sometimes competing traditions, both of which are part of America's political heritage. The first is the tradition of religious and personal freedom. The second is a tradition that assigns government responsibility for guarding the public moral space in which all must live. A good part of constitutional law consists in reconciling these two ideas. What is the appropriate balance in the case of abortion?

X. Government's Legitimate Concerns

One idea deployed in both the majority and dissenting opinions in *Roe* might have seemed mysterious: that a state has an interest in "protecting human life." I have now assigned a particular sense to that idea. A community has an interest in protecting the sanctity of life—in protecting the community's sense that human life in any form has enormous intrinsic value—by requiring its members to acknowledge that intrinsic value in their individual decisions. But that statement is ambiguous. It might describe either of two goals, and the distinction between them is extremely important. The first is the goal of responsibility. A state might aim that its citizens treat decisions about abortion as matters of moral importance, that they recognize that fundamental intrinsic values are at stake in their decision, and that they decide reflectively, not out of immediate convenience but out of examined conviction. The second is the goal of conformity. A state might aim that all its citizens obey rules and practices that the majority believes best capture and respect the sanctity of life, that they abort only in circumstances, if any, in which the majority thinks abortion is appropriate or at least permissible.

These goals of responsibility and conformity are not only different; they are antagonistic. If we aim at responsibility, we must leave citizens free, in the end, to decide as they think right, because that is what moral responsibility entails. If, on the other hand, we aim at conformity, we deny citizens that decision. We demand that they act in a way that might be contrary to their own moral convictions, and we discourage rather than encourage them to develop their own sense of when and why life is sacred.

The traditional assumption that states have a derivative interest in preventing abortion, which I have rejected, submerges the distinction between the two goals. If a fetus is a person, then of course the state's dominant goal must be to protect that person, just as it protects all other people. The state must therefore subordinate any interest it has in developing its citizens' sense of moral responsibility to its interest that they reach, or at least act on, a particular moral conclusion: that killing people is wrong.

But when we shift the state's interest, as we have, to its interest in protecting a particular intrinsic value, then the contrast and opposition between the two goals moves into the foreground. The sanctity of life is, as I said, a highly contestable value. What it requires in particular cases is controversial: when a fetus is deformed, for example, or when having a child would seriously depress a woman's chance to make something valuable of her own life. Does a state protect a contestable value best by encouraging people to accept the value *as* contestable, with the understanding that they are responsible for deciding for themselves what it means? Or does the state protect that value best by itself deciding, through the political process, which interpretation is the right one, and then forcing everyone to conform? The goal of responsibility justifies the first choice; the goal of conformity the second. A state cannot pursue both goals at the same time.

I can think of no reason, grounded in a plausible conception of either equal concern or basic liberty, why government should not aim that its citizens treat decisions about human life and death as matters of serious moral importance. The benefits of such a policy are evident and pervasive. So in my view the Constitution allows states to pursue the goal of responsibility; but only in ways that respect the distinction between that goal and the antagonistic goal of wholly or partly coercing a final decision. May a state require a woman contemplating abortion to wait twenty-four hours before the operation? May it require that she receive information explaining the gravity of a decision to abort? May it require a pregnant teen-age woman to consult with her parents, or with some other adult? Or a married woman to inform her husband if she can locate him? Must the government provide funds for abortion if, and on the same terms as, it provides funds for the costs of childbirth for those too poor to bear those costs themselves? Constitutional lawyers have tended to discuss these issues as if they were all governed by *Roe*, as they would be if the only pertinent issue were whether a fetus is a person. If that were the only issue, and if *Roe* is right that a fetus is not a constitutional person, then on what ground could a state require women contemplating abortion to wait, or to discuss the question with an adult? On what ground could Congress aid women who wanted to bear their fetuses but not those who wanted to abort?

Much of the media discussion about how far the Supreme Court has amended *Roe* in its recent decisions presupposes that questions about responsibility and questions about conformity are tied together in that way. That explains why the Court's decision in *Webster*[40] was widely viewed as in itself altering *Roe*,[41] why the New York Times said that the Third Circuit's recent *Casey* decision upholding a comprehensive Pennsylvania regulatory statute assumed that *Roe* would soon be overturned,[42] and why so many commentators expect the Supreme Court, which has agreed to review the Third Circuit decision, to use that opportunity further to narrow *Roe* or perhaps to overrule it altogether, even though the Court requested parties only to brief issues the Third Circuit had actually addressed.[43]

Many of these commentators say that *Roe* gave women a fundamental right to abortion, which states need a compelling reason to curtail, and that *Webster* undermined *Roe*, and *Casey* will undermine it further, by allowing states to curtail the right without such a reason. But when we understand *Roe* as I suggest, this analysis becomes too crude. The fundamental right *Roe* upheld is a right against conformity. It is a right that states not prohibit abortion before the third trimester, either directly or through undue burdens on a woman's choice to abort. *Roe* itself did not grant a right, fundamental or otherwise, that states not encourage responsibility in the decision a woman makes or that states not display a collective view of which decision is most appropriate.

It is a further question, certainly, whether a particular regulation—say, a mandatory waiting period or mandatory notification or consultation—makes abortion much more expensive or dangerous or difficult to secure, and so does unduly burden the right against conformity.[44] And of course I agree that it would be naive to read the Court's recent decisions as carrying no threat to *Roe* at all. The past statements of at least four justices, and the likely views of the two newest appointees, are threatening indeed. But we do no favor to the crucial right *Roe* recognized by insisting that

---

[40] *Webster v Reproductive Health Services*, 492 US 490 (1989).

[41] Professor Tribe, for example, says that "[i]f constitutional law is as constitutional law does, then after *Webster*, *Roe* is not what it once was." Tribe, *Abortion* at 24 (cited in note 36).

[42] See Michael de Courcy Hinds, *Appeals Court Upholds Limits For Abortions*, NY Times A1 (Oct 22, 1991), discussing *Planned Parenthood v Casey*, 947 F2d 682 (3d Cir 1991), cert granted in part by 60 USLW 3388 (1992), and in part by 60 USLW 3446 (1992). In fact the majority opinion in *Casey* assumed the distinction between responsibility and conformity I defend in the text, and interpreted Justice O'Connor's "undue burden" test in *Webster*, 492 US at 529-31 (O'Connor concurring), to presuppose that distinction as well.

[43] See, for example, Sheryl McCarthy, *Climactic Battle Is at Hand*, Newsday 5 (Jan 22, 1992); *Washington Brief*, Natl L J 5 (Feb 3, 1992).

[44] In *Casey*, the Third Circuit, claiming to follow Justice O'Connor, proposed that the pertinent test should be whether the regulation imposed an "undue burden" on a woman's right to have an abortion if after reflection she wished one. 947 F2d at 695-97, 706-07.

every decision pro-life groups applaud is automatically another nail in *Roe*'s coffin.

The real question decided in *Roe*, and the heart of the national debate, is the question of conformity. I said that government sometimes acts properly when it coerces people in order to protect values the majority endorses: when it collects taxes to support art, or when it requires businessmen to spend money to avoid endangering a species, for example. Why (I asked) can the state not forbid abortion on the same ground: that the majority of its citizens thinks that aborting a fetus, except when the mother's own life is at stake, is an intolerable insult to the inherent value of human life?

XI. Conformity and Coercion

I begin my reply to that question by noticing three central and connected reasons why prohibiting abortion is a very different matter from conservation or aesthetic zoning or protecting endangered species. First, the impact on particular people—pregnant women—is far greater. A woman who is forced by her community to bear a child she does not want is no longer in charge of her own body. It has been taken over for purposes she does not share. That is a partial enslavement, a deprivation of liberty vastly more serious than any disadvantage citizens must bear to protect cultural treasures or to save troubled species. The partial enslavement of a forced pregnancy is, moreover, only the beginning of the price a woman denied an abortion pays. Bearing a child destroys many women's lives, because they will no longer be able to work or study or live as they believe they should, or because they will be unable to support that child. Adoption, even when available, may not reduce the injury. Many women would find it nearly intolerable to turn their child over to others to raise and love. Of course, these different kinds of injury are intensified if the pregnancy began in rape or incest, or if a child is born with grave physical or mental handicaps. Many women regard these as not simply undesirable but terrible consequences, and would do almost anything to avoid them. We must never forget that a great many abortions took place, before *Roe v Wade*, in states that prohibited abortion. These were illegal abortions, and many of them were very dangerous. If a woman desperate for an abortion defies the criminal law, she may risk her life. If she bows to it, her life might be destroyed, and her self-respect compromised.

Second, it is a matter of deep disagreement within our culture, as I said, what someone who is anxious to respect the intrinsic value of human life should therefore do about abortion. There is no parallel disagreement in the case of the other values I mentioned. No one could plausibly claim that respect for future generations sometimes means leaving the planet uninhabitable for them or that respect for animal species sometimes means allowing their extinction. When the law requires people to make sacrifices for those values, it requires them, at most, to sacrifice for something that they do not believe to be important, but that the rest of the community does. They are not forced to act in ways that they think are not only disadvantageous to them but ethically wrong.[45] A woman who must bear a child whose life will be stunted by deformity, or a child who is doomed to an impoverished childhood and an inadequate education, or a child whose existence will cripple the woman's own life, is not merely forced to make sacrifices for values she does not share. She is forced to act not just in the absence of, but in defiance of, her own beliefs about what respect for human life means and requires.

Third, our convictions about how and why human life has intrinsic importance, from which we draw our views about abortion, are much more fundamental to our overall moral personality than the other convictions about inherent value I mentioned. They are decisive in forming our opinions about all life-and-death matters, including not only abortion but also suicide, euthanasia, the death penalty and conscientious objection to war. Their power is even greater than this suggests, moreover, because our opinions about how and why our *own* lives have intrinsic value crucially influence every major choice we make about how we should live.[46] Very few people's opinions about architectural conservation or endangered species are even nearly so foundational to the rest of their moral personality, even nearly so interwoven with the other major structural convictions of their lives.

These interconnections are most evident in the lives of people who are religious in a traditional way. The connection between their faith and their opinions about abortion is not contingent but constitutive: their convictions about abortion are shadows of more general foundational convictions about why human life itself is im-

---

[45] Of course, government sometimes forces people to do what they think wrong—to pay taxes that will be used to fight a war they think immoral, for example. But in such cases government justifies coercion by appealing to the rights and interests of other people, not to an intrinsic value those who are coerced believe requires the opposite decision.

[46] See Ronald Dworkin, *Foundations of a Liberal Equality*, in 11 *The Tanner Lectures on Human Values* 1 (Utah, 1990).

portant, convictions at work in all aspects of their lives. A particular religion, like Catholicism, could not comprehensively change its views about abortion without becoming a significantly different faith, organized around a significantly different sense of the ground and consequences of the sacrosanct character of human life. People who are not religious in the conventional way also have general, instinctive convictions about whether, why and how any human life—their own, for example—has intrinsic value. No one can lead even a mildly reflective life without expressing such convictions. These convictions surface, for almost everyone, at exactly the same critical moments in life—in decisions about reproduction and death and war. Someone who is an atheist, because he does not believe in a personal god, nevertheless has convictions or at least instincts about the value of human life in an infinite and cold universe, and these convictions are just as pervasive, just as foundational to moral personality, as the convictions of a Catholic or a Moslem. They are convictions that have, in the words of a famous Supreme Court opinion, "a place in the life of its possessor parallel to that filled by the orthodox belief in God . . . ."[47]

For that reason we may describe people's beliefs about the inherent value of human life, beliefs deployed in their opinions about abortion, as *essentially* religious beliefs. I shall later try to defend that claim as a matter of constitutional interpretation: I shall argue that such beliefs should be deemed religious within the meaning of the First Amendment. My present point is not legal but philosophical, however. Many people, it is true, think that no belief is religious in character unless it presupposes a personal god. But many established religions—some forms of Buddhism and Hinduism, for example—include no commitment to such a supreme being. Once we set aside the idea that every religious belief presupposes a god, it is doubtful that we can discover any defining feature that all but only religious beliefs have. We must decide whether to classify a belief as religious in a less rigid way: by asking whether it is similar in content to plainly religious beliefs.[48] On that test, the belief that the value of human life transcends its value for the creature whose life it is—that human life is objectively valuable from the point of view, as it were, of the universe—is plainly a religious belief, even when it is held by people

---

[47] *United States v Seeger*, 380 US 163, 166 (1965).

[48] Kent Greenawalt, *Religion as a Concept in Constitutional Law*, 72 Cal L Rev 753 (1984); George Freeman III, *The Misguided Search for the Constitutional Definition of "Religion"*, 71 Georgetown L J 1519 (1983).

who do not believe in a personal deity. It is, in fact, the most fundamental purpose of traditional religions to make exactly that claim to its faithful, and to embody it in some vision or narrative that makes the belief seem intelligible and persuasive.

Religion in that way responds to the most terrifying feature of human life: that we have lives to lead, and death to face, with no evident reason to think that our living, still less how we live, makes any genuine difference at all. The existential question whether human life has any intrinsic or objective importance has been raised in many ways. People ask about the "meaning" or "point" of life, for example. However it is put, the question is foundational. It cannot be answered by pointing out that if people live in a particular recommended way—observing a particular moral code, for example, or following a particular theory of justice—this will make them, individually or collectively, safer or more prosperous, or that it will help them fulfill or realize their human nature, as understood in some particular way. The existential question is deeper, because it asks why any of that matters.

In that way beliefs about the intrinsic importance of human life are distinguished from more secular convictions about morality, fairness and justice. The latter declare how competing interests of particular people should be served or adjusted or compromised. They rarely reflect any distinctive view about why human interests have objective intrinsic importance, or even whether they do.[49] That explains why people with very different views about the meaning or point of human life can agree about justice, and why people with much the same views about that religious issue can disagree about justice dramatically. Of course many people believe that fairness and justice are important only because they think that it is objectively important how a human life goes.[50] But their particular views about what justice requires are not, for that reason, themselves views about why or in what way that is true.

Religions attempt to answer the deeper existential question by connecting individual human lives to a transcendent objective value. They declare that all human lives (or, for more parochial

---

[49] John Rawls, for example, distinguishes his own and other theories of justice from what he calls comprehensive religious or ethical schemes; political theories of justice, he says, presuppose no opinion about what is objectively important. In particular, they presuppose no opinion about if or why or in what way it is intrinsically important that human life continue or prosper, though of course political theories of justice are compatible with a great variety of such opinions. See John Rawls, *Justice as Fairness, Political not Metaphysical*, 14 Phil & Pub Aff 223 (1985).

[50] See Dworkin, *Foundations of a Liberal Equality* (cited in note 46).

religions, the lives of believers) have objective importance through some source of value outside human subjective experience: the love of a creator or a redeemer, for example, or nature believed to give objective normative importance to what it creates, or a natural order understood in some other but equally transcendental way. People who think that abortion is morally problematic, even though a fetus has no interests of its own, all accept that human life is intrinsically, objectively valuable. Some think that human life is intrinsically important because it is created by a god, others because human life is the triumph of nature's genius, and others because human life's complexity and promise is in itself awe-inspiring. Some people in each of these groups believe that because human life has intrinsic importance abortion is always, or almost always, wrong. Others in each group have reached a contrary conclusion: that abortion is sometimes necessary in order truly to respect life's inherent value.[51] In each case the belief affirms the essentially religious idea that the importance of human life transcends subjective experience.

XII. The Right of Procreative Autonomy

These three ways in which abortion is special, even among issues that involve claims about inherent value, suggest an interpretation of the much-discussed constitutional right of privacy. That constitutional right limits a state's power to invade personal liberty when the state acts, not to protect rights or interests of other people, but to safeguard an intrinsic value. A state may not curtail liberty, in order to protect an intrinsic value, (1) when the decisions it forbids are matters of personal commitment on essentially religious issues, (2) when the community is divided about what the best understanding of the value in question requires, and (3) when the decision has very great and disparate impact on the person whose decision is displaced.[52]

I should say again (though by now you will be tired of the point) that the principle of privacy I just defined would not guarantee a right to abortion if a fetus were a constitutional person

---

[51] *McRae*, 491 F Supp at 690-702. I develop this point at length in the forthcoming book I mentioned earlier.

[52] I do not mean that no stronger constitutional right of personal autonomy can be defended as flowing from the best interpretation of the Constitution as a whole. Indeed I think a significantly stronger right can be. But I shall not defend any principle broader than the more limited one just described, because that principle is strong enough to ground a right of privacy understood to include a right to procreative autonomy.

from the moment of conception. The principle is limited to circumstances in which the state claims authority to protect some inherent value, not the rights and interests of another person. But once we accept that a fetus is not a constitutional person, and shift the ground of constitutional inquiry to the different question of whether a state may forbid abortion in order to respect the inherent value of human life, then the principle of privacy plainly does apply.

It applies because ethical decisions about procreation meet the tests the principle provides. That is why procreative decisions have been collected, through the common law method of adjudication, into a distinct principle we might call the principle of procreative autonomy. That principle, understood as an application of the more general principle of privacy, provides the best available justification for the Court's decisions about contraception, for example. In the first of these cases—*Griswold v Connecticut*[53]—the Justices who made up the majority provided a variety of justifications for their decision. Justice Harlan said that laws forbidding married couples to use contraceptives violated the Constitution because they could only be enforced by police searching marital bedrooms, a practice that struck him as repulsive to the concept of ordered liberty.[54]

This justification was inadequate even for the decision in *Griswold*—a prohibition on the purchase or sale of contraceptives could be enforced without searching marital bedrooms, just as a prohibition on the sale of drugs to or the use of drugs by married couples can be enforced without such a search. And it was plainly inadequate for the later decisions in the series. In one of these, Justice Brennan, speaking for the Court, offered a different and more general explanation. "If the right of privacy means anything," he said, "it is the right of the *individual*, married or not, to be free from government intrusion into matters so fundamentally affecting a person as the decision whether to bear or beget a child."[55]

I take the principle of procreative autonomy to be an elaboration of Brennan's suggestion. It explains the sense in which individual procreative decisions are, as he said, fundamental. Many decisions, including economic decisions, for example, have serious

---

[53] 381 US 479 (1965).

[54] Id at 500 (Harlan concurring) (referring to his dissent in *Poe v Ullman*, 367 US 497, 539-45 (1961)).

[55] *Eisenstadt v Baird*, 405 US 438, 453 (1972) (emphasis in original).

and disparate impact. Procreative decisions are fundamental in a different way, because the moral issues on which a procreative decision hinges are religious in the broad sense I defined. They are issues touching the ultimate point and value of human life itself. The state's power to prohibit contraception could plausibly be defended only by assuming a general power to dictate to all citizens what respect for the inherent value of human life requires: that it requires, for example, that people not make love except with the intention to procreate.

The Supreme Court, in denying the specific power to make contraception criminal, presupposed the more general principle of procreative autonomy I am defending. That is important, because almost no one believes that the contraception decisions should now be overruled. It is true that Bork had challenged *Griswold* and the later decisions in speeches and articles before his nomination.[56] But during his hearings, he hinted that *Griswold* might be defended on other grounds.[57]

The law's integrity demands, as I said, that principles necessary to support an authoritative set of decisions must be accepted in other contexts as well. It might seem an appealing political compromise to apply the principle of procreative autonomy to contraception, which almost no one now thinks the states can forbid, but not to apply it to abortion, which powerful conservative constituencies violently oppose. But the point of integrity—the point of law itself—is exactly to rule out political compromises of that kind. We must be one nation of principle: our Constitution must represent conviction, not the tactical strategies of justices anxious to satisfy as many political constituencies as possible.

Integrity does not, of course, require that justices respect principles embedded in past decisions that they and others regard as *mistakes*. It permits the Court to declare, as it has several times in the past, that a particular decision or string of decisions was in error, because the principles underlying those decisions are inconsistent with more fundamental principles embedded in the Constitution's structure and history. The Court cannot declare everything in the past a mistake: that would destroy integrity under the pretext of serving it. It must exercise its power to disregard past

---

[56] See, for example, Robert H. Bork, *Neutral Principles and Some First Amendment Problems*, 47 Ind L J 1, 7-10 (1971).

[57] Nomination of Robert H. Bork to be Associate Justice of the Supreme Court of the United States, Hearings Before the Senate Committee on the Judiciary, 100th Cong, 1st Sess 250 (Sep 16, 1987). See Ethan Bonner, *Battle for Justice* 221-22, 260 (Norton, 1989).

decisions modestly. But it must also exercise that power in good faith. It cannot ignore principles underlying past decisions it purports to approve, decisions it would ratify if asked to do so, decisions almost no one, not even rabid critics of the Court's past performance, now disapproves or regards as mistakes. The contraception cases fall into that category, and it would be both dangerous and offensive for the Court cynically to ignore the principles presupposed in those cases in any decision it now reaches about abortion.

So integrity demands general recognition of the principle of procreative autonomy, and therefore of the right of women to decide for themselves not only whether to conceive but whether to bear a child. If you remain in doubt, then consider the possibility that in some state a majority of voters will come to think that it shows *disrespect* for the sanctity of life to continue a pregnancy in some circumstances—in cases of fetal deformity, for example. If a majority has the power to impose its own views about the sanctity of life on everyone, then the state could *require* someone to abort, even if that were against her own religious or ethical convictions, at least if abortion had become physically as convenient and safe as, for example, the vaccinations and inoculations states are now recognized as having the power to require.

Of course, if a fetus were a person with a right to live, it would not follow from the fact that one state had the right to forbid abortion that another would have the right to require it. But that does follow once we recognize that the constitutional question at stake in the abortion controversy is whether a state can impose a canonical interpretation of the inherent value of life on everyone. Of course it would be intolerable for a state to require an abortion to prevent the birth of a deformed child. No one doubts, I think, that that requirement would be unconstitutional. But the reason why—because it denies a pregnant woman's right to decide for herself what the sanctity of life requires her to do about her own pregnancy—applies with exactly equal force in the other direction. A state just as seriously insults the dignity of a pregnant woman when it forces her to the opposite choice, and the fact that the choice is approved by a majority is no better justification in the one case than in the other.

XIII. Textual Homes

My argument so far has not appealed to any particular constitutional provision. But, as I said, the general structure of the Bill of Rights is such that any moral right as fundamental as the right of procreative autonomy is very likely to have a safe home in the Constitution's text. Indeed, we should expect to see a principle of that foundational character protected not just by one but by several constitutional provisions, because these must necessarily overlap in the way I also described.

The right of procreative autonomy follows from any competent interpretation of the Due Process Clause and of the Supreme Court's past decisions applying that clause. I have already indicated, in my discussion of the contraception cases, my grounds for that claim. I shall now argue, however, for a different and further textual basis for that right. The First Amendment prohibits government from establishing any religion, and it guarantees all citizens the free exercise of their own religion. The Fourteenth Amendment, which incorporates the First Amendment, imposes the same prohibition and the same responsibility on the states. These provisions guarantee the right of procreative autonomy. I do not mean that the First Amendment defense of that right is stronger than the Due Process Clause defense. On the contrary, the First Amendment defense is more complex and less demonstrable as a matter of precedent. I take it up because it is, as I shall try to show, a natural defense, because it illuminates an important dimension of the national debate about abortion, and because the argument for it illustrates both the power and the constraining force of the ideal of legal integrity.

Locating the abortion controversy in the First Amendment would seem natural to most people, who instinctively perceive that the abortion controversy is at bottom essentially a religious one. Some of you may fear, however, that I am trying to revive an old argument now rejected even by some of those who once subscribed to it. This argument holds that since the morality of abortion is a matter of controversy among religious groups, since it is declared immoral and sinful by some orthodox religions—conspicuously the Catholic Church—but permissible by others, the old idea of separation of church and state means that government must leave the subject of abortion alone. That would indeed be a very bad argument if states were permitted to treat a fetus as a person with rights and interests competitive with the rights of a pregnant woman. For the most important responsibility of government is to identify the differing and sometimes competing rights and interests of the people for whom it is responsible, and to decide how these rights may best be accommodated and these interests best served. Government has no reason to abdicate that responsibility just because (or when) organized religion also takes an interest in those matters. Religious bodies and groups were among the strongest campaigners against slavery, and they have for centuries sought social justice, the eradication of suffering and disease, and a vast variety of other humanitarian goals. If the distinction between church and state barred government from also taking up those goals, the doctrine would paralyze government altogether.

But we are now assuming that the issue whether a fetus is a person with rights and interests of its own has already been decided, by secular government, in the only way that issue can be decided under our constitutional system. Now we are considering a different constitutional issue: whether states may nevertheless prohibit abortion in order to endorse a controversial view about what respect for the intrinsic value of human life requires. That is not an issue about who has rights, or how people's competing interests should be balanced and protected. If states are forbidden to prohibit conduct on the ground that it insults the intrinsic value of human life, they are not therefore disabled from pursuing their normal responsibilities. On the contrary, it is one of government's most fundamental duties, recognized throughout Western democracies since the eighteenth century, to insure that people have a right to live their lives in accordance with their own convictions about essentially religious issues. So the reasons for rejecting the bad argument I described are not arguments against my suggestion that the First Amendment forbids states to force people to conform to an official view about what the sanctity of human life requires.

We must now consider arguments for that suggestion. It is controversial how the Establishment and Free Exercise Clauses should be interpreted, and the Supreme Court's rulings on these clauses are somewhat unclear.[58] I cannot offer an extended consideration of those rulings here, and my immediate purpose is not to compose a full and detailed legal argument for the First Amendment defense, but rather to indicate the main structural lines of that defense. Any satisfactory interpretation of the Religion Clauses of the amendment must cover two issues. First, it must fill out the phrase "free exercise of religion" by explaining which features make a particular belief a religious conviction rather than a non-religious moral principle or a personal preference. Second, it must interpret "establishment" by explaining the difference between secular and religious aims of government.

---

[58] See Greenawalt, 72 Cal L Rev 753 (cited in note 48); Freeman, 71 Georgetown L J 1519 (cited in note 48).

Difficult cases arise when government restricts or penalizes conduct required by genuinely religious convictions, but for the secular purpose of serving and protecting other people's interests.[59] Such cases require courts to decide how far the right of free exercise prevents government from adopting policies it believes would increase the general secular welfare of the community. It is a very different matter, however, when government's only purpose is to support one side of an argument about an essentially religious issue. Legislation for that purpose which substantially impaired anyone's religious freedom would violate both of the First Amendment's Religion Clauses at once.

Of course, if a fetus were a constitutional person, with interests government is obliged and entitled to protect, then legislation outlawing abortion would fall into the first of these categories even if convictions permitting or requiring abortion are genuinely religious in character. Such legislation would plainly be constitutional: rights of free exercise would not extend to the killing of a fetus any more than they extend to human sacrifice in religious ritual. But a fetus is not a constitutional person. If people's convictions about what the inherent value of human life requires are religious convictions, therefore, any government demand for conformity would be an attempt to impose a collective religion, and the case would fall into the second category.

What makes a belief a religious one for purposes of the First Amendment? The great majority of eighteenth-century statesmen who wrote and ratified the Constitution may have assumed that every religious conviction presupposes a personal god. But, as the Supreme Court apparently decided in *United States v Seeger*, that restriction is not now acceptable as part of a constitutional definition of religion, in part because not all the major religions represented in this country presuppose such a being.[60] Once the idea of

---

[59] We can regard the Supreme Court's decision in *Smith v Employment Division*, 494 US 872 (1990), as an example of that kind of case, whether or not we agree with the decision.

[60] 380 US 163. The Court in that case construed a statute rather then the Constitution. But since the Court's decision contradicted the evident statutory purpose, commentators have assumed that the Court meant to imply that the statute was constitutional only if so construed.

In a recent book, which I received while this Article was in galleys, Professor Peter Wenz argues for a ground of distinction between religious and secular opinions that is different from the two possible distinctions I mention here (which he calls "epistemological"). He accepts the traditional view, that the argument over abortion is about whether a fetus is a person, but insists that the question whether an early fetus is a person is a religious one because it cannot be decided "entirely" on the basis of "methods of argumentation that are

religion is divorced from that requirement, however, courts face a difficulty in distinguishing between religious and other kinds of conviction. There are two possibilities: a conviction can be deemed religious because of its content—because it speaks to concerns identified as distinctly religious—or because it has very great subjective importance to the person who holds it, as orthodox religious convictions do for devout believers. In *Seeger*, the Court suggested that a scruple is religious if it has "a place in the life of its possessor parallel to that filled by the orthodox belief in God of one who clearly qualifies for the exemption."[61] That statement, taken by itself, is ambiguous. It might mean that a conviction is religious if it answers the same questions that orthodox religion answers for a believer, which is a test of content, or that it is religious if it is embraced as fervently as orthodox religion is embraced by a devout believer, which is a test of subjective importance.

The opinion as a whole is indecisive about which of these two meanings, or which combination of them, the Court intended, and the ambiguity has damaged the development of constitutional law in this area. In any case, however, a subjective importance test is plainly inadequate, by itself, to distinguish religious from other forms of conviction, or indeed from intensely felt preferences. Even people who are religious in the orthodox way often count plainly non-religious affiliations, like patriotism, as equally or even more important. Some test of content is at least necessary, and may be sufficient.

I argued, earlier, that a belief in the objective and intrinsic importance of human life has a distinctly religious content. Convictions that endorse that objective importance play the same role, in providing an objective underpinning for concerns about human rights and interests, as orthodox religious beliefs provide for those who accept them. Several of the theologians the Court cited in *Seeger* made the same claim. The Court called the following statement from the Schema of a recent Ecumenical Council, for example, "a most significant declaration on religion": "Men expect from the various religions answers to the riddles of the human condi-

---

integral to our way of life." Peter Wenz, *Abortion Rights as Religious Freedom* 131 (Temple, 1992). I agree with the conclusion he reaches: that the abortion debate is primarily a religious one governed by the First Amendment. But his test is not acceptable, because government must make and impose decisions on a wide variety or moral issues about which people disagree profoundly, and which cannot be decided on empirical grounds or by appeal to any convictions shared by everyone or by methods that are in any other way "integral" to any collective way of life.

[61] Id at 165-66.

tion: What is man? What is the meaning and purpose of our lives?"[62]

I can think of no plausible account of the content a belief must have, in order to be religious in character, that would rule out convictions about why and how human life has intrinsic objective importance, except the abandoned test that requires a religious belief to presuppose a god. It is, of course, essential that any test of religious content allow a distinction between religious beliefs, on the one hand, and non-religious political or moral convictions, on the other. I have already suggested, however, how the belief that human life has intrinsic objective importance, and other beliefs that interpret and follow directly from that belief, differ from most people's opinions about political fairness or the just distribution of economic or other resources.[63]

We can see the distinction at work in the Supreme Court's disposition of the conscientious objector cases. In *Seeger*, the Court presumed that the Constitution would not allow exempting men whose opposition to all war was based on theistic religion but not men whose similar opposition was grounded in a non-theistic belief. In *Gillette*, on the other hand, the Court upheld Congress's refusal to grant exemption to men whose opposition to war was selective, even to those whose convictions condemning a particular war were supported by their religion.[64] Though the Court offered various practical grounds for the distinction, these were unpersuasive. The distinction can in fact be justified—if it can be justified at all—only by supposing that though a flat opposition to all war is based on a conviction that human life as such is sacred—which is a distinctly religious conviction—selective opposition is at least normally based on considerations of justice or policy, which justify killing in some cases but not others, and which are not themselves religious in content even when they are endorsed by a religious group. As the Court said,

> A virtually limitless variety of beliefs are subsumable under the rubric, "objection to a particular war." All the factors that might go into nonconscientious dissent from policy, also might appear as the concrete basis of an objection that has roots in conscience and religion as well. Indeed, over the realm of pos-

---

[62] See *Draft Declaration on the Church's Relations with Non-Christians*, in Council Daybook 282 (Vatican II, 3d Sess, 1965), quoted and cited in *Seeger*, 380 US at 181-82 & n 4.

[63] See text accompanying notes 49-51.

[64] *Gillette v United States*, 401 US 437.

sible situations, opposition to a particular war may more
likely be political and nonconscientious, than otherwise.[65]

So the popular sense that the abortion issue is fundamentally a
religious one, and some lawyers' sense that it therefore lies outside
the proper limits of state action, is at bottom sound, though for
reasons somewhat more complex than is often supposed. It rests on
a natural—indeed irresistible—understanding of the First Amendment: that a state has no business prescribing what people should
think about the ultimate point and value of human life, about why
life has intrinsic importance, and about how that value is respected
or dishonored in different circumstances. In his reply, Posner objects that if my view of the scope of the Free Exercise Clause were
correct, government could not forbid "an aesthete to alter the exterior of his landmark house."[66] But he has misunderstood my view:
he apparently thinks that I use a test of subjective importance to
identify religious convictions. He points out, as a *reductio ad ab-
surdum* of my argument, that "economic freedom *is* a religion" to
a variety of libertarians,[67] suggesting that taxation, which libertarians find particularly offensive, would on my argument violate their
religious freedom.

I argued, however, that convictions about the intrinsic value of
human life are religious on a test of content, not subjective importance. A law forbidding people to tear down Georgian houses does
not raise essentially religious issues, no matter how much some
people would prefer to build post-modern pastiches instead, because that law does not presuppose any particular conception of
why and how human life is sacred, or take a position on any other
matter historically religious in character.[68] It is even plainer that
my argument would not justify exempting Milton Friedman from
tax on grounds of his free-market faith. Government collects taxes
in order to serve a variety of secular interests of its citizens, not to
declare or support a particular view about any essentially religious

---

[65] Id at 455 (footnotes omitted). The Court also endorsed, as on a careful view supporting the distinction between universal and selective opposition, the government's claim that
opposition to a particular war necessarily involves judgment that is "political and particular" and "based on the same political, sociological, and economic factors that the government necessarily considered" in deciding whether to wage war. Id at 458 (citing government's brief).

[66] Posner, 59 U Chi L Rev at 444 (cited in note 9).

[67] Id at 443.

[68] Such laws do raise other issues about intrinsic value, and in some extremely unusual
circumstances might violate a more powerful form of the principle of privacy than the weak
form I described and defended.

matter. It is, of course, true that some people resist paying taxes for reasons that do implicate their convictions about the intrinsic value of human life. Some people refuse to pay taxes to finance war on that basis, for example. In such cases compulsory taxation does plausibly impair the free exercise of religion. But the problem falls into the first of the two categories I distinguished, and the appropriate balancing sustains the tax, given the limited character of the infringement of free exercise and the importance of uniform taxation.

I conclude that the right to procreative autonomy, from which a right of choice about abortion flows, is well grounded in the First Amendment.[69] But it would be remarkable, as I said, if so basic a right did not figure in the best interpretation of constitutional liberty and equality as well. It would be remarkable, that is, if lawyers who accepted the right did not think it fundamental to the concept of ordered liberty, and so protected by the Due Process Clause, or part of what government's equal concern for all citizens requires, and so protected by the Equal Protection Clause. Posner is amused that different scholars who endorse a right of procreative autonomy have offered a variety of textual homes for it: he says that in my account, *Roe v Wade* "is the Wandering Jew of constitutional law."[70] But of course, as he would agree, it is hardly an embarrassment for that right that lawyers have disagreed about which clause to emphasize in their arguments for it. Some constitutional lawyers have an odd taste for constitutional neatness: they want rights mapped uniquely onto clauses with no overlap, as if redundancy were a constitutional vice. Once we understand, however, that the Bill of Rights is not a list of discrete remedies drawn up by a parsimonious draftsman, but a commitment to an ideal of just government, that taste makes no more sense than the claim that freedom of religion is not also liberty, or that the protection of freedom for everyone has nothing to do with equality.

---

[69] I should mention a complexity. I have been arguing that many women's decisions about abortion reflect convictions, which may well be inarticulate, about whether abortion or childbirth would best respect what they believe intrinsically valuable about human life. That is not necessarily true of all women who want abortions, however, and the free exercise claim might therefore not be available, as a matter of principle, for everyone. But states could not devise appropriate and practicable tests for discriminating among women in that way, and in any case prohibition would be the establishment of an essentially religious position, even in cases when it worked to outlaw abortion for someone whose grounds were not religious in any sense.

[70] Posner, 59 U Chi L Rev at 441 (cited in note 9).

XIV. DIGNITY AND CONCERN

I pause for a brief summary. We must abandon the traditional way of understanding the constitutional argument about abortion. It is not an argument about whether a fetus is a person. It is rather a dispute about whether and how far government may enforce an official view about the right understanding of the sanctity of human life. I described a constitutional right—the right of procreational autonomy—which denies government that power. I suggested that this right is firmly embedded in our constitutional history. It is the best available justification of the "privacy" cases, including the contraception cases. Those cases are conventionally understood as residing, by way of textual home, in the Due Process Clause of the Fourteenth Amendment. I argued that they might also rest on the Religion Clauses of the First Amendment.

Posner suggests that my argument is more powerful construed holistically, that is, as an argument about what the Constitution as a whole requires. I do not, as I said, see a difference between clause-by-clause and holistic interpretations of the Bill of Rights. But I nevertheless accept the spirit of his suggestion—that it is important to notice the place the right I have been describing holds not only in the structure of the Constitution, but in our political culture more generally. Cardinal in that culture is a belief in individual human dignity: that people have the moral right—and the moral responsibility—to confront for themselves, answering to their own conscience and conviction, the most fundamental questions touching the meaning and value of their own lives. That assumption was the engine of emancipation and of racial equality, for example. The most powerful arguments against slavery before the Civil War, and for equal protection after it, were framed in the language of dignity: the cruelest aspect of slavery, for the abolitionists, both religious and secular, was its failure to recognize a slave's right to decide issues of value for himself or herself. Indeed the most basic premise of our entire constitutional system—that our government shall be republican rather than despotic—embodies a commitment to that conception of dignity.

So the principle of procreative autonomy, in the broad sense, is a principle that any remotely plausible explanation of our entire political culture would have to recognize. It is also a principle we would want our Constitution to contain even if we were starting on a clean slate, free to make any constitution we wanted. I want to guard against an interpretation of my argument that I would disown, however. It does not suppose that people either are or should be indifferent, either as individuals or as members of a political community, to the decisions their friends or neighbors or fellow citizens or fellow human beings make about abortion. On the contrary it recognizes several reasons why they should not be indifferent. As I have already noticed, individual choices together create a moral environment that inevitably influences what others can do. So a person's concern for his own life, and for that of his children and friends, gives him a reason for worrying about how even strangers treat the inherent value of human life. Our concern that people lead good lives is not naturally limited, moreover, nor should it be, to concern for our own lives and those of our family. We want others, even strangers, not to lead what we regard as a blighted life, ruined by a terrible act of desecration.

But the most powerful reason we have for wanting others to respect the intrinsic value of human life, in the way we think that value demands, is not our concern for our own or other people's interests at all, but just our concern for the value itself. If people did *not* think it transcendently important that human lives not be wasted by abortion, then they would not have the kind of commitment my argument assumes people do have. So of course Americans who think that almost all abortion is immoral must take a passionate interest in the issue: liberals who count such people as deranged busybodies are insensitive as well as wrong. Nevertheless, we must insist on religious tolerance in this area, as in other issues about which people once cared just as passionately and in the same way, and once thought sufficiently important to wage not just sit-ins but wars. Tolerance is a cost we must pay for our adventure in liberty. We are committed, by our Constitution, to live in a community in which no group is deemed clever or spiritual or numerous enough to decide essentially religious matters for everyone else. If we have genuine concern for the lives others lead, moreover, we will also accept that no life is a good one lived against the grain of conviction, that it does not aid someone else's life but spoils it to force values upon him he cannot accept but can only bow before out of fear or prudence.

XV. *Roe* Reconsidered

We must now take a fresh look at *Roe v Wade. Roe* did three things. First, it re-affirmed a pregnant woman's constitutional right of procreative autonomy, and declared that states do not have the power simply to forbid abortion on any terms they wish. Second, it recognized that states nevertheless do have a legitimate interest in regulating abortion. Third, it constructed a detailed regime for balancing that right and that interest: it declared, roughly, that states could not forbid abortion for any reason in the first trimester of pregnancy, that they could regulate abortion in the second trimester only out of concern for the health of the mother, and, finally, that they could outlaw abortion altogether after fetal viability, that is, after approximately the beginning of the third trimester. We must inspect those three decisions against the background of our argument so far.

Our argument confirms the first decision. The crucial issue in the constitutional abortion controversy is not whether a fetus is a person—*Roe* was plainly right in holding that a fetus is not a person within the meaning of the Constitution—but whether states have a legitimate power to dictate how their members must respect the inherent value of life. Since any competent interpretation of the Constitution must recognize a principle of procreative autonomy, states do not have the power simply to forbid abortion altogether.

Roe was also right on the second score. States do have a legitimate interest in regulating the abortion decision. It was mysterious, in *Roe* and other decisions, what that interest was. Our account identifies it as a legitimate interest in maintaining a moral environment in which decisions about life and death, including the abortion decision, are taken seriously, treated as matters of moral gravity.

It remains to consider whether *Roe* was right on the third score. Does the trimester scheme it announced allow states to pursue their legitimate interests while adequately protecting a pregnant woman's right of autonomy? That trimester scheme has been criticized as arbitrary and overly rigid, even by some lawyers who are sympathetic to the narrowest decision in *Roe*: that the Texas statute was unconstitutional. Why is the point of viability the crucial point? We might put that question in two ways. We might ask why viability should mark the earliest time at which a state is entitled to prohibit abortion. If it can prohibit abortion then, why not earlier, as a majority of citizens in some states apparently wish? Or we might ask why viability should mark the end of a woman's right to protection. If a state cannot prohibit abortion before viability, then why may it prohibit it after that point? Both questions challenge the point of viability as arbitrary though from different directions. I shall first pursue the second form of the question. What happens at viability to make the right I have been describing—the right of procreative autonomy—less powerful or effective?

Two answers to that question might figure in any defense of the *Roe v Wade* scheme. First, at about the point of viability, but not much before, fetal brain development may be sufficient to allow pain.[71] So at the point of viability, but not much before, a fetus can sensibly be said to have interests of its own. That does not mean, I must emphasize, that a state is permitted to declare a fetus a person at that point. The question who is a constitutional person, with independent constitutional rights in competition with the rights of others, must be decided nationally, as I argued. But a state may nevertheless act to protect the interests even of creatures—animals, for example—who are not constitutional persons, so long as it respects constitutional rights in doing so. So at the point of viability, the state may claim a legitimate derivative interest that is independent of its detached interest in enforcing its collective conception of the sanctity of life.

Second, choosing the point of viability gives a pregnant woman, in most cases, ample opportunity to reflect upon and decide whether she believes it best and right to continue her pregnancy or to terminate it. Very few abortions are performed during the third trimester—only about .01 percent[72]—and even fewer if we exclude emergency abortions necessary to save a mother's life, which almost no one wants to prohibit even near the end of pregnancy. It is true that a very few women—most of whom are very young women—are unaware of their pregnancy until it is nearly complete. But in almost all cases, a woman knows she is pregnant in good time to make a reflective decision before viability. That suggests that a state does not violate most women's right to choose by insisting on a decision before that point, and it also suggests an important reason why a state might properly so insist.

It is an almost universal conviction that abortion becomes progressively morally more problematic as a fetus develops towards the shape of infanthood, as the difference between pregnancy and infancy becomes more a matter of location than development. That widespread conviction seems odd so long as we suppose that whether abortion is wrong depends only on whether a fetus is a person from the moment of conception. But the belief is compelling once we realize that abortion is wrong, when it is, because it

---

[71] See Grobstein, *Science and the Unborn* at 54-55 (cited in note 37).

[72] *Facts in Brief: Abortion in the United States* (Alan Guttmacher Institute, 1991). See also Stanley K. Henshaw, *Characteristics of U.S. Women Having Abortions. 1982-83*, in Stanley K. Henshaw and Jennifer Van Vort, eds, *Abortion Services in the United States: Each State and Metropolitan Area, 1984-85* 23 (Alan Guttmacher Institute, 1988).

insults the sanctity of human life. The insult to that value is greater when the life destroyed is further advanced, when, as it were, the creative investment in that life is greater. Women who have a genuine opportunity to decide on abortion early in pregnancy, when the impact is much less, but who actually decide only near the end, may well be indifferent to the moral and social meaning of their act. Society has a right, if its members so decide, to protect its culture from that kind of indifference, so long as the means it chooses do not infringe the right of pregnant women to a reflective choice.

Taken together, these two answers provide, I believe, a persuasive explanation of why government is entitled to prohibit abortion, subject to certain exceptions, after the sixth month of pregnancy. But do they provide an answer to the question asked from the other direction? Why may government not prohibit abortion earlier? The first answer would not justify any much earlier date, because, as I said, the central nervous system is not sufficiently developed much before the end of twenty-six weeks of pregnancy to admit of pain.[73] But must that be decisive? The second answer does not depend on attributing interests to a fetus, and, by itself, seems an adequate justification of state power to prohibit abortion after a sufficiently long period. Would women not have a sufficient opportunity to exercise their right of autonomy if they were forbidden abortion after just five months? Four? Three?

Blackmun chose a point in pregnancy that he thought plainly late enough to give women a fair chance to exercise their right, in normal circumstances, and that was salient for two other reasons, each captured in the overall explanation I gave. As I said, viability seems, on the best developmental evidence, the earliest point at which a fetus might be thought to have interests of its own, and the point at which the natural development of a fetus is so far continued that deliberately waiting until after that point seems contemptuous of the inherent value of life. These three factors together indicate viability as the most appropriate point after which a state could properly assert its interests in protecting a fetus's interests, and in responsibility. Blackmun's decision should not be overruled. So important a decision should not be overruled, after nearly twenty years, unless it is clearly wrong, and his was not clearly wrong. On the contrary, the arguments for choosing viability as the key date remain impressive.

---

[73] See note 37.

But it is important to acknowledge that a different test, bringing the cut-off date forward by some period, would have been acceptable if it had afforded women enough time to exercise their right to terminate an unwanted pregnancy. Of course, the earlier the cut-off time, the more important it would be to provide realistic exceptions for reasons the mother could not reasonably have discovered earlier. Suppose that the Court had substituted for the fixed scheme of *Roe*, not another fixed scheme, but rather a constitutional standard drafted in terms of overall reasonableness, which the federal courts would enforce case-by-case. Such a standard might have provided, in effect, that any prohibition would be unconstitutional if it did not provide women a reasonable time to decide upon an abortion after discovering that they were pregnant, or after discovering medical information indicating defects in the fetus or an increased risk to the mother of pregnancy, or other facts pertinent to the impact of childbirth on their lives.

In the end, as Blackmun no doubt anticipated, the Court would have had to adopt more rigid standards that selected at least a *prima facie* point in pregnancy before which prohibition would be presumptively unconstitutional. But the Court might have developed those standards gradually, perhaps deciding, in the first instance, that any statute that forbade second-term abortions would be subject to strict scrutiny to see whether it contained the exceptions necessary to protect a woman's right to a reflective choice. That approach still would have struck down the Texas law in *Roe*. It would also strike down the equally strict laws that some states and Guam have recently adopted, each hoping to provide the lawsuit that will end *Roe*.

Would it make much practical difference if the Supreme Court now substituted such a case-by-case test for *Roe*'s rigid structure? A case-by-case test might not, in fact, much reduce legal abortion. In 1987, only ten percent of abortions took place in the second trimester,[74] and many of these were on medical or other grounds that would still be permitted in any legislation acceptable under the more flexible test I have described. If a more flexible test were adopted, publicity might bring home to more women the impor-

---

[74] The U.S. Bureau of the Census reports that ten percent of the 1,559,100 abortions performed in 1987 occurred at thirteen or more weeks gestational age. U.S. Department of Commerce, Economics and Statistics Administration, Bureau of the Census, *The Statistical Abstract of the United States* 71 (111th ed 1991). Since about .01% of all abortions are performed after twenty-four weeks, see note 72 and accompanying text, it can be inferred that about 9.99% of the abortions performed in 1987 occurred in the second trimester.

tance of deciding and acting early. Medical developments in the technology of abortion might soon increase the percentage of very early abortions anyway. For instance, the abortion pill being developed in France, RU 486, which permits a safe abortion at home early in pregnancy, will allow pregnant women a more private method of abortion, if they decide and act in a timely way.[75] Of course, no statute that banned that pill would be constitutional, even under the more flexible standard.

I believe, as I said, that *Roe v Wade* should not be substantially changed. The line it draws is salient and effectively serves the legitimate state purpose of promoting a responsible attitude toward the intrinsic value of human life. But the most important line, as I said, is the line between that legitimate goal and the illegitimate goal of coercion. It will be disappointing, but not intolerable, if *Roe* is amended in some such way as I have been discussing. But it would be intolerable if *Roe* is wholly reversed, if the constitutional right of procreative autonomy is denied altogether. Some of you already think that recent appointments to the Court, and recent decisions by it, signal a dark age for the American constitutional adventure, that this symposium should have been convened as a wake, not as a celebration. I hope that your bleak judgment is premature. But it will be confirmed, spectacularly, if the Supreme Court declares that American citizens have no right to follow their own reflective convictions in the most personal, conscience-driven and religious decisions many of them will ever make.

---

[75] The RU 486 pill may in any case defuse the public controversy by reducing the need for abortion clinics that act as magnets for protesters, as in Wichita.

ACKNOWLEDGMENTS

Langer, William L. "Infanticide: A Historical Survey." *History of Childhood Quarterly* 1 (1974): 353–65. Courtesy of the editor.

Dellapenna, Joseph W. "The History of Abortion: Technology, Morality, and Law." *University of Pittsburgh Law Review* 40 (1979): 359–428. Reprinted with the permission of the University of Pittsburgh Law School. Courtesy of the Yale University Law Library.

Ashe, Marie. "Zig-Zag Stitching and the Seamless Web: Thoughts on 'Reproduction' and the Law." *Nova Law Review* 13 (1989): 355–83. Reprinted with the permission of the *Nova Law Review*. Courtesy of the Yale University Law Library.

Byrn, Robert M. "An American Tragedy: The Supreme Court on Abortion." *Fordham Law Review* 41 (1973): 807–62. Reprinted with the permission of the *Fordham Law Review*. Courtesy of the editor.

Means, Cyril C., Jr. "The Law of New York Concerning Abortion and the Status of the Foetus, 1664–1968: A Case of Cessation of Constitutionality." *New York Law Forum* 14 (1968): 411–515. Courtesy of the Yale University Law Library.

Means, Cyril C., Jr. "The Phoenix of Abortional Freedom: Is a Penumbral or Ninth-Amendment Right About to Arise from the Nineteenth-Century Legislative Ashes of a Fourteenth-Century Common-Law Liberty?" *New York Law Forum* 17 (1971): 335–410. Courtesy of the Yale University Law Library.

Thomson, Judith Jarvis. "A Defense of Abortion." *Philosophy and Public Affairs* 1 (1971): 47–66. Copyright (1971) by Princeton University Press. Reprinted by permission of Princeton University Press. Courtesy of the editor.

Posner, Richard A. "Legal Reasoning from the Top Down and from the Bottom Up: The Question of Unenumerated Constitutional Rights."

University of Chicago Law Review 59 (1992): 433–50. Reprinted with the permission of the University of Chicago Law School. Courtesy of the Yale University Law Library.

Dworkin, Ronald. "Unenumerated Rights: Whether and How *Roe* Should be Overruled." *University of Chicago Law Review* 59 (1992): 381–432. Reprinted with the permission of the University of Chicago Law School. Courtesy of the Yale University Law Library.

≡Contents≡
of the Series

THE CONSTITUTION AND THE FLAG
VOLUME 1
The Flag Salute Cases
VOLUME 2
The Flag Burning Cases

PRAYER IN PUBLIC SCHOOLS
AND THE CONSTITUTION, 1961-1992
VOLUME 1
Government-Sponsored Religious Activities
in Public Schools and the Constitution
VOLUME 2
Moments of Silence in Public Schools and the Constitution
VOLUME 3
Protecting Religious Speech in Public Schools:
The Establishment and Free Exercise Clauses in the Public Arena

GUN CONTROL AND THE CONSTITUTION
Sources and Explorations on the Second Amendment
VOLUME 1
The Courts, Congress, and the Second Amendment
VOLUME 2
Advocates and Scholars: The Modern Debate on Gun Control
VOLUME 3
Special Topics on Gun Control

SCHOOL BUSING
Constitutional and Political Developments
VOLUME 1
The Development of School Busing as a Desegregation Remedy
VOLUME 2
The Public Debate over Busing
and Attempts to Restrict Its Use

ABORTION LAW IN THE UNITED STATES
VOLUME 1
From Roe v. Wade to the Present
VOLUME 2
Historical Development of Abortion Law
VOLUME 3
Modern Writings on Abortion